SEEDS OF LIBERTY

The American Mind in Art:

The Peale Family, painted by Charles Willson Peale.

[By courtesy of the New York Historical Society, New York City]

SEEDS OF
Liberty

THE GENESIS OF THE
AMERICAN MIND

By MAX SAVELLE

"... for the seeds of liberty are universally found there,
and nothing can eradicate them."

—BENJAMIN FRANKLIN.

NEW YORK ALFRED A. KNOPF 1948

uS

57737

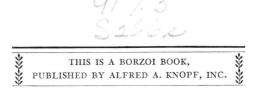

FIRST EDITION

TO

IRENE

NOTE : Chapter Nine of this book, entitled "Of Music, and of America Singing," was written by Mr. CYCLONE COVEY.

PREFACE

" As an Historian, every Thing is in my province."

WILLIAM DOUGLASS.

THIS book was written, primarily, for the average American citizen. It is an attempt to answer, in a broad and tentative way, the question of what was the origin of the American way of life, and when, why, and how the first pattern of American culture took the form and the design that it did. It seeks to draw together, in one integrated whole, the major threads and motifs that appeared in the tapestry of early American thought. And as the spectrum runs through all the colors, from infra-red to ultra-violet, and yet is one, so, too, may the earliest American mind be described as containing many shades of opinion and ideals, from those of the most rabid Tory Anglophile to those of the most libertarian frontier radical, shading one into another to form one complex but growing unity.

I hope, of course, that scholars may not disapprove of this enterprise. It is based strictly upon eighteenth-century expression, including both the writings and the artistic products of the people of mid-eighteenth-century America. There are relatively few monographs covering the special aspects of the problem here considered, and where there were studies on particular aspects of the intellectual life of that period I have occasionally found reason to differ with their conclusions. On the other hand, it has been my deliberate desire to present the thinking of that generation, in so far as possible, in that generation's own words. Thus I have used a good many quotations, some of them fairly lengthy, in order to get the exact meaning, as well as the flavor, of the writers. All but one quotation in the book is from someone who lived in America at the time ; similarly, every portrait, and every illustration of whatever sort, was originally made by that generation. These illustrations, in fact, are documents ; often they are more expressive of the minds of their creators than words could ever be ; and they are presented here as historical documentation, as first-hand, direct expressions of American thought, precisely as the quotations are presented. Thus a Copley portrait or a photograph of a Georgian house is printed here, not as the art expert or the architect might do it, but rather as historical evidence ; because the portrait or the house, more than anything that even Copley or the builder could say, presents to us a documentation of what Copley thought painting ought to be or the standard, economic, social, intellectual, or æsthetic, that the house-builder set for himself when he set about building his home.

In other words, this is an effort to let the mind of the eighteenth-century Americans speak for itself, and present, as it were, its own historical evidence. Beyond that, however, it is the historian's task to do what none of those men could do, in the way of relating these phenomena to each other and to the complicated whole of which they were small parts. I have generalized, therefore, on the basis of what they said, in an effort to interpret that generation to ours. In numerous cases, I may have erred ; but that is a probability that every historian must face, especially when he undertakes to paint upon a canvas as broad as this. Many of these general statements are made here, so far as I know, for the first time ; a good many of them, too, differ substantially from positions hitherto generally accepted. But I believe they are all justified by the evidence, critically examined, and I make them deliberately. I cannot hope, therefore, to avoid the criticism of historians who may doubtless be better qualified than I to speak on certain specialized aspects of this subject. But then, as I said before, this book is written for the layman.

It is admittedly a bold thing for one student to try to present an adequately accurate picture of all the varied aspects of the mind of a people, painting as well as economics, philosophy and religion as well as politics, literature as well as social thought, and their relationship with one another. Yet no partial picture might be presented : for to present only a part of a picture, no matter how accurately, is inevitably to distort, or completely miss, a fair and accurate conception of the whole.

Perhaps any effort by a single man to survey in its entirety the mind of America in the twentieth century would be inconceivable, because there is hardly one man capable of understanding all the major aspects of modern life even well enough to write the most superficial survey. But any twentieth-century American who has had introductory training in the physical, biological, and social sciences and in arts and letters can understand just about everything that anybody in the eighteenth century had to say, and in many cases better than men of that century understood it themselves.

Every American schoolboy knows something of the deeds and the greatness of Washington, Jefferson, the Adamses, Hamilton, and Madison ; but relatively few know anything about the fathers of that generation, or, what is far more important, that it was the fathers of the Revolutionary generation who really formulated the American way of life for which that generation fought. The Revolution was, in fact, essentially a civil war fought for a recognition and acceptance, by the mother coun-

try and the world, of the new pattern of culture that had been established by those who preceded the young men who made independence
a practical reality : the older generation, who, while the Revolutionary
generation was still in its teens, formulated and brought to maturity the
ideal of life and liberty that those younger men were to find worth fighting for.

The pattern of American culture was approaching maturity in the
interim of peace between King George's War and the Seven Years' War ;
and that maturity crystallized in the self-conscious, national self-realization that flowered in the 1750's and '60's. Such things cannot, of course,
be accurately dated ; but it is perfectly clear that the thirteen English
colonies on the continent of North America were asserting themselves
with enormous vigor and clarity and with increasing self-assurance at
the mid-century. The decades before and after 1750 constitute the period covered by this book. I have attempted to find every important figure who flourished in the period between 1740 and 1760 and to find out
what he was thinking, and, where possible, why he thought as he did.
In general, this has meant that I have generally ignored men born after
1730, and have considered, of those who were active and productive before that date, only those without a discussion of whom an understanding of the later period would be too difficult. There are some exceptions,
notably in the fields of literature and painting ; for in these areas it was
the young men — many of whom, indeed, were still in their teens — who
gave the mind of America its first genuinely native expression, precisely
in the 1750's. Similarly, I have tried to avoid getting involved too deeply
in the heats and controversies of the years following 1760 or 1764, although it has been necessary to carry some parts of the story down to
1770 or even later to show the logical completion of the long-term development of certain of the themes in American colonial thought. In
general, it has been my desire to catch the mind of the Americans in the
mood in which it stood in the period of calm British-American self-consciousness before the abnormal strains of controversy arose to disturb
that mood. For that was the "normal" mood of the Americans at the moment of their highest colonial development. Similarly, I have not attempted to describe all the men who were thinking and writing or creating works of art in the period described, but rather to select the most
outstanding and most typical of them. The book, therefore, makes no
pretense to being exhaustive.

By the same token, there is no effort made here to present an exhaustive bibliography of the hundreds of titles that might be listed. The
source of every quotation is given in the notes for those who desire it.
Similarly, the note to the reader at the end of every chapter will furnish
a very few titles, selected partly on the basis of their significance, but

also because they are interesting enough in their own right to be worth the general reader's attention, to enlarge his enjoyment and understanding of this period of our history.

It is a pleasure to acknowledge my indebtedness to the many institutions and persons who have given me their assistance in this enterprise. First of all, my thanks are due to the Library of Congress, in Washington, and particularly to Dr. Luther Evans, its director, and the staffs of nearly all the divisions of the Library, who rendered me such long-suffering and effective aid. Similarly, my thanks are due to the Boston Museum of Fine Arts, the Massachusetts Historical Society, the Fogg Museum of Art at Harvard University, the Worcester Museum of Art, Yale University, the Metropolitan Museum of Art, the New York Historical Society, the Historical Society of Pennsylvania, Princeton University Library, the Maryland Historical Society, the National Gallery of Art, the Corcoran Art Gallery, the American Antiquarian Society, the Smithsonian Institution, the Frick Art Reference Library, and the Cleveland Museum of Fine Arts, for permission to print photographs of paintings or objects in their collections. I am particularly indebted to Mrs. Jerome M. Graham for permission to print a photograph of Benjamin West's portrait of Mrs. William Gibbes, née Ann Atwood.

I am grateful for the counsel and advice of Mr. Frederick E. Brasch, of the Library of Congress, who read parts of the manuscript and gave me many valuable criticisms, to Mrs. Dwight Hutchinson, who rendered valuable editorial and critical assistance at every stage of the writing, and to Mr. Richard P. Cecil, whose careful and critical reading saved me from many an egregious blunder.

Mr. Cyclone Covey, of Reed College, wrote the chapter devoted to early American music ; I am grateful to him for his willingness to undertake this painstaking study. Without his collaboration the discussion of that essential and important facet of the early American mind could not have been as adequate as it is. For that chapter Mr. Covey wishes to acknowledge his indebtedness to Richard P. Cecil, Lola Covey, Spencer H. Norton, John Jacob Niles, Herbert Weinstock, Samuel P. Bayard, Gene Lavengood, E. E. Dale, James R. Lawson, Ferenc Molnar, D. Sterling Wheelright, Warren D. Allen, and Robert and Virginia Langdon ; and to the following for permission to quote from their publications : Oliver Ditson Company, The Macmillan Company, John Lomax, Eloise Hubbard Linscott, Thomas Y. Crowell Company, Alfred A. Knopf, and J. Fischer & Bro.

To all these and many others my appreciation goes out fully. It should be stated, however, that responsibility for all errors of fact and interpretation that may appear is mine alone.

MAX SAVELLE

University of Washington 1948

CONTENTS

Contents

Contents

xvi   Contents

ILLUSTRATIONS

SEEDS OF LIBERTY

Introduction

"What, then, is the American, this new man?"

M. G. St. J. de Crèvecœur.

THERE probably does not exist in all human history another case of the rise of a new culture whose record is so nearly complete and well documented as is that of American civilization right from the beginning. For the Europeans who founded this new civilization brought their own with them and planted it, as it were, in a blank space where there was no pre-existing culture to absorb it or even seriously to influence it. If any culture should have reproduced exactly that of its parent country, this one should; yet after the passage of a century and a half the culture those first Europeans had planted here was sharply differentiated, in many respects, from that of the mother country, and the people who had produced that culture were a new people.

The process of adaptation and growth along new lines, in the course of which a distinctly American way began to appear, began with the strokes of the first English ax that bit its way into the trunk of an American tree standing on American soil. Its first clearly defined results, however, were not surely to be observed until toward the end of the seventeenth century, in the lifetime of the second and third generations of men and women actually born on American soil. And the new society and its new ways did not achieve full maturity until toward the end of the first half of the eighteenth century.

The thirteen British colonies on the continent of North America that eventually seceded from the British Empire to become the United States of America were only a fragment of the broad, world-wide frontier of Europe overseas, and just a segment of the British frontier in America; but their patterns of culture were differentiated, by 1750, both from that of the mother country and from each other. It is easily conceivable, indeed, that the three or four differentiated culture-patterns formed in the original thirteen colonies might have crystallized, eventually, into as many independent, sovereign nations, had the formative conditions that tended to draw them all together operated less strongly. For the sectional differences and antagonisms were sharp; it was the force of common antagonisms and conflicts against French and

[3]

Indians on one side and resentment against the dominance of the mother country on the other, supplementing the cohesive forces of intellectual, social, and economic exchange, that finally fused them into one.

The culture that the first Europeans brought with them, the cultural endowment of America at its birth, was, of course, European. More exactly, it was English. For they came from the England of Queen Elizabeth and James I and Charles I, the England of Shakespeare and Bacon and Milton. Queen Elizabeth died in 1603, to be succeeded by James I, from Scotland; and the Thirty Years' War, which was not to be without its influence upon America, began in 1618. Jamestown was thus founded four years after Elizabeth's death, and the Pilgrims landed in Cape Cod Bay two years after the beginning of the Thirty Years' War. But England was still suffering from internal parliamentary growing-pains, and her parliamentary suffering was aggravated by the bitter conflict of the warring Protestant sects that had sprung from the English revolt from Roman Catholicism; and in the course of this conflict the extreme English Calvinists, the Puritans and Presbyterians, once the persecuted dissidents from Anglicanism, achieved control of the English state under the leadership of Oliver Cromwell, only to lose it when, after his death, England in 1660 turned back to her Stuart rulers and relaxed from the rigid moral tension of the Puritan era, to which she never again reverted. Thereafter new forces were to change the texture, if not the pattern, of English life. For the great Sir Isaac Newton presented to the world the scientific basis for a new philosophy of the stars and a new outlook on human life. And the colonies, now prospering and profitable, were beginning to place such a demand for English goods upon English manufactories as to give great impetus to the industrialization of English society, already begun. But by the end of the seventeenth century the culture of the colonies was obviously diverging from that of the mother country, and while they eagerly took unto themselves the whole of Newtonian science, the social and intellectual effects of English industrialization left them practically untouched, and the Anglican restoration in religion was only partial in its effects upon America, for reasons that will appear.

The inheritance of the American colonies at their birth was thus only a part of what England might have given. For the colonies were settled at a moment of economic, social, and political unrest in England; and the first immigrants from there who came to America were those who were suffering from economic distress or the religious persecution that was being inflicted upon the dissident Calvinistic Puritans by the official Calvinistic Anglican Church. Thus the inheritance was strongly colored by Puritanism, in both the north and the south. For although the establishment of Anglicanism in Virginia, along with the Old Dominion's sympathy for the Stuart cause, and the appearance of a tobacco aristocracy in Virginia and Maryland opened the door for the infiltration of Restoration culture and manners into the south, the force of that part of the inheritance known as Puritanism was strong even there; while in the north it was profound, all-absorbent, and decisive. Similarly, the Europeans who settled in Dutch New Amsterdam were also Calvinists, of another shade, and there, too, the Calvinistic mood in culture prevailed.

There probably never was a century, in fact, in the entire history of western civilization, when the deeply felt religion of the average man was as powerful a determinant of human history as in the seventeenth century. And while the practical motives of the first-comers to the colonies were extremely mixed, including especially the desire for economic gain and social status and the ambition to political power, it was religion that dominated the realm of ideas; every human activity and its rationalization, at least for the men and women who came to America, was forced to fit into an ideological system the plan of which was laid by the religious concept of the universe and man's place in it.

Yet even though religion did dominate men's thinking, religion alone was not, and probably could not have been, entirely or even chiefly responsible for the founding of a British Empire in America. It is a well-known fact that the people who founded English colonies in the West Indies and the south did not emigrate for primarily religious reasons; it was only in New England that religion was a major motive, and it was so only among a minority even there. The fact is that the great majority of the settlers came for economic reasons to escape depression and economic hardship in England and to get a new economic start in America. The greatest lodestone, to nearly all of them, was land: the opportunity, that is, to get and to possess land of their own. Naturally, therefore, economic ideas were of first-rate and fundamental importance in the first beginnings of their settlements; naturally, also, their economic ideas were in complete harmony with their religion. This is not the place to debate whether their deeply felt religious convictions were but the rationalization of their economic desires; the important thing is that Calvinistic religion and the Protestant economic ideal that developed with England's commercial expansion were parts of the American cultural inheritance that fitted together like hand and skin.

Also organically united in the seventeenth-century ideology were religion and politics. For if economic thought envisaged permitting a limited range of individualism within a grand pattern of economic statism, politics, too, followed the concept and the pattern of the newly absolute, integrated state; and church and state were the two arms of sovereignty. Similarly, the ideological patterns of the social structure and social thought were organically attached to economics, religion, and politics. Thus the concept of society followed closely the pattern of statism in economics, in politics, and in religion, and permitted a highly limited social individualism within a broad, but fixed and stratified, social plan.

Literature, art, music, and philosophy followed and expressed the pattern of statism. Only science had begun to bore from within to undermine the restrictions placed upon the human mind and soul by predestinarian Calvinism and monolithic statism. This it did, almost unconsciously, by first breaking the long-accepted and revered patterns of the physical universe and then sowing in the wind the faith that man's mind, freed from restrictions of any sort, whether economic, religious, political, or other, could be depended on to discover truth — a new truth of reason and observation that would replace the false truths of so-called revelation.

The ideological inheritance of the first colonists in America contained all these things; but they were fused together into a unity that, allowing for all variations and exceptions, revolved about the central core of statism: civilization and culture according to plan. It also contained the single revolutionary element of science, which, at the beginning no more than a spark, was nevertheless to generate the intellectual explosion that was in part, at least, to set the mind of modern man free.

Such was the inheritance of the first-comers. But that inheritance was English; and America was to receive another heritage of ideas from those who came later, the myriads of men and women who came from the non-English parts of western Europe. These were the Scots, the Irish, the French, the Jews, the Swiss, and the Germans who were to flow into America in the eighteenth century, bringing with them their own ideological heritage to add to those of Dutchmen and Swedes who were already here, and all of them to fuse with that brought over by the English.

Thus to religious Calvinism was added the leaven of pietism; and upon intolerant religious statism was brought to bear the corrosive force of religious individualism, which could only move the whole toward religious toleration. To the English language and literature was added the enriching and broadening influence of foreign words and ideas; and to English styles in architecture and painting were added the suggestions of Dutch, French, and German forms. To the English heritage of ideas was added a body of culture that was different from it ; the children of America were doubly and trebly the heirs of European civilization.

But the multiple heritage of America from Europe could not alone build a culture in America. For the ideas brought from Europe were but the raw material poured into a crucible in which something new was to be formed. The crucible was the land ; and the fusing heat that melted and molded the elements into something new was the experience of the people on the land.

The men and women who founded the seedling communities from which was to grow this nation erected their huts in a land that was completely virgin, a land as yet untouched and unmolded by European hands. To be sure, savage Indians roamed the primeval forest that covered the land to the very ocean's edge, and these savage Indians were to contribute their own ingredients to the amalgam that was to be American civilization ; but the land was new, and fresh, and to all practical purposes empty ; and the first founders had no old and firmly established civilization to subdue, no fixed and static culture with which to compromise their own. They started at the beginning, in a new soil, with no prejudices, no institutions, no priesthoods, no laws to hold them back except those they brought with them. The very freedom from old-established restraints was an augury that the people here to be born should be free and should develop freely along lines that were peculiarly their own. Even the intolerances and rigidities in their own intellectual baggage could not resist the native freedom of the first frontier, and began to wither away within a decade of their landings.

The land that was to be the matrix of America was a plain, a rolling coastal plain that sloped eastward, facing the rising sun, from the crest of the Allegheny Mountains, which stretch from the Gaspé Peninsula in the Gulf of St. Lawrence to the headwaters of the muddy, sluggish rivers that flow through Georgia to the Gulf of Mexico ; eastward to the broken, indented shores of the blue Atlantic. That plain was one plain ; the people that grew there was to become one people, made of many ; and the civilization that was theirs in 1750 was basically one, though shaded profusely and heavily by many varieties of opinion and of feeling.

In the north, New England was marked by rock-bound shores and matchless forests of white pine, spruce, fir, hemlock, and hickory. The rocky, uneven soil was uncongenial, except, perhaps, in the lower valley of the Connecticut. This soil, the conglomerate dumpings of the glacial age, yielded only grudgingly, through patient, endless toil, an adequate supply of the settler's daily bread. But the forests were full of animals that could be used for food and for their pelts' sake ; the forests themselves were a living, timeless invitation to a breed sprung from English seamen to build new boats and ships. But the invitation was the more inviting because the sea, just offshore, literally teemed with fish that could be had for the merest dropping of a line and, better still, could be sold in all the corners of the basin of the Atlantic. It was no accident, therefore, that the Americans who lived in that part of the matrix-plain should grow to be a family of fishermen, farmers, lumbermen, builders of ships, and traders. Nor is it odd that this race of merchants should have harvested wealth from the sea and its highways and, along with wealth, the ideas from other lands that inevitably travel with the bales in the holds of ships.

Between the low Housatonic range, marking the eastern border of the Hudson valley, and the valley of the Susquehanna lies another sort of soil and climate. For here are three great fertile valleys, the Hudson, the Delaware, and the Susquehanna; and the soils along the rivers in those valleys are among the best for farming in North America. The climate, too, less rigorous than in New England, invites the farmers of four seasons to grow wheat, rye, and flax, and easily to raise their fowl, hogs, cattle, and horses, for food, for labor, and for profit. These rivers, too, were the gateways to the west — the west beyond the mountains from which the Indians and the traders brought pelts and skins over the passes and down the rivers, to be piled in the warehouses of New York and Philadelphia for shipment overseas. As in New England, nature aided man in deciding what he would do for a living; and man aided nature in making this land bring forth its fruits in profusion. Here was a region of farmers, and the merchants to harvest their surplus food-products and to traffic with the Indians for furs.

Southward, again, around the shores of Chesapeake Bay and along the deep, slow rivers that flow into it, nature presented another scene. The soil was not quite so good, perhaps, as farther north; but the climate was warmer and milder, and the growing-season longer; and because John Rolfe could show that the Indians' smoking weed could be made to grow in his garden and pay good profits, the workers on the farms along those rivers began to grow it, and tobacco became the foundation of an entirely different society. Thus did the Indian, all unknowing, exercise his first great influence upon the course of the white man's history.

Southward once more, beyond the swamps that line the shores of Roanoke, the soil thins out still more until, when it reaches the Florida peninsula it is largely sand, suitable for growing citrus at a later day, but not yet offering a base for large-scale agriculture, except for the rice that could be grown in the swamps near tidewater and the indigo that might be grown a little farther inland. The scrubby, short-leaf pine on the pine-barrens, however, was rich in sap that might be made into pitch and tar and turpentine, and the hills beyond the fall-line were thickly populated with deer, whose skins might be used to make a soft and pliable leather for shoes and rugged clothing.

To the westward, inland, along the eastern slope of the mountains that shut off this coastal plain from the unknown west, lay the uplands of the piedmont and, on beyond, the great valley that lies in broken segments between the Blue Ridge and the higher Allegheny Mountains. This land, indeed, is different from the seacoast ; for it is high, cool, fertile, and well watered. Except for the fragments of this great valley that may be said to extend into New England — in the more clearly marked stretches of it that run from the Adirondacks southwestward to the headwaters of the Tennessee — it is a farmer's paradise. And it was to these hills and valleys of the piedmont and the mountains, along the Mohawk, the Juniata, the "West Branch," the Susquehanna, the Shenandoah, the upper reaches of the Great Kanawha, the Holston, and the upper Tennessee that the Germans, the Scots-Irish, and other non-English ingredients of the melting-pot made their way, to build a new frontier, repeating again the founding of civilization anew in a land where none had been before, and building out of their own peculiar experience a set of institutions and ideals that were to clash with those of the older east in the first conflicts between the American "west" and "east."

Such was the geographical matrix of America. And as the north, middle, south, and west were different from each other, so the societies that grew there were different, in mind and spirit. Yet as the great Atlantic plain was one, broken and diversified though it was, so the people of the matrix were also one ; for the great common denominator of all the people, and all their cultural variations, was freedom.

The inevitable adaptation of the inherited way of life to the new environment was clearly and unmistakably under way within a generation or so of the first settlement. Thus by 1660 New England had already discovered that the lines of least resistance and greatest profit were the lines that followed the sea, taking advantage of the two great natural resources of the region, the myriads of fish in the ocean just offshore and the unrivaled forests upon the land, which furnished a great and universally salable commodity on the one hand and the lumber for ships in which to carry it on the other. The Puritans and the Pilgrims were not compelled to choose commerce based on the fisheries as their basic economic activity, but it was certainly the most natural thing in the world for them to seize upon this "main chance" in their environment. And if their Puritan ideology fitted this virgin economic situation as glove fits hand, that only made it easier still for ideas and activities to march together to produce the bourgeois Puritan culture of the godly commonwealth.

To the south, in the same brief decades, Virginia and Maryland had discovered that their own "main chance" lay in the cultivation of tobacco; and by 1660 the process had begun by which the society of the Chesapeake area was to become a land- and slave-owning society,

Centers of Colonial American Culture: Boston, about 1743.
[From the *American Magazine,* Boston, 1743]

based upon a new variety of plantation economy. And if the ideology of the Anglican courtly aristocracy of the Stuart epoch in England promoted what was to the newly rich plantation-owners of Virginia the good life of courtliness and sophistication, here, too, it was easy for experience and idea to march together to produce the cavalier society of the tideland plantations. North Carolina, founded in the Roanoke tidelands, gradually took up and followed Chesapeake tideland models, both of economy and of culture. Similarly, too, when the rice plantations of South Carolina sprang up around its metropolis, Charleston, the rice-planters copied the Chesapeake model of culture, but with important variations in the direction of greater urban commercialism, dictated by Charleston's location as a focus of a lucrative Indian trade.

In New York and New Jersey, and later Pennsylvania and Delaware, fertile soil and balanced climate presented a congenial choice to Dutch, English, and German farmers, to make sure that it was not without reason that these were called the "bread colonies"; but practicable water highways deep into the heart of a fur-bearing continent offered another choice also, the rich opportunity for profit and wealth to be derived from trade in pelts with the Indian savages of the inland. But great grants of land produced a landed aristocracy in New York, and proprietary and other speculators in land amounted to almost the same thing in Pennsylvania. So commerce was added to farming, and vast landholdings to both, to complicate the economy of the middle colo-

Centers of Colonial American Culture: Charleston, about 1760.
[By courtesy of the New York Public Library]

nies; while here, too, the phenomenal melting-pot of ideas and religions, even more complicated than the economy itself, operated upon the formation of a culture in such a way as to make civilization more rich, more fertile, and more varied in this area than elsewhere, as well as more fluid, and even, it may be, more free.

It will be readily seen that, in the process of adaptation to the new world, the cultures that were arising in these areas were sharply different from each other, although hardly as different as they were from that of the mother country. What was the reason for those differences? Was it climate and soil alone? Hardly. For it could never be denied that the Puritan fathers' conception of what a culture ought to be had a profound effect upon the cultural mood of New England, even for centuries, quite apart from economic considerations. New England culture was the result of ideas working upon the environment; following the lines of least resistance, to be sure, but steering the movement of history along a clear and well-determined line. The product, as it was about 1750, was certainly not English; nor was it anything else in the world that was foreign to that land. It was American.

Likewise, the urbane, sophisticated culture of the southland was no arbitrary or inevitable outgrowth of the cultivation of tobacco; but the cultivation of that weed did make the plantation system easy; and the plantation system made it easy for the plantation-owners to indulge

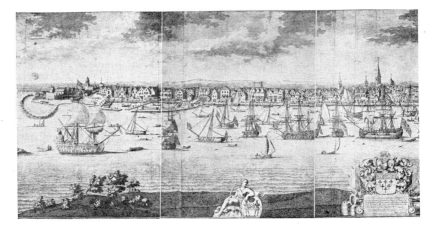

Centers of Colonial American Culture : New York, about 1746.
[By courtesy of the Library of Congress]

their courtly taste for urbanity and sophistication and more or less deliberately to make urbanity the basic element in their cultural pattern. Nothing exactly like the southern plantation culture of 1750 existed in England, or anywhere else in the world, for that matter. It was in many ways distinctive; clearly the product of ideas at work upon the environment and the developing economy, it certainly was not a European culture : it was American.

Again, it seems satisfactorily clear that the culture of New York and New Jersey or that of Pennsylvania, as of 1750, could not have been duplicated anywhere else in the world. Nor could it be said that those cultures — for they were in some ways different even from each other — were merely the product of the economic situation alone. For the ideas of the Quakers and the Germans and the Dutch exercised at least strong directive influences upon the formation of the patterns of culture there. Moreover, the civilization of the middle colonies at the middle of the eighteenth century was not English or European; it was American.

These culture-nuclei, these different ways of life, were neither the duplicates of any other that had ever existed anywhere, nor yet the simple product of the environment. Nor, indeed, were they the product of the simple addition of ideas and environment. They were the product of a living process, as of a man using the knowledge and the ideas he had brought with him into a new land, using some, changing some, discarding others, and, when necessary, inventing new ones. It was this living, day-by-day activity, the employment of thought in action, and neither

Centers of Colonial American Culture : Philadelphia, about 1750.
[By courtesy of the New York Public Library]

ideas alone nor environment alone, that eventually produced the peculiarly American mind. This was a living experience, peculiar to that time and place ; and it is experience that generates ideas.

But if the internal experience of a community generates its characteristic ideas and culture, it is its external experience that develops its self-consciousness. It is external experience or relationships, also, that may drive it into antagonism toward its neighbors or draw it into a harmony or even a unity with them. Thus, despite the differences between the young American communities, there were certain experiences common to all of them that were operating strongly, about the year 1750, to overcome their differentness and to draw them together into a common, or at least a federal, unity.

Basic among those forces were the economic, social, and intellectual exchanges that had become commonplace between the colonies to stimulate a keen interest in each other. Much more important, however, was the presence of Indian and French enemies upon the western borders of nearly all the colonies, enemies standing astride the coveted treasure of the western lands. The presence of the common enemies, thwarting a common purpose, was probably more powerful as a force to draw them together than any other. Yet the uniting power of the fear of those enemies was only a little less powerful, but a great deal less persistent, than the slowly growing realization that the colonies had a great, compelling common problem in their relations with the mother country. It was the consciousness of the French menace that drew them toward each other in the 1750's to drive the French out of the continent; it was the sudden realization of the oppressive nature of their common relationships with the mother country that drew them together after the French war was over to send England and the British menace down the way the French had gone.

Thus the forces of union, already at work in 1750, overcame the tendency toward particularism and drew the colonies into a sort of alliance that was to demand from the mother country full autonomy within the British Empire and, failing that, to proclaim themselves independent sovereign states. It was about the middle of the eighteenth century that the new culture-pattern of the Americans, the product of many factors, reached for the first time a stage of maturity that entitled them either to call themselves a people or to demand from the rest of the world a recognition of that maturity.

Basic to everything, probably, was the population — the people themselves — and the fact that by this time they were probably more thoroughly mixed than any other people in the western world. To that factor must be added the ideological inheritance. The essential element in it was English, to be sure; but so many non-English sets of ideas had been added by 1750 that it certainly could no longer be called purely English, any more than it could be called purely anything else. Yet the European element in the process of making an American culture was strong and gave both color and variety to the new ideological complex that was appearing. At the same time, a third formative factor, the most important, probably, of all the new world factors, was the physical environment to which this mixed people and their mixed ideological inheritance had to adapt themselves. For if some of the old ideas might work in America, most of them did not, at least without a great deal of modification to suit the new time and place; and the modifications themselves had to differ, as between those of the north and those of the south and those of the middle colonies. But the environment was not merely physical: the presence of fur-bearing animals in the forests exercised a significant influence upon important parts of the American economy and society and their culture. But even more important, as a fifth formative factor, was the presence of the indigenous savage Indians in possession of the land; and the necessity for a struggle of epic proportions to dispossess them completely had profound effects upon American civilization, then as later. Add to that the rivalry of the equally expansive and ambitious French empire blocking the way of the American Britons to the enjoyment of the continent as they conquered it in their endless struggle with the red-men ; that, too, profoundly influenced the thinking of the Americans, political, religious, and cultural, and galvanized them into a self-consciousness that was the first sure mark of their becoming a nation. The American culture of the 1750's, then, was not English. It was British, to be sure, about as twentieth-century Canadian culture is British. But it was, in fact and in essence, a culture different from anything else in the world. By that time it was American.

"What, then, is the American, this new man ?" asked St. John de Crèvecœur, a French savant who had settled in the colonies. And then he answered his own question :

> He is an American, who leaving behind him all his ancient prejudices and manners, receives new ones from the new mode of life he has embraced, the new government he obeys, and the new rank he holds. . . . Americans are the western pilgrims, who are carrying along with them that great mass of arts, sciences, vigour, and industry which began long since in the east ; they will finish the great circle. . . . The American is a new man, who acts upon new principles ; he must therefore entertain new ideas, and form new opinions. From involuntary idleness, servile dependence, penury, and useless labour, he has passed to toils of a very different nature, rewarded by ample subsistence. — This is an American.[1]

NOTE TO THE READER

There are a good many books written by modern scholars to describe the life of the Americans of the colonial period, and you can find them listed in any good textbook. I imagine, however, that you are likely to enjoy, a great deal more than any of these modern works, the only book of the sort written by a man who lived at the time. This is Dr. William Douglass's *A Summary, Historical and Political, of the British Settlements in North America*, written as a series of articles in Boston in the 1740's and published together in 1752. Dr. Douglass was a man of magnificent prejudices, so you must not accept everything he says as literally true ; but his book has the advantage of breathing the living mood of the period, which is the one that we are to discuss here.

There are two modern books dealing with our period that I should like particularly to recommend. One of them is Lawrence H. Gipson's *The British Empire before the American Revolution* (6 vols. to date ; New York, 1936–   ), of which I believe volumes II, III, and IV may be of greatest interest to the average American. Do not be afraid of the fact that it is in sev-

[1] Michel Gilliaume St. Jean de Crèvecœur : *Letters from an American Farmer* (London, 1782), pp. 51–3.

eral volumes ; it is all interesting reading. Besides, you do not have to read all of it : every chapter stands alone.

The other book is a delightful little bibliographical essay called *An American Bookshelf, 1755* (Philadelphia, 1934) written by Lawrence C. Wroth. This little study is an entertaining and highly informative descriptive list of the books that the average educated American was likely to be reading in the period between the third and fourth Anglo-French "intercolonial" wars. You will find it a highly useful and instructive essay on the reading-habits of our forefathers.

CHAPTER I

Of the Ways of God with Men— and of Men with God

"It is practical religion, the love of God, and a life of righteousness and "charity, proceeding from faith in Christ and the gospel, that denom-"inates us good men and good christians."

JONATHAN MAYHEW.

ELIGION is both rational and irrational. Rationally, it is the ordinary man's explanation of what is : that is, religion is the common man's philosophy. As an irrational phenomenon, it has generally been, historically, an emotional reaction of the human animal to the universe in which he lived; a reaction that was rooted deep in his emotional nature and was unexplainable except in terms of a mystical or æsthetic feeling of — or yearning for — oneness with the powers that make the universe go or with the universe itself. It has not always been a matter of morals; on the contrary, among primitive peoples the gods or nature spirits were often thought to be just as immoral, or amoral, as human beings, if not more so.

The religion of Europe during the Middle Ages was Roman Catholicism, which had not yet divested itself of belief in miracles, in witchcraft, or in a geocentric universe. In its emotional content it had derived largely from St. Augustine, but by the thirteenth century it had absorbed much of the rationalism of Plato and Aristotle, to become, on its rational side, the religion of Thomas Aquinas and Dante. Institutionally, the religious life of western Europe was now organized in the Roman Catholic Church, which had as its head the pope, who was thought to be the vicegerent of God on earth. But for the common man of the Middle Ages, religion was a set of customs and a fearful faith in gods and devils that beset him at every turn, and which could be controlled — more or less — only if one humbly followed the instructions of the village priest, local representative of the universal authority of the pope, which could — and did — force even kings to their knees in dreary penance when they strayed from the papal way. Medieval Christianity was thus composed of two streams, the emotional, prophetic and pietistic, represented by Augustine, Bernard of Clairvaux, Francis of Assisi, and the common people on the one side, and the rationalistic institutionalized Catholicism of Abélard, Aquinas, Dante, and the papal hierarchy on the other.

For Augustine, God was an absolute, personal sovereign, of inflexible and unchallenged will. The ultimate purpose of the whole universe, indeed, was to show forth the glory, the majesty, and the goodness of God. God had created man as a good being in God's own image; but man had sinned, and had thereby lost the power of being or doing good without God's aid. Thus all men were blinded by sin; but God, in his mercy, had chosen to restore some men to their original goodness and fellowship with himself by extending to them his grace. These, the elect, were thus predestined — since God, in his omniscience, had planned it all from eternity — to be saved. All others were predestined to eternal damnation for their sins.

In the course of the centuries, however, and especially after the rediscovery of Aristotle, this rigid doctrine of predestination was modified, and in the doctrines of the church less emphasis was placed upon the complete sufficiency of God's grace and more upon rational behavior in compliance with the system of the seven sacraments of baptism, confirmation, the eucharist, penance, extreme unction, holy orders, and matrimony. Thus, under the direction of the village priest, the common man of the thirteenth or fourteenth century might consider himself "saved" if he dutifully and sincerely performed these "good works."

The Protestant revolt, when it came, was a revolt from this priestly religion of good works back, as the Protestants thought, to a more primitive Christianity that rested squarely upon the individual's salvation by divine grace, directly vouchsafed to him by God, and received by him only when he achieved a complete faith in God's goodness and mercy. But the logical application of any of the varying degrees of individualism in the Protestant beliefs would of necessity involve, if not the complete dissolution of the priesthood and the papacy, at least a great weakening of its prestige and ultimate authority, and this the church could hardly be expected to accept.

In the pronouncements of the Council of Trent, which ended its work early in 1564, the major positions of Roman Catholicism were restated as follows: The Council first reaffirmed the validity of the Nicene Creed, which was a statement of the basic Catholic understanding of the Christian epic. It then listed the beliefs that had come to elaborate the original creed, such as acceptance of the apostolic authority of the Roman Church and its priesthood, especially in the interpretation of the Bible, the seven sacraments, the miracle of the mass (the belief, that is, that the bread and wine of the mass are miraculously transformed into the actual body and blood of Christ), the belief in purgatory, the veneration of images of Christ, the Virgin Mary, and the saints, and the belief that salvation is to be achieved only through the Roman Catholic Church, and so on. Every good Catholic was expected to accept this position ; and the last act of the Council was a double curse upon heretics, including, of course, all Protestants. Such was the basic doctrine of the Catholic religion that was brought to America ; and it changed little, either in the colonial period or later, except by the addition of the two doctrines of the immaculate conception and papal infallibility.

By the fifteenth century the religion of pope, priest, and sacrament was the accepted religion of western Europe, apparently unchallenged. Heresies had, indeed, ventured to differ from the accepted doctrines, but the papal church, by rigorous, ruthless persecution, excommunication, or massacre, had managed to still the voices of the dissidents. But not for long. For just a century after John Hus had been betrayed and burned for his dissent (1415), another and greater dissenter had arisen, in the person of Martin Luther, a renegade monk, who was to crack the institutional structure of western Catholicism to its foundations.

The movement that Luther started was called the Protestant revolt and the Catholic reform that took place as a healthy reaction to the revolt — of which the Council of Trent was a part — was called the Counter-Reformation. Taken together, the Protestant revolt and the Catholic reform constituted the so-called Reformation, one of the most significant events in the history of human thought and institutions. Significant as it was, however, the actual changes in religion that occurred as part or result of the Reformation were relatively superficial. For western Europe remained Christian : all the multitude of divisions, Protestant and Catholic alike, retained the essential features of the Christian epic. The chief controversies gradually resolved themselves into questions whether salvation of the individual was to be achieved by good works, with a little faith, as with the Catholics; by faith alone, as with Luther ; or by faith dependent upon divine grace, as with Calvin. Thus the Protestant revolt quickly produced two major divisions of Protestants who hated each other almost as much as they hated Catholicism, and from these two soon sprang two others, the literal-minded Anabaptists and the related pietist sects on the one side, and the latitudinarian, rationalistic, Calvinistic Anglicans on the other. The seventeenth century thus opened with five major groups of Christians in western Europe, all of which were of great significance, direct or in-direct, for the future development of Anglo-America.

The most conservative of these were the Catholics. The Council of Trent had reaffirmed Catholic doctrine pretty much as it had been during the Middle Ages; the militant order of the Society of Jesus, or the Jesuits, had been organized to carry forward the crusade of the "true" Catholic religion; and the church court of the Inquisition had been revived to continue the battle against heresy in the countries that had not been completely lost to the Protestants. Even Catholicism, how-ever, was not without its internal divisions, and something closely akin to Calvinism appeared within the fold in the form of Jansenism, only to be stamped out by the ruthless persecution of the Jesuits.

Martin Luther, archtype of the reformers, was a German cleric whose rebellion began as a trifling debate over the unscrupulous sale of indulgences by the church and its agents. Challenged to defend him-self, and under the influence of his own subjective religious experi-ences, Luther quickly arrived at a rationalization of his position that swept away most of the sacraments, the intermediary priesthood, and the papacy and, proclaiming the doctrine of salvation by faith alone, elevated the validity of the Bible as the only necessary guide to the will of God. Needless to say, this set of ideas completely and thoroughly undermined the entire institutional structure of the Catholic Church, and it is not at all surprising that the church tried desperately to crush him and his doctrines as it had crushed the Cathars before him. But Luther had the support of the new and modern forces of nationalism and bourgeois commercialism, and he bound both of them to his own cause of religious reform; together they succeeded in taking the north-ern parts of Europe almost completely out of the Catholic fold.

But Luther would not be taken too literally, especially if it threat-ened the vested interests of his allies. Thus he pronounced an anathema upon the Anabaptists, who took advantage of Luther's success to pro-claim a more radical return to primitive Christianity, and assisted with all his might in suppressing this somewhat communistic threat at the institutions of bourgeois property.

For the Anabaptists, so called because they rejected the validity of infant baptism, required, first of all, a personal profession of faith in Jesus Christ before baptism, which was performed by total immersion, as Christ was said to have been baptized. Taking literally Christ's state-ment that he came not to destroy, but to save, the Anabaptists believed in religious liberty for all, and steadfastly opposed the use of force — thus becoming doctrinal pacifists. Taking their cue from the earliest Christians, they preached the revolutionary doctrines of economic equality and communal ownership of property; and while they retained a congregational form of church organization and discipline, they steadfastly maintained the essentially individual position that a man's answerability in matters of religion was to God and God alone. These Christian radicals were the spiritual forebears of the Mennonites, the Baptists, and the Quakers, who were to play such important roles in the later development of religion in America.

But Martin Luther's great rival was John Calvin, called "The Protestant Pope" of Geneva. For Calvin, a French lawyer turned reformer, was much more logical than Luther. From Augustine he borrowed the ideas of the omniscience and unchallengeable will of God, original sin, predestination, and salvation by faith dependent upon divine grace. But Calvin, in his return to the Augustinian stream of prophetic religion, rejected the doctrine of the mass, substituting for it the idea of the "spiritual" presence of Christ in the bread and wine, and calling it simply the "Lord's Supper." He retained only this sacrament and the sacrament of baptism, rejecting such "priestly" devices as confirmation, holy orders, and extreme unction and making matrimony merely a civil contract, ordained and approved by God. In the place of the Catholic hierarchy he organized the "visible church" as a body of individual believers held together by their common faith and governed by a "presbytery of elders." Practically, too, he identified the church with the civil community, and taught that government of the civil state should rest in the hands of the "elect," who would then be empowered to see to it that God's will was done in the community and that evil was stamped out. Naturally enough, Calvin himself became the effective head of the government in Geneva when his doctrines were accepted there, and he ruled it with a rod of iron.

If the pietism of the Anabaptists was a literal application of the logical implications of Luther's revolt, Anglicanism was the result of an effort to "Calvinize" the Anglican Catholicism that had been the product of Henry VIII's break with the papal hierarchy in England. Henry had hardly altered Catholic doctrine; he had merely rejected the pope's authority and set up his own for the church in England — aside from his confiscation of church property for his and his followers' benefit. But the "Elizabethan Settlement," arranged under Henry's daughter and from which emerged the Church of England and its doctrine contained in the so-called Thirty-nine Articles, was the product of a doctrinal revolution precipitated largely by the influence of John Calvin upon the English reformers.

As defined in the Thirty-nine Articles, the Anglicanism that became the established religion in Virginia followed fairly closely the ideas of Calvin. Thus the Articles proclaim the essential features of the Holy Trinity, the epic of Christ's death and resurrection, the authority of the Scriptures, original sin, salvation by faith, election and predestination. The church, for the Anglican, was a "congregation of faythfull men," and the sacraments were only two, baptism and the Lord's Supper. Baptism was regarded as a sign of "Regeneration of New-Birth"; the bread and wine of the Lord's Supper were the body and blood of Christ "only after an heavenly and spirituall maner." The point at which the Anglicans parted company with the Calvinists was the priesthood; for the Anglican Church retained its own hierarchy of bishops, priests, and deacons, while rejecting the Catholic requirement of celibacy in the priesthood. The queen (or king) of England was made the head of the Church of England, but only in civil matters; spiritual authority was eventually vested in the archbishop of Canterbury.

Thus Anglican Protestantism differed from the Calvinistic brand chiefly in matters of organization and administration. As this division of Protestantism developed, however, the Anglicans tended to become more and more rationalistic in their religious attitudes, allowing greater latitude for individual judgment in such questions as, for example, the interpretation of the Scriptures. It was over these two questions of "latitudinarianism" versus "literalism," and "priestly authority" versus "congregational authority," that the Anglican Church was itself split, and that the Puritans, almost completely Calvinistic, eventually seceded from it.

These, then, were the parent religions — Catholicism, Lutheranism, Anabaptism, Calvinism, and Anglicanism — that were to furnish the religious seedlings that, already well grown and strong, were to be planted in America; but under the influence of the American environment, physical, social, and intellectual, they were to experience many modifications, so many and so radical, indeed, as sharply to differentiate many of their offspring from the parent stock.

CALVINISM IN EUROPE AND AMERICA

The Englishmen who came to America in the third and fourth decades of the seventeenth century came from an England that was moving out of the Elizabethan era into the era of Puritanism. This movement, this changing of the mind of England, was somewhat abrupt; but it was an integral part of that great groundswell of opinion already described as the Protestant revolt from Roman Catholicism. That heavy groundswell, however, had its origin in the emotions and minds of individuals and groups long since disappeared from the European scene; and Puritanism, to be understood, must be traced back to its origins, which are to be found in the far-away dawn of civilization among the peoples of the ancient east. For Puritanism is essentially a mood, an introspective mood that rests upon the idea of sin and the conviction that man himself is essentially evil or sinful and that human decency and progress can be achieved only by an eternal and rigorous self-discipline.

The greatest "Puritan" among the early medieval Christians was Augustine, Bishop of Hippo, who was himself profoundly influenced by Manichæan ideas and who was the direct ideological ancestor, as it were, of the English and American Puritans of the seventeenth century. He, too, was challenged by the problem of evil in the world, and found the answer in the concept of sin : "and I sought [he says] where is evil . . . and it was manifested unto me, that those things be good, which yet are corrupted. . . . That evil then which I sought, wherever it is, is not any substance : for were it a substance, it should be good. . . . And I enquired what iniquity was, and found it to be no substance, but the perversion of the will, turned aside from Thee, O God, the Supreme, towards these lower things. . . ." [1]

During the later Middle Ages western Christianity became institutionalized in the Roman Catholic Church ; and salvation, from being, as with Augustine, an intensely personal, emotional experience, became a function of the church, performed by the priesthood, purchased more by the performance of good works, as represented by the sacraments, than by any experience of the heart. Philosophy, in the various branches of Scholasticism, sought to rationalize the drama of salvation in terms derived chiefly from Aristotle, and faith tended to become less important for an understanding of God and his ways than reason. There were recrudescences of the Puritanical spirit, however, from time to time, as in the monastic reforms initiated by Bernard of Clairvaux in France, who insisted that faith is superior to reason and that the mystical experience of salvation as experienced by Augustine was more dependable as a guide to God than either reason or good works alone. Thus throughout the history of western religions there runs the two and often conflicting streams of the prophetic and the priestly, of faith and reason (or good works). The Protestant revolt, and especially Calvinism, was essentially a revolt and a resurgence of the prophetic mood, the mood of mysticism and faith in a direct relationship between a man and his God.

English Puritanism, in which we of America are most interested, started as a movement to "Calvinize" the Anglican branch of Protestantism. This was partially accomplished in the so-called Thirty-nine Articles. But the Calvinists in England were not satisfied with the retention of certain ritualistic practices in the Anglican Church, its episco-

[1] Augustine, Bishop of Hippo : *The Confessions of St. Augustine* (E. B. Pusey, trans., New York, 1910), pp. 123, 135, 137.

pal organization, or its relatively broad latitudinarianism in matters of faith and doctrine, and sought to purify it of these vestiges of "popery." It was because of their efforts at purification of the Anglican Protestant Church that they first were called Puritans. It was not long, however, before they began to be persecuted by the official Anglican Church, and small groups of them decided to emigrate to America, where they hoped to establish in the wilderness of Massachusetts a Christian commonwealth patterned after that at Geneva.

The American Puritans, radical outcasts from Anglicanism, followed, in their religious doctrines, the teachings of Calvin. Thus, for them, as for Augustine and Calvin before them, God was omnipotent, omniscient, absolute, with a close personal interest in the affairs of every human being. He had created man in his own image, as an originally good and pure soul. But man had sinned; he had disobeyed God, and, as the fruit of knowledge, he had acquired the ability to know good and evil. God, for man's sin, had blinded him to good, had deprived him of the capacity to choose good, and had condemned him to eternal damnation in hell-fire. Only because of his infinite mercy had God relented and selected some men to be restored to the knowledge of God's goodness. Man himself received this salvation through faith in God, but even his faith was the gift of God's grace.

But not only were some men to enjoy this mystic union with God. They were also to become the instruments and the agents of God's work here on earth. Following the instruction they had from God in the Bible, which they understood to be God's literal word, they felt themselves charged to organize themselves as believers, and those leaders who came to America felt themselves especially directed to set up such a civil and religious society as should follow God's instructions faithfully and literally in their "New Zion." Nothing, absolutely nothing, was to be allowed to interfere with the purity of religion or society in New England. God's will was to be done, and no compromise; in New England, at least, God could depend upon his people to conduct themselves as he intended.

The Puritans in Massachusetts and in England, however, never went as far as the Calvinists or Presbyterians at Geneva did in setting up an institutionalized church, but clung, despite repeated efforts to institutionalize Puritanism in one solid church organization, to their basic principle of congregational autonomy. This "Congregationalism" became the basis, indeed, of their civic and political institutions; so that their political units, locally the towns, were essentially church congregations; and their state was a representative federation of towns — or churches.

It was easy, too, for the Puritans to feel they were the chosen people of God and to develop a certain feeling of superiority to other groups. This made for a sort of incipient nationalism in Massachusetts. In England, Cromwell combined the capitalistic and Protestant individualism of the merchants, the mercantilism of the merchant class, the anti-Catholic feeling of England generally, and the feeling of superiority of the Puritans to produce a state of mind that was probably the most completely nationalistic in England's history prior to the nineteenth century. Naturally enough, the Puritans who set up the godly societies of New England, who were even more strongly convinced of their special place in God's favor and purposes, displayed a comparable, but entirely separate, quasi-nationalism in New England.

The Puritans were, of course, not the only nationalists in the western world, for there were Spanish and French nationalists also. But the Puritans' conviction that they were the modern chosen people of God made them, probably, the most ardent nationalists of their time.

Puritanism was thus a religion and a way of life, essential to which was the dual idea of the omnipotence of God and the depravity of man. It must be thought of as a deliberate effort, by fervently convinced men, to reform the world and bring it back to the way of life originally intended by God. It was a reform, moreover, on a world scale; the commonwealths of England and Massachusetts were but the first steps toward such a reform as would put the control of the world's affairs in the hands of the regenerate, the saved, the men who knew God's mind; under their direction evil would at last be eradicated from human affairs, goodness would prevail, and the earthly society would march steadily forward toward the millennium of the control of sin, if not complete victory over it, before the final trump, and the establishment of a society that, if not exactly a heavenly city, would be as perfect and as godly as the persistence of sin in the unregenerate would allow. Puritanism as a religion was a religion of the regenerate heart; but as a social and political system it was an effort to raise humanity, as it were, by its bootstraps, out of the morass of sin upwards toward God.

For the convinced Puritan believer, the Puritan way was anything but sordid and ugly. On the contrary, it was a mood of heavenly beauty, a sort of rationalized mysticism that led him into the exquisite security of complete surrender of oneself to God's will. Puritanism at its best was thus a genuine effort to live according to an ideal. God was good and beautiful; if life could only be made to be as God intended, life itself, here and now, would also be good and beautiful. For the Puritan, for example, drinking was no sin. Did not Christ change water into wine? The sin lay only in drunkenness, or overindulgence — in giving in to the evil impulses of Satan. Sex was not evil, but good, for

God had made it; evil, or sin, lay only in using sex for pleasure not permitted by God's rules. Those who could not understand the rules had to be watched; and it was this necessity for keeping the unregenerate under control in the name of righteousness that led to many of the more sordid, unlovely aspects of Puritanism. But those aspects were only the imperfections of the application of an ideal. For it must never be forgotten that, for the Puritan, Puritanism was a heroic and titanic effort literally to live according to the most superlatively beautiful idea he knew, which was the idea of the will of God.

The next-door neighbors of the Puritans of New England were the Dutch in New Amsterdam. They, too, were Calvinists, of the so-called Dutch Reformed persuasion, even though they permitted a greater measure of religious freedom than existed in any other colony on the continent except Rhode Island. The Swedes and Danes along the Delaware, who had been absorbed by New Netherland before the English engulfed them all, were Lutheran, and furnished a nucleus for the growth of Lutheran Protestantism in the middle colonies later on; but Lutheranism, although important, never became one of the major influences in early American intellectual life.

Anglicanism, on the other hand, was a major intellectual influence throughout the colonies south of Pennsylvania, especially in the seventeenth century before the great influx of British and Scottish dissidents and German pietists into Pennsylvania and the southern back-country. Anglicanism, indeed, established as the official religion in Maryland, Virginia, and the Carolinas, was essentially Calvinistic in doctrine, as already explained. But it was latitudinarian in doctrinal outlook and episcopal and aristocratic in institutional structure, as befitted the urbane, rationalistic, and aristocratic mind of the emerging planter aristocracy resting upon the slave-supported plantation economy of the southern tidewater. And the southern aristocracy that was taking shape precisely in the decades of the Stuart restoration in England, with all its courtly trappings and Anglican establishment, consciously copied much of the English fashion, in the realm of religion as well as in those of culture and social ideal.

The two prevalent systems of religious ideas in the English colonies in the middle of the seventeenth century, Puritanism and Anglicanism, were thus both essentially Calvinistic in doctrine. They differed widely as to the nature of orthodoxy and the mechanisms for maintaining it and as to church or ecclesiastical organization. But each in its own way was committed to the principles of the authoritarian state and the idea that the church is a religious arm of the state, as well as to the social principle that men are born unequal — that some are born to lead society and others to follow.

Religion, in fact, permeated every branch of human thought, and, broadly speaking, no one even questioned the general assumption that things as they were, aside from the machinations of sinful men, were so as part of the eternal plan and purpose of God. Religion was thus the great common denominator of the mind of the first two or three generations of Englishmen in America, despite the fact that religion alone was never, for any considerable number, the sole or even the chief cause for migration to the new world. Furthermore, the preponderantly Calvinistic and Puritan ideas and faiths of this religion, quite apart from economic or political or other forms of self-interest, were to have an immeasurably profound effect upon the American mind as it developed through the centuries.

The Religions of Scientific Rationalism

Puritanism, then, was a psychological phenomenon that moved history. It was a mood, a subjective, introspective mood, that worked itself out in religion, and from that into society, politics, ethics, philosophy, literature, and art, in the first half of the seventeenth century; and it was probably the high-water mark of the Protestant revolt. But the utopia of Puritanism began to decay almost as soon as it was established; for human nature could not be expected to live for long at such a high tension of idealism, especially in the face of the earthy, all-absorbing practical necessities of life on the American frontier and of the corroding influence brought to bear upon the uncritical faith of the Puritans by the implications of Newtonian science or the comparative study of non-European religions by the eighteenth-century rationalists.

Puritanism had taken root in America, nevertheless. It took its own forms, to be sure, and soon lost its doctrinal purity. But as a mood of self-control, self-discipline, self-direction, it was firmly rooted in the American experience and in the emerging American mind of the eighteenth century, and from New England as a center it has radiated its influence in American civilization, for good or ill, from that day to this; and the end is not yet.

At the same time the implications of science and the broadened perspective of European knowledge of the world and its inhabitants gave rise to a new, more naturalistic and humanistic outlook and produced a group of new religious theories, which, taken together, are called Deism, and a new faith, the faith in the unlimited capabilities of human reason, to replace the ancient faith of blind, unquestioning intellectual docility.

At the same time, too, the restoration of Anglicanism to its place of political establishment in England and in the southern colonies that occurred with the restoration of Charles II in 1660 gave that faith a position of authority and strengthened respectability, even in New England. And as the latitudinarian mood of Anglicanism was somewhat more congenial to the free play of human reason and common sense than Calvinism, it won a number of distinguished converts, especially among the aristocrats and the Anglophiles. Closely associated, as it was, with the crown in England and with English officialdom in America, its growth was doubtless retarded by the suspicion under which it fell as the Americans became more self-confident and self-assertive at the time of the eventual conflict with the mother country. Yet Anglicanism was not uncongenial to the moods of the new rationalism, and individual Anglicans, if not Anglicanism itself, were deeply influenced by it. The liberalization of Anglicanism that took place in the eighteenth century is thus to be linked with that same naturalism and nationalism that produced Deism.

The rationalization of Puritanism : the seeds of Unitarianism

The rationalization of Puritanism began in Boston itself, toward the end of the seventeenth century. Very early in the history of the Puritan commonwealth, indeed, the rigorous demands of Puritanism had been found impracticable, and an official compromise had been made in 1662, in the so-called "half-way covenant," according to which those who could not honestly claim to have experienced "conversion" or "regeneration" could be members of the churches and have their children baptized, but could not partake of the Lord's Supper or participate in the congregational elections. This compromise was tantamount to a confession that there were not enough people who had the personal experience of regeneration to carry on the Puritan ideal of a commonwealth of the "elect," and that meant, in effect, that the ideal of a Puritan utopia was a failure.

But its greatest significance, probably, lay in the fact that the majority of ordinary people simply did not consciously experience regeneration. Without the sort of emotional excitement that was to come later in the Great Awakening, but which was a profound departure from the essential rationalism of the Puritans, such an experience was contrary to the nature and inclinations of normal human beings. But to admit this fact, however tacitly, meant the opening of a breach in the wall of the Puritan utopia, in the name of human nature, that could never be healed. This break was soon widened by the Synod of 1680, which adopted the Savoy Declaration of the English Congregationalists (1658), which modified the Westminster Confession of Faith in such a way as to introduce a much more tolerant attitude toward differences of opinion, and to allow churches to admit members without forcing them to make public confessions of faith and regeneration. It was even argued, by such men as Solomon Stoddard, that admission of technically unregenerate Christians to the Lord's Supper might have the effect of inducing in them the desired conversion. But the real decay of Puritanism began with the mild, rationalistic criticism of its more rigorous doctrines by some of the Puritan leaders themselves.

It was Thomas Brattle, businessman, and his brother William, who was a tutor at Harvard and minister at the Cambridge Church, who, together with John Leverett, later president of Harvard College, organized the liberal Puritan dissidents in Boston by the creation of the Brattle Street Church in 1699, with Benjamin Coleman as their minister. The Brattle Street congregation, while it professed adherence to the Westminster Confession, yet admitted to baptism and to the communion "persons of visible sanctity," but from whom no public relation of the experience of regeneration was required, and all persons who had been baptized were to have the right to vote in the church elections. More important still, perhaps, was the changed attitude of this congregation, for in its preaching and in its publications its emphasis was directed increasingly toward God's mercy, while less and less emphasis was placed upon the inflexibility and the rigorousness of divine justice. The organization of the Brattle Street Church, indeed, marked the parting of the ways for New England Puritanism; for it was the beginning of the liberalization and the humanization of Puritan doctrine that led directly, if very gradually, toward the rationalism of New England Unitarianism.

As might have been expected, the publication of the doctrine and policy of the Brattle Street Church aroused a storm of opposition from the conservative Puritans. The Brattle Street congregation marched steadily forward, however, and, when Increase Mather and his son Cotton tried to set up a sort of presbytery as a mechanism for whipping the liberal churches into line, the Brattle Street Church was joined in its resistance to the movement by many other churches, which under the eloquent leadership of John Wise, pastor of Ipswich Church, held fast to their precious and long-established congregational autonomy. Wise's philosophy of church and civil government was especially significant, in that it gave the final *coup de grâce* to the old Puritan philosophy of state government in the hands of the elect, and made of the church merely "a religious society," the chief end of whose government was, like that of the state, to "cultivate humanity, and promote the happiness of all, and the good of every man in all his rights." [2]

Wise marked a step in the gradual turning of religion, in the America

[2] John Wise : *Vindication of the Government of the New England Churches* (Boston, 1772), p. 40.

of the eighteenth century, away from the stern injunction to show forth the glory of God toward the more congenial business of promoting the happiness of man. This was a revolution that was going on in religion in England as well as in America, and the American intellectual and religious leaders were strongly influenced by the ideas they discovered in England. This borrowing of English ideas in religion is also an instance of the provincial attitude that marked the awakening of the Americans to cultural self-consciousness in the eighteenth century; it is to be considered along with the comparable borrowings in the realms of literature, political and economic theory, music, science, art, and philosophy that were taking place at the same time.

The trend toward liberalism in religion throughout eighteenth-century America was generally termed "Arminianism." The term, which was rather loosely used, had originally sprung from the fact that Jacob Arminius, a professor of theology at the University of Leiden at the beginning of the seventeenth century, had taught a doctrine of free will as opposed to the rigorous predestinarianism of John Calvin, and had claimed that man is saved by good works *and* faith, instead of by faith alone. These doctrines gave the actions and decisions of man himself much more importance in the drama of salvation than the doctrines of predestination allowed, and were discovered by the leaders of the New England liberalism to be exceedingly congenial to their own developing way of thought. It was not, however, so much the actual ideas of Arminius that characterized the new "Arminianism" as its generally humanistic attitude; many of the leaders of religion in England, even among the Anglican divines, had accepted this "reasonable" attitude, and through them, particularly such preachers as the quasi-Deist Samuel Clarke, John Tillotson, Archbishop of Canterbury, and the humanist philosopher Francis Hutcheson, it found its way to America, where the soil was in fact already prepared.

Another "heresy" condemned by the Puritan die-hards was Pelagianism, derived from Pelagius, who had held that men are good, not sinful. Still another heretical doctrine that was splitting the rationalistic clergy from those who clung to the Puritan system — or thought they did — was what was known as Arianism. This was a doctrine that went back to the ancient Arius, who denied that Christ was of the same substance as God — a distinction that, if it did not actually deny Christ's divinity, at least made him inferior to the Father.

All three of these doctrines appeared first, apparently, among the rationalistic Anglican preachers of England; but this Anglican rationalism found its way into the minds and the sermons of a number of the New England preachers who were occupying pulpits formerly filled by the most rigorous Puritans.

Among the most distinguished of the first true exponents of the new liberalized and humanized religion in New England was Jonathan Mayhew, minister of the West Church in Boston. Strongly influenced by Samuel Clarke and other English exponents of the Enlightenment, Mayhew openly acknowledged his Arminianism and preached a "natural" religion. God, for him, was a kindly sovereign, who "governs his great family, his universal Kingdom, according to those general rules and maxims which are in themselves most wise and good, such as the wisest and best kings govern by . . . perfect goodness, love itself, is his very essence, in a peculiar sense; immeasurable, immutable, universal and everlasting love."[3] This was a far cry from the stern, literal-minded God of the literal-minded Puritans, and it shows both the influence of Newtonian science and the humanitarianism of the Enlightenment.

The logical implication of the natural religion of the radical wing of the English Newtonians involved the rejection of both revelation and the doctrine of the divinity of Christ, a position that logically anticipated Unitarianism. Jonathan Mayhew, in Boston, skirted the edges of Unitarianism without ever clearly explaining it. For him, God was a God of love; salvation was largely a matter of moral striving for goodness; God rewards the well-doers and punishes those who willfully do evil. For religion, with Mayhew, is no longer complete submission to God's inscrutable purpose for God's unspeakable glory, but, rather, a religion of love, for the promotion of human happiness, which was the true and kindly purpose of the benevolent God:

> We must suppose that the *end* of all God's commandments, must be the advancement of the happiness of his creatures, and not for his own. . . . Piety, or the love of God is the first and principle thing in religion. . . . The love of our neighbour . . . necessarily flows from the love of God. . . . It is practical religion, the love of God, and a life of righteousness and charity, proceeding from faith in Christ and the gospel, that denominates us good men and good christians. . . . Not any *enthusiastic fervors* of spirit — Not a firm *perswasion* that we are *elected* of God, and that our *names are written in the book of life.*[4]

Mayhew, under the influence of Newtonianism and Dr. Samuel Clarke, taught that there is a "natural" difference between right and wrong. Truth and right are real parts of nature, as real as matter itself. And "since *truth* and *right* have a real existence in nature, independent on the *sentiments* and *practices* of men, they do not necessarily follow the multitude, or major part: nor ought we to make *number* the cri-

[3] Jonathan Mayhew: *Two Sermons on the Nature, Extent and Perfection of the Divine Goodness* (Boston, 1763), pp. 23–4, 44.
[4] Jonathan Mayhew, *Seven Sermons* (Boston, 1749), pp. 133–46.

terion of the true religion. Men are fickle and various and contradictory in their opinions and practices : but truth and moral rectitude are things fixed, stable and uniform, having their foundation in the nature of things." [5] God was a God of a Newtonian universe — a God of love and of reason, of natural order and natural goodness.

Here was a deep and bitter conflict in religion, the conflict between the Puritan God of glory, dominating and subjecting all existence, in-

Leaders of American Religious Thought : Jonathan Mayhew.
Mezzotint by Richard Jennys.

[By courtesy of the Museum of Fine Arts, Boston]

cluding man, for his own sake, and the rationalistic God of goodness and mercy, the creator and lawgiver of the universe, to be sure, but one who leaves man free, within the framework of natural laws, to work out his own destiny. Rationalism was not only freeing men's minds ; it was freeing their souls as well.

Nor was Mayhew alone in his naturalism, his rationalistic religion of benevolence. There were many Americans who had so far departed from the Puritan tradition as to make the happiness of man, rather than the glory of God, the chief desideratum of religion — even of God himself. Charles Chauncy, a contemporary and colleague of Mayhew's, carried the implications of the benevolence of God even farther than Mayhew. He, too, was deeply influenced by Samuel Clarke, and ac-

[5] Ibid., p. 117.

cepted Clarke's statement that "'Tis goodness that finishes the idea of *God*, and represents him to us under the lovely character of the *best* as well as greatest Being in the universe. . . . Immense and eternal goodness, goodness all powerful and all-wise, goodness invested with supreme dominion, and tempering the rigor of unrelenting justice: This is indeed the description of a Perfect Being; a character truely worthy of God!"[6]

Chauncy could not stomach the Puritan doctrine of predestination, which, in addition to its implied doctrine of the moral helplessness of man, logically appeared to him to make God the author of evil. God is good, not evil, and goodness in God "is the *same thing* with goodness in all other intelligent moral beings." Far from placing his own glory above the happiness of men, God in his goodness wishes only the happiness of mankind. Man is "an *intelligent moral agent;* having within himself an *ability* and *freedom* to will, as well as to *do*, in opposition to necessity from any extraneous cause whatever."[7] God, "the Supreme Being . . . communicates good by *general laws*, whose operation he does not counter-act, but concurs with, in a *regular uniform* course." Evil, he says, was "introduced by *ourselves*, against the manifest *tendency* of those laws which [God] was pleased to establish, in order to effect [the world's] *greater good*, so far as it could reasonably and wisely be done. And that this end is not accomplished, is wholly chargeable to that *abuse* of our faculties, whereby we have perverted the *tendency* of those laws, which would otherwise have operated to its taking effect."[8] God is good, and operates through natural laws for the promotion of human happiness. Evil is man-made, the effect of man's misuse of his rational faculties. And the way to combat evil is by reasonable, practical benevolence, which is also the way and the plan of God.

Obviously the implications of these ideals were little short of revolutionary. The Puritan concept of an arbitrary, self-centered, and glory-loving God is gone, and with it the Puritan concept of original sin and the corrupt nature of man. In their place is the concept of a loving and benevolent God, who directs the universe according to a dependable plan; man, from being utterly contemptible in the eyes of God, is dignified, rational, good — capable of sharing the good life and living it. The end of life and of religion is human happiness, which is available to all by the use of reason. Here, on the eve of the American Revolution, was a religion of faith in men.

---

[6] Quoted by Charles Chauncy in his *The Benevolence of the Deity, Fairly and Impartially Considered* (Boston, 1784), Introduction, p. iv.

[7] Ibid., title page.

[8] Ibid., pp. 67, 68–9.

It would be a mistake, however, to think of the religious rationalism of Mayhew and Chauncy as ending for all time the Puritan outlook. For Puritanism was essentially an effort to control human destiny by the elimination or control of sin or evil. This effort at control differed from the plan of the religious rationalists chiefly in its belief that the will of God for the betterment of the world was to be read literally in the words of the Bible, whereas Mayhew and Chauncy believed the divine will was to be achieved by a rationalistic conformity with the divine "plan" of the universe. So far as actual conduct was concerned, both Mayhew and Chauncy expected human beings to behave almost as circumspectly as their Puritan forebears; not because God had explicitly commanded it so, but simply because it was "reasonable." Puritanism, in other words, did not die with Mayhew and Chauncy; it merely shifted its ground from "revelation" to "reason." The attitude of mind that expected men to control their affairs and their destiny by control of themselves in the conduct of their private lives remained.[9]

The link between Newtonianism and religion was explicit in many of the leaders of American religious thought. Jared Eliot, of Connecticut, found no conflict between science and revelation; both, for him, were the witnesses of God:

> When we lift up our Eyes to the Heavenly Bodies over our Heads, behold their Motions, consider their Magnitude, Distance, and Influences, can we think them other than the Works of some Intelligent Being? View this lower World, the Stability of some parts of it, the Mutability of other, the Beauty and Harmony of all, can we think these things came by Chance? . . . The characters of a Divine Being [are] written so plainly upon the face of this visible Creation that he that runs may read it: it is written as with the pen of Iron and with the point of a Diamond.[10]

Ebenezer Gay, preaching the Dudleian lecture at Harvard in 1759 on "natural religion," found that man's impulses to religion are a part of his nature; the force of righteousness was part of the natural system of the universe; morality was like the force of gravity: "There may be something in the intelligent moral world analogous to Attraction [the force of gravity] in the material System — something that inclines and draws Men toward God, the Centre of their Perfection, and consummate Object of their Happiness; and which, if its Energy were not obstructed, would as certainly procure such Regularity in the

---

[9] See, for example, Mayhew's *Christian Sobriety: Being Eight Sermons on Titus II. 6.* (Boston, 1763), and Chauncy's *Benevolence of the Deity*, Part III.

[10] Jared Eliot: *The Two Witnesses; or, Religion Supported by Reason and Divine Revelation* (New London, 1736), p. 8.

States and Actions of all intelligent Beings in the spiritual World, as that of Attraction doth in the Positions and Motions of all the Bodies in the material World."[11]

Samuel Quincy, preaching in Charleston, expressed a similar doctrine of rationalism in religion :

> Christianity is then a rational Religion, and those who deny it can, or ought to be maintained upon rational Principles, do in Effect give it up. For is not Reason the only Faculty of the Soul that God has given us, to render us capable of Religion : And would Men persuade us to lay it aside, in order to become more religious ? A monstrous Absurdity! 'Tis true, Reason is fallible, weak, and liable to be imposed on : But still it is the only Guide we have to direct us in our Searches after Truth ; for without it we could neither distinguish Good from Evil, nor Truth from Falshood, and might as well embrace a false Opinion, as a right one ; and could be no more accountable to our Maker for the one, than for the other.[12]

Science and rationalism were one in their influence on religion. And their chief effect in America was to make the minds and the souls of men more free. Naturally enough, an almost inevitable by-product of this ideal was the growth and spread of a true religious toleration — of which more later.

Samuel Johnson and the Anglican upsurge

If rational discontent with the old, monolithic Puritanism of their fathers led Mayhew and Chauncy into a position closely approximating Unitarianism, it led another New England divine, Samuel Johnson, out of Congregationalism entirely, into the more rationalistic Church of England.

For Samuel Johnson, educated at Yale, had discovered, in the "well-chosen library of new books collected by Mr. Dummer, agent for the Colony [of Connecticut]," the writings of Bacon, Boyle, Newton, Tillotson, Locke, and others of the English Enlightenment, and the discovery changed his entire way of life. This "conversion," together with his unhappiness over the provincialism and the doctrinal squabblings of the New England Congregationalists, led him in 1722 to become an Anglican and to take orders in the English Church.

Johnson was one of the more dramatic exemplars of the American "discovery of England" in the eighteenth century. He immediately became one of the exponents of that "colonialism" which looked upon all things American as primitive and unrefined, as compared with the cul-

---

[11] Ebenezer Gay : *Natural Religion Revealed* (Boston, 1759), p. 13.
[12] Samuel Quincy : *Twenty Sermons* . . . (Boston, 1750), p. 12.

ture of England, and he consciously set about to raise the level of the culture of his native land. This "colonial" or "provincial" attitude was typical of the more conservative elements in American cultural life. The discovery of the higher culture of other nations may be, perhaps, a necessary phase in the process of awakening to the possibility of producing a rational culture of one's own; in any case this is just what happened, not only to Samuel Johnson but also to many other Americans like him.

Johnson, under the influence of the new rationalism and particularly of Bishop George Berkeley, who carried his particular type of rationalism straight into idealism, adopted Berkeley's subjective idealism as his own. His philosophy, however, was of less importance to him than his religion, and it was as an Anglican divine and as an educator that he thought of himself as doing his most significant work.

Johnson, like Chauncy and Mayhew, was repelled by extreme Calvinism. Like them, too, he profoundly distrusted the emotional religious fervor that swept up and down the colonies in the years following his contact with Berkeley, and he consciously set himself to combat the "enthusiasm" that marked the so-called Great Awakening and its leaders. But he was far too conservative to follow "such loose thinkers as Mayhew, who can scarcely be accounted better christians than the Turks. . . ."[13] His own solution of the religious problem was a sort of middle course between the Scylla of Puritan predestinarianism and the Charybdis of Mayhew's extreme rationalism. He would not deny the existence of sin and the necessity for regeneration; but he would not accept the Calvinistic helplessness of man either. "May not one who is not yet thus entirely devoted to God, be brought by the assistance of common grace to be serious and really solicitous for salvation; so as being deeply sensible of his own guilt and weakness, earnestly to cry to God for help and to strive in earnest that he may be qualified for God's help?"[14] Salvation was necessary, to be sure; but it was to be earned, or, at least, God's willingness to help the sinner was to be won by earnest effort on the sinner's part. God is personally interested in every human being, and will help him; if everything is fatally predestined by God, what real encouragement is there for a man to strive to be good, and what justice could there be in punishing him for behavior that he cannot avoid?

Here, again, is a certain rationalism in religion. More than with Mayhew and Chauncy, it is the old drama of salvation, but restated in terms of human dignity rather than depravity. Salvation becomes a

[13] Herbert and Carol Schneider, eds.: *Samuel Johnson, President of King's College, His Career and Writings* (4 vols., New York, 1929), I, 346.
[14] Ibid., IV, 179–80.

process of regeneration that embodies, in religious guise, the eighteenth century's belief in progress and the perfectibility of man through education. But Johnson was no republican like Chauncy. He believed in order, discipline, and respect for the powers that be, and the Anglican Church seemed to him to be an effective way of maintaining order and discipline in religion while preserving the right of the individual to work out his own salvation within the churchly institution; he even hoped and labored for the day when an Anglican episcopacy might become a religious bond binding the colonies to the culture of the mother country.

The yearning for a closer religious tie with England was of course not peculiar to Johnson. The Anglican Church was either officially established or occupied a favored position in the colonies of New York, Virginia, North Carolina, South Carolina, Georgia, and Maryland, and many good Anglicans believed that its ineffectiveness was due to the fact that there was no episcopal authority in America to supervise and direct its work. Thus efforts were made from the beginning of the eighteenth century onward to have a bishopric established in the colonies, and Samuel Johnson was one of the leaders of the movement. "Pray, my lord," he wrote to the Archbishop of Canterbury, primate of England, "will our dear mother country have no bowels of compassion for her poor depressed, destitute children of the established church (a million of them) dispersed into these remote regions?" [15]

The establishment of an American bishopric was opposed by some in England, on the ground that such a step would be one taken in the direction of American independence; that, in other words, keeping the episcopal see for America in London was one means of keeping the Americans in a due sense of subjection to England. To this shortsighted argument Johnson replied that the exact contrary was likely to be true. This argument, he wrote to the Archbishop of Canterbury as early as 1737, "is certainly so far from being an objection that [it] is a very great reason why we should be provided for, and that as speedily as possible; since they are the dissenters only, of whom there is a vast body, (by much the prevailing number) in these colonies, from whom there can be any apprehension, and from whom there may in time be reason for it; they being generally people of anti-monarchial as well as anti-episcopal principles; while, on the other hand, any imagination of independency [from] England, or any tending thereunto, is what is abhorred of all the people of our church in these plantations." [16]

But the Anglicans in America were not as united in their loyalty as Johnson thought. The Anglican pastors in the southern colonies had fallen into disrepute with their northern brethren, who probably exag-

[15] Ibid., I, 361.   [16] Ibid., I, 88.

gerated their worldliness, and even Johnson himself had to admit that the southerners were not anxious to accept the discipline of an American episcopate or a closer tie with England. "The southern clergy," he wrote in 1765, "as far as I can learn [are totally averse to bishops]. They are now their own masters, quite independent of the people, and therefore do not choose a Master! Besides, its too notorious that no bishop, unless a very abandoned one, would put up with the lives they generally lead." [17]

Anglicanism was, indeed, a house divided, with a pro-bishop and an anti-bishop party. Johnson's description of the situation was not strictly accurate, for the more democratic parishes of the church, particularly in the southern colonies, were coming increasingly to control their pastors. The Reverend Jonathan Boucher complained bitterly of the insistence of the parishes upon the right to elect their curates regardless of the bishops; it was a practice that had become general throughout the south. The provincial legislature of South Carolina passed a law to protect the clerics from the vicissitudes of this nascent parish democracy by providing that, once elected, pastors could not be removed. But the parishes evaded the law by employing no pastor unless he first agreed not to ask for permanent election to the rectorate, and even then only for a year at a time. For, the Bishop of London's commissary in Charleston ruefully reported, "the Principles of most of the Colonists in America are independent in Matters of Religion, as well as republican in those of Government." [18] Thus was democracy creeping into religion, even Anglicanism, the most aristocratic religion of them all.

The more conservative Anglican leaders, like Johnson, believed fervently that the establishment of an American bishopric would bring order to the church in America, would have a salutary effect upon the sobriety and the morality of the people, and would encourage a stronger loyalty among the Americans toward England, to counterbalance, as Johnson had said, the independent, "anti-monarchial" tendencies of the vast number of American dissenters. The more radical, democratic wing of the Anglicans, however, were not at all convinced of the necessity for an American episcopate; indeed, many Anglicans, even, distrusted the ceremonial ritual of the church. They, as Americans, were practical men: as Robert Carter put it, "Let others take what courses they please in the bringing up of their posterity, I resolve the principles of our holy religion shall be instilled into mine betimes;

[17] Quoted in William W. Sweet : *Religion in Colonial America* (New York, 1942), p. 70.
[18] Library of Congress : Fulham MSS. [transcripts] No. 230 ; Charles Martyn to the Lord Bishop of London, Charleston, S.C., October 20, 1765.

as I am of the Church of England way, so I desire they should be. But the high-flown up top notions and the great stress that is laid upon ceremonies, any farther than decency and conformity, are what I cannot come into the reason of. Practical godliness is the substance — these are but the shell." [19]

The clergy of Virginia and Maryland, indeed, just prior to the Revolution, apparently feared an Anglican episcopate in America as an agency of British control. The "left wing" of Anglicanism in America was moving toward greater simplicity in ritual and more local autonomy in church government. It was this wing that probably most genuinely represented the American mood in religion. On the other hand, Johnson and others who believed like him felt that the establishment of an American episcopate would do more than merely restore efficiency to an inefficient establishment. Theirs was a sort of "provincial" or "colonial" state of mind, a feeling of inferiority and a sense of cultural dependency derived from a discovery of the imagined greater richness and maturity of the mother culture. The "Toryism" of the right-wing Anglicans, therefore, was a sort of renascent patriotism for England and things English, as distinguished from the newly emergent patriotism of America for America and the American way.

Needless to say, the American rationalists, led by Mayhew and Chauncy, fought the idea of an American episcopate with all their power, especially after 1765. It was very easy for them to see in such a step another effort of the mother country to establish over the colonies an unwarranted extension of its control, and they cited certain instances of lobbying and interference in American affairs by the Anglican Society for the Propagation of the Gospel in Foreign Parts to prove their point. Such a move toward the strengthening of those Anglican and Tory forces that stood in natural opposition to the American trend toward autonomy might not have had any significant effect upon the course of events, but it certainly was easy for the Americans to believe it would.

The opposition to the proposed Anglican episcopate is thus to be linked with the political struggle of the provincial assemblies for increased autonomy, on the one side, and with the American trend toward democracy, even within the church itself, especially in the southern colonies, on the other. As William Smith put it, in his *History of New York*, written in the 1750's :

> . . . the body of the people, are for an equal, universal, toleration of protestants, and utterly averse to any kind of ecclesiastical establishment. The dissenters, though fearless of each other, are all jealous of

[19] Louis B. Wright, ed.: *Letters of Robert Carter, the Commercial Interests of a Virginia Gentleman* (San Marino, 1940), p. 25.

the episcopal party, being apprehensive that the countenance they may
have from home, will foment a lust for dominion, and enable them, in
process of time, to subjugate and oppress their fellow subjects. . . .
For though his majesty has no other subjects upon whose loyalty he
can more firmly depend, yet an abhorrence of persecution, under any
of its appearances, is so deeply rooted in the people of this plantation;
that as long as they continue their numbers and interest in the assembly, no attempt will probably be made upon the rights of conscience,
without endangering the publick repose.[20]

One of the most robust and vigorous of the seeds of liberty in America,
surely, was that of liberty in religion!

Deism

If Mayhew and Chauncy are called Unitarians rather than Deists
it is because they retained, despite their essential rationalism, their beliefs in many of the more irrational elements of revealed Christianity.
The more radical English Deists, and their followers in America, discarded everything about religion that could not be made to conform to
the dictates of reason. Thus they took the position that religious ideas
should be tested by the scientific method just as all other ideas should,
and, having discarded all that could not stand the test of reason, these
Deists retained only three basic concepts, which they claimed were
common to all religions. These were the belief in one omnipotent God,
the belief that God's plan for the universe includes virtuous living for
men, and the belief in a life after death in which the virtuous in this
life will be rewarded and evil-doers punished. For these extremists
revelation was completely ruled out of the scheme of things: the universe operates according to the laws of nature laid down by God,
which God himself does not violate; it is man's business to find out by
the use of his reason, given him for the purpose, what the laws of nature and nature's God are, and to live accordingly.

This radical Deism made little headway in America until near the
middle of the eighteenth century, although Benjamin Franklin had absorbed the ideas of Anthony Collins and Lord Shaftesbury even before he left Boston for Philadelphia at the age of seventeen. Franklin
became more thoroughly acquainted with the ideas of Deism as a
typesetter in London, and it was in answer to William Wollaston's
Dissertation on Natural Religion that he wrote his youthful *Dissertation on Liberty and Necessity, Pleasure and Pain,* in which he attempted, as he later described it, "to prove the doctrine of fate, from
the supposed attributes of God." In it he took the position that God,
being infinitely good and wise, had created the best possible world;

[20] William Smith, Jr.: *History of New York* (Albany, 1814), pp. 334–5.

evil did not exist; everything that happened was the result of God's inflexible edicts expressed in natural law : even the idea of the continuance of personality after death was rejected. Franklin soon abandoned this extreme position, however, and repudiated his youthful "erratum." [21] In fact, this early pamphlet was hardly more than an intellectual exercise in close reasoning, as was the unpublished pamphlet on prayer, written in 1730, in which he logically demolished the validity of prayer and the entire argument that the universe and all things in it were ordained of God. In 1728 he formulated his *Articles of Belief and Acts of Religion,* which was another result of speculative thinking that produced an astonishing but reasonable sort of polytheism, for, he says, "I believe that Man is not the most perfect Being but one, rather that as there are many Degrees of Being his Inferiors, so there are many Degrees of Being superior to him." [22]

But Franklin soon discovered that speculation and pure logic are likely to prove barren. "The great uncertainty I found in metaphysical reasonings disgusted me, and I quitted that kind of reading and study for others more satisfactory." In his violent reaction against the inflexibility of Calvinism he had swung to the opposite extreme of Deism, only to fall back, eventually, upon the customary position of the moderate Deists because — and this is typical of Franklin — it was more practicable! As he says :

> I grew convinc'd that *truth, sincerity* and *integrity* in dealings between man and man were of the utmost importance to the felicity of life. . . . Revelation had indeed no weight with me, as such; but I entertain'd an opinion that, though certain actions might not be bad *because* they were forbidden by it, or good *because* it commanded them, yet probably these actions might be forbidden *because* they were bad for us, or commanded *because* they were beneficial to us, in their own natures, all the circumstances of things considered. [23]

Franklin's religion thus became a sort of religious pragmatism. True, he restated his beliefs, late in life, to Ezra Stiles, as follows :

> I believe in one God, creator of the Universe. That he governs it by his Providence. That he ought to be worshipped. That the most acceptable Service we render to him is doing good to his other children. That the soul of Man is immortal, and will be treated with Justice in another Life respecting its Conduct in this. These I take to be the fundamental Principles of all sound Religion, and I regard them as you do

---

[21] Benjamin Franklin : *The Life and Writings of Benjamin Franklin,* edited by Albert H. Smyth (10 vols., New York, 1905–7), I, 277.

[22] Reprinted, ibid., II, 91–100.

[23] Ibid., I, 296.

in whatever Sect I meet with them. As to Jesus of Nazareth, my Opinion of whom you particularly desire, I think the System of Morals and his Religion, as he left them to us, the best the World ever saw or is likely to see; but I apprehend it has received various corrupting changes, and I have, with most of the present Dissenters in England, some Doubts as to his Divinity.[24]

Which was nothing more than the position generally held by the Deists. Still, for Franklin religion was always, after his early speculative years, more a matter of practice than of theory; for, as he wrote to his father in 1738, "the Scriptures assure me, that at the last day we shall not be examined what we *thought*, but what we *did;* and our recommendation will not be, that we said, *Lord! Lord!* but that we did good to our fellow creatures." [25]

This Deism was shared by many of the American scientists and other intellectual laymen. Archibald Kennedy, of New York, was typical of this group. For him:

Religion . . . however distinguished, or disguised, is nothing more, nor nothing less, than a sincere Belief in *One supreme intelligent Being*, the Author and Preserver of all Things. . . . Love your God, pay him those Acknowledgments due, with a Spirit of Sincerity and Truth; and treat your Neighbour, that is, the whole Race of Mankind, with Charity and Meekness, as you would incline they should treat you, in every Circumstance of Life. Here is all that is truly essential in Religion; and what most profess, but few, very few, practice.[26]

The only American Deist to write a full-length and systematic outline of his beliefs was Ethan Allen, of Connecticut and Vermont. Allen's book was actually published after the Revolution; but it seems to have been based upon thinking he had done as a young man in Connecticut. Allen was a son of the frontier, and his Deism, which reaches the proportions rather of a philosophy than of a religion, derives from a combination of his early instruction and his experiences in the hard and practical life in the Vermont settlements. As a youth he apparently heard of the English rationalists through Thomas Young, an itinerant physician, by whom his rebellion against orthodox Calvinism, and specifically against Jonathan Edwards, was abetted and encouraged; and it was probably in collaboration with Young that Allen first planned to put his beliefs into writing. But his early bent toward rationalism was probably strengthened by the observations of the natural world by his precocious mind in the course of his long and active life in war and

[24] Ibid., X, 84; cf. I, 340–1.
[25] Ibid., II, 215.
[26] Archibald Kennedy : *A Speech said to have been Delivered Some Time Before the Close of the Late Sessions* (New York, 1755), pp. 22–3.

peace in the sparsely settled wilderness of the upper Connecticut Valley. His one rule, he says, was that "I have invariably endeavored to make reason my guide through the whole contents of the system, and expect that they who read it, will approve or disapprove it, as they may judge, whether it accords with that original principle or not." [27]

Allen knew very well that the orthodox would attack him for his radical, anti-Puritan rationalism. "But I am a hardy Mountaineer," he wrote, "and have been accustomed to the ravages and horrors of War and Captivity, and scorn to be intimidated by threats; if they fright me, they must absolutely produce some of their tremendous fire, and give me a sensative scorching." [28] The frontiersman had worked out his religious system of reason and nature for himself, and the frontiersman was ready to defend it, come hell-fire and brimstone!

Allen's religion was simply this: There is one God:

> The Laws of Nature having subjected mankind to a state of absolute dependence on something out of, and manifestly beyond themselves . . . gave them the first conception of a superior principle existing. . . . But this sense of dependency, which results from experience and reasoning on the facts . . . has uniformly established the knowledge of our dependence . . . which necessarily involves or contains in it the idea of a ruling power, or that there is a GOD, which ideas are synonimous.[29] [God is] unchangeably and infinitely just and good, as well as infinitely wise and powerful. . . . Of all possible systems infinite wisdom must have eternally discerned the best, and infinite justice, goodness and truth approved it, and infinite power effected it. . . . This conclusion is meant to respect the creation and providence of God only, and not to affect the liberty of man, or to infringe the morality of his actions.[30] . . . The eternity and infinity of God necessarily imply the eternity and infinity of creation and providence. . . . : This doctrine of eternal creation and providence, as also the infinitude of it, may give offence to such persons who may read this book, and who have habituated themselves to trace their genealogy from Adam as the first rational finite being.[31]

Beings, including men, are finite; they are parts of an infinite and eternal succession of finite beings. But

> The providence of God supports the universe, and enables rational agents to act in certain limited spheres with a derived freedom. . . .
> To suppose the conduct or demeanor of mankind to have been prede-

---

[27] Ethan Allen: *Reason the Only Oracle of Man* (Bennington, Vt., 1784), p. vi.

[28] Quoted in C. Woodbridge Riley: *American Philosophy, the Early Schools* (New York, 1907), p. 46.

[29] Allen, op. cit., pp. 25–6.

[30] Ibid., p. 37.

[31] Ibid., pp. 62–3.

termined by God, and affected merely by his providence, is a manifest infringement of his justice and goodness in the constitution of our mental powers . . . [and, further,] it is injurious to the divine character . . . as it would make God the author of moral evil . . . or exclude moral evil from the universe.[32]

God is interested in human behavior; good actions are pleasing to him and evil actions are displeasing. Men are distinguished from the "natural" or "animal" world precisely by their rational power to exercise moral choice, and evil results from the conscious choice of evil actions. But evil, or sin, is finite, and relative to the finite limitations of human nature. The Puritan doctrine of eternal damnation is therefore untenable, since sin is not infinite, and since it would be incompatible with the infinite goodness of God. On the contrary, rational man is in a constant state of self-improvement; his evil choices result in his unhappiness, his good choices result in "happifying" his life and he learns and progresses toward goodness by his experience. This process of improvement, this rational progress, through "agency and probation" will continue, Allen thought, in the life after death.

It will be seen from all this that Allen's religion was a religion of nature and reason. Typical of the eighteenth century, it embodied the faith of many eighteenth-century intellectuals in a universe governed by the laws of nature, in the ability of human reason to understand and live according to those laws, and in the continuing progress of human improvement, even after death. His rejection of the absolutism of Puritanism and his faith in the adaptibility and progressive improvement of human nature by the use of reason, or intelligence, was substantiated by his experiences on the American frontier. Allen, like so many other Americans, borrowed the ideas of European thinkers that seemed, on the one hand, to explain and justify the American experience and, on the other, to be borne out by it.

Of the scientists, Cadwallader Colden was unquestionably the most radical in his religious beliefs. For the study of the universe, which led him to the theory that he explained in his book, *The Principles of Action in Matter,* brought him so far toward a completely materialistic explanation of the universe as almost to rule any supernatural agency out of it entirely. In his *First Principles of Morality,* published in 1746, he had offered a materialistic form of hedonism according to which the virtues derive from men's desire to avoid pain and enjoy pleasure. As his philosophy developed, he came to believe that intelligence is a sort of substance, or mind, that is coextensive with matter and that exercises an influence upon the individual mind to produce the sort

[32] Ibid., pp. 83, 88.

of reactions presently called instinctive. In this he seems to have been a sort of pantheist; but he evaded that accusation, too, and admitted that there must have been a great creator of the universe, and that there was some activating force in it that might be called intelligence, or at least some substance with power to act on its own volition. But, as he wrote to Alexander Garden, of Charleston, in 1757, "I cannot conceive power or action or property without some thing which has that power or something which acts and this thing I call Substance. I have no other notion or conception of substance but as the substratum of power and action and if this be desired I cannot conceive how the existence of any substance or thing can be proved distinct from the Supreme Being." [33]

Colden entered into a long and profound correspondence with Samuel Johnson, the idealist, over the problems of religion and philosophy. Johnson invited him to take the short step necessary to become an Anglican idealist like himself; but this Colden was unwilling to do. Johnson wrote to him, nevertheless, and not without a certain satisfaction: "You suppose indeed an active medium which you call matter intervening between the Deity and our Minds perceiving, to the action of which in perceiving they are passive; which . . . does not affect me, so long as you allow all action throughout all sensible Nature to derive originally from Him [God]." [34]

Colden thus turned out to be a sort of materialistic Deist, who, although he did not give up the idea of a great creator-intelligence as the "first cause" in the universe, yet went far beyond the other Deists in the direction of pure materialism. His position, resting as it did upon what he believed to be the findings of Newtonian science, was probably the most radical one reached in colonial America.

THE CONSERVATIVE REACTION

But the conservatives in religion, the true religious descendants of seventeenth-century Calvinism, whether Puritan or Anglican, were not disposed to give up the old way in the face of the inroads of Arminianism, Arianism, Pelagianism, or even plain rationalism, without a fight. And there rose up prophets of the old order to save the way of their fathers from oblivion, and the world from its own consequent destruction.

Of these, for example, Joseph Bellamy set out to save "true religion" from both the diluting effect of rationalism on one side and the con-

[33] Cadwallader Colden: *The Letters and Papers of Cadwallader Colden* (*Collections of The New York Historical Society*, Vols. L–LVI, LXVII–LXVIII), V, 153–4.

[34] Ibid., III, 399.

suming fire of "enthusiasm" on the other. For him, true religion "consists in a real Conformity to the Law, and in a genuine Compliance with the Gospel." [35] Needless to say, this meant the law of the Old Testament and the gospel of the New, interpreted as Bellamy thought the Puritan fathers would have interpreted it.

A much more powerful and more strategically placed defender of Israel was Thomas Clap, president of Yale. Clap made Yale the defensive center of the old faith, and he was supported by the fellows of the college, who officially reaffirmed their adherence to the Saybrook abridgment of the Westminster Confession of Faith and their determination that the college should propagate the doctrines contained in this statement of the Puritan creed; future presidents and fellows would be required to adhere publicly to this creed, and if they changed their minds, they would be expected to resign. Students of the college were required to go to the sermons based upon the old way; even Anglican students were permitted to go to their own church only on communion days; and in 1752 Yale created a professorship in divinity, as explained in the Saybrook creed, to protect the boys against the corrosive influences of both rationalism and Anglicanism.

Clap examined all the new doctrines — free will, happiness as the end of life, the innate goodness of man, the negative nature of sin, and so on — and rejected them all as perversions of the true doctrine. As for the toleration being preached by Mayhew and the other liberals, "if every particular Person has a Right to judge for *himself*; then surely *publick Bodies* and *Communities of men* have a Right to judge *for themselves*, concerning their own publick State and Constitution; the Qualifications of their own Ministers and Instructors; and what Doctrines they would have preach'd to themselves and to their *Posterity.*" [36] In other words, if the Puritan community decided it would exclude all who disagreed with it, it had a right to do so. It appeared to him that there was a body of absolute, unalterable truths represented by Puritanism that were being destroyed by the newfangled ideas. Those who supposed there were no fundamental principles for salvation, he was sure, destroyed the fundamentals of the Christian religion. Either those fundamental truths were right or there was no such thing as religion. For himself, he said:

For my Part, I have critically and carefully, and I think, with the utmost Impartiality, examined into the Doctrines contained in our Cate-

[35] Joseph Bellamy: *True Religion Delineated; or, Experimental Religion, as distinguished from Formality on the one Hand, and Enthusiasm on the other* . . . (Boston, 1750), p. 247.
[36] Thomas Clap: *A Brief History and Vindication of the Doctrines Received and Established in the Churches of New England* (New Haven, 1755), p. 25.

chism and Confession of Faith, and believe they are fully and plainly contained in the sacred Oracles of Truth, perfectly agreeable to Reason, and harmonious with each other; and that most of them are of the utmost Consequence to the Salvation of the Souls of Men. And therefore look upon myself in Duty bound, to do all that lies in my Power, to continue and propagate those Doctrines; especially in the College [Yale] committed to my Care, since that is the Fountain from whence our Churches must be supplied.[37]

But the greatest of all the defenders of the faith of the Puritan fathers was Jonathan Edwards, pastor of the church at Northampton, Massachusetts, the greatest theologian and philosopher that colonial America was to produce.

Edwards had come to the church at Northampton in 1726 as assistant to his grandfather, the elderly Solomon Stoddard. He had been educated for the ministry at Yale and had passed through a singularly intense personal religious experience, an experience that seemed to him to justify a belief in the necessity for conversion. It was not, however, a dramatic emotional crisis in his life, but rather what he called "a new Sense of Things." As a result of this "conversion" he had come to see God everywhere and had given himself up wholly to God. This experience was the key to both his religious work and his philosophy; for he dedicated his life to bringing the beauty of similar conversions to other men, and his philosophy was elaborated to explain his conviction that God, and the working of God's mind, were to be seen in everything in the universe.

Edwards's own conversion was the sort of mystical experience that he believed God was pleased to vouchsafe to all his elect; and it was this emphasis upon the individual and his mystical experience of God that made Edwards's preaching so effective. He was never a thundering evangelist, however. Quite the contrary; for with quiet voice and very few gestures he led his hearers to a sense of their need of salvation by simple, logical persuasion, fortified by illustrations drawn, without being too specific, from their daily experience. Edwards was a quiet man, and most of his sermons deal with the beauties of religion and of the Christian life, and the principles underlying them; it was only in moments of revivalism that he preached the awful consequences of sin in the relatively few sermons for which he is popularly remembered. The following passage is typical of Edwards at his best:

The beauty of trees, Plants, and flowers with which God has bespangled the Earth is Delightsome, the beautiful frame of the body of Man, especially in its Perfection is Astonishing, the beauty of the moon and stars, is wonderfull, the beauty of highest heaven, is transcendent, the

[37] Ibid., p. 37.

Excellency of angels and the saints in light, is very Glorious, but it is all Deformity, and Darkness in Comparison of the higher Glories and beauties of the Creator of all.[38]

He had come into contact with Newtonian science at Yale ; he understood it, and was something of a scientist in his own right. But the

Leaders of American Religious Thought : Jonathan Edwards. Portrait by Joseph Badger.
[By courtesy of Yale University Art Gallery]

wonders of the universe portrayed by science were for him only the revealed wonders and transcendent beauties of God. It would be a mistake, therefore, to think of Edwards as only a terrifying preacher of hell-fire and damnation. Serious he was, and earnest, to a degree seldom equaled even in that New England of serious men. But the dominant theme in his religion is beauty, rather than ugliness ; the goodness of God, rather than the sinfulness of men. And the old Puritan system seemed to him to be the only one that rested logically upon that beauty, holiness, and glory.

As religion was the great and all-dominating theme in his own life,

[38] Quoted in Ola Winslow : *Jonathan Edwards* (New York, 1940), p. 139.

he aspired to awaken his congregation to a sense of the importance it ought to have with them. The trouble had begun, Edwards thought, in the so-called half-way covenant of 1662, by which the Puritan fathers, faced with a decline in church membership, had agreed to admit to a sort of half-way membership persons who had been baptized but could not testify to full and complete conversion. Presently, some ministers and churches, particularly the Brattle Street Church in Boston, had begun to admit to the communion table these "half-way" members, those who "owned [or accepted] the covenant" but who could not testify to their visitation of divine grace. Edwards's own grandfather, Solomon Stoddard, had begun the practice in Southhampton, in the hope that the communion might be used as an agent to conversion as well as a sacrament for those in full church membership.

But conversion, for Edwards, was the central core of the entire Christian experience, and communion was the sacred symbol of the fellowship of those who had been converted. He therefore felt not only that it should be restricted to those who had testified to their conversion and been accepted, but also that church membership should be restricted to those who had passed the church's test. At the same time, the wave of rationalistic "Arminianism" that was making headway among the intellectual leaders of New England was seriously undermining the old Puritan doctrine of predestination; while to the southward, in New Jersey and Pennsylvania, the Tennents had already begun to demonstrate the possibilities of revivalistic preaching among the common people when it played upon the emotions and the direct relationship of the individual to his God. It was probably a combination of motives, therefore, his interest in bringing the beauty of God to his people, his desire to defend the Puritan ideal of the glory of God, as he understood it, and his desire to capitalize upon the popular mood of revival, that inspired Edwards, in 1731, in a sermon that attracted widespread attention, to take a stand in defense of Calvinism against the "fashionable new divinity" of the rationalists. In this, his first published sermon, he reiterated the Calvinist position that God is all-powerful and that the happiness of man derives from showing forth God's glory; even man's yearning for God's grace is given him by God in the first place :

> There is an absolute and universal dependence of the redeemed on God. The nature and contrivance of our redemption is such, that the redeemed are in every thing directly, immediately, and entirely dependent on God : they are dependent on him for all, and are dependent on him every way. . . .
> And it is from mere grace that the benefits of Christ are applied to such and such particular persons. Those that are called and sanctified

are to attribute it alone to the good pleasure of God's goodness, by which they are distinguished. He is sovereign, and hath mercy on whom he will show mercy. . . .

The redeemed have all their *inherent* good in God. . . . They have spiritual excellency and joy by a kind of participation of God. They are made excellent by a communication of God's excellency. God puts his own beauty, *i.e.* his beautiful likeness, upon their souls. . . . The saints are beautiful and blessed by a communication of God's holiness and joy, as the moon and planets are bright by the sun's light. . . .

Hence those doctrines and schemes of divinity that are in any respect opposite to such an absolute and universal dependence on God, derogate from his glory, and thwart the design of our redemption. . . . They own a partial dependence on Christ, as he through whom we have life, as having purchased new terms of life, but still hold that the righteousness through which we have life is inherent in ourselves, as it was under the first covenant. Now whatever scheme is inconsistent with our *entire* dependence on God for all, and of having all of him, through him, and in him, it is repugnant to the design and tenor of the gospel, and robs it of that which God accounts its lustre and glory.[39]

This sermon attracted the immediate and enthusiastic attention of the conservative clergy. Here, they imagined, was a young man who would revivify a moribund Puritanism. It is clear from this sermon that Edwards was, indeed, opposed to the new "doctrines and schemes of divinity," because they seemed to rob God of his glory, his greatest attribute, and encourage presumption in man. And when it began to appear that God was stirring the people deeply toward a new seriousness, a new consciousness of things divine, he found it easy to believe that this was God's answer to the "Arminianism" and other heresies that were troubling the church in Israel.

This was the beginning of what he called a "very great awakening" among the people of all the colonies; and he at first looked upon the emotional phenomena that went with these stirrings as clearly the handiwork of God. As both preachers and hearers began to go to extreme excesses, however, and as the older churches began to be divided between the "old lights" and the "new lights," Edwards found it necessary to caution his people against spurious prophets and misleading experiences. He still looked upon the Great Awakening as God's counter weight against Arminianism; but he distrusted the "wild enthusiastical Sort of People," and especially deplored their tendency to separate from the old churches and set up new ones. But these things, for Edwards's life work, were not really significant; for him the question was still in 1749, after the crest of the Great Awakening had passed: "Whether . . .

---

[39] "God Glorified in Man's Dependence," in Jonathan Edwards : *The Works of Jonathan Edwards,* edited by Edward Hickman (2 vols., London, 1840), I, 3–7.

any ought to be admitted to the Communion and Privileges of Members of the visible Church of Christ in compleat Standing, but such as are in Possession, and in the Eye of the Church's Christian Judgment, godly or gracious Persons?" [40] And in his *Humble Inquiry*, published that year, he insisted, with all the power of the scripture at the command of his highly logical mind, that church membership should be restricted to those who could make a profession of real piety and that the sacrament of the Lord's supper should be closed to all but these saints who had been accepted into church membership. In other words, he thought of his life work as being the defense and vindication of Puritan Calvinism; his evangelism, powerful and dramatic though it was, was relatively incidental and unimportant.

But rationalism was on the march. Strict Calvinism was on the defensive against the attacks both of the rationalists and of the "enthusiasts," and Edwards had no idea of abandoning the battle. Since the conflict with Arminianism centered on the rationalists' attacks upon the Calvinists' doctrine of predestination and their apparent denial of the freedom of the human will, Edwards published what may well be his greatest work, *A careful and strict Enquiry into the modern prevailing Notions of . . . Freedom of the Will* (Boston, 1754).

In this book he carried the fight to the enemy; and with a logic that was as flawless as it was ultimately futile, he pointed out the inconsistencies of the doctrines of the rationalists — the essential goodness of man, the freedom of the human will to choose between good and evil, the claim that Calvinism makes God the author of sin, and all the rest. Basing his definition of the will upon John Locke, he assumed that man is a free moral agent; but since God has an absolute and certain knowledge of the actions of moral agents, as well as everything else in creation, it followed "of necessity" that individual men would choose good or evil and that God knew which they would choose. It could not be otherwise, indeed; for if God foresaw a man choosing one way and then, when the time came, the man chose something else, that would be, in effect, upsetting God's prior knowledge, which was unthinkable. Thus God's foreknowledge had the effect of a decree, although it was not actually a command: men did good or evil as God expected them to; but they did it as free agents, and were therefore praiseworthy or guilty according to their choice. So God, after all, was not the author of sin. Man was dependent upon him, to be sure, and God actually permitted him to commit sin, just as he permitted the crucifiers of Christ to commit that dreadful act. But he did not cause sin, any more than the sun,

---

[40] Jonathan Edwards: *An Humble Inquiry into the Rules of the Word of God, Concerning the Qualifications Requisite to a Compleat Standing and Full Communion in the Visible Christian Church* (Boston, 1749), p. 1.

which is a source of light and heat, causes darkness and cold; sin was
the result of man's own inability to choose good without God's guiding
assistance.

Edwards thus sustained what he thought was the Calvinistic doctrine of the human will as a free agent acting according to the "cer-
tainty" of God's expectations. But he was not yet through with his defense; and four years later he completed, just prior to his death in 1758,
his defense of the Calvinist doctrine of original sin, which was published
posthumously. The task of defending this tenet of Calvinism, however,
was not nearly so arduous as that of defending the doctrine of predestination. It is clear from mere observation, he said, that the wickedness of
men is "a prevailing effective Tendency in their Nature, to that Sin and
Wickedness, which implies their utter and eternal Ruin." [41] But the
testimony of the senses and of history is corroborated by the testimony
of the Bible, which, after all, is the final authority; and Edwards mar-
shals the Biblical evidence to prove his case. But the positive, beautiful side of the doctrine of original sin is its obverse side, the doctrine of
redemption; and this unspeakably beautiful drama of salvation is his
final and, as he thought, crushing, answer to the Pelagians. It seemed
to him that men were so obviously wicked, so patently in need of salvation, and, on the other hand, that the record of Christ's incarnation and
purchase of salvation for men was so clear, and the mystical experience
of salvation so sublimely convincing, that the denial of the doctrine
could only arise from ignorance and error.

Edwards was without doubt the greatest preacher and religious con-
troversialist that eighteenth-century America produced. He fought a
valiant fight, and did more than any other man, perhaps, to make Puritanism appear beautiful and reasonable: he was to Puritan theology
what Edward Taylor was to Puritan literature. But he was fighting
against his own time. Rationalism was on the march, and not Edwards
and Clap and all the others who sought to save Puritanism could stem
that tide. As a matter of fact, Edwards himself, more or less influenced
by the new rationalism that he had absorbed in the Yale library, was a
child of his time, and in both his philosophy of mystical idealism on the
one side and his appeal to emotionalism on the other he departed from
the theology and the practice of strict Puritanism in manners and to a
degree that would almost certainly have scandalized the Puritan fathers.

No, his reaction, the conservative reaction generally, like all such reactions, deluded itself: it could not have gone back to the original Puritanism, even if it had had no opposition. For the minds of the very
reactionaries themselves were too far advanced beyond those of their

[41] Jonathan Edwards: *The Great Christian Doctrine of Original Sin Defended* . . . (Boston, 1758), p. xv.

fathers. Given the eighteenth-century climate of opinion, the reaction was inevitably doomed to failure.

THE RELIGION OF THE COMMON MAN: THE SECTS

It would be a great mistake to assume that even a majority of the people followed the rationalistic religious leadership of Mayhew, Chauncy, Franklin, or Allen. The educated people, who could follow the arguments of these religious thinkers or who concerned themselves with the intellectual problems of religion, were relatively few. For most of the people religion was still the emotional and uncritical belief in God and the effort to do his will handed down to them by their fathers and grandfathers. The Enlightenment did have its effect upon the common people, especially through the rationalism and the Newtonianism of the almanacs; but its effect upon the religion of the common people was probably slight. Many of these people, particularly the non-British immigrants, carried on their religion without visible change; among the poor native Americans, the Scotch-Irish, and some of the Germans along the frontier, the middle of the eighteenth century was marked by an outburst of emotional, evangelical religion that was to some degree a protest against the coldness of that very rationalism that was splitting the older churches on the higher levels of leadership.

As for the great body of quiet, humble, and immigrant Americans, it will be recalled that at the beginning of the Protestant revolt there were many people who took the implications of Luther's teachings quite literally, and there sprang up a sect known as the Anabaptists who sought to get back to the pure, simple religion of the early Christians, with its supposed emphasis upon personal redemption, and who therefore revived the practice of adult baptism as an outward sign and symbol of the inward change. The central feature of this religious way was the inward, emotional experience of the individual and the direct relationship of the individual with God. Thus, while some of its leaders were educated men, many of them were entirely uneducated and depended upon direct inspiration in their preaching, and its appeal was generally to the poor and illiterate, who found in it an emotional escape from the sordidness and drabness of their daily lives.

A number of the sects that came from Germany to America in the late seventeenth and early eighteenth centuries were offshoots from the Mennonites, the original followers of Menno Simons. Menno, a Dutch Catholic priest who was converted to the doctrines of the Anabaptists, and particularly to the doctrine of the "inner light," succeeded in reorganizing some of the remnants of the Anabaptists after the wars of persecution against them, and his followers found refuge in Switzerland and Holland. There were other groups, however, of which some were influenced by Menno and some were not, who developed similar beliefs and practices, generally centering on the pietistic experience of the individual believer. Such were the Schwenkfelders, followers of Casper Schwenkfeld, and the Dunkers, or German Baptists. This pietism found expression even within the Lutheran Church itself, when Philipp Jacob Spener, a Lutheran pastor, began about 1670 to organize little societies for the promotion of "piety" among the members of his church. One of these pietistic Lutherans was Count Zinzendorf, who gave refuge to a group of Moravians, at a settlement on his estate called Herrnhut. The Moravians were followers of John Hus, whose revolt from Rome antedated even that of Luther ; but they had much in common with the other so-called pietist sects.

The first of these groups to come to America was made up of Mennonites, who came to Pennsylvania from Crefeld, on the lower Rhine, in 1683. Their leader was Francis Daniel Pastorius, a devoutly religious lawyer from Frankfurt am Main. From Germantown, which was their first settlement, the Mennonites spread westward through Pennsylvania, and Lancaster County became another center of Mennonite settlement, whose population came chiefly from the Rhenish Palatinate. Probably about twenty-five hundred Mennonites had come to America by the middle of the eighteenth century. Closely akin to the Quakers in their beliefs, they found themselves in a congenial atmosphere. Their greatest significance, however, lies in the fact that they led the way for so many other pietistic sects from the continent of Europe.

For the Mennonites were followed to America by many other religious radicals in the early eighteenth century. Thus the Dunkers, who used a spectacular form of adult baptism, in which the convert was immersed three times face forward in a flowing stream, once for the Father, once for the Son, and once for the Holy Ghost, and who followed the custom of washing one another's feet as a sign of humility, founded their first church in Pennsylvania in 1723. The Dunkers produced a number of important leaders, the most distinguished of whom was Christopher Sauer, the German printer of Germantown ; on the eve of the Revolution they numbered an estimated seven hundred souls in the thirteen colonies, most of whom were in Pennsylvania. One of their leaders, Conrad Beissel, broke off from the main Dunker movement to found the religious community at Ephrata, which was organized along somewhat communistic lines in its economic life, and where an attempt was made to get along without sex altogether. Following the convictions of their leader, who numbered among his great blessings the fact that God had "preserved him from the allurements of the female sex," the men and women of this community were housed in separate dormitories and were expected to live in monastic celibacy, since, according to Beissel, "the married state had originated in sin." Needless to say, although Beissel attracted a number of distinguished followers, the Ephrata community was never very significant in the religious history of America.

The Baptists came to America from both Germany and England. The English Baptists were in general agreement with the Calvinists; they differed chiefly in their rejection of infant baptism in favor of adult baptism of believers and in their advocacy of religious freedom, both of which points they seem to have acquired from the Dutch Mennonites. These Baptists, the "Regular" or "Calvinistic" Baptists, found themselves in a fairly congenial atmosphere in Puritan New England, although Roger Williams, who became one of them, found it convenient to move with his followers to Rhode Island because of his outspoken criticism of the lack of religious freedom in Massachusetts Bay.

The followers of John Smyth, however, rejected the Calvinistic doctrine of predestination and insisted upon the freedom of the will; they also insisted upon religious liberty and the complete separation of church and state. The numbers of this branch of the Baptists, which came to be known in America as the Freewill Baptists, were greatly increased as a result of the Great Awakening. Because of their insistence upon the individual's direct relationship with God, their emphasis upon faith and salvation, and their mystical emotionalism, the Freewill Baptists were closer to the other mystical sects than to the Calvinists.

The most important of the mystical sects in America were the Quakers. The Society of Friends, as they were called, was founded by George Fox, an English mystic who, whether consciously or unconsciously, had absorbed many of the ideas of the Mennonites. The Quakers soon became the most persecuted sect in England under the Restoration, and it was as a follower of Fox and his ideas that William Penn became a Quaker and devised his plan for a colony based upon Quaker ideas of toleration.

The Quaker faith is to the twentieth-century mind probably the most beautiful and saintly among all the welter of creeds in western Christendom of the seventeenth century. As Robert Barclay put it, the Quakers dismissed all high-flown philosophy and all institutional forms, and took the position that God had "laid aside the wise and the learned and the disputers of this world, and hath chosen a few despicable and unlearned instruments as he did fishermen of old, to publish his pure and naked truth, and to free it of those mists and fogs wherewith the clergy hath clouded it." Rejecting even the idea of a ministry and all formal sacraments, they carried the idea of individualism in religion to its logical conclusion. For them, such things as baptism, atonement, and communion were inward things of faith and the spirit. These people were not rationalists; just the contrary: for their whole system depended upon the super-natural relationships between the individual soul and God, and that relationship could not be seen by others. Its only outward expression was through the meek and humble behavior of the believer and his testimonial, when the "inner voice" moved him to speak, in Quaker meeting. The most pious and effective speakers were sometimes singled out as specially chosen mouthpieces of the spirit, and were sent about the country testifying to others. Aside from these, however, the Quakers were entirely without a ministry; they explicitly rejected the idea of a paid or professional religious leader as something that contradicted the very nature of religious experience.

William Penn had described the sect of which he was a member as follows:

> . . . That which people had been vainly seeking without, with much pains and cost, they . . . found within, where it was they wanted what they sought for, viz. the right way to peace with God. For they were directed to the light of Jesus Christ within them as the seed and leaven of the Kingdom of God. . . .
>
> First, repentence from dead works to serve the living God. . . .
>
> From hence sprang a second doctrine they were led to declare, as the mark of the prize of the high calling to all true Christians, viz. Perfection from sin, according to the scriptures of truth [that is, salvation, or new birth]. . . .
>
> Thirdly, this leads to an acknowledgment of eternal rewards and punishments.[42]

From these simple doctrines sprang others: love for each other and for all men, even one's enemies, the "sufficiency of truth-speaking . . . without swearing" or taking oaths, complete pacifism, refusal to pay tithes for an established church or ministry, and "not to respect persons." Titles, vain gestures, and compliments of respect they regarded as sinful, "though to virtue and authority they ever made a deference." They "used the plain language of thee and thou" to everybody, "whatever was his degree among men." They practiced silence, "having very few words upon all occasions." In their desire to avoid superfluity and excess, "they forebore drinking to people, or pledging of them, as the manner of the world is: a practice that is not only unnecessary, but . . . a provocation to drink more than did people good. . . ." They employed neither priest nor magistrate in marriage; the man and the woman involved merely took each other as husband and wife in the presence of the others to witness publicly that the voice of God within

[42] William Penn: *A Brief Account of the Rise and Progress of the People Called Quakers* (12th ed., Manchester, 1834), pp. 13, 18–20. For a more precise statement, see Penn's *Primitive Christianity Revived in the Faith and Practice of the People Called Quakers,* edited with a foreword by James M. Brown (Philadelphia, 1877).

them had joined them inwardly. In their search for simplicity and sincerity they wore the plainest of clothes; they spoke softly, simply, and as seldom as possible; and they listened, with the attitude of true tolerance, to the words of all men, even the humblest; for the words of the lowliest might be the words of God.[43'] Slavery, indeed, they could not countenance; every human soul was free, in the eyes of God, and equal in preciousness to all others; the enslavement of one soul by another was a violation of every principle of their belief, but especially their doctrine of brotherly love.[44]

Such were the beliefs and the practices of "the people called Quakers," of whom the most eloquent in eighteenth-century America was John Woolman. Born in the frontier community of Northampton, in New Jersey, he became a tailor. Becoming prosperous, he laid his business aside for considerable periods of time and visited the Indians of Pennsylvania and the Quaker communities all over the colonies, testifying to the doctrine of the "inner light" and combating the injustices of social and economic inequality, especially the institution of slavery. Woolman's *Journal* has been called a "classic of the inner life." His simple, pure religion of love is implicit in everything he wrote. He states it most clearly, perhaps, in his epistle to the Quakers of America, written when finally he went to England just before the Revolution to help the work of the Friends of the mother country:

> To be convinced of the pure principle of Truth, and diligently exercised in walking answerable thereto, is necessary before I can consistently recommend this principle to others, and I often feel a labour in spirit, that we who are active members in Society, may experience in ourselves the truth of those expressions of the Holy One, "I will be sanctified in them that come nigh me." Lev. x. 3. In this case my mind hath been often exercised when alone, year after year, for many years, and in the renewings of Divine Love, a tender care hath been incited in me, that we who profess this inward Light to be our teacher, may be a family united in that purity of worship, which comprehends a holy life, and ministers instruction to others. . . .
>
> The necessity of an inward stillness, hath under these exercises appeared clear to my mind. In true silence strength is renewed, the mind herein is weaned from all things, but as they may be enjoyed in the Divine Will, and a lowliness in outward living, opposite to wordly honour,

---

[43] Ibid., pp. 20–34.

[44] John Woolman: *Considerations on Keeping Negroes . . .* reprinted in Amelia Mott Gummere, ed.: *The Journals and Essays of John Woolman* (New York, 1922), pp. 334 ff. William Penn did not believe in the equality of Negroes with whites before the law. But he apparently did believe the essential equality of men in the eyes of God. Cf. Edward C. O. Beatty: *William Penn as Social Philosopher* (New York, 1939), pp. 184–5. Disapproval of Negro slavery became more universal among the Quakers after Penn's time.

becomes truly acceptable to us. In the desire of outward gain, the mind is prevented from a perfect attention to the voice of Christ, but in the weaning of the mind from all things but as they may be enjoyed in the Divine will, the pure Light shines into the soul. . . .[45]

Here, among the Quakers, was a religion of Christian love carried to its logical conclusion. Like the Puritans, they believed that if the true principles of Christ's religion could be sincerely and humbly applied by his followers, the confusions and the vanities of the world would disappear; unlike the Puritans, they would bring into being the utopia by pure love rather than by pure will. Unhappily for the world, the Quaker way was just about as impracticable, the nature of man being what it was, as the Puritan way. Utopia was not to be achieved either by love or by law.

Yet the doctrines of the Quakers and their kindred sects were very close to the hearts of many simple, kindly folk in colonial America who placed a greater value upon the generous and friendly impulses of religion than upon its conflicting and confusing dogmas. Among the common people of America, and especially among the settlers along the frontier, people seldom knew what they believed; they only knew what they felt. Feeling, as a historical force, was probably more powerful, among the masses of the people, than thought.

The Great Awakening

If Anglicanism, rationalism, and Deism were characteristic of the religious life of the intellectuals among the socially elite; if the "old lights" in the Congregational, Presbyterian, and Dutch Reformed churches were the religious conservatives among the middle class and the well-to-do; and if the pietistic sects expressed the religious feelings of the lowly English and European social orders; then the religious and social phenomenon known as the Great Awakening was a great democratic outpouring among the poorer, less-educated native Americans of the towns and the frontier. John Wise had preached the natural equality and natural liberty of all men, and he had won his fight for a continuance of democratic government in the churches. But his victory was a negative one: the Congregational form of government was retained in the Congregational churches, but the theories of equality and democracy were forgotten in the rise of rationalism in New England and the south and the battle of the conservatives against it.

Yet the primitive dynamics of human feeling were not to go unheard, and the resurgence of emotionalism in religion was both a protest

[45] John Woolman: *An Epistle to the Quarterly and Monthly Meeting of Friends* (London, 1772), reprinted in *The Journal and Essays of John Woolman,* Amelia Mott Gummere, ed. (pp. 473–87), pp. 477, 478–9, 483–4, 486, 487.

against the over-intellectualization of the old religions and a psychological and social outburst that was to lay the positive foundation for a religious development that was new. For the common people of the colonies had little of the erudition of the great ones of the world to go by : they had only their feelings, and those feelings were to be an important and explosive element in the outlook on life of the eighteenth century as well as of subsequent generations of Americans.

The old established religions, as the seventeenth century turned into the eighteenth, were apparently losing their contact with the common people, just at the moment when they were being overhauled intellectually by those leaders who accepted the implications of the new science. Somehow the religions of the Puritans and the Anglicans seemed cold and impersonal and not very useful to the people on the farms and along the frontier who had little time, preparation, or patience for fine-spun theological argument. They needed a religion that was vital, moving, personal, the sort of thing that was characteristic of the sects that were now pouring into Pennsylvania. Religion had "cooled off"; on the other hand, there was nothing in America as yet to take its place as an outlet for human emotional and social energy. Anyone who could "warm religion up" again, and renew it as a vital force among the uneducated masses had an almost boundless opportunity lying ripe and ready before him. A group of such leaders, or revivers, appeared in America in the third decade of the eighteenth century.

It was probably no accident that the wave of revivalism known as the Great Awakening had its beginning in the middle colonies, where the pietism of the sects had demonstrated what a warm, personal thing religion could be. The emotionalism of the revival went to much greater extremes than the quietism of the sects, however ; for the "new lights" of the revival were to work themselves up into paroxysms of emotional fervor that all too often actually reached the stage of pathological violence.

The first notable revivalist was a pastor of the Dutch Reformed Church, Theodore J. Frelinghuysen. He had come to America in 1720, to become pastor of a semi-frontier community in New Jersey, and he, a German pietist, soon scandalized his more well-to-do parishioners, while he delighted the poorer, less conservative members of his flock. He preached a religion of inward feeling and conversion ; and despite the organized opposition of his superiors he succeeded in deeply stirring most of his people and in bringing about many "conversions."

At about the same time, whether under Frelinghuysen's influence or some other, William Tennent, a Presbyterian, began a sort of revival not far away in Pennsylvania. Starting out with the idea of educating his own sons, Tennent found himself the head of a "Log College" on his farm at Neshaming. Tennent and his disciples preached a flaming revivalism, and their influence quickly spread through eastern Pennsylvania and in New Jersey, where they joined forces with Frelinghuysen. But the revivalism of the Tennents split the Presbyterian Church as Frelinghuysen had split the Dutch Reformed Church, and the conservative Presbyterian ministers tried desperately to head off the revival by enacting church legislation that would prevent these "Log Cabin"-trained ministers from preaching. These efforts, by and large, were entirely unsuccessful.

The revivalists marched forward. Everywhere they preached individual salvation for sinners who repented, hell-fire and damnation for the unregenerate who refused to hear the voice of God in their souls — including the "unregenerate ministry." Back in old England a similar reaction against intellectualism in religion had broken out among the poor. The basic reasons for revivalism there were probably much the same as the reasons for it in America; but the revival in America was probably more widespread and deep-seated, and it was almost certainly more violent. The two greatest of the English revivalists were John Wesley and George Whitefield, and both of them contributed to the power with which the Great Awakening swept across English America.

Wesley, an introspective, zealous Anglican pietist from Oxford, came to Georgia as a missionary in 1735, shortly after the founding of that colony. He was disgusted by his failure to impress the Indians, and turned his talents toward his white neighbors, with hardly more success. After a visit to Germany, however, where he absorbed much of the emotionalism of the Moravians, he returned to England with greater power and success. There he set in motion the so-called Methodist revival, and from there he sent a number of his followers to America.

The greatest of these visiting revivalists was George Whitefield, who arrived in Delaware in 1739, just as the work of Frelinghuysen and the "Log Cabin" evangelists was reaching its height. Whitefield was without doubt one of the most effective popular preachers of all time; but his success in America was due no less to the fact that the mood of revivalism had already been prepared for him by lesser men. Technically an Anglican, he found the leaders of the dissenting sects more congenial than the Anglican pastors, and it was chiefly from dissenting pulpits that he preached. Starting from Philadelphia, he preached his way across New Jersey and back again. Thereafter, on a series of journeys to and in America, he preached to enormous crowds in every colony from Massachusetts to Georgia.

That Whitefield was amazingly effective, there can be no doubt.

Franklin, who in 1743 poked fun at Whitefield as a "spiritual shaver and trimmer," only to become a close friend of his later on, described the preacher's work and the effect of his preaching as follows :

The multitudes of all sects and denominations that attended his sermons were enormous, and it was matter of speculation to me, who was one of the number, to observe the extraordinary influence of his ora-

Leaders of American Religious Thought : George Whitefield.
A portrait attributed to Joseph Badger.
[By courtesy of the Fogg Museum of Art, Harvard University]

tory on his hearers, and how much they admir'd and respected him, notwithstanding his common abuse of them, by assuring them they were naturally *half beasts and half devils.* It was wonderful to see the change soon made in the manners of our inhabitants. From being thoughtless or indifferent about religion, it seem'd as if all the world were growing religious, so that we could not walk thro' the town in an evening without hearing psalms sung in different families of every street. . . . I happened . . . to attend one of his sermons, in the course of which I perceived he intended to finish with a collection, and I silently resolved he should get nothing from me. I had in my pocket a handful of copper money, three or four silver dollars, and five pistoles in gold. As he proceeded I began to soften, and concluded to give the coppers. Another stroke of his oratory made me asham'd of that, and determin'd me to give the silver ; and he finish'd so admirably, that I empty'd my pocket wholly into the collector's dish, gold and all.[46]

The evangel that so aroused Whitefield's audiences was a message of sin and repentance :

> I say, generally : — For, as God is a sovereign Agent, his sacred Spirit bloweth not only on whom, but when and how it listeth. There-fore, far be it from me to confine the Almighty to one Way of acting, or say, that all undergo an equal Degree of Conviction : — No, there is a holy Variety in God's Methods of calling home his Elect. But this we may affirm assuredly, "That, wherever there is a Work of true Con-viction and Conversion wrought upon a Sinner's Heart, the Holy Ghost, whether by a greater or less Degree of inward Soul-trouble, does that which our Lord Jesus tells the Disciples, in the Words of the Text, that he should do when he came. . . . Be humble, therefore, O Believers, be humble : Look to the Rock from whence you have been hewn ; — extol *free Grace ;* Admire *electing love,* which alone has made you to differ from the rest of your Brethren. — Has God brought you into Light ? Walk as becometh children of Light. Provoke not the Holy Spirit to depart from you. . . . Rejoice, but let it be with Trembling. — As the Elect of God, put on, not only Humbleness of Mind, but Bowels of Compassion ; and pray, oh pray, for your unconverted Brethren ! [47]

Thus, with an ascending crescendo of emotional persuasiveness, Whitefield appealed to his hearers to hear God "calling home his Elect." His theology was never very clear ; it contained elements of both Calvinism and Arminianism ; but Whitefield was never as con-cerned with fine points of doctrine as with inducing in his hearers the joy of uncritical conversion. In contrast with the Tennents and the other fiery Presbyterians, he was all persuasiveness, and was probably the more successful because of that.

Whitefield insisted that Christ's evangel was shared equally by all ; salvation was the same for the rich as for the poor : and the poor flocked to hear him.

> For these rabble, my Lords, have precious and immortal Souls, for which the dear Redeemer shed his precious blood, as well as the great and rich. These, my Lords, are the publicans and harlots that enter into the kingdom of heaven, whilst self-righteous professors reject it. To

---

[46] Franklin : *Writings* (Smyth, ed.), I, 354–5, 356.
[47] George Whitefield : *Nine Sermons* (Edinburgh, 1742), pp. 157, 159–60, 173.

shew such poor sinners the way to God, to preach to them the power of Christ's resurrection ; and to pluck them as firebrands out of the burning, the Methodist preachers go out into the highways and hedges. If this is to be vile, by the help of my God, I shall be more vile ; neither count I my life dear unto myself, so that I may finish my course with joy, and be made instrumental in turning any of this rabble to righteousness.[48]

He even preached the salvation of Negroes, and rebuked the slave owners for keeping their slaves in ignorance and religious darkness : "God is the same to-day, as he was yesterday, and will continue the same forever. He does not reject the prayer of the poor and destitute, nor disregard the cry of the meanest negroes. . . ."[49] This was essentially an equalitarian doctrine ; it was a sort of religious democracy ; and it could not fail to give an impetus to the upward-looking impulses of the poor and the disfranchised everywhere. But not only that : any man could preach ; learning was hardly necessary ; the essential thing was a genuine movement of the spirit.

In 1740, Whitefield made a tour — a "procession" would be a better word — through New England. He was welcomed in Boston, where he preached to enormous crowds on the Common and "in the fields." His success in stirring men was phenomenal, though the cool-headed Jonathan Mayhew could write of him : "I heard him once, and it was as low, confused, puerile, conceited, ill-natured, enthusiastic a performance as I ever heard."[50] Such voices on sour notes were relatively few, however, and Whitefield moved on to Northampton, where he stayed with Jonathan Edwards for four days. Whitefield records the visit to Edwards's church : "When I came into his Pulpit, I found my Heart drawn out to talk of scarce any thing besides the Consolations and Privileges of Saints, and the plentiful Effusion of the Spirit upon the Hearts of Believers. And, when I came to remind them of their former Experiences, and how zealous and lively they were at that Time, both Minister and People wept much ; and the Holy Ghost enabled me to speak with a great deal of Power."[51]

After Whitefield, the Tennents came to New England ; and by 1741 the religious fervor of that section was at fever heat. It was in the midst of this second wave of revivalism, prepared for him by others, that Jonathan Edwards began again to stir up the fears of his audiences and to call again to sinners to repent and hear the voice of God. This time,

[48] George Whitefield : *The Works of the Reverend George Whitefield, M.A.* (4 vols., London, 1771), IV, 139.
[49] Ibid., III, 39.
[50] Quoted from the *Diary of Rev. Daniel Wadsworth* (Hartford, 1894), p. 56, in Winslow, op. cit., p. 185.
[51] Quoted in ibid., p. 87.

however, the same sort of thing was going on all over New England — all over most of the continental colonies, indeed — and the common people in America were rolling, as it were, in a frenzy of salvation.

It was at Enfield, on July 9, 1741, that Edwards preached the revivalist sermon that is generally taken as perhaps the most typical sermon of the Great Awakening in New England, and has been chiefly responsible for his misplaced and misleading popular reputation as a preacher of hell-fire and brimstone. In this sermon, "Sinners in the Hands of an angry God," he says :

> There is nothing that keeps wicked men at any one moment out of hell, but the mere pleasure of God. . . .
>
> We find it easy to tread on and crush a worm that we see crawling on the earth ; so it is easy for us to cut or singe a slender thread that any thing hangs by : thus easy it is for God, when he pleases, to cast his enemies down to hell. What are we, that we should think to stand before him, at whose rebuke the earth trembles, and before whom the rocks are thrown down ? . . .
>
> They [sinners] *deserve* to be cast into hell. . . .
>
> They are already under a sentence of condemnation to hell. . . .
>
> They are now the objects of that very same *anger* and wrath of God, that is expressed in the torments of hell. . . . The wrath of God burns against them, their damnation does not slumber ; the pit is prepared, the fire is made ready, the furnace is now hot, ready to receive them ; the flames do now rage and glow. The glittering sword is whet, and held over them, and the pit hath opened its mouth under them. . . .
>
> The *devil* stands ready to fall upon them, and seize them as his own, at what moment God will permit him. They belong to him ; he has their souls in his possession, and under his dominion. . . . The old serpent is gaping for them ; hell opens its mouth wide to receive them ; and if God should permit it, they would be hastily swallowed up and lost. . . .
>
> The God that holds you over the pit of hell, much as one holds a spider, or some loathesome insect, over the fire, abhors you, and is dreadfully provoked . . . you are ten thousand times more abominable in his eyes, than the most hateful venemous serpent is in ours. . . .
>
> There is reason to think, that there are many in this congregation now hearing this discourse, that will actually be the subjects of this very misery to all eternity. . . . And it would be a wonder, if some that are now present should not be in hell in a very short time, even before this year is out. And it would be no wonder if some persons that now sit here, in some seats of this meeting-house, in health, quiet and secure, should be there before to-morrow morning. . . .[52]

[52] Jonathan Edwards : *Works* (Hickman ed.), II, 7–12.

The effect that this quiet, sickly man had upon his hearers was little short of phenomenal. He was always a student of human psychology, and it is difficult to avoid the conclusion that he deliberately piled image upon image, reiteration upon reiteration, fear upon fear, to drive the people to a sense of the necessity of throwing themselves upon God. In any case, he was successful; so successful, in fact, that the people were driven quite to hysteria. One of those who heard him described the scene thus: ". . . before the sermon was done — there was a great moaning & crying out through ye whole House — What shall I do to be Sav^d — oh I am going to Hell — Oh what shall I do for Christ &c. &c. So y^t ye minister was obliged to desist — ye shrieks & cry^s were piercing & amazing . . . & Several Souls were hopefully wrought upon y^t night. & oh ye cheerfulness and pleasantness of their countenances y^t receiv^d comfort. . . ."[53]

But what, in all soberness, was the religion that Edwards went to such lengths to induce in his followers?

Essentially, strange as it may seem, it was Puritanism at its loveliest and best. For opposite to the pit stood the refuge to which he would have driven them, the unspeakable beauty and happiness of life with God. Let them surrender to God; let them accept the utter dependence upon God that he had preached in his sermon at Boston in 1731, and they would be happy. For him, religion was beauty, and a means to beauty, the beauty of knowing God. If he sought to frighten men into seeking God it was because, by so doing, they could escape from evil and to that degree drive Satan out of the world.

In other ways, however, Edwards had departed radically from the Puritanism of the Puritan fathers. To begin with the most obvious difference, Edwards's appeal to the emotions, the "enthusiasm," of his followers would never have had the approval of the fathers. For them, God saved by grace freely given and not earned. Nothing that the believer could do would influence God's decision, since God, being perfect, is above influence; conversion, when it came, was emotional, to be sure, but disciplined by rational conviction. Edwards probably would not have admitted that the "enthusiasm" of his converts influenced God, but his encouragement of "enthusiasm," deliberately provoked by the appeal to fear, was still a wide departure from the rational discipline of orthodox Puritanism. Indeed, despite his own rational presentation of it, his appeal was to the emotions rather than to reason; his lifelong study of the mind was secondary to his lifelong objective of stimulating religious emotions; his "psychology" was a ra-

[53] Quoted from the Diary of Stephen Williams, printed in Oliver Means: *A Sketch of the Strict Congregational Church of Enfield, Conn.* (Hartford, 1899), p. 19, in Winslow, op. cit., p. 192.

tional means to an emotional end. But he was not an extremist, and often viewed with some concern the physical excesses of the "enthusiasts," and he felt it necessary at last to caution his followers to avoid spurious signs and false preachers, as already related. His caution was the product of cool, objective thinking about the remarkable phenomena that had occurred, and he was forced to conclude that mere pathological emotional orgies were not necessarily signs of God's handiwork. Yet when all allowances were made for the dross, he felt sure that this great movement among the people was God's doing, the divine answer to the fatal influences of Arminianism: "So I look upon myself called on this Occasion to give my Testimony, that so far as the Nature and Tendency of such a Work is capable of falling under the Observation of a By-stander . . . this Work has all those Marks that have been spoken of; in very many instances, in every Article; and particularly in many of those that have been the Subjects of such extraordinary Operations, all those Marks have appeared in a very great Degree."[54] He therefore placed his stamp of approval upon it; we believe in it, he said, but let us be sure it is the work of God before we surrender to it.

The significant thing about Edwards's part in the Great Awakening was that he, the most intellectual of all the revivalist preachers, looked upon it, not as a democratic emotional drive for salvation based upon the free will of the converted — far from it — but, rather, as a movement inspired by God for combating rationalism and the very free-will doctrines of the Arminians that many of the revivalist preachers themselves had adopted. Thus Edwards, while a leading participant in the Great Awakening, was not really of it. For him it was essentially defensive; for the others it was a great forward upsurge of the human spirit.

The Great Awakening in the middle colonies and New England ran its course among the common people of the towns and among the farmers. In the southern colonies, on the other hand, its appeal was to the poor whites and the frontiersmen along the Alleghenies and the piedmont; here, even more than elsewhere in the colonies, the Great Awakening was a frontier phenomenon. It was in the south that social and economic changes were most extreme; it is probably true that the greater intensity of the Great Awakening in this region was due to the fact that it offered an avenue of emotional and social "escape" to those who needed it most.

Thus in the back-country of Virginia and the Carolinas, where the German pietists were mingling with the Scotch-Irish Presbyterians,

---

[54] Jonathan Edwards: *The Distinguishing Marks of a Work of the Spirit of God* (Boston, 1741; London reprint, 1742), pp. 46–7.

Whitefield and the "Log Cabin" evangelists like William Robinson and Samuel Davies found a ready hearing. As elsewhere in the colonies, the appearance of "new light" preachers brought about splits in all the old churches, and a bitter religious controversy, especially in Virginia, over the question whether the evangelists should be allowed to preach

Leaders of American Religious Thought : Samuel Davies. A portrait made from a contemporary print by James Massalon in 1874.
[By courtesy of Princeton University]

at all. The most renowned of these southern evangelists was Samuel Davies, who was closely identified with the founding of the Presbyterian college at Princeton and later became its president. Davies was one of the most effective preachers of his time, and became the champion, in the 1750's, of religious liberty against the official intolerance of Virginia in favor of the established Anglicanism. Davies, a Presbyterian, rejected the accusation of the "old lights" and of the Anglicans that he was one of the "itinerants" and "incendiaries" among the people; but he, like Edwards, concluded that despite the irregularities that had doubtless taken place, the Great Awakening had brought about a "visible Reformation of life" in many people and must be regarded as redounding to the glory of God.[55] Be that as it may, Davies himself was one of the most significant figures in both the Great Awakening in the south and the struggle for religious liberty there.

Contemporaneously with the rapid spread of "new light" Presbyterianism, there appeared in the south a relatively new group of revivalists in the persons of certain Baptist preachers, who, under the influence of revivalism and George Whitefield, deserted the "Regular" Baptists of the older Calvinistic type, to preach the more appealing and more "Arminian" doctrines of emotional personal conversion.

The center of southern Baptist revivalism was Sandy Creek, in western North Carolina, where Shubal Stearns and Daniel Marshall, both converts from Congregationalism and followers of Whitefield, set up their homes and began to preach in 1755. From this place as a center spread the Baptist doctrine; and up and down the frontier country the uneducated, often illiterate Baptist preachers went, scornful of learning, preaching a gospel of sin and salvation, and their converts were soon numbered in thousands. Thus the Baptists, like others, were split into "old lights" and "new lights," and it was the "new lights" who eventually became the most numerous sect along the American frontier, especially in the south. While their theology was not very rigid, and beliefs were left largely to the individual conscience, they held to the basic Christian ideas of an omnipotent and omniscient triune God, the evil nature of man, and the necessity for salvation through faith in Christ — a salvation that was open to all who would repent of their sins and receive it.

The significance of the Baptists, however, lay less in their theology than in their belief in religious equality, in their insistence upon complete separation of church and state, and in their demand for complete religious freedom. They were, after the Quakers — whose successors, in many ways, they were — probably the most democratic of all the sects in America. Political democracy was as yet in an embryonic stage in America; religious democracy, on the other hand, had definitely made its appearance, among the poor and rough frontiersmen of the old west. Religious democracy thus anticipated political democracy in a very large fragment of the American mind of the mid-eighteenth century. But democracy in any form was still anathema to the great of the world; few, if any, of the leaders of American thought and politics dreamed of the influence that the mood of the Baptists would have upon later American society, politics, and religion.

The Great Awakening, then — that wave of emotional religious fervor which swept the length and breadth of the Atlantic seaboard and the in-

---

[55] Samuel Davies: *The Impartial Trial, impartially tried, and convicted of Partiality* (Williamsburg, 1748), p. 1 *et passim.*

land frontier in the third, fourth, fifth, and sixth decades of the eighteenth century, which reached its crest in 1740–1 but continued through the 1750's — was more than an outpouring of religion. Indeed, when the tide had receded and men had generally returned to soberness, institutionalized religion was, perhaps, weaker in the colonies than ever before. Certainly there were more sects ; if religion had been broken into segments by the Protestant revolt of the sixteenth century, it was atomized now by the Great Awakening of the eighteenth. Yet for all its doctrinal bickering, most of which the common people understood not at all, the Great Awakening was an appeal to individual self-consciousness. For the common man it was a moment of discovery — or rediscovery — of himself. He had value in the eyes of God ; God, indeed, was definitely and consciously interested in him as a person. This religion was the opposite extreme from the rationalized, impersonal religion of the Deists ; it did not call for reason : it demanded only feelings, and that the common people could understand. That it should have made its appeal to the poor, the ignorant, the workers, and the frontiersmen is easy to understand. For inherent in it was an appeal to a sense of individual worth, which is the essence of democracy. Democracy in religion was not democracy in politics ; but it did appeal to the common people's sense of what, in the light of their own experience in the shop, on the farm, and in the frontier wilderness, was right. And when there was democracy in religion, in that as yet strongly religious age, democracy in politics could not be far behind.

It goes almost without saying that the emotionalism, the crudities, the pathological excesses of the participants in the Great Awakening should have aroused the disgust of both the religious conservatives and the intellectual liberals, and that one of its intellectual by-products was its condemnation by them.

The outspoken criticism of the "old light" clergy by George Whitefield and his awakening colleagues set a precedent of criticism and controversy that tended to dispel the aura of sacrosanctity that had surrounded the clergy, and encouraged thought and discussion by the laity in a manner that would have scandalized its grandfathers. The religious sects were split many ways, and the net result was probably a lowering, rather than a raising, of intellectual standards in religious thought. In general the intellectual effects of the Great Awakening were negative ; but in its encouragement of the habits of criticism in the laity, even criticism of the ministers, and in its great new emphasis upon the worth of the individual and his thought, no matter how humble he might be, it contributed two of the most significant intellectual elements to the synthesis that was to eventuate in genuine religious and intellectual democracy.

The "old light" clergy, whether liberal or conservative, were on the defensive, and they condemned, with all the power at their disposal, this to them unspeakable development. It was those crack-brained preachers like Whitefield, Tennent, and John Davenport who seemed to be to blame, and the conservatives fought the revivalists both by warning their own congregations against such goings-on and by direct attack upon the revivalists themselves.

One of the most outspoken champions of the opposition was Charles Chauncy, of Boston. Chauncy did not hesitate to write to Edwards, Whitefield, Davenport, and others and take them to task for the mischief he thought they were doing in tampering with the minds and emotions of the people. To Davenport, for example, he wrote bluntly, in an open letter :

> I doubt not, you verily think, God sent you hither ; and that your preaching here is by *immediate* commission from *him :* But others must be excus'd, if they han't the same tho't of the matter. . . . Suffer me, Sir, to take this opportunity, to beseech you in the bowels of Christ Jesus, and as you regard your own soul, to review your conduct in this matter of *rash, and uncharitable* judging.[56]

His own congregation Chauncy instructed to beware of "enthusiasm" : "No greater mischiefs have arisen from any quarter. . . . Popery it self han't been the mother of more and greater blasphemies and abominations. It has made strong attempts to destroy all property, to make all things common, *wives* as well as goods. . . . It has made men fancy themselves to be *prophets* and *apostles ;* yea, some have taken themselves to be Christ Jesus ; yea, the blessed God himself." [57] Keep calm, and use your minds, he said ; rely on the Scriptures for sane guidance in religion, but, most of all, "Make use of the *Reason* and *Understanding* God has given you. . . . Next to the *Scripture,* there is no greater enemy to *enthusiasm,* than reason." [58]

Chauncy stood for the rationalists everywhere, and the controversy between him and the "enthusiasts" marked a deep cleavage in the American mind — a cleavage between rationalism and emotionalism, between the control of human conduct by "the reason and understanding God has given you" and behavior by undisciplined mood and impulse. Nor was the controversy an isolated phenomenon ; for it was linked to the social and economic and political cleavages that were differentiating — if not very clearly — east from west, rich from poor.

The rationalism of Chauncy and his colleagues was in this sense

---

[56] Charles Chauncy : *Enthusiasm Described and Caution'd Against* (Boston, 1742), pp. ii–iv.
[57] Ibid., p. 15.
[58] Ibid., p. 3.

conservative : that despite its departure from the strict doctrines of the fathers it was entirely sympathetic with the Puritan insistence upon rationally controlled behavior and distrust of compromise with the emotions and undisciplined impulse in any field. On the other hand, the "enthusiasts" not only departed often from the strict tenets of seventeenth-century Calvinism : they were also radicals in their egalitarianism, in their individualism, and in their penchant for democratic forms in church government. In this sense, therefore, the religious manifestation known as the Great Awakening must be seen as one of the deep psychological forces at work in American society that were moving, even against the rational convictions of many of the intellectuals, in the direction of democracy.

The Growth of Religious Freedom

Complete legal freedom of conscience in matters pertaining to religion has been called "the most striking contribution of America to the science of government." [59]

This may be true ; it is at least fairly certain that there were more different varieties of Christianity in the English colonies in America, and that they enjoyed in most colonies a greater degree of toleration, than was the case anywhere else in the world. Not only were they allowed to exist, however : the belief in individual religious freedom was already an established and important article of conviction in the American mind.

The ideas of religious toleration and of religious freedom were not themselves originally religious doctrines. Nor have they derived solely, or even primarily, from religious thought. In almost no religion has the idea of religious toleration or a belief in religious freedom been a tenet of the religion itself. On the contrary, most Christian religions have denied the validity of both religious toleration and religious freedom, both implicitly and explicitly ; whether on the basis of sheer logic or on the grounds of evangelical expediency, it is difficult to see how they could have done otherwise. In America, where the ideas of both toleration and religious freedom had their most rapid growth in early modern times, religious toleration was at first a product of practical circumstances. But if "toleration" was a product of expediency and frontier conditions, true religious freedom was probably the child of the eighteenth-century rationalism that arose from the spread of early modern science, coupled with the sort of religious individualism that was implicit in the doctrines of certain religious sects, notably the American Quakers and Baptists.

[59] Sanford H. Cobb : *The Rise of Religious Liberty in America* (New York, 1902), p. vii.

To the generation of men that first settled America, an alliance of an institutionalized church with the state was a natural, even necessary, condition of social and political organization. In every state in Europe, the state itself was allied with a state church, which was expected to enhance with its dogmas and its rituals the glory and the majesty of the state and, with its powerful sanctions, to buttress the authority of the state among the common citizens. The established church, in other words, was an instrument of the authoritarian state. Practically, the close alliance of church and state produced a great deal of intolerance and persecution. For sects or individuals who had the temerity to disagree with established dogma were regarded as dangerous, not only to the church, but to the state also. Thus the persecutions of Catholics in England in the sixteenth century and the persecutions of Quakers in the seventeenth were in large part the result of fear that these sects, if allowed to prosper, would surely endanger the existing order, not only in intellectual and religious life, with a consequent destruction of English ideals, but even the state itself. Not only was "popery" akin to witchcraft in the eyes of the English Protestants : the survival of Mary Stuart was a constant threat that England, by the devious machinations of Mary's church, might be brought under the domination of Spain. Similarly, a century later, not only did the Quakers constitute a threat to the established Anglicanism, but also, because they would not take oaths or hold the great of this world in proper awe, they were regarded as being a threat to the stability of all authority, even of the English state itself.

Official intolerance in religion was therefore the negative side of the religious aspect of the seventeenth-century "monolithic" state. The state church was a part of the state mechanism : *cujus regio, ejus religio;* the citizen paid allegiance to the church just as he did to the state. If a man were a citizen of a state, a member of the national society, he was expected to conform to that society's religion; if he could not, he was not fully a citizen : he was potentially dangerous and was encouraged to get out.

Intolerance, indeed, official and unofficial, usually rests upon fear. Fear for one's own cherished ideals or fear for the security of the political and social order that embodies those ideals in reality. It was precisely because of their fear for the safety and the permanence of their own godly commonwealth that the Puritan fathers chased Roger Williams and Ann Hutchinson out of Massachusetts. Not only were their own religious convictions and ideals at stake : the whole social and political structure that they had built about those ideals must inevitably topple if Williams's ideals were allowed to prosper in Massachusetts. Wrote Nathaniel Ward for the Massachusetts Puritans with quaint eloquence in *The Simple Cobbler of Aggawam*: "How all Religions should enjoy their Liberty, Justice its due regularity, Civill cohabitation moral honesty, in one and the same Jurisdiction, is beyond the Artique of my comprehension. If the whole conclave of Hell can so compromise, exadverse, and diametriall contradictions, as to cosmopolitize such a multimonstrous maufrey of heteroclytes and quicquidlibets quietly; I trust I may say with all humble reverence, they can doe more than the Senate of Heaven." [60]

To the official Puritan mind, the toleration of dissent within the holy commonwealth was simply inconceivable. Similarly, because the Anglican Virginians feared the political effects of Lord Baltimore's Catholicism upon the dominion they had founded, they discouraged him from settling in Virginia. Similarly, too, it was fear for the maintenance of the established order that led to such intolerant persecution of dissenters from the Dutch Reformed religion — Quakers and Catholics — as there was in Dutch New Netherland and English New York.

Even while America was being settled, however, the question of the validity of state interference in private religion was attracting the attention of thoughtful men, both in Europe and America. Sir Henry Vane, who had experienced the official intolerance of the Massachusetts Commonwealth before his return to England, was probably the foremost advocate of tolerance there in the middle of the seventeenth century. In his opinion, "the magistrate had no right to go beyond matters of outward practice, converse, and dealings in the things of this life between man and man." At the same time John Milton was also concluding that religious toleration was both reasonable and desirable; but even Milton would not go so far as to permit religious liberty to Roman Catholics. Oliver Cromwell himself asked: "Is it ingenuous to ask for [religious] liberty and not to give it?" Yet Cromwell would not allow papists to hold office, and prohibited the Anglican Book of Common Prayer. Jeremy Taylor, too, as an Anglican, wrote an eloquent plea for religious tolerance in the period of Cromwellian authoritarianism; but he promptly forgot his principles of toleration as soon as the Anglicans returned to power in the baggage train of Charles II.

What all these writers were after was the principle of freedom from interference in religion by the state. They did not get so far as to develop a thorough, logical theory of complete freedom of conscience; their chief emphasis was upon the political aspects of tolerance, and their chief conclusion was that tolerance of dissenting religions was no danger to the state. They were all contemporaries of Roger Wil-

[60] Nathaniel Ward: *The Simple Cobbler of Aggawam in America*, quoted in Perry Miller and Thomas H. Johnson: *The Puritans* (New York, 1938), p. 232.

liams; he was personally acquainted with all or most of them, and certainly was familiar with their works; his own most important works were written while in their midst in England.

The Restoration of the Stuarts to the throne of England in 1660 brought with it the re-establishment of the Church of England as the religious arm of the state and, along with it, a revival of discrimination and persecution against dissenters. But by this time the mystical Quaker doctrine of the "inner light" was beginning to have a following, while at the other end of the social and intellectual scale the rationalism of such men as Baron Herbert of Cherbury and the poet John Dryden had begun, by a comparative study of religions, to lay the foundation for a genuine doctrine of religious toleration. Thus the aristocratic William Penn, articulate advocate of religious toleration among the Quakers, writing from the point of view of the persecuted, wrote in 1670 that the civil persecution of religious dissent was contrary both to the teachings of Christ and to "the privilege of nature and principle of reason." By contrast, Thomas Hobbes, greatest of the materialists, had rejected all religions and could therefore consider them objectively; such toleration as he felt was a matter of almost pure indifference. But with the growth of rationalism alongside of the forces that were to produce the "Glorious Revolution" of 1688 religious toleration began to be justified on more and more rationalistic grounds, and there was developed a rationalistic explanation that reached its best expression in John Locke's *Letters on Toleration.*

But if intolerance is the monstrous offspring of emotional and political fears for the safety of established ideals, the earliest forms of toleration were also the weakling children — if better favored — of fears, all too well justified, of what might happen to the newer religious conviction if the absolutism of the state were allowed to go unchallenged. The first forms of tolerance were thus nearly all defensive rather than progressive in their essential purpose. Yet they gave dissent a limited sort of freedom for growth, and merely by holding the line against official state intolerance they showed the force of ideas upon history and constituted a significant milestone on the long, hard, still unended uphill climb of man toward the freedom of the human mind.

Roger Williams was the first outspoken advocate of religious toleration in America; and he spoke as an American emissary, as it were, of the limited toleration then receiving a hearing in England. For his colleagues in England who favored religious toleration desired to justify it chiefly for themselves in the face of the persistent authoritarianism of Anglicanism; and Williams, sharing their enlightenment, was inspired to invoke its arguments to defend himself and those who were suffering from the same persecution by the official intolerance of the fathers of Massachusetts Bay.

The Maryland Toleration Act of 1649, made by far lesser men than Roger Williams, illustrates even more clearly than he does the defensive nature of that stage in the growth of the infant idea of religious toleration. For the Maryland Toleration Act was primarily for the protection of Catholics against the insults and persecutions of the Maryland Protestants; what would happen to any who diverged too widely from the tenets of these two officially recognized Christian groups was grimly accented by the grisly provision of the act, inserted at the insistence of the Puritans in the assembly, that anyone who denied the divinity of Christ should be punishable by death.

There existed, then, a certain amount of religious toleration in America at the end of the seventeenth century; but there was as yet little or no true religious freedom. For toleration itself is negative: it involves enduring that which cannot be prevented, or that to which society is indifferent. Religious freedom, on the other hand, is positive: for it means that a man's mind is free, and that, as to religion, he may believe or not believe, grow religiously or not grow, as his own convictions lead him to do. But mere religious freedom is itself negative in nature and relatively unimportant in the intellectual history of a people so long as this freedom of thought is freedom only in religion or so long as it means only that the individual is free to think as he pleases. This freedom becomes significant and a genuinely positive force in human history only when it is applied to thought in every realm explorable by the human mind, and only when it becomes a base upon which may be constructed social progress.

Such intellectual freedom as a basis of human progress has existed only rarely and to a relative degree in the history of western civilization. But one of those times was that when it began to be a reality — still in a relative degree only — in America in the eighteenth century. Such as it was, the incipient intellectual freedom of the eighteenth century in America was one of the most important of the bases upon which the American way of life was built; without it, indeed, American democracy could probably never have been born.

Religious intolerance still raised its ugly head, and often, in the colonies in the eighteenth century. Yet there were certain factors in the American experience that were making steadily and surely for the birth of an idea — the concept of a positive religious freedom. The very multiplicity of sects, in the first place, the greater variety of religions here than anywhere else in the world, practically forced upon the Americans the convictions that, on the one side, diversity of religions might not be a threat to the maintenance of order and authority, and that, on the other, any one sect must allow the others to live if it would live itself. Thus the mere facts of the existing situation produced a sort of "live and let live" attitude that was preparatory to something more creative.

The Great Awakening, for example, gave a strong religious impetus to the growth of the idea of religious toleration. George Whitefield was scornful of narrow religious differences on points of doctrine; in one of his sermons he exclaimed: "Father Abraham, who have you in heaven? 'Any Episcopalians?' 'No.' 'Any Presbyterians?' 'No.' 'Any Baptists?' 'No.' 'Any Methodists, Seceders, or Independents?' 'No, No!' 'Why who have you there?' 'We dont know those names here. All who are here are Christians.' Oh, is that the case? Then, God help me! and God help us all to forget party names and to become Christians in deed and truth." [61]

On the other hand, there was much in the quiet, undramatic convictions of the sects, particularly the Quakers, that, by implication at least, could only lead logically to the principle of toleration. For if the voice within a man is the voice of God, he not only has a divine right to speak, but also, and probably more important, has a divine right to be heard. Thus implicit in the practices of the Quaker meeting, if not explicit in the Quaker theology, is the germ of true and genuine religious freedom. For if it is the voice of God that speaks, it may bring its most sublime truths to the human race through its most humble members, and woe to the society that turns a deaf ear to God's truth, no matter where spoken. This sort of religious freedom, and only this, might be the basis for further progress; for it not only recognized that the new, divine instructions to men for their future improvement might be transmitted by any man: it provided the mechanism and commanded the attitude by which the new and the better way might be learned and applied to human life. The idea of progressive enlightenment as a result of religious freedom was expressed by Woolman:

> There have been in times past severe persecutions under the English government, and many sincere hearted people . . . suffered death for the testimony of a good conscience, whose faithfulness in their day hath ministered encouragement to others, and been a blessing to many who have succeeded them. Thus from age to age the darkness being more & more removed, a channel at length, through the tender mercies of God hath been opened for the exercise of the pure gift of the gospel ministry, without interruption from outward power. . . .
>
> We stand in a plan of outward liberty, under the full exercise of our conscience towards God, not obtained but through great and manifold

[61] Quoted in Alice M. Baldwin: *The New England Clergy and the American Revolution* (Durham, 1928), p. 58 n. 35.

afflictions of those who lived before us. There is gratitude due from us to our heavenly Father. There is justice due to our posterity. Can our hearts endure or our hands be strong if we desert a cause so precious ; if we turn aside from a work under which so many have patiently laboured ?" [62]

It was typical of Woolman that he did not expatiate upon the nature of freedom of conscience. It was a precious thing, but it was simply a gift of God to men that had been hardly won through the sufferings of many. Through the freedom, now, of those who would minister to others in the name of God, society and posterity would be benefited. But it was a sign of God's goodness, not primarily a natural law. Woolman thinks that others are in error, and the Quakers right ; but he gladly listens to, and sweetly reasons with, those others ; while he is sure that the doctrine of the inner light, now being free from persecution and hindrance, will, if listened to and followed, bring mankind to an ever greater happiness. The achievement of freedom of conscience marks one stage, for him, in human progress. Let us use it and build upon it for the promotion of further progress.

But if in the Quaker doctrine there was implied the divine right to be heard as well as the divine right to speak, that doctrine was never clearly explicit or self-assertive. The contribution of the Quakers to the great cause of religious toleration, therefore, significant as it was, fell short of being a positive doctrine. Much more positive at least in its assertiveness, was the New England school of religious rationalists ; for the advent of science and scientific rationalism had thrown an entirely new light upon the problem of religious freedom. The searchers after natural order in everything found it in religion, as elsewhere ; and the comparative study of the religions of the world was leading the Deists and the rationalists, who had already discovered that God was a deity of mechanics and natural law in the universe, to see in the great "common" points of "natural religion" a core about which all religions seemed to revolve. Given this simple, universal core, it was easy to believe that all religions, from even Catholicism to the Indians' primitive animism, were but varying expressions of man's universal, "natural" propensity to worship and a recognition of the apparent fact that God "naturally" expects human worship. Given this naturalistic outlook, it easily became a matter of "natural right" for a man to adopt whichever mode of worship best suited his own rational convictions.

From this point it was only a short step for the rationalists to move onward from the concept of the "natural right" of every man to worship God as he thought best to the belief that it was actually his duty to figure out his religion for himself : "So that it is not left to the op-

62 Woolman : *Journal* (Gummere, ed.), pp. 482, 483.

tion of christians whether they will relinquish their natural liberty in religious matters, or not; they are commanded to assert it. God has given us abilities to *judge even for ourselves what is right*: and requires us to improve them. He forbids us to *call any man master upon earth*. And as he has forbidden us to submit implicitly to the dictates of any man, so he has also explicitly forbid all Christians to assume or usurp any authority over their brethren." [63]

Furthermore, continues Jonathan Mayhew, those who interfere with this right and this duty are interfering with the manifest intentions of God:

> They are encroachers upon the natural rights of mankind, because it is the natural right and priviledge of every man to make the best use he can of his own intellectual faculties — They set up their own authority in opposition to that of almighty God, because God has not only given us liberty to examine and judge for ourselves; but expressly required us to do it — They are enemies to truth, and the gospel of Jesus Christ; because free examination is the way to truth, and the gospel in particular, gains ground the faster, the more its doctrines and evidences are examined. — While other tyrants enslave the bodies of men, these throw their chains and fetters upon the mind, which was *born free;* and which ought not to be *in bondage to any man:* but only to the *Father of Spirits.*[64]

The basis for toleration among the religious rationalists, then, was a sort of Newtonian naturalism; man's right to religious self-determinism was as perfectly inherent in the natural order of things as the law of gravity itself. Man, according to Ebenezer Gay:

> hath a Principle of Action within himself, and is an Agent in the strict and proper sense of the Word. The special Endowment of his Nature, which constitutes him such, is the Power of Self-determination, or Freedom of Choice; his being possessed of which is self-evident. . . . And this inward Judgment which every one passes on his own Actions, is enforced with another Principle, which belongs more or less to our common Nature, viz. a Regard to the Judgment that is passed upon our Conduct by other Beings; especially Beings whose Favour or Displeasure is of any Importance to us.[65]

What a far cry this rational toleration was from the authoritarian intolerance of the Puritan fathers! But it was widespread, not only among the rationalistic clergy but also, and probably more commonly, among enlightened laymen. Dr. William Douglass favored religious toleration on rational grounds — although he still had doubts about the

---

[63] Jonathan Mayhew: *Seven Sermons* (Boston, 1749), p. 56.
[64] Ibid., pp. 57–8.
[65] Ebenezer Gay: *Natural Religion Revealed* (Boston, 1759), pp. 12–13.

Catholics. And Archibald Kennedy, in a theoretical address to his son, said :

> I allow you Freedom of Conscience, to think, and judge for yourself;
> and I likewise allow you Freedom, if not entirely from all Manner or
> Influence, yet from the Dominion of human Authority, in thinking and
> judging for yourself. I am so much for Liberty in these Matters that con-
> cerns us, as reasonable Beings, that I must recommend to you, on the
> other Hand, a third Sort of Freedom ; that is, a Freedom from Pride, Sin-
> gularity, and the Spirit of Contradiction. . . . As for my own Part, I have
> no Notion, of Religion's passing by Descent, or Inheritance, as Estates
> do ; nor am I for craming my Religion down my Child's Throat. This,
> in my humble Opinion, would be a Species of Persecution : If he has
> good sense, and capable of judging, let him chuse.[66]

The ideal of intellectual and religious freedom was certainly a common ideal among the Americans of the mid-eighteenth century. But
it was the scientists who, in the last analysis, made of the ideal a
positive and constructive intellectual principle. The natural-rights doctrine of individual judgment preached by Mayhew and Gay was, to
be sure, a positive doctrine of inalienable right in men. But even this
natural-rights doctrine of religious freedom did no more than leave a
man within his rights. Such a doctrine of religious freedom was hardly
more than a rationalization of indifference. What did it matter what
a man believed ? It was of no importance, anyway, so long as he did
not disturb the public peace. If the rationalists made this a matter of
natural right, they merely substituted a positive "natural right" for
Roger Williams's negative "God does not require." But the scientists
went farther and explicitly added to the principle of the right to think
and speak freely the principle of the duty to listen to others and of
the right to be heard. It was Benjamin Franklin who first put succinctly the principle of a learner's humility as the constructive obverse of the principle of intellectual freedom, in a letter he wrote to
his father in 1738 :

> When the natural weakness and imperfection of human understand-
> ing is considered, the unfavorable influence of education, custom, books,
> and company upon our ways of thinking, I imagine a man must have a
> good deal of vanity who believes, and a good deal of boldness who af-
> firms, that all the doctrines he holds are true, and all he rejects are false.
> And perhaps the same may be justly said of every sect, church, and so-
> ciety of men, when they assume to themselves that infallibility, which
> they deny to the Pope and councils.

[66] Archibald Kennedy : *A Speech Said to have been Delivered Some Time
Before the Close of the Late Session, by a Member Dissenting from the Church*
(New York, 1755), pp. 28–9.

I think opinions should be judged of by their influences and effects; and, if a man holds none that tend to make him less virtuous or more vicious, it may be concluded he holds none that are dangerous; which I hope is the case with me. . . .

But, since it is no more in a man's power to *think* than to *look* like another, methinks all that should be expected from me is, to keep my mind open to conviction, to hear patiently, and examine attentively, whatever is offered me for that end.[67]

Here was Franklin's pragmatism at work, and his simple natural-ism. But this remark contains the logical justification not only of genu-ine toleration in religion, but also of constructive intellectual freedom in every realm of thought. For his fundamental attitude is one of learn-ing, rather than the imposition of the truth as he saw it upon others, or the mere negative enjoyment of his own brand of truth, as it were, in a vacuum. For him, human progress depended upon the exchange of ideas; and religious freedom and intellectual freedom meant es-sentially a freedom of exchange in ideas: a freedom to give and a freedom — nay, an obligation — to receive. That this was true he felt sure because it produced a supremely beneficial result in the spread and intensification of human enlightenment and human happiness.

As of the 1750's, America was not yet free of intellectual and re-ligious persecution; practice lagged behind theory. But even in prac-tice the British colonies in America were probably more advanced than any other part of the world. Jonathan Mayhew, in a burst of pa-triotic feeling, rejoiced in 1750 that, "GOD be thanked, one may, in any part of the *British* dominions, speak freely (if a decent regard be paid to those in authority) both of government and religion; and even give some broad hints, that he is engaged on the side of Liberty, the BIBLE and Common Sense, in opposition to Tyrany, PRIEST-CRAFT and Nonsense, without being in danger either of the *Bastile* or the *In-quisition.*"[68]

Franklin, as late as 1772, comparing the New England colonies with old England, could still show that the colonies were more de-voted to the principles and the practice of toleration than the mother country:

In New England, where the legislative bodies are almost to a man dissenters from the Church of England.

1. There is no test to prevent churchmen [Anglicans] from holding offices.

2. The sons of churchmen have the full benefit of the universities.

[67] Benjamin Franklin: *The Works of Benjamin Franklin*, edited by Jared Sparks (10 vols., Boston, 1840), VII, 6.

[68] Jonathan Mayhew: *Discourse on Unlimited Submission* (Boston, 1750), preface, p. v.

3. The taxes for the support of public worship, when paid by church-men, are given to the Episcopal minister.

In Old England,
1. Dissenters are excluded from all offices of profit and honor.
2. The benefits of education in the universities are appropriated to the sons of churchmen.
3. The clergy of the Dissenters receive none of the tithes paid by their people, who must be at the additional charge of maintaining their own separate worship.[69]

Conclusion: The Religious Seeds of Freedom and Democracy

The religion of the Americans of the mid-eighteenth century, as distinguished from the almost uniform cold grey Calvinist, Anglican, Dutch Reformed, and Puritan of the seventeenth, was characterized by the multiplicity of shades of belief rather than fundamental differences of belief. For all, or nearly all, were Christians; even the Deists retained the Christian ethic if not the Christian mythology. Toleration was more advanced in theory than in practice; but the theory was highly developed; the American mind was almost universally committed to it, from one end of the colonies to the other. Rationalism dominated the religious thinking of the sophisticates; conservative Calvinism the thought of the middle class; evangelism, with little real thought of any sort, was the motive force in the religious life of the poor, the illiterate, and the frontiersmen.

This situation was the product of the same three basic formative factors that were determining the nature of American culture in its other aspects. Calvinism, which was the major item in the religious inheritance of the Americans from Great Britain, had undergone a profound, even revolutionary modification under the force of rationalism, derived from science, and under the formative compulsion of the frontier experience. Even the faiths of the pietists had begun to feel the effects of these two forces, although the German religions had as yet, by 1750, hardly been in America long enough to show much change. Thus the inheritance remained as a sort of core of religious belief; but it had been greatly modified under the stresses of rationalism and of the American environment. And it was now something that was to all intents and purposes new. Nowhere, except among the most conservative groups, was seventeenth-century Calvinism preserved in anything closely resembling its original pristine purity. The religious life that was American was new, a sort of end-product of the fusion of original inheritance, new science, and frontier experience.

69 Franklin : *Works* (Sparks ed.), II, 116–17.

But that is not all. This residuum of religious experience in America was of a piece with the corresponding ideological end-products of the economic, social, and political experiences. Religion was but one facet of a larger whole of which the thought-forms dealing with economics, society, and politics were other facets; as were also, indeed, philosophy, literature, art, and music. And the shadings of religion followed, if somewhat irregularly, the shadings of social and political status and ideals. Rationalism in religion was characteristic of those areas and those groups where science was most active, and was to be found most consistently among the most highly educated. Most of the religious rationalists were also political and economic rationalists; it can hardly be any accident that so many of the leaders of the American Revolution belonged to this group, although it is true that a few of them became Tories. The split among the rationalists came between those who thought of freedom from British restraint, in religion as in politics, to be justified in natural law, on one side, and those who found the natural order of things in the religious and political and social system that bound America to the crown of England.

Many perhaps most, of the Americans who remained loyal to Britain when the crisis came were Anglicans who were not greatly affected by rationalism. The members of the "Assembly party" who slowly and consistently, in the 1750's, were building up the strength of the assemblies, were of the middle classes in society and followed a relatively undiluted Calvinism, whether Anglican, Presbyterian, or Puritan-Congregational, in their religion.

The parts of American society that were most radical in religion and politics were the poor and the frontiersmen. This is clearly shown by the course of the Great Awakening; but it is also shown by the fact that these were the people who were most actively interested in political and social leveling, as they were the part of American society that, with certain peculiar exceptions, was least loyal to the British connection.

Similarly, the spread of the ideal of intellectual freedom among the people apparently followed the course of religion. The most intolerant in religion appear to have been generally the most reactionary in social and political thought, although there were exceptions. On the other hand the ideal of toleration was strongest and clearest among those who, like the scientists, were most liberal and rational in religion or among those of the radical democratic sects, such as the Quakers and the Baptists, who believed in religious toleration because they were so strongly individualistic.

It would be a mistake, of course, to push this pattern of connections between religious, social, political, and economic thought too hard. In general, however, the connection is genuine and valid : the pattern of the religious facet of the American mind repeated, in a general way, the patterns of the other facets. By and large, it was the pattern of a developing freedom.

NOTE TO THE READER

A vast quantity of books and pamphlets was produced by the religious mind of eighteenth-century Americans. As a matter of fact, the average man probably read more sermons than any other form of literature. Of the religious books, the following are probably the most representative of the various facets of the religious thought of the Americans, and the most interesting in their own right.

Of the writings of the rationalists, Jonathan Mayhew's *Seven Sermons* (Boston, 1749), Charles Chauncy's *The Benevolence of the Deity* (Boston, 1784), and Samuel Quincy's *Twenty Sermons* (Boston, 1750) are probably the most outstanding. I find Ethan Allen's *Reason the Only Oracle of Man* (Bennington, Vt., 1784), a really exciting statement of the Deists' position ; it is now available in a facsimile edition.

On the side of the conservatives, Thomas Clap's *A Brief History and Vindication of the Doctrines Received and Established in the Churches of New England* (New Haven, 1755) is one of the most significant; but the writings of Jonathan Edwards, published as *The Works of Jonathan Edwards,* edited by Edward Hickman (2 vols., London, 1840), are equally important. For the Great Awakening, Edwards's Enfield sermon gives a good idea of what was going on, but Edwards was never really typical of the revivalists. Besides, Edwards's writing is often fairly difficult reading, although some of his more literary pieces are in beautiful, clear prose. The most available of the awakeners' or "new lights'" writings, probably, are the sermons of George Whitefield (*The Works of the Reverend George Whitefield, M.A.* 4 vols., London, 1771). The sermons of John Davenport or Gilbert Tennent are expressive of the "new light" mind, but they are relatively difficult to find. Samuel Davies was the most distinguished "new light" preacher in the south ; his sermons have been collected as *Sermons on Important Subjects* (3 vols., London, 1792).

Samuel Johnson's *Autobiography* relates his conversion to Anglicanism, as well as his reactions to many other experiences, and his letters are of great interest. His philosophical works are difficult going, however. See Samuel Johnson : *Samuel Johnson . . . His Career and Writings;* edited by Herbert and Carol Schneider (4 vols., New York, 1929). The *Autobiography* and the letters are in Volume I ; his life and writings as a churchman are presented in Volume III.

The best survey of religion in eighteenth-century America is probably W. W. Sweet's *Religion in Colonial America* (New York, 1942).

CHAPTER II

Of the Universe of Nature and of Reason: Newtonian Science

"Oh! let it never be said in this city, or in this province, so happy in its

"climate, and its soil, where commerce has long flourished and plenty

"smiled, that science, the amiable daughter of liberty and sister of opu-

"lence, droops her languid head, or follows behind with a slow un-

"equal pace. I pronounce with confidence this shall not be the case,

"but, under your protection, every useful kind of learning shall here

"fix a favorite seat, and shine forth in meridian splendor."

JOHN MORGAN.

F the Christian religion was the most ancient ele-
ment flowing into the intellectual matrix of Amer-
ica, "Newtonian" science was the most modern.
Nor was it any less important, probably, in the
formation of the American mind; indeed, the so-
called Newtonian concept of the universe, including man, colored and influenced most of the think-
ing, religious and other, that was going on. For not only did science
have a profound effect upon the development of the religious outlook;
the concepts and the language of science were also carried bodily into
the realms of literature and philosophy, economics, sociology, and politics.

Science, as well as religion, demonstrates clearly the fact that the
affairs of men are not always determined by crude self-interest alone.
For there have been important developments in the course of human
affairs — such, for example, as the decreased rate of infant mortality —
that have been brought about, in the last analysis, by the work of the
human mind, by the pragmatic application of disciplined observation
and thought to human problems; in short, by science. There were

[84]

many such developments, large and small, in the eighteenth century; and they were new. For the eighteenth was the century in which New-tonian science began to make itself felt as a force in the determining of human destiny; and as a new and practical learning it had an enor-mous appeal for the Americans, a new and practical people. It is true, of course, that the developing American ideas in the realms of eco-nomics, social phenomena, and politics, derived as they were from first-hand experience in the new world, were largely sincere rationaliza-tions of self-interest elaborated in the light of that experience. But the American outlook on life, in these closely interwoven areas of thought as in all others, was deeply conditioned by ideas drawn from other areas, and particularly from science.

EARLY MODERN SCIENCE IN EUROPE AND AMERICA

Modern science was born, as it were, in the same years that saw the birth of America. Born together, out of the fullness of western civiliza-tion, they grew up together and probably enjoyed a greater interaction upon each other than was the case in any other of the areas of intel-lectual life. Certainly European science and scientific rationalism had more direct influence upon the American mind of the eighteenth cen-tury than any other set of European intellectual phenomena except re-ligion; and, by the same token, American influence upon European thought, such as it was, was almost uniquely in the field of science — at least until American political ideas, based upon the pseudo-scientific concepts of natural law and natural right, began to affect continental European thinking toward the end of the century. The general effects of science upon the American mind, also, were such as tended to make it more secular, more this-worldly, more rationalistic, more ingenious. Especially the last: for in this aspect of the American mind the forces of the frontier and the influence of science combined to produce the most "ingenious," inventive people in the world.

The generation of Europeans who first settled the eastern seaboard of North America was also the generation that first discovered the uni-verse revealed by modern science. For this was the generation of Johann Kepler, Galileo Galilei, Francis Bacon, William Harvey, Robert Boyle, and René Descartes; and these were soon to be followed by Sir Isaac Newton, Gottfried Wilhelm Leibniz, and Hermann Boerhaave. Thus while the colonists at Jamestown and Plymouth were struggling for the mere assurance of physical survival, Johann Kepler was per-fecting his mathematical demonstration of the validity of the Coperni-can theory of the solar system, and Galileo Galilei was making the dis-coveries and writing the books on astronomy and physics that brought him into head-on collision with the Catholic Church. In England, William Harvey was carrying on the experiments with chicken embryos that were to lead to the demonstration of the circulation of the blood in the human body, and Robert Boyle was about to begin the work that eventually led to a new concept of the chemical composition of matter. Presently, about the time of the settlement of Pennsylvania, Isaac Newton was to invent calculus at about the same time as Gottfried Wilhelm Leibniz, in Germany, and to discover the law of gravitation. Science, in the hands of these men and a multitude of others, was opening a new vision of the material universe to the human mind; and others were soon to apply the scientific principles and method to human society and the human mind as well as to the human body.

It was Francis Bacon, writing at the moment of the first American beginnings, who had expressed the spirit of the new learning: "Now the true and lawful goal of the sciences is none other than this: that human life be endowed with new discoveries and powers." And René Descartes exulted that

> It is possible to attain knowledge which is very useful in life, and instead of that speculative philosophy which is taught in the schools [Scholasticism], we may find a practical philosophy by means of which, knowing the force and the action of fire, water, the stars, heavens, and all other bodies that environ us, as distinctly as we know the different crafts of our artisans, we can in the same way employ them in all those uses to which they are adapted, and thus render ourselves the masters and possessors of nature.[1]

Not only did the new science suddenly open to men a new vision of the world: its most revolutionary achievement, probably, was its discovery of a method, the method of induction, to replace the backward-looking reliance on Aristotelian authority that had characterized the Middle Ages: a new method by which, it seemed, every secret of nature and of the universe might eventually be laid bare before the mind of man. Not only that, Francis Bacon knew knowledge to be power: not only could men know the world; they might also control it, become "the masters and possessors of nature" for the benefit of mankind. This was the new philosophy of science: the philosophy of power over nature for the good of men. And this idea, tucked away in the intellectual baggage of the first settlers of America, was to grow and flourish "as a mustard seed." How congenial it was to the new world of America and the frontier was to be demonstrated in every one of the facets of the developing American mind.

The most profoundly significant figure to appear in the annals of

---

[1] René Descartes: *Discourse on Method,* quoted in John H. Randall, Jr.: *The Making of the Modern Mind* (New York, 1940), p. 224.

science in the century of American settlement was Isaac Newton, an almost exact contemporary of William Penn. Newton, a mathematical genius, developed the integral calculus, and this led him into the study of gravity. Meanwhile he became interested in optics, with resultant studies in the nature of color and his adoption of the corpuscular theory of light. The most characteristic aspect of these studies was probably his insistence upon mechanical explanations of all the phenomena that could be expressed in mathematical terms. It was this line of thought that brought about his greatest contribution to science when applied to the force of gravity operating upon the bodies in the solar system. Newton's law of gravity, that bodies attract each other directly in proportion to their mass and inversely in proportion to the square of their distances from each other, as applied to the solar system, was worked out in detail in his great *Philosophiæ Naturalis Principia Mathematica*, generally known as Newton's *Principia*, published in 1687, five years after Pennsylvania was founded; and this book became the basic text for mathematical, physical, and astronomical study for two hundred years.

The intellectual epoch initiated by Newton's work, not without reason called the Newtonian age, was as much influenced, probably, by the implications of his discoveries as by the discoveries themselves. For whereas Bacon and Descartes had given science a method, Newton gave it a superb basis for generalization: the concept of mechanical natural law. For it was easy for scientists — and easier for pseudo-scientists — to jump from the demonstration of the law of gravity to the idea that there were other laws; that the universe, in fact, including man, was completely ruled by natural law. From this point it was just one easy step to the belief that man, having discovered one of the laws, could discover the others, and by living in accordance with them could raise himself and his institutions indefinitely toward perfection. It followed logically that the way to learn the laws of nature was by education; and education, from an instrument for training the mind to perceive and understand God's eternal will, became a mechanism for the inculcation of the great principles of nature and the promotion of the dignity, nobility, and perfectibility of men on the earth here and now.

That the implications of the new science must inevitably bring it into conflict with the accepted positions of the established religions, both Catholic and Protestant, went almost without saying; and the instinct of the Catholic Church was sound when it vaguely saw in Galileo the ideological symbol of its own revision, if not of its eventual destruction. Many men, seeing this, revised their religious convictions to fit the apparently incontrovertible facts exposed by science. So the age of modern science also initiated the modern phase of the conflict of rationalism with religion, a conflict that was just opening in Catholic Italy as the Protestant émigrés from England set sail for America.

Not that the first-comers to America realized it, or even dreamed it. Had they imagined, indeed, the extent to which the scientific explanation of the universe was to reason away many of their most cherished convictions as to the secret ways of God, they probably might have rejected science in perfect horror. But they did not feel the least premonition of real conflict. For them, God had created the universe. It mattered little whether God worked his wonders by the Ptolemaic system or the Copernican. The first notable scientist to appear in America was John Winthrop, Jr., son of the famous Puritan Governor of Massachusetts and himself the Governor of Connecticut. Winthrop owned what was probably the first telescope in English America — which he presented to Harvard College about 1676 — and devoted much serious attention to chemistry, medicine, astronomy, and witchcraft. He was probably the first American member of the Royal Society.[2] And when doughty old John Davenport, one of the founders of New Haven and himself a devotee of the old science, heard of the new Copernican Almanac published at Harvard by Zechariah Bridgen in 1659, he merely commented: "let him injoy his opinion; and I shall rest in what I have learned, til more cogant arguments be produced."[3] At least, he was willing to be shown. Bridgen sensed the probability that the readers of his almanac might resist the Copernican theory of the universe explained in it because of the obvious discrepancy with the Bible account of the creation, and took care to anticipate that opposition by an appeal to reason :

> Those objections that are back't with Divine authority, although they are most weighty, yet by the maintayners of this Systeme, are not let pass without an answer, the breif whereof is
> That the Scriptures being fitted as well to the capacity of the rudest mechanick, as of the [a]blest Philosopher, do not intend so much propriety and exactness, as playnes and perspicuity ; and in Philosophical truths, therein contayned, the proper literal sense is always subservient to the casting vote of reason.[4]

This was indeed a bold stand to take, to say that the literal words of the Scriptures were subservient to the final decision of human rea-

---

[2] Fredrick E. Brash : *The Royal Society of London and Its Influence upon Scientific Thought in the Colonies* (Washington, 1931), pp. 5 ff.

[3] Quoted in Samuel E. Morison : *The Puritan Pronaos* (New York, 1936), p. 240.

[4] Quoted in Samuel E. Morison : "The Harvard School of Astronomy in the Seventeenth Century," *New England Quarterly*, VII (1934), p. 12.

son. Revolutionary, in fact; but it was hardly challenged because to the Puritans of that day it did not matter very much how God performed his works; the important thing was that he performed them, according to his own plan. The remarkable thing was that Bridgen could set up reason as the intellectual court of highest appeal among a people who had hitherto been such inflexible literalists in their interpretation of the Bible. Yet Bridgen's appeal to reason and John Davenport's tolerance did not affect the main fact that the science of the Puritans was merely a way of understanding God and his handiwork. The universe was God's creation; he had a plan for it, and any unusual occurrences in it were but manifestations of God's moving purpose. Samuel Danforth, for example, discussing a comet that appeared in the heavens in 1665, rejected the older idea that comets were "exhalations" from the earth and, in almost modern fashion, found them subject to natural law. But God, in this case, was only using his own natural laws to convey a message, relative to his purposes with men, to human beings:

I. *This Comet is no sublunary Meteor or sulphureous Exhalation, but a Celestial Luminary, moving in* the starry Heavens. . . .

IV. *This Comet is not a new fixed Star, but a Planetick or Erratick Body, wandring up & down in the etherial firmament under the fixed stars.* . . .

Unto these and some other no less threatening Visitations, is superadded this strange and fearful Appearance in the Heavens, which is now seconded by a new Appearance this Spring, concomitant to the translation of our Honoured and Aged Governour, Mr. *John Endicot,* from hence to a better world: By all which doubtless the Lord calls upon *New England* to awake to repent. . . .[5]

Danforth was not sure, exactly, how, but it was "doubtless" a call from God to New England to repent; of one thing he was certain: God's plan and purpose were behind it. Increase Mather, a sort of amateur scientist and the greatest of the second generation of Puritan preachers, echoed Danforth's position, for he, too, could take a naturalistic position with regard to the comets; but he could not leave them without pointing out their relationship to God's interest in men: "It concerns us then, to hearken to the voice of the Lord therein; who by such tremendous Sights is speaking awfully to the children of Men. Hear then *Heaven's Alarm* this day. . . .[But] The Lord's threatening's are not absolute; but conditional." So far as we in America are concerned, "it is possible we may escape the Evils threatened thereby, if we duely hearken to the voice of God therein. . . . If Repentance

[5] Miller and Johnson: *The Puritans,* pp. 738–9.

intervene, the Evils which otherwise must be looked for, may be diverted." [6] God worked in naturalistic ways, perhaps, his wonders to perform, but they were none the less messages to men; science became, in effect, a way of understanding God's warning; it was distinctly subservient to the main business of nature and man alike, which was the glorification of God.

Increase Mather's naïve Puritan harmonization of science with religion was enthusiastically seconded by Cotton Mather, his son:

> *Philosophy* [science] is no *Enemy*, but a mighty and wondrous *incentive* to *Religion.* . . . If Men so much admire Philosophers, because they *discover* a small Part of the *Wisdom* that made all things; they must be stark blind, who do not admire that *Wisdom itself.* . . . The great GOD is infinitely *gratified* in beholding the Displays of His own infinite *Power,* and *Wisdom,* and *Goodness,* in the Works which He has made; but it is also a most acceptable Gratification to Him, when such of His Works as are the *rational Beholders* of themselves, and of the rest, shall with devout Minds *acknowledge* His Perfections, which they see shining there.[7]

Cotton Mather was surprisingly modern, indeed, in his attitude toward the new ideas of science, as is abundantly shown by his *Christian Philosopher*, which is an agreeable survey of certain fields of natural science, and in his sponsoring of inoculation for smallpox. But he was always a Puritan: The world of nature is the visible handiwork of God, the material documentation of God's plan for men. For example, with regard to the magnet: "God forbid that I should be, *Tam Lapis ut Lapidi Numen isse putem* [such a stone as to attribute divine authority to a stone]. . . . But then it would be a very agreeable *Homage* unto the Glorious GOD, for me to see much of Him in such a wonderful *Stone* as the MAGNET. They have done well to call it the Loadstone, that is to say, the *Lead-stone: May it lead me unto Thee, O My God and My Saviour! Magnetism* is in this like to Gravity, that it leads us to GOD, and brings us very near to Him." [8]

SCIENCE IN EIGHTEENTH-CENTURY AMERICA
The physical sciences

The subservience of science to religion could not last. The frontier was making for a greater secularism in life itself, and science was making ineluctably for a greater rationalism in thought of all kinds, with

---

[6] Increase Mather: *Heaven's Alarm to the World* (Boston, 1682), pp. 24, 32–3.

[7] Cotton Mather: *The Christian Philosopher;* excerpts printed in Kenneth B. Murdock, ed.: *Selections from Cotton Mather* (New York, 1926), pp. 286, 292, 351–2.

[8] Ibid., p. 314.

religion having, perforce, either to adapt itself to science or lose altogether its influence as an ideological force in American society. For Newtonian science was on the march.

Science, or "natural philosophy," as it was called, was largely in the hands of amateurs in the eighteenth century. The only professional

Newtonian Science in America: Professor John Winthrop. A portrait by John Singleton Copley.
[By courtesy of the Fogg Museum of Art, Harvard University]

scientists were the physicians and a scattering of college professors. The professors, however, trained as they were in Newtonian mathematics and the scientific method, made profoundly important contributions to the advancement and the spread of Newtonian science generally. Because, too, of their more rigorous scientific discipline, these professionals were generally more exact in method and in language than the amateurs. Franklin, of course, the greatest amateur of them all, must be excepted. Of the professionals, the greatest were John Winthrop of Harvard, William Small of William and Mary, and the self-taught David Rittenhouse, who became professor of astronomy at the University of Pennsylvania during the Revolution, in the year in which John Winthrop died.

Professor John Winthrop was a scion of the family of the first governor of Massachusetts. He was elected to the Hollis Professorship of Mathematics and Natural Philosophy at Harvard in 1738, and he filled that chair with brilliance until his death in the midst of the American Revolution, 1779. His work of experiment and teaching ranged over the entire field of the physical sciences, astronomy, geology and seismology, mathematics, chemistry, and electricity. He introduced the calculus to Harvard students, and corroborated the work of Franklin in electricity. He thought of science as the servant of man, to be used for his improvement; with regard to Franklin's lightning-rods he wrote : "It is as much our duty to secure ourselves against the effects of lightning as against those of rain, snow, and wind, by the means God has put into our hands." [9]

But Winthrop's greatest claim to fame rests upon his work as an astronomer and seismologist. He was particularly interested in eclipses, and he had occasion to observe a series of transits, which he described in print. The first of these studies was an observation of a transit of Mercury, which was made in 1740, and this was followed by observations of another transit of Mercury in 1743 and the transits of Venus in 1761 and 1769. The papers describing this work were sent to the Royal Society, in London, and published in its *Philosophical Transactions*. Winthrop himself was elected to the society.

What was probably the first publicly supported scientific expedition in this country was led by Winthrop to Newfoundland, in 1761, for the observation of the transit of Venus. The enthusiasm of this usually cautious scientist was aroused by the perspective of the universe opened to the human mind by the study of astronomy, and he exclaimed : "How Astronomy transports us into distant Futurity !" [10] More specifically, however, he looked upon the study of the transit of Venus as helping to solve certain very definite problems then facing astronomers : "The comparison of the observations made in the N. W. parts of the world with those in the S. E. when all of them come to be laid together, will give the true path of Venus, abstracted from parallax, by which means, the quantity of the parallax will at length be discovered. The right determination of which point will render this year 1761 an ever memorable æra in the annals of astronomy." [11] Winthrop's

[9] Quoted in J. M. Davis and P. L. Sharpe : *Science* (New York, 1936), p. 1226.
[10] John Winthrop : *Relation of a Voyage from Boston to Newfoundland, for the Observation of the Transit of Venus, June 6, 1761* (Boston, 1761), p. 17.
[11] Ibid., p. 21.

interest in these studies of the transit of Venus was directed especially toward determining the parallax of the sun, in order to calculate its distance from the earth. Incidentally, however, he was also conscious of the importance these observations would have upon the more accurate determination of longitude. The expedition to Newfoundland in 1761 was a great success; in view of the impossibility of getting exactly accurate instruments and exactly controlled conditions for its observations, it is remarkable that he was able to accomplish as much as he did. He gave a distillation of the results of his studies of Venus over a period of several years in two public lectures in 1769, at which time he explained the practical value of the solution to the problem of the parallax and predicted that the next transits of Venus over the sun would be in A.D. 1874 and 2004. The twentieth century, he said, would pass without an opportunity to view this spectacle! As a result of his observations, he found that the distance from the earth to the sun was approximately 94,030,000 miles. (At the present day the distance, on the average, is considered 92,900,000 miles.)

But "natural philosophy" meant all of the modern "physical sciences" as well as mathematics and astronomy, and included both geology and meteorology. Winthrop made systematic observations in both these last-named fields, and his interest, especially in geology, was dramatically stimulated by the earthquake of 1755.

New England had had a series of earthquakes prior to that year, and they had provoked a great deal of scientific speculation. Paul Dudley, for example, a fellow of the Royal Society, had attributed earthquakes to an undulating motion of the earth's crust. But Dudley did not understand the cause of the motion, and felt there must be some connection between earthquakes and the weather:

> Our earth might be disposed to or prepared for the earthquake that followed; first by a long continued Drought and extreme heat, whereby the Earth became more porous and abounded with Exhalations or Vapours inflamed, and which afterwards being shut up by the succeeding great Rains and Frost, and thereby hindered from an ordinary and easy Passage through the Pores and Common Vents of the Earth, worked so much more forcibly and terribly upon one another.[12]

Dr. William Douglass also interested himself in this problem of the cause of earthquakes and the connection, if any, between earthquakes and the weather. He could find no such connection; but he did send a careful description of the earthquake of 1727 to Cadwallader Colden in New York, and estimated its center to have been "somewhere in the Wilderness N W of our Settlements, and that [although the area of the

---

[12] Royal Society, *Philosophical Transactions*, XXXIX, 63–73.

quake] gradually decreased towards the S W and S E, to the N E it must reach a great way because it was violent 130 miles N E of Boston." [13] The Reverend Thomas Prince, however, was not nearly so scientifically objective in his sermon, inspired by this same earthquake, entitled *Earthquakes the Works of God and Tokens of his just Displeasure.* He did, to be sure, attempt to explain the natural or "secondary" causes of the quake, but he, like his Puritan forebears, was still chiefly concerned with its relationship to the purposes of God. God had constructed the earth with subterranean caverns filled with "sulphureous" particles ready to explode like gunpowder and shake the earth whenever the divine wisdom thought it desirable. In fact, says Prince, "what we call the *Laws of Nature* are only the usual Methods in which He is pleased to Work in the World; and from which He sees not cause to depart but in some extraordinary Cases where his usual manner of working cannot reach his Designs." [14] This early harmonizer of science and religion found the concept of natural law not at all uncongenial to him; indeed, even the atomic theory — which he had borrowed from Boyle — seemed entirely acceptable to him. The important thing was that when God was angry, as he often was, "The smallest Atoms of Matter are of themselves as Dead and unable to fly off from each other as the greatest Rocks in the World. . . . That mighty and invisible Cause [God] which moves them is every where always Present, attending these numberless and most minute materials, and moving them all in the most regular and intelligent manner." [15]

When in 1755 New England suffered another major earthquake, John Winthrop published some of his observations upon it, attributing it to a wavelike undulation of the crust of the earth, more or less as Dudley had described it: "It appears, that our buildings were rocked with a kind of angular motion, like that of a cradle; the upper parts of them moving swifter, or thro' greater spaces in the same time, than the lower; the natural consequence of an undulatory motion of the earth." [16] He did not attempt to draw a connection between the earthquake and the weather; but he expressed by implication a certain skepticism regarding the old Dudley thesis. The most striking characteristic of Winthrop's study was its cool, scientific attitude with regard to this phenomenon, in the midst of a flurry of sermons and pamphlets purporting to show that the earthquake was a sign of God's wrath. Many of the outstanding New England divines sought to improve the occasion for the purposes of their ministry; and Thomas

[13] *Colden Papers,* I, 235.
[14] Thomas Prince: *Earthquakes the Works of God and Tokens of his just Displeasure* (Boston, 1727), pp. 12–13.
[15] Ibid., p. 13.
[16] *Philosophical Transactions,* L, 12–13.

Prince, now the elder statesman among them, reprinted his sermon of 1727; but by this time Franklin's lightning-rods had made their appearance, and "this reverend philosopher," as Winthrop called him, added a note to the sermon that attributed the quake to them.[17]

Another, somewhat less dramatic aspect of Winthrop's work in astronomy was his observations of comets and meteors. Here, too, his descriptions of the phenomena were coolly objective and rational, although he generally assured his students and his audiences that ultimately, of course, the great first cause of all natural phenomena was God. As he said in one of his eulogies of Newton that the great significance of Newton's study, as of all natural philosophy, was that it "pointed out the fundamental law which the alwise CREATOR has established for regulating the several movements in this grand machine." [18]

John Winthrop may probably be called the first truly great and representative native American scientist. But he was not only a "laboratory" scientist and professor; he was also a great popularizer, and always interested in ways and means of making science useful to his fellow men. It was this success in spreading a knowledge of science and an interest in it that led a group of his students to found, in 1780, the American Academy of Arts and Sciences, which was patterned somewhat after the American Philosophical Society in Philadelphia. He received, in 1773, the first honorary degree ever awarded by Harvard University, and participated in the great break with the mother country as scientific adviser to the government of Massachusetts, particularly in questions referring to engineering problems, munitions, and supply. Thus did the laboratory scientist and his science serve the causes of practical human betterment, of intellectual freedom, and of political independence.

Less of a laboratory astronomer and physicist than John Winthrop IV, but more of a theorist than either Winthrop or Benjamin Franklin, Cadwallader Colden, Lieutenant-Governor of New York, made a number of astronomical studies and advanced certain theories of the universe that made him unquestionably one of the ablest scientists of the American colonies. Colden's interests ranged the entire field of human learning, and he performed the remarkable feat of producing a number of important essays and books while immersed in the bitter and boisterous conflicts of New York's provincial politics. Despite his scientific writings and studies, however, Colden was apparently never elected to the Royal Society — possibly because he dared to appear to criticize the great Sir Isaac Newton. His scientific training was in medi-

17 Thomas Prince : *Earthquakes the Works of God and Tokens of his just Displeasure* (Boston, 1755), appendix.
18 Winthrop : *Relation of a Voyage . . . to Newfoundland,* p. 6.

cine, and he wrote much in that field. But he corresponded with Linnæus and Alexander Garden in the field of botany, with Peter Collinson and Benjamin Franklin in the field of physics, and with all these and a host of others in the field of medicine and chemistry. As a mathematician he wrote *An Introduction to The Doctrine of Fluxions,* and as a physicist he wrote pamphlets on *Light and Color, The Cohesion of the Parts of Bodies,* and numerous others.

Colden and Franklin carried on a vigorous correspondence, on medical subjects as well as physics, and Franklin sent Colden copies of the notes he made on his own electrical studies in the 1740's. At one time, about 1746, Franklin conceived the idea that the easterly voyages across the Atlantic were shorter than the westerly voyages because the diurnal motion of the earth hastened the ship eastward and retarded it on the westerly voyage. Colden was of the opinion that the motion of the earth had little or no importance : less, surely, than the resistance of the water; and he decided that the water's resistance to the ship was less on the eastward voyage because of the tides, which, following the moon, reach their high-water mark at a more easterly point each day, favoring the ship; whereas this same phenomenon, he thought, served to retard the ship on the westerly voyage ! Franklin was at the moment planning to publish a "philosophical miscellany," and Colden was so sure of his idea that he offered to support it in Franklin's publication. It was not until about 1769 that Franklin learned of the retarding and accelerating effects of the Gulf Stream from a Nantucket sea-captain then in London, and that particular problem was resolved.

But whereas Franklin's interest was always centered chiefly in the practical aspects of science, Colden's interest centered chiefly in theory; and it was in the realm of theoretical physics that he wrote his most ambitious scientific book, *The Principles of Action in Matter,* printed in London in 1751. Several earlier editions of this work had been published, in New York, London, and even Leipzig and Hamburg; but the edition of 1751 was the definitive one. In the opinion of Colden himself, this was his greatest work. In short, he wrote : "I think that I can demonstrate the theorem [of gravitation] in Sr Isaac Newtones Principia from these Principles. . . . I am in hopes it may likewise be of use to explain some other Phænomena besides Gravitation of which none of the Philosophers have hitherto been able to give any tollerable account." [19]

In other words, if Newton had demonstrated the existence and the force of gravity, Colden would go farther and explain the nature of this force and how it operated. He knew that he would be regarded as foolhardy in attempting to supplement Newton; but he was so con-

[19] *Colden Papers,* VIII, 336.

vinced that he had found the solution to this problem that he was determined to face the criticism.

His theory is original and very suggestive. For he believed that gravitation was a force exerted by an elastic, contractive form of matter that he called ether, which permeates the entire universe. Curiously enough, in arriving at this idea he seems to get pretty close to a sort of "field theory" of gravitation : "the force of gravitation towards any body being at every distance reciprocally [inversely] as the squares of the distance, seems to shew, that gravitation is the effect of some emanation from the attracting body : for the force of the emanation of any vertue, proceeding from any body . . . is at every distance reciprocally, as the squares of the distances. . . . But this no way lessens the difficulty : for how can we conceive, that an emanation or motion from any body, can make another move toward it?" [20] He answers his own question by suggesting that the ether is a sort of universal cohesive agent; any "field" of operation of this force is most intense where other forms of matter, such as those composing a planet, are bound together, and the force operates least intensely in the great semi-void spaces between. This, he thought, explained the Newtonian law that gravity operates inversely as the squares of the distances between bodies. The most significant aspect of the idea was Colden's concept of a universal, elastic form of matter whose contractile force in one area was nicely balanced, in the case of any given body or mass, by its own contractile force operating from some other mass or masses in another area.

Colden's book itself is obscure, highly technical, and difficult to follow ; and some of his demonstrations do not seem to be consistent with his theory ; even Franklin confessed it was not clear to him. Colden's hope that he had improved upon Newton's explanation of the basic principles of gravitation was never realized in the general acceptance of his idea ; yet the idea itself was regarded as highly original, and was widely read in intellectual circles all over the western world. The idea of an active ether had been suggested, toward the end of the seventeenth century, by the Swiss Jacques Bernouilli, but it is hardly probable that Colden had heard of it.

Colden was greatly interested in the nature of light, also, and entered into an interesting exchange of ideas on the subject with Franklin. He believed in a sort of corpuscular theory of light, and that all bodies emanate light, even though we may not always see it.

Light is a substance or being essentially distinct from what we commonly call matter or body ; they have nothing in common between them, ex-

[20] Cadwallader Colden : *An Explication of the First Causes of action in Matter ; and of the Cause of Gravitation* (New York, 1745), p. 36.

cept that we consider or conceive both as consisting of quantity, that is, that in the same space there may be a greater or less quantity of either. . . . Light has no power of attraction [i.e., gravity], though it be attracted by resisting matter. The vibrations of a fluid will in no manner ex-

Newtonian Science in America: Cadwallader Colden. A portrait by Matthew Pratt.

[By courtesy of the New York State Chamber of Commerce]

plain the phenomena of light, as is very expressly pointed out in Sir Isaac Newton's *Optics;* . . . again, the separation of the distinct parts of light, which excite in us the different and distinct sensations of colors, and which, once separated, always remain the same, proves that these sensations cannot be produced by the vibrations of any medium supposed to convey the action of light from the luminous body.[21]

[21] Franklin : *Works* (Sparks ed.), VI, 115–16.

To which Franklin could only reply :

I must own, I am much in the *dark* about *light*. I am not satisfied with the doctrine, that supposes particles of matter called light, continually driven off from the sun's surface, with a swiftness so prodigious ! . . . May not all the phenomena of light be more conveniently solved, by supposing universal space filled with a subtile elastic fluid, which, when at rest, is not visible, but whose vibrations affect that fine sense in the eye, as those of air do the grosser organs of the ear ? We do not, in the case of sound, imagine that any sonorous particles are thrown off from a bell, for instance, and fly in straight lines to the ear ; why must we believe that luminous particles leave the sun and proceed to the eye ? [22]

But Colden continued to develop his position, for he believed that his theory of light substantiated his explanation of the nature of gravitation. In fact, the logic of his theory of the material structure of the universe demanded a third sort of matter or "being" that could be furnished, he thought, only by the nature of light. For if the more obvious forms of matter were called the "resisting" type of matter, and if ether were considered as "reacting" or contractile matter, then light was a third sort of "being," if not "matter" which, since the rays of light interpenetrate one another, could not possibly be made up of solid particles. This third sort of "being" or "power" he described as a "moving" medium ; for "wherever we discover light we discover motion ; and if we eliminate motion from our concept of light the concept itself collapses. Light, therefore, is in some mysterious way the vehicle for the communication of motion to the two other classes of matter, bringing to the ether the power of contracting and to mass the power of resisting. It is a distinct susbtance from matter" ; and "It is easy to conceive . . . that light is the moving power or the principle of motion." [23] Finally, he said : "On the whole, I am strongly possessed with an Opinion, that all the phenomena in Nature can be deduced from [these] three distinct & essentially different powers or Beings. The Resisting power in Matter, the Moving power in Light, & the Reacting power of the universal Medium [ether]. That the Phenomena of every System . . . may be deduced from the combined Actions of these three simple powers, under the direction of an Intelligent Being." [24]

Thus Colden's theoretical physics led him straight into philosophy ; and that, in turn, reacted upon his religion. But he seems to have conceived of his "Intelligent Being," the directing principle of the universe,

[22] Ibid., V, 285–6.
[23] Cadwallader Colden : "Introduction to the Study of Philosophy" ; manuscript, New York Historical Society ; pp. 11–16.
[24] Colden : "An Inquiry into the Principles of Vital Motion" ; manuscript, New York Historical Society ; p. 35.

as somehow resident in the universe, rather than outside, and "it never opposes or acts contrary to the material powers." Colden's philosophy will be explained in another place; suffice it to say here that he carried his scientific thinking much farther in the direction of a logical explanation of the ultimate physical structure of the universe than any other colonial scientist.

The best-known and in some ways the greatest of the American physicists was "the ingenious Doctor Franklin." Franklin was less of an exact, mathematical scientist than either Winthrop, Colden, or David Rittenhouse, but he stood, even more clearly than they, in the American tradition of self-education and scientific accomplishment built upon native ingenuity. For Franklin was both scientist and inventor. He probably invented more useful "gadgets" than any other American before Thomas A. Edison, and his scientific experimenting and study took him into many fields, from oceanography through physics to chemistry, meteorology, geography, and medicine. But the most sensational and original scientific studies he ever made were in the field of electricity; and his book on the subject, a collection of letters and papers first published by Peter Collinson of the Royal Society and later gathered together under the title *Experiments and Observations on Electricity Made at Philadelphia,* was one of the most widely read and discussed books ever written on a scientific subject.

Franklin's interest in electricity was awakened about 1746 when he saw in Boston some electrical demonstrations performed by a "Doctor Spencer." Upon his return to Philadelphia he tried his hand at electricity with some apparatus sent the Library Company by Peter Collinson of London, to which Franklin added all of Spencer's equipment, which he purchased. From that time on, for several years, he and several of his friends, most notably Ebenezer Kinnersley and Philip Syng, spent most of their time conducting experiments with electricity, manufacturing for themselves the additional equipment that they needed. Presently they were also manufacturing equipment for Cadwallader Colden, who had started experimenting on his own account.

Franklin and his collaborators actually discovered much that was new, and reported their discoveries to Peter Collinson, through whose agency Franklin's letters were made known to the Royal Society and presently to the scientists on the continent of Europe. Indeed, the greatest contribution made by America to European thought in the eighteenth century was precisely this set of reports of the experiments in electricity being carried on in Philadelphia. Among the contributions made by Franklin and his group was the demonstration that pointed conductors were more effective than blunt ones in the transmission of electrical charges across gaps. Of greater importance was Franklin's description of electricity as "positive" and "negative," and of still greater importance was his discovery that the charge in a Leyden jar is negative on the inside and positive on the outside and that the two charges bal-

Newtonian Science in America: Benjamin Franklin. A mezzotint portrait by Edward Fisher after an oil portrait by Mason Chamberlin.

ance each other. By a series of careful experiments, described in his letters to Collinson, Franklin also discovered that the actual charge of the jar resides in the glass, rather than in the metal outside or in the tinfoil inside.

The great and dramatic climax of Franklin's work with electricity came with his famous kite-demonstration of his theory that lightning was electricity. That theory had already been confirmed by others, however, and Franklin himself had already given it — as usual — a practical application by the invention of the lightning-rod. The famous kite merely gave a dramatic and popular emphasis to a set of discoveries and theories whose significance was already widely recognized.

Even before he began his work in electricity Franklin had made a series of studies of heat and ventilation that resulted in his invention of the so-called "Pennsylvania fireplace," the chief function of which was a more economic conservation of the heat thrown off by the fire within the stove. But his studies of heat and evaporation in the atmosphere led him to speculate on the nature of "fire," which he seems to have identified with "heat." He concluded that it was a "fluid," like electricity. As he wrote to Dr. John Lining, of Charleston, who was conducting some experiments of his own :

> Allowing common fire, as well as electricity, to be a fluid capable of permeating other bodies, and seeking an equilibrium, I imagine some bodies are better fitted by nature to be conductors of that fluid than others ; and that, generally, those which are the best conductors of the electrical fluid, are also the best conductors of this ; and e contra. . . .[25]
>
> Thus, as by a constant supply of fuel in a chimney, you keep a warm room, so, by the constant supply of food in the stomach, you keep a warm body ; only, where little exercise is used, the heat may possibly be conducted away too fast ; in which case such materials are to be used for clothing and bedding, against the effects of an immediate contact of the air, as are, in themselves, bad conductors of heat, and, consequently, prevent its being communicated through their substance to the air. . . . Clothing, thus considered, does not make a man warm by giving warmth, but by preventing the too quick dissipation of the heat produced in his body, and so occasioning an accumulation.[26]

At this point Franklin got fairly close to the theory of metabolism, a problem on which both Dr. Lining of Charleston and Cadwallader Colden in New York were working at nearly the same time.

Franklin's scientific and inventive interests led him into the field of public health, ventilation, the theory of medicine, meteorology, geology, chemistry, astronomy, physics, and aeronautics. As the most widely known and recognized American scientist of his time he was elected to the Royal Society in 1756 and to the French Academy of Sciences in 1772. He was a great rationalist, with the rationalist's faith in man's ability to learn and to use his knowledge for human betterment. Yet he was not entirely averse to a sort of speculative thinking that might be dignified by the name of theoretical physics, and in his discussion of light with Cadwallader Colden he came remarkably close to the theory of the conservation of matter :

[25] Franklin : Works (Sparks ed.) VI, 205.   [26] Ibid., VII, 208–9.

If the Sun is not wasted by Expence of Light, I can easily conceive that he shall otherwise always retain the same Quantity of Matter, tho we should suppose him made of Sulphur constantly flowing. The Action of Fire only *separates* the Particles of Matter, it does not *annihilate* them. . . . And if we could collect all the Particles of burning Matter that go off in Smoke, perhaps they might, with the Ashes, weigh as much as the Body before it was fired ; and if we could put them into the same Position with regard to each other, the Mass would be the same as before ; and might be burnt over again.[27]

Franklin eschewed formal philosophy and made no effort to construct a systematic explanation of the universe upon the basis of his scientific discoveries. His interest in science was primarily utilitarian : he wished to use science for the improvement of man's condition. His interest was thus a pragmatic interest : in science, as in all his thinking, his test of the validity of any scientific knowledge was its usefulness. And in this, like his neighbor John Bartram, he was eminently American ; for it was precisely this pragmatic attitude toward all things that, probably more than anything else, distinguished the thinking of the Americans from that of their foreign contemporaries.

Franklin attracted the interest of a number of younger men, who helped him with his experiments or who, distant from Philadelphia, repeated them and confirmed his findings. Ebenezer Kinnersley and Philip Syng, in Philadelphia, contributed much to his work ; and Kinnersley in particular became famous as a lecturer on electricity and "natural philosophy" from one end of the colonies to the other, including the West Indies.

Another amateur physicist who was worthy of note was James Bowdoin of Boston, who graduated from Harvard in 1745. Though his career lay in the fields of business and politics, Bowdoin was greatly interested in science, and was influenced by both John Winthrop and Benjamin Franklin, with whom he corresponded regularly. He was especially interested in electricity and in the problem of the nature of light. He repeated Franklin's experiments in both fields, but showed his own originality by disagreeing with him in the field of optics, holding to the corpuscular theory of light as against Franklin's wave theory. He also attempted to calculate the speed of light upon the basis of a distance of the earth from the sun estimated at some eighty million miles — a figure soon to be corrected by John Winthrop.

Bowdoin entered into a discussion with Franklin relative to the luminosity of ocean water at night (that is, its phosphorescence). Seamen had suggested to him that it might be caused by the putrefaction of the organic matter in the ocean, since a dead fish may show this luminosity

[27] *Colden Papers*, IV, 322.

at night; but Bowdoin preferred to believe that it was caused by tiny luminous animalcula. Franklin, early in his studies of electricity, believed that the luminosity of the sea was caused by electricity, and that somehow this was the probable ultimate source of lightning. Bowdoin disputed this hypothesis, and Franklin, after a series of experiments with sea-water, was compelled to abandon it. Bowdoin's explanation of the sea's luminosity now appeared to him reasonable.

Later in life, in the midst of the American Revolution, Bowdoin joined with other "philosophers" of New England to found, in 1780, the American Academy of Arts and Sciences, becoming its first president. In his inaugural address he gave eloquent testimony not only to his own scientific interest, but to the scientific outlook of most eighteenth-century scientists :

> When we contemplate the works of nature, animate and inanimate, connected with our earth ; observe the immense number and variety of them ; their exquisite beauty and contrivance ; and the uses to which they are adapted : — when we raise our view to the heavens, and behold the beauteous and astonishing scenes they present to us — unumbered worlds revolving in the immeasurable expanse ; systems beyond systems composing one boundless universe ; and all of them, if we may argue from analogy, peopled with an endless variety of inhabitants : — When we contemplate these works of nature, which no human eloquence can adequately describe, they force upon us the idea of a Supreme Mind, the consummately perfect author of them, —
> > *"That universal spirit, which informs,*
> > *Pervades, and actuates the wond'rous whole.*[28]

Dr. John Lining, of Charleston, who achieved considerable note in the realm of medicine as well as that of electricity, wrote of his own repetitions of Franklin's kite-experiment :

> The flow of the electric fluid, or the matter of lightning, was so rapid and copious down the line, near 700 feet long, to the key appended at the lower end of the line, that from thence I obtained sparks of lightning as thick and as long as the first two joints of a man's little finger, and these as quick one after another, as I could bring the loop of a wire, which I used for that purpose, within about two inches of the key ; And the snappings from the key were so smart and loud, that they were heard at the distance of at least two hundred yards. A ten ounce phial coated [Leyden jar] was then properly suspended by the key, that it might be charged, but the flux of the electric matter down the line, was so copious, that the phial was charged almost as soon as it was hung to the key, and the surcharge continued flying off, for a considerable time, from the end of the phial's hook, making a very loud hissing noise. I then endeavoured, with-

[28] *Memoirs of the American Academy of Arts and Sciences,* I, 20.

out taking the phial off the key, to discharge it in the usual manner ; but as soon as I brought the loop of the wire towards the coating of the phial, I received such a shock up to my shoulder, that I failed in the attempt, and before I could be furnished with a longer wire to discharge the phial, without receiving a shock, all the electric fluid, or lightning in the clouds was drawn from them, and discharged in the air, with a hissing noise from the extremity of the vial's hook.[29]

Still another younger contemporary, who was probably second only to John Winthrop as an astronomer, was David Rittenhouse, of Philadelphia. Rittenhouse, starting as a farm boy, was almost completely self-taught. His native ingenuity and inventiveness led him first into the self-directed study of mathematics and the profession of clock- and instrument-maker. He built the first orrery in America in 1767. Like John Winthrop at Harvard, he was interested in longitude and the movement of the planets, and he conducted, in 1769, under the auspices of the American Philosophical Society, a famous triangulated observation of the transit of Venus, which resulted in a surprisingly accurate estimate of the distance of the sun from the earth and a discovery of the atmosphere surrounding the planet Venus. In 1768 Rittenhouse began work on the Norriton Astronomical Observatory, the first of its kind in Pennsylvania.

Rittenhouse, like Winthrop, was inspired by the vision of the limitless horizons of human knowledge, and the significance of the rational study of nature for the increase of human happiness. In 1775, in an oration before the American Philosophical Society — just on the eve of the Revolution — he rose to heights of eloquence as he brought his theory of a "plurality of worlds" to the service of the American struggle against England :

> The doctrine of a plurality of worlds, is inseparable from the principles of Astronomy ; but this doctrine is still thought by some pious persons, and by many more I fear, who do not deserve that title, to militate against the truths asserted by the Christian religion . . . . But neither religion nor philosophy forbids us to believe that infinite wisdom and power, prompted by infinite goodness, may throughout the vast extent of creation and duration, have frequently interposed in a manner quite incomprehensible to us, when it became necessary to the happiness of created beings of some other rank or degree.
>
> How far indeed the inhabitants of the other planets may resemble man, we cannot pretend to say. If like him they were created liable to fall, yet some if not all of them, may still retain their original rectitude. We will hope they do : the thought is comfortable. . . . If their inhabitants resemble man in their faculties and affections, let us suppose

[29] *Gentleman's Magazine* XXIII, 431.

that they are wise enough to govern themselves according to the dictates of that reason their creator has given them, in such manner as to consult their own and each other's true happiness, on all occasions. . . . We will hope that their statesmen are patriots, and that their kings, if that order of beings has found admittance there, have the feelings of humanity. — Happy people! and perhaps more happy still, that all communication with us is denied. . . . None of your sons and daughters, degraded from their native dignity, have been doomed to endless slavery by us in America, merely because their bodies may be disposed to reflect or absorb the rays of light, in a way different from ours. . . . Even British thunder impelled by British thirst of gain, cannot reach you.[30]

America unquestionably produced a galaxy of brilliant physical scientists in the middle of the eighteenth century; there were many more of them than can be named here. Nearly every educated man who interested himself in nature at all dabbled in physics and chemistry, magnetism, meteorology, and earthquakes, even while his own more important contributions to thought might be in the field of medicine or religion or literature.

The biological sciences

The biological sciences received greater attention in the south than in the north. This may have been due to the longer and more comfortable season for outdoor observation in the southern colonies, as against the long, cold winters and relatively short summers of the north. The persistent New England preoccupation with explanations of first causes, also, witnessed by the passage-at-arms between Thomas Prince and John Winthrop, may have tended to discourage somewhat purely descriptive biological science, although both William Douglass and Jared Eliot were devoted to the principles of careful observation and description, and Winthrop himself was perhaps the most exact and careful descriptive scientist in America. Whatever the explanation, the biological sciences produced more written literature in the south, particularly if Pennsylvania be included, than any other branch of "natural philosophy," and by far the greater number of biologists and botanists.

Of the early students of botany in the colonies, two of the most notable were John Clayton and John Banister, of Virginia. Clayton's garden on his estate, Windsor, was filled chiefly with the plants of Virginia, and his book, *Flora Virginica*, was devoted almost entirely to them. Clayton, who became the first president of the Virginia Society for the Advancement of Useful Knowledge, wrote two volumes on American

[30] David Rittenhouse: *An Oration Delivered February 24, 1775, before The American Philosophical Society* . . . Printed in William Barton: *Memoirs of the Life of David Rittenhouse* (Philadelphia, 1813, pp. 563–77), pp. 565–6.

plant life, but they were accidentally destroyed by fire and never published.

Clayton's fellow Virginian John Banister, rector of the church at Appomattox, was a devout, rationalistic scientist. He, too, was especially interested in the plants and animals of Virginia and wrote a number of papers for the *Philosophical Transactions* on the insects, snails, and plants of Virginia, including one on the snakeroot, a plant that was thought to be effective for preventing the evil effects of rattlesnake poisoning.

One of the earliest experimental biologists in the colonies was James Logan, of Philadelphia, who was also a distinguished mathematician. Logan had an experimental garden and interested himself, among other things, in the study of sex in plants. He was able to demonstrate conclusively the essential necessity of what he called the "male seed" in the propagation of Indian corn. As a result of his experiments he was convinced that "None of the Grains will grow up to their Size, when prevented of receiving the *Farina* [pollen] to impregnate them, but appear, when the Ears of Corn are disclosed, with all the Beds of the Seeds, or Grains, in their Ranges, with only a dry skin on each, about the same Size as when the little tender Ears appear fill'd with milky Juice before it puts out its Silk.[31]

But the greatest botanist in America was John Bartram of Philadelphia, the Quaker. Completely self-taught but handicapped by a lack of technical training, Bartram was yet able to gather in his garden a notable collection of plants, American and foreign, and to win the respect and admiration of such well-known European botanists as Linnæus, Peter Collinson, and Peter Kalm. Kalm, who visited Philadelphia in 1748, said of him : "He has acquired a great knowledge of natural philosophy and history, and seems to be born with a peculiar genius for these sciences. . . . We owe to him the knowledge of many rare plants which he first found and which were never known before. . . . I, also, owe him much, for he possessed that great quality of communicating everything he knew." [32]

Bartram's interest in plants was lifelong; as he wrote to Collinson in 1764, "I had always since ten years old a great inclination to plants, and knew all that I once observed by right, though not their proper names, having no person nor books to instruct me." [33] His friends encouraged his interest, however, and no less a person than James Logan bought him botanical books. He eventually built his home on the banks

[31] *Philosophical Transactions*, XXXIX, 195.

[32] Peter Kalm : *Peter Kalm's Travels in North America*, edited by Adolph B. Benson (2 vols., New York, 1937), I, 61–2.

[33] Quoted in William J. Youmans : *Pioneers of Science in America* (New York, 1896), p. 26.

of the Schuylkill, where he laid out a garden of some five acres for his observations and experiments. There he collected all the native plants he could find, and sent seeds and cuttings to people in Europe, particularly Peter Collinson. With the assistance of his English friends, he made a number of expeditions into the interior of the continent and southward to Florida for making observations and collections. He did not find many Americans interested in botany, but one in particular, Colonel William Byrd II of Virginia, showed great interest in his studies and exchanged notes and comments with him. He also corresponded with Cadwallader Colden and with Alexander Garden.

As an experimental botanist Bartram was particularly interested in sex in plants, and experimented with cross-fertilization. He succeeded, by his own account, in producing types of coloration in flowers that had not been known before. But his scientific interest was not limited to botany : he collected insects, birds, eggs, and fossils, and he suggested to Dr. Garden the possibility of making a "subterraneous map" — by which he seems to have meant a sort of geological map. He was a better botanist than zoologist, however ; for he was sensitive about handling living things, such as mice and snakes, to the point of squeamishness.

> As for the Opossums, I can't endure to touch them, — or hardly look at them, without sickness at stomach ; and I question whether any beast of prey is so fond of them as to kill them for food ; and as they make but little resistance, but by their loathsome scent, few creatures will kill them for sport, except dogs. But if Wolves or Panthers should chase them, they can creep into less holes — in a hollow tree, or between rocks, than their pursuers can : or if suddenly surprised, there is a tree or bush mostly at hand, where they can be secure ; for they can run to the extremity of a horizontal branch, and lap their tail-end round a slender twig, by which they will hang, pendulous, out of the reach of larger animals.[34]

Bartram was a plant enthusiast and an experimenter, but he cared little for exact record and precise classification. His great vocation was the discovery of new plants and making them grow. Alexander Garden wrote of him, somewhat patronizingly :

> His garden is a perfect portraiture of himself, here you meet w^t a row of rare plants almost covered over w^t weeds, here with a Beautifull.Shrub, even Luxuriant Amongst Briars, and in another corner an Elegant & Lofty tree lost in common thicket — on our way from town to his house he carried me to severall rocks & Dens where he shewed me some of his rare plants, which he had brought from the Mountains &c. In a word he disdains to have a garden less than Pennsylvania & Every den is an Arbour, Every run of water, a Canal, & every small level Spot a Parterre,

[34] William Darlington : *Memorials of John Bartram and Humphrey Marshall* (Philadelphia, 1849), p. 197.

where he nurses up some of his Idol Flowers & cultivates his darling productions.[35]

Bartram, despite his handicaps as a self-trained naturalist, was a typical exponent of the intellectual outlook of his time. Like Franklin, Colden, Allen, Byrd, and many others, he was a rationalist, with a great faith in the power of the human mind to learn the facts about the universe and to use them for man's improvement. As a rationalist, though a Quaker, he was impatient of ignorance and superstition, and could express himself with forthright critical vigor. As he himself said : "When we are upon the topic of astrology, magic, and mystic divinity, I am apt to be a little troublesome, by inquiring into the foundation and reasonableness of these notions — which thee knows, will not bear to be searched and examined into."[36] He reached the honorable climax of a full and successful life in being named American botanist for His Majesty George III.

Cadwallader Colden was second only to Bartram as a botanist, and was probably much more exact in method. Colden studied and classified the plants around his home, Coldengham, and carried on an active correspondence with the great European botanists. He was also a friend of Alexander Garden, with whom he exchanged ideas, seeds, and specimens.

Dr. Garden, whose home was in Charleston, S.C., was hardly less distinguished than Bartram and more exact in his technical, scientific method. A physician by training, he was a close friend of Cadwallader Colden and exchanged botanical notes with him, as he did with Bartram. He also carried on a regular correspondence with Linnæus, Peter Collinson, and Gronovius. He was elected a member of the Royal Society of Upsala in 1763 and a fellow of the Royal Society in 1773. Garden studied carefully the flora and fauna of Carolina, which he classified, and he contributed to the proceedings of the Royal Society a paper on the electric eel. It was for him that the "gardenia" was named by John Ellis, the English naturalist.

Garden's interest was chiefly in the description and classification of plants, although he was also interested in their medicinal properties. To Colden he expressed his position thus :

In a letter from the Ingenious *Huxham* he greatly regrets that Botanists should attend so much to the Nomenclature of Plants & so little to their own virtues and Qualities, had they done this says he their observations would have been of more general use to mankind. I entirely join issue [agree] with him if we consider Botany as subservient to Medicinal purposes, but I imagine most Botanists study it (at least in its greatest extent) as a branch of Naturall History & I doubt not too for the advance-

[35] *Colden Papers*, IV, 472.   [36] Quoted in Youmans, op. cit., p. 29.

ment of *Analogy & Comparative Anatomy,* in both of which it is certainly . of the greatest & most singular use. He would have Botanists not only re-marking the Species of each plant but also the nature as far as possible, of each individual [plant ;] for this I think he is entirely right.[37]

Thus Garden, while he insisted upon careful technical description, conceived of his science largely in terms of its utility. In this he was in entire accord with most of his American colleagues.

William Byrd of Virginia, who died in 1743, was hardly a systematic botanist, though his observations were keen and careful and his notes copious. His *History of the Dividing Line,* written in 1728, is full of de-scriptions of the flora and fauna of the Virginia-Carolina backwoods, coupled with rationalistic and often humorous comments upon them. For example, on the native ipecacuanha :

> In the Stony Grounds we rode over we found great Quantity of the true Ipocoacauna, which in this part of the World is call'd Indian-Physick. This has Several Stalks growing up from the Same Root about a Foot high, baring a Leaf resembling that of a Straw-Berry. It is not so strong as that from Brazil, but has the same happy Effects, If taken in Some-what a larger Dose. It is an excellent Vomit, and generally cures intermit-ting Fevers and Bloody Fluxes at once or twice taking. There is an abund-ance of it in the upper part of the Country, where it delights most in a Stony Soil intermixt with black Mold.[38]

Zoology, like botany, was hardly differentiated from the rest of "nat-ural philosophy." Bartram, for example, nursed and studied his animals with almost as great interest as his plants, although his Quaker tender-ness prevented him from killing animals for scientific examination. He was convinced, nevertheless, that animals have intelligence and sensibil-ities not unlike those of human beings : "I am . . . of the opinion that the creatures commonly called brutes possess higher qualifications, and more exalted ideas, than our traditional mystery-mongers are willing to allow them."

But the most monumental book on American plant and animal life, by far, and the most widely read, was Mark Catesby's *Natural History of Carolina, Florida, and the Bahamas.* Catesby, an Englishman, spent a number of years in the southern colonies gathering data and making drawings, and his book is a beautiful collection of line engravings, in color, accompanied by descriptive notes and an appendix that deals largely with the Indians.

Catesby was apparently interested chiefly in birds, for most of his

[37] *Colden Papers,* V, 2.
[38] Byrd : *History of the Dividing Line and Other Tracts* (2 vols., Richmond, 1866), I, 85.

drawings are devoted to them. His description of the "Red-Bird" [cardinal] was as follows:

> In Bigness it equals if not exceeds the Sky-Lark. The Bill is of a pale red, very thick and strong. A black List [band] encompasses the Basis of it. The Head is adorned with a towring Crest, which it raises and falls at Pleasure. Except the Black round the basis of the Bill, the whole Bird is scarlet, though the Back and Tail have least Lustre, being darker and of a more cloudy red.
>
> The hen is brown ; yet has a tincture of red on her Wings, Bill and other parts. They often sing in Cages as well as the Cocks. These Birds are common in all parts of *America,* from *New-England* to the *Capes* of *Florida,* and probably much more South. They are seldom seen above three or four together. They have a very great Strength with their Bill, with which they will break the hardest Grain of *Maiz* with much facility. It is a hardy and familiar Bird. They are frequently brought from *Virginia* and other parts of *North America* [to England] for their Beauty and agreeable Singing, they having some Notes not unlike our Nightingale, which in *England* seems to have caused its Name of the *Virginia-Nightingale,* though in those Countries [the colonies] they call it the *Red-Bird.*[39]

Catesby was also interested in animals, insects, reptiles and plants. His drawings of fauna are almost always accompanied by drawings of typical flora.

Catesby described the rattlesnake thus :

> The colour of the head of the rattlesnake is brown, the eye red, the upper part of the body of a brownish yellow, transversely marked with irregular broad black lists [bands]. The rattle is of a brown colour, composed of several horny membranous cells of an undulated pyramidal figure, which are articulated one within the other, so that the point of the first cell reaches as far as the basis or protuberant ring of the third, and so on ; which articulation being very loose, gives liberty to the parts of the cells that are inclosed within the outward rings to strike against the sides of them, and to cause the rattling noise heard when the snake shakes its tail.
>
> This snake is the largest and most terrible of all the viper kind ! Some of them are 8 feet long, and weight about 8 or 9 pounds. Its bite is most deadly, If the fangs penetrate a vein or artery, inevitable death ensues in less than two minutes. When the bite is in a fleshy part, it must be immediately cut out to stop the current of the poison.[40]

Catesby's book, though expensive, was widely used in America. It was revised by George Edwards in 1754, and served as a foundation

[39] Mark Catesby : *The Natural History of Carolina, Florida, and the Bahama Islands* (2 vols., London, 1731, 1743, and 1748), I, 38.

[40] Ibid., II, 41.

for Edwards's own *Natural History of Birds* and *Gleanings from Natural History*,[41] to which some Americans, including William Bartram,
John Bartram's greater son, contributed.

If scientific agriculture may be called applied botany and zoology,
then the Reverend Jared Eliot of Connecticut may be called one of the
foremost American biological scientists of the eighteenth century. Eliot

The Biological Sciences in America: "The Rattlesnake."
[From Mark Catesby: *The Natural History of Carolina* . . . II, appendix,
pl. 41]

carried on a steady correspondence with John Bartram. He was, moreover, one of the colonies' most assiduous utilizers of scientific knowledge. In his *Essays* he describes the drainage of swamps and the value
of reclaimed swamp land for crops; manures; the revitalization of the
soil by crops, like clover; the breeding of sheep; diseases of wheat;
the general increase of agricultural production; crop diversification;
and agricultural implements. Like Franklin, he tested all knowledge by
its utility: "*Experimental Philosophy* being founded in Nature and
Truth is obtained no way, but by Time and Diligence: The *Knowledge* of *Things Useful* are gained by little and little. We are not to ad-
mire or despise Things meerly because they are new: but value Things

[41] Published together, in five volumes, London, 1802–5.

or disregard them just so far as they are found (by *Experience* that faithful Instructor) to be useful or unprofitable." [42]

Yet, for all his utilitarianism, Eliot was not beyond a little rhapsody, now and then, upon the æsthetic values in this applied botany, zoology, and chemistry: "Behold it [the drained swamp] now cloathed with sweet verdant Grass, adorned with the lofty wide spreading well-set In-

The Biological Sciences in America: "The American Bison."
[From Mark Catesby: *The Natural History of Carolina* . . . II, appendix, pl. 20]

dian-Corn; the yellow Barley; the Silver coloured Flax; the ramping Hemp, beautified with fine Ranges of Cabbage; the delicious Melon, and the best of Turnips, all pleasing to the Eye, and, many, agreeable to the Taste; a wonderful Change this! and all brought about in a short Time; a Resemblance of Creation, as much as we, impotent Beings, can attain to, the happy Product of Skill and Industry." [43] Knowledge, scientific knowledge, was for him power and the creator of

[42] Jared Eliot: *Essays upon Field Husbandry in New England,* edited by Harry J. Carman and Rexford G. Tugwell (New York, 1934), p. 24.

[43] Ibid., pp. 96–7.

beauty; further, it was an avenue of insight into the marvelous wisdom of God.

Eliot sent one of his inventions, a planting machine or drill, to James Logan, the Quaker botanist of Philadelphia, and on July 25, 1756 Logan wrote to Eliot: "I have had the opportunity of reading thy Several

The Biological Sciences in America: "The largest Carolina Moth"
and the shrub "Great Anona."

[From Mark Catesby: *The Natural History of Carolina* . . . II, pl. 86]

Essays on Husbandry, and altho' we have had many Authors that have wrote on the English Methods of Farming, Yet it does not altogether agree with our Climate, and I Can assure thee that it Gives me Great pleasure to See any Gentlemen taking the Pains in our American Parts thou Seems to do, & afterwards make Publick his Experiments for the Benefit of his Country men and Neighbors, and think the Farmers of Your Countrey are Greatly obliged to thee." [44]

The only rival of Eliot's *Essays upon Field Husbandry in New England* was a book called *American Husbandry*, published anonymously

[44] Quoted by Rodney H. True in the Introduction to Eliot's *Essays*, p. 1.

on the eve of the American Revolution. It has been attributed to Dr. John Mitchell, to Arthur Young, and to others ; whoever the author was, this book, with its accurate description of American agricultural conditions and practices and its trenchant criticisms of American ways, should be regarded as a major contribution to the literature of sys-

The Biological Sciences in America : "The Laurel Tree (Magnolia) of Carolina."
[From Mark Catesby : *The Natural History of Carolina* . . . II, pl. 61]

tematic agriculture in America and as one of the manifestations of the "scientific" agriculture that was developing in almost all the colonies. It criticized the Americans for their careless use of the land, resulting in soil-exhaustion, for their unscientific treatment of their livestock, and for their neglect of the proper use of manures. With regard to the farmers of Pennsylvania, for example, it says :

> Their system is the first thing that demands attention, because a thousand evils flow from this alone : instead of exhausting their lands with perpetual corn crops, as long as it will bear them, they certainly ought to throw in corn with such moderation as never to exhaust the soil ; to inter-mix crops of pease, buckwheat, turneps, cabbages, potatoes, clover, and lucerne. . . . They know not how to raise dung, from the circumstances of their cattle running abroad all the winter ; for where cattle are not confined, no dung can be made. The want of dung makes them

solicitous for such land, and at the same time much confines their culture; with plenty of it, all their crops would be far more considerable.[45]

Similar criticisms and suggestions appear throughout the book, and
show the author to have been a genuine scientist, judged by eighteenth-
century standards. And the eventual popularity of the book shows it to
have had an almost universal appeal to the mind of the author's contemporaries.

This increasingly scientific attitude toward agriculture was typical
of the thought of the eighteenth century. The most notable of its exponents in America was John Randolph, of Virginia, who, besides being
a jurist and political philosopher of distinction, was also a scientific
gardener. Randolph's book, called *Randolph's Culinary Gardener*, was
a sort of handbook of instructions to those who would raise kitchen
vegetables, including directions for the use of manure, the building of
hotbeds, the planting and care of the vegetables, and so on.

Meanwhile, papers on agricultural subjects appeared in the proceedings of the learned societies that flourished just before and during the
Revolution. Scientific agriculture was clearly coming to be recognized
as one of the branches of "natural philosophy"; it was particularly congenial to the Americans because of its nature as science and ingenuity
applied to the practical business of living; and especially because at
this point science touched and became part of agriculture, which was
the basic activity of most Americans, and the land, which was the object of their deepest emotional attachment.

Anthropology

There was no science in the eighteenth century that actually gloried
in the name of anthropology; yet there were numerous speculations
that had as their aim the description of the human animal, both physi-
cally and culturally. Of the first kind, there were such speculations as
those of Dr. John Mitchell, in Virginia, which, prompted by the presence of so many black people, sought to explain differences of skin-
color in terms of climate. He tried to relate the differences of color to
Newton's studies of light and color. This problem, he says, "supposes
the Knowledge of the Causes of Colours in general; so that if I can deduce the Colour of the Skin from its structure, &c. in the same manner,
and for the same Reasons, from which the great *Newton* deduces the
Colours of other Substances, it is all I can pretend to, which will be as
much as that Branch of Philosophy will permit."[46] He did not succeed

---

[45].*American Husbandry*, edited by Harry J. Carman (New York, 1934), pp.
125–6.

[46] *Philosophical Transactions*, XLIII, 130.

very well, although he did satisfy himself that the black color of the
Negro skin does not proceed from black humors or fluids in their bodies. He concluded, rather lamely, that the influence of the sun has
much to do with it, but that the ways of life of the people also contribute to the differences as between, say, Indians and Negroes; "and
the Ways of Living, in Use among most Nations of white People, make
their Colours Whiter, than they were originally, or would be naturally." [47]

It was only natural that among the American people, constantly exposed as they were to contacts, pleasant and otherwise, with the Indians, there should have developed an interest in the Indian way of
life. This interest seems to have increased as the speculative interest in
western lands developed toward the mid-century. At the same time,
with the wave of imperialism that swept England about mid-century,
there developed in the mother country a great interest in things American that provided a market for anthropological description. Thus the
writings of Lewis Evans, John Mitchell, John Bartram, and Cadwallader Colden descriptive of the west and of the Indians commanded a
wide and ready sale in England as well as in America.

Colden's book *The History of the Five Indian Nations* of Canada
was first published in 1747, and was almost the only book in English
that attempted to describe the history and the life of the American aborigines. He drew heavily, in the anthropological parts of the book,
upon older French authors, and very little upon his own close experience and contacts with the Indians. Yet the book is a dependable, if
uneven, history of the relations between the English and the Iroquois
and contains a number of documents relative to that history that must
have been highly interesting to the readers of the time. The high point
is reached in the description of the meeting of Governor George Clinton with the Indians at Albany in 1746, at which Colden himself was
present, in which Clinton engaged the Indians to enter the war against
the French on the side of England. Imperfect as it is, the book presents
a mass of information relative to the Indians that was, as Franklin said,
extremely useful to everybody interested in the frontier, Anglo-French
and Anglo-Indian relations, and the expansion of the British Empire.

The *Observations* of John Bartram, published in 1751, supplemented Colden's book. Bartram described some of the habits of the Indians and then attempted to answer the problem of their origin. He
noted three theories of the origin of the Indians, one of which was
shrewdly suggestive of the one later accepted as correct: "Again, it is
not unlikely but there may be land most of the way from *America* to
Japan, at least islands, separated only by narrow channels, and in sight,

[47] Ibid., XLIII, 131.

or nearly so, of one another,"[48] across which they may have crossed from Asia to America. For his own part, however, Bartram preferred the theory that supposed the Indians to be descendants of the scattered Carthaginians, who had supposedly crossed the Atlantic from Africa to Brazil and then spread northward!

Bartram's interest in the Indians and their habits was of a part with his scientific interest in plants and animals. Consider, for example, his description of an Indian *"pawawing"*:

> They cut a parcel of poles, which they stick in the ground in a circle, about the bigness of hop poles, the circle about five foot diameter, and then bring them together at the top, and tie them in form of an oven, where the conjurer placeth himself; then his assistants cover the cage over close with blankets and to make it still more suffocating, hot stones are rolled in; after all this the priest must cry aloud, and agitate his body after the most violent manner, till nature has almost lost all her faculties before the stubborn spirit will become visible to him, which they say is generally in the shape of some bird. There is usually a stake drove into the ground about four foot high and painted. I suppose this they design for the *winged airy Being* to perch upon, while he reveals to the invocant what he has taken so much pains to know. However, I find different nations have different ways of obtaining the pretended information. Some have a bowl of water, into which they often look, when their strength is almost exhausted, and their senses failing, to see whether the spirit is ready to answer their demands. I have seen many of these places in my travels. They differ from their sweating coops, in that they are often far from water, and have a stake by the cage, yet both have a heap of red hot stones put in.[49]

Benjamin Franklin also should perhaps be included in any list of American students of anthropology, since he made at least one very respectable study of population and its increase and made a few speculative remarks with regard to race and color. But Franklin's thought along these lines sprang from an interest that was much more sociological than anthropological. Anthropology as such could hardly be said to have existed in more than the most primitive embryonic form.

Medicine

Medical science in colonial America was in some ways not very far advanced beyond Galen and Aristotle. Yet much progress had been made in other ways, since Andreas Vesalius opened the era of modern medicine by the publication of his *De humani corporis fabrica* in 1543.

[48] John Bartram : *Observations . . . made by Mr. John Bartram in his Travels from Pensilvania to Onondago, Oswego and the Lake Ontario, in Canada* (London, 1751), p. 76.
[49] Ibid., p. 32.

For the decades of settlement in America were the decades of Harvey and Boyle in England, and the appearance of Cartesian and Newtonian science was bound to have an enormous effect upon the theory of disease.

The medical theory of the Middle Ages had been a corrupt form of Galenism and Aristotelianism. Galen's physiological scheme involving the three sets of spirits, "natural" (liver), "vital" (heart), and "animal" (brain), was combined with the old Hippocratic-Aristotelian concept of the four "humors" or liquids in the body — blood, phlegm, black bile, and yellow bile — which must be kept in proper balance for the preservation of health. It was a sort of synthesis of these theories that was followed by the practicing physicians of the seventeenth century in America.

But the vision of a mechanical explanation of the universe was thought to include man, and the mechanical explanation of the human body and its functions was attempted by Descartes in his *De homine* (1662) and, with more success, in the next century by La Mettrie in his *L'Homme machine*. At the same time the growth of chemical concepts led such physicians as Franciscus Sylvanus at Leiden to place great emphasis on the "alkaline" and "acid" elements in the body, and on "fermentation." Medical practice was improved and extended by such new medicines from the colonial world as ipecacuanha, quinine, and tobacco. Finally, to all these new influences was added that of men like Hermann Boerhaave, also of Leiden, who introduced the principles of clinical observation and insisted upon close and careful regard for the observed facts, and such a famous practitioner as Dr. Thomas Sydenham, in England, who also insisted upon the "natural history" of disease, and who had great influence in America. Thus while the theory of medicine was still exceedingly primitive, even in the eighteenth century, the practices of medicine were beginning to feel clearly the impact and the influence of scientific methods and attitudes.

By the end of the seventeenth century experimental medicine was making itself felt in America, and it received a dramatic filip to its development with the discovery of the method of preventing smallpox by inoculation, just after the turn of the century. This discovery was first made by the Turks, and its use by them was observed by an Englishwoman, Lady Mary Wortley Montagu, who described it to her friends in England at about the same time as it was reported to the Royal Society. It was through the *Transactions* of the Royal Society that it came to America, for Cotton Mather read of it there and prevailed upon Dr. Zabdiel Boylston to practice it. The introduction of inoculation was achieved only against the bitter opposition of the conservative and the religious, however; for the pious saw in the visitation of smallpox an act of God, and its prevention, even if successful, as an interference with God's divine purpose. The death of a patient from inoculation, moreover, was regarded as murder, and punishable as such. Boston was soon convinced; but the conflict spread through all the colonies as the practice spread, and even Benjamin Franklin was drawn into it with the following versified comment in *Poor Richard's Almanack*:

> *God offered to the Jews salvation,*
> *And 'twas refused by half the nation;*
> *Thus (though 'tis life's preservation)*
> *Many oppose inoculation.*[50]

Franklin, writing in London in 1759 at the request of Dr. William Heberden, reviewed the history of inoculation in the colonies and concluded that the deaths from inoculation must be reckoned at about one in one hundred, whereas the deaths in the frequent epidemics that swept the colonies amounted to about one in nine or ten. As to the popular attitude toward the practice, however, even at that late day, he had to acknowledge a considerable amount of conservatism:

Notwithstanding the now uncontroverted success of Inoculation, it does not seem to make that progress among the common people in America, which was at first expected, *Scruples of conscience* weigh with many, concerning the *lawfulness* of the practice, and if one parent or near relation is against it, the other does not choose to inoculate a child without free consent of all parties, lest in case of a disastrous event, perpetual blame should follow. . . . The *expence* of having the operation performed by a Surgeon, weighs with others, for that has been pretty high in some parts of America; and when a common tradesman or artificer has a number in his family to have the distemper, it amounts to more money than he can well spare. . . . A small Pamphlet wrote in plain language by some skilful Physician and published, directing what preparations of the body should be used before the Inoculation of children, what precautions to avoid giving the infection at the same time in the common way, and how the operation is to be performed . . . might be encouraging parents to inoculate their own children, be a means of removing that objection of the expence, render the practice more general, and thereby save the lives of thousands.[51]

The controversy over inoculation brought into prominence Dr. William Douglass. This irascible savant was a trained physician, having studied medicine at Edinburgh, Leiden in the days of Boerhaave, and Paris, presenting a sharp contrast with the "medical parsons" like Jared Eliot, who, despite their devotion and diligence, were really educated

[50] *Poor Richard's Almanack,* 1737.
[51] Quoted in Francis R. Packard : *The History of Medicine in the United States* (New York, 1931), p. 93.

as theologians and cared for the sick only by virtue of the fact that they were the most highly educated men in their communities. Douglass had settled in Boston about 1718 and had become one of the city's most celebrated practitioners; but he was opposed to inoculation, and he lost no time in saying so, in a series of pamphlets directed against the practice. Yet he was not unable to learn, and was compelled by its obvious effectiveness to admit the validity of it. As he himself explained in his great *Summary*:

> The novel practice of procuring the small-pox by inoculation, is a very considerable and most beneficial improvement in that article of medical practice. It is true, the first promoters of it were too extravagant, and therefore suspected in their recommendations of it; . . . these considerations made me, 1721, not enter into the practice, until further trials did evince the success of it; but now after upwards of thirty years practice of it in Great-Britain, and the dominions thereto belonging, we found that the small-pox received by cuticular incisions has a better chance for life and an easy decumbiture; that is, the small-pox so received is less mortal, and generally more favourable, than when received in the accidental or natural way, by inspiration, deglutition, pores of the skin, and the like.[52]

In the years 1735 and 1736 there appeared in Boston an unfamiliar disease that seemed to center in an infection of the throat and may have been scarlet fever or diphtheria, but probably the latter. Douglass wrote a pamphlet describing it, which he entitled: *The Practical History of a New Epidemical Eruptive Military Fever* . . . (Boston, 1736), and a group of prominent physicians, asked to investigate it, reported that it did not seem so serious as some other epidemics, and that "As formerly, so now again after many Months Observation, we conclude, that the present prevailing Distemper appears to us to *proceed from some Affection of the Air, and not from any personal Infection receiv'd from the Sick, or Goods in their neighborhood.*"[53] In his pamphlet Douglass described the disease, to which he found children particularly susceptible, and invited an exchange of information upon it. Whether he ever received any is not of record; but in the absence of any concept of the germ theory of disease, it was hardly probable that a cure would be found.

Douglass gave his life to his profession, finding time to write pamphlets on paper money and his *Summary*, and came to his end heroically battling the smallpox in Boston in the great epidemic of 1752.

Cadwallader Colden was also a trained physician. He had studied

---

[52] William Douglass: *Summary, Historical and Political, of the British Settlements in North-America* (2 vols., Boston, 1749–52), II, 406–7.

[53] Quoted in Packard, op. cit., p. 99.

medicine at Edinburgh and as a young man had been associated with a group of scientists and mathematicians in England. He had come to America in 1716 and practiced medicine in Philadelphia until his removal to New York in 1720, after which he was almost constantly in the employ of the crown, while apparently continuing at the same time his practice of medicine and his studies of the medical properties of plants along with his many other scientific and literary pursuits. It is difficult, indeed, to understand how he carried on so many highly exacting activities simultaneously.

Colden's medical treatises included studies of cancer, smallpox, tar water, yellow fever, the effect of climate on disease, and voluminous commentaries contained in his correspondence with Dr. William Douglass and Dr. Alexander Garden, and in Europe Linnæus, Gronovius, and Collinson. Colden's medicine was a mixture of the modern with the antiquated. He was ahead of his times, for example, in his conviction that diet had a great deal to do with such diseases as scurvy : "As to the reason of the children of the people of Europe (not the native Indians) losing their teeth so commonly I attribute it entirely to the Scurvy of which scarce one family in this Country is free. . . . In former times they had little fresh Provision or Sallad so that they were obliged to feed on salt meet allmost the whole year." [54] But if his theories of diet were advanced, some of his ideas about other medical matters were exceedingly naïve. Such, for example, was his enthusiasm for tar water :

> Tho' I expected no visible & speedy good effect of [tar water] as intended only as a preventive of . . . Gout & Gravail yet it Soon had an unexpected Effect. . . . After three or four days useing the tarr water, I found that my Looseness was gone, was not troubled with wind as before I got a keen appetite Such as I remember not to have had these twenty years, and Do venture upon roots & Greens again without finding the Like Consequences from them as before — as it has had this unexpected effect I intend to Continue it in hopes it may have the effect I intended. [55]

Colden's most distinguished medical writing was probably that which he did on the subject of yellow fever. He was of course ignorant of the germ theory of disease, but he came amazingly close to the correct empirical explanation of the source of the fever. For he attributed it to the noxious exhalations of stagnant pools and swamps. Clear, deep pools, he said, were not sources of contamination ; nor were pools of salt water ; "but the more saturated they are with mud and slime, especially with the dead carcasses of insects or of beasts, or other nastiness,

[54] *Colden Papers,* IV, 261.   [55] Ibid., III, 108.

or of sulphureous or arsenical minerals, the more mischievous they are; and the greater variety in the Places situated on the north side of those slimy wet places, are more unhealthy than those on the south side of them, because the warm moist southerly winds increase the fermentation, and consequently the quantity of noxious vapours rising from it, and carries them to the northward." [56]

One of Colden's collaborators in the study of yellow fever was Dr. John Mitchell, of Virginia, where there took place an epidemic about the same time as the New York epidemic of 1741–2. Mitchell studied this disease carefully, and sent his findings to Colden through their friend Benjamin Franklin. This paper, which was also seen later by Benjamin Rush, was not published until 1814; but both Colden and Rush found it useful. In it Mitchell defined the yellow fever as "a pestilential fever proceeding from a *contagious miasma sui generis,* which inflames the stomach and adjacent viscera, obstructs the biliary ducts, and dissolves the adipose humours." [57]

He then went on to describe the course of the disease thus :

> 1. The fluids [of the body] are manifestly dissolved from the beginning by the miasma of the disease, and are much more so by the effects of the fever succeeding it. 2. The blood is much accelerated in its motions, when it is thin, dissolved, hot and acrid. . . . 3. The solids [of the body] are not rigid, and the body dense and imperspirable, as in most other acute continual fevers; they are rather lax than weak . . . but they are to be drawn into spasms and convulsions, as weak fibers generally are, by the heated, accelerated acrimonious humours, especially in the more sensible membrane about the præcordia. 4. Hence a stagnation or inflammation in those membranes, especially the stomach and contiguous viscera. . . . These bring on an universal spasm or systolic motion of all the nervous membranous parts; hence the arteries are contracted of nigh to a continued systole, as is felt by the pulse, which makes the dissolved blood, lymph, and bilious, oily humours stagnate in the extreme capillaries; whence mortification of the inflamed parts.[58]

Here Mitchell is still working upon the theory of humours, or balanced liquids and solids in the body; the balance is upset by the degenerating effects upon them of the "miasmic vapours" in the air. His interest is in the pathology of the disease rather than in its prevention or an effort to find its source, while Colden was interested in its origin outside the human body and the mechanism of communication. But Mitchell, too, concluded that it was caused by the inhalation of air-

[56] Cadwallader Colden : "Observations on the Fever which prevailed in the City of New York in 1741 and 2, written in 1743" (printed in the *American Medical and Philosophical Register,* I, 310–24), pp. 320–1.

[57] *American Medical and Philosophical Register,* IV, 182.

[58] Ibid., IV, 205–6.

borne vapors; his best practical suggestion was for the drainage of the swamps or ponds from which the vapors arose. This is typical of eighteenth-century medicine: often the doctors arrived at perfectly sound practices for prevention of disease just by observation, without knowing exactly why their means were effective.

Dr. Mitchell gave up his practice in Virginia on account of his health and returned to England in 1746. But his interest in American natural history, medicine, and geography continued to influence the thinking of both Americans and Englishmen for many years thereafter.

John Tennent, also of Virginia, was a well-known doctor and writer on medical questions. He, too, was a devotee of the liquids-solids-balance theory. He recommends "a moderate Use of Spirituous Liquors, which would in a great Measure thin the Blood." The cure of pleurisy, for example, seemed to him to depend upon decreasing the blood's "viscuity"; anything that achieved this end would be effective: bloodletting, blisters, emetics, or "an Infusion of Stone-horse Dung and Castor, Glisters, Sudorifics, Diaphoretics, and Purges."[59] By the same token, the learned doctor thought he might also prescribe rattlesnake root for pleurisy, since it was well known that this plant cured the bite of a rattlesnake by thinning the blood, unduly thickened by the bite! Bloodletting, indeed, was universally practiced, and for this same reason, the desire to restore the balance of liquids and solids in the body. Needless to say, there probably were many patients who died of loss of blood, rather than disease, as apparently was the case with Samuel Davies, president of Princeton.

In Charleston the medical profession in the 1750's was ornamented by the names of Dr. Alexander Garden, who was perhaps best known as a botanist, and Dr. John Lining, who was botanist, physicist, and physiologist. While Lining also achieved some note as an experimenter with electricity, his best and most original claim to fame rested on his experiments upon himself made in an effort to determine the effects of climate upon health, a set of experiments and observations that brought him close to the field of metabolism. As he explained it, "What first induced me to enter upon this Course, was that I might experimentally discover the Influences of our different Seasons upon the Human Body; by which I might arrive at some more certain Knowledge of the Causes of our epidemic Diseases, which as regularly return at their stated Seasons, as a good Clock strikes twelve when the Sun is in the Meridian; and therefore must proceed from some general Cause operating uniformly in the returning different Seasons."[60]

In the course of his observations he regularly weighed himself and

---

[59] John Tennent: *An Essay on the Pleurisy* (Williamsburg, 1742), p. 10.
[60] *Philosophical Transactions*, XLII, 492.

his intake of food morning and evening, measured the quantity of his perspiration, took his pulse morning and evening, weighed his excreta, and measured his urine; at the same time he took careful observations of the temperature, direction and force of the wind, clouds, the quantity of rainfall, barometer readings, humidity measurements with a home-made hygroscope, and so on.

After the series of experiments was all over he wasn't quite sure what he had proved. But he believed he was on the right track to something important:

> The Deductions from these tables . . . appear to me to point out the physical Principles, from whence we may account for the Production of these epidemic Diseases of the different Seasons, which are not infectious. For are not these the Effects of different Constitutions of the Air on human Bodies? And are not the Increments and Decrements of the sensible and insensible Excretions . . . the only Index of the Changes produced in the human Constitution, by Vicissitudes of the Weather? [61]

This was a widely held opinion, that non-infectious diseases were caused by conditions in the air. Even infectious diseases were made more or less malignant by the seasonal changes in the atmosphere. Dr. Tennent of Virginia, it will be remembered, believed that pleurisy was more deadly in the winter than in the summer because the colder air of the winter caused the blood to flow more slowly, and all the medical experimenters, from Charleston to Boston, concluded at one time or another that disease was caused by foul conditions of the air. This was one of the dominant ideas, indeed, among the students and practitioners of medical science.

In the realm of medical theory, however, as in the realm of theoretical physics, it was Cadwallader Colden who went farthest in the direction of working out a logical explanation of the ultimate cause of disease. Needless to say, of course, in a time when the germ theory was still unheard of, Colden's explanation could not have been any real explanation; the important thing is that he had the originality and the courage to make a reasonable attempt to explain *why* disease was communicated by the air, and just what the process was by which it operated in the human body. His answer to this problem was arrived at as a part of his broader, more philosophical attempt to explain the nature of organic life itself: life, or "vital motion," is the result of a sort of "fermentation," which is the product of the operation of mind upon matter; and the preservation of health depends upon keeping the vital fermentations in their regular and natural order. Heat stimulates these fermentations; cold decreases them; exercise also promotes them. But

[61] Ibid., XLIII, 319.

"in preserving health no less regard must be had to the mind : for . . . it is evident, that great care should be taken, that it be not diverted from the direction it has over all the vital functions, & experience may convince us, that it is diverted by violent appetites and passions." [62] Disease, then, was the result of faulty fermentation; and in suggesting the importance of the relationship of mental phenomena and conditions to health and disease Colden went farther in the direction of the modern scientific attitude toward the mind and its relationship to health than any other American before Benjamin Rush. Colden's entire work in the theory of disease, indeed, probably represented the most advanced thinking in that field in eighteenth-century America.

The most distinguished physician in the Philadelphia of the mid-century generation was Dr. John Kearsley, who thought of himself as the man who first introduced inoculation for smallpox to that city. But Kearsley's position in the scientific and intellectual life of Philadelphia was most significant, probably, because he was the teacher and leader of the remarkable group of younger doctors that made that city the most advanced medical center on the continent. Among this group were Dr. Thomas Bond, who with Franklin's aid organized the Philadelphia hospital, Thomas Cadwallader, who wrote a well-known pamphlet called *An Essay on the West-India Dry-Gripes* (Philadelphia, 1745) and who was one of the first to attempt to use electricity in the treatment of disease, Dr. William Shippen, and Dr. John Redman, who was in turn the teacher of the even more famous John Morgan and Benjamin Rush.

John Morgan represents more clearly, perhaps, than any other physician in America, the direct importation and influence of foreign ideas in this branch of science. He represents also, probably, the high point reached by medical science in the colonies prior to the Revolution. Born in Philadelphia in 1735, he graduated from the college there with its first four-year class in 1757. After studying medicine for a while with Dr. John Redman and serving as a medical officer in the Seven Years' War, he went abroad to study, first at the University of Edinburgh and then at London. He was elected a member of the Society of Belles-Lettres at Rome, and an Associate Fellow of the Académie Royal de Chirurgie at Paris. He returned to America in 1764, to see whether, as he said, "I can get my living without turning apothecary or practitioner of surgery." [63]

In his inaugural address as the first "Professor of the Theory and

---

[62] Cadwallader Colden : "An Inquiry into the Principles of Vital Motion," manuscript, New York Historical Society, pp. 22–3.
[63] Quoted in Packard, op. cit., p. 342.

Practice of Medicine in the College of Philadelphia," Dr. Morgan made an eloquent plea for the teaching of science in the universities, and particularly the teaching of medicine. For, he said, "a thirst for knowledge and a spirit of inquiry are natural to man,"[64] and the way to pro-

Medicine in Colonial America: Dr. John Morgan. A portrait by Angelica Kaufman.

[By courtesy of the University of Pennsylvania]

gress lies in gratifying and encouraging these impulses. Yet this may not be done alone; and the self-taught scientific quacks, especially in the field of medicine, are to be shunned as one would shun the plague:

> The industry of many centuries have already been employed to bring Physic to that degree of perfection at which it is now arrived. It will still require a long time to remove the obscurities which yet veil many parts of it. The application of many, amongst the greatest of men, has hitherto been insufficient to clear up all our doubts in medicine. How then can it

[64] John Morgan : *A Discourse upon the Institution of Medical Schools in America* (Philadelphia, 1765), p. 3.

be supposed that any one, untutored in this art, can by his own natural abilities ever reach the bounds of what is already known of it? [65]

The physician, says Dr. Morgan, must strictly practice according to the scientific method : "Observation and physical experiments should blend their light to dissipate obscurity from medicine. This is the more needful, as nature commonly offers herself to our notice under a cloud, and requires that we should follow her steps with scrupulous attention, watch all her motions, and trace her through every meander she makes, in order to discern clearly the tract she keeps in." [66]

As for the study of medicine itself, Dr. Morgan broke it down into its component disciplines : "Anatomy, Materia Medica, Botany, Chymistry, the Theory of Medicine, and the practice," and advised prospective doctors to specialize. Physiology, for example, a branch of medical theory, he explained as "the application of natural philosophy to Anatomy, and may very well be defined *A philosophic knowledge of the human body, or a science of all the conditions arising from the structure of its parts.* It has a foundation both in Anatomy and Philosophy," whereas "Pathology treats of the *vital,* animal, and natural functions in a morbid state, as Physiology does in a sound healthful condition. It traces out the seat of diseases, examines their causes and effects, shews their differences, explains their symptoms, and all the different phenomena, which result from various affections of the system, it prognosticates the event, and indicates the general method of treatment." [67]

Thus were medicine and "philosophy" (that is, general science) linked together; and Dr. Morgan, who was unquestionably the greatest medical teacher of pre-Revolutionary America, links science in general and medicine in particular to the Newtonianism that pervaded almost every realm of intellectual life.

Finally, Morgan held up a bright and nationalistic vision of the future of science in America :

We live on a wide extended continent of which but the smallest portion, even of the inhabited part, has yet been explored. The woods, the mountains, the rivers and bowels of the earth afford ample scope for the researches of the ingenious. In this respect an American student has some considerable advantage over those of Europe, viz. The most ample field lies before us for the improvement of natural history. The countries of Europe have been repeatedly traversed by numerous persons of the highest genius and learning. . . . This part of the world may be looked upon as offering the richest mines of natural knowledge yet unriffled, sufficient to gratify the laudable thirst of glory in young inquirers into nature.[68]

[65] Ibid., p. 21.
[66] Ibid., p. 22.

[67] Ibid., p. 12–13.
[68] Ibid., pp. 52–3.

Dr. Morgan, born and raised in America, had received his education and early medical training here; and he had added to that the finest medical study that could be had in Europe. His intellectual outlook was thus a synthesis of American and European experiences; he was thus one of the finest exponents of the American mind: rationalist, doctor, educator, and Anglo-American patriot.

With the inauguration of Morgan, the medical course in the College of Philadelphia got under way, and under Morgan's stimulating guidance it expanded rapidly. Dr. William Shippen, Jr., was appointed professor of anatomy and surgery at the college in September 1767, and he and Dr. Morgan combined their talents to provide a curriculum for a "Bachelor's Degree In Physic." Each candidate for the degree was expected to know Latin, Mathematics, and certain branches of "Natural and Experimental Philosophy." Chiefly, however:

> Each student shall attend at least one course of lectures in Anatomy, Materia Medica, Chemistry, the Theory and Practice of Physic, and one course of Clynical Lectures, and shall attend the Practice of the Pennsylvania Hospital for one year.[69]

Hitherto, prospective professional physicians had learned their trade by apprenticing themselves to already practicing doctors. Now, just on the eve of the American Revolution, medical education had achieved the maturity, in form, at least, of the modern medical curriculum of laboratory, science, theory, and clinical practice. For this John Morgan, more than any other one man, was responsible.

While the antiquated theory of disease was the great and fatal nucleus of medicine in the eighteenth century, yet the doctors made genuine progress in the realm of practice nevertheless. Thus the conviction that disease was spread by noxious air led to the draining of swamps and the establishment of rules of quarantine. The general scientific respect for observed facts permeated the profession and led to a more careful clinical observation and history of actual cases. Dr. William Douglass seems to have organized the first medical society in New England for the exchange of findings and ideas, and John Morgan organized the Philadelphia Medical Society in 1766. The organization of the Pennsylvania hospital was a shining example — not imitated until after the Revolution — of the progress that was being made toward the improvement of medical facilities. All over the colonies the doctors were botanists themselves and they encouraged others to study botany, with the express purpose of discovering the medical properties of plants. Thus Garden, Mitchell, Douglass, and Colden all advanced the study of an embryonic materia medica; and one of John Bartram's

[69] Quoted in Packard, op. cit., p. 355.

most important essays was the preface that he wrote to Thomas Short's *Treatise on such Physical [medical] Plants, as are generally to be found in the Fields or Gardens in Great Britain* (London, 1751).

The science of medicine in colonial America as hitherto described was one of the intellectual prerogatives of the rich and socially elite. But medicine was far from being the exclusive and monopolistic mystery that it later became; and if almost any barber could still consider himself a surgeon, so any midwife or any farmer could prescribe for his stock, his family, or himself. In fact, there was still a brisk exchange among friends of "recipes" for this or that malady. But the most popular emporium of medical knowledge for the poor and the self-medicators was the almanac, the universal encyclopedic intellectual Mercury of the common people.

Nathaniel Ames, for example, lectured his readers on diet and the importance of proper air in health; and *Poor Richard*, likewise, brought morsels of medical thought to its readers. For example, in the issue for 1756 there appears this item:

> In the Fifth Volume of the *Edinburgh Medical Essays,* the following Medicine is called a *Specific* for the Dysentery or bloody Flux, viz.
>
> *Mix an Ounce* of Glass of Antimony, finely powdered, *with a Drachm of yellow Wax: Keep* [heat] *it in an Iron Ladle over a slow clear Charcoal Fire about Half an Hour, continually stirring it with an Iron Spatula, until the Wax is all consumed, and ceases to emit Fumes. It will then be of the Colour of Snuff. Power* [powder] *it fine, and keep it in a Bottle for Use. Dose, from six to ten Grains, till you find Relief.*[70]

Yet so far as the almanacs were concerned, remedies and prescriptions that were offered to their readers were generally no better and no worse than those used by the physicians themselves. As a matter of fact, many of them were the same; many were taken from the medical journals, as in this case. Self-medication was encouraged; Franklin even recommended self-inoculation, as has already been remarked. Doctors were held — perhaps not without some reason — in suspicion; and Poor Richard probably expressed the general popular attitude when he said, in his almanac, that "God cures, and the doctor takes the fee." Or Roger Sherman when he said in his almanac that "Physicians easily can tell, advice to others, when themselves are well."

On the other hand, there was a lot of attention paid to astrology in the almanacs, a recognition of the common belief that there was a close connection between the constellations of the zodiac and health. At the same time, also, the colonies were a quack's paradise. The newspapers were studded with advertisements of patent medicines and

[70] *Poor Richard Improved, 1756.*

cure-alls : Bostock's Elixir, Turlington's Balsom, Eau de Luce, and many others. William Smith, the historian, complained that quacks had overrun the colonies, and bemoaned the absence of regulations. And William Douglass, always provocatively outspoken, felt impelled to complain that

> In our plantations, a practitioner, bold, rash, impudent, a lyar, basely born and educated, has much the advantage of an honest cautious modest gentleman — In general, the physical practice in our colonies is so perniciously bad that excepting in surgery, and some very acute cases, it is better to let nature under a proper regimen take her course . . . than to trust to the honesty and sagacity of the practitioner. . . . Frequently there is more danger from the physician than from the distemper ; [this is] a country where the medical practice is very irregular.[71]

This critical feeling towards quackery was widespread; and Virginia had the honor of passing what was probably the first law against illegal and irresponsible medical practitioners, in 1736. Quackery, indeed, was on the decline ; and the work of such physicians as Douglass, Mitchell, Lining, and Morgan was bringing medicine steadily forward into its modern scientific and clinical attitudes.

In general, then, it may be said that, despite the stalemate of theory, medical practice was making great strides forward ; new medicines, like quinine, had proved their value ; dissection of human bodies was making for a more scientific knowledge of anatomy, a beginning was made at the establishment of hospitals, medical societies, and medical schools. Most of all, the true scientific attitude of observation of facts was working steadily and surely to produce better clinical records and more scientific study of disease, and to dispel the gloom of ignorance and superstition and quackery that still pervaded this area of human thought. Thomas Cadwallader expressed a thoroughly modern attitude when he wrote that "All hypotheses, unless they agree with facts, are delusive and vain ; and I believe it will be readily granted, that had the writers of former ages confined themselves more to practical observations, some diseases, the *Opprobria Medicorum*, would have been better understood."[72]

Medicine, too, was coming of age.

GEOGRAPHY AND THE WESTWARD MOVEMENT

The science that, next to agriculture, probably lay closest to the vital core of the American experience was geography. For the Americans

---

[71] Douglass : *Summary, Historical and Political*, II, 351.
[72] Thomas Cadwallader : *An Essay on the West-India Dry Gripes* (Philadelphia, 1745), p. 18.

had been dependent upon applied geography, from their first crossings of the ocean and the exploring and surveying of their lands to the tactical problems presented by the intercolonial wars and the great vogue of map-making and map-reading that was a natural intellectual aspect of the westward movement of population. This movement reached its flood about the middle of the eighteenth century; and at that time there were published in America a number of maps of the continent, or parts of it, that are surprising for their accuracy and detailed information.

But the science of geography, like all the other sciences, had not been born full-grown. It had had to develop, as had astronomy and medicine. But the beginnings of modern geography go farther back than either of these, probably for the simple reason that it is such a practical science and so necessary to the conduct of everyday affairs. Thus the beginnings of modern observational geography, as distinguished from the fantastically theoretical geography of the classical Ptolemy, probably should be dated from the small outline maps that the Italian ship captains carried in their *portolani*, or small notebooks of navigation. With the advent of the age of exploration and the expansion of European civilization overseas, geography became a matter of vital interest to nearly every educated man in western Europe. The map-makers were busy expanding and making more accurate their maps of the world, and new scientific projections, such as that of Gerard Mercator, were invented to meet the problem of portraying the spherical surface of the earth on flat paper. The study of navigation was steadily improved; the accurate determination of longitude was finally made possible by the development of the chronometer late in the seventeenth century; but the first accurate measurement of a degree of longitude was made by Jean Picard only in 1770. Sea-travel was becoming more and more dependable. Meanwhile such scientific explorers as Samuel Champlain were steadily accumulating accurate geographic data, and these descriptive data were being meticulously collected by such men as the Reverend Richard Hakluyt in England. It was no accident, therefore, that Hakluyt should have been one of the sponsors of Sir Walter Raleigh and a member of the first Council for Virginia. Thus the generation of Englishmen that saw the settlement of Anglo-America was one that was marked by a keen popular and scientific interest in this most popular of the sciences, and by an interest in the overseas world of the colonies, the "new world," that culminated, finally, in the classic *History of European Colonies and Commerce* by G. T. F. Raynal, published in 1770.

But the experience of the settlers in America was one to accentuate certain aspects of this popular interest in geography. For as a society of farmers, and one that was constantly expanding into new lands to the westward, an acquaintanceship with the rudiments of surveying and climatology, of map-reading and map-making, and a consciousness of the problems of physical, animal, and ethnological geography (at least with regard to the Indians) became a part of the intellectual equipment of practically every man, and even, often enough, men who could hardly read and write.

The popular and scientific interest in geography flourished in the middle of the eighteenth century, at the moment when the westward movement, that profoundly significant social phenomenon, was reaching the crest of the Alleghenies and beginning to flow down the other side, thus opening to the expansive people of the older colonies a vision of the new world of the "western waters."

There was a sharp difference, however, between the interest of the British "imperialists" in American geography and that of the people moving westward; and the two notable maps of the colonies published in 1755 represent those two differing points of view. For the British Board of Trade, echoing the interests not only of the expansionists in Great Britain but of the American imperialists as well, commissioned Dr. John Mitchell, who had lived for so many years in Virginia, to make a map of the colonies that would show the fullest extent of the British territorial claims in North America. Thus Mitchell's *Map of the British and French Dominions* (1755) was an official map, and constituted a part of British official propaganda for the support of British claims in the diplomatic contest for the control of North America then going on between Britain and France. It was accurate, it was based on official British documents, and it presented the British claims at their fullest extent. Its significance for the Americans, however, lay in the satisfaction with which it was received by such American imperialists as William Shirley, William Livingston, Archibald Kennedy, and others. In the minds of the American Tory imperialists, this map was far superior to that of Lewis Evans, published in the same year, because Evans was less imperialist-minded, and because he even went so far as to recognize the right of the French to the land north of Lake Ontario.

Lewis Evans, as a geographer, was much closer than Mitchell to the needs and the interests of the American people. For Evans was closely concerned, in his own personal experience, with intercolonial boundary disputes, western land speculation, relation with the Indians, and actual western settlement. He made a map of the famous "walking purchase" of 1737, but his first important map was his *Map of Pensilvania, New Jersey, New York, and the three Delaware Counties*, based upon his own personal observations and published in 1749; this map immediately got him into trouble with the Penns, because it seemed to do them something less than justice in the size of Pennsylvania and to favor Maryland.

It was also criticized as being too crowded; so Evans revised it in 1752. Apparently it was widely used by travelers and settlers in the west.

Evans's greatest work was his famous *General Map of the Middle British Colonies in America,* which he published in 1755 together with a small handbook euphemistically entitled *Geographical, Historical, Political Philosophical and Mechanical Essays.* Evans presented a series of notes on the west in this handbook, and urged the establishment of colonies west of the mountains on the ground that they would serve as buffer states between the seaboard colonies and their French and Indian enemies. But Evans recognized the legitimacy of the French claim to the territory north of the Great Lakes; although he recognized the pressing nature of the Anglo-French rivalry, his chief interest was in the west itself, and in its settlement.

As a good Pennsylvanian, Evans supported the claims of his province to the upper part of the Ohio Valley against those of Virginia, and he was employed in 1750 by the Pennsylvania government to go to the west and observe the movements of the Ohio Company of Virginia as well as to map and appraise the country for Pennsylvania. He may or may not have made the journey necessary for carrying out his instructions, but his great map of 1755 seems to have been in large measure the fulfillment of his commission. His map showed in detail the English settlements in the Pennsylvania back-country as of about 1754. It is indicative of the wide current interest in such things that he was able to use, in addition to his own observations, materials that he gathered from others — traders, surveyors, settlers, travelers like his comrade John Bartram, and colonial agents like Conrad Weiser. It is also indicative of the popular interest in his map that it went through eighteen English editions before 1800.

But Evans's honesty brought down upon his map and himself the criticisms of several powerful groups of interests. He was opposed to the great land companies and warned against them, thereby winning their undying hatred; his acknowledgment of the French title to Canada brought upon him the ire of the imperialistic expansionists; his emphasis upon the great significance of the Ohio Valley brought upon him the criticism of those who thought Acadia or Canada more important; his tactless suggestion that Massachusetts was contemplating independence provoked the wrath of that colony. The imperialists, especially, took great umbrage at Evans's map and attacked him in the *New York Mercury* and in a pamphlet called *A Review of the Military Operations in North America,* published in London in 1757, on the ground that he was disloyal to the British interests in the territory north of Lake Ontario and unfairly critical of William Shirley's mili-

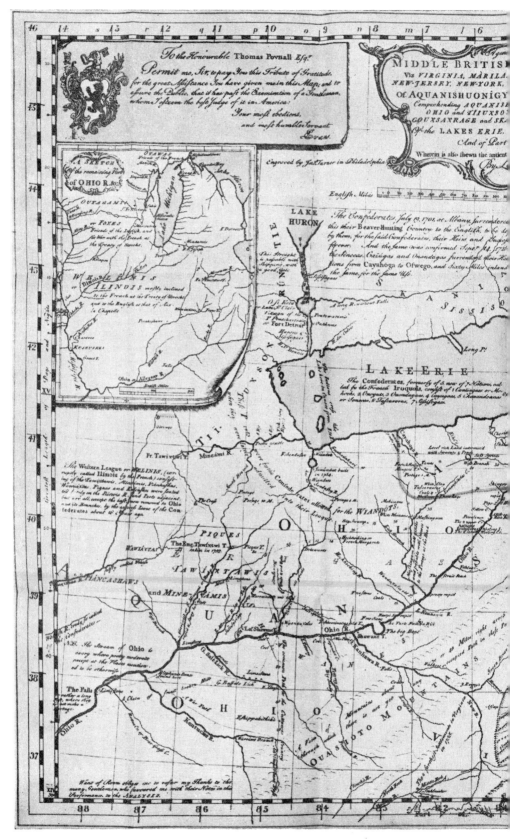

Geography in America : Lewis Evans's M[ap]
[From *Pennsylvania A[...]*]

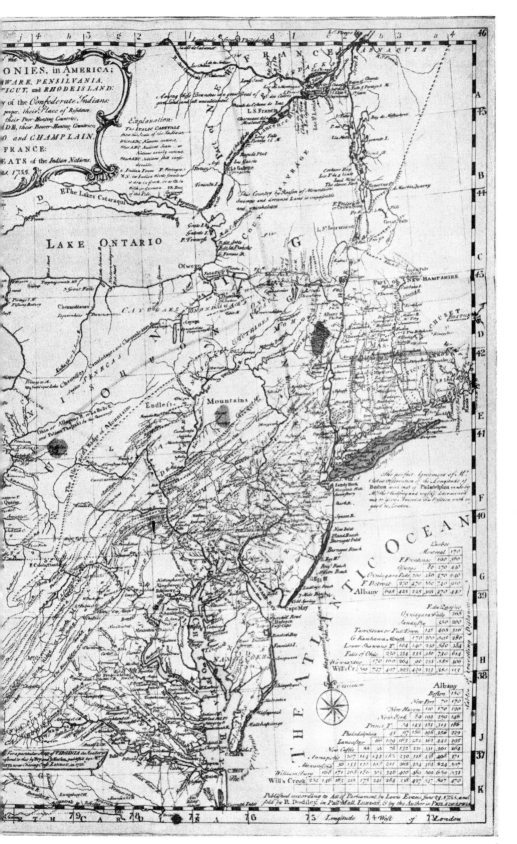

the "Middle British Colonies in America."

Geography in America: W. Scull's "Map of the Province of P─────"

Science

tary career. Evans justified himself, with his accustomed vi
Essays, Number II, and had somewhat the best of the argu
significance of the discussion, however, lay in the clarity wit
illustrated and contrasted the divergent interests and views c
moderate and less militaristic exponents of the westward
as against the more aggressive ideas and intentions of the n
perialists.

The important thing was the great popular interest in
and the way in which the study of the geography of that
linked to American provincial and private speculative enter
is also illustrated by the expedition to the Ohio Valley by C
Gist made in 1750 under the auspices of the Ohio Compa
report on the geography of the area was not published until
link between imperialistic military geography and the geog
terests of commercial and speculative groups concerned with
ward movement of population also became quite clear with
of Thomas Hutchins after Canada and the eastern half of t
sippi Valley had been ceded to Great Britain by the Treaty c
1763. Hutchins, in fact, built his studies of the west on those
Thomas Pownall's *Topographical Description of North Amer*
don, 1776), also, was hardly more than a revision of Evans's
essays of 1755.

Cadwallader Colden should be mentioned as a student
raphy, both physical and human. His *History of the Five I*
tions contained a map of the Iroquois country, probably mad
self. Certainly his work as surveyor-general of the province
York must have given him the technical facility as well as tl
edge of his work. Colden's lifelong friend and correspondent
liam Douglass was also interested in geography and project
and description of New England, which never reached fruiti

Geography, for the observers of the eighteenth century,
largely geology. Bartram, Evans, Franklin, Garden, and Doug
all very much interested in the structure of the earth as wel
surface and its flora and fauna. These primitive geologists w
cially intrigued by the presence of sea-shells near the tops o
legheny Mountains, and all too often succumbed to the temp
explain that phenomenon by the Biblical account of the floo
however, had an idea of his own :

> These Mountains . . . furnish endless Funds for Systems an
> ries of the World, but the most obvious to me was, that this Ea
> made of the Ruins of another, at the Creation. Bones and Shell
> escaped the Fate of softer animal Substances, we find mixt with

Materials and elegantly preserved in the loose Stones and rocky Bases of the highest of these Hills.[73]

The interest of the Americans in geography was widespread and genuine; for it sprang from one of the profoundest experiences of a rapidly multiplying and expanding people. And like their new interest in their own history, it must also be linked to their emerging self-consciousness; even more obviously, the interest in American geography is to be linked, in both England and America, to the advent of the climactic phase of the epic, century-long struggle of Great Britain and France for the control of the continent.

THE SCIENCE OF THE PEOPLE

The almanac, purveyor of scientific and quasi-scientific medicine to the common people, was no less a purveyor to them of Newtonian science in general — with, also, a steady diet of astrology and other pseudo-scientific materials.

Astrology was a matter of widespread popular interest; and the ordinary man reposed as much faith in the predictions he imagined he could read in the various conjunctions of the planets and the constellations as he did in the predictions of eclipses of the sun and moon that the almanac carried for each year. Every arrangement of the planets and the constellations relative to each other was believed to have its significance for the race in general, and in particular for the individuals born under those "signs" and combinations. Furthermore, these astrological combinations were thought to have great influence upon human health, business enterprises, crops, and general fortune, good or ill. Similarly, the various phases of the moon, carefully and accurately predicted in the almanac for the entire year, were thought to have great influence over the affairs of men. It was recognized as a well-known fact that crops planted in the inauspicious phases of the moon would not prosper, and certain aspects of that heavenly body were thought to indicate, if not to cause, positive catastrophe. The almanac-writers did not hesitate to predict the weather for the entire year; this they did with a safe margin of accuracy, for they could predict with confidence that February would have a considerable amount of snow and that July would have a hot spell.

Yet this hodgepodge of astrology, superstition, and guesswork was balanced by a large fund of genuinely scientific information — the calculations of the tides, the phases of the moon, and the calendar were generally quite accurate, mathematically, as were predictions of eclipses. Much of the medical information was sound, also. At the

[73] Quoted in Lawrence H. Gipson: *Lewis Evans* (Philadelphia, 1936), p. 12.

same time, the almanac-writers, particularly Franklin and Ames, glorified Newton and the other scientists in verse and essay, thus introducing Newtonianism to the lowest ranks of literate society. For example,

Popular Science (and astrology) in colonial America: "The Anatomy of Man's Body as govern'd by the Twelve Constellations."
[From *Poor Richard's Almanack, 1749*]

Poor Richard Improved for 1756 carried a series of verses eulogizing the scientists. Here are some samples:

> *Astronomy, hail, Science heavenly born!*
> *Thy Schemes, the Life assist, the Mind adorn.*
> *To changing Seasons give determin'd Space,*
> *And fix to Hours and Years their measur'd Race*
> *The point'ng Dial, on whose figur'd Plane,*
> *Of Times still Flight we Notices obtain;*
> *The Pendulum, dividing lesser Parts,*
> *Their Rise acquire from thy inventive Arts.*

Th' acute Geographer, *th'* Historian *sage*
By Thy Discov'ries clear the doubtful Page
From marked Eclipses, Longitude perceive,
Can settle Distances, *and Aera's give.*
From his known Shore the Seaman distant far,
Steers safely guided by thy Polar Star ;
Nor errs, when Clouds and Storms obscure its Ray,
His Compass makes him as exact a Way.

Cassini next, and Huygens, like renown'd,
The moons *and wondrous Ring of* Saturn *found*
Sagacious Kepler, still advancing saw
The elliptic motion, *Natures plainest Law,*
That Universal acts thro' every part.
This laid the Basis of Newtonian Art.
Newton! vast mind! whose piercing Pow'rs apply'd
The Secret Cause of Motion first decry'd ;
Found Gravitation was the primal Spring
That wheel'd the Planets round their central King.[74]

Franklin evidently expected his thousands of readers to understand "elliptic motion," gravitation, Saturn's ring, and the like.

Nathaniel Ames's *Astronomical Diary* for 1755 carried two essays on air and diet for the edification and instruction of his readers :

OF AIR

The Air which fills our raptur'd Breasts with Joy, supports all Natures Sons with Life, without whose Energy the Blood of Man and Beasts would soon become a drossy Tide, and all the Efforts of the active Heart, would be unable to propell the purple Currant thro' its secret mazy Channels. Sometimes the Planets dart their Influence down ; or from the Earth's wide Womb strange Plagues arise and contaminate the Æthereal Tracts of Air, which stains the blue Serenity of Heaven with Death in various Shapes.

Breathe not the air of *Cities*, where breathless Winds imbibe Effluvia, from the Sick and Dying, from the Dead, from Docks and Dunghills ; where Thousands of Lungs with Exhalations foul, sate the Air with strange Corruption, and make that vital Element a nauseous Mass, enough to spoil and corrode that weak and tender Organ thro' whose flexible Tubes the putrid Salts of all obscene corrupt offensive Things are carried to the Blood.[75]

This was Ames's way of putting into popular language what the doctors all believed to be the dangerous role played by the air in the

[74] *Poor Richard Improved,* 1756.
[75] *An Astronomical Diary : or an Almanack for the year of our Lord Christ,* 1755.

transmission of disease. It was essays such as these that brought the findings of science to the layman.

John Bartram, America's greatest botanist, helped Franklin to popularize botanical science through his *Poor Richard's Almanac* by

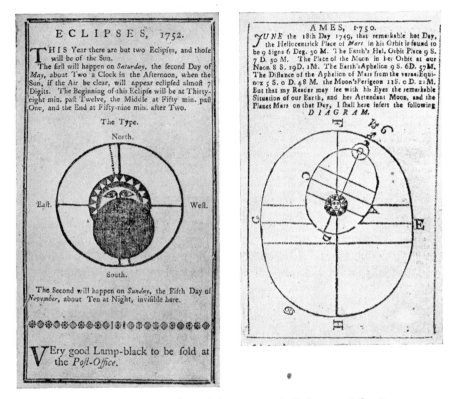

Popular Science in colonial America: *a*) *Eclipses of the Sun.*
b) *The movements of the heavenly bodies.*

[a) From *Poor Richard Improved*, 1752. b) From Nathaniel Ames *Astronomical Diary*, 1750]

writing an essay for the 1749 issue on the subject of the red cedar. But this was not merely science; it was also something useful; for Bartram, like many others, was convinced that the red cedar was one of America's most useful trees. Thus Bartram points out the fact that the rapid rate of settlement is destroying the American forest, especially oak, which is the wood used, for example, for fencing. But oak, moreover, is a slowly growing tree and rots relatively rapidly. Red cedar, on the other hand, matures rapidly, rots more slowly than oak, and may be grown, as it were, at home. In his essay he gives directions for planting and care of these trees.

Some of the scientific essays and diagrams in the almanacs were surprisingly technical and advanced. Such, for example, was the one on the juxtaposition of the earth and Mars on May 18, 1749, which appeared, with a diagram, in Ames's *Astronomical Diary* for 1750, and, much less difficult to understand, the diagram of an eclipse that appeared in *Poor Richard Improved* for 1752.

But if the almanacs were popularizers of science, so were the newspapers, which published essays on scientific subjects. Some of these essays were fantastic, to say the least. Consider, for example, the essay on lightning that appeared in the *South Carolina Gazette*, written by one who apparently refused to be taken in by Franklin's radical ideas : air, says the essayist, is an exhalation of vapor from the earth ; we can be sure of it, because our senses tell us it is so. The air is mixed with other vapors, nitrous, aluminous, sulphureous, etc. ; and these vapors accumulate in the clouds. When the clouds are sufficiently charged with such vapors, they become heavy, approach the earth, and discharge their contents with rain and lightning :

> On this occasion the several exhalations, which were before dispersed through the atmospherical ocean, are collected and brought into contact, which, as they consist of very opposite and heterogeneous principles, a luctus and effervescence must arise when the saline and acid particles mix with such as are sulphureous, which will rush on each other with smart vibratory and repercussive motions, whereby a sufficient degree of heat will be generated, to kindle the sulphureous parts, by which the vitriolic and nitrous salts will be instantaneously accended, and as those consist of very active and elastic principles they dilate themselves on being inflamed with a vast expansion, so that a flash will immediately burst forth from the cloud with great explosion, setting fire to whatever matter of the same kind it meets with in its course, so that lightning is often seen to branch itself out and run in different directions.[76]

Not all the scientific material in the newspapers was drivel of this sort, however. Much of it was sound ; and the same paper that printed this fantastic essay on the lightning of vitriolic and nitrous salts also printed the reports of Franklin's electrical experiments.

Science was often material for daily conversation ; just as often it made up the content of personal letters of laymen. The lively young Eliza Lucas, for example, interested, as always, in everything, comments on the scientific happenings of her day in one of her letters

[76] *South Carolina Gazette,* June 17, 1751.

thus : "I cant conclude yet till I have told you I saw the Commett Sir I Newton foretold should appear in 1741 — wc^h. in his oppinion is that, that will destroy the world, how long it may be travelling down to us he does not say but I think it does not concern us much as our time of action is over at our death." [77] A few weeks later she wrote the same friend again :

> By y^r. enquiry after the Commett I find y^r. curiosity has not been strong enough to raise you out of your bed so much before your usual time as mine has been. but to answer your queries — The Comett had the appearance of a very large Starr with a tail to my sight about 5 or 6 foot long its' real magnitude must really be prodigious. The tail was much paler than the comett itself. not unlike the milky way. . . . The light of the comett to my unphilosophical eyes seems to be natural and all it's own how much it may really borrow from the sun I am not astronomer enough to tell — [78]

Newtonian science, then, was the common possession of all, or nearly all, the people. But the scientific mind of the Americans was not restricted to the Newtonian theoretical sciences of nature, or even to the combination of Newtonianism and astrology and speudo-science that weighed down the almanacs. For the Americans were an eminently practical people, and their applied science and inventions were probably more characteristically American than any other aspect of American scientific thought. It was thus no accident that Franklin, one of America's greatest scientists, was also its greatest inventor, or that his most important inventions arose out of his scientific studies. Thus the lightning-rod was the product of his studies of electricity; his "Pennsylvania Fireplace" resulted from his study of heat; his bifocal spectacles grew out of his study of optics; his "musical armonica" out of his experiments with sound. Similarly, Jared Eliot invented a number of agricultural implements, and Cadwallader Colden invented "a new method of printing," a sort of mimeographing process; Thomas Godfrey about 1730 invented a sextant to meet his needs, and Benjamin West discovered the principle of the camera obscura.

The Americans were an ingenious, inventive people. They had to be; especially the frontiersmen : for they were often miles from settlements where tools, harness, furniture, or other utensils could be bought; and they generally had no money with which to buy them, in any case. Yet the need for a new sort of gadget was continually presenting itself to the frontier people; often their very survival depended upon their inventing something to meet the need, and quickly, or

[77] Eliza Lucas Pinckney : *The Journal and Letters of Eliza Lucas,* edited by Harriott Pinchney Holbrook (Wormsloe, 1850), p. 8.
[78] Ibid., pp. 9–10.

upon their ability to seize quickly an opportunity that presented itself by means of some invention. The daily experience of the Americans on farm and frontier literally forced them to become an inventive, adaptable people. This explains why travelers were constantly com-

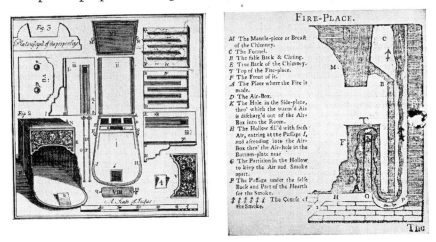

Applied Science and American inventiveness: Drawing for "The Pennsylvania Fireplace."

[From Benjamin Franklin, *An Account of the Newly-Invented Pennsylvania Fireplace* (Philadelphia, 1744)]

menting upon American ingenuity; as one of them put it, "every village has its genius [inventor]."

CONCLUSION: THE SCIENCE OF PRAGMATISM AND FREEDOM

The great new ingredient flowing into the American mind of the eighteenth century was Newtonian science and its concomitant rationalism. This stream strongly affected the development of every other aspect of intellectual life: economic thought, social thought, politics, religion, literature, and philosophy. Furthermore, Newtonian science permeated the thinking of every social or intellectual class.

This eighteenth-century science was marked by certain attitudes and methods. It rested upon observed facts, and about the middle of the century the scientists had come to understand the usefulness of the controlled experiment. At the same time the scientists elevated the ideals of objectivity, self-criticism, and the free exchange of information and theory. William Douglass, severe critic of others that he was, especially in his economics and his politics, yet was anxious to exchange scientific criticism with other scientists, and, more important still, he was capable of changing his mind. Franklin, in a letter for Douglass, addressed to John Perkins, expressed the scientist's attitude in 1752:

> I am indebted for your preceding letter, but business sometimes obliges me to postpone philosophical amusements. Whatever I have wrote of that kind are really, as they are entitled, but *Conjectures* and Suppositions; which ought always to give place, when careful observation militates against them. I own I have too strong a *penchant* to the building of hypotheses; they indulge my natural indolence. I wish I had more of your patience and accuracy in making observations, on which alone true philosophy can be founded. And, I assure you, nothing can be more obliging to me, than your kind communication of those you make, however they may disagree with my preconceived notions.[79]

The eighteenth-century scientists were deliberately seeking for generalizations. They hoped and expected to find the laws governing all the realms of nature, and all but a very few believed that these laws would be found to be the laws of God. All, or nearly all, stood in profound awe before the spectacle of a law-bound, God-created universe. In the words of Alexander Garden, for example:

> A few days will I hope compleat my happiness in that affair [love], but as to real happiness, which cannot possible consist in Any thing but in a knowledge of the beautifull order disposition & harmony of the three Kingdoms here & the other parts of this System in its higher Spheres, which at last leads us Gradually to the Great Eternall & first Cause — as to this happiness I say, I expect to grow in it daily while you & such Ingenious members of Society continue to favour me w[t] your Correspondence, which not only informs my judgment but rouses all the faculties and powers of my mind to exert themselves in endeavoring to imitate & follow such Examples & Patterns.[80]

The method was the method of free investigation, free exchange of ideas, and free mutual criticism. One of the most striking characteristics of this intellectual outlook, indeed, was its devotion to a true intellectual fredom and its humility in the name of learning, one scientist from another. It was this ideal that motivated the Royal Society of London, of which many of the American scientists were fellows, and it was this same ideal that prompted Franklin to propose the organization of the American Philosophical Society. This society contained a number of scientists who were not members of the Royal Society; it was somewhat self-consciously an American organization, and Franklin, in proposing it, expressed its purpose thus:

[79] Franklin: *Works* (Sparks ed.), VI, 120–1.
[80] *Colden Papers*, V, 41.

The first drudgery of a settling new colonies, which confines the attention of people to mere necessaries, is now pretty well over ; and there are many in every province in circumstances, that set them at ease, and afford leisure to cultivate the finer arts, and improve the common stock of knowledge. To such of these who are men of speculation, many hints must from time to time arrive, many observations occur, which if well examined, pursued, and improved, might produce discoveries to the advantage of some or all of the British planations, or to the benefit of mankind in general.[81]

It was this emphasis upon the utilitarian aspect of their science, probably, that was most typical of the American attitude. It was this emphasis, also, that led to the organization of other societies for the promotion of "useful" knowledge, as well as the museums in Charleston and Philadelphia. But there was a certain rationalistic self-consciousness present in the mind of the Americans, also. As Franklin wrote to Colden in 1753, "I see it is not without Reluctance that the Europeans will allow that they can possibly receive any Instruction from us Americans."[82]

This science, and the rationalistic outlook that accompanied it, was finding its way into education, to the dismay of such conservatives as Thomas Clap, president of Yale. Harvard, under the leadership of John Winthrop in the Hollis Professorship, was a center of Newtonian science ; William and Mary, a hotbed of rationalism, was distinguished by the work of William Small, and "natural philosophy" occupied important places in the curricula of the College of Philadelphia and King's College in New York. Even Yale, despite Clap's resistance to the new religions, both of the right and of the left, gave countenance to natural philosophy and the discussion of Newtonian topics in the students' theses. Princeton, organized for the teaching of ministers, was less science-conscious than the others, and actually went into a phase of reactionism at the moment when William and Mary was reaffirming its faith in the freedom of science and of teaching in its new charter of 1758.

It would be difficult to exaggerate the importance of Newtonian science and rationalism in the development of American intellectual life. For it influenced every realm of thought, from economics to religion, literature, and philosophy, and it affected the lives and the minds of all the people, of all social classes, from the wealthiest to the poorest, and from the settled society of the seaboard to the restless itinerants of the frontier. The sweep of science in America was part and parcel of the so-called Enlightenment of Europe ; at the same time, in

[81] Franklin : *Works* (Sparks ed.), VI, 14.
[82] *Colden Papers*, IV, 382.

its wide popularization, in the emphasis upon utility, and in its application to the practical, daily affairs of life by the ingenuity of the Americans, it was peculiarly American. Like all the other phases of American thought, it was part of the general mood of western civilization as a whole, but it was a part that was differentiated by certain characteristics that were peculiarly American.

The conflict of science with religion that was not yet completely visible lay not in the scientific explanation of the structures and the mechanism of the universe, which the religious might easily accept as the creation of God in one mighty week, but rather, in a relatively minor detail, the question of first cause and immediate cause of natural phenomena, or whether God ever set aside the natural laws he laid down for the regulation of the universe. For the reactionaries interpreted comets and earthquakes and other natural phenomena as signs from God : God, in the carrying-out of his plan for men, might intervene directly to strike a man dead with lightning or to heal a child who was incurably ill. It was upon this point, indeed, that the real conflict arose. For the scientists tended to ignore the questions of first cause and divine purpose in their descriptions of natural phenomena. Thus when John Winthrop IV, in the middle of the eighteenth century, reported that earthquakes are caused by undulations in the earth's crust, he stirred up the excited denunciation of such religious leaders as Thomas Prince and Mather Byles, who insisted that such natural phenomena were indicational of God's mood, to say the least. Said Byles :

> No Doubt natural Causes may be assigned for this Phenomenon. An imprisoned Vapour too closely pent, or too strongly compressed in the Caverns beneath, will, thro' a natural Elasticity, abhor Confinement, dilate and expand, swell and heave up the Surface of the Earth, producing a Tremor and Commotion, till [it] either finds Vent, or from some other Cause, it is smothered, and its Violence abated. . . .
>
> But we must not imagine from hence, that an Earthquake, because it may be accounted for on Philosophical [scientific] Principles, is a casual Event, or that some Chance has happened unto us. It is God at Work, tho' he works by the Intervention of second Causes. . . .
>
> The supream Being first appointed & regulated the Laws of Nature, with infinite Wisdom & uncontroulable Sovereignty. He overrules them all, suspends or alters them as he pleases. . . . He formed our Globe of such a Constitution as to be liable to Earthquakes. And he produces them at such Times, in such Places, and in such Degrees of Violence & Severity, as are most for his Glory, and best calculated to accomplish the Designs of his Providence, in the Government of the natural and the moral World.[83]

[83] Mather Byles : *Divine Power and Anger displayed in Earthquakes* (Boston, 1755), pp. 4, 5, 7–8.

But it was Thomas Prince who most ardently took up the cudgels for the cause of religion. Earthquakes might have natural causes; they might also be caused by human monkeying with the forces of nature. Take lightning-rods, for example : who in New England had not been cursed by Franklin's presumptuous rods? Thus:

> The more *Points of Iron* are erected round the *Earth*, to draw the Electrical Substance out of the *Air;* the more the *Earth* must needs be charged with it. And therefore it seems worth of consideration, whether *any Part* of the *Earth* being fuller of *this terrible Substance*, may not be more exposed to *more shocking Earthquakes.* In Boston are more erected than any where else in *New England;* and Boston seems to be more dreadfully shaken. O! there is no getting out of the Mighty hand of GOD! If we think to avoid it in the *Air*, we cannot in the *Earth :* Yea it may grow more fatal; and there is no safety anywhere, but in his *Almighty Friendship* through CHRIST the Mediator, and by *heartily Repenting* of *every* Sin and *hearty embracing* the *Saviour,* in *all his offices,* and upright Living to Him.[84]

Prince, when he read Winthrop's explanation of the earthquake, was pleased with it, and in a letter to the *Boston Gazette*, somewhat pontifically expressed his approval. He took the scientist to task, however, for his scientific objectivity. For whatever the immediate cause of earthquakes, the first cause was God, and it seemed to him that Winthrop had neglected his plain duty in not using this awful manifestation of God's majesty and power to recall men to a due sense of their dependence. Furthermore, Winthrop had not, apparently, taken into consideration the explanation of earthquakes that Prince had written back in 1727. To which Winthrop replied in fine irony : "Had I known of this learned Sermon in season, I might have adorned my discourse with another illustrious name, besides those of Newton, Boyle, &c. I might at the same time have corroborated *that particular* in it, which relates to the existence of subterraneous caverns, by the testimony of an unexceptionable witness, who 'in *accounting* for these natural *causes*,' as he by a remarkable peculiarity of phrase expresses himself, goes no farther than he has seen with his eyes." [85]

As for science and religion, he says, "The consideration of a DEITY is not peculiar to *Divinity*, but belongs also to *natural Philosophy.* And indeed the main business of natural Philosophy is, to trace the chain of natural causes from one link to another, till we come to the FIRST CAUSE ; who, in Philosophy, is considered as presiding over, and con-

[84] Thomas Prince : *Earthquakes the Works of God and Tokens of his just Displeasure* (Boston, 1727 ; reprint, with added note, 1755), appendix.

[85] John Winthrop : *A Letter to the Publishers of the Boston Gazette* (Boston, 1756), p. 1.

tinually actuating this whole chain and every link of it; and accordingly, I have ever been careful to give my discourses this turn." [86]

But it seemed to Winthrop that Prince was drawing new proofs of the continued agency of God, merely by making new suppositions with regard to earthquakes, especially by supposing, without the slightest evidence, that earthquakes might be caused by lightning-rods; and he took the "reverend philosopher" severely to task. He felt that he must rebuke publication of the thoroughly unscientific Prince's ideas and his irresponsible use of his pseudo-scientific findings to disturb the people unnecessarily. He was glad that Prince was willing to accept his explanation of earthquakes, but especially, he said, "I cannot but esteem it an high felicity to have rescued this worthy Divine from the pains which had seized him, when he wrote his Poscript about the *iron-points;* and by him, consequently a great number of others, especially of the more *timorous Sex* (so extensive is his influence!) who have been thrown into unreasonable terrors, by means of a too slender acquaintance with the laws of electricity." [87]

The upshot of all which was that Prince wrote one more public letter, in which he said: "I freely forgive his Treatment of me," and then proceeded to propose that the colonial legislature give Professor Winthrop a pension! [88]

But the great significance of the intellectual chastising administered to the "reverend divine" by the professor of science lay in the scientist's rebuke to the religious pseudo-scientist who distorted science for the purposes of religion. For the intellectual method championed by Winthrop was the method of rationalistic objectivity and observation; despite his own devout religious feeling, he was unwilling either to moralize upon the findings of science any farther than those findings themselves would warrant or to distort them for the purpose of arousing religious feeling in the people. At the same time, his defense was a defense of his fellow scientist Franklin, whose studies of electricity had been so grossly misinterpreted by the divine.

This dramatic exchange between religion and science was not the only one. A large wing of the more conservative colonists was disturbed by the inroads of rationalism, scientific or otherwise, and were rising to defend the old religious way. But America was a more tolerant country than most, and the scientists could thank their stars that they were free. As Franklin wrote to Cadwallader Colden relative to the latter's radical theories of the universe: "It is well we are not, as poor Galileo was, subject to the Inquisition for philosophical heresy.

---

[86] Ibid., p. 2.
[87] Ibid., p. 7.
[88] *Boston Gazette,* February 23, 1756.

My whispers against the orthodox doctrine, in private letters, would be dangerous; but your writing and printing would be highly criminal. As it is, you must expect some censure; but one heretic will surely excuse another." [89]

NOTE TO THE READER

Of the writings of the Americans in science, Benjamin Franklin's *Experiments and Observations on Electricity* (London, 1769) is doubtless the most interesting. The latest edition of these letters and essays is one edited by J. Bernard Cohen (Cambridge, 1941).

John Winthrop's little pamphlet *Relation of a Voyage from Boston to Newfoundland* (Boston, 1761) is a very interesting account of this famous expedition to Newfoundland to observe the transit of Venus, of the care taken to make the observations accurate, and of the observations themselves. It is a fine expression of the scientific attitude and normal scientific practice of the time.

Benjamin Franklin's *An Account of the New Invented Pennsylvania Fireplace* (Philadelphia, 1744) is an interesting example of the way in which Franklin turned his studies of heat to a practical end.

Cadwallader Colden's *Principles of Action in Matter* (London, 1751) is an important scientific writing; but I warn you, it is difficult reading; it was too much so for most of his contemporaries and is worse for us of the twentieth century.

A very significant book for the history of medicine was John Morgan's *Discourse upon the Institution of Medical Schools in America* (Philadelphia, 1765); for in this little book Dr. Morgan not only laid down the basic plan for American medical education; he also advocated specialization and laid down the lines it was to follow.

By far the most impressive book of a popular scientific nature dealing with America was Mark Catesby's *The Natural History of Carolina . . .* (Vol. I, London, 1731–43). This large book, with its beautiful colored engravings, was widely read by the Americans of that generation who could afford to buy it, although it is relatively unknown today. It was revised and reprinted by George Edwards in 1754 and again in 1771. Some of the drawings of the later edition were made by William Bartram, son of the Quaker botanist.

One of the most delightful little books of a scientific nature emanating from this period is John Bartram's *Observations on the Inhabitants, Climate, Soil, Rivers . . . made by Mr. John Bartram, in his Travels from Pensilvania . . . to . . . the Lake Ontario* (London, 1751). It is more like anthropology than descriptive biology, however.

Lawrence H. Gipson has edited the writings of Lewis Evans under the

[89] Franklin : *Works* (Sparks ed.), V, 287.

title of *Lewis Evans* (Philadelphia, 1939). This book also has a masterly introductory biographical note and reproductions of Evans's maps. Furthermore, it is a fine example of book-making.

Mr. Frederick E. Brasch, of the Carnegie Institution, has written several pioneer essays on Newtonian science in America in the eighteenth century. The best known of these is *The Royal Society of London and Its Influence upon Scientific Thought in the American Colonies* (Washington, 1931).

Of later books on early American science there are practically none; but there is a chapter on science among the Puritans in Samuel E. Morison's delightful *The Puritan Pronaos* (New York, 1936). In the Brown University Library there is an unpublished Ph.D. dissertation by Winthrop Tilley, entitled "The Literature of Natural and Physical Science in the American Colonies from the Beginnings to 1765." This is the only thing of the sort that I have seen; it proved very helpful to me in the writing of this chapter.

CHAPTER III
Of the Meaning of Existence:
Philosophy

"The great uncertainty I found in metaphysical reasonings disgusted

"me, and I quitted that kind of reading and study for others more sat-

"isfactory. . . . I grew convinced that Truth, Sincerity and Integrity

"in Dealings between Man and Man, were of the utmost Importance

"to the Felicity of Life. . . . O that moral Science were in as fair a

"way of Improvement, that Men would cease to be Wolves to one

"another, and that human Beings would at length learn what they now

"improperly call Humanity."

—BENJAMIN FRANKLIN.

PHILOSOPHY is the supreme effort of the human mind to understand the universe, itself, and the meaning, if there is any, of existence. It is the apogee of the pyramid of human learning and thought, the great integrator of all that men know. For it is the great synthesis, the great "pulling together," the great systematization of the knowledge and the aspirations of a people, or an age, or a culture. Philosophy is the great synthesis of the human mind; and so it was in the seedtime of America. And if religion was the oldest and most deeply seated element in the formation of an American intellectual synthesis, and science the newest, American philosophy itself was the product of a sort of fusion of these two, modified by the ideas and ideals driven into the minds of the colonists by the facts, pleasant and unpleasant, of their daily experience on the land and in the forest.

Yet the various segments of American colonial society found different syntheses to fit their own group or local experiences and aspirations. As in other aspects of their thinking, the philosophical outlook of the first Americans changed from that of the fathers, Winthrop, John Cotton, or John Smith, to that of the sons and grandsons, Edwards, Chauncy, Allen, Franklin, Witherspoon, and Jefferson. From the brittle idealism of Calvinism, framed to justify the fixed concepts of society of, say, 1640, it changed to the flexible naturalism that was more expressive of the mind and spirit of the late eighteenth century. But it did not change as a single unit. The mood of the well-to-do northern merchants or of the aristocrats of the tidewater lands and cities of the south, or the outlook of the more explosive and dynamic sects of the settled frontier, remained typical of those classes of people.

Philosophy, however, described as systematic thinking, was the possession neither of the middle class nor of the underprivileged. These classes of people, wherever they were, were neither prepared nor sufficiently interested in abstractions to discuss systematically and formally such problems as the nature of being or how men know. This highly intellectualized business was the prerogative, rather, of the educated intellectual elite, of whom there were in America, as elsewhere and always, relatively few. The ideas of the philosophers did, indeed, as always, filter down to those of the spadesmen who had an ear to hear and a mind to perceive; and, as always, these ideas did have a perceptible influence upon the course of history. But it was, after all, the philosophers who did the philosophizing, and of these there were not many.

The seedling philosophers who did appear in America in the eighteenth century belong to about four groups, their membership in which was largely determined by their individual social and geographic origins and the conditions of their experience, whether educational or other. Thus the most conservative philosophers were those who, like Cotton Mather, tried to preserve the philosophical Puritanism of their fathers, or Jonathan Edwards, who, in a similar effort in the name of Calvinism, moved into a new philosophical idealism that would probably have been neither recognized nor accepted by his Puritan forebears. Edwards, indeed, belongs in a second group of thinkers, who, profoundly influenced by the incontrovertible findings of science, found an escape from its implications in the Berkeleian idealism that in effect denies the existence of matter altogether. Of this way of thinking, also, was Samuel Johnson, first president of King's College. The third group to be noted was that group of thinkers who, like Ethan Allen, Benjamin Franklin, and Thomas Jefferson, accepted the findings of science and forced their philosophy, which came to be known as Deism, to fit the universe of natural law even if that meant stripping God of much of the old-time picturesqueness of his personality. A fourth small group, made up of men like Cadwallader Colden, was materialistic to the point of ruling God out of the universe almost altogether — though they all hedged at this extreme implication of their philosophies. John Witherspoon, president of Princeton and philosopher of "common sense" in the name of practical realism, rejected the extremes both of materialism and of idealism, and tried to restore the old-time religious explanation of the universe and man to a position of philosophical respectability; and because it went neither too far to the right nor too far to the left, this philosophy, the philosophy of "common sense," became the one to which most Americans adhered.

One other line of thought must be mentioned, which, though it did not in the eighteenth century achieve the status of a philosophy, yet did spring from the day-to-day experience of the Americans and provided, as it were, the experiential germ-plasm of the later American philosophy of pragmatism. This was the intellectual product of the fact that Americans, by and large, had to make their living with their hands and that no tool or practice was worth keeping unless it proved its validity by its usefulness in the struggle to survive and prosper. There was no formal pragmatism in the eighteenth century, but Benjamin Franklin was essentially a practicing pragmatist all his life and in most of his thought and probably should be considered as such. Thus the picture of philosophy in eighteenth-century America is a changing, complex mosaic of Puritanism, idealism, materialism, realism, Deism, and — in embryo — pragmatism.

THE EUROPEAN BACKGROUND

The great philosophical heritage of the seventeenth century was Scholasticism, which, though it varied from school to school and from philosopher to philosopher, was essentially an effort to interpret the universe in terms of the Christian epic in such a fashion as to make it appear reasonable to the human mind. Or, put in another way, Scholasticism, as found in its greatest exponent, Thomas Aquinas, was a systematic philosophical effort to harmonize the Christian faith in the plan and the works of God with the findings of human reason. Taking the explanation of the nature of the universe given by Aristotle as the final and authoritative statement, Scholasticism sought by the deductive method to harmonize experience with the Aristotelian generalization; it was thus essentially authoritarian, and the great agency objectifying the philosophy was the authoritarian medieval Catholic Church.

Of all the European philosophers, aside from Calvin himself, who influenced the history of thought in America, it was probably Pierre de la Ramée, or Peter Ramus, who lived and wrote in France in the middle of the sixteenth century, who most profoundly affected the out-look of the Puritan colonies. For Ramus had attacked Aristotelian Scholasticism as early as 1536, and had become a Protestant in 1561; and he had built up a system of logic that, carried to Calvinistic Cambridge University by his followers, was to have a profound influence upon the Cambridge-trained English Puritans, including those who were to lead the Puritan migration to America. Ramus was a humanist, and he borrowed much of his thought and his method directly from the ancients. But his thought was essentially Platonic rather than Aristotelian, for he found the universe to be a structure of idealistic order: nature was the handiwork of the God of order; truth itself, the truth of God, was revealed in nature and the Bible; logic was the instrument by which the mind of man deduced from those sources the truth of God. Ramus's conception of the universe was Platonic in that he saw the material world as an orderly reflection of the ideas in God's mind. Men's understanding of it was deduced, insofar as man was capable of understanding it at all, by the method of logic, which with Ramus amounted to a clear and lacelike pattern of ideas corresponding to the pattern of the universe, springing from the orderly system of God's own mind. Thus the Puritan found the logical pattern of the universe all laid out for him, a pattern, indeed, that corresponded exactly to his own idea of what God's orderly universe was likely to be.

But the advent of Copernican science shook both the Aristotelian and the Platonic explanations of the universe to their core, and Giordano Bruno earned a martyrdom for himself in 1600 by having the courage to see and to expound the philosophical implications of the heliocentric universe and the rule of natural law. It was Francis Bacon of Elizabethan England who, though neither scientist nor philosopher himself, made the first clear rationalization, in his *Novum Organum*, of the inductive method of reasoning that was to prove to be the method both of modern science and of modern philosophy. Thus if modern science demolished the Aristotelian physical universe of the schoolmen, the inductive method replaced their deductive method; and philosophy, perforce, entered upon a new era.

René Descartes was the first philosopher of the scientific age, for it was he who sought first to apply the methods of science to philosophy. Thus, wiping his mind clean of all the contradictory opinions of the philosophers who had preceded him, Descartes took as the basis of his system the obvious and incontrovertible argument: "I think, therefore I am." From this it was easy for him to deduce the axioms that it is man's nature to think and that what the mind thinks, intuitively and clearly, is true. But the mind thinks clearly and intuitively of perfection, and aspires to it; and since man's own mind and the world are imperfect, the only source of this intuitive idea of perfection is God. Therefore God exists.

Descartes thus proves the existence of God, to his own satisfaction — by the mathematical method of geometry and his original conviction that the human mind can find the truth intuitively. This took him away from induction to a form of intuitive rationalism; but the logic was the logic of mathematics. In his effort to build a new philosophy upon the Copernican concept of the universe and mathematical logic, he had hardly done more than devise a new and more beautiful Platonism, which, however, in its essential features was actually older than the Aristotelian Scholasticism it sought to replace. Gottfried Leibniz, the greatest German philosopher of the seventeenth century, was another exponent of the rationalist school.

The third great European philosopher of the seventeenth century was Benedict Spinoza, a Jewish thinker who had absorbed the Cartesian system as well as his ancestral Hebraism and had conversed much with the pietistic Mennonites of his native Holland. The effect of this combination of influences upon him was a sort of pantheism, which found God to be a spirit immanent in the universe revealed by science. But Spinoza had no followers, and his beautiful pantheistic philosophy of the universe stood alone and solitary among the various new schools of thought, almost without influence anywhere, and certainly with none in America.

While the Puritans of England were learning their Ramean Platonism to carry it to New England, there had appeared one of the ablest philosophers England ever produced : Thomas Hobbes, who uniquely produced a philosophy unmixed with theology, a materialism untainted, as it were, by the presence of God. Hobbes admitted the validity of both science and reason as instruments for the apprehension of knowledge; but as all knowledge is subjective, it is also all one, and the same set of concepts that deals with the physical universe must also deal with the phenomena of human life. He thus significantly unified all knowledge into one system, and applied to the state and to society the language, the method, and, by implication, the rationalistic optimism, of natural science. The significance of this synthesis for later "rationalism" — used here as meaning a faith in the ability of the human mind, learning through the senses, to know external reality by the methods of science — is easy to see. For him everything, including even the human mind and its functions, was only matter; thought rested upon the foundation of sense impression, and would be impossible without it. Thus Hobbes was the greatest and most thoroughgoing exponent of the scientific-rationalistic revolution in philosophy; and though he shocked and aroused his contemporaries, parts of his philosophy were adopted by the thinkers who came after him, and his influence upon the development of English thought was profound.

John Locke, for example, the greatest English philosopher after Hobbes, took much from him, without losing his own deistic religion. Thus he based his thinking upon the Copernican-Newtonian universe as revealed by science, and accepted the principles of natural law in human affairs. His best-known work, aside from his political writings, was his *Essay Concerning the Human Understanding,* written primarily to validate the findings of science as the basis and method of the new learning, in which he elaborates an epistemology based upon sensationalism — that is, the belief that all knowledge is acquired through the senses. Locke thus became the great apologist for science and its place in the thinking of the eighteenth century; and his work seemed to justify the current faith in the scientific explanation of the universe and in man's ability through his reason to understand it and to improve his own condition by living in conformity with natural law.

For the thinkers of a radical turn of mind, Locke's epistemology provided a set of premises upon which to build a philosophical system that would go to the logical conclusion implied by material science. It was therefore seized upon by a group of French rationalists to justify a philosophy of complete materialism, a school of thought of which the greatest exponent was Paul Heinrich Dietrich, the Baron d'Holbach. His most important book was *Le Système de la nature,* in which he explained all the phenomena of the universe, human as well as material, psychological as well as physical, in terms of matter and motion. For him the entire universe was matter, and nothing but matter. Life and thought are but manifestations of a sort of fermentation of various sorts of matter. The only evidence we have of real existence is the sense impressions brought along the nerves to the brain; these impressions are true evidences of external reality transmitted to the brain from the nerve-ends; and the only real existence is thus that to be observed by the human senses in the universe of matter, of which man himself is an integral part. So far as man and his psyche are concerned, the materialistic hypothesis was developed by J. O. de La Mettrie, in his book *L'Homme machine,* in which he explains thought as a purely materialistic phenomenon.

But while Locke was willing to admit that some knowledge may be acquired by direct inspiration from God, the obvious conclusion from his system was that all knowledge, of whatever sort, is strictly subjective; that is, that it exists only within ourselves. This furnished the opening needed by those who feared the materialistic implications of the new sensationalism and rationalism, and the Anglican Bishop Berkeley of Cloyne, in Ireland, turned the fact of the subjective nature of knowledge into the basis for a proposition that this knowledge, these ideas of things, were, after all, the only reality, and were but extensions of the mind of God into the mind of man. Matter, for him, did not exist; the only reality was idea. His philosophy, therefore, has been called idealism.

But the same Lockian principle of the subjectivity of knowledge furnished an equally good opening for the opposite extreme, also. For if all knowledge is subjective, then the knowledge of God, who is external to ourselves, is also subjective. Logically, therefore, we cannot be sure that anything exists outside ourselves: we must accept what our senses tell us and what we believe we know by pure reason or by inspiration only on the faith that it is so; for we cannot prove it. Such was the extreme logical conclusion of the Lockian position pointed out by David Hume, and is called philosophical skepticism — as well it might be.

But human beings were hardly to be expected to accept this discouraging philosophy as a basis for living, and the reaction was prompt and effective. It appeared, most significantly for America, in the form of the so-called Scottish realism of John Reid, the great philosopher at the University of Edinburgh, which was brought to the colonies by John Witherspoon, where it was taught at Princeton as the philosophy of "common sense." According to Reid, the human mind can know truth in three different ways: by the sensory impressions, by the moral sense of, say, right and wrong, which needs no outward prompting, and by direct inspiration from God. This is borne out by experience, and it seems only common sense to accept it as so; furthermore, this way of treating the question how men know, while it does not reject the findings of material science, does not impose any revolutionary rejection of the Christian concept of the universe or the Christian epic, either. Essentially conservative, therefore, while accepting a certain amount of scientific rationalism, it was easy to accept; it is no accident that it became so popular in the colonies.

Such, then, was the cycle through which European philosophy moved from Ramus to Hume and back to Reid. All, or nearly all, of these new schools of thought had their influence upon the developing mind of British America.

PHILOSOPHY IN AMERICA: PURITANISM

The basic philosophy of the first settlers in America was Calvinistic Puritanism, which, as philosophy, was a sort of Augustinian Platonism that had been revived by Calvin and given a logical pattern by Peter Ramus.

Puritanism, indeed, must be regarded as both a religion and a philosophy. It was more a religion than a system of thought, but it was also a fairly systematic explanation of the nature of existence, and as such it not only represented its own time, but also gave the mind of the first Americans a cast that had to be overcome before America could produce an indigenous philosophy of its own. Better still, it might be said that the philosophy of Puritanism was the European root upon which, transplanted into the new world, was grafted a new and American outlook on life.

The Puritans' philosophical explanation of the physical universe and of man's relationship to it were not essentially different from the medieval system of thought expressed by the poet Dante and the philosopher Thomas Aquinas. There was still much of Aristotle in the Puritan's study of physics; and the idealism of both Puritanism and Anglicanism accepted the medieval assumption of the unity of knowledge and a medieval, Dantesque hierarchy of values through which, from the lowest to the highest, the soul might ascend to the highest, supreme good, which was God. Yet the Copernican revision of Ptolemy had commanded the respect of the Puritan philosophers, and they accepted it. Science, as exemplified by their great contemporary Galileo, was not of prime interest to them, but they did not discourage it. Some of them, indeed, became enthusiastic exponents of the Copernican-Keplerian-Newtonian system. After all, the chief business of both man and the natural universe was to show forth God's glory. What mattered it whether that glory were focused through a Ptolemaic lens or a Copernican? And if it suited God's purpose or his glory to change or temporarily alter the order of the universe by a miracle, that too was in complete harmony with the basic explanation of things, which rested, in the last analysis, upon the purpose of God.

Thus the basic absolute in the Puritan's philosophy was the purpose in the mind of God. To this degree the Puritan was a Platonist; yet he differed radically from Plato in his conviction that, where Plato had found the absolutes unknowable except vaguely and partially as by the reflection of a shadow on a wall, the Puritan could at least know some of the truth in God's mind by reason of the opening of his eyes that took place at the moment of salvation. For him the mind and purpose of God was the one all-pervading absolute in the universe; the explanation of every phenomenon in the universe, including man, was to be found in the way in which that phenomenon showed forth or conformed to that purpose. Here again the thinking of the Puritan philosophers was essentially deductive, essentially scholastic. But where the scholastic philosopher placed his great emphasis upon the efficacy of human reason for the understanding of truth, whether the truth of nature or the truth of man or the truth of God, with faith taking a relatively minor place, the Puritan placed his great emphasis upon the essential necessity of divine grace, the free gift of God, before the human reason through faith could grasp the truth of God at all. After the receipt of illuminating grace and the establishment of faith, the Puritan man could understand, according to his own way of thinking, more of God's truth than even the most rationalistic of the scholastics would have allowed.

It was the influence of the subjective mood, the overwhelming consciousness of human sin, that made this so. Sin, for the Puritan, was a rebellion against God's truth that produced intellectual blindness in the sinner; and the visitation of divine grace upon him opened his eyes to truth. The valid, but mostly inferior, activities of reason followed after that.

Puritanism was thus a dualistic philosophy of the ideal, the nonmaterial reality, on the one hand, and material reality on the other. As the supreme embodiment of the ideal good, God had created everything in the universe, including man, whom God had created in his own image. But man had presumed to rival God in knowledge and for his sin had been blinded forever to the vision of God's spiritual loveliness. He was the slave of his material nature and incapable of knowing spiritual beauty; but God, in his goodness, had chosen, for his own greater glory, to redeem a portion of the human race, freeing those individuals from their spiritual blindness; the rest of humanity he condemned to eternal torment as their just punishment. Thus the philosophical dualism of the Puritans was also a religious dualism. Philosophy was theology; and in this dualistic philosophy was at once the whole explanation of existence and its meaning, and the complete drama of human life forever. In such a system material existence is real; but material reality is of a lower order than spiritual reality. Man has both sorts of reality within himself; but sin has blinded him to true spiritual reality, and it is not until God opens his eyes that he can rise out of his material nature into his spiritual, which brings him close to God, who is pure spirit.

It is this idealistic dualism of Puritanism as a philosophy that provided the intellectual framework for the Puritan utopia; but it was of even greater historical significance than that; for the Puritans' moral dualism filtered into the American mind to such an extent as to influence American history for centuries. And the end is not yet.

By the beginning of the eighteenth century the large outlines of the Puritan philosophy were being worn away by the corrosive intellectual influences of science and rationalism and the secularizing influence of daily experience on the frontier. Yet there were some who refused to be shaken and maintained their adherence to the Puritan absolutes, come what might. Of these defenders of the old Puritan way, it was Thomas Clap, president of Yale, who held most consistently to the original Puritan doctrine, in his philosophy as well as in his religion. He accepted the Platonic-Ramean Puritan system of the universe without much elaboration or revision. While he wrote much of a defensive religious nature, his philosophical writings were largely confined to the field of ethics, and he wrote a handbook of ethics, based upon the Puritan ideology, for the students of Yale. In this little book, called *An Essay on the Nature and Foundation of Moral Virtue and Obligation,* he defined virtue as "a Conformity to the *Moral Perfection of God;* or it is an Imitation of God, in the moral Perfections of his Nature, so far as they are imitable by his Creatures."[1] This definition is perfectly expressive of the old Puritan philosophy; Clap distinguishes between "internal or real virtue," which is a thing of the mind and conformable to the perfections of God's own nature, and "external or apparent virtue," which seems to be the outward, visible expression of "inward" virtue; in reality, however, it is not so, but "proceeds from some *lower* Motive, such as Self-Interest, Honour, Fancy, or the like."[2] It is the obligation of all rational creatures to seek to conform to the moral perfection of God:

> For as God is the most perfect Being, so the most *perfect State* of any other Being, must consist in being *like to him.* . . . The Perfection, therefore, of a rational Creature, must be to *continue* in that *perfect* state in which he was created: But to *lose* any Part of it, or to acquire any *contrary* Disposition or Quality is a Defection from the most *perfect Pattern and Standard,* and a Destruction of the Works of God. This . . . is also called *Moral Depravity or Sin,* and as it is the first Principle of wrong Action, it is called *Original Sin.*[3]

Clap's ethics were thus a part of his larger Puritan philosophy; and his effort to preserve and make clear that philosophy in the minds of his students was a part of his valiant effort to hold the Puritan line, without compromise, against the infiltration of the implication of science and rationalism. As was the case with many of his contemporaries, his philosophy was subservient to his religion. But he was an anachronism: the set of the tide of the times was against him, and though he made a deep impress upon the minds and the ethical outlook of many classes of Yale students, he was foredoomed to essential failure.

[1] Thomas Clap : *An Essay on the Nature and Foundation of Moral Virtue and Obligation; being a Short Introduction to the Study of Ethics* (New Haven, 1765), p. 3.

[2] Ibid., p. 7.

[3] Ibid., pp. 8–9.

The Idealism of Jonathan Edwards

Puritan idealism was not essentially different from the idealism that underlay the religion of Anglicanism. Both these philosophical structures, indeed, had appeared as parts of the same Calvinistic revival of Augustinian Platonism. Essentially similar in their philosophy, Puritanism and Anglicanism rested upon the basic assumption of an absolute and perfect God, whose glory constituted the be-all and the end-all of existence. Both the Anglican and the Puritan were rationalists, given the consummation of the act of salvation (which depended not at all upon reason, but upon the grace of God and the faith of the saved). But the Puritan used his reason to deduce the meaning of the Bible and events and things by a fixed logical system that followed closely that of Peter Ramus, in terms of an assumed and accepted, fixed, and explicit purpose of God. The Anglican, however, while he accepted the purpose of God as the great moving force in nature and in man, allowed a great deal of freedom to the human reason in the search for an understanding of how God operated to carry his purposes into effect. For the Puritan, God had spoken in the Bible, and nowhere else; his words were to be taken literally; and the business of man's reason was to find the meaning of the words, in order to understand as much of God's purpose as he had chosen to reveal in them and to perfect ways and means of giving effect to God's purpose in the everyday life of this world. For the Anglican, the Bible was only one of the ways in which God had spoken; and since it had been written down by human hands, it was regarded as a human document, with human limitations, and not necessarily to be taken literally. Further, the will of God might also be found expressed elsewhere, and it was the business of human reason to find and study these other expressions as well as the Bible.

Now, the adaptation of religion to the new experiences growing out of the rise of science, the secularization of outlook, and the expansion of the American frontier has already been discussed. The adaptation of the Puritan philosophy of ethical idealism to the "age of reason" followed along similar lines. Indeed, the adaptation and restatement of philosophy was actually carried out by the same leaders who were working in the problems of religion. Thomas Clap has already been noticed; Jonathan Edwards and Samuel Johnson, two of the great adapters of religion, were also the two greatest adapters of philosophy.

Jonathan Edwards has even been called the greatest systematic thinker that America has ever produced. Born into Puritan New England at a time when Puritanism was losing its dominant position in the philosophical mind of America, Edwards devoted his life to the purpose of restoring it. Curiously enough, Edwards's elaboration of Puritan Platonism carried him, by his own native reasoning, straight into a position almost identical with that of the Berkeleian idealists, albeit, apparently, quite independently of Berkeley. That Edwards was profoundly influenced in his thinking by the discoveries and the implications of modern science seems evident by the fact that he read both John Locke's *Essay Concerning the Human Understanding* and Ralph Cudworth's *The True Intellectual System of the Universe*, and that he himself wrote upon scientific subjects in the spirit of the eighteenth century and even projected an essay upon natural science. His philosophy, however, was based upon neither science nor theology, but chiefly upon his own experience.

Edwards himself considered his life work as more concerned with religious experience than with philosophy. His philosophical thinking was the result of his efforts to arrive at a more perfect understanding and appreciation of God's beauty and grandeur; philosophy was only auxiliary to theology. In fact, he recognized the philosophical idealism at which he arrived as having little or no practical importance, since, as he says, to "find out the reason of things, in Natural Philosophy, is only to find out the proportion of God's acting. And the case is the same, as to such proportions, whether we suppose the World only mental, in our sense, or no."[4] Nevertheless, it is as a philosopher that Edwards is most widely remembered and respected. And his philosophy, a sort of mystical idealism, is the first great system of thought that can be said to have arisen natively out of the American soil and the American experience.

At the age of fourteen, as a Yale College sophomore, Edwards had read John Locke's *Essay Concerning the Human Understanding* and had probably been prompted by it to write his "Notes on the Mind," in which the basic propositions of his philosophy are laid down: "As to Bodies . . . they have no proper Being of their own. And as to Spirits, they are the communications of the Great Original Spirit; and doubtless, in metaphysical strictness and propriety, He *is*, as there is none else. He is likewise Indefinitely Excellent, and all Excellence and Beauty is derived from him, in the same manner as all Being. And all other Excellence is, in strictness, only a shadow of His."[5] Thus Edwards is a pure idealist: matter, as such, does not exist. The conception or idea of anything that appears in our minds is a "communication" of the idea in God's mind, or part of it: For Edwards, "That which truly is the Substance of all Bodies, is the infinitely exact, and precise, and perfectly stable Idea, in God's mind, together with his stable Will that the same shall gradually be communicated to us, and

<hr/>

[4] Edwards : *Works*, I, 94, 669–70.   [5] Ibid., I, 700.

to other minds, according to certain fixed and established Methods and Laws : or in somewhat different language, the infinitely exact and precise Divine Idea, together with an answerable, perfectly exact, precise and stable Will, with respect to correspondent communication to Created Minds, and effects on their minds."[6] In other words, nothing really exists except the idea of the thing in God's mind ; it exists for us only in so far as the idea of it appears in our minds ; but both our minds and the ideas in them are reflections, or extensions, of the mind of God. But this line of reasoning led Edwards into an interest in psychology, in an effort to find out how the human mind operated ; for sin had clogged up the human mind's communication, as it were, with its original source, which was the mind of God ; and though God still "communicated" ideas to the individual human mind, the mind, cut off from its guiding principle, the beauty and the holiness of God, could not but wander around in confusion until God, in his goodness, opened the individual understanding again to the light by the process of salvation. Edwards's philosophy, and his psychology, were both subservient to his religion, which was, after all, an irrational, emotional response to his vision of the loveliness of God. The important thing, for him, philosophically, was the concept of the universe as being idea — God's idea — and of everything else, including the apparent sensory perceptions of matter, as only the complex manifestations of the infinite variety of ideas in God's mind.

Because of his dominant concern with the practical psychology of the soul, Edwards never formulated his idealistic philosophy in a systematic treatise. His chief concern was a revival and a reinvigorating of the Calvinistic doctrines of the total depravity of man and of the necessity for divine grace. His interest in psychology was subservient to that, just as his interest in philosophy was ; incidentally, however, his interest in psychology may be regarded as one evidence of the effect upon him of the new science. Edwards was a child of the Enlightenment, as Berkeley was a child of the Enlightenment, and though he fought hard for a return to Calvinistic Puritanism, it was by emotional methods that would have revolted the rationalistic souls of the Puritan fathers and with a philosophy which went much farther toward pure idealism than the Platonism of even the Puritan fathers would have dreamed of going. Times had changed. The American frontier was destroying the purity and the effectiveness of Puritanism among the people ; and the scientific outlook had distorted it and prevented its loyal acceptance in its original form, even in the mind of Edwards himself. Edwards, whether he realized it or not, was of the eighteenth century ; even had he succeeded in establishing his idealism in the

[6] Ibid., I, 671.

minds of his people, it still would not have been the original philosophy of Puritanism. Thomas Clap was, indeed, trying to preserve the genuine philosophy of Puritanism; but Edwards was trying, all unwittingly, to establish a philosophy that, so far as the Puritans were concerned, was essentially something new.

Berkeleian Idealism in America: Samuel Johnson

Samuel Johnson, who has already been mentioned as a religious leader, was one of Jonathan Edwards's contemporaries whose outlook on life and the universe was quite similar to that of Edwards himself. His major interest, as was that of Edwards, was in religion, and his philosophy was thus an effort at intellectual justification of his religious faith and purpose. Both Johnson and Edwards, indeed, were defenders of religion in the early stages of the Enlightenment; their philosophies are honest and significant efforts to bring religion into harmonious relationship with the new science.

Johnson, educated at Yale, first made his acquaintance with philosophy as it was in the Scholasticism of the Yale curriculum. He soon read Bacon, Newton, and Locke, however, and it was probably in large measure because of them that he was converted to Anglicanism from the Congregationalism in which he was raised. His first effort at philosophical writing was a sort of encyclopedia of philosophy, which in its mature form clearly showed the influence of the "nature-philosophers." The greatest single influence in his life, however, was that exercised by Bishop George Berkeley, the greatest English philosopher in the generation immediately following that of John Locke, who visited New England in 1729.

Under the influence of Berkeley, Johnson became an idealist. According to this way of explaining existence, the reality of things consists in their being perceived by the mind. Nothing exists except when perceived by the mind in the form of a mental image or idea. But the ideas of individual things did not originate in the individual mind; they were extensions — or reflections — of the general ideas, the "archtypes" of things, in the mind of God. As he put it:

> Our minds may be said to be created mere *tabulæ rasæ*; i.e., they have no notices of any objects of any kind properly created in them, or con-created with them: yet I apprehend, that in all the notices they have of any kind of objects, they have an immediate dependence upon the Deity, as really as they depend upon Him for their existence; i.e. they are no more authors to themselves of the objects of their perceptions, or the light by which they perceive them, than of the power of perceiving itself; but that they perceive them by a perpetual intercourse with that

great Parent Mind, to whose incessant agency they are entirely passive, both in all the perceptions of sense, and in that intellectual light by which they perceive the objects of pure intellect.[7]

This followed Berkeley's line of argument and is quite similar, in general conception, to Edwards's explanation of thought and ideal reality. But Johnson elaborated upon Berkeley's basic concept and suc-

American Philosophers: Samuel Johnson. A portrait by John Smibert.

[By courtesy of Columbia University]

ceeded in proving to his own satisfaction that the "archetypes," or ideas of things in the mind of God, are universal and eternal, that there thus exists in the divine mind of God a "system of universal nature," and that the things we see and feel and hear are but so much of the true system of existence as God pleases to reveal to us:

Not that it is to be doubted but that there are archtypes of these sensible ideas existing, external to our minds; but then they must exist in some other mind, and be ideas as well as ours; because an idea can resemble nothing but an idea; and an idea ever implies in the very nature of it, relation to a mind perceiving it, or in which it exists. But then those

[7] Samuel Johnson : *Writings,* II, 374.

archtypes or originals, and the manner of their existence in that eternal mind, must be entirely different from that of their existence in our mind . . . in Him, as originals; in us, only as faint copies; such as he thinks fit to communicate to us, according to such laws and limitations as he hath established, and such as are sufficient to all the purposes relating to our well-being, in which only we are concerned.[8]

All of which sounds a good deal like Plato and the Platonic absolutes; but Johnson was a monist: all real existence was idea; there was no other sort. Thus he could not distrust daily experience; it was both valid and trustworthy, since the ideas of particular things in our minds are directly from the mind of God.

It is easy to see how such a philosophy could bring to him the comfortable conviction of the constant immanence of God in every individual, a conviction that seemed to be the answer to the Deists' idea of a remote, impersonal watchmaker-God of a universe of perfect law and order. The rational justification of this conviction was for Johnson the highest function that philosophy could perform.

Johnson, then, like Edwards, was a product of the Enlightenment in America acting upon an older Calvinism. He did not reject the findings of science; he only sought to make them fit into the general concept of a personal God. Himself a product of the second-generation frontier at Guilford, Connecticut, he found medieval Scholasticism uncongenial. He reacted violently against the low condition of learning on the frontier, and his discovery of Boyle, Newton, Barrow, and other English scientists was to him "like a flood of day to his low state of mind." His conversion to Anglicanism was in a sense a triumph for the Enlightenment, for which his mind was doubtless prepared by the utilitarian influences of frontier life. But the triumph was not complete; he could not go all the way. For he could not surrender his conviction of the personal, intimate immanence of God instilled in him in childhood by his Congregational deacon father. He thus could not accept the philosophy of Deism although he did accept a quasi-Deistic system of ethics. His philosophy had to justify his religious convictions. His philosophical idealism was the answer to his dilemma.

THE PHILOSOPHICAL ASPECTS OF DEISM

The philosophies of Edwards and Johnson were essentially reactionary; for they were elaborated to preserve the older Calvinistic faith in the immanence of God in a God-dominated universe in the face of the corrosive influence of the implications of science and rationalism. They are to be considered a sort of philosophical complement to the at-

---

[8] Ibid., II, 376–7.

tempt of religious and social conservatives like President Clap of Yale to preserve the way of the Puritan fathers. But where Clap was a true reactionary, attempting to revive Puritan philosophy as it actually was, the idealism of Edwards and Johnson was so profound a modification of Puritanism as to constitute a new philosophy, subservient to religion, which in effect forced the findings of empirical science into a ready-made notion of the universe as idea that could be accepted without surrendering or substantially modifying the Christian epic. Philosophy, with them, was called in to the defense of the old-time religion.

It was not so, however, with those thinkers who accepted the philosophical implications of science and rationalism and allowed themselves to be led by those implications — up to a certain point — wherever it might lead them. These philosophers, the Deists, were unwilling to admit with Hobbes that the findings of science and reason eliminated God from the universe entirely; but they were willing to admit almost everything else.

The Enlightenment won its greatest victories in America in those philosophers who accepted the philosophical ideas of Deism. For Deism was not only the scientists' religion already described; it was also a philosophical response to the implications of Newtonian science, and it found a ready acceptance in many of the hard-headed practical men produced by the conditions of the "natural world" on the American frontier.

The first response of the European philosophers — Descartes, Spinoza, Leibniz — and the Puritans to the implications of the science of Bacon, Galileo, and Newton had been an attempt, or a series of attempts, to harmonize the newly discovered mechanical aspects of nature with the older basic conceptions of Aristotelian Christianity. But their philosophy was generally deductive; that is, it started with the assumption of a first cause, or God, and fitted the findings of experimental science into the concept of this God who is as infinite as the universe, or who, as with Spinoza, is the principle of order inherent in the universe itself. All of these systems, except Spinoza's pantheism, were built upon a medieval dualism of matter and spirit, body and soul, evil and good.

The attempts of these philosophers to harmonize the new findings of science with the old assumptions of medieval Christianity prepared the way for Deism, which reversed the process and sought to harmonize religion with the scientific facts of nature; furthermore, whereas the seventeenth-century philosophers were in one way or another theistic, accepting the idea of divine intervention in the affairs of men, Deism went one step farther in the acceptance of the mechanistic explanation of the universe, to the point where it relegated God to the position of a supermechanic who had invented the mechanism and set it going, and then sat back and let it work out its own destiny according to the laws he had laid down for it.

There were, of course, many forms and shades of Deism, both in Europe and in America. It was, indeed, rather a "natural religion" than a philosophy, and it has already been described as such. As a philosophy, however, it began by replacing the old cosmology with the more up-to-date one revealed by science, and it built its philosophical structures upon that. And if the universe was a universe of law, the natural laws governing it applied to man as well as to the lower animals, the earth, and the cosmos. Thus the philosophy of Deism sought to find the answer to the problem of "what is" in the record of the natural world alone. Reality was the material reality of the universe, and man's reason became the mechanism by which, through the simple processes of science, men might bring themselves to a satisfactory knowledge of reality. Thus the Deistic philosophers were rationalists, in the newer sense that they had faith in the ability of the human reason to discover reality and to use it for the perfection of men. Challenged to defend their naturalistic ontology and its implications against the doctrines of innate ideas held by Descartes and Leibniz, they accepted John Locke's sensationalism as a sufficient epistemology; a sufficient answer, that is, to the question of how men know. For Locke succeeded, to the satisfaction of most of the Deists, in demonstrating that sense perception is the true avenue for the acquisition of knowledge and, therefore, the truth about the universe, and that the scientific knowledge upon which their ontology was built was trustworthy and could be depended upon.

The philosophy of Deism, the rationalization of Newtonian science, found many exponents in British America; and if idealists such as Edwards and Johnson made philosophy the handmaiden of theology, the Deists forced their religion to fit their Newtonian conceptions of the nature of existence. For them the "natural" structure of the universe, and its laws, came first. But since the universe obviously exists, it must have had a creator: therefore there had to be a first cause, or "prime mover," or creator; and the beginning of the Deistic position was there. As President Edward Holyoke of Harvard put it:

> There were three opinions as to the existence of the world. One was that it was from Eternity, & Plato, it seems, was the Father of it, and though it flowed from God as Raies do from the Sun . . . another opinion as to the Existence of the world, was that it came into this beautiful Form, by Chance, or a fortuitous concourse & jumble of Atoms, This is by all known to be the Philosophy of Epicurus. . . . But the most prevailing Opinion . . . was, *that the world had a beginning, &*

was form'd by some great and excellent Being whom they called God. And this indeed is a tho't that is perfectly agreeable to Reason.[9]

Given this first creative act by God, the universe itself was purely material, regulated and controlled by natural law. The most thorough-going Deists looked upon human reason as one of the mechanisms of natural law, and ethics became a code of human conduct based upon the idea of the application of reason to the natural laws of right or proper human behavior. Benjamin Franklin carried this principle to its logical conclusion in his *Articles of Belief and Acts of Religion*, in which he proves logically that evil cannot exist, that men are inherently good, and that all are, therefore, equal in the sight of God. But there were few who had the courage or the conviction to go that far. Even Franklin himself was too much of a hard-headed realist to accept the unanswerable conclusion of his own logic. The conditions of human life might, in general, be determined by the laws of nature, as laid down by God; but Franklin could not escape the evidence he saw all about him that men did choose actions that by their results ought to be called evil or good. Evidently men did have the power of choice; therefore they must have the power in large measure to determine their own fate. He was too practical a man to believe otherwise; the American experience that proved the point was too strong in him. Franklin, indeed, was somewhat disillusioned by his early contact with formal philosophy, and he gradually lost his love for Plato. He did not lose his faith in the Newtonian order; but he did abandon his youthful logical determinism in favor of a faith that the human will is naturally endowed with a large measure of freedom. He became the practical philosopher within the general framework of Deism, and his philosophy underlay all his behavior — a philosophy that might perhaps be called "Deistic pragmatism." Of which more later.

If Franklin and his ideas were a typical product of the rise of the seaboard city, the city of Philadelphia, in the new world of America, Ethan Allen was just as typically a product of the American frontier, the frontier of Vermont. His life was spent in warfare, intercolonial conflict, and frontier settlement; but he found time to think about nature and nature's God and finally published the results of his thinking in 1784 in his *Reason the Only Oracle of Man*.

Allen, like Franklin, was largely self-taught, and was primarily a rationalist. As he says in the preface to his book:

In the circle of my acquaintance . . . I have generally been denominated a Deist, the reality of which I never disputed, being conscious I

[9] Quoted in Woodbridge Riley: *American Thought from Puritanism to Pragmatism* (New York, 1915), pp. 59–60.

am no Christian. . . . And as to being a Deist, I know not strictly speaking, whether I am one or not, for I have never read their writings; mine will therefore determine the matter.[10]

Here was a son of the frontier who, though he had heard of the Deists and the empiricists and had doubtless discussed their ideas with Thomas Young, had read few books and built his philosophy almost purely upon his experience in the Connecticut valley. He was convinced that reason was the only adequate and trustworthy guide to human life. Almost without knowing it, he placed himself squarely in the school of the eighteenth-century rationalists. Of greater significance, perhaps, was the apparent fact that his was a philosophy of nature which, given its first slight impetus in his intellectual youth, flowered and matured in the natural world of the American frontier.

Although Allen's work was essentially religious in the sense that it was his contribution to the laudable effort "to reclaim mankind from their ignorance and delusion . . . concerning God and his providence" and although his Deism was essentially a religion — a religion that might perhaps be called "naturalistic rationalism" — yet like other Deistic systems it rested upon the typical Deistic philosophical assumptions. For Allen accepted without question the Newtonian concept of the world machine, governed by natural law. The world of nature was for him the orderly manifestation of God, and human reason was the mechanism, provided by God, by which men are able to acquire some comprehension of God as revealed in nature. The universe, for him, was infinite, since God, its creator and governor, was infinite, omniscient, and omnipotent. But God does not violate his own natural laws; and since God is perfect, his creation and his laws must be perfect, and the world, therefore, is the best of all possible worlds. But the most original part of Allen's philosophical system appears in his belief in "an absolute plenum of intelligent entity" that is coextensive with the universe, and in the idea that man's soul is both rational and immortal by reason of its participation in this universal plenum. Evil exists in the world, but evil is not infinite; it is, indeed, the result of men's failure to be guided by reason, and men may achieve happiness and overcome evil precisely by the use of reason. "I am persuaded," he said,

that if Mankind would dare to exercise their reason as freely on those divine topics, as they do in the common concerns of life, they would, in a great measure rid themselves of their blindness and superstition, gain more exalted ideas of God and their obligations to him and one another, and be proportionally delighted and blessed with the views of his moral government, make better members of society, and acquire many power-

[10] Allen : *Reason the Only Oracle*, preface.

ful incentives to the practice of morality, which is the last and greatest perfection that human nature is capable of.[11]

Ethan Allen, then, by his acceptance of the mechanistic universe, his belief in a remote creator-God, his empiricism, and his faith in human reason and the perfectibility of man, was a typical eighteenth-century Deist. Having read as few books as he seems to have done, and having based his philosophy largely upon his own experience and his own observation of the world of nature about him, it is somewhat surprising that his thought agreed as closely as it did with the Deistic thinking of his contemporaries. It was an age of Deism, however, and Allen probably learned much from conversation. In any case, it is probably not too much to say that Allen, the first clearly articulate native American Deist, expressed much of the radical wing of the philosophical thinking that was going on in his time along the American frontier.

Generally speaking, Deism was the most radical philosophical mood to attain any wide currency in America. Its strongest hold was upon the minds of the faculties and students of the colonial colleges, especially in the south. This was particularly true of William and Mary, the attitude of which toward philosophy, under its charter of 1758, and despite its political difficulties, probably made it the most liberal college in British America. William Small, who occupied the professorship of mathematics and natural philosophy at that college was a philosophical radical of the deistic school and had a profound effect upon the thinking of such students as John Page and the young Thomas Jefferson.

MATERIALISM

The implications of eighteenth-century Deism, pushed to their logical conclusion, led directly to materialism. For if the universe were a machine, and man a part of it, man was a machine too. And if what our senses tell us is true, and only that, then a belief in God is untenable, since there is no sensory evidence of God to be found anywhere. The only reality is that revealed by the senses, which is matter. Thus matter is the only reality; man is only one form of matter, and man's mind is only a sort of electro-chemical machine for registering sensory impressions and deriving from them the principles of human behavior. This philosophy, which accepted Newton's cosmology and Locke's epistemology as its logical premises, was known as materialism, of which Thomas Hobbes (who actually antedated both Newton and Locke) was the earliest and most radical exponent in England. It was particularly strong in France, where it found expression in the eight-

---

[11] Ibid., pp. 24–5.

eenth century in the writings of Claude Adrien Helvétius, Paul Heinrich Dietrich d'Holbach, Julien Offrey de La Mettrie, and others.

The only important American materialist of the eighteenth century prior to the Revolution was Cadwallader Colden, of New York, whose scientific attainments have already been related. Colden was a materialist and, like other materialists, took Newton as his starting-point, although he believed he had found an explanation for gravitation where Newton had failed. He was also a follower of Thomas Hobbes; but unlike Hobbes and the French extremists he admitted the possibility of spiritual being while he denied human capacity for knowing anything about it. Unlike other materialists, too, while they thought of matter as being passive and inert, he thought of certain forms of matter as being active. Matter, he believed, extends throughout the universe in one of three types: "resisting" matter, "moving" matter, and "reacting" matter, or æther, which penetrates the two others; and each type presents its own type of action or force. The entire universe was thus to be understood in terms of these three types of matter, and "That the Phenomena of every System . . . may be deduced from the combined Actions of these three simple powers, under the direction of an Intelligent Being." [12]

Up to this point Colden was moving in the realm of theoretical physics, but the conclusion that the universe is directed by some sort of intelligent being introduces a philosophical consideration. Not necessarily theological or metaphysical, however; for although Colden believed the complex operations of matter in the universe called for some sort of direction, and that comprehension of that power might be beyond the ken of human beings, yet he was not ready to admit that that direction was necessarily supernatural. In fact, one of his last philosophical papers boldly suggested that the force of intelligence might reside in one of the three forms of matter, or "force," that he had described. [13]

Perhaps drawing the original idea from the French materialists, Colden had interested himself, both as doctor and as philosopher, in "fermentation" as the essential activity in organic life. He had observed the fertilization of the ovum by the spermatozoon, the "fermentation" of yeast, and other phenomena that seemed by their "intestine motion" to produce others that were ultimately different from themselves; and he had also observed that this "intestine motion" seems always to be accompanied by heat. Therefore, he asked, "may it not be concluded,

[12] Cadwallader Colden: *The Principles of Action in Matter, the Gravitation of Bodies, and the Motion of The Planets, explained from these Principles* (London, 1751), pp. 157–67.
[13] Cadwallader Colden: "An Inquiry into the Principles of Vital Motion," manuscript, New York Historical Society, p. 35.

that an intestine motion or fermentation of the fluids, in the earth for Vegetables, or in the Uterus or contents of the egg for animals is absolutely necessary for their life or vital motion ?" [14] Similarly, the digestion of food and the circulation of the blood proceed by the process of fermentation; but the veins, created to accommodate the blood, are built with little valves and other mechanisms to promote the process :

> Hence it follows that the Operation of *Intelligence* or of some Intelligent being is necessary in the [formation] of animals and vegetables. The intelligent being does not give motion nor resist motion, otherwise there can be no use of any matter or Material Powers. . . . The Characteristic of the Intelligent being is to act with some view or purpose, and therefore to direct is the proper operation of Intelligence. . . . The intelligent being may, in some sense, be considered as the artificer, and the material powers as the tools necessary for performing the work.[15]

But how does this intelligence operate in the universe of matter ? Something like this : fermentation, which is the essential factor in "vital motion," is not a material phenomenon, but is the product of the interaction of intelligence and matter. Nor is it peculiar to living things, or even to the earth. Now the minute particles of bodies are similar to the great bodies, like the particles of light thrown off by the sun. Some of these particles of bodies may themselves be tiny suns; and these tiny suns may be the "leaven" that promotes the vital motion, or fermentation in vegetables and animals. In other words, Colden seems to have been feeling his way toward the idea that the source, or at least the mechanism, of intelligence may be these tiny particles or "suns" that were universally dispersed through the universe. He did not quite complete his philosophical system; but he seemed to be moving in the direction of somehow identifying light with intelligence, and of concluding that intelligence, or "intelligent being," was universally existent throughout the universe. Intelligence, thus conceived, would be a fourth sort of "being," or existence, directing the other three, but without any supernatural attributes. If this interpretation of Colden's thought is correct, then he was a thoroughgoing "naturalist," if not "materialist"; and he was the only one of any distinction in the colonies.

Philosophies of the Middle Class: "Common Sense"

The philosophies of Jonathan Edwards and Samuel Johnson, who were philosophers of reaction, the defenders and preservers of Calvinistic Puritanism and Anglicanism, failed of their purpose; they had no

[14] Ibid., p. 4.   [15] Ibid., p. 10.

considerable following, largely because their respective idealisms were too abstruse, too remote from the outlook of the ordinary man, too nearly impossible for the laity to understand. For most ordinary Americans reacted to the logic-chopping of the philosophers either, as Franklin did, by abandoning it altogether or by saying in effect: "a plague

American philosophers: John Witherspoon. A portrait by Charles Willson Peale.
[By courtesy of Princeton University]

on all your houses" and by following for themselves the principles that seemed to be most in accord with "common sense," the principles of the so-called Scottish realism, as adapted to the American intellectual environment by John Witherspoon.

This common-sense reaction against the analytical philosophies of idealism, Deism, and materialism first came to this country, in nebulous form, in the intellectual baggage of some of the Presbyterian Scotsmen who swarmed to America in the mid-eighteenth century, and in books by the thinkers of the Scottish school that had reached American colleges and philosophers by the 1750's. It became an important factor in American intellectual life, however, only after John Witherspoon became president of the College of New Jersey (Princeton) in 1768. And Princeton has been the great source and center of it ever since.

Witherspoon, indeed, was the most notable of the American realists of the Scottish persuasion, although he cannot be said to have been a great philosopher. For, sprung from a long line of Scottish covenanters, he was too close to his Presbyterian intellectual background to swing to any very radical philosophical extreme. There were a good many fine points, too, that had been pointed out by his master, Reid, that he never grasped with adequate precision. But the important fact is that Witherspoon, the administrator and man of action, based his life and his great influence upon a philosophy built upon plain common sense. One of the attractive features of this philosophy, indeed, was the ease with which the ordinary practical-minded layman could understand it and accept it. And this was probably the reason why it has been called, perhaps incorrectly, "pre-eminently the American philosophy." [16]

Accepting the natural and material world of the senses as real, then, Witherspoon also felt sure of a spiritual reality in the universe that was to him equally self-evident, and he explained man's relationship to it in terms of a dualism that seemed to him to be completely obvious:

> Considering man as an individual, we discover the most obvious and re-markable circumstances of his nature, that he is a compound of body and spirit. . . . The body and spirit have a great reciprocal influence one upon another. The body on the temper and disposition of the soul, and the soul on the state and habit of the body. The body is properly the minister of the soul, the means of conveying perceptions to it, but nothing without it. . . . The faculties of the mind are commonly di-vided into these three kinds, the understanding, the will, and the affec-tions; though perhaps it is proper to observe, that these are not three qualities wholly distinct, as if they were three different beings, but dif-ferent ways of exerting the same principle. It is the soul or mind that understands, wills, or is affected with pleasure and pain.[17]

The human understanding, he says, has truth for its objective: "The discovering things as they really are in themselves, and in their rela-tions one to another." Of the will, the great function is choice: "All the acts of the will may be reduced to the two great heads of desire and aversion, or in other words, chusing and refusing." The affections, sometimes called passions, "may be called strong propensities, im-planted in our nature, which of themselves contribute not a little to bias the judgment, or incline the will." [18]

So much for the problems of epistemology. As for ethics and the problems of human conduct:

[16] J. Woodbridge Riley: *American Philosophy; The Early Schools* (New York, 1907), p. 476.

[17] John Witherspoon: *Lectures on Moral Philosophy*, edited by V. L. Collins (Princeton, 1912), pp. 8–10.

[18] Ibid., pp. 10, 11, 12.

The nature and will of God is so perfect as to be the true standard of all excellence, natural and moral : and if we are sure of what he is or commands, it would be presumption and folly to reason against it, or put our views of fitness in the room of his pleasure ; but to say that God, by his will, might have made the same temper and conduct virtuous and excellent, which we now call vicious [as some of the Deists do], seems to unhinge all our notions of the supreme excellence even of God himself.[19]

Upon this base Witherspoon built his philosophy of morals, ethics, and conduct. Here was a simple rationalization of the universe, of God, and of human nature that any "sensible" person could understand and accept without surrendering the long-established basic predispositions of the old-time religion. It was an intellectual reaction both against the "immaterialists," like Berkeley, Edwards, and Johnson, on the one side, and the "materialists," like Franklin, Allen, or Colden, on the other. It was a way of thinking that was easily acceptable to most Americans, and it succeeded, therefore, probably more than any other one thing, in checking or retarding the spread of idealism in New England, Deism in the middle colonies, and materialism in the south. For to Princeton as an educational center soon came students from all the sections, especially the south and west, and Princeton, through them, cast the bread of "realism" upon the American waters. Be that as it may, the "common sense" philosophy of "realism" was the great stabilizer of American thought until the transcendentalism and pragmatism of the nineteenth and twentieth centuries arose to disturb it again.

The Philosophy of Poor Richard: Embryonic Pragmatism

The philosophical systems hitherto described were borrowed, as it were, from Europe, and then remolded nearer to the American desire under the stress of the American social and physical environment. But there was one mental outlook — which, indeed, as yet could hardly be called a philosophy — that was peculiar to America ; that, in fact, had arisen largely and directly as a result of the experience of this new people in their new land. For lack of a better name it may be called pragmatism, although it should be carefully recognized that no formal or intellectually respectable philosophy of pragmatism as yet existed; Americans were as yet far from being ready to depart that far from their long-established intellectual habits and inhibitions.

Yet the American experience had been a practical one ; men had been able to conquer the wilderness because they had adapted themselves to it. In the course of their adaptation they had been forced to

[19] Ibid., p. 28.

discard many of their old ways of life and adopt or invent new ones. And most of the mechanisms for survival in the frontier struggle were tested and accepted or rejected in the light of their effectiveness in that stern struggle to survive. Men fell into the habit of inventiveness — for the control of the environment for their own benefit; and the Americans fell naturally into the habit of evaluating every new idea or invention in terms of its functional validity or usefulness. Did it successfully perform the function for which it was invented or proposed? Then accept it. Did it not? Then reject it.

It would of course be an error to suppose that this attitude was entirely original with the Americans. A century earlier Francis Bacon had seen the vision of a body of truth acquired by the scientific method that would be considered worthy of acceptance only in so far as it promoted human welfare. Yet it appears safe to say at least that the American experience had created in the Americans a "practical" habit of mind that was not duplicated elsewhere. The almanacs were full of it, especially *Poor Richard*: "God helps them that help themselves"; "Fools make feasts, and wise men eat them"; "A ploughman on his legs is higher than a gentleman on his knees"; "It is hard for an empty bag to stand upright"; and so on.[20] Or, in the style of Nathaniel Ames: "Happy would be the Times if all would strive to mend their Lives"; "The Fire of Contention destroys the publick Good"; "good Projections without Resolution and action, will produce no good Effects"; "A selfish spirit ruins the Interest of the Publick"; and the like.[21]

From this attitude of practical functionalism toward everyday things it was but a short step to the examination even of customary morality and the "eternal verities" in the light of their functional validity in the lives of men. It was probably no accident, therefore, that Franklin proposed to write a great work on the "Art of Virtue," which, unfortunately, he never completed, in which the chief doctrine was to be that it was "every one's interest to be virtuous, who wished to be happy even in this world";[22] or, as he stated his idea more clearly in another place:

I grew convinc'd that *truth, sincerity* and *integrity* in dealings between man and man, were of the utmost importance to the felicity of life; and I formed written resolutions . . . to practice them ever while I lived. Revelation had indeed no weight with me, as such; but I entertained an opinion, that, though certain actions might not be bad, *because* they were forbidden by it, or good *because* it commanded them, yet probably those actions might be forbidden *because* they were bad for us, or

[20] Franklin : *Works* (Sparks ed.), II, 94–103.
[21] Nathaniel Ames : *An Astronomical Diary* (1755).
[22] Franklin : *Works* (Sparks ed.), I, 115.

commanded *because* they were beneficial to us, in their own natures, all the circumstances of things considered.[23]

To this idea he returned again and again, throughout his life.

Nor is this a mere morality, or system of shrewd peasant cleverness. Franklin early abandoned formal philosophy and unfortunately never made any detailed or systematic statement of his whole philosophy. Yet these statements represented in him a set of profound convictions and a genuine sense of values : health and wealth were not desirable merely because they were useful ; Franklin was also interested in knowing *why* they were desirable and useful. He finds the answer to this question in the fact that health, wealth, and wisdom make men "free and easy" — free from vice, from economic servitude, from superstition and intolerance, free to use their time and their talents for the common benefit of mankind.

A list of Franklin's virtues is in one sense but a new and secularized version of the Puritan discipline of an earlier age, a discipline by which the condition of mankind might be consciously and deliberately improved. Thus Franklin's pragmatism, such as it was, had this in common with the Puritanism that preceded it and with the pragmatism that was to follow : that it was a philosophy of deliberate self-improvement, by control of self coupled with control of nature. His experience and the experience of his American contemporaries was one to dictate this sort of philosophy above all others ; and the American devotion to the ideals of freedom of enterprise, individualism, thrift, the self-made man, are only other and more popular expressions of the same outlook. Franklin, more than any other early American philosopher, was the exponent and the philosophical first fruit of the American experience on the American soil.

CONCLUSION: THE GESTATION OF PHILOSOPHY IN FREEDOM

American philosophy, then, was a product of three factors : the religious inheritance from Calvinism ; the modification of the Aristotelian concept of the material universe forced upon the western mind by the findings of modern science ; and the day-by-day experiences of the Americans in the market, on the farm, and on the frontier. Some able American minds, like Edwards and Johnson, devised philosophical systems to preserve their religions against the destructive impact of science ; others, like the Deists and Colden, accepted the philosophical implications of science and reshaped their theology to fit their Newtonian ontology ; others still, like Witherspoon, refused to be greatly

[23] Ibid., I, 76.

moved away from their theological preconceptions, one way or the other; finally, in the practical outlook of the Americans was to be seen the first small beginning of a brand new attitude toward the world, toward knowledge, and even toward the nature of truth itself.

The importance of this attitude should not be exaggerated. It is of much more importance to emphasize the fact that philosophy, almost without exception, stood in a position of subservience to religion. Science had forced upon theology a new concept of the physical universe, to be sure; it had, indeed, induced several new concepts of God's position relative to the universe. But God's ultimate authority over both the universe and the affairs of men was questioned, if at all, only by a very few. Religion was still the most powerful and dominant single force in the realm of ideas and feelings.

At the same time, the developments in religion, science, and philosophy alike seem, in a broad, general way, to have followed the lines of intellectual and social division. Thus science and rationalism in religion appear to have reached their highest development among the intellectual elite and the social aristocracy; the reactionaries in religion and philosophy stemmed from the conservative middle class among townsmen and farmers; the radicals in philosophy and religion were apparently the poor, the frontiersmen, and self-made men like Allen and Franklin. It may not be too much to say, therefore, that the philosophy or, rather, the outlook on life that seems most completely to have derived from the actual experience of the Americans, on the soil of America, was the mood of an incipient pragmatism.

Be that as it may, it seems clear that each of these American philosophies, whether grouped by geographic section or by social class, was the distillation of ideas from experience — that is, derived from the old inheritance, the pounding of the environment, and the conservative force of already established American patterns. In the realms of systematic thought, as in economics, politics, or art, the ideological product was the product of experience. And if the ideological systems in the realm of philosophy differed from each other as they differed in those other realms of thought, it was because the individual and group experiences that generate the ideas differed in the first place. And if there were many philosophies, as there were many religions, it was probably because great diversity made for freedom and mutual toleration, and because freedom, in turn, made for diversity.

NOTE TO THE READER

Because of the fact that nearly all American thinking was still strongly dominated by religion, there were few purely philosophical works written in the Anglo-American colonies in the eighteenth century. Philosophy, with only one or two exceptions, was completely in the service of religion. Jonathan Edwards is the outstanding example; his *Notes on the Mind* are most easily available in *The Works of Jonathan Edwards* (edited by Edward Hickman, 2 vols., London, 1840) and other editions of his collected works. His famous book on the freedom of the will, entitled *A Careful and Strict Enquiry into the modern prevailing Notions of That Freedom of Will which is supposed to be essential to Moral Agency* (Boston, 1754), was the nearest he ever came to a systematic philosophical treatise. As reading-matter, it is anything but light.

Samuel Johnson's *Elementa philosophica* was almost the only formal explanation of a philosophical position written in America. It was written for his students and is fairly easy to read and understand. It is most easily available in *Samuel Johnson, His Career and Writings* (edited by Herbert and Carol Schneider, 4 vols., New York, 1929; II, 359–515). A much more attractive little piece, showing the connection between philosophy and the good life, is *Raphael, or the Genius of the English America* (ibid., II, 521–600). Johnson also wrote an *Encyclopedia of Philosophy* and a *Synopsis of Natural Philosophy*, both of which are printed in the Schneider edition of his works; they are not recommended, however, as books to be read for the sheer pleasure of it.

Some of the essays of John Witherspoon have been collected and published as *Lectures on Moral Philosophy* (edited by Varnum L. Collins; Princeton, 1912). This is a pleasant and interesting little book and gives a good statement of the so-called "philosophy of common sense."

Benjamin Franklin's philosophical writings are fragmentary and scattered. He did not write much of that sort of thing; he did not think it very useful; and early in life he decided to devote his attention to the practical and the useful. He was a fairly profound thinker, nevertheless; it is a pity he never put his philosophy of existence into complete and systematic form.

Ethan Allen's book, *Reason the Only Oracle of Man*, which states the Deists' position, has been mentioned in the chapter on religion.

The one thinker of America who may be said to have freed his philosophy from the cramping influence of religion was Cadwallader Colden. The basic concept of the universe upon which he built his thought was expressed in his *Principles of Action in Matter* (London, 1751); but unfortunately he never really thought through his system to its logical conclusion. He apparently was moving in that direction in the last years of his life; for there are several manuscripts, more or less fragmentary, which approach a final statement of complete materialism, in the collections of the New York Historical

Society. It is a pity he never completed his system ; it is also a pity that these late manuscripts have never been published.

Of the modern books, of which there are not many, I. Woodbridge Riley's *American Philosophy, The Early Schools* (New York, 1907), is by far the most satisfying. It is a bulky tome, and it is often difficult reading ; but it is accurate and penetrating and well repays the effort required in reading it.

CHAPTER IV
Of Land, of Labor, and of Economic Freedom

"Freedom and protection are most indisputable principles whereon the

"success of trade must depend, as clearly as an open, good road tends

"toward a safe and speedy intercourse; nor is there a greater enemy to

"trade than constraint."

—BENJAMIN FRANKLIN.

HE basic and most vital activities of the human animal are probably those which are concerned with the business of getting a living—that is, with acquiring food, shelter, and clothing. This, the economic side of human life, is not, perhaps, the highest or most refined expression of the human spirit, but it is basic to all the others, and closely connected with them. The artist and the philosopher and the scientist have to have food, shelter, and clothing before they can devote their lives to their highly intellectual callings; and their attitude toward their work will often, if not always, be affected by the manner in which they acquire these more mundane goods and by their feeling of security or insecurity with regard to them. Similarly, the outlook of a whole people with regard to economic matters will often be strongly influenced, if not actually determined, by the manner in which they provide for their economic needs, and their economic ideas are likely to color, even strongly to influence, their thinking about other matters. There are relatively few philosophers or artists in any given society, with the result that there are relatively few persons who have ideas with regard to the somewhat esoteric problems of philosophy and art. But every individual in a society is concerned with the problems of making a living, and he must, perforce, do a certain amount of thinking about it. Thus the economic problem is practically universal; and ideas with regard

to it, however primitive and simple, are likely to be more common among the people than with regard to any other problem of human life — with the possible exception of sex. It is certainly a historical fact that the vast majority of the Englishmen who came to America in the first half of the seventeenth century were moved most forcibly by economic motives. It is probably safe to say also that economic ideas occupied more of their thinking than any other kind, and that the first foundations of America, especially the economic foundations, were given their color and their fiber by those economic ideas, brought over by the first English colonists.

The Old Way, in Europe and America

Most of the people who came to America in the seventeenth century came primarily to get land. There were, of course, a multitude of motives in their minds, and the motives in the mind of any single individual were almost always mixed. A few came purely to escape religious persecution; some came to escape political disorder or the threat of war; and some came purely for adventure's sake or for the pursuit of quick wealth to be derived from piracy. But it is probably true that the great mass of inarticulate, uncelebrated, and unsung men and women who emigrated from England, and later from the Continent, to build new homes in America did so because they had heard that there was land here. Land, and yet more land, a limitless supply of "God's waste"; all to be had for the taking. This was the lodestone that drew them, above all other things, to America.

For to them land was the basis and the mark of wealth and well-being. It had been so for ages, certainly for centuries; and the love of the land and respect for it was rooted in the land itself, far back in the nebulous beginnings of medieval feudalism. In England, however, as elsewhere in Europe, the land, while still the distinguishing mark of fortune, was no longer an adequate source of wealth for the support of the feudal aristocracy. For commerce was becoming the dominant activity for the production of wealth, and the rise of commerce and the discovery and exploitation of new lands overseas that resulted from it in turn provided a sharp impetus, in the form of markets, materials, and precious metals, to further expansions and the accumulation of yet greater stores of surplus wealth ready for investment. The declining feudal aristocracy turned to commerce for financial support, and linked its fate to that of the rising commercial bourgeoisie. It thus came about that some of the economic ideals of the feudal aristocracy, such as love of the land, and respect for the land as the badge of wealth and social status, became associated with the newer bourgeois ideals derived from commerce. The two sets of ideas often conflicted with each other;

but as commerce continued to expand, and the ideals of the city-dwellers began to break the bands of guild-restriction and the law-merchant, the merchant bought land, and the loosening ideas of bourgeois economic individualism began to absorb and incorporate the love of the land and the ideals that sprang from it into the bourgeois ideology.

Presently religious considerations were injected into the development of economic theory by the revolt of large groups of the bourgeois businessmen against the restrictive influences of the economic theory of the medieval Catholic Church; for the church had forbidden the taking of interest. Why was it a sin for the wealthy merchant to lend some money to a needy colleague, taking in return for the convenience extended a small interest charge, so that the transaction would be beneficial to both? It came to pass that many of the Protestants, resenting either the economic theory of the church or its taxgathering proclivities, were confirmed in their Protestantism because it seemed to encourage their economic individualism. Religious individualism was merged with economic individualism, to become the religious side of the mercantilist outlook on life.

The Puritan doctrines of individualism, indeed, had found their most willing believers and advocates among the new bourgeoisie of the cities. Thus Calvinism spread most rapidly among the merchant towns of France, Holland, and Scotland; and Calvinistic Puritanism in England and America was strongest among the merchants and the lesser bourgeoisie generally. It is no accident, therefore, that the Puritans found it easy to reject the authoritarian restrictions placed upon commerce and finance by the medieval church and to substitute for them regulations presented by the state, especially when it was controlled by the Puritans themselves. The taking of interest, for example, was now condoned, and not only was a man in business considered as having been "called" to that sort of a "ministry," just as the shoemaker or the church pastor was "called" by divine wish into those pursuits, but prosperity was actually thought to be a mark of God's favor upon a man in his calling.

The Puritans did not, of course, discard all the medieval economic concepts in favor of the rugged individualism of a later day. For they never lost sight of the social aspects of economic life and made strenuous efforts, in both old England and New England, to preserve the principle of the just price and the reasonable wage by laws that sought to regulate prices and prohibit monopoly, speculation, and the ruthless exploitation of labor. Obviously, while Puritanism made its appeal by its positive encouragement of individual enterprise, this individualism was one that existed within the bounds of state-regulated social welfare. Men became wealthy, to be sure, and as often as not by sharp practice; but in theory, at least, to the men of the Reformation in England and America the possession of wealth was a sort of stewardship for which the possessor would be held strictly accountable to God. For the Puritan, at least, the state was not so much a positive mechanism for the promotion of the welfare of the individual within it as an institution inspired by God for the curbing of the excessive "self-love," greed, and sinful excess of men left to their own devices. Men were economically willful as well as otherwise; the state was God's institution for the curbing of economic sin.

Historically, the modern state had arisen as a product of the joint struggles of nationalistic kings for power and of town merchants for freedom from the control or restrictions of feudal lord and Catholic bishop; and the monarchies of western Europe about the year 1600 were to a large degree the creatures of the mercantile interests. The state policies of mercantilism, therefore, were above all calculated to promote the financial interests of both king and merchant, who were, in fact, often business partners in the same commercial enterprise. But mercantilism was broader than that; for the mercantilists believed sincerely that if the wealth of the state were built up by the successful maintenance of a favorable balance of trade, everybody in the country would benefit. And since the state's mercantile wealth could best be promoted by an over-all state policy, the individual, while he was encouraged in his individual enterprises, was expected to conform strictly to the mercantile policy laid down by the government.

Now, this mercantilism which had taken hold of the economic mind of western Europe by 1600 was a sort of nationalistic capitalism; but the mercantilism of the Virginia Company and the Massachusetts Bay Company was not yet the mercantilism of the Great Navigation Act and the Board of Trade, both created in 1696. For mercantilism at this early stage was still naïvely "bullionism"; and its general tenets may be described somewhat as follows:

The individual is motivated by self-interest; this self-interest — this economic individualism — must be encouraged, but it must not be allowed to get out of bounds. The medieval church had recognized much the same basic principle; but whereas the church had laid down an elaborate set of rules to control self-interest on the basis of the abstract principles of justice, right, and the like, mercantilistic thought took the more utilitarian view that self-interest should be limited only by the common, or social, good. But the state had now supplanted the church as the chief agent for the common good in the lives of men; therefore it was the state that must regulate economic life, both internal and external, in the interest of all the citizens. Further, the state, as a body of all the citizens, was thought of much as an individual who makes a profit by selling more than he buys, by which he acquires gold and silver, or money wealth, given him in payment of the balance due him. The state was motivated by the same self-interest as the individual, and acted in similar fashion, except that the state felt no responsibility whatever to the society of states or to any other authority outside itself. Thus it was believed that the state must promote national exports and discourage national imports; and if this involved the creation of great monopolies of trade or of regional areas, such as a Muscovy Company, an East India Company, a Virginia Company, or a Massachusetts Bay Company, it was because the state created them theoretically for the common good, which was supposed to be best served by prohibiting competition and further restricting the freedom, within those areas, of individual enterprise.

Colonies, however, were regarded as having special values for the state's economic life, since they would both provide markets, to absorb much of the national export, and supply raw materials, to be used either in the manufacture of more exportable products or for direct re-export. Furthermore, the supply of raw materials from the colonies would, in many instances, relieve the dependence of the mother country upon foreign countries for supplies of those materials which might be cut off in time of war. The development of the colonies might be expected to absorb surplus population and to provide bases for raiding-operations against the commerce and the colonies of rival states.

Thus reasoned Richard Hakluyt, one of the Elizabethan sponsors of English colonial expansion, who was largely instrumental in the first founding of Virginia. Hakluyt was an eloquent clergyman, and not exactly an economist; but he was prompted by the profit-seeking Sir Walter Raleigh, and his views were those of many of his mercantile contemporaries. Some of these merchants were writing economic theory along the lines suggested by Hakluyt; but they soon went far beyond him in their thinking. The most important of these, probably, were Edward Misselden and Thomas Mun. Mun, especially, a member of the East India Company, was interested in the colonial aspects of mercantilism, and his *England's Treasure by Forraign Trade*, written in the year in which Massachusetts was settled, is one of the classics of mercantilist writing.

For Mun, the wealth of a country derives from the profit it makes on its foreign trade. Imports should not be discouraged, especially if the imported commodities can be re-exported at a profit; the export of bullion, if it is for the purchase of imports that can be re-exported, is beneficial. Mun believed that English commerce should be carried in

English ships, and that a prosperous foreign commerce would increase the value of land and the products of the land. But he recognized that state regulation might go too far; he favored the greatest possible amount of freedom for individual trades within the framework of general regulation. Both Mun and Sir Josiah Child, who published his *New-Discourse of Trade* at about the time when Carolina was being settled, emphasized the idea of the general balance of trade as against the balances of particular trades. This idea underlay much of the English policy of regulation of colonial trade; later it emerged as the idea of the self-sufficient empire in which the various colonial areas were expected to specialize in the commodities they could best produce as their contribution to the welfare of the whole. It was William Wood, whose *Survey of Trade* was published in 1718, who gave fullest recognition to the value of the contribution of the colonies to the general balance of trade of the Empire. All the colonies, for Wood, were copartners with the mother country and with each other in building up the commerce, and therefore the wealth, of the Empire as a whole. In general, the colonies would be expected to supply raw material to each other and to the mother country; the mother country would supply the Empire with manufactured goods. The growth of manufactures, indeed, had by this time introduced the idea of protectionism into mercantilist thought, and the manufactures of the colonies were either closely regulated or actually prohibited in order to prevent colonial competition with the mother country in this field.

Obviously, the mother country was the greatest beneficiary, as well as the directive head, of the mercantilist Empire; and where the interests of mother country and colonies conflicted, it was the colonies that must be sacrificed. On the whole, however, the mercantilist system, through all its development, was a system of economic nationalism, or statism, in which individual or local enterprise was encouraged, to be sure, but in which the state, with its over-all national policy, took supreme precedence over both individual and locality. It was not until toward the third quarter of the eighteenth century that the physiocrats and Adam Smith began to apply the principles of natural law to economic phenomena to produce the European theories of free trade. But by that time the Americans were producing a theory of their own.

Such, then, was the mercantilist background of economic thought in the England from which the first settlers of America emigrated. Massachusetts and Virginia were founded in the day of Thomas Mun, Pennsylvania in the day of Sir Josiah Child, Georgia in that of William Wood. This mercantilism, however much it differed from merchant to merchant and from decade to decade, had this constant idea : that the economic welfare of a people depended upon commerce, and that commerce should be regulated, if not actually controlled, by the centralized state for the benefit of the whole people.

Naturally enough, the earliest English colonists brought with them these ideas; and it is no accident that New England Puritanism, with its religious individualism limited by the intolerant authoritarianism of the oligarchy of the elect, found perfectly congenial the capitalistic economic individualism limited by the authoritarian mercantilist state. The economic thought of the leaders of the Puritan state in Massachusetts was the counterpart, in economics, of Puritan authoritarianism in religion. Thus the Puritans, when they set up their godly commonwealth in Massachusetts, enacted law after law to regulate economic conduct. They regulated and inspected weights and measures, inns, mills, and markets; lest the baker cheat his customers, they set up an assize of bread; lest the brewer poison his, they established an assize of beer; and lest employer and laborer defraud each other, they regulated prices and wages and prohibited, in somewhat medieval style, such antisocial practices as the "forestalling" and "engrossing" of commodities.

For, to begin with, man was inherently sinful. Self-interest in itself was not reprehensible, but man's sinful nature was such that he was almost certain to carry his self-interest to the excessive point of cheating his neighbor and harming the community — and thereby obstructing the purposes of God — if not restrained. Puritan mercantilism is thus a religious, a godly mercantilism. But within the limitations placed upon him by the state the individual was encouraged to exert himself in industry, in thrift, and in imagination to improve the condition of his business. And God would smile upon the industrious and the thrifty and give them wealth; but he would frown upon the wasters and idlers and the frivolous and would reduce them to inferior positions and thrust them into outer darkness of poverty. In the words of Cotton Mather: "as for those who Indulge themselves in Idleness, the Express Command of God unto us, is, That we should let them Starve." [1]

The Puritans believed that material prosperity, like all other good things of life, was ordained of God. It was the abuse of it, the worship of gain for its own sake, covetousness, miserliness, and the like, that were reprehensible. God bestowed his favor upon his chosen; and though the preachers warned against the sins of materialism, they could not deny that New England's prosperity was a part of God's plan. If the people abused the divine generosity toward New England, as Michael Wigglesworth put it, God himself could only ask:

[1] Quoted in E. A. J. Johnson: *American Economic Thought in the Seventeenth Century* (London, 1932), p. 31.

Is this the people blest with bounteous store,
By land and sea full richly clad and fed,
Whom plenty's self stands waiting still before,
And powreth out their cups well tempered?
For whose dear sake an howling wilderness
I lately turned into a fruitfull paradeis? [2]

If the economic thinking of Puritan New England was a theological and ethical mercantilism, the economic thinking of the southern colonists, while much less articulate, was no less mercantilistic; it was only less theological — less inclined, that is, to relate all economic life to the plan and desires of God — and more inclined to explain economic phenomena upon relatively more utilitarian and mundane grounds. Thus the combination of economic individualism with state control of economic life was not peculiar to New England; a similar line of thought is to be observed in New York, in Pennsylvania, and in Maryland and Virginia down to about the end of the seventeenth century and even into the eighteenth. It was a local variation of this line of thought, for example, that led the Virginia Legislature to try to control the production and the prices of tobacco and to make repeated attempts to legislate into existence warehouses or even towns that, before the march of settlement into the piedmont, the colony did not need. It was this general attitude, too, that caused Robert Beverley, the colonial amateur historian-economist of Virginia, to deplore, just at the turn of the eighteenth century, the indifference of the Virginia Assembly toward the promotion of manufactures.

Beverley roundly condemned Governor Francis Nicholson of Virginia for encouraging the mother country to prohibit the colony from manufacturing cloth, which, he says, "is desiring a charitable law, that the planters shall go naked." Requiring the colony to buy its manufactured goods from England, he thought, was equivalent to a required importation of "foreign [English] labor incorporated into goods." [3] It should be pointed out, of course, that Beverley was not advocating free trade; he was merely asking the substitution of a Virginia brand of mercantilism in Virginia for the English brand. For he believed that Virginia should be made as nearly economically self-sufficient as possible, and that the government of the colony should follow an aggressive policy of economic regulation, protection, and control to make it so. At the same time, his suggestion that the colony should be allowed to determine its own economic destinies was, indeed, highly prophetic of the future.

[2] Quoted in Miller : *The New England Mind*, p. 474.
[3] Robert Beverley : *History of Virginia* (reprint, Richmond, 1855). pp. 56–62, 82–4, *et passim*.

In general, then, the economic mind of the first two generations of the founders of America was essentially mercantilistic. It was dominated by a set of economic ideas that recognized the sanctity of private property, especially in land, and a certain amount of individual economic freedom. But this way of thinking distrusted, with a still medieval distrust, an unrestrained individualism and favored a large measure of state control, both for the negative restraint of individual greed and for the positive promotion of the common good. The faith that economic welfare would automatically be achieved if economic life were left completely free had not yet appeared; the state was expected to promote provincial economic self-sufficiency by all possible means. Economic thinking was largely ethical in outlook, especially in New England, and recognized economic inequality as part of God's plan for men. Wages, therefore, must be neither too low nor too high, since insufficient wages would be conducive to suffering and possibly immorality, while excessively high wages would be likely to encourage extravagance. The elements making for the dissolution of this static "old way" of economic thought were already present before the end of the seventeenth century; but some of it, especially its ethical outlook, was carried down into the more secular, utilitarian eighteenth.

This small-scale, ethical, and provincial "statism" was not of a piece with English mercantilism. Far from it: the colonists learned very soon after their first arrival that English colonial policy was not always favorable to their interests. Their colonial mercantilism, or statism, was something of their own, often, if not generally, running counter to English statism because their interest ran counter to England's. The change in ideal that was to come was not purely, or even chiefly, change from an English to an American ideology; it was, rather, a change from American ideology, involving a provincial statism, regulation, protection, encouragement, control, and the rest, toward an ever greater degree of freedom — for the individual and for commerce as a whole. The American way in economics, then, when it finally found the orientation that suited it best, was the way of freedom; not yet complete freedom, to be sure, but essentially freedom. It was this that made it American; and the trend toward freedom was deeply rooted in the American experience.

The American Way: Agrarianism

The economic ideas that had been brought to America by the first settlers were thus the ideas of early mercantilistic statism. But those ideas could not long prevail in the American wilderness, even as provincial or colonial statism; for there were new conditions to be met, and new conditions demanded new ways of meeting them. Even within a short generation of the foundation of the colonies, both the northern and the southern settlements had begun to develop along economic lines that ran counter to the mercantilistic colonial policies of the mother country, and the Massachusetts General Court could write that it considered the Navigation Acts "an invasion of the rights, liberties, and properties of the subjects of his Majesty in the colony, and [that] . . . the laws of England were bounded within the four seas, and did not reach America."[4] Sir William Berkeley, Governor of Virginia, protesting against the inclusion of tobacco in the list of enumerated articles in the Navigation Act of 1660, complained bitterly "that forty thousand people should bee empoverished to enrich little more than forty merchts, who being the onely buyers of our Tobacco, gives us what they please for it."[5] In 1671, he wrote again that the handicaps placed upon Virginia commerce were

> Mighty and distructive by that severe Act of parliament wch excludes us from haveving [sic] any Commerce wth any Nacõn in Europe but our owne, Soe that wee cannot add to our plantacõn any Comodity that growes out of itt, as olive trees, Cotton or Vines, besides this wee Cannot procure any skilfull Men for our now hopefull Comodity Silke, For it is not lawfull for us to carry a pipe Staf or a Bushell of Corne to any place in Europe out of the King's dominions. If this were for his Maty Service or the good of his Subjects wee should not repine w^{t}ever our Sufferings are for it. But on my Soule it is the Contrary for both.[6]

So far as Virginia was concerned, English mercantilism was a violation of the colony's interest ; more important still, it seemed to Sir William that both Virginia and the mother country would benefit more from a policy of greater commercial freedom. The fact is, of course, that natural economic conditions in both New England and Virginia seemed to demand freedom : freedom to sell in the best market and to buy in the best ; and if that meant trade with the Dutch, in the long run both the mother country and the colonies would benefit thereby. Such were the free-trade implications of Sir William's pronouncement.

The colonies were not yet able successfully to resist English mercantilistic imperialism. The colonial protests were significant, none the less ; for they clearly documented the fact that the economic develop-

---

[4] Quoted in Thomas Hutchinson : *The History of the Colony and Province of Massachusetts-Bay, edited by Lawrence Shaw Mayo* (3 vols., Cambridge, Mass., 1936), I, 272.

[5] Quoted in George L. Beer : *The Old Colonial System* (2 vols., New York, 1912), I, 112–13.

[6] Ibid., I, 113–14.

ment of the colonies was bringing with it a new way of thinking in economic matters, an "American way," which was bound, sooner or later, to conflict with the "European way" of the mother country.

By the end of the first half of the eighteenth century this process of differentiation in economic life and thought had gone on to the point where it could be said that there existed in America a way of thinking in economics that was almost completely at variance with English mercantilism and that, while it retained some of the old ideas, diverged so far from the English ideology as to be now distinctly American. The new ideas were not held uniformly by all the people in the colonies, of course. For every community had its own outlook; every class emphasized certain ideas of its own; even every individual was likely to differ from his neighbors in his answers to the economic problem. This characteristic, indeed — this freedom and diversity of thought — was one of the most remarkable aspects of the American way. Yet there was considerable solidarity within groups, and there were certain broad common denominators that marked the American economic mind wherever it was to be found.

Love of the land

The most profound and most universal element in the American economic mind of the eighteenth century was love of the land. For the Americans were an agrarian people. The land was the chief source of food and sustenance, the basis of human welfare, the fountain of wealth. But more than anything else it was the sure foundation of individual economic freedom. This love and respect for the land, inherited in the first place from land-minded England, had been intensified and doubly justified by the experience of the Americans. Most of them had come to America poor, landless men; they had got land almost for the taking; they had cultivated it and had won their way by it, literally hundreds of thousands of them, to economic security and independence, even, in many cases, to a measure of opulence.

The recognition of land as the source and the badge of wealth stemmed from the feudal age, as has been noted; but individual ownership in freehold was a modern development. Furthermore, while progress had been made in England away from the old feudal system of landholding toward a modern form, that progress, at the time of the settlement of America, had hardly gone farther than the commutation of the old feudal dues into money payments called quit-rents. This form of landholding, called "free and common socage," was transmitted to America, and some form of quit-rent system existed in all the colonies except those of New England. In that section, where the original charter grants were made to corporations that either were commercial companies or were closely patterned after them, the land was granted to the colonizing corporations outright, and the corporate governments, in turn, granted the land outright to the communities, or towns, who granted it in like fashion to the settlers.

Thus the first breach in the old system was made in the corporate colonies. The modern tendency toward freehold was also accelerated by the frontier conditions, even in the proprietary colonies, where the collection of quit-rents was extremely difficult and where it was easy for the settler to "squat" on the land without benefit of legal deed and to defy everybody, including the proprietor or the King, to throw him off. Moreover, the legal acquisition of the land was relatively easy, since several of the provinces granted "headrights" of fifty acres or more to immigrants or those who imported them, and it was not unusual for an employer to give an indentured servant land upon termination of the indenture. In some of the provinces the headright system had been given up in favor of outright sale at small fees, and this, too, encouraged individual landownership.

Thus it is possible to say that individual ownership of land, with quit-rents or without, was much easier in America than in Europe. And since most of the immigrants who came to America in the colonial period were chiefly attracted by the prospect of free or easily obtainable land, and since such a large proportion of the immigrants did actually achieve a competence because of the free cultivation of the land, it is easy to understand why a love of the land was so deeply rooted in the minds and hearts of the bulk of the American people.

The theme is repeated over and over again. The love of the land is expressed by all classes of people, in all the sections of the colonies. Thus the Reverend William Smith, of Pennsylvania, reports that the German immigrants "are extremely ignorant, and think a large Farm the greatest Blessing in Life."[7] In more prosaic terms the author of *American Husbandry* observed the same phenomenon :

> In the plantations every man, however low his condition and rank in life, can obtain on demand, and [by] paying the settled fees, whatever land he pleases, provided he engages to settle on it in ten years a number of white persons ; and when he has got his grant, it is a freehold to him and his posterity for ever. . . .
>
> The pleasures of being a land owner are so great, and in America the real advantages so numerous, that it is not to be wondered at that men are so eager to enjoy [them], that they cross the Atlantic ocean in order to possess them ; nor is it judicious to draw comparisons between our British wastes and these, between which there is no analogy in

---

[7] William Smith : *A Brief State of the Province of Pennsylvania* (second edition, London, 1755 ; reprinted as *Sabin's Reprints*, No. IV, New York, 1865), p. 31.

those essential circumstances that are the foundation of the great population of America.[8]

But the Americans' love of the land was most eloquently voiced by St. John Crèvecœur :

The instant I enter on my own land, the bright idea of property, of exclusive right, or independence exalt my mind. Precious soil, I say to myself, by what singular custom of law is it that thou wast made to con-

Creative industry in America: from wilderness to cultivation; from log cabin to mansion.

[Contemporary engraving from *Scenographia Americana*]

stitute the riches of the freeholder? What should we American farmers be without the distinct possession of that soil? It feeds, it clothes us, from it we draw even a great exhuberancy, our best meat, our richest drink, the very honey of our bees comes from this privileged spot. No wonder we should thus cherish its possession, no wonder that so many Europeans who have never been able to say that such portion of land was theirs, cross the Atlantic to realize that happiness. This formerly rude soil has been converted by my father into a pleasant farm, and in return it has established all our rights; on it is founded our rank, our freedom, our power as citizens, our importance as inhabitants of such a district.[9]

---

[8] *American Husbandry*, edited by Harry J. Carman (New York, 1939), pp. 178–9.
[9] Crèvecœur : *Letters from an American Farmer* (London, 1782), pp. 25–6.

The land was the fountainhead of freedom — freedom from poverty and want, freedom from the arbitrary exactions of a feudal overlord, freedom from humility of economic and social status. The Americans loved their land with both their minds and their hearts, because it was the land that made them free.

The agrarian economic outlook

Among a people made up predominantly of farmers who believed so ardently in the basic importance of their industry and the land that supported it, it was almost inevitable that there should arise an agrarian philosophy of economics. Such a philosophy was implicit in the crude ideas of the farmers and in the rough and hackneyed saws of the almanacs; and Benjamin Franklin, acute observer and pragmatic philosopher that he was, could wax lyrical about the life of the farmer:

THE COUNTRY MAN

Happy the Man whose Wish and Care
A few paternal Acres bound,
Content to breathe his native Air,
In his own ground.

Whose Herds with Milk, whose Fields with Bread,
Whose Flocks supply him with Attire,
Whose Trees in Summer yield him Shade,
In Winter Fire.

Blest, who can unconcernedly find
Hours, Days and Years slide soft away,
In Health of Body, Peace of Mind,
Quiet by Day.

Sound Sleep by Night; Study and Ease
Together mixt; Sweet Recreation;
And Innocence which most does please
With Meditation.

Thus let me live, unseen, unknown,
Thus unlamented let me die,
Steal from the World, and not a Stone
Tell where I lie.[10]

The American's attachment to his land was, indeed, both emotional and intellectual — what manifestation of "mind" is not? — but his philosophy of life was far from being mere sentimentality. And there arose

[10] *Poor Richard Day by Day; pithy paragraphs from the writings of Benjamin Franklin* (Philadelphia, 1917), p. 81.

a number of Americans who outlined this agrarian philosophy in highly intellectual terms. The most notable agrarian thinker of the colonies, probably, was Jared Eliot, pastor, "clerical physician," and experimental farmer, of Killingworth, Connecticut, whose *Essays upon Field-Husbandry in New England* constitutes a classic expression of the American agrarian mind. Eliot recognized the difference between England and America, so far as agriculture was concerned, and the necessity for new ways of thought applicable to the American environment : "There *are sundry Books on* Husbandry *wrote in* England : *Having read all on* that *Subject I could obtain ; yet such is the difference of Climate and method of Management between them and us, arising from Causes that must make them always differ, so that those Books are not very Useful to us. Besides this, the Terms of Art made use of are so unknown to us, that a great deal they Write is quite unintelligible to the generality of* New England *Readers.*" [11]

Eliot was writing for farmers, in the hope that his essays would prove useful. He drew his materials from experience, his own and that of others ; in fact, he wrote, "Our Reasonings and Speculations without Experience are delusory and uncertain. It used to be the Saying of an old Man, *That an Ounce of Experience is better than a Pound of Science.*" [12] Eliot was, in fact, an experimental agricultural scientist ; and most of his writing falls within that branch of thought. Much of his thinking, however, is also generally economic in character, and it is that which chiefly concerns us here. For Eliot was the spokesman of an agrarian economic philosophy that expressed the mind of his farmer fellow-Americans, a philosophy based upon the idea that land is the basis of all true production, and that agricultural industry is the basis of all wealth :

Wealth or Riches may be considered as nominal or real, natural or artificial. . . .

Husbandry and Navigation are the true Source of natural or real Wealth. Without Husbandry, even Navigation cannot be carried on ; without it we should want many of the Comforts and Conveniences of Life. Husbandry then is a Subject of great Importance, without which all Commerce and Communication must come to an End, all social Advantages cease, Comfort and earthly Pleasure be no more. Nay, this is the very Basis and Foundation of all nominal or artificial Wealth and Riches. This rises and falls, lives or dies, just in Proportion to the Plenty or Scarcity of real Riches or natural Wealth. . . .

Husbandry is the true Mine from whence are drawn true Riches and real Wealth. [13]

[11] Eliot : *Essays upon Field-Husbandry in New England,* p. 3.
[12] Ibid., p. 15.
[13] Ibid., pp. 98–9.

Here is a clear statement of the agrarian theory of economic life : the whole structure of human life and society, as it now is, rests upon agriculture. This was Eliot's idea; but the most significant aspect of his idea is that it expressed the thinking of so many of his fellow Americans.

But it was Benjamin Franklin, colonial America's "universal phi-

Leaders of American agriculture: Jared Eliot. A contemporary portrait.

[Reproduced in *Century*, V, 437]

losopher," who formulated the agrarian philosophy in its most complete terms. Both Eliot and Franklin anticipated the physiocrats, but it was Franklin who came closest to an original expression of the complete physiocratic doctrine and the most effective American expression of it. The clearest single formulation of his ideas, in his *Positions to be Examined, Concerning National Wealth,* was written after he had read the physiocrats' writings, but it was only one of many expressions of his developing agrarianism. In this statement Franklin's agrarian economic philosophy becomes crystal-clear. His argument runs thus :

1. All food or subsistence for mankind arises from the earth or waters.
2. Necessaries of life, that are not food, and all other conveniences, have their values estimated by the proportion of food consumed while we are employed in procuring them.
3. A small people, with a large territory, may subsist on the productions

of nature, with no other labor than that of gathering the vegetables and catching the animals.

4. A large people, with a small territory, finds these insufficient, and, to subsist, must labor the earth, to make it produce greater quantities of vegetable food, suitable for the nourishment of men, and of the animals they intend to eat.

5. From this labor arises a *great increase* of vegetable and animal food, and of materials for clothing, as flax, wool, silk, &c. The superfluity of these is wealth.[14]

Thus wealth, for Franklin, derives primarily from the land; and

6. *Manufactures* are only *another shape* into which so much provisions and subsistence are turned, as were equal in value to the manufactures produced. This appears from hence, that the manufacturer [laborer] does not, in fact, obtain from the employer, for his labor, *more* than a mere subsistence, including raiment, fuel and shelter; all which derive their value from the provisions consumed in procuring them.[15]

Franklin not only ascribes the production of all wealth to agriculture; he also suggests that value is determined by an agrarian standard and he is faintly prophetic of Ricardo in his idea that industrial wages tend to stand persistently at the level of mere subsistence. Since his explanation of the nature of wealth leads him into a discussion of value, he goes on to find the determinant of value to be the amount of agrarian labor required for the production of food. Franklin had already arrived at the labor theory of value as early as 1729; now, with his adoption of the physiocratic doctrines, he defines this determinant as agrarian labor. Finally, he says:

There seems to be three ways for a nation to acquire wealth. The first is by *war*, as the Romans did, in plundering their conquered neighbours. This is *robbery*. The second is by *commerce*, which is generally *cheating*. The third by *agriculture*, the only *honest way*, wherein man receives a real increase of the seed thrown into the ground, in a kind of continual miracle, wrought by the hand of God in his favor, as a reward for his innocent life and his virtuous industry.[16]

Here, then, is the basic idea in the economic thinking of an agrarian people. The Americans loved their land; they respected it for what it did for them, and they built their economic thinking upon it. Here, in Jared Eliot and Benjamin Franklin, are the basic economic ideas that were held more or less consciously and explicitly, about the middle of the eighteenth century, by the vast majority of Americans. Some,

[14] Franklin : *Works* (Sparks ed.), II, 373–4.
[15] Ibid., II, 374.
[16] Ibid., II, 376.

like Crèvecœur and even the great Franklin himself, could wax sentimental about it. But the American mind was made of much more than sentiment : it was also a body of hard, carefully thought-out convictions, based upon the almost universal practical experience of the Americans themselves. And from this basic position, that wealth, in the last analysis, derives from agriculture and the land, were derived the American ideas of the eighteenth century as to commerce, money, value, and the like, as well as the more abstract virtues of industry, thrift, intelligence. Finally, and above all, it was out of their experience, coupled with such thinking as this, that the Americans formed their ideal of an economic system based upon individual initiative nurtured in almost complete economic freedom.

Economic ideals of landed aristocracy

In the agrarian American society of the eighteenth century the most aristocratic element was made up of the great tobacco-plantation owners of Virginia and Maryland and the rice and indigo merchant planters of South Carolina. These groups, with economic interests that differed widely and in many ways from those of the farmers and frontiersmen, had a set of economic ideas and ideals that were peculiarly their own. The broad common denominator of the American economic mind almost everywhere was freedom, to be sure, but men of different economic groups interpreted the principle differently. For the great majority of the people, the farmers, freedom meant agrarian freedom ; for the mercantile interests the idea of freedom turned upon commercial freedom ; for the masses of common men and workers struggling upward the ideal of freedom meant the freedom to rise that comes from the equality of economic opportunity. Naturally, for the landed gentry of the south, freedom meant something else again.

Theirs was a plantation economy based on slavery, and the complex commerce of commodity exchange so typical of the northern commercial cities was absent. Yet the great planters all knew that their prosperity depended upon the sale of their commodities, and they were keenly conscious of market conditions, the laws governing commercial relations, and the intricacies of foreign exchange. These great agrarian capitalists were, indeed, essentially merchants. Their staple commodity in trade was tobacco or, in South Carolina, rice, indigo, and the deerskins emanating from the Indian trade. But these staples were supplemented by many others, such as wheat and Indian corn, livestock, fruit, iron, naval stores, and lumber produced on or near the plantations. Considerable quantities of these commodities were sold to visiting ships as supplies, and some were exported to England and the West Indies.

The trade in Negroes was practiced by many of the planters for the profit there was in it. For example, William Byrd of Virginia was what might have been called a "wholesaler" in the trade in indentured servants and slaves; he spoke of servants and slaves as any other merchant might speak of cords of wood or sacks of flour :

> I know not how long the Palatines are sold for, who do not Pay Passage to Phyladelphia, but here they are sold for Four years and fetch from 6 to 9 Pounds and perhaps good Tradesmen may go for Ten. If these Prices would answer, I am pretty Confident I could dispose of two Shiploads every year in this River : and I myself would undertake it for Eight [per] cent on the Sales, and make you as few bad Debts as possible. This is the Allowance Our Negro Sellers have, which sell for more than Double these People will, and consequently afford twice the Profet.[17]

It is to be noted that Negroes were considered more valuable, since their services were permanent, while those of white servants were only for four years; and that Byrd sold on commission.

Slavery as an economic institution was of course approved; but these men looked down upon labor. They considered themselves superior to other men : labor was not for them; it was just another commodity, to be bought and sold in the form of slaves or indentured servants. Slaves, of course, were considered a valuable economic asset :

> Negroes being a property for life, the death of slaves in the prime of youth or strength, is a material loss to the proprietor ; they are therefore, almost in every instance, under more comfortable circumstances than the miserable European, over whom the rigid planter exercises an inflexible severity. They [the white servants] are strained to the utmost to perform their alloted labour ; and from a prepossession in many cases too justly founded, they are supposed to be receiving only the just reward which is due to repeated offences.[18]

Even the most aristocratic planters of the tidewater were shrewd, profit-minded businessmen. Such men as Robert Carter of Virginia or Henry Laurens of South Carolina (who was primarily a merchant) had economic interests quite similar to those of the merchants of Boston and New York, and their ideas on economic matters were likely to be, with local variations, much the same. Their thinking, although never systematized and always implicit in their writings rather than explicit, revolved about a set of ideas that accepted and justified their system.

---

[17] William Byrd to Mr. Andrews of Rotterdam, in *A Documentary History of American Industrial Society*, edited by John P. Commons, Ulrich B. Phillips, Eugene A. Gilmore, Helen L. Sumner, and John B. Andrews (10 vols., Cleveland, 1910), I, 374.

[18] William Eddis ; *Letters from America*, ibid., I, 343.

Thus they believed in private property, slavery, and freedom for their own commerce. They believed in a certain amount of state aid, however, for they passed and supported laws protecting Virginia tobacco against the competition of inferior grades from North Carolina, laws for the encouragement of manufactures, and laws for the establishment of ports and warehouses. At the beginning of the eighteenth century they were still rather strongly of the state-aid or mercantilistic school of thought, and in a moment of depression in the midst of Queen Anne's War they called upon the Queen for aid with an argument that is mercantilist to the core:

> If Tobacco wont yield them sufficient to cloath them with the manufactures of Great Britain, they must apply themselves to manufactures of their own, to the utter neglect of Tobacco, the Trade of which must be intirely lost. And can it ever be for her Majesty's Service or for the Interest of her Subjects to drop a Trade so vastly beneficial as that of Tobacco; A Trade that every year employs so many Ships, & is so fruitfull a Nursery for Seamen: A Trade that Sets so many poor People at work both in Great Britain & America: That occasions so great a demand Yearly of British Manufactures; and consequently so greatly improves the Value of the Land that produces those Manufactures; and above all a Trade which so abundantly helps to Balance the Commerce of Great Britain with foreign Parts, which wou'd otherwise every year drain mighty Sums of Specie from Thence.[19]

But this was special pleading, to win the help of the British government in a special case. As the eighteenth century wore on, the economic outlook of the planter aristocracy moved steadily toward the principle of economic *laissez faire*. A debtor class, constantly in debt to their London factors, they were essentially of the "easy-money" persuasion, although they were also creditors. And while they never lost their interest in profits, they came to be somewhat careless of money for its own sake, although financial honesty came to be a high point of honor with them. Andrew Burnaby described them as extravagant, and quite willing to overdraw their credit: "The display of a character thus constituted, will naturally be in acts of extravagance, ostentation, and a disregard of economy; it is not extraordinary therefore, that the Virginians outrun their incomes; and that having involved themselves in difficulties, they are frequently tempted to raise money by bills of exchange, which they know will be returned protested, with 10 per cent. interest."[20]

[19] William Byrd: *History of the Dividing Line and other Tracts.* (2 vols., Richmond, 1866), II, 208.
[20] Andrew Burnaby: *Burnaby's Travels through North America,* edited by Rufus R. Wilson (New York, 1904), p. 55.

At the same time, the Virginians of the tidewater were beginning to chafe under the mercantilist restrictions of the mother country; for the British colonial system kept them almost completely under the thumbs of the London tobacco factors to whom they were in debt, and many of the planters attributed their ills to this fact. The solution, they believed, would be freedom to sell their tobacco where they could get the best prices and buy their supplies where they were cheapest. Burnaby, good Englishman that he was, wrote of them in 1759: "In matters of commerce they are ignorant of the necessary principles that must prevail between a colony and the mother country; they think it a hardship not to have an unlimited trade to every part of the world. They consider the duties upon their staple as injurious only to themselves; and it is utterly impossible to persuade them that they affect the consumer also." [21]

But it was not merely ignorance of the "necessary principles" of the relations between mother country and colony that made the Virginians increasingly free-traders. It was their experience, and the circumstances in which they found themselves — factors that Burnaby, or any other Englishman, for that matter, could not fully understand. What the Virginians desired was autonomy, or self-determination, and this desire flared into brilliant expression by Patrick Henry in connection with the famous "Parsons' Cause," which achieved its dramatic significance over the question whether the crown could directly override a Virginia law regulating a minor and insignificant detail of its own economic life. When the controversy over taxation of the colonies by Parliament began to loom dark on the horizon in 1764 and 1765, Richard Bland could ask: "why is the Trade of the Colonies more circumscribed than the Trade of Britain? . . . Their Commerce ought to be equally free with the Commerce of *Britain*, otherwise [taxation of American trade] will be loading them with Burthens at the same time that they are deprived of Strength to sustain them." [22]

But it remained for the planter Thomas Jefferson to phrase, at the time of crisis, the free-trade convictions of his class as they corresponded perfectly with the mercantile liberalism expressed to the northward by Franklin. On the eve of the Revolution, in 1774, Jefferson put it succinctly and definitely: "That the exercise of a free trade with all parts of the world, possessed by the American Colonists, [was theirs] as of natural right, and . . . no law of their own had taken away or abridged [it]." [23] The planters had come to see eye to eye, in basic eco-

[21] Ibid., pp. 56–7.

[22] Richard Bland : *An Inquiry into the Rights of the British Colonies,* edited by E. G. Swem (Richmond, 1922), pp. 25–6.

[23] Thomas Jefferson : *A Summary View of the Rights of British America* (Williamsburg, 1774), p. 8.

nomic questions, with their mercantile northern neighbors : the essential theory in their economic outlook was freedom — freedom that was theirs by natural law. Freedom, that is, for their system ; freedom from English restraint or meddling ; the social question of human freedom involved in Negro slavery as an economic institution was not, directly at least, involved.

But there was one more aspect of the thinking of the southern gentry that was looking toward freedom from restraint ; and this they shared with many of their wealthy compeers of the commercial north : their speculative interest in the land. This widespread interest of the wealthy in all the colonies was only natural in a country and at a time when population was increasing and expanding westward so rapidly that the price of land was skyrocketing by the middle of the century ; and Alexander Mackraby reported in 1768 that it was almost a proverb in Philadelphia that "Every great fortune made here [Pennsylvania] within these 50 years has been by land." [24]

This driving interest in land-speculation was in itself a practical matter, almost purely an enterprise for the making of money. But it had certain effects upon the American economic mentality that were not without significance. For the boom in speculation and deals in land, most of it issued, now, in fee simple, could only enhance the idea of private property, and it gave a further impetus to the demise of feudal tenures in America. But there was another way in which this land-speculation reacted upon American economic thought. For whereas the mercantile interests generally were clearly committed to the principles of individual, small-scale enterprises and looked with fear and distrust upon large-scale enterprises that smacked of monopoly, the American land companies generally adopted the corporate, stockholding form of combination for their purposes and reintroduced this form and idea to American economic practice — and respectability.

But the greatest ideological significance of the speculative ventures of the great landowners in all the colonies probably lay in the fact that, in the face of increased English control of lands in the American west after 1763, the American land-speculators became increasingly distrustful of English policy. This distrust seemed confirmed, in the years preceding the Revolution, by the apparent tendency of English official policy to favor small holdings in America while encouraging such large groups of English land-speculators as that which promoted the great Vandalia project. Land-speculators in many of the colonies, but especially in the south, became suspicious of England and devised a set of

[24] Alexander Mackraby : "Philadelphia Society before the Revolution ; Extracts from Letters of Alexander Mackraby to Sir Philip Francis," *Pennsylvania Magazine of History and Biography*, XI, 277.

ideas that fixed the authority over the land, as over commerce, by natural right in the local provincial "parliament," or legislature. This set
of ideas, too, reached its culminating, classical expression in Jefferson's
Summary View: "America was not conquered by William the Norman,
nor its lands surrendered to him, or any of his successors. Possessions
there are undoubtedly of the allodial nature." [25]

Title to the land was thus grounded in the laws of nature. Economic and political thought combined to show that the land of America, like its commerce, should be free from the restraining hand of Britain; and that the sovereign control of the land, as of commerce, must
rest in the hands of the representatives of the people in their legislatures. In Virginia, as elsewhere among the southern aristocracy, the
groundwork in economic thought was laid, even as early as the mid-
century, for the assertion of the ideals of both economic and political
self-direction.

The American Merchant versus English Mercantilism

The America of the mid-eighteenth century was thus a predominantly agrarian society, with a correspondingly agrarian philosophy of
economic life. The wealth of this society had been produced, primarily,
by the cultivation of the soil; and the accumulation of actual capital
wealth by agrarian production, supplemented by the fisheries and the
fur trade, seemed visibly and concretely to support the agrarian economic ideas to which the Americans generally held. But the basic
agrarian wealth of the country was enhanced and expanded by the exchange of the products of one region or colony with another, and by
the sale of surplus agrarian products, together with fish and furs,
abroad. Of the agrarian products, the most important were wheat and
flour, tobacco, rice, indigo, and (in the West Indies) sugar. Among the
colonies and within the Empire, commerce was relatively free, ham-
pered only by certain import and export duties, which varied from place
to place, and by certain other local restrictions. But colonial commerce
with the world outside the Empire was under a good many severe restrictions placed upon it by the mother country in the interest of English mercantilist policy.

By and large, the greatest volume of trade from the seaboard colonies was with the mother country and the British West Indies. But the
balance of exchange with the mother country was always unfavorable,
and it was made much more so by the English Navigation Acts and the
so-called Acts of Trade. On the other hand, the trade of the colonies

[25] Jefferson: *Summary View,* p. 20.

with the rest of the world was distinctly favorable, and by the year 1760 the value of American exports was almost double that of the imports. This flourishing colonial commerce centered in the burgeoning colonial cities, Boston, Newport, New York, Philadelphia, Baltimore, Norfolk, and Charleston, and with the growth of commerce and commercial towns there also had appeared a class of men, the merchant bankers of these cities, who made their livelihood by trade. It was easy for these men, the merchants, to see that it was to their interest to sell where prices were high and to buy where prices were low. This meant freedom to trade directly, wherever and however they thought best. But the British mercantile system was always there, limiting their market for tobacco, indigo, rice, beaver-skins, naval stores, and other products to England, while prohibiting or limiting the colonial manufactures of such commodities as woolens, hats, and iron with the objective of forcing the colonies to buy these products from England. The colonial merchants, indeed, where they did import Dutch or French or other European goods, were required to import them by way of England in order that English middlemen might reap profits on these deals and that the foreign price of the goods might be raised to the level of English prices to discourage foreign competition. Obviously, there existed a profound conflict of interest between the needs of the colonial merchants for freedom and the English policy of restriction. The consequence was resentment and evasion on the part of the Americans, and a more or less clearly expressed desire to be free from British commercial restriction. It was almost inevitable that out of these circumstances there should arise an American philosophy of commercial freedom to supplement the agrarian libertarianism of the farmers. Already in 1721 some of the colonies had protested to England in the name of free trade against its mercantilist policies. The protest had been voiced by Jeremiah Dummer, agent for Massachusetts in England: "Oppression is the most opposite thing in the World to Commerce, and the most destructive Enemy it can have. . . . Governours have in all Times, and in all Countries, bin too much inclin'd to oppress: And consequently, it cannot be the Interest of the Nation to increase their Power, and lessen the Liberties of the People." [26]

But the official attitude of England, represented by the colonial governors, was something very different from the colonial concept of freedom. For them, the interests of the mother country came first; the colonies were expected, in gratitude for their existence and the mother country's protection, to be willing to sacrifice their own interests and

[26] Albert B. Hart, ed.: *American History Told by Contemporaries* (4 vols., New York, 1898), II, 137.

take second place to that of England. Governor William Keith, of Pennsylvania, writing in 1728, best represents this theory, which was re-echoed again and again by other colonial governors :

> Every Act of Dependant Provincial Governments ought . . . to Terminate in the Advantage of the Mother State, unto whom it owes its being, & Protection in all its valuable Priviledges, Hence it follows that all Advantageous Projects or Commercial Gains in any Colony, which are truly prejudicial to & inconsistent with the Interests of the Mother State, must be understood to be illegal, & the Practice of them unwarrantable, because they Contradict the End for which the Colony had a being, & are incompatible with the Terms on which the People Claim both Priviledges & Protection.[27]

It is true, of course, that practically all the colonies retained certain mercantilistic practices in the eighteenth century, whether in the form of import and export duties, discrimination in favor of the colony's shipping, regulation and fiscal protection of production, or some other. It is true, also, that most of the early thinking of the Americans, as they felt their way toward freedom of trade, was nebulous in the extreme, with many old mercantilist ideas persisting in the midst of a new set of concepts that had commercial freedom as their basic common denominator. Such, for example, was the case with the writer who, as *Amicus Reipublicæ*, set forth his ideas in 1731 in the pamphlet *Trade and Commerce Inculcated*. Commerce, for him, is more fundamental for the production of wealth than agriculture or labor :

> *Trade or Commerce is principally necessary to a people flourishing in the World.*
> Altho' the Wealth and Flourishing of a People depends upon Diligent Labour as the Efficient of its Substance, or as a Cause without which it cannot be ; yet Labour will not be improved to any considerable degree of Wealth, without the advantage & encouragement of a profitable *Commerce*. In all Labour there is profit ; for Profit is the final Cause of Labour ; and as there cannot be much profit by Labour without *Commerce*, so *Commerce* is the Cause of Profit by Labour, and consequently the cause of Labour, that is of the abundant Labour in order to Wealth and Flourishing. [No country has everything it needs.] And since each Country has but its peculiar Commodities to be raised in abundance, *Commerce* is necessary to a suitable distribution and digesture of it, holding it in value, and therefore necessary to the encouragement and support of Labour.[28]

[27] Printed in William Byrd : *History of the Dividing Line, and other Tracts,* II, 215.

[28] Amicus Reipublicæ [pseud.] : *Trade and Commerce Inculcated . . .* (Boston, 1731), pp. 2–3.

"Amicus" recognized that labor is the creator of the commodities exchanged in trade, and he understood clearly the strength of the appeal of the motive of private profit; but though labor were to create great stocks of commodities, and those commodities constituted a certain value in themselves, yet there would be no real expansion of wealth unless they were exchanged. A little farther on he states emphatically that a "free and liberal" commerce is very profitable to any state. But despite his vision of a free commerce he is essentially a mercantilist in his statism:

> *Trade* or *Commerce*, is an Engine of State, to draw men in to business, for the advancing and ennobling of the Rich, for the support of the Poor, for the strengthening and fortifying the State; and when it is wisely conducted and vigorously carried on, it is the King of Business for increasing the Wealth, Civil Strength, and Temporal Glory of a People. . . .
>
> It is the Bounty, Pomp, and Grandeur, peculiar to a free and vigorous carrying on in *Trade*, that ordinarily makes good Business for Labouring men. . . .
>
> [A] People may be possessed of a Fruitful Rich Country, and yet for want of good Regulations, and [state?] Policy in *Trade*, the business of the Country (considered in the mean) will be rendered greatly disadvantageous and unprofitable, as to any enlarged undertaking.[29]

The result of "Amicus'" thinking, such as it is, is a mixture of mercantilism with an embryonic economic liberalism. He had evidently read Franklin's pamphlet on paper money; and he agreed that there should be an expanding currency to facilitate an expanding economy; but he believed that a supply of currency would be acquired if the balance of trade were kept favorable; this, he thought, could be managed by undervaluing commodities and overvaluing money, or lowering the prices of exports to the point where they might be "dumped" abroad in sufficient quantities to keep the foreign balance of payments always favorable. This, of course, could only be done by the state. Thus he is essentially a mercantilist, a manipulator; although he might have called himself a manipulator for freedom. Yet the basic interests of colonial commerce were clearly leading toward the concept of freedom of commerce, and this concept gradually loomed more important in colonial economic thought than provincial interference or regulation.

The growth of free-trade ideas is to be noted fairly clearly in the thinking of Franklin. For example, when he published his *Modest Enquiry into the Nature and Necessity of a Paper Currency*, Franklin still retained the mercantilist conception of the balance of trade and the de-

---

[29] Ibid., pp. 4, 6.

sirability of a limited amount of state interference for maintaining a favorable balance. By 1747, however, he had come to see the complicated nature of this problem and went clearly on record for at least a modified form of free trade. At that time, in a letter to Jared Eliot, he advised against a proposed imposition of import duties of the colony of Connecticut to defray the costs of the then current war. For after all, he says, such import duties are always paid by the consumer; further, they would be very difficult to enforce against smugglers; and they would be likely to provoke retaliatory duties by other colonies. Implicit in his argument is the principle of free trade between the colonies, although he does admit that if the proposed import duties should have the effect of protecting and encouraging manufactures in the colony, thereby relieving it of the necessity of buying some of its manufactured goods outside, that would be an advantage.

As Franklin's thinking progressed, he gradually went completely over to the doctrines of freedom in commerce. He scoffed at the mother country's fear of colonial competition and opposed its mercantilist efforts at regulation of colonial economic life. In 1751, in his *Observations concerning the Increase of Mankind and the Peopling of Countries,* he said:

> The danger . . . of these colonies interfering with their mother country in trades that depend on labor, manufactures, &c., is too remote to require the attention of Great Britain.
>
> But in proportion to the increase of the colonies, a vast demand is growing for British manufactures, a glorious market wholly in the power of Britain, in which foreigners cannot interfere, which will increase in a short time even beyond her power of supplying, though her whole trade should be to her colonies; therefore Britain should not too much restrain manufactures in her colonies. A wise and good mother will not do it. To distress is to weaken, and weakening the children weakens the whole family.[30]

But manufactures, although desirable, did not, according to Franklin, actually produce any wealth. Neither did commerce:

> The Value of Manufactures arises out of the Earth, and is not the Creation of Labour as commonly supposed.
>
> When a grain of Corn is put into the Ground it may produce ten Grains. After defraying the Expence, there is a real Increase of Wealth. — Above we see that Manufactures make no Addition to it, they only change its Form. — So Trade, or the Exchange of Manufactures, makes no Increase of Wealth among Mankind in general; no more than the Game of Commerce at Cards makes any Increase of money among the

[30] Franklin: *Works* (Sparks ed.), II, 314.

Company tho' particular Persons may be Gainers while others are Losers. But the clear Produce of Agriculture is clear additional Wealth.[31]

Thus Franklin returns to his agrarianism in his discussion of manufactures and commerce; but these branches of economic life must be free:

> Suppose a country, X, with three manufactures, as *cloth, silk, iron,* supplying three other countries, A. B. C. but is desirous of increasing the vent [sale], and raising the price of cloth in favor of her own clothiers.
> In order to this, she forbids the importation of foreign cloth from A.
> A, in return, forbids silks from X.
> Then the silk-workers complain of a decay of trade.
> And X, to content them, forbids silks from B.
> B, in return, forbids iron ware from X.
> Then the silk-workers complain of a decay of trade.
> And Y forbids the importation of iron from C.
> C, in return, forbids cloth from X.
> What is got by all these prohibitions?
> *Answer.* — All four find their common stock of the enjoyments and conveniences of life diminished.[32]

Franklin's agrarianism and his free-trade ideas were one. He was himself a merchant, and he saw that the interests of merchants and farmers were all bound up together in the principles of freedom. He believed in economic freedom because his experience and his observations taught him that economic freedom was more conducive to human prosperity and happiness than over-regulation or control.

Franklin's belief in the desirability for commercial freedom was shared by the mercantile interests generally, although not always with Franklin's complete rejection of mercantilism and English economic control. Thomas Hutchinson of Massachusetts, for example, gave expression to the same idea, but he saw no way out but by submission to English control for the sake of English protection:

> It was hard parting with a free open trade to all parts of the world which the Massachusetts carried on before the present charter. . . . It is owing, in a great measure, to the taxes, duties and excises, the consequences of an enormous load of debt, that the manufactures of England come dearer to us than those of other countries. Great part of this debt was incurred by our immediate protection. Shall we think much of sharing in the burden when we have been so great sharers in the benefit? There is no way in which we can more effectually contribute to the na-

[31] *Remark on Chap. XI. of the Consid.ns on Policy, Trade, &c.*, printed in Lewis J. Carey: *Franklin's Economic Views* (Garden City, 1928), pp. 144–6.
[32] Franklin: *Works* (Sparks ed.), II, 366.

tional relief than by submitting to regulation and restraints upon our trade, and yet no way in which she should be so little sensible of it.[33]

Free trade is desirable, yes; but it must be sacrificed in the interest of the Empire as a whole, of which England is both the head and the protector. To arrive at this conclusion Hutchinson used the mercantilists' own argument of regional specialization within a self-sufficient empire and the rationalists' argument of the design of nature:

> The great creator of the universe in infinite wisdom has so formed the earth that different parts of it, from the soil, climate, &c. are adapted to different produce, and he so orders and disposes the genius, temper, numbers and other circumstances relative to the inhabitants as to render some employments peculiarly proper for one country, and others for another, and by this provision a mutual intercourse is kept up between the different parts of the globe. It would be folly in a Virginian to attempt a plantation of rice for the sake of having all he consumes from the produce of his own labour, when South-Carolina, by nature, is peculiarly designed for rice, and capable of supplying one half the world. Old countries, stocked with people, are ordinarily best adapted to manufactures. Would it be the interest of New England, whilst thin of people, to turn their attention from the whale, cod, mackarel and herring fishery, their lumber trade and ship building, which require but few hands compared with many other sorts of business, to such manufactures as are now imported from Great Britain, or to take their sons from clearing the land and turning an uncultivated wilderness into pleasant and profitable fields, and set them to spinning, weaving and the like employments?[34]

No, let New England stick to its fishing, to its lumbering, and to the farms on its expanding frontier. Nature itself prescribed the law of specialization and evidently designed New England's specialty to be fishing. By the same token, nature designed South Carolina for producing rice, and, apparently, England for manufacturing the articles the colonies could not produce as well, in addition to the function of regulating and protecting these mutually interdependent specialized parts of the Empire. Hutchinson was at heart a free-trader, and his argument is as perfect an argument for free trade as it is for submission to British economic control for the sake of the self-sufficient Empire; but his loyalty to England and the King's majesty, and his conviction that the interest of the colonies was bound up with the welfare of the Empire as a whole prevented him from going to the logical conclusion of his own argument: "the state from whence we sprang [Eng-

[33] Hutchinson: *History . . . of Massachusetts Bay* (Mayo ed.), II, 342–3.
[34] Ibid., II, 343.

land] and upon which we still depend for protection, may justly expect to be distinguished by us, and . . . we should delight in and contribute to its prosperity, beyond all other parts of the globe." [35]

Thus did the American conservative reflect, in 1768, the policies of English mercantilism and the thought more or less consciously, of the English mercantilist William Wood. But Hutchinson was a voice of the minority, not the majority, of his countrymen. Franklin had already spoken for most Americans, and Pelatiah Webster was to reiterate it in Philadelphia just after Jefferson was voicing the same idea for his planter neighbors of the south. As Webster put it, bluntly, "Freedom of trade, or unrestrained liberty of the subject to *hold or dispose of* his property as he pleases, is absolutely necessary to the prosperity of every community, and to the happiness of all individuals who compose it." [36] In the realm of commerce, as elsewhere, the essential principle in the American ideal was freedom.

MONEY AND VALUE

One of the most troublesome issues in the development of American economic thought in the eighteenth century was that raised by the problem of a circulating medium of commerce. All the colonies were steadily expanding their capital wealth, both agricultural and commercial, and this expansion created a growing need for a medium of exchange. Generally speaking, in the seventeenth century silver coin was almost the only monetary medium ; but money was scarce in the colonies, and commodities and commodity certificates were used in the absence of coin. Some of the merchants of Boston hit upon a scheme for circulating merchants' notes for local purposes, but apparently with only limited success.

The expanding commerce of the colonies complicated the problem, for while the balance of external trade was generally favorable, the trade with the mother country was unfavorable, and this unfavorable balance had to be rectified by the export of coin, by invisible exports such as travel, education, or residence in England, or by the transfer of credits to England from other areas where the balance of payments was favorable. In the eyes of many of the colonists it was the exportation of coin that made money so scarce in the colonies, although there were some who saw the problem in its more complex nature and realized that the phenomenal expansion of the colonial economy alone would have made coin scarce, even without any exportation of it. There were also some who realized that, once the use of paper money

[35] Ibid., II, 343.
[36] Pelatiah Webster : *Political Essays on the Nature and Operation of Money, Public Finances, and Other Subjects* (Philadelphia, 1791), p. 9.

was begun, the cheaper paper aggravated the scarcity of coin by driving the hard money into hiding.

In any case, in the first quarter of the eighteenth century most of the colonies began to issue paper money to supply the very real need for a circulating medium, and long before the Revolution they were all doing it. Some of this paper money took the form of provincial government notes covered by future collections of taxes; some colonies issued currency against silver plate; and some of the money was simply "fiat money" with no promise of redemption. Some of the colonies, notably Pennsylvania, were cautious and businesslike in the issue and retirement of money; others, notably Rhode Island, threw discretion to the winds and printed paper money indiscriminately.

That the employment of paper money was of great benefit to the colonies in the long run there can hardly be any question; but in an age when the benefits of paper money were just being discovered and the laws of finance and credit were not at all understood, it was inevitable that many mistakes should be made. In the colonies where the paper was printed most carelessly, especially in New England, the paper dropped to a fraction of its face value, with a resultant chaos in business. Many of those who witnessed the loss of money by the inflation of paper turned against it entirely, while others were divided as to whether money should be issued and guaranteed by the government, which was inevitably affected by politics, or by private banks. Among the latter, again, there was a sharp division between those who favored banks whose money would be based on silver and those who favored bank-notes secured by land.

This problem of a circulating medium was new, both in England and in America, and the Americans had little or no precedent to go by. They were compelled to think their way through to a set of convictions by the hard way of experience. Their first ideas were often naïve and

A TABLE for the more ready casting up of Coins, in Pennsylvania.				
No.	Ps. Eight. £ s. d.	Spanish Pistoles. £ s. d.	English Guineas. £ s. d.	Moidores. £ s. d.
1	0 7 6	1 7 0	1 14 0	2 3 6
2	0 15 0	2 14 0	3 8 0	4 7 0
3	1 2 6	4 1 0	5 2 0	6 10 6
4	1 10 0	5 8 0	6 16 0	8 14 0
5	1 17 6	6 15 0	8 10 0	10 17 6
6	2 5 0	8 2 0	10 4 0	13 1 0
7	2 12 6	9 9 0	11 18 0	15 4 6
8	3 0 0	10 16 0	13 12 0	17 8 0
9	3 7 6	12 3 0	15 6 0	19 11 6
10	3 15 0	13 10 0	17 0 0	21 15 0
11	4 2 6	14 17 0	18 14 0	23 18 6
12	4 10 0	16 4 0	20 8 0	26 2 0
13	4 17 6	17 11 0	22 2 0	28 5 6
14	5 5 0	18 18 0	23 16 0	30 9 0
15	5 12 6	20 5 0	25 10 0	32 12 6
16	6 0 0	21 12 0	27 4 0	34 16 0
17	6 7 6	22 19 0	28 18 0	36 19 6
18	6 15 0	24 6 0	30 12 0	39 3 0
19	7 2 6	25 13 0	32 6 0	41 6 6
20	7 10 0	27 0 0	34 0 0	43 10 0
30	11 5 0	40 10 0	51 0 0	65 5 0
40	15 0 0	54 0 0	68 0 0	87 0 0
50	18 15 0	67 10 0	85 0 0	108 15 0
60	22 10 0	81 0 0	102 0 0	130 10 0
70	26 5 0	94 10 0	119 0 0	152 5 0
80	30 0 0	108 0 0	136 0 0	174 0 0
90	33 15 0	121 10 0	153 0 0	195 15 0
100	37 10 0	135 0 0	170 0 0	217 10 0

EXPLANATION.

Find your Number in the first Col. under No. and right against the same you have the Sum of that Number of Pieces of Eight, Spanish Pistoles, English Guineas, Moidores. But if your Sum cannot be found at one View, it must be taken at two or more Operations.

Money in the colonies: "A Table for the more ready casting up of Coins, in Pennsylvania."

[From *Poor Richard's Almanack*, 1749]

almost always confused, but out of the confusion appeared two fairly defined positions : that which favored the issuance of as much paper money as might be needed, and that which either opposed it entirely or would permit the use of paper only under the strictest and most conservative sort of coverage and control.

Among those who favored the issuance of money by the government, Benjamin Franklin was by far the most distinguished; of those who favored private banks John Colman of Massachusetts was perhaps best known; of the theoretical opponents of paper money, Dr. William Douglass of Boston was by far the most able and eloquent. In general, the pro-paper position was about as stated by Franklin in 1729. To begin with, says Franklin, "*There is a certain proportionate quantity of money requisite to carry on the trade of a country freely and currently ; more than which would be of no advantage in trade, and less, if much less, exceedingly detrimental to it.*" [37] The scarcity of money, he says, is extremely detrimental to healthy economic life, for the following reasons :

First. *A great want of money, in any trading country, occasions interest to be at a very high rate. . . .*
Secondly. *Want of money in a country reduces the price of that part of its produce which is used in trade. . . .*
Thirdly. *Want of money in a country discourages laboring and handicraftsmen . . . from coming to settle in it, and induces many that were settled to leave the country, and seek entertainment and employment in other places, where they can be better paid. . . .*
Fourthly. *Want of money in such a country as ours, occasions a greater consumption of English and European goods, in proportion to the number of the people, than there would otherwise be.*[38]

Here Franklin states and defends the quantity theory of money. Of course, he says, the general employment of paper money will be opposed by the money-lenders who receive exorbitant interest charges on their loans; by land-speculators who hope to purchase more land later ; and by lawyers, because people "will have less occasion to run in debt, and consequently less occasion to go to law and sue one another for their debts." Despite the objections of these vested interests, however, Franklin concludes that

since a plentiful currency will be so great a cause of advancing this province in trade and riches, and increasing the number of its people ;

[37] Benjamin Franklin : *A Modest Inquiry into the Nature and Necessity of a Paper Currency ;* printed in Franklin : *Works* (Sparks ed.), II, 254–77. This quotation is from II, 255.
[38] Ibid., II, 255–9.

which . . . will occasion a much greater vent and demand for [English] commodities here; and allowing that the crown is the more powerful for its subjects increasing in wealth and number, I cannot think it the interest of England to oppose us in making as great a sum of paper money here, as we, who are the best judges of our own necessities, find convenient. And if I were not sensible that the gentlemen of trade in England, to whom we have already parted with our silver and gold, are misinformed of our circumstances, and therefore endeavour to have our currency stinted to what it now is, I should think the government at home had some reasons for discouraging and impoverishing this province, which we are not acquainted with.[39]

But the English were probably not misinformed; nor was England prepared to admit that we Americans were "the best judges of our own necessities." Quite the contrary, indeed, as will appear.

Franklin's economic theory — to say nothing of his logic — was often faulty, from the point of view of the modern science of economics; but as a practical man he saw the practical utility of paper money; such a simple factor, for example, as the greater ease of handling paper as against heavy sacks of coin seemed to him to be of considerable importance. The great problem was to keep up the value of the paper; and this he would do both by supporting the bills by something of intrinsic worth, such as gold or silver, and by the prestige of the government and a requirement that the paper be acceptable as legal tender.

Not all the advocates of paper money shared precisely all of Franklin's ideas; but his general position that the economic growth of the colonies made absolutely necessary some such medium of exchange certainly represents the opinion of the generality of Americans.

Bitterly opposed to the issuance of paper money was the irascible physician Dr. William Douglass, of Boston. Douglass was conscious of the operation of Gresham's law, and saw in silver alone the most stable medium of exchange:

Silver itself is a Merchandize, and being the least variable of all others, is by general Consent made the Medium of Trade . . . a trading Country must have regard to the universal commercial Medium, which is Silver; or cheat, and trade to a Disadvantage. . . . There can therefore be no other proper Medium of Trade, but Silver. . . . The Debitor Party (I am ashamed to mention it) being the prevailing Party in all our Depreciating-Paper-Money Colonies, do wickedly endeavor to delude the unthinking Multitude, by perswading them, that all Endeavours of the Govenour [sic], or Proposals and Schemes of private Societies, to introduce a Silver Medium, or a Credit upon a Silver Bottom, to prevent the honest and industrious Creditor from being

[39] Ibid., II, 263.

defrauded; are Impositions upon the Liberty and Property of the People.[40]

Douglass was definitely a hard-money man. He never achieved a positive philosophy of money, but he knew what he did not like, and — quite intelligently — why : because, he said, "as it always happens, a bad Currency drove away the good Currency." He pointed out the mischiefs that had arisen in Massachusetts because of the depreciation of the currency : real wages had decreased as the amount of paper money increased ; the merchants of England were defrauded ; widows, orphans, other funds at interest, "and all other creditors" had lost money, both in interest and in their principal, by depreciation ; the price of silver had risen, and silver itself had been driven out of circulation.

While nobody at that time fully understood the mysteries of credit and its power, Douglass realized that it could not be abused :

No Country can have an indefinite or unlimited Credit ; the further a Country endeavours to stretch its Credit beyond a certain Pitch, the more it depreciates. The Credit of a Country may be compared to that of a private Trader ; if his Credit is equal to 100,000*l.* Sterl. his Notes of Hand for 100,000*l.* will be as good as Silver ; if it be known that he passes Notes of Hand for 200,000*l.* Sterl. their full Credit will be suspected and eventually be worth no more than his real Credit 100,000*l.* Sterl : if he can be supposed to utter 500,000*l.* Bills for notes, his 5*l.* Note will be worth only 20s Sterling . . . the more Paper Money we emit our real Value of Currency or *Medium* becomes less, and *what we emit beyond the Trading Credit of the Country does not add to the real Medium, but rather diminishes from it, by creating an Opinion against us, of bad Œconomy and sinking Credit.*[41]

Here Douglass gets very close to a national-fund theory of credit. He also warns against the abuse of public credit by self-seeking politicians, and, finally, against the moral effect of easy money, not only upon debtors, but upon creditors as well : "All Shame and Modesty is banished even in the Creditors ; who tho' formerly a modest forbearing Man, is now obliged to Dun incessantly or lose his Debt." [42]

Douglass denied that paper money prevented high interest rates and showed that prices increased, rather than the contrary, because of it. He refuted the contention of some of the pamphleteers that the export of silver made paper money necessary ; but as a solution of the problem presented by the export of silver, which he recognized, he

[40] William Douglass : *A Discourse Concerning the Currencies of the British Plantations in America* (Boston, 1740). Reprinted in American Economic Association : *Economic Studies*, II (1897), 259–375, pp. 293–5.

[41] Ibid., II, 328–9.

[42] Ibid., II, 333.

could only advance the mercantilist argument of the favorable balance of trade : "no Country can want a true real Medium of Trade, while their Exports exceed their Imports : Let us then lessen our Imports by our Frugality, and add to our Exports by our Industry ; and we shall have no occasion for this *chimerical ill founded Medium, Paper Money.*" [43]

Douglass believed, too, that the best way to support government and its money was by taxation in hard money ; and, he said, "every Emission of Paper Credit Called Money, is laying a heavy Tax upon us." Nor is paper money necessary for the payment of debts : it is absurd to imagine that a Government finds Money for its People, it is the People who by their Trade and Industry, provide not only for their own Subsistence, but also for the Support of the Government, and to find their own *Tools* or *Medium* of Trade." [44] He was thus also definitely opposed to "priming the pump."

Douglass did not deny that the expansion of the colonial economy made an increase in the circulating medium necessary ; he only insisted that paper was no medium. There could be only one "true" medium for him, and that was silver. Silver, too, would be plentiful if the colonies would just establish a favorable balance of trade. As a matter of fact, Douglass was even willing to use a certain amount of paper, so long as it was adequately backed by silver. His anger and sarcasm were directed only at those who would more or less consciously print and force upon the public paper money that must inevitably decline in value because not guaranteed by any commodity of intrinsic worth. He saw quite clearly that easy money could be used by the debtor classes to defraud the creditors and that, in the long run, an uncontrolled flood of easy money was likely to be more detrimental than beneficial to colonial economic life.

The hard-money position was vindicated in Massachusetts with the provision for the retirement of the outstanding paper in 1749, and the passage by Parliament of the Colonial Currency Act in 1751 effectively prevented the New England colonies from issuing any more paper money. The interference of the mother country in the colonial money situation, notably in strangling the Massachusetts Land Bank in 1740, in the Colonial Currency Act of 1751, and in the extension of this act to all the colonies in 1764 favored the colonial hard-money party. But the majority of the Americans were not of this party. Whether or not paper money of any type was economically sound, the Americans, predominantly agrarian and predominantly debtors, were also predominantly in favor of it. Many of them learned caution in the manipulation of money and credit, but they still believed that paper money had

[43] Ibid., II, 340.   [44] Ibid., II, 342–3.

been and still was an important and extremely beneficial aid in the rapid and successful economic expansion of the colonies. As Franklin insisted, in 1764, the use of paper money in Pennsylvania had been successful, and of unmeasured benefit in the economic expansion of that colony. Pennsylvania's currency had remained relatively stable over a period of some forty years and had demonstrated in use its superiority as a medium of exchange even over gold and silver. He concluded that

> On the whole, no method has hitherto been formed to establish a medium of trade, in lieu of Money, equal, in all its advantages, to bills of credit, funded on sufficient taxes for discharging it, or on land security of double the value for repaying it at the end of the term, and in the meantime made a GENERAL LEGAL TENDER. The experience of now near half a century in the middle colonies, has convinced them of it among themselves, by the great increase of their settlements, numbers, buildings, improvements, agriculture, shipping, and commerce. And the same experience has satisfied the British merchants, who trade thither, that it has been greatly useful to them, and not in a single instance prejudicial.[45]

The careful use of paper money had been fully justified, in his opinion, by its results. A little later, Franklin collaborated with Governor Thomas Pownall of Massachusetts in the preparation of a plan for an all-American intercolonial currency, to be printed in England, which would avoid the difficulties attendant upon the great variety of currencies issued by the different colonies. Such a colonial currency would have been a long step in the direction of a colonial monetary union; but nothing came of the plan.

The discussion of money inevitably carried the colonial economists into the problem of value. Franklin, in 1729, had found labor to be the ultimate measure of value: "As Providence had so ordered it, that not only different countries, but even different parts of the same country, have their peculiar most suitable productions; and likewise that different men have geniuses adapted to a variety of different arts and manufactures: therefore *commerce*, or the exchange of one commodity or manufacture for another, is highly convenient and beneficial to mankind." But commodities cannot be exchanged directly; and, "to remedy such inconveniences, and facilitate exchange, men have invented MONEY, properly called a *medium of exchange*, because through or by its means labor is exchanged for labor, or one commodity for another." Gold and silver have long been used as this medium, and the value of all other commodities measured by them. "But as silver itself is of no certain permanent value, being worth more or less according

---

[45] "Remarks and Facts relative to the American Paper Money"; Franklin: *Works* (Sparks ed.), II, 354.

to its scarcity or plenty, therefore it seems requisite to fix upon something else, more proper to be made a *Measure of values,* and this I take to be *labor.*" [46]

Here Franklin states his version of the labor theory of value. He measures the value of silver, like everything else, in terms of labor; further, the price of silver, determined by the labor required to produce it, should be the same as that of a quantity of, say, wheat produced by the same amount of labor. He thus identifies value and price, and "the riches of a country are to be valued by the quantity of labor its inhabitants are able to purchase, and not by gold they possess." But wages go up or down according to the supply of money available; supply and demand enter into the matter; and Franklin returns to his belief that, while real value depends upon labor, prices and wages are affected by the supply of money, of which, for the maintenance of the optimum level of prices and wages, there should be an adequate but not excessive supply.

Franklin was almost alone among the colonials in his thoughtful consideration of value, prices, and wages. Jared Eliot touched upon it, vaguely identifying value, nominal and real, with wealth, nominal and real; nominal or artificial wealth being "those things which derive all, or the greatest Part of their Value, from Opinion, Custom, common Consent, or a Stamp of Authority, by which a Value is set; such as Silver, Gold, Pearls, precious Stones, Pictures, Bills of Credit. Some of these things have a Degree of intrinsick Value in them, but not in any Proportion to the Value to which they are raised by Custom of Consent. . . . But many things in high Esteem have no intrinsick Worth at all." On the other hand, "Natural or real Wealth are [such] things as supply the Necessities or Conveniences of Life: These are obtained from the Earth, or the Sun; such as Corn, Flesh, or Fish, Fruit, Food and Raiment." [47] Husbandry, the creator of real wealth, is thus also the creator of real, as distinguished from nominal, value. But Eliot went no farther in the direction of the theory of value.

William Douglass, also, apparently confused value with wealth: "All Commerce naturally is a *Truck Trade,* exchanging Commodities which we can spare (or their Value) for Goods we are in want of." [48] But Douglass, too, was confronting a condition of fact rather than theory, and his capacity for economic theory was hardly adequate to the task of solving the fundamental problem.

On this new and vital problem of a circulating medium for the ex-

[46] Franklin : *Works* (Sparks ed.), II, 263–5.
[47] Eliot : *Essays Upon Field Husbandry in New England,* pp. 98–99.
[48] Douglass : *A Discourse Concerning the Currencies of the British Plantations* . . . , loc. cit., II, 293.

panding colonial economy, then, the American mind was divided. The agrarians, in general, disagreed with the merchants; the easy-money thinkers stood against the hard-money school. Those who favored pub-lic-issue money stood against those who favored private-bank issue. These divisions rested squarely upon economic interests, real or im-agined, and reflected the divisions of American society and politics that were to persist for over a century. But a still greater significance lay in the fact that the paper-money problem pitted the American mind against the mind of England and those Americans, such as Thomas Hutchinson and William Douglass, who represented the English view-point here. America was essentially an area of easy-money thinking, and England was essentially hard-money: the determination of Eng-land to impose its monetary ideas upon the colonies in 1740, 1751, and 1764 contrary to the ideas derived from the Americans' own experience crystallized an ideological conflict that was a profound and important element in the growth of the mind of America toward the maturity that was some day to demand that it be master in its own house.

Labor, the Thrifty Virtues, and the Self-Made Man

Most of the first settlers in America had been working-men. In-deed, aside from the contributions of the middle-class Puritans who seized the leadership in New England and a few English aristocrats who came to Virginia and Maryland, it may safely be said that Amer-ica was built by laboring men. And as cities and farms were built by manual labor; as America became a people predominantly made up of small farmers, a respect for labor and the laborer became almost as deeply rooted in the American mind as the love of the soil itself. This attitude is reflected in the writings of Franklin, Crèvecœur, Eliot, and many others; but the respect for labor and the laboring man that char-acterized nearly all the Americans except the great plantation-owners of the south is perhaps best expressed by Philip Fithian, just on the eve of the Revolution:

> In New-Jersey Government throughout, but especially in the Counties where you have any personal acquaintance, Gentlemen in the first rank of Dignity & Quality, of the Council, general Assembly, inferior Magis-trates, Clergy-men, or Independent Gentlemen, without the smallest fear of bringing any manner of reproach either on their office, or their high-born, long recorded Families associate freely & commonly with Farmers & Mechanicks tho' they be poor & industrious. Ingenuity & in-dustry are the Strongest, & most approved recommendations to a Man in that Colony. . . . In our Government [colony], the laborious part of Men, who are commonly ranked in the midling or lower Class, are

accounted the strength & Honour of the Colony ; & the encouragement they receive from Gentlemen in the highest stations is the spring of Industry, next to their private advantage.[49]

Opportunity was great, and abundantly within the reach of any man who could exploit to his own profit a share in the expansion that was going on. Many a cabin-boy, by the easy, multiple turnovers of the triangular trades, rapidly became wealthy ; many a frontiersman, by a little shrewd buying and selling of land, made a fortune ; many a farmer, indeed, or journeyman, by catching hold of a small fragment of the universal expansion, achieved comfort and a competence. It was no accident that out of a rapidly expanding commerce, as out of a rapidly expanding frontier, the belief in self-help, the ideal of the self-made man, and the faith in progress should have embedded themselves in the minds of the Americans. These ideas sprang from the American's actual daily experience ; they were true and valid because the individual and social achievements, repeated over and over again, had proved them so.

Throughout Benjamin Franklin's writings there run the doctrines of thrift, industry, honesty, and individual initiative. *Poor Richard's Almanack* is full of wise sayings for the encouragement of these virtues, for Franklin was convinced that material comfort was basic to human happiness and spiritual freedom. In the *Almanack* for 1758 he compiled a discourse made up of these sayings, called "Father Abraham's Speech," which runs, in part, as follows : *"The Sleeping Fox catches no Poultry. . . . Sloth makes all things difficult, but Industry all things easy . . . and Early to Bed, and early to rise, makes a Man healthy, wealthy, and wise. . . . He that lives upon Hope will die fasting. . . . He that hath a Trade hath an Estate. . . . At the working Man's House Hunger looks in, but dares not enter . . . little Strokes fell great Oaks."* And so on.

But to industry is to be added frugality :

> *Many Estates are spent in the Getting.*
> *Since Women for Tea forsook Spinning and Knitting,*
> *And Men for Punch forsook Hewing and Splitting.*

"A small Leak will sink a great ship. . . . Fools make Feasts and wise Men eat them. . . . Silks and Satins, Scarlet and Velvets . . . put out the Kitchen Fire." And to frugality is added honesty : *"The second Vice is Lying, the first is running in Debt. . . . Lying rides upon Debt's Back. . . . But Poverty often deprives a Man of all spirit and*

[49] Philip Vickers Fithian : *Journal and Letters, 1767–1774,* edited by John R. Williams (Princeton, 1900), p. 285.

Virtue." Finally, "*Experience keeps a dear School, but Fools will learn in no other, and scarce in that.*" [50]

The appeal of this little statement was demonstrated by its widespread popularity. As Franklin says in his *Autobiography*:

> The piece, being universally approved, was copied in all the newspapers of the American Continent, reprinted in Britain on a large sheet of paper, to be stuck up in houses; two translations were made of it in France, and great numbers bought by the clergy and gentry, to distribute gratis among their poor parishioners and tenants. In Pennsylvania, as it discouraged useless expense in foreign superfluities, some thought it had its share of influence in producing that growing plenty of money, which was observable for several years after its publication.[51]

The mere fact of its universal popularity, indeed, is indicative that it expressed what great numbers of the people were thinking.

Here, embedded in this collection of homely proverbs, is an interpretation of ethics that is at least negatively materialistic. Franklin never went so far as to become a thorough materialist in his philosophy, either of economics or of ethics or of anything else, but his constant and profound preoccupation with the practical led him to see, perhaps more clearly than any other man of his time, the connection between the material, practical things of life and the more abstract world of ideas and ideals. In this, too, he was typically — perhaps more than typically — American. As he says, "I therefore filled all the little spaces [in my Almanack], that occurred between the remarkable days in the Calendar, with proverbial sentences, chiefly such as inculcated industry and frugality, as the means of procuring wealth, and thereby securing virtue; it being more difficult for a man in want to act always honestly, as, to use one of those proverbs, *it is hard for an empty bag to stand upright.*" [52]

It should always be remembered, however, that there was in the colonies a considerable number of people who reacted against the materialistic outlook expressed by Franklin; pious souls who placed spiritual welfare above material prosperity. Such a preacher of economic humility was John Woolman, of New Jersey.

Woolman was far from being an economist; he was a profoundly religious man, and all his thinking, whether economic or social, was of one heavily religious piece. Thus when he thought in terms of the material necessities of life, his ideas revolved around his conviction that the individual must practice humility and contentment with little, and

---

[50] *Poor Richard Improved* (1758), preface.
[51] Franklin: *Works* (Sparks ed.), I, 122–3.
[52] Ibid., II, 101.

resist the temptation to accumulate wealth. Hence, he says, "such Buildings, Furniture, Food, and Raiment, as best answer our Necessities, and are the least likely to feed that selfish Spirit which is our Enemy, are the most acceptable to us. In this State the Mind is tender, and inwardly watchful, that the Love of Gain draw us not into any Business which may weaken our Love to our Heavenly Father, or bring unnecessary Trouble to any of his Creatures." [53]

Yet if wealth accumulates as he saw it do, even among his Quaker contemporaries, it must be treated as a steward might treat a charge from God and be used for the benefit of men : "Wealth desired for its own sake Obstructs the increase of Virtue and large possessions in the hands of selfish men have a bad tendency, for by their means too small a number of people are employed in things useful, and therefore some of them are necessitated to labour too hard, while others would want [lack] business to earn their Bread, were not employments invented, which having no real use, serve only to please the vain mind." [54]

But Woolman is not merely a pious wisher for a more Christian distribution and administration of wealth. He has a practical solution, based upon what he calls the "right use of things," which looks curiously like a sort of Christian socialism :

> The Creator of the earth is the owner of it. He gave us being thereon, and our nature requires nourishment, which is the produce of it. As he is kind and merciful we, as his creatures, while we live answerable to the design of our creation, are so far Entitled to a convenient Subsistence, that no man may justly deprive us of it. . . .
>
> Were all superfluities, and the desire of outward greatness laid aside, and the right use of things universally attended to, such a number of people might be employed in things useful, as that moderate labour, with the Blessing of Heaven, would answer all good purposes relating to people and their Animals, and a Sufficient number have time to attend to proper Affairs of Civil Society. . . .
>
> Where men have great Estates, they stand in a place of Trust. To have it in their power, without difficulty, to live in that fashion which occasions much labour, and at the same time confine themselves to that use of things Prescribed by our Redeemer . . . for men possessed of great Estates to live thus, requires close attention to *Divine love*.
>
> Men of large estates, whose hearts are thus enlarged, are like Fathers to the poor, and in looking over their Brethren in distressed circumstances, and considering their own more easie condition, they find a Field for humble meditation, & feel the strength of those obligations they are under to be kind and tender-hearted toward them. Poor men eased of their burthens, and released from too close an application to

[53] Woolman : *Journal and Essays* (Gummere ed.), p. 393.
[54] "A Plea for the Poor," ibid., p. 402.

business, are at Liberty to hire others to their assistance, to provide well for their Animals, and find time to perform those duties amongst their Acquaintances, which belong to a well guided Social Life.[55]

Thus for Woolman all wealth belongs in the last analysis to God. Every man is entitled to a subsistence drawn from the earth's resources, and the conscientious wealthy man must see to it that his employees have it. Further, the proper administration of the earth's wealth will not only provide a subsistence for everybody, but will result in short hours of labor, occupations and labor suitable to the laborer, and sufficient leisure time to permit proper civic and religious activity.

But Woolman was less in step with the practical realism of America than Benjamin Franklin; for America was a materialistic country, in the sense that practically all the people were engaged in the pursuit of wealth, even Woolman's Quaker friends, and were in no mood to restrain themselves. On the contrary, it is probably safe to say that the vast majority of the people shared, to one degree or another, Franklin's conviction that material prosperity is an essential foundation of true virtue.

The American mind was thus not deeply divided on the basic questions relative to the economic life and ideals of the individual. For this was a hard-working, industrious, frugal people, building material wealth and a civilization where none had been before. Their experience indicated to them that civilization rested upon material wealth, and therefore, in the minds of most, the two things went together. Even in the mind of Woolman both the economic happiness and the spiritual welfare of the people depended upon "the right use of things," which was almost the same as saying an equitable distribution of wealth. But where Franklin placed the responsibility for the acquisition of wealth squarely upon the shoulders of the individual, working from the bottom upwards in a world of relatively free competition, Woolman depended much, and much too piously, perhaps, upon the Christian humanitarianism of the wealthy, working from above downward, for such a distribution of wealth as would guarantee a subsistence for all. Woolman may have been the more profound of the two in recognizing the lengths to which human greed unrestrained by religion or a sense of social responsibility would go in the direction of exploiting other human beings for gain, but Franklin was certainly more realistic — and more "American." Woolman is strongly reminiscent of the Puritans in his accent upon ethical responsibility in economic affairs; Franklin believes in much the same thrifty virtues, but both virtue and responsibility are for him desirable chiefly because they are useful, in the

[55] Ibid., pp. 403–5.

long run, rather than merely ethical, and because, in the long run they give the individual the greatest possible amount of freedom.

It is no wonder, American conditions being what they were, that the ideal of the self-made man should have become a sort of epitome of the various American virtues of industry, thrift, frugality, and intelligence. Franklin probably expressed the sentiment of nearly all the Americans of his day when he said: "I fear the giving mankind a dependence on any thing for support, in age or sickness, besides industry and frugality during youth and health, tends to flatter our natural indolence, to encourage idleness and prodigality, and thereby to promote and increase poverty, the very evil it was intended to cure; thus multiplying beggars instead of diminishing them." [56] Or to put it in the more positive and idealistic terms that Crèvecœur put in the mouth of America welcoming the immigrant: "If thou wilt work, I have bread for thee; if thou wilt be honest, sober, and industrious, I have greater rewards to confer on thee — ease and independence. . . . Go thou and work and till; thou shalt prosper, provided thou be just, grateful and industrious." [57] In other words, opportunity and freedom are provided for you; the responsibility for achieving the happiness that springs from the use of them is your own.

FRONTIER AND RADICAL RUGGED INDIVIDUALISM

The most important single factor in the development of the American mind of the eighteenth century was probably the frontier, a frontier of settlement that at the mid-century lay, from Maine to Georgia, along the foothills and the valleys of the broken Allegheny chain of mountains. The frontier, as an economic situation, was one that placed a great premium for success upon individual initiative, shrewdness, and vigor; and the people who settled the frontier were generally persons possessed of these qualities, often enough to a rough extreme; the very conditions of the frontier made it a hotbed of individualism, even of the type called "rugged."

The population of the frontier settlements was made up largely of Scotch-Irish and Germans. Of the Scotch-Irish in Pennsylvania James Logan wrote in 1724: "These bold and indigent strangers, saying as their excuse when challenged for titles that we had solicited for colonists and they had come accordingly," and asserting that "it was against the laws of God and nature that so much land should be idle while so many christians wanted it to work on and to raise their bread." [58]

[56] Franklin: *Works* (Sparks ed.), II, 368.
[57] Crèvecœur: *Letters from an American Farmer*, pp. 86–7.
[58] Quoted in Charles A. Hanna: *The Scotch-Irish* (2 vols., New York, 1902), II, 62–3.

These earlier immigrants from Ulster were aggressive to the point of ruthlessness, and intolerant to a degree; and they brought their aggressive individualism to the frontier, where it flourished among their sons in that congenial soil. They hated England and had no use for English economic regulations; and they showed little or no respect for the laws requiring them to pay quit-rents to an English proprietor; they paid only on compulsion.

The Germans, on the other hand, while hardly less fiercely attached to their land, were probably somewhat more docile, and settled in communities, which, however, probably placed only a little less emphasis upon the individual virtues than did the Scotch-Irish.

There is little or no explicit expression of economic thought from the frontier. Travelers agreed, however, that the economic outlook of the frontiersmen was one of rough, often unscrupulous, and aggressive individualism. Here the ideal of the self-made man was often best exemplified by those who were successful; but the success of these stood alongside the failure of those who were content to live in squalor. At the same time it must be remembered that the spirit of co-operation was strong among these men, and many a rugged individual owed a part, at least, of his prosperity to the co-operation of his neighbors in the raising of his house, the harvesting of his hay, and the husking of his corn. By and large, however, the economic life and ideology of the frontier was the ideal of rugged individualism writ large.

Conclusion: the Seeds of Economic Freedom

A review of the economic mind of the Americans of the mid-eighteenth century, while it reveals a considerable variety of ideas, even antagonisms, relative to superficial problems, presents a fairly unified body of thought as to the fundamental economic facts of life. This body of thought was basically agrarian in outlook, but its agrarianism was supplemented by a body of thought relative to commerce which, despite the persistence of petty provincial mercantilism and rivalries, was moving toward the doctrines of free trade. Needless to say, these trends in the American mind brought it into a position of antagonism vis-à-vis England and its mercantilist policies of interference in, and control of, colonial economic life. Furthermore, the more deeply rooted the American doctrines of economic freedom and independence from external control became, the more profound became the ideological rift between the colonies and the mother country.

Basic to the American economic outlook was the now ingrained conviction of economic individualism. From the acquisition of land in freehold to the oft-demonstrated practicability of the ideal of the self-made man in commerce and the satisfactions of life on the frontier, the experience of the Americans had taught them conclusively not only that economic individualism was the most satisfying sort of economic ideal, but also that it was practicable and worth fighting for. At the same time, the testing and proving of economic experience had made of the Americans a pragmatic people. Franklin, of course, was the most typical exponent of the American habit of testing everything, even ideas, by its results. At the same time, also, it should not be forgotten that the Americans of the eighteenth century had inherited a strong religious idealism, and economic thought was still strongly colored by this religious bent. Woolman, Franklin's neighbor and contemporary, is perhaps most eloquently expressive of this persistent ethical content in economic thought, but even Franklin felt it and preached it in the midst of his "Poor-Richardism." As Father Abraham said, "This Doctrine, my Friends, is *Reason* and *Wisdom*; but after all, do not depend too much on your own *Industry*, and *Frugality*, and *Prudence*, though excellent Things; for they May all be blasted without the Blessing of Heaven; and therefore ask that Blessing humbly, and be not uncharitable to those that at present seem to want it, but comfort and help them. Remember *Job* suffered and was afterwards prosperous." [59]

This American agrarian individualism, mixed with pragmatism and idealism, was moving toward a general ideal of economic freedom. Of course there were many exceptions, by region, by class, and by political group: the colonial "Tories," in particular, were willing to force their economic ideas into an accommodation with British mercantilism at the sacrifice of the native American ideal. But the Americans were probably the freest people in the world; the land and their experience had made and were making them free. It is no wonder that they should have believed in freedom. Both in agriculture and in commerce wealth was developing so rapidly that almost any young man who had a modicum of intelligence, industry, thrift, and frugality might achieve financial success. America, in those days, was full of self-made men who had started life as cabin-boy, indentured servant, or squatter in the wilderness. They had done it. They knew it could be done — by others as well as by themselves. And as the future of American expansion was limited only by a continent that for them had as yet no limit, their optimism, their faith in progress, was boundless. America was *ne plus ultra* the country of the self-made man nurtured in freedom.

If the common denominator in the American economic mind was the ideal of freedom, the common question was "freedom for whom, from whom?" The answer was generally freedom from English interference; though to the frontiersmen it might mean freedom from the

<hr>

[59] *Poor Richard Improved* (1758), preface.

merchant money-lenders of the cities; and for such victims of speculation and political exploitation as the Regulators of the Carolinas, it
might mean freedom from the voracious land-speculators of the tidewater. Generally speaking, it was England that was looked upon as
the great economic oppressor; it was from England that freedom must
be obtained. This was not, of course, a mood of revolution as yet; but
it was a mood of smoldering resentment; and the ideal of economic
freedom lay deep beneath the surface when the time came to demand
freedom — complete freedom — in all things, political and otherwise.

NOTE TO THE READER

Michel Gilliaume St. Jean de Crèvecœur was a French savant who lived
at Carlyle, Pennsylvania, for a number of years prior to the American Revolution. He observed life on the American frontier and described it, often in
sentimental terms; later on, he became somewhat disillusioned. His book,
however, *Letters from an American Farmer,* is one of the best contemporary descriptions of the more ideal apects of American life. It is available
in several editions, and is still extremely interesting reading.

Jared Eliot's *Essays upon Field Husbandry in New England* is another
highly interesting and entertaining book. It is now available in an attractive
edition edited by Harry J. Carman and Rexford G. Tugwell (New York,
1934). Similarly, *American Husbandry,* published anonymously on the eve
of the American Revolution, has been reprinted in a new edition edited by
Harry J. Carman (New York, 1939). It is probably the best description of
American agriculture written in the eighteenth century.

There is no good contemporary description of American commerce, unless Dr. Douglass's *Summary, Historical and Political,* be considered such.

John Woolman's *Journals and Essays,* have already been suggested in
connection with religion. The *Journal* is almost a classic, and the essays
printed with it in the edition made by Amelia M. Gummere are full of
Woolman's pietistic social and economic thought. Those essays, too, are
very well worth reading.

Of the secondary books, *History of the Domestic and Foreign Com-
merce of the United States* (2 vols., Washington, 1915), by Emory R. John-
son and others, is probably the best for the history of commerce, as Percy
W. Bidwell's and John I. Falconer's *History of Agriculture in the Northern
United States, 1620–1860* (New York, 1941), is the best for agriculture.
The first volume of Joseph Dorfman: *The Economic Mind in American
Civilization* (2 vols., New York, 1946), discusses the economic thought of
the eighteenth-century Americans.

CHAPTER V

Of Society and Social Freedom: Social Thought

NY human society is likely to be organized along lines that follow economic groupings; and social thought tends to follow, even to rationalize, economic interests. But the human motives that make for social organization are not solely economic. The biological nature of man as a bi-sexual animal doubtless lies close to the foundations of human society in its more primitive forms of family, phratry, clan, or tribe. Other impulses, also, such as the vaguely defined human gregariousness or the religious impulse to group worship, must be taken into consideration in any explanation of social institutions or social thought, quite apart from simple economic needs or impulses. Thus while most human societies have fairly clear-cut economic patterns, and those patterns tend to determine social groupings, it would be a mistake to say that economic interest, whether of the group or of the individual, is the sole determinant of social institutions or that ideas with regard to society are mere rationalizations of economic self-interest. Far from it. The thinking of the Americans, which at once expressed and justified what was probably the freest society of the world in the eighteenth century, was the product of a set of experiences that included much that was basically economic, to be sure; but much of American social thought also was drawn from religion, from common purposes of defense or education, or from the newly appeared Newtonian science and humanitarianism.

[228]

THE OLD WAY, IN EUROPE AND AMERICA

The society of the England out of which came the first settlers of America was that of the reign of Queen Elizabeth and the early Stuarts. This was a society of sharply differentiated social classes, each class resting upon its own economic base. The old medieval aristocracy, which derived its power and social prestige from its ownership of the land, was still strong; strong enough, in the time of the Great Rebellion, to resist for six years on the field of war the military power of the Puritan bourgeoisie and small farmers, and to restore Charles II when the inevitable reaction set in and Charles indicated a willingness to compromise with the merchants. The landed aristocracy was thus still the dominant element in English society, although the ultimate decisive power in the executive and political life of the country was fast slipping into the hands of the rival social class, the mercantile bourgeoisie. This rival class, with which the English aristocracy warred off and on for a century for the control of English life, only to surrender to it and form an alliance with it in the end, was made up of merchants and small businessmen, some of whom were also farmers near the towns, and many of whom were Puritans in religion. The English yeomanry, still an important element in English society, was generally overshadowed and dominated by the landed gentry, although there was a broad, almost unbridgeable social gulf between the two classes. In the rising cities, under the shadow of the merchant princes, the journeymen and servants constituted the lowest class of respectables, beneath which there were only the riffraff and the slaves.

It was a society that accepted the rigid stratification of social class as a matter of course and accepted the authority, the superiority, and the condescension of the wealthy upper classes without question. For among the people of the England under the early Stuarts, the philosophy of social inequality was so generally accepted that no one ever thought to challenge it. It is true that the members of the commercial class demanded and received a recognition of their social status, which they improved by marriage or the purchase of land and titles when they could; theirs was still a status, however, that left them in a rival position inferior to that of the older aristocracy.

This was the century of such thinkers on social questions as Francis Bacon, Robert Filmer, Jeremy Taylor, John Milton, and Thomas Hobbes, all of whom were flourishing in the decades during which North America was first being permanently settled. Later in the century Algernon Sidney, William Penn, and John Locke appeared, with a somewhat modified social and political outlook. All of these, with the possible exception of Locke, identified society with the state, and the state with government; it is therefore difficult to separate their social thinking from their political ideas — as is the case, indeed, with most men of that age, including the Americans. They were, in fact, more concerned with that new, modern phenomenon, the state, than they were with the structure of society. But in order to make reasonable their explanation of the state, they had to derive it from its social origins.

Thus Filmer, the darling of the English Tory aristocrats, justified the absolutism of the king in terms of what he fancied to have been the origin of kingship in the authority of the father over the primitive family. The tribe and the nation were for him only enlarged families, and in each there was a hierarchy of social status that went hand in hand with the hierarchy of political power. Far from being equal, for Filmer men were unequal by nature, and by nature incapable of surviving without the benevolent control and protection of their betters. Jeremy Taylor, likewise, Anglican minister and royalist, was inclined to accept stratified society as divinely ordained and the duty of the individual to obey authority as a natural part of the divine plan: "For a private spirit to oppose the public," he says, "is a disorder greater than is in hell itself."

But Filmer and Taylor hardly did more than describe what they saw. It was Thomas Hobbes who attempted to get to the root of the matter by examining the fundamental nature of society as it is derived from the nature of man himself. Hobbes was a much more powerful thinker than either of the others, and his great work on the state, *Leviathan*, is a classic. Hobbes, too, recognized the absolutism of the state, but based his argument, not on the will of God, but on the bestial nature of man. It is man's selfish, cruel, ruthless nature, according to Hobbes, that forces him, in sheer self-defense, to form a society to which he surrenders both freedom and equality; once in it, however, once having accepted the social compact, he must submit to the social will without question; indeed, without recourse or escape.

Sidney and Harrington were relatively republican in their political outlook; Sidney attempted to refute Filmer, and Harrington, in his hostility to Hobbes, ignored the idea of the social compact. By the time when William Penn began to formulate his ideas and John Locke wrote his apologetics for the Whig revolution, the idea of the depravity of man had given place to the idea of human benevolence and natural rights. These men accepted the idea of the formation of society by compact, but it was a compact that was not so much an outright surrender of natural freedom as a positive mechanism involving the delegation of individual and group sovereignty to promote human welfare.

Yet all these men were aristocrats in their social outlook; all, in one way or another, accepted the stratified society. Filmer was the extreme divine-right Tory; the Whig Locke admitted the propertied middle class to a place in the social sun. But all accepted sharp divisions of social class and status and failed to allow even for a fluid social movement, much less for social equality. Even John Milton, the Puritans' own poet philosopher, would have provided more intellectual and ethical and religious freedom, but only for the elect, the chosen of God — never for what he called the "rabble."

These were the vaguely defined ideas of society that were current in the England of the first American settlements. It is no wonder that the first-comers should have brought them to America. It is even symbolic of this transportation of ideas that John Winthrop, doughty Puritan Governor of Massachusetts Bay, should have written on shipboard enroute to America his famous *Modell of Christian Charity*, in which he claims divine sanction for social inequality in the following terms: "God Almightie in his most holy and wise providence hath soe disposed of the Condicion of mankinde, as in all times some must be rich some poore, some highe and emminent in power and dignitie; others meane and in subieceion."[1] And William Hubbard, born in England but a member of the first class to graduate from Harvard, expressed the same idea to his people, a generation after Winthrop, in more elaborate language:

In the firmament of the air, may we not see the lofty eagle in his flight far surmounting the little choristers of the valleys? . . . And hath not the same Almighty Creator and disposer of all things made some of the sons of men as far differing in height of body one from the other, as Saul from the rest of the people. . . . It is not then the result of time or chance, that some are mounted on horseback, while others are left to travell on foot. That some have with the Centurion power to command, while others are required to obey, *the poor and the rich meet together, the Lord is the maker of them both.* The Almighty hath appointed her that sits behind the mill, as well as him that ruleth the throne. . . . The fearful and the weak might be destroyed, if others more strong and valiant, did not protect and defend them. The poor and needy might starve with hunger and cold, were they not fed with the morsells, and warmed with the fleece of the wealthy. Is it not proved by experience, that the greatest part of mankind, are but as tools and Instruments for others to work by, rather than any proper Agents to effect any thing of themselves: In peace how would most people destroy themselves by slothfulness and security? In war they would be destroyed by others, were it not for the wisdome and courage of the Valliant. . . . Nothing therefore can be imagined more remote either

[1] Miller and Johnson: *The Puritans*, p. 195.

from right reason, or true religion, than to think that because we were all once equal at our birth, and shall be again at our death, therefore we should be so in the whole course of our lives.[2]

No ; the organized, stratified society was not only right and proper · it was ordained by God. It was even necessary to the survival of mankind ; to challenge it would be to challenge God's plan for the protection and the happiness of his people.

Cotton Mather was still preaching the same idea at the turn of the century :

> If a man cannot keep out of a *Low and Mean Condition*, without a plain *wrong to the Estates of other Men*, he is then most Evidently called of GOD into a *Low and Mean Condition*. . . . Thy *Straits* are what the Glorious God has ordered for thee. . . . If God confine a Man unto a *Low and Mean Condition*, the Man should Labour for a sweet *Contentment* with his *Low and Mean Condition*. . . . Let a Man get a *Spirit* suited unto his Condition. . . . Let him cheerfully entertain the Opportunities which his being *made Low*, and falling into Decay, gives him to express his Patience, his Humility, his Resignation, and Glorify God.[3]

These people accepted the fixed, stratified society ; let a man be content with the social status that God had given him, and not expect much change : such presumption would be a manifestation of sinful pride, which would be all too likely to precede the well-known fall, both in the eyes of God and in those of one's neighbors. A few there were who did it, of course, and successfully defied the admonitions of their parsons to accept their low status contentedly ; but these were the as yet scattered pioneers of American social fluidity. For a century and more New England clung to its faith in a divinely planned society of fixed classes, ruled over by a sort of Puritan aristocracy.

This was not an English landed aristocracy, however : it was a new, mercantile aristocracy produced in New England by the conditions of New England economic and social life. From lower-middle-class clerks, lawyers, and parsons, the Puritan leaders and their descendants, augmented by the self-made men who had not been content to accept nonentity in a stratified society, had become a New England aristocracy, as different from the aristocracy of England as they were from their aristocratic cousins in the tobacco- and rice-raising plantation areas of the south. They held to the old ideas of the stratified society ; but they applied them to a society that was new.

---

[2] Ibid., pp. 248–9.
[3] Cotton Mather : *Fair Dealing between Debtor and Creditor* (Boston, 1716), pp. 13, 14.

Meanwhile, to the southward in Virginia, there was appearing an aristocratic society of a different sort. For from a society of yeomen farmers in the middle of the seventeenth century Virginia had become, by the end of that century, a quasi-feudal, aristocratic society based upon Negro slavery. The yeomen, to be sure, had brought their ideas about society from England, and they paid great respect to their own burgeoning aristocracy as it emerged, just because they did not question its legitimacy. The new Virginia aristocrats aped the landed nobility of England; and their thinking, at this early moment in their development, was copied after that of the Tory aristocrats and country gentlemen of the old country. This Chesapeake aristocracy was not imported, either, but arose in America out of the conditions of the Maryland and Virginia tidewater areas; similarly, the aristocracy of South Carolina as it developed was a product of local conditions. It was no accident, therefore, that the southern aristocracies should have developed an outlook on life that rationalized and justified their social institutions and their own social status.

These Virginia, Maryland, and South Carolina "gentlemen" made a conscious effort to pattern their civilization after that of the landed gentry in England, and borrowed many of their ideas from it. But there were a number of elements in their thinking that differentiated their way from the English, and even revealed certain deep ideological antagonisms to it. At the same time, too, the growth of New York as a commercial center, coupled with the policy of giving away great landed estates along the Hudson River, had resulted in the appearance of an aristocracy there. The thinking of the New York aristocracy was quite comparable to that of Boston or Charleston, with local variations.

The development of American society in the seventeenth century, then, was marked by the acceptance of an old set of ideas, imported from England, and the effort everywhere to force the new American society, as it developed, into the framework of those aristocratic ideals. In some instances, as in New England, this was successful, or, as in Virginia, more than successful. By and large it was a set of social ideas and ideals that would have fixed an imitation of the caste system upon American society and would have formulated a set or sets of ideas to rationalize it. And to a considerable degree it succeeded and took root among the new American aristocracies of north, middle, and south. Yet the ideal of a fixed, inflexible aristocratic society was not congenial to America; and the same conditions that made possible so much individualism in economic life encouraged the sort of social movement that made an American aristocratic caste system impossible to maintain.

THE AMERICAN WAY

The outlook of the first-comers to America with regard to the nature and the structure of society was thus the outlook of an age that, despite the social ferment going on in Europe, still believed in a static, stratified society and attributed the existing order of things either to the plan of God or to some sort of social compact formed by our primitive ancestors while still in a "natural" state. But the social ideology that was brought to America in the seventeenth century had to contend with the corrosive influence of the frontier; and the phenomenal expansion of commerce in the colonies created, almost daily, new rich men to challenge the vested social interests of the first order of bourgeois aristocrats of the north, while the ranks of the southern aristocracy were steadily augmented by the men who were clever enough, by land-speculation or by careful business methods, to build up for themselves the wealth in land that was the key to the highest social status. But that was not all: the influx, early in the eighteenth century, of a vast horde of continental Europeans who were hungry for land and better social status added a still more powerful leaven of social change to the influence of agricultural and commercial expansion. Finally, the advent of science and humanitarianism, with the ideas of the natural man with inalienable natural rights, the worth of the individual, and the rational prospect of human progress, brought with it a complex of intellectual and emotional experiences that made a modification — even democratization — of the American social mind almost inevitable.

Yet the ideals of aristocratic society had taken root in the older parts of America and flourished. In the eighteenth century, despite the fact that the truly American ideal of social fluidity had begun to mark the social mind of the vast majority of Americans from Maine to Georgia, the aristocratic outlook on life was already firmly entrenched among the landed gentry in all the colonies, as also among the wealthy older families of the commercial cities of the seaboard. The aristocratic ideology of the landed gentry rested upon wealth derived from the land and human slavery; the aristocratic mood of the merchants rested upon wealth derived from trade. The aristocratic ideal, as historical fate would have it, did not turn out to express the true social genius of America. But if that genius lay in the fluidity derived from an unlimited amount of free land and the melting-pot, it had to struggle desperately against the retarding influence of a native American aristocracy and its ideals — ideas that made up a large and significant part of the eighteenth-century American social mind.

Aristocracy of the land, and its concomitant, slavery

By the middle of the eighteenth century, then, America had its own landed aristocracy. This landed class shared the control of society in New England and the middle colonies with the merchant aristocracy of the cities, with which, indeed, it was closely identified. In the southern colonies the landed aristocrats were the unchallenged rulers of society. Social classes were sharply differentiated everywhere. The divisions in agrarian society in New England were described, just before the American Revolution, by the author of *American Husbandry*:

> The most ancient settled parts of the province New England . . . contain many considerable land estates, upon which the owners live much in the style of country gentlemen in England. . . . Here therefore we see a sketch of one class of people that has a minute resemblance to the gentlemen in England who live upon their own estates, but they have in some respects a great superiority : they have more liberty in many instances, and are quite exempt from the overbearing influence of any neighbouring nobleman, which in England is very mischievous to many gentlemen of small fortunes.[4]

In other words, the New England aristocracy was not burdened with the complicated ties of feudalism that remained in England. Their taxes were low, and they paid no tithes or "rates" for the support of the poor.

> The next class of the country inhabitants of which I am to describe is the farmers. . . . These countrymen in general are a very happy people ; they enjoy many of the necessaries of life on their own farms, and what they do not so gain, they have from the sale of their surplus products. . . . These freeholders of small tracts of land which compose the greatest part of the province, have, almost to a point, the necessaries of life and nothing more, speaking however according to our ideas of life in Europe.[5]

As to the third social class :

> Respecting the lower classes in New England, there is scarcely any part of the world in which they are better off. The price of labour is very high, and they have with this advantage another no less valuable of being able to take up a tract of land whenever they are able to settle it.[6]

This state of affairs made the workers very industrious, and beggars practically nonexistent. For industry and diligence practically any worker could look forward to the sure reward of improved economic

[4] *American Husbandry*, pp. 46–7.
[5] Ibid., pp. 49–50.
[6] Ibid., p. 52.

and social status that would come to him from ownership of his own land.

The most important point in all this is the fact that the stratification of society into three classes "gentlemen," "farmers," and "lower classes," was accepted by everybody as a matter of course. The aspect that made it characteristically "American" was the fact that it was so much easier here than in England to pass from one class into another, from a lower into a higher. And while the author of *American Husbandry* was chiefly concerned with life on the land, it may also be said that this characteristic was just as marked among the mercantile classes of the towns, "gentleman" or "mister" (merchant), "goodman" (small shopkeeper), and "Jones" or "Smith" (worker), as among the agrarian classes here described.

In the southern colonies the aristocracy was made up of the great plantation-owners; for the rest, the Negro slaves constituted the lowest stratum of society, separated from their white masters by an impassable gulf; while in the foothills and valleys of the Allegheny highlands to the westward there had appeared a society of small farmers made up of thrifty, industrious Germans and adventurous Irishmen who generally opposed slavery and stood, in their own social status, in the position of a sort of middle class below the level of the tidewater aristocracy.

The landed gentry of the south, though it took many of its ideas from England, was native to America and arose out of American conditions. For where large grants of land had been made to private individuals, those individuals were placed in a position to exploit the great influx of immigrants, white and black, and, either by a system of rentals or sale of land at high prices with long-term payments or by the mechanisms of slavery, to become wealthy at the expense of those who actually developed the land. This was a new and fluid situation created by the new land; and the formation, out of these new landowners, of a new and powerful American aristocracy was a consequence of the new situation.

This class took shape first in Virginia, where it was already, in the last quarter of the seventeenth century, developing a self-consciousness like that of William Fitzhugh, who panted after the outward and visible manifestations of the quality:

> I thank God I am plentifully supplied with servants of all conditions to serve me in all my occasions, therefore would not have you put yourself to the charge or trouble of procuring or sending me any in, well knowing it lies out of the course of your business and concerns. But again, as I said last year, I should be heartily glad of your picture and our coat-of-arms fairly and rightfully drawn, not as on the steel seal that

came here, if you cannot find any advantageous opportunity of shewing me the original. . . . We live here very plentifully without money, and now tobacco is low I shall be very hard put to it to purchase £ 10 for to supply our mother.[7]

During the eighteenth century this "first social order" grew in wealth, power, and self-satisfaction. Philip Fithian, tutor in the family

Williamsburg, capital of the Virginia aristocracy. The "Bodleian Plate."

[By courtesy of the Library of Congress]

of Robert Carter of Nomini Hall, describes their social attitude, and the relation of social attitude to wealth, as follows: "The very Slaves in some families here, could not be bought under 30000 £. Such amazing property, no matter how deep it is involved, blows up the owners to an imagination, which is visible in all, but in various degrees according to their respective virtue, that they are exalted as much above other Men in worth & precedency, as blind stupid fortune has made a difference in their property; excepting always the value they put upon posts of honour, & mental acquirements."[8]

But aristocratic thinking was more explicit than that, for there was

[7] Quoted in Louis B. Wright: *The First Gentlemen of Virginia* (San Marino, 1940), p. 60.

[8] Fithian: *Journal*, pp. 286–7.

an actual social theory of aristocracy, in all the colonies. Jonathan Boucher, for years a tutor in tidewater Virginia and later Anglican rector in Annapolis, Maryland, put the aristocratic philosophy of society into formal terms in a sermon he preached to his congregation just before fleeing from Annapolis on the eve of the Revolution:

> This popular notion, that government was originally formed by the consent or by a compact of the people, rests on, and is supported by, another similar notion, not less popular, nor better founded. This other notion is, that the whole human race is born equal; and that no man is naturally inferior, or, in any respect, subjected to another; and that he can be made subject to another only by his own consent. . . . In hardly any sense that can be imagined is the position strictly true. . . . Man differs from man in every thing that can be supposed to lead to supremacy and subjection, *as one star differs from another star in glory.* It was the purpose of the Creator, that man should be social: but, without government, there can be no society; nor, without some relative inferiority and superiority, can there be any government. A musical instrument composed of chords, keys, or pipes, all perfectly equal in size and power, might as well be expected to produce harmony, as a society composed of members all perfectly equal to be productive of order and peace. . . .
>
> Any attempt, therefore, to introduce this fantastic system into practice, would reduce the whole business of social life to the wearisome, confused, and useless task of mankind's first expressing, and then withdrawing, their consent to an endless succession of schemes of government.[9]

This belief in the inequality of man was typical of the aristocrats, almost wherever found. Since they believed in the inequality of men, and since their experience in life seemed to demonstrate it, they found it easy to believe in slavery. Black men were inferior to whites in the natural order of things, they thought; and they took Negro slavery and their own position of superiority as a matter of course. Slavery, indeed, they believed actually to be beneficial to the Negroes who were brought by it out of savagery into civilization: "Their Work . . . is not very laborious; their greatest Hardship consisting in that they and their Posterity are not at their own Liberty or Disposal, but are the Property of their Owners; and when they are free, they know not how to provide so well for themselves generally; neither did they live so plentifully nor (many of them) so easily in their own Country, where they are made slaves to one another, or taken captive by their Enemies."[10]

[9] Jonathan Boucher: *A View of the Causes and Consequences of the American Revolution* (London, 1797), pp. 514–16.
[10] Hugh Jones: *The Present State of Virginia* (London, 1724), p. 37.

The Negroes — their owners claimed — were treated well; if not out of kindness, at least because it was good business. As Richard Cashin instructed his plantation manager in 1759 :

> The care of negroes is the first thing to be recommended that you give me timely notice of their wants that may be provided all Necessarys : The breeding Wenches more particularly you must Instruct the Overseers to be Kind and Indulgent to, and not force them when with Child upon any service or hardship that will be injurious to them & that they have every necessary when in that condition that is needful for them, and the children to be well looked after and to give them every Spring & Fall the Jerusalem Oak seed for a week together & that none of them suffer in time of sickness for want of proper care.[11]

And Boucher, again, was able to rationalize the system to his own satisfaction :

> The condition of the lower classes of mankind everywhere, when compared with that of those above them, may seem hard; yet on a fair investigation, it will probably be found that people in general in a low sphere are not less happy than those in higher sphere. I am equally well persuaded in my own mind that the negroes in general in Virginia and Maryland in my time were not upon the whole worse off nor less happy than the labouring poor in Great Britain. . . . As for the abstract question of the right that one part of mankind have to make slaves of another . . . suffice it to say that I think the discussion of it of less moment to the interests of mankind in general than is commonly imagined. Slavery is not one of the most intolerable evils incident to humanity, even to slaves.[12]

There were some, indeed, who went so far as to attribute the importation of Negro slaves into America to the direct will of God. For, after all, were they not in Africa in a condition of darkness, ignorance, superstition, and slavery to one another ? And might it not be reasoned, as one author wrote for the *American Magazine,* that "for their deliverance from this wretched condition, God . . . made them and their expediency known to the enterprizing *Europeans,* when their assistance was requisite for clearing and tending the *American* uncultivated wilderness ; for which end they are inspired with a spirit of captivating and selling, instead of killing those that fall into the power of their *Headmen* amongst them; to be purchased and transported by the means or permission of the African company established in London." [13]

[11] *Documentary History of American Industrial Society,* I, 110.

[12] Jonathan Boucher : *Reminiscences of an American Loyalist* (Boston, 1925), pp. 97–8.

[13] [William Smith ?] : "History of the War," *American Magazine,* I, No. 7 (April 1758), p. 401.

There were many Americans, however, who for sociological or humanitarian reasons saw the anachronistic character of slavery, and some of these were to be found even among the aristocrats. Henry Laurens of Charleston, though in his lifetime he bought and sold thousands of Negroes, hated the institution, chiefly on religious grounds, as he said in a famous letter to his son at the beginning of the Revolution :

> You know, my dear son, I abhor slavery. I was born in a country where slavery had been established by British kings and parliaments, as well as by the laws of that country ages before my existence. I found the Christian religion and slavery growing under the same authority and cultivation. I nevertheless disliked it. In former days there was no combating the prejudices of men supported by interest ; the day I hope is approaching when, from principles of gratitude as well as justice, every man will strive to be foremost in showing his readiness to comply with the golden rule. . . . I am devising means of manumitting many of [my slaves], and for cutting off the entail of slavery.[14]

Thomas Jefferson, also, saw the evils of slavery and its influence upon the society in which he lived. He, too, thought he saw reason to hope for a better day :

> There must doubtless be an unhappy influence on the manners of our people produced by the existence of slavery among us. The whole commerce between master and slave is a perpetual exercise of the most boisterous passions, the most unremitting despotism on the one part, and degrading submissions on the other. Our children see this, and learn to imitate it ; for man is an imitative animal. . . . And with what execrations should the statesman be loaded, who permitting one half the citizens thus to trample on the rights of the other, transforms those into despots, and these into enemies, destroys the morals of the one part, and the amor patriæ of the other. . . . With the morals of the people, their industry also is destroyed. For in a warm climate, no man will labour for himself who can make another labour for him. This is so true, that of the proprietors of slaves a very small proportion indeed are ever seen to labour. I think a change already perceptible since the origin of the present revolution. The spirit of the master is abating, that of the slave rising from the dust, his condition mollifying, the way I hope preparing, under the auspices of heaven, for a total emancipation, and that this is disposed, in the order of events, to be with the consent of the masters, rather than by their exterpation.[15]

[14] Henry Laurens : *Correspondence of Henry Laurens, of South Carolina,* edited by Frank Moore (New York, 1861), pp. 20–1.

[15] Thomas Jefferson : *Notes on the State of Virginia* (n. p., 1782), pp. 298–300.

But Laurens and Jefferson were not representative of their class. They were, indeed, members of a new generation of republican-minded patriots who were moved by the emotions of a war for human freedom. Their ideas were the climactic outburst of long years of development among a few generous-minded aristocrats; it did not, certainly, represent the mind of the vast majority of the great slave-owners of the mid-century. On the contrary, those men believed in the inequality of men, even among the whites; their belief in slavery was taken for granted and without discussion. It was only such northern social radicals as Franklin and Woolman who ventured even to discuss that great social institution, much less to criticize it. Social inequality was entrenched in the institutions and in the minds of the American aristocracy. To them the system seemed in accord with the laws of nature; and slavery was a part of the system.

Aristocracy in the towns

If the amassing of wealth in the form of land and its products had resulted in the appearance in the rural areas of the colonies of a landed gentry with distinct and clear-cut ideas of social superiority, the accumulation of wealth in the counting-houses of the merchants in the seaboard cities had become the foundation upon which had risen an aristocracy of merchants with a corresponding idea of their own social quality and superiority over the common man.

In Boston, "where the Lowells talk to the Cabots, and the Cabots talk only to God," as in all the New England coast-line cities, the lines of social cleavage were clearly and firmly drawn. Those merchant families which had acquired wealth early had assumed the prerogatives of high social place and, starting from the principles laid down by the Puritan fathers, had developed a set of ideas that naturally justified their own position and power. The principles of a stratified society were very congenial to them, and they put those principles to practical use. John Quincy Adams wrote of the education of his famous father, then at Harvard, that "The distinction or ranks was observed with such punctilious nicety, that, in the arrangement of the members of every class, precedence was assigned to every individual according to the dignity of his birth, or to the rank of his parents. John Adams was thus placed the fourteenth in a class of twenty-four, a station for which he was probably indebted rather to the standing of his maternal family than to that of his father."[16]

In church, too, the belief in rigid class distinctions was still applied. Colchester, Connecticut, for example, copying the practice of the large

[16] John Adams : *The Works of John Adams,* edited by Charles Francis Adams (10 vols., Boston, 1856), I, 14.

towns, voted the pew closest to the pulpit "to be first in dignety, the next behind it to be 2ᵈ in dignety & the foremost of the long seats to be third in Dignety," and humble Richard Hazzen, of Haverhill, Massachusetts, was embarrassed because he had "no place to sit but upon courtesy of Mr. Eastman or crowding into some foreseat too honorable for me"; [17] so he was allowed to build a pew for himself at a properly humble spot in the church.

The mind of the merchant "gentleman," with its assumption of social superiority over the "inferior sort," was seldom explicitly stated. It was a mood, an assumption, taken for granted and accepted by everybody, although murmurings of discontent at the sharpness of social divisions were beginning to be heard from the new working classes in all the seaboard cities. The stratification of society was clear, in the cities as well as in the plantation areas. Cadwallader Colden's description of New York society was probably both accurate and typical, although it should be remembered that landed aristocracy and merchant aristocracy were more closely blended in New York and Charleston, say, than they were in the more purely plantation type of society in Maryland and Virginia :

> The People of New York are properly Distinguished into different Ranks.
>
> 1st. The Proprietors of the large Tracts of Land, who include within their claims from 100,000 acres to above one Million of acres under one grant. . . .
>
> 2nd. The Gentlemen of the Law make the second class in which properly are included both the Bench and the Bar. Both of them act on the same Principles, and are of the most distinguished Rank in the Policy of the Province.
>
> 3rd. The merchants make the third class. Many of them have rose suddenly from the lowest Rank of the People to considerable Fortunes, & chiefly by illicit Trade in the last War. They abhor every limitation of Trade and Duty on it, & therefore gladly go into every Measure whereby they hope to have Trade free.
>
> 4thly. In the last Rank may be placed the Farmers and Mechanics. Tho' the Farmers hold their Lands in fee simple, they are as to condition of Life in no way superior to the common Farmers in England ; and the Mechanics such only as are necessary in Domestic Life.[18]

Colden's information should have been accurate, since he was in intimate personal contact with the situation he described ; the greatest significance in his description of New York society, however, probably

[17] Quoted in William B. Weeden : *Economic and Social History of New England, 1620–1789* (2 vols., Boston, 1890), II, 529.

[18] Cadwallader Colden : *Colden Letter-Books* (*Collections of the New York Historical Society*, Publication Fund Series, Vols. IX–X), II, 68.

lies in the clear light it throws both upon the attitude of the Tory aristocrat toward the upstart merchants, and upon the close relationship that existed between economic and social status and economic and social thought. The same thing may be said of political thought, too ; for it was these same upstart merchants, associated with some of the "gentlemen of the law," who were making so much trouble for Colden and the royal officers generally in the name of provincial-assembly autonomy and freedom from English restraints upon colonial trade.

As for slavery, most of the merchant aristocrats had slaves and took the institution for granted. While there was some humanitarian agitation against slavery by such Quaker radicals as John Woolman, most of the mercantile gentry agreed with the writer who quoted the book of Genesis to show that white men have divine sanction for their dominion over black men. Negroes, wrote this one, are not even of the same species as white men ; and "who will not allow that God formed them with horses, oxen, dogs, &c for the benefit of white people alone . . . to labor with their other beasts in the culture of tobacco, indigo, rice, and sugar ?" [19]

Urban aristocracy tended to merge with the aristocracy of landed wealth. Generally, as soon as a merchant had amassed a sufficient fortune in trade, he bought lands and a country house and became a country "gentleman." Naturally enough, his ideas on society, when he had any, tended to follow the line of thought that was typical of the established landed gentry.

Immigrant, farm, and frontier

The most typical aspect of American society, however, was its fluidity ; and, as a result, the sort of social thought most typical of the American mind was a set of ideas and sentiments that justified — even glorified — that fluidity. The germ of this idea was to be found among the immigrants and the small farmers, and on the frontier. For it was in these social areas that the forces of the melting-pot and the leveling effects of free land were most powerfully at work.

Out on the fringes of settlement, where men were building homes in the forest with their own hands and protecting them by their own bravery and cunning, the responsibility for survival rested upon the individual himself. A premium was placed upon individual strength, individual courage, individual inventiveness, individual initiative. A man had no "calling" ; or he had all of them. On the frontier a new sort of social individualism was born ; and with it was born a new sort of individual equality and a new sort of individual freedom. And the new ideal came to be not one of status, but one of change, improvement,

[19] *Pennsylvania Packet,* November 3, 1773.

progress, agrarian economic freedom, and social contentment made possible by the ownership and cultivation of the land.

With the frontier there was combined another profoundly significant factor in the process of differentiating American society and social thought from that of the mother country. That new element was the enormous influence of non-English immigrants that flowed into the colonies in the first half of the eighteenth century, among whom were hundreds of thousands of Germans, Scotch-Irishmen, Frenchmen, and Jews. These "foreigners" brought with them, of course, a heritage of social thought and institutions that derived from their homelands, and these non-English ideals were poured into the crucible of the American social mind to color it and flavor it in non-English ways. The result was an amalgam in which were fused three major influences : the English inheritance, the "foreign" addition, and the social tendencies of the frontier.

The mere fact of being immigrants, settled in more or less homogeneous groups along the frontier, exercised a powerful influence upon the social thinking of this portion of the Americans. For the feeling of the immigrants was a mixture of relief at having escaped the dangers and humiliations of Europe, a determination to get on in the world, a sometimes exultant optimism, and a faith, which grew with every success, in the boundless future of the society with which they had cast in their lot. Some of them were disillusioned in America, to be sure, and were bitterly disappointed with the life they found here; others, lacking the energy and the persistence necessary for success, degenerated when they got outside the pale of social control. But by and large the immigrants' experiences and their successes made of them a simple, industrious, and forward-looking people, with a great faith in themselves and in the country.

This was particularly true of the Germans. The Reverend Andrew Burnaby, traveling on the frontier along the Shenandoah River in 1759, described them thus :

I could not but reflect with pleasure on the situation of these people ; and think if there is such a thing as happiness in this life, that they enjoy it. Far from the bustle of the world, they live in the most delightful climate, and richest soil imaginable ; they are everywhere surrounded with beautiful prospects and sylvan scenes ; lofty mountains, transparent streams, falls of water, rich valleys, and majestic woods ; the whole interspersed with an infinite variety of flowering shrubs, constitute the landscape surrounding them : they are subject to few diseases ; are generally robust ; and live in perfect liberty : they are ignorant of want, and acquainted with but few vices. Their inexperience of the elegancies of life precludes any regret that they possess not the means of enjoying them : but they possess what many princes would give half their dominions for, health, content, and tranquillity of mind.[20]

They possessed much more than tranquillity of mind, however, for they had brought their individualistic religions to America with them, and their music ; and they created a literature of their own. All of which they contributed to the growing mind of America.

The immigrant in American society : "A View of Bethle[he]m, the Great Moravian Settlement in the Province of Pennsylvania."
[From *Scenographia Americana*]

Literally hundreds of thousands of poor immigrants, indentured servants, criminals, and artisans, in a total population of about a million and a half, had come to America from the non-English parts of Europe to get a new economic start in life. They had improved their social status, many of them, far above what it could have been in Europe, because they had acquired and improved land of their own. Here, again, Crèvecœur, in his description of the American, expresses in somewhat romantically overdrawn terms the ideal of the social status of the immigrant farmer :

Whence came all these people ? They are a mixture of English, Scotch, Irish, French, Dutch, Germans, and Swedes. From this promiscuous breed, that race now called Americans have arisen. . . .

[20] Andrew Burnaby : *Burnaby's Travels through North America*, edited by Rufus R. Wilson (New York, 1904), pp. 73–4.

In this great American asylum, the poor of Europe have by some means met together, and in consequence of various causes. . . . Every thing has tended to regenerate them ; new laws, a new mode of living, a new social system ; here they are become men. . . .

I could point out to you a family whose grandfather was an Englishman, whose wife was Dutch, whose son married a French woman, and whose present four sons have now four wives of different nations. . . . The Americans were once scattered all over Europe ; here they are incorporated into one of the finest systems of population which has ever appeared, and which will hereafter become distinct by the power of the different climates they inhabit. The American ought therefore to love this country much better than that wherein either he or his forefathers were born. Here the rewards of his industry follow with equal steps the progress of his labour; his labour is founded on the basis of nature, *self-interest;* Can it want a stronger allurement? Wives and children, who before in vain demanded of him a morsel of bread, now, fat and frolicsome, gladly help their father to clear those fields whence exuberant crops are to arise to feed and to clothe them all ; without any part being claimed, either by a despotic prince, a rich abbot, or a mighty lord.[21]

Crèvecœur saw, and recognized, the process of the American melting-pot and its social significance. He recognized, too, the mixture of factors that were working together to produce a new and freer society. And he was deeply moved by what he saw. Not all Americans shared his idealism and his enthusiasm, for the elements in the melting-pot were not immediately fused, and there was some friction between them before the fusion took place. The English old-timers, somewhat naturally, resented the newcomers, and there developed a certain "nativism" among them that was probably the first thing of its kind in American history. Thus the Reverend William Smith, in his description of Pennsylvania, written in 1755, not only expressed resentment against the Germans in that province but saw them as an actual international menace :

And, indeed, it is clear that the *French* have turned their Hopes upon this great Body of Germans. They have now got Possession of the vast and exceedingly fruitful Country upon the *Ohio,* just behind our *German* Settlements. They know our *Germans* are extremely ignorant, and think a large Farm the greatest Blessing in Life. Therefore, by sending their *Jesuitical* Emissaries among them, to persuade them over to the *Popish* Religion, they will draw them from the *English,* in Multitudes, or perhaps lead them in a Body against us. This is plainly a Scheme laid by the *French* many Years ago, and uniformly pursued till this Time, with the greatest Address ; being the true Cause of their con-

---

[21] Crèvecœur : *Letters from an American Farmer,* pp. 48, 49, 51, 52, 53.

tinual Encroachments, and holding their Countries by *Forts,* without settling them. When they come near enough to have Communication with our *Germans,* it will be much more their Interest to plant their Colonies, by offering the said *Germans* easy Settlements, than by bringing new Hands from Europe; for by such Means they not only get an Accession of People who are accustomed to the Country, but also weaken us, in Proportion as they strengthen themselves.[22]

Even such a judicious observer as Benjamin Franklin did not escape the pangs of nativism, and he burst out in protest against the tide of "Palatine boors" that threatened to Germanize America : "And since detachments of English from Britain, sent to America, will have their places at home so soon supplied and increase so largely here; why should the Palatine boors be suffered to swarm into our settlements, and, by herding together, establish their language and manners, to the exclusion of ours ? Why should Pennsylvania, founded by the English, become a colony of aliens, who will shortly be so numerous as to Germanize us instead of our Anglifying them, and will never adopt our language or customs any more than they can acquire our complexion ?"[23] Franklin's nativism persisted for some years; but he could not overlook the strength of the Germans, or their contributions to American economic, social, and intellectual life. He moved, therefore, from what appeared to be a desire to exclude them entirely, in 1751, to a proposal that they be distributed through all the colonies rather than concentrated in Pennsylvania :

> I am perfectly of your mind, that measures of great temper are necessary with the Germans; and am not without apprehensions, that, through their indiscretion, or ours, or both, great disorders may one day arise among us. Those who come hither are generally the most stupid of their own nation, and, as ignorance is often attended with credulity when knavery would mislead it, and with suspicion when honesty would set it right; and as few of the English understand the German language, and so cannot address them either from the press or the pulpit, it is almost impossible to remove any prejudices they may entertain. . . .
>
> In short, unless the stream of their importation could be turned from this to other colonies, as you very judiciously propose, they will soon so outnumber us that all the advantages we have, will in my opinion, be not able to preserve our language, and even our government will become precarious. . . . Yet I am not for refusing to admit them entirely into our colonies. All that seems to me necessary, is, to distribute them more equally, mix them with the English, establish

---

[22] William Smith : *A Brief State of the Province of Pennsylvania* (London, 1775), pp. 29–30.

[23] Franklin : *Works* (Sparks ed.), II, 320.

English schools, where they are now too thick-settled; and take some care to prevent the practice, lately fallen into by some of the ship-owners, of sweeping the German gaols to make up the number of their passengers. I say, I am not against the admission of Germans in general, for they have their virtues. Their industry and frugality are exemplary. They are excellent husbandmen, and contribute greatly to the improvement of a country.[24]

Yet the nativism of "old" Americans hardly retarded the influx of immigrants. Nor could it prevent their mingling with their neighbors and imbibing respect for the man of the soil. There was going on, indeed, in all parts of America except the aristocratic plantation areas and the more conservative social strata of the cities, a leveling process that tended more and more toward social equality and included even the foreigners who could demonstrate, by their own accomplishments, their social worth. This process was described by Philip Fithian, contrasting New Jersey with tidewater Virginia:

> The Levil which is admired in New-Jersey Government, among People of every rank, arises, no doubt, from the very great division of the lands in that Province, and consequently from the near approach to an equality of Wealth among the Inhabitants, since it is not famous for trade. . . . Hence we see Gentlemen, when they are not actually engaged in the publick Service, on their farms, setting a laborious example to their Domesticks, & on the other hand we see labourers at the Tables & in the Parlours of their Betters enjoying the advantage, & honour of their society and conversation.[25]

This social leveling was the true social genius of America.

Of course, aristocrats like Jonathan Boucher lamented this state of affairs. It was such a corruption, it seemed to him, of true culture: "Man is a creature of habits," he wrote; "when therefore it is considered that in America men do not as in Europe associate daily with those of their own kindred and neighbourhood only, but with fellow-creatures from every quarter of the globe; it will not be thought so surprising that they should not be so apt to cultivate those amities and charities which are elsewhere deemed of such moment to the welfare and comfort of the social life."[26] As for Philadelphia, that focal point in the melting-pot, "the people [of Philadelphia] too are like their town, all very well, but nothing more. One is as good as another, and no better; and it is in vain to look for anything like character among them. In one point, not contented with being not agreeable they are al-

[24] Ibid., VII, 71–3.
[25] Fithian : *Journal and Letters*, pp. 285–6.
[26] Boucher : *Reminiscences of an American Loyalist*, p. 99.

most disagreeable : the almost universal topic of conversation among them is the superiority of Philadelphia over every other spot on the globe." [27]

It was Crèvecœur again who put this social ideal of the Americans of the frontier and the melting-pot into words :

> What attachment can a poor European emigrant have for a country where he had nothing? The knowledge of the language, the love of a few kindred as poor as himself, were the only cords that tied him : his country is now that which gives him land, bread, protection, and consequence : *Ubi panis ibi patria*, is the motto of all emigrants. What then is the American, this new man? He is either an European, or the descendant of an European; hence that strange mixture of blood, which you will find in no other country. . . . *He* is an American, who leaving behind him all his ancient prejudices and manners, receives new ones from the new mode of life he has embraced, the new government he obeys, and the new rank he holds. He becomes an American by being received in the broad lap of our great *Alma Mater.* Here individuals of all nations are melted into a new race of men, whose labours and posterity will one day cause great changes in the world. Americans are the western pilgrims, who are carrying along with them that great mass of arts, sciences, vigour, and industry, which began long since in the east; they will finish the great circle. . . . The American is a new man, who acts upon new principles; he must therefore entertain new ideas, and form new opinions. From involuntary idleness, servile dependence, penury, and useless labour, he has passed to toils of a very different nature, rewarded by ample subsistence. — This is an American. [28]

Women and the Family

If the tide of American social thought was running strongly in the direction of social equality and social freedom, it was also bringing with it a new concept of the family and the position of women in society. For the eighteenth-century Americans had advanced far beyond the ideas of the Puritans, who believed with John Winthrop that "the woman's own choice makes such a man her husband; yet being so chosen, he is her lord, and she is subject to him, yet in a way of liberty, not of bondage; and a true wife accounts her subjection her honor and freedom, and would not think her condition safe and free, but in her subjection to her husband's authority." [29]

The family, of which the mother was but one of the subservient members, was one of the creations of God for the better regulation of

---

[27] Ibid., p. 101.

[28] Crèvecœur : *Letters from an American Farmer,* pp. 51–3.

[29] Miller and Johnson : *The Puritans,* p. 207.

human affairs. As Deodat Lawson put it, the father is the head of the family by God's will; but not only that, the father, *"the Master of the Family,* is as it were the SOUL *of the Family,"* and correlates relationships of all its members. The father is a sort of patriarch, and is responsible to God for the spiritual as well as the physical welfare of the family : *"The Master of the Family, hath an Especial Betrustment, with all the* SOULS *in the Family, and must* One Day *be Accountable* for them." Finally, *"The Foundation of a whole People or Kingdoms* Reformation, or Defection, Religion, or Rebellion, *is laid in Families.* Families are the Constituent Parts of Nations, and Kingdoms; hence as Families are *Well* or *Ill Disciplined,* so will the whole be *Well* Disposed, or *Ill Inclined.* . . . Such as carry themselves *Ill* in the Family, will not be likely to Demean themselves *Well* in the *Common-Wealth."* [30]

Cotton Mather shared this Puritan outlook upon the family as the basic unit of a society built according to the plan of God. For, he said, "As the Great God, who at the Beginning said, *Let US make man after our Image,* hath made man a *Sociable* Creature, so it is evident, That *Families* are the *Nurseries* of all Societies ; and the First Combinations of mankind. *Well-ordered Families* naturally produce a *Good Order* in other *Societies."* [31]

In other words, the family is the divinely ordained basic unit of society. This way of thinking was accepted by everybody, including the women, and in all the colonies; few women, if any, ever dreamed of questioning the established order.

In the southern colonies, as in New England, the women among the first settlers were expected to occupy a position of helpful subservience to their husbands, and were not averse to hard manual labor, even in the fields among the men. As the chambermaid complains in *The Sot-Weed Factor,*

> *now at the Hoe,*
> *I daily work, and Barefoot go,*
> *In weeding Corn, or feeding Swine,*
> *I spend my melancholy Time.* [32]

Legally, even as late as the eighteenth century, a wife had no individual existence apart from her husband. Under the English common law, which was generally accepted in the colonies in the absence of statutes, according to Mr. Justice Blackstone, one of the greatest of

[30] Deodat Lawson : *The Duty & Property of a Religious Householder* (Boston, 1693), pp. 1, 30, 31, 51.

[31] Cotton Mather : *A Family Well Ordered* (Boston, 1699), p. 3.

[32] Ebenezer Cook : *The Sot-Weed Factor* (London, 1708 ; reprint, 1865), p. 7.

English legal commentators, "by marriage the husband and wife are one person in law; that is, the very being or legal existence of the woman is suspended during the marriage, or at least is incorporated and consolidated into that of her husband. . . . For this reason a man cannot grant anything to his wife, or enter into covenant with her; for the grant would be to suppose her separate existence." [33]

As for children, they were expected to give unquestioning obedience to their parents, particularly the father; under the laws of certain colonies obstinately disobedient children were even punishable by death, although there appears to be no record of any actual execution of such a penalty. Unmarried persons were both distrusted and pitied, and the individual man, woman, or child was known and socially placed according to his family relationships. Marriage itself was regarded as a civil contract in the northern colonies, but in the south, where the Anglican Church was established, it was a religious function, and one of the prerogatives of the clergy.

But if matrimony and the family were ordained by God, they were nevertheless strongly economic in nature. A wife and sons and daughters, in a land where food and the materials for shelter and clothing were more plentiful than either hired labor or money, every strong hand to help the farmer, the frontiersman, or the merchant was a substantial economic asset. At the same time the responsibility of the husband for the support of his wife carried with it the right to expect as large a dowry as she or her family could afford, and downright bargaining over the terms of the marriage contract was taken as a matter of course.

Yet though the wife was "subject" to her husband, and though even the most highly placed dames in early American society were expected to be engaged in some useful activity in the service of their husbands or their families every waking moment, women were appreciated as very necessary and useful members of that social microcosm. They worked, cooked, knitted, made soap, dipped candles, spun and wove the cloth for the family clothing, which they made, milked cows, kept the kitchen garden, helped with the husking, and taught the children their letters and their manners. Woman's place was in the home, but it was a definitely important place. Many women, indeed, who came to America as indentured servants, after serving out the four or five years of their contracts, married well and rose to positions of high social status and esteem. As one of the card-playing ladies in *The Sot-Weed Factor* spitefully says to another:

[33] Quoted in Wyllistine Goodsell: *A History of Marriage and the Family* (New York, 1934), pp. 359–60.

> . . . *tho' now so brave,*
> *I knew you late a Four-Years Slave;*
> *What if for Planter's Wife you go,*
> *Nature designed you for the Hoe.*[34]

American conditions were making it possible for women to rise in
social status, exactly as they were making it possible for men; and by
the middle of the eighteenth century the position of women had improved far beyond what it had been at the beginning. Among the aristocracy, at least, their position was now that of queenly supervisors of
the plantation or the great merchant house, hostesses and social companions for their husbands, guides and teachers for their high-bred
children — and alas, all too often, card-playing, gossiping wasters of
time and their husbands' money.

The position of the wives of the great social planters was a particularly distinguished one. For, aristocratic to the core, and often badly
spoiled, they nevertheless presided over the planters' households with
grace and charm. The planter's wife was a sort of symbol of morality
and social authority; she was the "mother" of the community, including her own children, and she ministered to all, slaves as well as whites,
in sickness, childbirth, accident, and social distress; she was the center
of service and attention, especially from the "gentlemen," and she became the symbol about which was growing up the tradition of southern chivalry. Yet although the women of the well-to-do classes now
performed much less physical labor than those of the middle and lower
classes, it would be a mistake to think of them as idle. For, as one traveler put it with regard to the women in Maryland in 1745:

> The women are very handsome in general and most notable house-
> wives; everything wears the Marks of cleanliness and Industry in their
> Houses, and their behavior to their Husbands is very edifying. You
> cant help observing, however, an Air of Reserve and somewhat that
> looks at first to a Stranger like Unsociableness, which is barely the
> effect of living at a great Distance from frequent Society and their
> Thorough Attention to the Duties of their Stations. . . . The girls
> under such good Mothers generally have twice the Sense and Discretion
> of the Boys. Their Dress is neat and Clean and not much bordering
> upon the Ridiculous Humour of the Mother Country where the
> Daughters seem Dress'd up for a Market.[35]

All through the colonies women were becoming freer. More and
more women engaged in business or managed the affairs of their men-
folk. Some, indeed, like Eliza Pinckney, of South Carolina, achieved

[34] Cook: *The Sot-Weed Factor*, p. 21.
[35] Quoted in Alice Morse Earle: *Colonial Dames and Goodwives* (New
York, 1924), pp. 15–16.

real distinction. Eliza managed her father's plantation, where she successfully introduced the cultivation of indigo, studied shorthand, wrote verses, read such novels as *Pamela,* and even dabbled in science and the law. Said the gay Eliza, describing her work of making wills for her poorer neighbors, "If you will not laugh too immoderately at me I'll trust you with a secrett : I have made two Wills already. I know I have done no harm for I conn'd my lesson very perfect, and know how to convey by Will Estates real and personal and never forget in its' proper place him and his heirs for Ever." [36] Furthermore, she took under her wing "a parcel of little Negroes whom I have undertaken to teach to read." [37]

Even in Puritanical New England the gradual secularization of outlook was making for more social freedom ; and a traveler in Boston in 1740 related that "both the ladies and gentlemen dress and appear as gay, usually, as courtiers in England on a coronation day or birthday. And the ladies here visit, drink tea, and do everything else in the height of fashion. They neglect the affairs of their families with as good a grace as the finest ladies in London." [38]

The increasing freedom of women and social manners was to be observed in many of the realms of life, including clothing. On the other hand it goes almost without saying that the increasing freedom for women that accompanied the secularization and the rationalization of manners was viewed with extreme alarm by many religious leaders and other serious-minded thinkers. Samuel Johnson, for example, in a philosophical commentary on his times entitled *Raphael, or the Genius of the English America,* gives a fine rationalistic explanation of the structure of society and the family, and of the derivation of morals. For, he says :

> the condition of mankind being such that they cannot be subsisted and propagated without marriages and affinities . . . and lastly since the love of your children and care for posterity is one of your strongest passions, and since their happiness must chiefly depend upon the good order, weal and prosperity of your country with which you leave them when you go off the stage ; this passion, one would think, can't but have a mighty force to engage every one to do all that he can to promote its general interests and public weal while he continues in it.[39]

But "Family government is grossly neglected in the country and this neglect is such a growing evil, that if it be not reformed in a little time,

---

[36] Eliza Lucas [Pinckney] : *The Journal and Letters of Eliza Lucas,* edited by Harriott P. Holbrook (Wormslee, Ga., 1850), p. 14.

[37] Ibid., p. 16.

[38] Quoted in Goodsell, op. cit., pp. 379–80.

[39] Samuel Johnson : *Career and Writings* (Schneider ed.), II, 544.

our youth will be utterly ruined and our commonwealth will sink into a confused jumble of untoward and ungoverned rebels." Was there ever a generation of oldsters that did not despair of the future if left in the hands of their tumultuous and freedom-loving young? Never, it seemed to Johnson, had the need for strict family discipline been so great as now, "when it is obvious that our youth are apace running headlong into all sorts of debauchery and uncontrolled indulgences, which I doubt not is, as you observe, chiefly owing to the fond indulgence of their parents." Let the parents not indulge the children, and let them set a good example; keep the children from bad company, and insist that they get home at reasonably early hours; and keep them busy, "forasmuch as idleness is a state of perpetual temptation."[40]

But Johnson, alas, despite his relatively progressive ideas in the field of education, was really falling out of step with his times; for with the secularization of society and the rationalization of thought, youth, too, was feeling, and enjoying, the new wind of freedom that was blowing into the very fabric of social thought.

Unquestionably the trend of the times in America was toward greater fluidity, more movement, greater freedom, for men, women, and children; and the American mind of the times was adopting the ideal of social movement as one of its accepted tenets. Yet in practical affairs the family, and respect for family connections, was a powerful force in American life and thought. It was the great aristocratic families, for example, who dominated, if they did not actually control, colonial politics as well as colonial society. In general, these families were grouped about the "court," or the provincial governor and his advisers, and there was an enormous amount of nepotism and intrigue among them.

But if the aristocratic families dominated both society and politics, it was the merchant, small-farmer, and professional middle-class families, especially the lawyers, who combined to dominate the assemblies and carry on the struggle for autonomy against prerogative; and some of these were marrying into the older families, with the result that some of the aristocrats found themselves allied with the "popular party" against the "court party." This phenomenon, also, caused governors like Cadwallader Colden considerable distress, and he reported this side of the picture with no little acerbity:

We have a Set of Lawyers in this Province as Insolent, Petulant and at the same time as well skilled in all the chicanerie of the Law as perhaps is to be found anywhere else. This requires Judges of ability & skill in the Law to restrain them who are not easily to be found in

[40] Ibid., II, 556, 557, 558.

this Place & at the same time disinterested for the distinguished Families in so small a Country are so united by intermarriages that in [but] few cases [can] a cause of any Consequence . . . be brought before a Judge who is one of these families in which he can be supposed entirely disinterested and free from connections with those interested. . . .[41]

It would be far from the truth to suppose that family connections and social considerations entirely determined the political thinking of either the "court party" or the "popular party." The fact was, indeed, that the old families had begun to be divided on the basis of political ideas, and this division on ideas ran counter to the older divisions that rested more largely upon family and personal leadership. But it was still true that social thinking and outlook were closely bound up with political thought, that both were closely bound up with economics.

The family, then, was of great importance to the mind of the Americans in the eighteenth century. For it was generally accepted as the basic unit of society, and it had been and still was a powerful force in politics. But family ties were not as strong as they had been a century earlier; they were more secular, and somewhat more relaxed. Finally, women were increasingly important in human affairs, and it would perhaps not be going too far to say that women were freer in America than anywhere else in the world. Morals, too, were based upon more rational principles rather than upon divine fiat; and youth, regarded by some with alarm and a yearning for the good old Puritan discipline, was by others trusted with the confidence that sprang from the rationalists' faith in progress and the unlimited capacities of the human mind. By and large, the times had changed: family relations, the position of women, moral standards, and the education of children were moving unmistakably in the direction of greater freedom.

THEORIES OF EDUCATION AND SOCIAL CONTROL

Education is often the clearest index to the social mind of a people, for it makes a deliberate effort to inculcate in the young the values the older generation holds most in reverence. It is at once progressive and conservative; for while it seeks to raise the level of intellectual standards of the future, it seeks to do so by a perpetuation of the values of the past. Each generation believes that it has achieved a higher degree of intellectual and cultural excellence than its predecessors; it seeks to perpetuate itself; but it seldom seeks, through education, deliberately to prepare its children to improve upon its own way

41 *Colden Letter Books*, I, 231.

of living. If the younger generation improve upon it, as they usually do, they accomplish that feat despite the education they receive from their elders rather than because of it.

Education, indeed, is generally an instrument of social policy, used by society for the perpetuation of itself and its ideals. In eighteenth-century America education was never an independent realm of thought in itself. For it was always a mechanism for the accomplishment of an objective rather than a philosophy; it was the instrument of one or other of the great human motives, such as social improvement, religion, science, or nationalism, but never a "discipline" in itself. The professional "educator" had not appeared.

Thus the educational ideas of America in the middle of the eighteenth century were ideas by which, progressive though they often were vis-à-vis their grandfathers', the fathers sought to make the sons like unto themselves : rationalists, practical men of affairs, or conservatives in intellect, as they were in their politics, their economics, and their society.

Educational thinking, at least in eighteenth-century America, clearly reflected the interests of social class and of economic ambition. Thus for the aristocratic classes education tended to be conservative and essentially classical in content, with intellectual cultivation as its chief aim. For the poor, however, who wished to take advantage of their American freedom to rise in the economic and social scale, education was a means to that end; and education began to show that typically American concern for and preoccupation with the practical and professional ends of education which was gradually and eventually to corrode and crowd out its cultural content, in some cases almost to the vanishing-point. Considered thus, by regions, a quick glance at American educational institutions and ideas at the mid-century reveals a picture of public schools for the poor and private academies for the rich in New England, denominational schools for the poor and private tutors for the rich in New York and Pennsylvania, parish schools — or none at all — for the poor and private tutors, with an occasional private school for the rich in the south. For the children of the wealthy in New England who went on to college, there were Harvard and Yale ; in the middle colonies King's College (1754), Princeton (1746), and the College of Philadelphia (1753) ; in the south, William and Mary.

In the first century of American settlement, theories of education saw it as an instrumentality for inculcating the ideals of conformity with the existing order. The clergy, to whose hands education was generally entrusted, were recruited from the ruling classes, and education, aside from the training of these leaders, was the business of teaching the lower classes to read the Bible, so as to understand God's plan with men, as interpreted in the pulpit, and at the same time to read and obey the laws laid down for them by their governors. Farther south, there was some doubt as to whether the poor should go to school at all; and while Governor Berkeley's extreme distaste for free schools was probably not truly representative of the mind of his generation, yet he probably represented the thought of many of the emerging Virginia aristocracy when he wrote, in 1671, that in matters of education in Virginia the planters followed "The same course that is taken in England out of towns; every man according to his ability instructing his children." [42] This meant that education in Virginia was left in the hands of the heads of families. There were almost no schools aside from a few endowed schools for orphan apprentices; indeed, it was hardly possible that there could be since the plantation system kept individual families so widely separated. The simple facts of economic and social existence almost forced the "family" system of education upon the Virginians. As the seventeenth century wore into the next, however, and the elements of fluidity appeared in economic life and society, as life became more secular, and as rationalism became increasingly important, the emphases in education began to change and to reflect these influences.

Education and Aristocracy

Social differences were still taken as a matter of course. Indeed, as a native American aristocracy began to emerge clearly in northern, southern, and middle colonies, the aristocratic factors in education became, if anything, stronger. The aristocrat was thought to be inherently superior to the yokel, whom it would be useless to try to educate. Education was thought of as graded to suit the gradations of society, and the whole aristocratic scheme of things was rationalized as having the divine sanction. Thus no less a person than the great Jonathan Mayhew thought the system perfectly in accord with nature and with God's intentions with regard to men:

> It is not intended in this assertion, that all men have *equal abilities* for judging what is true and right. The whole creation is diversified, and men in particular. There is a great variety in their intellectual faculties. That which principally distinguishes some men from the beasts of the field, is the different formation of their bodies. Their bodies are *human*, but they are in a manner *brute* all beside. . . . Those of the lower class can go but a little ways in their inquiries into the natural and moral constitution of the world. But even these may have the power of judging, in *some degree*. . . . From the most dull and stupid

[42] Quoted in Ellwood P. Cubberley: *Public Education in the United States* (Boston, 1934), p. 23.

of the human species, there is a continual rise or gradation, there being as great a variety in the intellectual powers of men, as in their bodily and active powers. . . . He that was *born like the wild asses-colt*, must needs continue to be so; or, at best, come to maturity, and grow up into an ass himself.[43]

For Cadwallader Colden, the main objective of education is to prepare young gentlemen for the gentlemanly life: "The chief objection to the college being in the country is, that the scholars cannot acquire that advantage of behaviour and address, which they would by a more general conversation with gentlemen. But this may be remedied by obliging them to use the same good manners towards one another, with a proper regard to their several ranks, as is used among well-bred gentlemen, and by having them taught dancing and other accomplishments, an easy carriage and address in company, and other exercises usually taught to gentlemen."[44] Colden was much more explicitly aristocratic, or "Tory," in his educational ideals than his friend and scientific colleague Franklin, and he became especially so after he became embittered by his struggle, as Lieutenant-Governor, with the "republican" tendencies of the New York Assembly. Even William Smith, provost of the Philadelphia Academy, believed that a distinction should be made between the education provided for those who were destined for the learned professions — who would doubtless be "gentlemen" — and those "design'd for the Mechanic Professions, and all the remaining People of the Country."[45]

But William Smith, while much more of a conservative in his social thinking than Franklin, was probably much less aristocratic in his educational ideas than Colden in New York or the aristocratic planters of the south. It was in the southern colonies, indeed, that the aristocratic ideal in education was most current. For the Virginia aristocracy educated its sons and daughters privately by tutors, before sending the boys to William and Mary or to England to complete their studies. Philip Fithian of New Jersey was a tutor in one of these Virginia aristocratic families, and his *Journal* contains an intimate picture of this sort of "family" education. Learning was held in vast respect by the aristocracy, and the tutor occupied a peculiar and important place in the community: "For example, if you should travel through this Colony [Virginia] with a well-confirmed testimonial of your having finished with Credit a Course of studies at Nassau-Hall; you would be rated, without any more questions asked . . . at 10,000 £; and you might

[43] Jonathan Mayhew: *Seven Sermons*, pp. 29, 32.
[44] Franklin: *Works* (Sparks ed.), III, 46.
[45] William Smith: *A General Idea of the College of Mirania* . . . (New York, 1753), p. 14.

come, & go, & converse, & keep company, according to this value ; and you would be despised and slighted if you rated yourself a farthing cheaper."[46] The planters themselves were often highly educated men. William Byrd, for example, educated in England, read Greek, Hebrew, Latin, Italian, and French, and owned — and used — what was probably the finest private library in the colonies. Robert Carter, of Nomini Hall, was another.

The tutorial ideal of education was expressed by Jonathan Boucher, friend of George Washington :

> Education is too generally considered merely as the acquisition of knowledge, & the cultivation of the intellectual Powers. And, agreeably to this notion, when we speak of a man well-educated, we seldom mean more than that He has been well instructed in those Languages which are the avenues to knowledge. But, surely, this is but a partial & imperfect account of it : & the aim of Education should be not only to form wise but good men, not only to cultivate the understanding, but to expand the Heart, to meliorate the Temper, & *fix the gen'rous Purpose in the glowing Breast.*[47]

This is the educational ideal of the Virginia gentleman : languages and information, to be sure ; but, beyond that, the cultivation of the human spirit, the essence of all true culture. A similar ideal was followed by the aristocrats of South Carolina, although the existence of Charleston as a large and flourishing city encouraged the development of private schools similar to those which were appearing in the northern cities. These urban private schools reflected the progressive trends in education rather more than the older classical academies ; appealing to an urban, mercantile clientele, their success, their very existence, depended upon serving the needs of the future merchant for training in such practical subjects as bookkeeping as well as the more cultural objectives of the gentleman.

The sons of the American aristocracy were going increasingly to the colleges of America as the eighteenth century entered upon its third quarter, and there they studied Latin, some Greek and Hebrew, and "natural philosophy," or science. For some, the prime objective was still religious ; as conservative President Clap of Yale wrote, in 1754, *"Colleges are Societies of Ministers,* for training up Persons for the Work of the Ministry. . . . The great design of founding this School [Yale], was to Educate Ministers in our *own* Way."[48] And even the relatively

---

[46] Fithian : *Journal and Letters,* p. 287.

[47] Jonathan Boucher : *Letters of Jonathan Boucher to George Washington,* edited by Worthington C. Ford (Brooklyn, 1899), p. 10. Abbreviated words have been spelled out.

[48] Quoted in Cubberley : *Public Education in the United States,* p. 265.

progressive Samuel Johnson, first president of the new King's College, felt it necessary to say, as he opened the college: "The chief Thing that is aimed at in this College, is, to teach and engage the Children to know God in Jesus Christ, and to love and serve him in all sobriety, Godliness and Righteousness of Life, *with a perfect Heart and a willing Mind;* and to train them up in all virtuous Habits, and all such useful Knowledge, as may render them creditable to their Families and

Higher education in British America: Yale College about 1770. An etching by Benjamin F. Buck after an engraving by Amos Doolittle.

[By courtesy of the Library of Congress]

Friends, Ornaments to their country, and useful to the publick Weal in their generations." [49] The prime objective was still a religious one; yet "useful Knowledge" and the socially "virtuous Habits" were joined with the religious aims, in the same sentence, in terms almost of equality.

Harvard, indeed, of the older colleges, was distinguished by the study of science under the Hollis Professorship, occupied illustriously by Isaac Greenwood (who was finally discharged because he was unable to overcome his propensity to drunkenness) and his more brilliant successor John Winthrop. Harvard showed extraordinary educational statesmanship in engaging the liberal Winthrop, but its relative religious modernism was also shown in 1760 by the permission given its students to attend the first Anglican church in Cambridge. Harvard, however, stood in the midst of a society where religious liberal-

[49] Ellwood P. Cubberley: *Readings in Public Education in the United States* (Boston, 1934), p. 92.

ism was being made fashionable by such forerunners of Unitarianism as Jonathan Mayhew and Charles Chauncy, whereas Yale stood true, still, to its founder's ideal of preserving the doctrines of simon-pure Congregationalism against the inroads of modernism.

Of the newer colleges, Princeton, founded in 1746 for the training of Presbyterian ministers, yet began its career with a proviso that no one there should be persecuted for conviction's sake. But Princeton's

Higher education in British America: Harvard College about 1726. Engraving by William Burgis.
[By courtesy of the Library of Congress]

curriculum contained little or no provision for natural science; its special interest was "divinity." As time went on, too, it became increasingly distrustful of the contemporary scientific rationalism and, true to its evangelical origin, sought for a time to exclude rationalism and all — or nearly all — its works from Nassau Hall's sacred precincts.

It was William and Mary College in Virginia, probably, that was the most liberal of all colleges founded before 1750. For it could rival Harvard in the proud possession of a chair of natural philosophy, and it could outdo Harvard, in 1758, in the specific provision for intellectual freedom made in its statutes of that year. As a matter of practice, too,

William and Mary's classes were already become brilliant forums for the discussion of scientific rationalism with regard to the natural world and the natural laws of politics. The liberalism of this southern college was partly due, probably, to the relative rationalism of contemporary Anglicanism, coupled with the stronger direct educational influence of England; probably, also, it was partly due to the fact that the study

Higher education in British America: Nassau Hall (Princeton) about 1749. An engraving by H. Dawkins.
[From *An Account of the College of New Jersey* (Woodbridge, N. J., 1764)]

of the law and the discussion of politics were predominantly, though not exclusively, the intellectual pursuits of the Virginia gentlemen. In any case, William and Mary reflected the intellectual fashions of the Virginia aristocracy; and it was probably no accident that Virginia was the mother of so many political statesmen of the natural-rights school.

The far south did not achieve its own college before the Revolution; although the gentlemen of Charleston did realize the need, and actually initiated a campaign, shortly after 1750, for the establishment of an academy that would be patterned after the one then getting started in Philadelphia, with a curriculum of "moral" or gentlemanly studies linked with such practical disciplines as agriculture, navigation, and astronomy.[50] Since the movement failed, the Charleston gentlemen continued to send their sons to William and Mary or the colleges farther north.

But of the six colleges existing in English America in 1755, the one that probably represented most closely the genius of American liberalism was the Philadelphia Academy and College, product chiefly

[50] *South Carolina Gazette*, August 6 and 13, 1750.

of the joint efforts and educational ideas of Benjamin Franklin and William Smith. Franklin's educational ideas were, if possible, more secular and they were certainly less aristocratic than those of his southern contemporaries. In his *Proposals Relating to the Education of Youth in Pennsylvania* (1749), Franklin admitted a certain embarrassment over the apparent conflict between the cultural ideal of edu-

Higher education in America: William and Mary College, Main Building. Built about 1700.

[By courtesy of the Library of Congress]

cation and the need for teaching "useful" subjects. Under ideal conditions, he said, students would be "taught *every thing* that is useful, and *every thing* that is ornamental. But art is long, and their time is short. It is therefore proposed, that they learn those things that are likely to be *most useful and most ornamental*; regard being had to the several professions for which they are intended." [51] It would be difficult to state more succinctly the modern ideal of education: practical ("useful"), cultural ("ornamental"), and professional.

But Franklin goes on to specify: as studies of a "practical" sort, writing, drawing, arithmetic, geography, chronology, morality, oratory, gardening, and commerce; for the enrichment of life, or cultural subjects, English literature and grammar, Latin, logic, history, ancient arts and customs, and natural science; for pre-professional studies, the

[51] Franklin: *Works* (Sparks ed.), I, 572.

languages requisite for the professions; "All intended for divinity, should be taught the Latin and Greek; for physic, Latin, Greek, and French; for law, the Latin and French; merchants, the French, German and Spanish,"[52] and so on.

All through the colonies the new emphasis on the secular, the practical, and the useful sides of education was becoming explicit

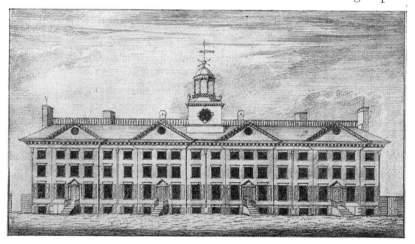

Higher education in British America: the King's College (Columbia College) building as it was completed in 1760.
[By courtesy of Columbia University]

and was written into the charters of many of the new schools and colleges. For example, the new King's College advertised the opening of its career with the statement that despite the religious objective already quoted, "it is to be understood, that as to Religion, there is no Intention to impose on the Scholars the peculiar Tenets of any particular Sect of Christians, but to inculcate upon their tender Minds, the great Principles of Christianity and Morality, in which, true Christians of each Denomination are generally agreed." Furthermore, on the practical side,

> it is further the Design of this College, to instruct and perfect the Youth in the learned Languages, and in the Arts of *Reasoning* exactly, of *Writing* correctly, and *Speaking* eloquently; And in the Arts of *Numbering* and *Measuring*, of *Surveying* and *Navigation*, of *Geography* and *History*, of *Husbandry, Commerce* and *Government;* and in the Knowledge of *all Nature* in the *Heavens* above us, and in the *Air, Water,* and *Earth* around us, and the various Kinds of *Meteors,* Stones, Mines, and Minerals, Plants and Animals [et cetera!] . . . And finally,

[52] Ibid., I, 572-4.

to lead them from the Study of Nature, to the knowledge of themselves, and of the God of Nature, and their Duty to him, themselves, and one another; and every Thing that can contribute to their true Happiness both here and hereafter.[53]

The similarity of this to Franklin's ideal is striking. For while devoutly religious in its emphasis upon human personality, it is tolerant in religion, secular in outlook, practical in content, and strongly conscious of the values of education for the promotion of the social ideal of human happiness.

The social ideal, the cultivation of "civic virtue," was now looked upon as the highest ideal of education. Even religion was now considered, at least in the minds of some, as being a useful and necessary part of education chiefly because it was expected to contribute to the achievement of this social educational aim. It was because of its value in this direction that Franklin placed so much emphasis upon the study of history; for, he said:

the general natural tendency of reading good history must be, to fix in the minds of youth deep impressions of the beauty and usefulness of virtue of all kinds, public spirit and fortitude. . . . History will also give occasion to expatiate on the advantage of civil orders and constitutions; how men and their properties are protected by joining in societies and establishing government; their industry encouraged and rewarded, arts invented, and life made more comfortable; the advantages of liberty, mischiefs of licentiousness, benefits arising from good laws and a due execution of justice. Thus may the first principles of sound politics be fixed in the minds of youth.[54]

Thus education, and particularly the study of history, was to be the agent, besides all these other objectives, for the teaching of the civic virtues, an understanding of one's own society, and the responsibilities of citizenship.

Archibald Kennedy of New York was quite clear on the point of making good citizenship the supreme end of education. For

The Intention and Design of Seminaries, in every Country governed by Laws, are to form the Minds of the Youth, to Virtue, and to make them useful Members of the Society, in whatever Station may be allotted to them, in Conformity to the Law of the Land. . . . In Countries, where Liberty prevails, and where the Road is left open for the Son of the meanest Plebeian, to arrive at the highest Pitch of Honours and Preferments, there never will be wanting great Emulation, and of Course great Men.[55]

[53] Quoted in Cubberley: *Public Education in the United States*, p. 93.
[54] Franklin: *Works* (Sparks ed.), I, 573–4.
[55] Archibald Kennedy: *A Speech Said to have been delivered* . . . , pp. 13–14.

And William Smith, in his description of the ideal college of "Mirania," said :

> The Object they kept always in Sight, was the easiest, simplest and and most natural Method of forming Youth to the Knowledge and Exercise of private and public Virtue ; and therefore they did not scruple to reject some Things commonly taught at Colleges ; to add others ; and shorten or invert the Order of others, as best suited their Circumstances. They often had this Sentence in their mouth . . . That the Knowledge of what tends neither directly nor indirectly to make better Men and better Citizens, is but a Knowledge of Trifles ; it is not Learning, but a specious and ingenious sort of Idleness.[56]

But whereas William Smith would provide one sort of education for the upper strata of society and another for the mechanics and the laborers, Samuel Johnson would have gauged education to suit the capacities of the individual, "in such a manner as that each of them should be pleased with and indulged and forwarded in their several pursuits, and none be forced to go against the grain of nature and current of inclination because the agreeableness and pleasure of doing anything is the great incentive to make proficiency in it." [57] This educational theory has, indeed, a very modern sound. Johnson, of course, would retain much of the classical in his ideal curriculum, along with the "useful." But he, too, placed the cultivation of the social virtues as the highest end of education. "Let therefore the great end of life be frequently inculcated from the very beginning of it, upon the minds of your youth, viz., that they are made and sent into the world to do good and be useful in it, and that therefore as their strongest passion should be the love of religion and their country, so they should bend all their studies and endeavors to this great end of rendering themselves useful to mankind in promoting their greatest interest and weal, both temporal and spiritual." [58]

This was a moment of a budding civic self-consciousness, even of nationalism. But it was a fine rationalistic and classical ideal of citizenship, which held "better Men and better Citizens" to be those who had achieved, along with their "useful" learning, the highest possible development of their own intellectual talents and the finest possible refinement of the individual personality. As Franklin put it :

> With the whole [of education] should be constantly inculcated and cultivated that *benignity of mind*, which shows itself in searching for and seizing every opportunity to serve and to oblige ; and is the foundation of what is called *good breeding*; highly useful to the possessor,

[56] Smith : *A General Idea of the College of Mirania*, p. 10.
[57] Johnson : *Career and Writings* (Schneider ed.), II, 566.
[58] Ibid., II, 569–70.

and most agreeable to all. The idea of what is *true merit* should also be often presented to youth, explained and impressed on their minds, as consisting in an *inclination*, joined with an *ability*, to serve with the blessing of God, to be acquired or greatly increased by *true learning*; and should, indeed, be the great *aim* and *end* of all learning.[59]

Educational trends toward democracy

William Smith's proposal to give even a minimum of cultural education to the future mechanics was more radical — more democratic, in fact — than the ideas of most of his contemporaries. For the education of the colleges, the academies, and the tutors was still the prerogative of the rich. The children of the poor and common people had to go elsewhere. In New England the famous public school still existed, but the wealthy sent their children to the academies, and the quality of the public schools had degenerated. In Pennsylvania, New Jersey, and New York the lower schools were largely in the hands of the religious denominations, especially the Quakers, the Moravians, and the Dutch Reformed churches. Along the frontier there were few schools or none at all until the ministers of the frontier churches, Baptist, Methodist, and Presbyterian, but especially the graduates of Presbyterian Princeton, began to keep school between Sundays. It was these young teaching preachers who founded the schools that were to become the academies of the Allegheny highlands. Naturally enough, education in these frontier schools was of a strongly religious cast; and these schools educated many of the future leaders of western democracy.

The most articulate advocates of education for the Negroes and the poor were the two Quaker friends Anthony Benezet and John Woolman. As one might expect, Woolman's emphasis in education was primarily religious. But some of his ideas have a surprisingly progressive ring:

> To encourage Children to do Things with a View to get Praise of Men, to me appears an Obstruction to their being inwardly acquainted with the Spirit of Truth. For it is the Work of the Holy Spirit to direct the Mind to God, that in all our Proceedings we may have a single Eye to him. . . . By cherishing the Spirit of Pride and Love of Praise in them, I believe they may sometimes improve faster in learning, than otherwise they would; but to take Measures to forward Children in learning, which naturally tend to divert their Minds from true Humility, appears to me to savour of the Wisdom of this World.[60]

The important objective of education, as of the rest of life, was the inner godliness that resulted from close attention and obedience to

[59] Franklin : *Works* (Sparks ed.), I, 566.
[60] Woolman : *Journal and Essays* (Gummere ed.), pp. 390–1.

the promptings of the Holy Spirit. Information as such, science, rationalism, professional training, none of these mattered so very much so long as education cultivated the individual's experience of God. To be sure, these things may be useful; but what doth it profit a man if he gain the whole world and lose his own soul? The only important thing is the soul and its progress toward God. Let education concentrate its efforts upon this great, pious, and mystical end.

Woolman criticized the schools of the colonies. Many teachers were burdened with responsibility for too many children; many teachers were selected who had too little true consecration to their work, or had too little preparation; many, he thought, actually did the children more harm than good. The school situation appeared to him a part of the social situation he had criticized on the ground of an unchristian distribution of wealth and a disregard for the "right use of things"; his educational thought becomes of a piece with his social thought. For, he said, "if those who have large Estates, were faithful Stewards, and laid no Rent nor Interest, nor other Demand, higher than is consistent with universal Love; and those in lower Circumstances would, under a moderate Employ, shun unnecessary Expense, even to the smallest Article; and all unite in humbly seeking to the Lord, he would graciously instruct us, and strengthen us, to relieve the Youth from various Snares, in which many of them are entangled." [61]

The chief objective of education, then, is to lead young people to a clearer union with God; it does have, also, a social aim: for its second objective is to cultivate brotherly love among men. Woolman's insistence upon putting piety above all other considerations appears to conflict with reason; for it would seem to imply that when a choice became necessary, as between piety and reason, piety must take precedence. So far as education was concerned, it would thus appear that Woolman favored training children to distrust reason and trust only their own mystical, non-rational emotions. But Woolman denied this: "That though to the Eye of Reason the difficulties appear great, in many places, which attend Instructing our Children in useful Learning, yet if we obediently attend to that wisdom which is from above, Our Gracious Father will open a way for us to give them such an Education as he requires of us." [62] He saw no conflict between his absolute, mystical faith and reason. He felt absolutely sure that the voice of God was in every individual. But so was reason, and since reason is also of God, there could be no conflict, except by a departure from the "true Christian spirit." The

[61] Ibid., p. 392. [62] Ibid., p. 430.

chief purpose of education was thus ultimately to keep reason and faith working together in true humility before God.

Woolman's thought on education is significant, not merely because he was individually a prophet of piety as a force in human living, but also because his ideas represented, in their essential pietistic emphasis, the educational thought of the multitude of pietists, German and others, including the frontier Methodists and Baptists, who had come to form so large a portion of American society. True to their pietistic principles, these sects consistently emphasized the individual; and this religious individualism doubtless contributed much power to the growth of individualism in American thought. Unfortunately, however, despite Woolman's denial, their strong emphasis upon pietistic emotionalism did tend to lead many to abandon or ignore the rational revelation as a guide to education and to life. Thus while pietism in education may be said to have contributed much to the American way of life in its emphasis upon individualism and the equality of men, its major effect among its devotees was probably in the direction of a flight from reason toward an emotionalism that has also been a powerful force in the development of the American mind, social and other.

In their emphasis upon piety in education and in life, however, the sects were but taking a fairly extreme position on an idea that was common to practically all Americans; that is, the belief in the social utility of religion. Over and over again, in letters, essays, school charters, and elsewhere, emphasis is placed upon the conviction that religious principles were the most effective promoter of decent behavior in the individual in society. Everybody — Colden, Franklin, Samuel Johnson, Edwards, Whitefield, Douglass, William Smith, Witherspoon, the Tennants, and the other leaders of American education — believed that the principles of religion — that is, the Christian ethic — were essential to society for the preservation of order and the promotion of the social good. But even this idea is a sign of the times : religion is no longer an essential ingredient of education simply because God requires that a man understand as much as he can of the divine plan ; it is essential to education now largely, if not chiefly, because it is socially and individually useful. The essentially pragmatic groundswell in American thought thus manifested itself in its harmonization of its sociology and its religion in education.

For the Negroes there was little or no education anywhere. There was, indeed, a strong feeling against educating them, since it was thought likely that education might give them a cause of, and the means for, revolt. Some slave-owners like Eliza Pinckney nevertheless undertook to teach the children of their slaves to read and write and an understanding of the simple essentials of Christianity. There were some northerners, too, who favored the establishment of schools for Negroes. Woolman favored it; but the leading sponsor of schools for Negroes was probably Anthony Benezet of Philadelphia, Woolman's lifelong Quaker friend and one of the moving spirits in the establishment of the Friends' School for Coloured Children, initiated in 1770.

Another social problem that involved education was the necessity for absorbing the new, inflowing elements in the melting-pot. Many colonial observers noted the "foreign" characteristics of the newcomers and, while recognizing the economic and social values of a rapidly expanding population, sought some means of adjusting the immigrants to the American way of life. William Smith, provost of the Philadelphia Academy, was deeply disturbed by this phenomenon, as was Franklin himself. Franklin wrote to Smith:

> Few of their children in the country know English. They import many books from Germany: and of the six printing-houses in the province [Pennsylvania], two are entirely German, two half German half English, and but two entirely English. They have one German newspaper, and one half-German. Advertisements, intended to be general, are now printed in Dutch [i.e., German] and English. The signs in our streets have inscriptions in both languages, and in some places only German . . . and I suppose in a few years [interpreters] will also be necessary in the Assembly, to tell one half of our legislators what the other half say.[63]

Franklin may have got his ideas for the Americanization of the Germans from Smith. Certainly the provost was greatly concerned with the problem of the Germans; and his conservative, Anglican distrust of the pacifism of the Quaker-dominated provincial assembly, supported by the German vote, made it appear to him as a threat at the very existence of the colony and even the Empire itself. It was for this reason that he proposed that this large, undigested mass of foreigners be culturally absorbed, and as soon as possible. Smith was probably the first professional educator to advocate a program of Americanization through the schools; but his recommendations touched more than education, and went much farther than the mild suggestions made by Franklin. Smith urged, anonymously, that certain definite steps be taken for the assimilation of the Germans. His first suggestion was that the Germans be denied the right to vote until they "have a sufficient Knowledge of our Language and Constitution"; the second was to establish "Protestant" ministry and schools in the

[63] Franklin: *Works* (Sparks ed.), VII, 71–2.

German settlements, "to instruct them in the Nature of free Government, the Purity and Value of the Protestant Faith; and to bind them to us by a common Language, and the consciousness of a common "interest." Smith's third suggestion was that all legal documents, such as bonds, contracts, wills, and the like, as also newspapers, almanacs, and other periodicals, be required by law to be in English. [64] Smith's program of Americanization, in fact, involved a political program as well as a reform of education.

The Americanization program of the provost of the academy was thus both educational and political; but it also had a significance that he hardly intended, or even imagined; for his proposals constitute the first serious suggestion of a program, educational or other, for the cultural absorption of foreigners into the Anglo-American way of life. That alone may properly be considered a step in the direction of democratization; taken along with Smith's other ideas on the education of all citizens, it makes Smith, conservative, "British" patriot that he was, one of the earliest serious thinkers toward educational democracy in British America.

Several years before Smith and Franklin were exchanging ideas on "Americanization" programs in education, there appeared one of the earliest important suggestions for a uniform, national system of public education. This suggestion came from the mind of the versatile Dr. William Douglass, who incorporated his idea in the proposal for an intercolonial union outlined in his *Summary, Historical and Political, of the British Settlements in North America.* For not only should the continental colonies be united; the central government, he thought, should be empowered to enact uniform electoral laws, laws regulating property-ownership, uniform guarantees of religious liberty ("Papists excepted"), a uniform system of courts, and a uniform network of public hospitals and public schools. He suggested that there be provided one public elementary school in each township, a grammar school in each shire or town, a college in each province, and, at some central location, "an University or Academy." In this continental university he proposed that curricula be provided for professional training in divinity, law, and medicine; the modern commercial languages; science, mathematics and belles-lettres; and, for the "gentlemen," riding, fencing, and dancing. Furthermore, students should be encouraged to travel; for "from School to College, from College to Travel, and from Travel into Business, are the Gradations of a liberal Education, but for Want of Effects the Link of Travel is frequently wanting." [65] At the same time Douglass made provision

[64] Smith : *A Brief State of the Province of Pennsylvania*, pp. 40-2.
[65] Douglass : *Summary, Historical and Political*, I, 256-7.

in his scheme for a plan of vocational education for poor children and orphans.

This striking scheme for a continental or national system of public education was highly remarkable as an indication of a realization of the need for educational facilities for all the people. Douglass still recognized the difference between "gentlemen" and others; but the idea of providing education for all who needed it was essentially democratic. Of equal significance, if not greater, was Douglass's conception of the problem as a national one : not only were a few Americans beginning to get a vision of education in the civic virtues for all the people; they were also beginning to conceive of an educational solidarity and unity that would overleap the intercolonial boundaries and bind the people of all the colonies together. Of course, Dr. Douglass's scheme had no practical outcome, although his book had a very wide circulation. The Americans were not yet ready to accept the idea much less do anything about it, any more than they were ready to accept the Albany plan for intercolonial union. The great significance of it lies in the fact that it was proposed at all.

The educational ideas of Smith, Franklin, Benezet, Woolman, and Douglass, taken together with the actual work being done in charity schools for the poor, the schools for Negroes, and the schools on the frontier, show the combined effects of eighteenth-century humanitarianism and rationalism, of the secularization of life, and of the influences of the frontier and the melting-pot upon American society and social thinking. If the educational ideas and ideals of the aristocratic elements in society reflect their social status and objectives, the educational thinking of these others show the ideals and the factors in American society that were making for social leveling and social change. Perhaps it may be accurately stated that the germ of social democracy in education lay in the dawning effort, all along the line, to give everybody, even the poorest, at least the minimum of an education. In its over-all characteristics educational thought was aristocratic, as society was aristocratic. Yet the leaven of a leveling tendency in education was present, especially in the areas where a social leveling was going on also. Everywhere, too, educational thought was looking upon education as an instrument of freedom — whether freedom from superstition and intolerance among the sophisticated or freedom from economic poverty, social inequality, and political oppression among the pioneers and the poor. Despite the fact that teachers were poorly paid, there was a great respect for literacy and learning, and the teacher was generally looked upon as a citizen of great social value. Nothing, said Franklin, was "of more importance for the public weal, than to form and train up youth in wisdom and virtue." Furthermore :

I think also, that general virtue is more probably to be expected and obtained from the education of youth, than from the exhortation of adult persons; bad habits and vices of the mind being, like diseases of the body, more easily prevented than cured. I think, moreover, that talents for the education of youth are the gift of God; and that he on whom they are bestowed, whenever a way is opened for the use of them, is as strongly called as if he heard a voice from heaven; nothing more surely pointing out duty in public service, than ability and opportunity of performing it.[66]

SOCIOLOGICAL THOUGHT

Of systematic thinkers on sociological questions there were but few in the colonies. There were few enough anywhere, indeed, for the serious study of human society as such was only just beginning. Yet a beginning had been made, and the influence of the new science and its rationalism was already making itself felt. For this was the age, after Hobbes, of Beccaria, Montesquieu, Diderot, Helvétius, and others; an age when the relations of man with man (and with woman) were beginning to be interpreted in terms of natural law and rational utilitarian values rather than in the language of eternal absolutes and divine will. Just how much influence these European thinkers had on America is uncertain; yet secularism, rationalism, and utilitarianism were characteristic of such sociological thought as there was in America, even when it had a strong religious coloring.

Benjamin Franklin and John Woolman were the only two thinkers in the English colonies who merit the name of serious, analytical students of society. Franklin, as usual, proved to be the most penetrating observer and commentator upon American sociological developments of his time. He was struck by the rapid increase of population, and, under the influence of Newtonian science, he sought to discover the natural laws governing sociological phenomena. Observing that the population of the colonies was doubling itself every twenty years, he nevertheless concluded that North America was so vast that "it will require many ages to settle it fully; and, till it is fully settled, labor will never be cheap here, where no man continues long a laborer for others, but gets a plantation of his own, no man continues long a journeyman to a trade, but goes among those new settlers, and sets up for himself, etc."[67]

In his explanations of the reasons for rapid increase of population, he anticipated Robert Malthus:

There is, in short, no bound to the prolific nature of plants or animals, but what is made by their crowding and interfering with each other's

---

[66] Franklin: *Works* (Sparks ed.), VII, 48.   [67] Ibid., II, 313.

means of subsistence. . . . Thus, there are supposed to be now upwards of one million English souls in North America, (though it is thought scarce eighty thousand have been brought over sea,) and yet perhaps there is not one the fewer in Britain, but rather many more, on account of the employment the colonies afford to manufacturers [laborers] at home. This million doubling, suppose but once in twenty-five years, will in another century, be more than the people of England, and the greatest number of Englishmen will be on this side of the water.[68]

Thus Franklin's naturalistic explanation of the increase of population led him to the belief that the population tends to increase without limit, so long as there is no limit to the "means of subsistence." In America, since there is no such limit, and there will not be for "ages," there will be an almost unlimited expansion of the population — a vision that aroused his exultant enthusiasm. But these facts, he believed, had, and would have, certain secondary effects upon American society: the price of labor would remain high, people would naturally prefer the freedom and self-sufficiency of the farm and, as a result, manufactures would be long in developing. Thus the economic life of the people, so long as there was enough land to go round, would be based on agriculture, and America would be preserved for centuries in its happy state as an agrarian society and would avoid the evils of industrialization and the industrial city. This is to say, in effect, that the economic activity of the Americans would be in large measure determined by the density of the population — assuming, perhaps incorrectly, that agriculture would be the natural first choice of the people where the population was sparse.

Franklin did not dream that the supply of free land would be exhausted and that America would be almost completely industrialized within little more than a century and a half after he wrote. Nor did he dream that the age following his own would be an age of collectivism rather than individualism. For his own age the operation of natural law that produced agrarian individualism seemed amply justified by the pragmatic test of the American experience; and he was the social philosopher of his age.

Franklin's idea that men would choose the agrarian life if they could was shared by many of his contemporaries. There were some, indeed, who suggested this supposed human preference as a basic motivation with which to save the British Empire from dissolution. For according to this way of thinking, if the desire for land was not gratified, the increasing population of America would turn to manufactures to rival and contend with those of Great Britain. America, if

[68] Ibid., II, 319.

the British mercantilist colonial policy was to succeed, must be kept an agricultural country. This is the argument of the author of *American Husbandry* for establishing new colonies in the American west; for "when land is difficult to be had or not good, owing to the extension of the settlements or the monopolies of the country, the poor must be driven to other employments than those which depend on land; manu-factureing, commerce, fisheries, &c. must then thrive in the natural course of things, unless some such measure as I have stated is put in practice in order to provide other employment. Such measures cannot be carried to the extent that is necessary with such an increasing people: the plan therefore to be adopted is certainly to prevent the future increase of the evil, by providing a motive for the fresh emigration of the people."[69] Apparently, the only way to preserve the Empire was by fostering a continued movement of the American people westward, thereby avoiding a congestion of population that must inevitably result in the development of industry, which would be fatal to Britain's overseas commerce.

A social thinker of a very different sort was John Woolman. For Woolman was a Quaker humanitarian and social reformer, and his abiding interest was in the condition of society rather than its nature. His efforts to explain social phenomena, therefore, were all directed toward finding an amelioration for human distress. His arguments are invariably based, not primarily upon natural law, although he does not ignore that, but upon considerations of human kindness and the benevolence of God:

> Wealth desired for its own sake Obstructs the increase of Virtue, and large possessions in the hands of selfish men have a bad tendency, for by their means too small a number of people are employed in things usefull, and therefore some of them are necessitated to labour too hard, while others would want business to earn their Bread, were not employments invented, which having no real use, serve only to please the vain mind. Rents set on lands are often so high, that persons who have but small substance are straitened in hiring a plantation and while Tenants are healthy, and prosperous in business, they often find Occasion to labour harder than was intended by our Gracious Creator.[70]

Woolman's appeal was to the power of the love of God: let employers be thoughtful of their employees; let the rich lay aside "superfluities" and other unnecessary trimmings to life; let only such labor be required of all men as to produce the things that are absolutely necessary for the maintenance of a simple, unadorned, Quaker standard of living. If these things are done, if the rule of

[69] *American Husbandry*, pp. 524–6.
[70] Woolman: *Journal and Essays* (Gummere ed.), p. 402.

brotherly love can be applied to economic and social relationships, men will be freed from drudgery and exploitation; life for man and beast will be easier, richer, more beautiful : the kingdom of God on earth will have come.

In some ways Woolman was the sheerest utopian dreamer; in others his vision of society anticipated some of the ideas later held by modern socialists : "Were all superfluities, and the desire of outward greatness laid aside, and the right use of things universally attended to, Such a number of people might be employed in things usefull, as that moderate labour, with the Blessing of Heaven, would answer all good purposes relating to people and their Animals, and a Sufficient number have time to attend to proper Affairs of Civil Society." [71]

Nor was Woolman's campaign against slavery, utopian as it may have been for his time, entirely impractical. Both Franklin and Woolman as well as many others were beginning to see the seamy sides of slavery and to advance certain basic ideas of humanitarianism and reform that were to culminate in the wave of antislavery sentiment that marked the idealistic side of the American Revolution. Franklin, as usual, writing in the proslavery world of 1751, approached the problem in an offhand mood of whimsical utilitarianism : "It is an ill-grounded opinion that, by the labor of slaves, America may possibly vie in cheapness of manufactures with Britain. The labor of slaves can never be so cheap here as the labor of workingmen is in Britain. Any one may compute it . . . . Why then will Americans purchase slaves ? Because slaves may be kept as long as a man pleases, or has occasion for their labor; while hired men are continually leaving their masters . . . and setting up for themselves." [72] As a matter of fact, he says :

the number of purely white people in the world is proportionably very small. All Africa is black or tawny ; Asia chiefly tawny ; America (exclusive of the new comers) wholly so. And in Europe, the Spaniards, Italians, French, Russians, and Swedes, are generally of what we call a swarthy complexion ; as are the Germans also, the Saxons only excepted, who, with the English, make the principal body of white people on the face of the earth. I could wish their numbers were increased. And while we are, as I may call it, scouring our planet, by clearing America of woods, and so making this side of our globe reflect a brighter light to the eyes of inhabitants in Mars or Venus, why should we, in the sight of superior beings, darken its people ? Why increase the sons of Africa, by planting them in America, where we have so fair an oppor-

[71] Ibid., p. 404.
[72] Franklin : *Works* (Sparks ed.), II, 314–15.

tunity, by excluding all blacks and tawnys, of increasing the lovely white and red? But perhaps I am partial to the complexion of my country, for such kind of partiality is natural to mankind.[73]

If Franklin was mildly nativist, he was also mildly racist. Both his nativism and his racism were based upon utilitarian considerations : he wished, most of all, to preserve this fruitful continent for his own people; and his utilitarianism was not untouched with sentiment. But he was a practical man; he knew that the tide of the times was against him, and he did not insist. But where Franklin's discreet criticism of slavery was based chiefly upon utilitarian considerations, the antislavery crusade of John Woolman was based upon religious considerations and humanitarianism. Woolman toured the colonies, from New England to North Carolina, preaching and conversing, in a single-handed campaign against the institution. While his basic argument was the religious one, yet he often invoked the theory of natural rights, and "believed that Liberty was the natural right of all men equally." [74]

Woolman was also quite capable of using the utilitarian argument with telling effect, and he turned the well-worn argument of the benefits of slavery to the black man back upon itself :

And I may here add, that another person, some time afterward mentioned the wretchedness of the Negroes [in Africa] occasioned by their intestine wars, as an argument in favour of our fetching them away for Slaves : to which I then replied, If compassion to the Africans, in regard to their domestick troubles, were the real motives of our purchasing them, That spirit of Sympathy being Attended to, would Incite us to use them kindly, that as Strangers brought out of Affliction, their lives might be happy amongst us, And as they are Human creatures, whose Souls are as precious as ours, and who may receive the same help & Comfort from the Holy Scriptures as we do, we could not omit suitable Endeavours to instruct them therein.[75]

But Woolman went farther. Not only should Negroes be free and treated kindly; not only were their souls equally precious with the souls of white men in the eyes of God; not only should they not be expected to labor more than the "true medium"; they were also, he thought, equally entitled with white men to a fair return on their labor. Here again Woolman gets pretty close to a sort of Christian socialism : "The Soyl yields us Support, and is profitable for man; & though some possessing a larger share of these profits than others,

73 Ibid., II, 320–1.
74 Woolman : *Journal and Essays* (Gummere ed.), p. 190.
75 Ibid., p. 191.

may consist with the Harmony of true Brotherhood, yet that the poorest people who are Honest, so long as they remain Inhabitants of the Earth are entitled to a certain portion of these profits, in as clear & absolute a sense as those who Inherit much, I believe will be agreed to by those whose hearts are Enlarged with Universal Love." [76]

Woolman sums up his whole argument against slavery in one simple principle: "Now when our minds are thoroughly divested of all prejudice in relation to the difference of colour, and the Love of Christ, in which there is no partiality, prevails upon us, I believe it will appear that a heavy account lies against us as a Civil Society for oppressions commited against people who did not injure us." [77] This is the basis of his whole social philosophy, in fact. He ably marshaled arguments drawn from the theory of natural rights, humanitarianism, "the right use of things," "pure wisdom," utility, and his own brand of economics, to explain and justify the sort of holy socialism he so ardently believed would please God and make men happy. But when all was said and done, "the love of Christ, in which there is no partiality," if honestly and thoroughly applied in practice, was philosophy enough; and it was a philosophy anybody could understand.

The contrast between Franklin and Woolman is clear: Franklin explained sociological phenomena as a rationalist, in terms of the natural laws governing such phenomena, without completely ruling out the influence of a supernatural first cause; Woolman explained society and its phenomena in terms of the wishes of the divine creator, and, while harmonizing reason and the voice of God, based his ideal of social behavior and relationships upon divine and brotherly love.

There was a middle ground, of course, represented by such men as Jonathan Mayhew, John Witherspoon and Samuel Johnson, which accepted the idea of natural law and the validity of human reason, but within the framework of the grand divine plan. So that Johnson, in the style of the religious rationalist and in conformity with his own philosophy of idealism, could write that

> every man is liable to more wants and necessities than he could of himself supply without the assistance of others . . . and the joint commerce of many and even distant nations, God having so ordered things that each different climate should produce some things peculiar to itself . . . and this seems designed on purpose to promote a general acquaintance, intercourse, faith and friendship among mankind; so that all the inhabitants of the whole globe are obliged to consider themselves on many accounts as one community. . . . It is therefore manifest that the great Author of your beings, by all these common sentiments, necessities and interests, affections, relations and depend-

[76] Ibid., pp. 424-5.   [77] Ibid., p. 437.

encies, has evidently designed to tie you together . . . as a system or whole made up of a vast number and diversity of members.[78]

If the more or less formal sociological thinking that was going on be linked with the anthropological observations that were being made, particularly with regard to the Indians, by such men as Bartram and Colden, it becomes clear that the Americans were becoming conscious of the problems of human society and institutions and were beginning to address themselves to those problems in the basic attitudes of observational science. Their explanations of the phenomena were of a part with their observations of the natural world and, generally speaking, were just about as rationalistic. The greatest significance in this line of thought, probably, lies in the fact that such a consideration of human problems as of a piece with the rest of the natural world had actually begun. In this sense the beginnings of sociological thought appear as an integral part of the development of eighteenth-century rationalism, as distinguished from the supernaturalism of the preceding century.

Conclusion: The Ideals of Social Freedom

Here, then, were the main outlines of the American social mind. Social thinking, of a piece with and inseparable from economic thought, tended to follow the lines of social division as social division tended to follow the lines of economic interest and competence. Economic status determined, to a large degree, social status; and social status dictated, for most men at least, the social idea. Thus the wealthy were aristocrats and thought in terms of aristocracy; the farmer who had risen from the European peasantry thought in terms of social movement, as did the frontiersman, to whom progress, economic and social, was a daily vision of reality.

But materialistic considerations were far from determining the whole of American social thought. For religion was still the great meliorator of the materialistic outlook: John Woolman was only the most articulate of a host of men who still felt the impulses of the worth of the individual in the eyes of God and of social responsibility in the name of religion. Many, also, like Crèvecœur, were humanitarian rationalists, products of the Enlightenment, who saw human beings as endowed in certain natural social rights motivated by the great common human mainspring of enlightened self-interest. Left to itself, natural, intelligent self-interest would bring into being the happiest society; but intelligent self-direction must be free and unhampered, to work out its social destiny along the most progressive and beneficial lines possible within the framework of nature.

[78] Samuel Johnson : *Career and Writings* (Schneider ed.), II, 543–5.

The American social mind was not without its essential social conflict. For just as the frontier debtor classes were advocates of easy money and suspicious and distrustful of the hard-money merchants, just so the rural small farmer and frontier social groups were beginning to resent the social superiority of the aristocrats. The conflict had little explicit manifestation; but the outbreaks of the Regulators toward the end of the colonial period were at least partly social in character; as was the remonstrance of the South Carolina frontiersmen to the Commons House of Assembly in 1767 against the neglect of them and their problems by the government. The remonstrance of the frontiersmen was coolly ignored by the aristocratic Assembly of South Carolina, and the frontiersmen, still awed by the superiority of class, did nothing about it. Social resentment on the frontier was real, but it was hardly strong enough yet to produce action; for the aristocrats were still in the seats of power, political, social, and intellectual.

On the other hand, there were certain great and unifying common denominators in American social thought which set it off from that of other societies and which were tending, despite surface divisions, toward a common unity of attitude and expression. Even the aristocrats were for the most part only a generation or two separated from the frontier social experience. They had risen to their social pre-eminence by the sweat of their fathers' brows and their own; their minds could not completely exclude the reality of social change by individual economic effort nor the ideal of social fluidity derived from that reality.

Thus the great common denominator of American social thinking was the ideal of social freedom—freedom to rise, that is—individualism, and social fluidity. If the Americans still believed in aristocracy, it was now, in theory at least, predominantly the sort of aristocracy that John Adams called "natural," an outlook based upon the ideal of an aristocracy of merit, of individual worth.

NOTE TO THE READER

The first and most obvious suggestion for reading in the field of social thought is Benjamin Franklin's "Observations Concerning the Increase of Mankind and the Peopling of Countries." This essay was written in 1751, but was first printed as an appendix to William Clarke's *Observations on the Late and Present Conduct of the French* (Boston, 1755). It is now easily available in all the standard collections of Franklin's writings.

A tract of a different sort, with a much more religious flavor, is Samuel Johnson's *Raphael, or the Genius of the English America,* printed in the Schneider edition of Johnson's *Career and Writings,* Volume II. This is a delightful and thought-provoking essay, dealing with the general problem of the good life and the good society, and includes stimulating thoughts on religious toleration, education, and the civic virtues.

John Woolman's *Journal and Essays* has already been suggested; it should be mentioned again here because the *Essays* in particular constitute a unique and in many ways original contribution to early American social thought.

In the realm of education William Smith's *An Idea of the College of Mirania* (New York, 1753), Franklin's *Proposals Relating to the Education of Youth in Pennsylvania* (Philadelphia, 1749), and Johnson's *Raphael* are the clearest and most interesting expressions of the new educational theory. At the same time, however, John Morgan's *Discourse upon the Institution of Medical Schools in America*, already mentioned in connection with the chapter on science, should be mentioned again here as laying down the lines for the development of American medical education.

Jonathan Boucher's writings are probably the clearest expression of the social philosophy of the American aristocrats. His books were not published until after the American Revolution, but the ideas and convictions expressed in them were formed in fifteen or twenty years prior to the Declaration of Independence. The two most important are his *Reminiscences of an American Loyalist* (Boston, 1925) and *A View of the Causes and Consequences of the American Revolution* (London, 1797).

Crèvecœur's *Letters from an American Farmer* and his *Sketches of Eighteenth Century America* (New Haven, 1935) are both delightful books, and give a charming literary picture of American society and social attitudes. They are probably the most readable of all the books mentioned here, although Crèvecœur was inclined to paint his pictures in somewhat over-romanticized colors.

Of the secondary works, the finest description of social life and manners in the colonies is the series by Thomas J. Wertenbaker called *The Founding of American Civilization*, in three volumes (New York, 1938–47).

Of the modern books on education, the monumental histories of Harvard University by Samuel E. Morison are by far the best, and they are, incidentally, beautiful exemplars of the book-making art. The two on the period of the seventeenth century are *The Founding of Harvard College* (Cambridge, 1935) and *Harvard College in the Seventeenth Century* (2 vols., Cambridge, 1936). A small, over-all history of Harvard is Morison's *Three Centuries of Harvard, 1636–1936* (Cambridge, 1936), which is a charming and highly entertaining essay.

CHAPTER VI

Of the State, of Government, and of the Natural Rights of Man: Political Thought

---

"The colonies have a complete and adequate legislative authority, and "are not only represented in their assemblies, but in no other man-"ner. . . .

"The power described in the provincial charters, is to make laws, "and in the exercise of that power, the colonies are bounded by no "other limitations than what result from their subordination to, and "dependence upon Great Britain."

DANIEL DULANY.

AS economic thought concerns itself basically with the material problems of human sustenance and shelter, and sociological thought has to do with human beings in their societal relationships with one another, so politics is the science of the institutions under which men organize themselves for political action and regulation. It is not always easy to distinguish between these three divisions of human institutions and thought, so intimately are they related; the thinkers of the seventeenth century, indeed, generally did confuse society with the state, and the state with government. But the state is neither society alone nor government alone; nor is a society, which is people, always a state, which is a political entity that may represent the political interests of many disparate groups of people. Similarly, the state, whose function is political, should not be confused with the nation, which is a socio-cultural phenomenon. Thus the state, as distinguished from society or the nation on the one hand and from government on the other, may be defined as a body politic, composed of one or more societal or national groups, functioning as a unit for the expression of the political interests and relationships of its members. Government, on the other hand, is nothing more than an institution, devised by the body politic, or the state, as a sort of mechanism for carrying out the political wishes of its members. The integral state, as a compact political entity, is a modern phenomenon; certainly it did not exist in the decentralized political world of the Middle Ages. It was emerging out of feudalism into its completed modern form as the accepted and typical political unit in Western civilization at just about the time when English America was first being settled.

Among the British American colonies in the eighteenth century, each colony was, as it were, a separate state, or body politic, in embryo. Yet it was not yet a completely sovereign state, for it bore a close but anomalous relationship to the rest of the British Empire, a relationship that involved a certain undefined political dependence upon Great Britain. The Empire as a whole could hardly be called a state, since it did not function as a political entity, but operated, rather, as an extremely heterogeneous congeries of separate colonies, possessions, territories, and provinces subject to Great Britain. Great Britain, on the other hand, was a state, since it existed and functioned as a political entity.

Just what the political relationship of the self-governing American provinces was to the state of Great Britain had never been explained. Very little thinking, indeed, had been done about it, and Britishers had generally assumed vaguely that the colonies, politically, were mere extensions of the British state, and that the government set up to administer the political affairs of Great Britain was more or less automatically also the government of the extensions of Great Britain in America. By the middle of the eighteenth century, however, it had become perfectly obvious to all who had an eye to see that this theory, however sound it may have been as theory, was not satisfactory in practice, especially to the Americans. For in the century and a half that had intervened since the colonies were founded the Americans had had, of sheer necessity, to assume a considerable amount of responsibility for the conduct of their own political affairs and to invent or devise mechanisms of government and ideas relative to politics to meet their needs, which now sharply distinguished them from the state, the government, and the political ideas of their cousins in Great Britain.

Yet the exact nature of the relationship between colony and mother country had never been defined. The British, in general, clung stubbornly to their old vague assumption that the colonies were extensions of the British state, whereas the new theory of the Americans was growing steadily, and almost without their being aware of it, toward a political theory whose logical conclusion could only be that the self-governing colonies were, in fact separate bodies politic in their own natural right, with all the attributes, within their own boundaries, of complete political sovereignty.

Not that there were more than a few Americans who saw the ultimate logic of the American position. But a few there were, on both sides of the question, who did. And, vague and indecisive as it was, most of the political thinking that was going on in the colonies in the middle decades of the eighteenth century was in the last analysis concerned with the effort to solve this problem.

THE OLD POLITICAL THEORY: THE ABSOLUTIST STATE IN EUROPE AND AMERICA

The seventeenth century is marked, in the political annals of western civilization, by the crystallization of the integrated sovereign state in its modern form. In the days of its first full-bloom emergence, however, while it was made up of all the people of France or all the people of England, it was still under the control of a relatively small minority; the masses of the common people were only just beginning to be barely conscious of the existence of the state and of the fact that they, as citizens, were part of it. The essential character of the state being its absolute sovereignty over itself and its individual citizens, the individual controlling the state found it easy to believe that that sovereignty derived, somehow, from himself. Thus kings like James I of England and Louis XIV of France found it easy to believe that the ultimate sovereignty of the state, which was a power derived in the last analysis from God, resided in themselves; and the vestigial feudal aristocracy, by this time reduced to a position of complete subservience to the king, were inclined to agree. Their theory of the divine right of kings, however, ran counter to the ideal of the rising commercial middle class, who resented the arbitrary management of state affairs by the king and felt an urgent desire to secure at least a share in its control for themselves. To counter the divine-right theories of the kings and their supporters, therefore, the middle class advanced the claim that sovereignty in the state derives from the people who make up the state, and that the king, while the symbol of that sovereignty, is himself subject to it. Naturally, for the middle class in England, the sounding-board for the voice of this sovereignty was Parliament, which was made up of the representatives of the people. Thus the political history of England in the seventeenth century was in large measure a see-saw struggle between those who found sovereignty to derive from God and reside in the king and those who insisted that it derived from the people and resided in Parliament. After the parliamentary republican Commonwealth and the failure of the compromise with divine-right monarchy in the Restoration, the parliamentary ideal finally triumphed in the "Glorious Revolution" of 1688–9.

The struggle in England, especially, generated a considerable amount of political theory. Sir Robert Filmer, in his *Patriarcha; or, The Natural Power of Kings*, elaborated and tried to justify the theory of the divine right of kings, basing his argument upon the idea that the king is a sort of "patriarch," or father, of his people; that his power, like the absolute power of the father over his family, or tribe, derives from the natural order of things created and supported by God's will.

Filmer's great opponent was Thomas Hobbes, who, in his great book *Leviathan*, derived the sovereignty of the state from the people, who, tacitly or explicitly, pool their sovereignty in the state by what he called a social compact. Men in a state of nature, according to Hobbes, are free, and they are equal. But they are selfish, savage, deterred from preying upon their fellows by nothing save the fear of retribution. Life in the state of nature, says Hobbes, is therefore "solitary, poor, nasty, brutish, and short." But men are guided by reason; and, prompted by their intelligence, they agree among themselves to surrender their individual freedom and sovereignty to a common authority over themselves for the sake of peace. Thus the state is set up by voluntary agreement, and it is endowed with the sovereignty formerly possessed by the individuals among the people. This authority is absolute, and it is not subject to criticism; it cannot alienate its authority nor is it answerable for its conduct in the last analysis, either to its citizens or to other states. Thus the state is absolute; and Hobbes's theory could be used to justify either monarchy or republic as a form of government. Its significance lay, however, in its logical derivation of the state from the people; and its naturalistic assumption of the original depravity of man.

John Milton, who was as Puritanically religious as Hobbes was atheistic, related his political ideals to the drama of salvation. He believed in a republican form of government, but he eventually concluded that the common people were just a depraved mob, and not to be trusted; the republic, apparently, was to be a republic controlled by the best people, the chosen few; depravity was the result of sin and darkness; enlightenment the result of salvation. Government is based upon the will of God: men were made in God's image; they are free so long as they exercise their freedom in accord with God's plan; if they choose to run counter to God's will, they deserve to lose their freedom, and they will; they thus become slaves by their own departure from God's plan for them. Milton's political theory thus resolves itself into a concept of a God-planned republic, with control in the hands of the elect, and freedom for the citizenry to do only those things that fit into the plan. These ideas, or ideas closely similar to them, were already being put into practice and expressed in theory in the Puritan commonwealth on the shores of Massachusetts Bay.

More significant than Milton, however, especially for later American political thought, were Algernon Sidney, who believed in a sort of aristocratic, mixed republic that would derive its magisterial power by delegation from the people, and James Harrington. Harrington's great work, *The Commonwealth of Oceana*, also advocated an aristocratic republic; he ignored the idea of the social compact, however, and his belief in written constitutions and the separation of powers in government found congenial receptivity among the Americans.

John Locke, apologist of the Glorious Revolution, marks the clear turn in theory away from the fixed, absolute state of Hobbes to one that could adapt itself to the changing wishes of the citizens. Starting with the idea of the social compact, Locke believed that, far from surrendering their natural rights, the participants in the compact by it guaranteed to themselves their natural rights of life, liberty, and property. The body politic formed by the compact could delegate its authority and power to government; but if the government ever failed to function as the body politic the people had originally intended, then the people could dismiss the government and get another — by force if necessary. Thus government, be it monarchy or republic, became the agent of the sovereignty of the state, or body politic, and was always answerable to it. It is no wonder that Locke's theory was found to be so congenial to the Americans when they finally decided to divest themselves of their king! But that is another story.

All these theories of the state were theories of aristocracy, or oligarchy — even Locke's. Yet there were certain religious radicals in England whose political thought, remotely derived, perhaps, from that of the German Anabaptists, contained the germ of ideas that were essentially democratic. Of these men the most notable were George Fox, leader of the Quakers, and John Lilburne, leader of the so-called "Levellers," and especially the latter. For while the equality of all men in the eyes of God was implicit in the religious doctrines and practices of the Quakers, Lilburne applied the doctrine of equality specifically to political problems. It seemed to Lilburne that since Adam and Eve were the parents of all, then all, men and women alike, were equal to each other as descendants of the original pair. Further, instead of deriving the state from the will of God, Lilburne derived it from the wishes of the people; for him it was in the people — all the people — that sovereignty in the state ultimately rested.

These ideas bear a remarkable resemblance both to the ideas of Samuel Pufendorf, in Germany, and to those of his later American disciple, John Wise; but they were far too radical for any considerable measure of acceptance as yet, either in Europe or in America. Democracy was anathema, in those days, everywhere; its earliest adoption in practice anywhere was probably in the primitive communities along the American frontier.

Pufendorf, the German, was a younger contemporary of John Locke. He accepted the idea of the social compact and the belief that men in a state of nature are free and equal; but, like Locke, he rejected the idea of the depravity of man and concluded that men formed the social compact, not defensively because they were evil, but positively and progressively, precisely because they were at least partially good and would use the state for the advancement of human happiness.

The theories of Lilburne, or even those of Pufendorf and Locke, with their emphasis upon natural rights, the pursuit of happiness, and the right of revolution, were a far cry from the rigid absolutism of the state in the theories of Filmer and Hobbes and Milton. And since those were the ideas that dominated political thought at the moment when America was being settled, those were the kinds of political ideas that were brought to America by the first generation of the founders.

The Puritans who founded New England thus came out of the school of political thought typified by Hobbes and Milton. Yet to them the state and its government were but parts of the great drama of salvation, and their political theory must be understood as referring always back to that. For to them the social compact was a religious compact, between each other and between themselves and God: "When *Jehojada* made a Covenant between the King and the people . . . that Covenant was but a branch of the Lords Covenant with them all, both King and people: for the King promised but to Rule the people righteously, according to the will of God: and the people to be subject to the King so Ruling. Now these duties of the King to them, and of them to the King, were such as God required in his Covenant, both of him and them."[1] And just as their ideas of society were conceived as parts of God's will with men, so also the organization of the people into a body politic and the form of the government set over them fell into the pattern of the divine plan. This idea, indeed, this concept of "plan," was the great cohesive principle that ran through all

[1] Quoted in Miller: *The New England Mind*, p. 415.

their thinking and gave it consistency. The Puritan was nothing if not consistent; at least, he consciously tried his best to be so.

The Puritan's attitude toward the state and his relationship to it was well expressed by John Winthrop in his "little speech" to the General Court in 1645:

> There is a twofold liberty, natural (I mean as our nature is now corrupt) and civil or federal. The first is common to man with beasts and other creatures. By this, man, as he stands in relation to man simply, hath liberty to do what he lists, it is liberty to evil as well as to good. This liberty is incompatible and inconsistent with authority, and cannot endure the least restraint of the most just authority. The exercise and maintaining this liberty makes men grow more evil, and in time to be worse than brute beasts. . . . This is that great enemy of truth and peace, that wild beast, which all the ordinances of God are bent against, to restrain and subdue it. The other kind of liberty I call civil or federal, it may also be termed moral, in reference to the covenant between God and man, in the moral law, and the politic covenants and constitutions, amongst men themselves. This liberty is the proper end and object of authority, and cannot subsist without it; and it is a liberty to that only which is good, just, and honest. . . . This liberty is maintained and exercized in a way of subjection to authority; it is of the same kind of liberty wherewith Christ hath made us free. . . . Even so, brethren, it will be between you and your Magistrates. If you stand for your natural corrupt liberties, and will do what is good in your own eyes, you will not endure the least weight of authority, but will murmur, and oppose, and be always striving to shake off that yoke; but if you will be satisfied to enjoy the civil and lawful liberties, such as Christ allows you, then will you quietly and cheerfully submit unto that authority which is set over you, in all the administrations of it, for your good.[2]

This might almost have been written by Hobbes but for its religious overtones. For Winthrop saw men in a natural state as little more than brute beasts; they had surrendered their "natural liberty," in accepting the authority of the state, in return for "civil liberty." Now that they were in the civil state they must obey it without question and without any recourse, except, as in the case of Roger Williams, to exile. The state was ordained by God in his plan for men, but effectuated by men themselves. And the state, thus set up according to God's plan and will, was absolute in its sovereignty over its citizens.

Nor was it a democratic state. For these were no democrats, these Puritans. As the Reverend John Cotton put it, "Democracy, I do not conceyve that ever God did ordeyne as a fitt government eyther for

[2] John Winthrop: *John Winthrop's Journal, History of New England*, edited by J. K. Hosmer (2 vols., New York, 1908), II, 233–9.

church or commonwealth. If the people be governors, who shall be governed? As for monarchy, and aristocracy, they are both of them clearly approved, and directed in scripture, yet so as referreth the soveraignitie to himselfe, and setteth up Theocracy in both, as the best forme of government in the commonwealth, as well as in the church." [3] God, indeed, was the real head of the state, and an autocratic head, at that; and government, whether monarchy or republic, was only an agent for God in advancing his plan with men. But government must govern. Both people and government were parts of the state; it was the business of one to govern; it was the business of the other to submit, to the greater glory of God and the better guidance of men. In any case, the state and its mechanisms were fixed, with a sharp, undemocratic distinction between government and governed. The religious qualifications for full citizenship restricted the governing class to a minority; yet, curiously enough, in the mechanism of the town meeting the Puritan state contained the instrument for its own eventual democratization.

If Puritan political theory of the absolute state was the intellectual offspring of Hobbes and Milton, the theory of the southerners was more nearly that of Filmer. For the sympathies of Virginia — with reservations — had been with Charles I against the Puritan republicans, and Sir William Berkeley, Governor under the Restoration, was nothing if not a royalist. Sir William was not alone in his insistence upon the unchallengeable authority of the state and the king; for when Nathaniel Bacon did dare to challenge it, the majority of the new planter aristocrats supported Sir William wholeheartedly. And these advocates of the fixed, authoritarian royalist state were the ancestors of the Virginia statesmen of the American Revolution!

The American Way

The first and most profound modification of the theory of the baroque state in America was its adaptation to the conditions of the new environment. For the adaptation of political ideas followed and shared the adaptation that was taking place in those relative to economics and society. Thus the immediate effect of the classless frontier was the invention of a new "territorial" basis of representation to replace the old "class" basis of the English parliaments. Since the American frontiers had no social divisions comparable to the English "Lords, temporal and spiritual," and "commons," the colonists were forced to find some other way, and the most obvious was representation by township; that is, by territorial unit. This territorial basis of representation became fixed in the American mind, and it provided the

[3] Miller and Johnson : *The Puritans,* pp. 209–10.

argument for many a frontier demand for a revision of representation in the provincial assemblies to accommodate the organization of the legislature to the expanding settlements in the west.

Another idea that got itself rooted in the American mind very early was the faith in written constitutions. This faith derived largely from the original colonial charters, which were actually contracts between the crown and the proprietors of the land, whether commercial companies like the Massachusetts Bay Company or individual proprietors like Lord Baltimore. But the provisions of these contracts, often enough cited to protect the proprietors or later the colonial governments from the king, also became guarantees of correct government to the freemen, or citizens, against the proprietor or the colonial government. The famous appeal of Watertown to the Massachusetts charter in 1633 was only one among many such cases. But this appeal to written constitutions was something new in the world, as yet peculiar to the Americans, and it never took root in England.

Thus the factors making for constitutional change and for a consequent revision of political thinking were present in the actual living-conditions of the settlers in the American scene right from the beginning. This is equivalent to saying that the frontier conditions in which they found themselves forced the settlers to invent new institutions and new ideas to meet and explain the problems of political life in the new world. But as the turn into the eighteenth century came, the advancing frontiers presented a still newer situation that demanded still further adaptation. For not only did the frontiersmen of the newer west demand representation; their greater remoteness from England, coupled with the admixture of great numbers of newcomers of non-English stock who were entirely without both a primary loyalty to England and the Englishman's sense of self-government and "the rights of Englishmen," definitely tended to diminish the Americans' willingness to accept dictation from England, and at the same time created the breach between the "conservative east" and the "radical west" that was the matrix of many American political parties and their ideals.

The influence of the American environment upon the evolution of political thought was strengthened by the rationalism in political thinking that was derived from Newtonian science and imported into America in the writings of Harrington and others, but especially of Locke. For the colonists, in the long struggle of their assemblies for a recognition of the right to have their own form of government based upon their American experience, found in the naturalistic theories of Locke the almost perfect philosophical rationalization of all that they were struggling for. The combination of the American experience with the imported ideas produced a political ideology that could not but conflict with the ideas of all those who represented the supremacy of the royal prerogative.

In the course of this conflict the representatives of the crown and those Americans who believed with them, forced to justify their own defense of the prerogative, developed a theory of their own relative to the state and government in colony and Empire which, while not precisely that of most Englishmen, gave a more or less rational explanation to their conception of the nature of the colonial state and its relation to the Empire. This group, known generally to the Americans as the "court party," was the group from which were to come those sincere men who, because of their convictions, felt compelled, when the day of the great decision came, to put their loyalty to the British constitution above their loyalty to the local constitutional theories of their neighbors, to be forever tarred with the opprobrium of the name of "Tories." Opposed to these Tory imperialists were the various groups who controlled the provincial assemblies. It was these groups, made up largely of members of the colonial assemblies and their supporters, who developed the American political theory that eventuated, after long and irregular but steady development, in the theory that each colony was a sovereign state in its own right, whether or not ruled over by the English kings. These men, the American "Whigs," were not democrats and did not believe in democracy; on the contrary, they feared democracy like the plague. Their theory was a theory of constitutionalism : the formation of the state by social compact, government derived from the people (the property-owners), and the legislature as the most powerful branch of government, the proper agency for the expression of the sovereign will of the people.

More radical still, intellectually even revolutionary, were numerous frontiersmen, some town laborers, and a few isolated thinkers who saw the vision of democracy, a vision just beginning to be made reality on the frontiers. Few of these men were articulate enough to make themselves heard, however ; and when they did they were looked upon as impossible radicals — at least until their theories began to command a following among a very few of the leaders of the Revolution.

As in economic life and in social life, the political mind of the eighteenth-century American was thus composed of a variety of schools of thought, representing different regions and different social classes. In broad outline, however, there were only three main positions : the "court party," the future "Tories," who recognized and accepted the supremacy of the English royal prerogative ; "the assembly party," the American "Whigs," who derived the American state, in the last analysis, from the American people rather than the English ;

and the frontier democratic elements who were pushing these naturalistic political concepts toward a belief in the equality of men and
a steadily broadening base of political control. The Negro slaves,
numerous as they were, and even if they had any concept of the state,
by reason of their economic and social status were entirely inarticulate.
Despite these differences, however, there was a surprising amount of
agreement among all groups of theorists as to the nature of the state,
the theory of natural law made manifest in the natural rights of Englishmen, constitutional restraints upon government, and the ultimate
derivation of sovereignty from the people. The differences were not
differences as to fundamentals until the moment of independence : they
were differences as to how the fundamentals should be worked out in
practice.

The "court party" : the Tory imperialists

England had given little or no thought to the colonial administration and the theory of the relationship between mother country and
colonies at the time when the English colonies in America were
founded. Aside from certain phrases in the Virginia charter of Sir
Walter Raleigh, some of the writings of Richard Hakluyt, and the organization of the first Virginia company, there was little or no thought
given to the political implications of the creation of an empire. Such
thinking as there of necessity had to be generally took for granted
the assumption that politically the colonies were extensions of England
and that the colonists were to be governed under the English constitution, just about like Englishmen in England.

Great Britain never produced a first-class thinker or a first-class
theory dealing with the political nature of the Empire prior to American independence. Yet the instructions to the colonial governor were
instinct with a set of ideas which, if never clear and always based
more upon expediency than upon consistent policy, did nevertheless
embody a sort of half-baked theory of the political dependence of the
colonies upon the mother country. It was in the colonies themselves,
apparently, that the best and clearest thinking along the lines of this
British or "Tory" point of view was done ; and this thinking, as it developed in both America and England, arose in fact as a sort of
defensive theory against the rising American demands for colonial
autonomy that were to culminate in nothing less than the theory of
an ultimate sovereignty resident in the people of the colonies themselves.

By the eighteenth century the colonists were already assuming
that the only way in which their precious inherent rights as Englishmen, including that of taxation only by their own representatives,

could be exercised was through their own elected assemblies. At the same time they were becoming conscious of the fact that they, so far from Britain and in a new situation, were better qualified to meet their peculiar political problems than the legislature or the governmental boards of England. This consciousness of the necessity for political adaptation, a concept that few people in England ever clearly grasped, was the ground of one of Jeremiah Dummer's chief arguments when he was called upon, as a colonial agent in 1721, to show cause why the liberal charters of the New England colonies should not be revoked : "As the reason is incontestable, so the Fact is apparent, that these [chartered New England] Governments, far from retrenching the Liberty of the Subject, have improv'd it in some important Articles, which the Circumstances of Things in Great Britain perhaps don't require, or won't easily admit. . . ."[4] The important thing, however, was the rights of Englishmen. At the time of the Andros riots in New England, Dummer continues, the Americans "were scoffingly told, *Those Things* [the rights of Englishmen] *would not follow them to the Ends of the Earth.* Unnatural Insult ! must the brave Adventurer, who with the Hazard of His Life and Fortune, seeks out new Climates to inrich his Mother Country, be deny'd those common Rights, which his Countrymen enjoy at Home in Ease and Indolence ?"[5]

But in exactly what did the rights of Englishmen consist ? How far had the colonists the authority to defend those rights locally in the colonies through their own legislatures ? And how far might they go in changing their local provincial political institutions in ways that seemed inimical to the constitution of Britain ? Nobody clearly knew.

The problem had become evident to the Americans fairly early in their history and became clearer as they continued to assume that the colonial assemblies possessed, as of inherent right, all or most of the authority, rights, and prerogatives of the English House of Commons in England. Hugh Jones, in his description of the Virginia House of Burgesses in 1724, describes this assumption without critical examination : The Burgesses, he said, "meet, choose a Speaker, &c. and proceed in most Respects as the *House of Commons* in England, who with the *Upper House,* consisting of the *Governor and Council,* make laws exactly as the *King* and *Parliament* do ; the laws being passed there [Virginia] by the *Governor,* as by the king here [England]."[6] A decade later, in 1735, the colonial position was made more explicit by the

[4] A. B. Hart, ed. : *American History Told by Contemporaries* (4 vols., New York, 1897), II, 133.

[5] Ibid., II, 135.

[6] Hugh Jones : *The Present State of Virginia* (London, 1724), p. 63.

South Carolina Commons House of Assembly when it resolved "That His Majesty's subjects in this province are entitled to all the liberties and privileges of Englishmen . . . [and] that the Commons House of Assembly in South Carolina, by the laws of England and South Carolina, and ancient usage and custom, have all the rights and priv-

Forums of American political debate : the Virginia provincial capitol, Williamsburg.

[By courtesy of the Library of Congress]

ileges pertaining to Money bills that are enjoyed by the British House of Commons." [7]

As the colonial assemblies not only assumed but extended the power inherent in the control of the purse, they came into head-on conflict with the colonial governors, royal and proprietary, whose activities, covered by the theory of the prerogative, they sought to restrict. This conflict precipitated an examination of the fundamental questions involved, and one of the classical answers to the problem of the political relationship of colonies to mother country was given by William Keith, Governor of Pennsylvania :

> From what has been said of the Nature of Colonies . . . [it is] plain that none of the English Plantations in America can with any reason or good sense pretend to claim an Absolute Legislative Power within themselves ; so that let their several Constitutions be founded on Ancient Charters, Royal Patent, Custom, Prescription or what other Legal

[7] Quoted in D. D. Wallace : *Constitutional History of South Carolina from 1725 to 1775* (Abbeville, S.C., 1899), p. 50.

Authority You please, yet still they cannot be possessed of any rightful
Capacity to contradict or evade the force of any act of Parliament
wherewith the Wisdom of Great Britain may think fit to effect them
from time to time, & in discoursing of their Legislative Power (improperly so called in a dependent Government) we are to consider
them only as so many Corporations at a distance invested with ability
to make Temporary By Laws for themselves agreeable to their Respective Situations & Clymates but no ways interfering with the Legal Prerogatives of the Crown or the true Legislative Power of the Mother
State.[8]

This was written in 1728. But it stated a principle always maintained by England, and eventually stated explicitly in the Declaratory
Act of 1766 : the principle, that is, that Parliament was the supreme
legislature for the entire Empire, and could legislate for all parts of it
on any question whatsoever. Without being quite clear about it in his
own mind, Keith was trying to resolve the dilemma presented by the
fact that Parliament was undeniably the legislative voice of the British
state, on the one side, and the equally obvious fact, on the other, that
the colonial assemblies were unquestionably representative of large
bodies of Englishmen. Either there was only one British state, with
Parliament as its legislature, of which all Englishmen everywhere
were subjects, or there were as many states as there were legislatures,
each one sovereign within itself. Keith, faced with this dilemma, could
only decide that there was only one state, Britain ; and that the colonial
assemblies could not possibly be legislatures at all, since there could
be only one legislature for the British state, and that was Parliament.

The position taken by Keith was shared by most of the colonial
governors, and even by many thoughtful Americans. But the assemblies
went right on extending their control of government — much, indeed,
as Parliament had done in England — until the governors, in their
panic, could see no outcome other than complete colonial independence. As Lieutenant-Governor George Clark blurted out to the New
York Assembly as early as 1741 :

But whether grown wanton by prosperity or whatever else it was they
began to divert from the example of the parliament, demanding to
have the nomination of a Treasurer . . . & being Indulged in this, they
soon grew in their demands . . . [and by] fixing on themselves ye dependence of the Officers for whom they provided (for men are naturally servants to those who pay them) they in effect subverted the
Constitution assuming to themselves one undoubted & essential branch
of his Majesty's Royal Prerogative. . . . [I hope now that] Sober and

[8] Printed in William Byrd : *History of the Dividing Line and Other Tracts,*
II, 219.

reasonable Councils will take place & the example of y^t august body, the parliament, will be the Rule of your future actions, this & only this will remove as to this province, a jealousy which for some years has obtained in England, that the plantations are not without thoughts of throwing off their Dependence on the Crown of England.[9]

The colonies of course had no thought of throwing off their allegiance to the crown; certainly not yet. But they were, indeed, moving toward a theory of legislative independence of Parliament and the Board of Trade; and the first thinker to point this out clearly was Archibald Kennedy, of New York, who did so in 1752. Surprisingly enough, however, in pointing out their independence of Parliament Kennedy could find no other logical alternative than to proclaim the colonies the personal, feudal demesne of the king, and therefore even more subject to the arbitrary unchallengeable power of the prerogative than they would be under Parliament's direct control; for this theory deprived them of even such protection as Parliament could or would give them. For, says Kennedy, like the Isle of Jersey,

We are Parcel of the Dominions of the Crown of England; we are no Part, nor ever were, of the Realm of England, but a peculiar of the Crown, and by a natural and necessary Consequence, exempted from parliamentary Aids. Thus you see our Dependence and the Reason of it, is altogether upon his Majesty's Grace and Favour. If we don't approve of our present System of Government, let us pray for a better: In the mean Time, let us not contemptuously treat those Favours the Crown has been pleased already to confer upon us.[10]

Furthermore, says Kennedy, since the colonial governments were the creation of the king for government of this handsome feudal estate, not only do instructions to his governors have the power of law, but he can even dissolve the colonial governments, including representative institutions themselves, if he sees fit to do so. As for the colonies and their governments,

We [the colony of New York] are no more than a little Corporation, in the same Manner as a Mayor, Aldermen, and Common-Council are impowered, by his Majesty's Letters Patent, to form Rules and Orders for the Government of a City, in its several Wards and Districts; even so; Tho' in somewhat a higher Degree, and more extensive Sphere; but all to the same Purpose is a Governor Council and Assembly, to govern a Colony, in its several Counties and Precincts, by the same Power: Every Law or Rule made, that is not peculiarly adapted to

[9] *Journal of the Legislative Council of the Colony of New York, 1691–1743* (Albany, 1861), p. 768.

[10] Archibald Kennedy: *An Essay on the Government of the Colonies* (New York), pp. 15–16.

their respective communities, has no Meaning; and every Law Made, that in any Shape clashes or interferes with the Laws of *Great-Britain*, are, *ipso Facto*, void. By this I understand, that the Liberties and Properties of *British* subjects abroad, established and cemented by the Treasure and Blood of our Ancestors, Time out of Mind, is not left to the caprice and Humour of a Colony Assembly.[11]

Thus by assigning the colonies to a feudal status and by an appeal to feudal political theory Kennedy proposed to protect the colonists — the rights of Englishmen, indeed! — from the capricious, disloyal behavior of the colonial assemblies.

This argument based on feudalism is the culmination of one of the possible developments of the position of William Keith. But it also opened the door to the radically opposite position: the complete legislative divorce of the colonies under the King from England and its Parliament, a position taken in fact by Richard Bland of Virginia a little over a decade later. The governors and their sympathizers, the "court party," were already on the defensive; and their thinking, from 1750 to 1774, was mostly a frantic effort to find logical reasons why the colonies should not demand the same sort of legislative domination of their governments that Britain had accepted, since these colonial Tories could see no middle ground between the complete theoretical sovereignty of the prerogative and the utter dissolution of the Empire in the independence of the colonies.

This was true in nearly all the colonies; the royal and proprietary governors were struggling desperately to hold the line against the advancing theory of assembly predominance in the provincial governments. But it was in the proprietary province of Pennsylvania that one of the most significant battles in this subtle warfare took place. For there the proprietary was, after all, a private citizen: the assembly might go farther, in its challenge to his "prerogative" than the assembly of a royal province would dare to go, especially if it did so in the name of a wish to make Pennsylvania a royal rather than a proprietary province. In any case the battle became bitter with the approach of war with France, and revolved about the strategic points of the issuance of paper currency, the legal authority of the proprietor's instructions to his Governor, the question of taxing the proprietor's lands for defense, and, most important of all, the question whether the proprietor could veto a law approved by his Governor. The assembly considered itself to be on the defensive against an advancing autocracy of the proprietor; the proprietor's party, on the other hand, believed that it saw in the assembly's claims to power a sinister expansion in

---

[11] Ibid., p. 14.

the direction of both democracy and independence, and that this tendency must be blocked at all costs. The great champion of the proprietary cause was William Smith, provost of the College of Philadelphia, whose *Brief State of the Province of Pennsylvania* is an eloquent, if extreme, statement of the reactionary position :

> Those who have made Politics their Study, know very well, that Infant Settlements flourish fastest under a Government leaning to the republican or popular Forms, because such a Government immediately interests every Individual in the common Prosperity, and settles itself at once on a broad and firm Basis. Moreover, the People being but few, and but small Profit in public Offices, the Government may also be administer'd without the Faction and Anarchy incident to popular Forms. But in Proportion as a Country grows rich and populous, more Checks are wanted to the Power of the People ; and the Government, by nice Gradations, should verge more and more from the popular to the mixt Forms. Thus it may happen that a Constitution which shall preserve *Liberty* and excite *Industry* in any Country, during its Infancy, shall be prejudicial to both, when Circumstances are altered.[12]

The chief cause of the trouble, Smith thought, was the Quakers, and their allies, the Germans, who were hardly to be expected to be loyal to English ideals anyway. For the Quakers, once in power, had extended their power rather than contracted it.

> Thus, in direct Contradiction to the Rule laid down above, the People, instead of being subjected to more Checks, are under fewer than at first ; and their Power has been continually increasing with their Numbers and Riches, while the Power of their Governors, far from keeping Pace with theirs, has rather been decreasing in the same Proportion ever since. The Consequence of this is clear. The Government, instead of drawing nearer to the *mixt Forms*, as it ought in Proportion to its Growth, is now, in fact, more a *pure Republic*, than when there were not ten Thousand Souls in it. The Inconveniences of this we now begin to feel severely, and they must continually increase with the Numbers of the People, till the Government becomes at last so unwieldy as to fall a Prey to any Invader, or sink beneath its own Weight, unless a speedy Remedy is applied.[13]

Gloomy, fearful prospect, indeed ! To such catastrophic endings were the state and government in Pennsylvania doomed unless the Quaker-derived tendency toward democracy was checked, and that soon !

Needless to say, the remedy was obvious : a reaction to more checks upon the power of the popular arms of government. And Smith

---

[12] Smith : *A Brief State of the Province of Pennsylvania*, p. 6.
[13] Ibid., pp. 8–9.

boldly proposed that Parliament pass a law requiring all members of the Pennsylvania Assembly to take the oath of allegiance to the King and to promise to defend the country against all enemies, and denying the vote to all until they could show a sufficient knowledge of "our Language and Constitution." These measures, he thought, would break the power of the Quakers and the Germans and place government again in the hands of the dependable conservative members of society. Such a law "would effectually rescue us from all the sad Train of Calamities I have pointed out; and without such Means, I see nothing to prevent this Province from falling into the Hands of the *French.*" [14]

William Smith and Archibald Kennedy were spokesmen of the extreme reactionary school of political thought, which in the 1750's thought of the colonies as being, in the natural order of things, subservient to the crown and its agents. For them the claims of the assemblies, moving steadily toward their logical conclusion in recognition of the provincial assembly as the most sovereign arm of government, were dangerous in the extreme and must in some manner be forestalled if catastrophe was to be avoided.

Thomas Pownall, Governor of Massachusetts Bay, was a more objective observer of this ideological conflict between the colonies and the parent state — more objective, perhaps, than most men of his time. Pownall dismissed the idea that the colonies had any intention or desire to become independent. But the problem must be settled, and soon; therefore, while the theory that the colonies were feudal fiefs might possibly be justified, the colonies did actually legislate for themselves, and some compromise of theory and practice based upon a recognition of this fact must be effected, he felt sure, before the colonies could be satisfied.

Pownall himself did not dare try to solve the legislative problem, one way or the other; but he did see it, and he stated it clearly. The question was "whether a subordinate legislature can be instructed, restricted, and controuled, in the very act of legislation? whether the King's instructions or letters from secretaries of state, and such like significations of his Majesty's will and pleasure, is a due and constitutional application of the governors, or of the royal negative? — The Colonists constantly deny it, — and ministry, otherwise such instructions would not be given, constantly maintain it." [15] Here was the core of the problem, so far as the question of the authority of the colonial legislatures went. Could the ministry in England instruct, limit, or direct Parliament in England? No. Then no more could it instruct

[14] Ibid., p. 43.
[15] Thomas Pownall: *The Administration of the Colonies* (London, 1765), p. 42.

the colonial legislatures, since they, the colonists insisted, had the same immunities and powers as Parliament.

It was against just such an argument as this that Thomas Hutchinson, American-born Governor of Massachusetts, had to struggle. For in that colony, as elsewhere, the crescendo of the "assembly party's" theory of colonial legislative autonomy came to its climax after the Stamp Act when the provincial assembly had the temerity to question Parliament's power to legislate for the colonies at all. The ten years following 1765 were marked by a succession of exchanges of political theory between the assembly and the Governor; and Hutchinson, like his fellow loyalists, felt that denial of legislative authority of Parliament over the colonies was really a denial of all British authority over them; this, he felt sure, could only mean independence: "I know of no Line that can be drawn between the supreme Authority of Parliament and the total Independence of the Colonies: It is impossible there should be two independent Legislatures in one and the same State, for although there may be but one Head, the King, yet the two Legislative Bodies will make two Governments as distinct as the Kingdom of England and Scotland before the Union. . . ."[16]

Hutchinson saw the distinction between the state as body politic and the legislature as the political organ of the state. But he felt sure one state could not have two such organs. If the colonists insisted upon the ultimate supremacy of their own legislature, it meant they were setting up a new state, and could mean nothing less. It did not occur to him, as it had to Franklin, that there might be two states, or several, each with its own legislature, all bound together by one unique symbol of their common nationality. Yet Hutchinson did apparently see more clearly, perhaps, than any other of the Tory thinkers that the fundamental question of the original nature of the state was involved, and that the logical conclusion drawn from the assemblies' argument was that the Americans had, indeed, already founded a group of new states in America. Hutchinson, caught on the horns of this dilemma, and not yet conceiving of the federative empire, could only take one logical way out: "His Majesty considers the British Empire as one entire Dominion, subject to one Supreme Legislative Power, a due submission to which is essential to the Maintenance of the Rights, Liberties and Privileges of the several Parts of this Dominion. . . ."[17]

This is the high point of loyalist political thinking prior to the American Revolution: the British Empire is one single state; it is derived from the British people, to be sure, but the British people all

---

[16] Thomas Hutchinson: *The Speeches of His Excellency Governor Hutchinson to the General Assembly of the Massachuestts Bay* (Boston, 1773), p. 11.
[17] Ibid., p. 84.

over the world; and the Parliament in England is their legislature. Logically Hutchinson was probably just as much right as the autonomists; but, unhappily for him, he could not make this theory fit with the practical situation or with the century-long political experience of the Americans. The best he could offer was a sort of compromise based on a generous modification of Keith's old position. For he was willing to admit that the governments of the colonies, "from their separate and remote Situation, require more general and extensive Powers of Legislation within themselves than those formed within the Kingdom, but subject, nevertheless, to all such Laws of the Kingdom as immediately respect them or are designed to extend to them. . . . " [18]

Which satisfied the assembly not at all, and left the argument just where it had stood for so many years. For this argument still left essentially unanswered the more profound question as to the nature of the Empire, whether as a feudal fief of the king, as one great imperial, sovereign state, or as a constellation of separate states. The feudal-fief theory of Kennedy and Pownall was unthinkable to the Americans, as Pownall knew very well it would be; and in the same year that he published his book Richard Bland, in Virginia, presented to the Tory thinkers the startling and dismaying theory that the colonies were completely separated, legislatively, from England and the English Parliament.

Franklin, indeed, had long thought of the Empire as one organic whole, and had once thought the solution of America's ills lay in having representation in the supreme imperial legislature; but he had discarded that idea at the time of the Stamp Act and Bland's theory of the new colonial state. It was Hutchinson's tragedy, and the tragedy of all the Tory imperialists, that now, on the eve of the great crisis, they still could not adapt their thinking to the simple and obvious facts — obvious, that is, to men like Bland and Franklin — that the concept of the idea as "one entire Dominion" was thoroughly dead, and that it was absolutely inapplicable to the American situation.

Jonathan Boucher, Anglican rector at Annapolis, was another Tory imperialist who simply could not fit the idea of colonial autonomy into his preconceived idea of the glorious authority of the crown. Seeing the growing impasse, he set himself earnestly to find the true explanation of the nature of the Empire. But what he found, just on the threshold of the Revolution, was not only a complete rejection of the natural-rights social-compact theory of the state, but a reversion to the divine-right theory of state and monarchy that he discovered in the writings of Sir Robert Filmer:

[18] Ibid., p. 5.

This popular notion, that government was originally formed by the consent or by a compact of the people rests on, and is supported by, another similar notion, not less popular, nor better founded. This other notion is, that the whole human race is born equal; and that no man is naturally inferior or, in any respect subjected to another; and that he can be made subject to another only by his own consent. . . . If

Forums of American political debate: the provincial capitol of Maryland at Annapolis.

[By courtesy of the Library of Congress]

(according to the idea of the advocates of this chimerical scheme of equality) no man could rightfully *be compelled to come in* and be a member even of a government to be formed by a regular compact, but by his own individual consent; it clearly follows, from the same principles, that neither could he rightfully be made or compelled to submit to the ordinances of any government already formed, to which he has not individually or actually consented. On the principle of equality, neither his parents, nor even the vote of a majority of the society . . . can have any such authority over any man. . . . The same principle of equality that exempts him from being governed without his own consent, clearly entitles him to recall and resume that consent whenever he sees fit; and he alone has a right to judge when and for what reasons it may be resumed.[19]

Thus did this trenchant critic of democracy demolish at one fell swoop — to his own satisfaction — Hobbes, Locke, the social-contract theory, and the ideas of the American liberals. That the state derived from the people or that government rested upon the common good seemed to him absurd. For him, state and government were created by a kindly and considerate God:

> It was not to be expected from an all-wise and all-merciful Creator, that, having formed creatures capable of order and rule, he should turn them loose into the world under the guidance only of their own unruly wills; that, like so many wild beasts, they might tear and worry one another in their mad contests for preeminence. . . . But as men were clearly formed for society, and to dwell together, which yet they cannot do without the restraint of law, or, in other words, without government, it is fair to infer that government was also the original intention of God, who never decrees the end, without also decreeing the means. . . . As soon as there were some to be governed, there were also some to govern: and the first man, by virtue of that paternal claim, on which all subsequent governments have been founded, was first invested with the power of government. . . . The first father was the first King: and if . . . the law may be inferred from the practice, it was thus that all government originated; and monarchy is it's most ancient form.[20]

Here was Filmer again, a century and a half after his death, speaking in America, in the voice of a sincere intelligent American who saw in the demands and the theories of his fellow Americans the dissolution of civic and religious authority and destruction of the British Empire.

Rebellion, for Boucher, was unthinkable. Passive resistance was as far as the unhappy citizen might go. For rebellion would be rebellion against God as well as the King. Furthermore, it would upset the natural order of things in society, and place in authority the uncouth rabble, to tread underfoot the aristocracy, the divinely ordained and benevolent leaders of men: "To encourage undistinguishing multitudes, by the vague term of resistance, to oppose all such laws as happen not to be agreeable to certain individuals, is neither more nor less than, by a regular plan, to attempt the subversion of the government: and I am not sure but that such attacks are more dangerous to free than to absolute governments."[21]

[19] Jonathan Boucher: *A View of the Causes and Consequences of the American Revolution* (London, 1797), pp. 514–16.
[20] Ibid., pp. 523–5.
[21] Ibid., p. 547.

The long effort of the Tory mind to find a philosophy of government that would fit the American case without destroying the Empire had been unable to hit upon any more proper theory than those of feudalism and Robert Filmer! One Tory imperialist, at least, was clear-headed enough to recognize the fact and to advocate a truce between the two conflicting ideologies that would, in effect, leave the solution of the problem to time. John Randolph, native-born royal attorney-general for Virginia, advocated such a truce. But Randolph was an aristocrat; he spurned the arguments of the rabble-rousers and warned his countrymen on the eve of the Revolution that insistence upon complete self-government would, in saving the colonies from the tyranny of Britain, throw them under the worse tyranny of the mob:

> The ignorant Vulgar are as unfit to judge the Modes, as they are unable to manage the Reins, of Government. . . . Cool reasoning seldom influences the Clamorous, but Men of Temper will always harken to it. To such Judges I appeal. . . .
>
> Our publick Happiness greatly depends on the People. Could they be induced to elect as their Representatives Gentlemen of Ability and Fortune, our Councils would have Weight, and our Cause be defended; but whilst they disregard these circumstances (which, it must be allowed, they sometimes do) and choose Members who cannot weigh Events in the Scales of Policy and Justice, but are led by Opinions as their Interests and Fancy direct them, Men who can be no great Losers in the general Wreck of the Constitution and Confusion of our Laws, our Assemblies, and, add to them, our Resolutions, Associations, &c., will have no Vigour or Influence against those whose Duty it is to obey them.[22]

Thus was social theory mixed with political theory, and economic ideas with both. The aristocratic-Tory-conservative-imperialist mind eventually failed to save British America for the Empire. As a set of ideas it greatly influenced the course of American history; but it was only a fragment, a refractory, reactionary fragment, if a large one, of the American mind; and its failure was merely a failure of a part of the American mind to prevent it from developing along lines that were truer to its own experience. The essential idea of the Tory imperialists, the idea that they all held in common, was their concept of the British Empire as one organic whole, whose sovereign government, of kings, lords, and commons, was the unchallengeable head and governor of that whole. Their tragic failure was the failure to see that ideas must follow facts, and to understand, as Bland and Franklin and Samuel Adams were acute enough to do, that the facts of life in America

[22] John Randolph: *Considerations on the Present State of Virginia* (n.p., 1774), pp. 15, 36.

simply could not be made to conform to any such outworn theory. The new world had made a new situation and a new experience, and the new experience could be rationalized only by new ideas. It was this that the Tory imperialists could not understand.

The "assembly party" : American constitutionalism

Ideas are never generated out of nothing; they are forged; forged out of the materials of inheritance upon the anvil of environment under the pounding of the hammers of time and experience. It was certainly so with the ideas of the great body of the early Americans : and where the inflexible ideas of the Tory imperialists were of unmalleable materials that refused to be reshaped by the American experience, the new ideas that more truly represented the American way of life were the product of the forging. The inheritance, the environment, and the American experience being what they were, the ideas, political, social, religious, or any other, that made up the American mind could hardly have been other than they were. But ideas are forged only slowly, and the ideas of the generation of 1750 were the product of over a century of such a process. Furthermore, while varying environments, physical and social, made for varying superficial characteristics in the American ideas thus generated, yet the unity of environment and experience, in that little plain between Georgia and Maine, the ocean and the mountains, was such that it gave a basic unity to the mind of those who lived there. And in none of the areas of their thinking is this clearer than in their political thought, fashioned by their common political experience.

It was in the colonial assemblies, more than anywhere else, that the native American political ideas had their principal growth. Certain ideas, like the belief in the social-compact origin of the state and in government by written constitution, went back at least as far as the *Mayflower* and Connecticut compacts and the various colonial charters. The occurrences that produced these documents, indeed, along with the documents themselves, should probably be taken as the first incidents in the long process of adaptation that was to produce a new political system. But it was in the representative assemblies that the argument worked itself out, in the dialectical conflict with the Tory ideas surrounding and supporting the royal prerogative, toward the climactic theories of American autonomism that preceded the final resort to independence. Curiously enough, the general trend of this development was one that more or less consciously sought to pattern American parliamentarianism after the British; in a pattern, that is, which tended directly, against the bitter opposition of the prerogative party, toward making the executive arm of the government eventually responsible to the legislature. If the American system did not eventuate in a parliamentary system of cabinet or executive responsibility to the legislature, it was certainly not because the Americans did not

Forums of American political debate : the Old State House, Boston.
[By courtesy of the Library of Congress]

want it so : it was, probably more than for any other reason, because of the partially successful opposition to that trend by the Tory-prerogative party and its ideas, which, while it failed to establish the unquestioned authority of the prerogative as it desired, did succeed in establishing certain checks and balances against the growing power of the assemblies. On the other hand, these weapons of obstruction, represented by the idea of an independent judiciary to check the executive, for example, were even adopted in the ideological armory of the assemblies themselves, when it suited their purpose. Thus the idea of checks and balances, introduced by the Tory imperialists, was partially accepted and used against them by the assemblies. It should be remembered, however, that the more or less conscious objective of the assemblies was complete control of government, in the fashion of the British Parliament, and that they accepted the idea of checks and balances only as a second-rate gain or lesser good when they failed to achieve that greater aim, as it were to "hold the line" in certain areas against the executive serving the "prerogative."

By the beginning of the eighteenth century the lower houses of the colonial assemblies had come to look upon themselves as smaller replicas of the British House of Commons, having all the rights and prerogatives of that house, especially in matters pertaining to the appropriation and disbursement of the people's money. It was the insistence of the Assembly of Pennsylvania upon just such a position that induced Keith's "corporations" theory of 1728, and it was similar exertions of power on the part of the New York Assembly that called forth Clark's "independence" blast in 1741 and Kennedy's "feudal-fief" theory of 1752.

But the assemblies knew what they wanted, and they extended themselves to the limit in order to get it. Their position, as described in 1743 with genuine insight by Governor Lewis Morris of New Jersey, was something like this : "The behavior of Assemblyes in this part of the world has induc'd some men to think that they aim at little less than grasping at the whole authority of the Government ; & the having or pretending to have the sole power of appointing the sallaries of ye Governor and officers, may by that means render them subservient to their purposes." [23] Similarly Governor William Shirley of Massachusetts wrote of the New York Assembly : "The Assembly seems to have left scarcely any part of His Majesty's prerogative untouched, and they have gone great lengths toward getting the government, military as well as civil, into their hands." [24]

The royal governors were alarmed. George Clinton, Governor of New York at the mid-century, described the assembly thus :

> They are selfish, and jealous of the power of the Crown, and of such levelling principles that they are constantly attacking its prerogative ; so that nothing but [the] Governor's independence [from assembly control] can bring them to a just sense of their duty to His Majesty and his service. . . . It is now become clear to me, that unless the

[23] Lewis Morris : *The Papers of Lewis Morris* (*Collections of the New Jersey Historical Society*), IV, p. 169.

[24] E. B. O'Callaghan, ed. : *Documents Relative to the Colonial History of the State of New York* (15 vols., Albany, 1856–67), VI, 436.

Legislature at home does take cognizance of their disobedience and indolence, and enjoin them to a more ready compliance to His Majesty's
Royal orders and instructions, I have but poor hopes of succeeding in
any affair, tho' ever so well concerted for His Majesty's service and
the Security of the Province.[25]

This story might be repeated, with local variations, with regard to
practically every province on the Atlantic seaboard. The assemblies,
naturally enough, would not admit any such subversive intentions. To
them what they were doing was defensive; defensive, that is, against
what they considered the unwarranted encroachments upon the people's rights by the agents of the crown.

Despite their protests, however, and although they often apparently
did not realize it themselves, the assemblies were steadily encroaching
upon the powers of the prerogative. William Smith, a pro-assembly
participant in the New York struggle, saw the implications, and in his
History of New York, first published in 1757, stated the case of the
assemblies, taking note at the same time of Kennedy's "feudal-fief"
theories:

Our representatives, agreeable to the general sense of their constituents,
are tenacious in their opinion that the inhabitants of this colony are
entitled to all the privileges of Englishmen; that they have a right
to participate in the legislative power, and that the session of assemblies here, is wisely substituted instead of a representation in parliament, which, all things considered, would at this remote distance,
be extremely inconvenient and dangerous. . . . The matter has been
often litigated with great fervency on both sides, and the example of
the British parliament [in making all the grants asked] urged as a precedent for our imitation. . . . [But] the particular state of this province
differs so widely from that of their mother country, that we ought not
in this respect to follow the custom of the commons. Our constitution,
as some observe, is so imperfect, in numberless instances, that the rights
of the people lie, even now, at the mere mercy of their governours; and
granting a perpetual [financial] support, it is thought, would be in
reality little less than the loss of every thing dear to them.[26]

The assemblies were claiming the rights of Parliament to make
laws, especially in matters relative to taxation. But they refused to
follow the example of Parliament by readily granting the money asked
of them by their governors, precisely because the governors felt no
responsibility to them. The great constitutional difference between
Parliament and the assemblies, indeed, lay in the fact that, whereas
the executive arm of government in England was in effect responsible

[25] Ibid., VI, 288.
[26] William Smith: *History of New York* (Albany, 1814), pp. 368–71.

to Parliament and had to command a majority of the votes in that body before it could even bring in a money bill, the executives in the American governments were theoretically in no way responsible to the colonial assemblies. It was precisely to establish some sort of responsibility to them that the assemblies were fighting. Had the American provincial assemblies been allowed to hold the colonial executives responsible as Parliament held the English ministry, they, too, would almost certainly have granted readily such requests as would then have been made to them. The history of the development of American political ideas in the eighteenth century is thus in large measure the history of the century-long effort to develop a theory that would make sense out of this anomalous situation.

The essential conflict between Tory-imperialist theory and American theory and practice was now beginning to be recognized by a good many Americans; and the struggle of the assemblies was beginning to prove a question of the alternatives in case the assemblies should ultimately fail to have their way. Would the assemblies have the right to resist the prerogative by force? It was an uncomfortable question to face; for the Americans were loyal to their King and to what they thought to be the English way of life; but some there were who had the courage to face it, at least in theory. Such a thinker was Jonathan Mayhew, Congregational pastor in Boston, who examined the problem of civil obedience in a sermon of 1750. In this famous sermon Mayhew decided that, though ordinarily civil obedience is due to "the higher powers," and that "disobedience to civil rulers in due exercise of their authority, is not merely *political sin,* but henious *offence* against *God and religion,*" yet "when they rob and ruin the public, instead of being guardians of its peace and welfare; they immediately cease to be the *ordinance* and *Ministers of God;* and no more deserve that glorious character, than common *pirates* and *highwaymen.*" [27]

This was strong language, in royally governed Massachusetts. Yet Mayhew went farther and drew the logical conclusion implied by his argument:

> If it be our duty, for example, to obey our King, merely for this reason, that he rules for the public welfare . . . it follows, by a parity of reason, that when he turns tyrant, and makes his subjects his prey to devour and to destroy, instead of his charge to defend and cherish, we are bound to throw off our allegiance to him, and to resist. . . . Not to discontinue our allegiance, in this case, would be to join with the sovereign in promoting the slavery and misery of that society, the wel-

[27] Jonathan Mayhew : *A Discourse Concerning Unlimited Submission and non-Resistance to the Higher Powers* (Boston, 1750 ; reprint, 1818), pp. 14, 25.

fare of which, we ourselves, as well as our sovereign, are indispensably obliged to secure and promote, as far as in us lies.[28]

And this was twenty-six years before the American Declaration of Independence! This is the theory of John Locke, of course, brought to America : the common good as the end of government, social contract, right of revolution, and all. But it fitted almost perfectly the case of the American provincial legislatures that were struggling more or less consciously for the supremacy of the people, through their representatives, over the governors with their theories of the supremacy of the prerogative.

In his pragmatism, in his making the "common felicity of the governed" the ultimate test of the validity of government, Mayhew was taking a typically American position; by the same token, he was taking a position as diametrically opposite as may be imagined from the fine-spun "feudal-fief" theory of Archibald Kennedy of New York enunciated two years later. As a rationalist, also, he demolished the theory of the divine right of kings nearly a quarter of a century before Jonathan Boucher tried to revive it.

> If we calmly consider the nature of the thing itself [absolute monarchy], nothing can well be imagined more directly contrary to common sense, than to suppose that *millions* of people should be subjected to the arbitrary, precarious pleasure of *one single man*. . . . Nothing but the most plain and express revelation from heaven could make a sober, impartial man believe such a monstrous, unaccountable doctrine. . . . The hereditary, indefeasible, divine right of kings, and the doctrine of non-resistance, which is built upon the supposition of such a right, are altogether as fabulous and chimerical, as transubstantiation; or any of the most absurd reveries of ancient or modern visionaries. . . . [Finally,] we may very safely assert these two things in general, without undermining government : One is, that no civil rulers are to be obeyed when they enjoin things that are inconsistent with the commands of God. . . . Another thing that may be asserted with equal truth and safety, is, that no government is to be submitted to, at the *expence* of that which is the *sole end* of all government — the common good and safety of society.[29]

Dr. Mayhew got pretty close to fundamentals. For to him the form of the government made little difference : the essential thing was the welfare of the people. He seems to have understood "society" to mean the aggregation of individual citizens joined together in a body politic or state, of which government was merely the agent or servant endowed with authority. Government derives from two sources, God and the common good of all the people. But it is God who moves the people

[28] Ibid., p. 29.   [29] Ibid., pp. 33, 35 fn.

to set up government in the first place : therefore the two sources are in fact one. As for the form of government, says Mayhew, the apostle Paul supposes this to be "left intirely to human prudence and descretion." Thus the people decide what sort of government they will have : the body politic, the state, is the people.

The significance of Jonathan Mayhew is that he is one of the earliest Americans to provide a religio-rationalistic basis for the expanding claims of the assemblies. John Wise, who had expounded a political doctrine based upon the concept of natural law forty years before, was probably a more profound thinker than Mayhew; but Wise was chiefly concerned with church organization. He was a theoretical democrat, preaching a doctrine of the equality of men, and neither Mayhew nor the assemblies were prepared, in 1750, to countenance such a doctrine. The American liberals were autonomists, beginning to derive their theory of the state from the American people themselves. But they were not democrats.

Even the doctrine of provincial autonomy was not yet fully developed or consistently adhered to. It is, indeed, doubtful whether many of the members of the colonial assemblies realized whither the steady expansion of their power was leading them. Needless to say, the assemblies were firmly convinced that they were merely protecting the rights of Englishmen. The right of Parliament to legislate for the colonies on questions other than taxation was universally admitted in the 1750's ; it was only against the encroachments of the executive arm of government in the name of the king's prerogative that they thought they were thus far contending ; the battle with Parliament had not yet begun. Even so, acts of Parliament that did not specifically mention the colonies were not regarded as applying to them. In 1757, for example, the Earl of Loudoun, at that time commanding the English army in America, was surprised that the Massachusetts assembly felt called upon to pass an act providing for the quartering of troops in public houses, since Parliament had already passed such an act. The assembly replied that the act passed by Parliament did not apply to the colonies, since it did not specifically say so. They did not, they said, question the right of the Parliament to make such a law ; and, they further assured Governor Pownall, "The authority of all Acts of Parliament which concern the Colonies, and extend to them, is ever acknowledged in the courts of law, and made the rule of all judicial proceedings in the Province. There is not a Member of the General Court, and we know of no inhabitant within the bounds of Government that ever questioned this authority." [30]

[30] Hutchinson : *The History of the Colony and Province of Massachusetts Bay,* III, 47–48 fn.

This was apparently an opposite position to that taken in the controversy with Hutchinson a few years later. Yet even this tenuous acknowledgment of "dependence" of the colonies upon the British Parliament was coming to be more a matter of words than of deeds; for in this same decade many of the colonists were denying this position of the Massachusetts Assembly. But what, in the view of the

Forums of American political debate: the provincial capitol of
Pennsylvania at Philadelphia (later called Independence Hall).
[By courtesy of the Library of Congress]

assemblies, was the nature of the political relationship between colonies and mother country? No one, not even the assemblies themselves, clearly knew.

One of the bitterest of the running battles in all this long struggle for the vague objectives of provincial-assembly autonomy was that which took place in Pennsylvania. William Smith's reactionary alarm at the "republican" tendencies of the Quaker-dominated assembly of that province has already been described; the assembly, on the other hand, represented by Thomas Galloway and Benjamin Franklin, insisted that it was on the defensive against the growing autocratic tendencies of the proprietor, the Governor, and their party. Galloway, for example, appealed to the "constitution": Smith's proposal for more checks upon the power of the people, he said, in effect demanded a violation of both the King's charter to William Penn and Penn's Charter of Liberties to the people of the colony, in which the power of the people was made part of the fundamental law. He denied that the power of the assembly had been increased, and boldly declared that if the Quakers, a minority group, were continued in a position of predominating power in the assembly, it was because their use of their power had been so eminently satisfactory to the people. The great fact that the Pennsylvania Assembly failed to realize was that their battle with the proprietor over constitutional principles was only one of many such battles going on in the colonies as part of a general movement toward a recognition of colonial legislative autonomy, or quasi-autonomy, as against any legislative control from England whatsoever, whether royal, parliamentary, or proprietary. The struggle was one that was common to all the colonies; there were local variations, but the basic constitutional idea involved was fundamentlly the same everywhere.

It was in Virginia that the logical conclusion of the assembly-autonomists' theory first flamed up in clear and unmistakable theoretical expression, in connection with the famous "Parsons' Cause" of the late 1750's, when the British government saw fit to veto a Virginia law regulating the form and value of the stipends of the Virginia clergy. For the Bishop of London indiscreetly called the action of the Virginia Legislature treason, because it modified a former law that had been approved by the King. Whereupon Richard Bland, taking a position essentially similar to that of Jonathan Mayhew ten years earlier, reminded the clergy that the ultimate test of government is not loyalty to the prerogative but the good of the people:

> The Royal Prerogative is, without Doubt, of great Weight and Power in a dependent and subordinate Government. . . . But, great and powerful as it is, it can only be exerted while in the Hands of the best and most benign Sovereign, for the Good of his People, and not for their Destruction. . . . The Royal Instructions ought certainly to be obeyed, and nothing but the most pressing necessity can justify any Person for infringing them; but as *salus populi est suprema lex,* where this necessity prevails, every Consideration must give Place to it, and even these Instructions may be deviated from with Impunity.[31]

A little later, Bland went a step farther, specifically rejecting the feudal-fief idea of the creation of the colonial governments by the prerogative of a fatherly king, and rejecting all laws not made by the elected representatives of the people:

[31] Richard Bland: *A Letter to the Clergy of Virginia* (Williamsburg, 1760), p. 18.

Under an *English* Government all Men are born free, are only subject to Laws made with their own Consent, and cannot be deprived of the Benefit of these Laws without a Transgression of them. . . . If then the People of this Colony are free born, and have a Right to the Liberties and Privileges of *English* subjects, they must necessarily have a legal Constitution, that is, a Legislature, composed in Part, of the Representatives of the People, who may enact Laws for the Internal Government of the Colony, and suitable to its various Circumstances and Occasions; and without such a Representative, I am bold enough to say, no Law can be made.[32]

This was a long step forward. But it was Patrick Henry, in connection with this same affair, who carried the principle of the autonomy of the provincial legislature to its logical conclusion. For Henry, arguing the rights of the legislature against the clergy, shocked the clergy and the conservatives everywhere by actually challenging the right of the crown to veto a colonial law at all. In his address to the jury in this celebrated case he was reported to have said: "that the Act of 1758 had every characteristic of a good law; that it was a law of general utility, and could not, consistently with what he called the original compact between the king and people . . . be annulled. . . . [And] that a king, by disallowing acts of this salutary nature, from being the father of his people, degenerated into a tyrant, and forfeits all right to his subjects' obedience."[33]

By some this doctrine was regarded as treason; yet Patrick Henry was merely claiming for the Virginia Legislature one of the principles of lawmaking just then coming to be enjoyed almost without question by the British Parliament itself, the principle that when Parliament passed a law it was accepted without question by the crown.

It was only a few short months after Patrick Henry's epoch-making speech that Parliament passed the so-called Sugar Act of 1764, which was followed by the Stamp Act of 1765, both of which were intended to draw money from the colonies by one form or another of taxation. This was the signal for a sudden protest, all up and down the colonies; more important still, these acts of Parliament called forth a flood of political theory that was marked, most significantly, by the final rejection of the right of Parliament to legislate on matters pertaining to the internal affairs of the colonies in any case whatsoever.

The doctrine of complete colonial legislative autonomy, at least in matters of taxation, was borne on a gale of legislative protests against the Stamp Act in the colonial assemblies. The first and most dramatic

[32] Richard Bland: *The Colonel Dismounted: or the Rector Vindicated* (n.p., 1764), pp. 21–2.
[33] Quoted in Moses Coit Tyler: *Patrick Henry* (Boston, 1887), p. 47.

of these was a set of resolutions introduced into the Virginia House of Burgesses by Patrick Henry:

> That His Majesty's liege people of this his most ancient and loyal Colony have without interruption enjoyed the inestimable right of being governed by such laws, respecting their internal polity and taxation, as are derived from their own consent, with the approbation of their sovereign, or his substitute [the Governor]; and that the same hath never been forfeited or yielded up, but have been constantly recognized by the kings and people of Great Britain. . . .
>
> That the General Assembly of this Colony have the only and sole exclusive right and power to lay taxes and impositions upon the inhabitants of this Colony, and that every attempt to vest such power in any person or persons whatever other than the General Assembly aforesaid has a manifest tendency to destroy British as well as American freedom. . . .
>
> That His Majesty's liege people, the inhabitants of this Colony, are not bound to yield obedience to any law or ordinance whatever, designed to impose any taxation whatsoever upon them, other than the laws or ordinances of the General Assembly aforesaid.[34]

The Virginia House of Burgesses toned down these resolutions before passing them in modified form. The general import was the same, however: the colony would make its own laws, at least where taxation was involved, and no outside authority was recognized as having the power to gainsay or overrule it. And the Massachusetts Assembly, a little later, invoked the great philosophical principles of natural law: "Life, Liberty, Property, and the Disposal of that Property with our own Consent, are natural rights. . . . The Preservation of these Rights is the great End of Government. . . . Hence is deducible, Representation: which being necessary to preserve these invaluable Rights of Nature, is itself, for that Reason, a natural Right, coinciding with, and running into, that great Law of Nature, Self-Preservation."[35]

This conviction was echoed up and down the colonies. And Daniel Dulany went so far as to say, in 1765: "The colonies have a complete and adequate legislative authority, and are not only represented in their assemblies, but in *no other manner*."[36] The South Carolina Assembly, along with those of other colonies, passed resolutions to the effect "That the People of this Province are not, and, from their local Circumstances, cannot be, represented in the House of Commons of Great-Britain: and farther, That, in the Opinion of this House, the

[34] S. E. Morison, ed.: *Sources and Documents Illustrating the American Revolution* (Oxford, 1923), pp. 17–18.

[35] Hutchinson: *The Speeches of His Excellency, the Governor . . .* p. 30.

[36] Daniel Dulany: *Considerations on the Propriety of Imposing Taxes in the British Colonies* (New York, 1765), p. 13.

several Powers of Legislation in America were constituted, in some Measure, upon the Apprehension of this Impracticability." [37]

This was almost, if not quite, the same thing as saying that the colonies were sovereign within their own boundaries, and that the sovereign right of the colonial legislature to pass laws controlling affairs within those boundaries could not be challenged by any outside power, not even England. Such an idea was little less than revolutionary; for it in effect said that the colony was a sovereign state. It was Richard Bland, again, who brilliantly put this American position into rational form. Furthermore, Bland has the distinction of apparently being the first American thinker to reduce the problem to its most fundamental terms, concluding that the colonies were, in fact, sovereign states, independent of Parliament and England, joined with Britain and the other members of the Empire only through loyalty to a common sovereign, the king:

Men in a State of Nature are absolutely free and independent of one another as to sovereign Jurisdiction, but when they enter into a Society, and by their own Consent become Members of it, they must submit to the laws of the Society according to which they agree to be governed; for it is evident, by the very Act of Association, that each Member subjects himself to the authority of that Body in whom, by common consent, the legislative Power of the State is placed: But though they must submit to the Laws, so long as they remain Members of the Society, yet they retain so much of their natural Freedom as to have a Right to retire from the Society, to renounce the Benefits of it, to enter into another Society, and to settle in another Country; for their Engagements to the Society, and their Submission to the publick authority of the State, do not oblige them to continue in it longer than they find it will conduce to their Happiness, which they have a natural Right to promote. This natural Right remains with every Man, and he cannot justly be deprived of it by any civil authority. . . . Now when men exercise this Right, and withdraw themselves from their Country, they recover their natural Freedom and Independence: The Jurisdiction and Sovereighnty of the State they have quitted ceases; and if they unite, and by common Consent take Possession of a new Country, and form themselves into a political Society, they become a sovereign State, independent of the State from which they separated. If then the Subjects of *England* have a natural Right to relinquish their Country, and by retiring from it, and associating together, to form a new political Society and independent State, they must have a Right, by Compact with the Sovereign of the Nation, to remove into a new Country, and to form a civil establishment upon the Terms of the Compact. . . . From

[37] *South-Carolina Gazetteer; and Country Journal,* December 17, 1765.

this Detail of the Charters, and other Acts of the Crown, under which the first Colony in *North America* was established, it is evident that the Colonists . . . [have always] had a regular Government . . . and were respected as a distinct State, independent, as to their *internal* Government, of the original Kingdom, but united with her, as to their *external* Polity. . . .[38]

Here it is, as clear as language can make it : Virginia is a sovereign state because a new one, founded freely and independently by men

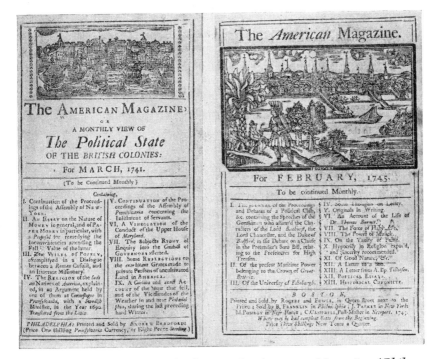

The popular literature of politics : The American Magazine (*Philadelphia, 1741*), *and* The American Magazine (*Boston, 1745*).

who left England and the authority of the English Parliament for the purpose. If Charles I had proclaimed that Virginia was bound directly to him, that did not mean, as Kennedy had insisted, that it was a feudal fief of the English crown, but, rather, that Virginia was a new and separate state, outside the reach of Parliament ; and this was borne out by the acceptance by Charles of the parliament the Virginians set

[38] Richard Bland : *An Inquiry into the Rights of the British Colonies* (1776), edited by Earl G. Swem (Richmond, 1922), pp. 9–10, 14, 20.

up for themselves. Virginia, then, was separate, completely self-governing in its internal affairs, associated with England and the other entities in the Empire only for common intercolonial, intraimperial, and international purposes.

It was only a short step from this to the blunt statement of Bland's young friend Thomas Jefferson: "That these [acts of Parliament] are acts of power, assumed by a body of men, foreign to our constitutions, and unacknowledged by our laws."[39]

In this, then, had the evolution of the theory of the American constitutionalists eventuated: that by the fact of their formation anew, in a wilderness, by their own sacred compacts among themselves and the acknowledged compacts with the king, they were new, separate states, sovereign by all the laws and rights of nature, bound to a common king, as a monarch only, in a federation of free states. This was not an idea devised at a moment's notice to meet a transient situation; it was, rather, the climactic flowering of a long process of ideological growth. The Americans knew the claims of the prerogative were ill-founded, unjust, and unworkable, because their experience in a century and a half of pounding their heads against it had driven home to them the now unshakable conviction that it was so. Bland, Dulany, and Franklin only gave final form to an idea toward which the Americans had apparently been moving, almost without realizing it, from the very beginning of their history. It was now as easy for the Americans to conceive of complete legislative autonomy, if not quite absolute sovereignty, within the British Empire as it was difficult for the Tory imperialists, who simply could not envisage a continuing Empire without the effective authority of Britain, including both that of Parliament and that of the sacred prerogative of the king. But therein lay the conflict of ideas that could only end, things being as they were, in the colonies successfully asserting and maintaining their sovereignty without, rather than within, the British Empire. It seems hardly necessary to point out that the ultimate objective was freedom, provincial freedom within the larger framework of imperial order. It remained for Franklin only to give logical expression to the ideal of such an empire.

The embryonic ideal of democracy

The ideas and ideals of democracy were apparently just about as anathema to the political mind of the majority of Americans in the eighteenth century as those of communism are to the twentieth. Yet there were a few intellectual leaders and a few communities, mostly on the frontier, whose ideas and practices found democracy, based

[39] Jefferson: A Summary View . . . p. 15.

upon the concept of the equality of men, to be not only in accord with the principles of natural law and reason, but also both practicable and desirable. And as political thought is generally found to be an integral part of the fabric of economic, social, and religious thought, it is not surprising to find that, generally speaking, the theories of political radicalism of the eighteenth century are to be found in those men who were also economic, social, or religious "levelers."

While allowance must be made for individual variance within, and divergence from, such patterns of thought, since the lines were never clearly drawn, it is remarkable almost to the point of obviousness that the men who held to the Tory-imperialist political theories based upon the idea of the sacrosanct nature of the prerogative were those who were most conservative in their economics, in their social thought, and in their religion. Similarly, the liberal autonomists in political theory were likely to be men who were also economic liberals, liberals in social thought (believing, that is, in a flexibility of social movement from class to class), and liberals in religion. The early American heralds of the democratic ideal were, generally speaking, men of humble social origin, living in relatively humble social and economic circumstances, devoted to economic individualism within the framework of frontier co-operation, and belonging to the relatively radical and individualistic religious sects. The thinkers who may be called democratic were only in a few instances as articulate as the leaders of the aristocratic and middle-class parties, partly because they were poor and uneducated; partly because they could not command as popular a hearing. Nor did they, probably, represent the majority of Americans; for the majority of Americans were probably represented by the assembly autonomists. Yet these humble democratic thinkers held the key to the American future.

The first notable native American democratic thinker was John Wise, pastor of one of the little frontier Congregational churches at Ipswich, Massachusetts. The practical occasion that called forth the expression of his political theory was a movement set on foot by certain members of the Massachusetts clergy to set up a sort of Presbyterian church government that would have a certain amount of control over the autonomous Congregational churches. Wise was earnestly opposed to this attempt at infringement of the old-time self-government of the churches, and he set forth his reasons for opposing it in a series of pamphlets that played a considerable part in the successful countermove to prevent the establishment of the Presbyterian scheme. Little as he seems to have expected or realized it, Wise's argument was much more significant as a statement of democratic political thought than as a defense of the old Congregational church government.

John Wise was probably the ablest political thinker to appear in America prior to the generation of the Revolution. Drawing his basic ideas from the German philosopher Pufendorf, he accepted the idea of the social compact, but while he also agreed that the state was created partly to protect men from their own savagery toward one another, he insisted that it was created for a positive purpose, by the operation of man's reason and social disposition; for the promotion, that is, of human welfare and happiness. Government, in his opinion, was created by men, although inspired in the mind of men by God: "It is certain civil government in general is a very admirable result of providence, and an incomparable benefit to mankind, yet must needs be acknowledged to be the effect of human free-compacts and not of divine institution; it is the produce of man's reason, of human and rational combinations, and not from any direct orders of infinite wisdom, in any positive law wherein is drawn up this or that scheme of civil government. . . . "[40]

The formation of the state, therefore, springs from the nature of man himself, which Wise described as follows :

> The prime immunity [or characteristic] in man's state, is that he is most properly the subject of the law of nature. He is the favorite animal on earth ; in that this part of God's image, namely, reason, is congenate with his nature, wherein by a law immutable, enstamped upon his frame, God has provided a rule for men in all their actions, obliging each one to the performance of that which is right, not only as to justice, but likewise as to all other moral virtues, the which is nothing but the dictate of right reason founded in the soul of man. . . .[41]

This rule of right reason is manifested, Wise says, by these qualities : "(1) a principle of self-love and self-preservation is predominant in every man's being. (2) a sociable disposition. (3) an affection or love to mankind in general."[42] Now, since man is marked by these natural and benevolent dispositions, as well as by his more malevolent characteristics, it follows that

> The second great immunity of man is an original liberty stamped upon his rational nature. He that intrudes upon this liberty, violates the law of nature. . . . [And this] native liberty of man's nature implies, a faculty of doing or omitting things according to the direction of his judgment. But in a more special meaning, this liberty does not consist in a loose and ungovernable freedom, or in an unbounded license of acting. . . . Man's external personal, natural liberty, antecedent to

[40] John Wise : *A Vindication of the Government of New England Churches* (fourth edition, Boston, 1860), p. 29.
[41] Ibid., p. 30.
[42] Ibid., p. 31.

all human parts or alliances, must also be considered. And so every man must be conceived to be perfectly in his own power and disposal, and not to be controlled by the authority of any other. . . .[43]

But if man is the subject of the law of nature expressing itself through reason, and if man is naturally free, the third characteristic of the natural man

is an equality among men; which is not to be denied by the law of nature, till man has resigned himself with all his rights for the sake of a civil state, and then his personal liberty and equality is to be cherished and preserved to the highest degree, as will consist with all just distinctions amongst men of honor, and shall be agreeable with the public good.[44]

Thus the state is hardly to restrain human liberty, but is created, rather, to cherish and protect it. As for the state itself, it is formed by the voluntary action of its members in associating themselves together.

Wise grasped the distinction between state and government more clearly than any other colonial thinker before Mayhew (who, by the way, though far from being a democrat, may have been influenced by Wise's ideas). The state is sovereign; and the state's sovereignty Wise found to reside in the people themselves: though they may delegate it to government, it always returns, by the law of nature, to them. With regard to the question of sovereignty, indeed, Wise anticipated the thinking of the assembly autonomists, since they, too, eventually came to the position that sovereignty is inherent in the people resident in the provinces. The great difference between him and them was their answer to the question: "Who are the people?" To the assembly autonomists "the people" were the substantial property-owners; had Wise's idea ever been introduced logically with practical politics (Wise himself probably would not have favored it), it would have meant at least all the male members of society, regardless of economic status or social rank.

Wise was far ahead of his time, with his doctrine of the natural equality of men and his advocacy of "a noble democracy," but he was closer to the true germ of American political thought than any other eighteenth-century American before Benjamin Franklin. For to most Americans of that century democracy was far from "noble" — it was unspeakable, unthinkable, and accursed.

The democracy theory of Wise appeared as a reaction against religious oligarchy; the democratic stirrings of the frontier were generated as practical reactions to political oligarchy. Between them another

[43] Ibid., pp. 33–4. [44] Ibid., p. 34.

and very important seed-root of democracy lay in the religious philosophy of the pietistic sects, particularly the Quakers. For if the core
of the mystical faith of the Quakers was the individual and his *rapport*
with God, and if all individuals were equal in the sight of God, any
influence that this theology may have had upon political thinking
could not fail to emphasize the worth of the individual and the general
principles of the equality of men in politics. But although William
Penn himself was a political philosopher of no mean gifts, and gave
Pennsylvania a good start in the direction of the relatively democratic
institutions that were to distinguish her, the Pennsylvania Quakers
never explicitly developed the democratic principles of their religion
in a theory of politics. They did tend, on the other hand, to apply
their ideas practically in the administration of the Pennsylvania government that they controlled for so long; it is at least worth considering whether Pennsylvania's relatively high degree of democracy was
not, as William Smith charged, in some measure due to their religion.
The Germans, whose religions were intellectually and psychologically
akin to Quakerism, followed the Quaker lead in practical politics. The
great leader of these people was Christopher Sauer, the printer and
publisher of Germantown, who published a German-language newspaper and a German-language almanac, and whose influence over his
fellow Germans was enormous. Sauer strongly favored the assembly
in its steady rise to power, but he was, if anything, in favor of more
democracy or "republicanism" rather than less. Sauer was a deeply religious man, and he believed, as did the Quakers John Woolman and
Anthony Benezet, that if the principles of Christ were followed in
human relationships, little enough of either government or law would
be necessary. Because he distrusted William Smith and the reactionary
party Smith represented, Sauer fought, successfully, against the setting
up of English schools in the German communities, thus preserving the
self-consciousness of the Germans and fanning the resentment of the
Americanizers.

The Quakers and the Germans believed alike, on political questions; but they produced no clear theory of the state. One thing, however, they did make abundantly clear, and that was their aversion
to war. Although the Pennsylvania Assembly did appropriate money
"for the use of the king," more or less under compulsion, for the purposes of the intercolonial wars, they made it perfectly plain that their
theory was opposed to war, and John Woolman even contemplated
refusing to pay taxes for warlike uses, even when appropriated by the
assembly. While the contribution of the Quakers to the developing
body of American political ideas was thus ostensibly of a negative,
defensive sort, yet by implication, in their logical persistence in their

essential principles of individual equality and the positive application of the principle of divine love in human relationships, their contribution was distinctly a positive one, and distinctly in the as yet hardly conscious groundswell of opinion toward democracy.

Similarly, it is also probably safe to say that the Great Awakening, with its fervent emphasis upon the individual and its implied distrust of high-born privilege and learning, gave a fillip to the democratic

Political cartoons: "The Paxton Boys a Farce." A satirical cartoon engraved in Philadelphia in 1764.
[By courtesy of the New York Historical Society]

stirrings among the poor who felt its impulse. Certainly the "new light" congregations that flowered in diversity after that great phenomenon, but especially the Baptists and the Methodists, were almost all democratic in organization and administration, with every member of the congregation having an equal voice with his fellows, and every congregation electing its own pastor.

Neither the democratic theories of John Wise nor the religious equalitarianism of the pietists had any clearly observable effect either upon purely political theory or upon political practice in the decades preceding that of the American Revolution. Yet the germ-cells of democracy lay in the American experience; and they grew. So that by the middle of the century the new mood began to be heard in the complaints of the frontiersmen against the usurpation of political power by the wealthy men of the east, and, more practically, in such things as the westerners' custom of electing their military leaders or in their demands for political reforms that would more adequately provide for their representation in the provincial assemblies and for better administration of justice in their villages. There were many such complaints and such demands; and while these protests were not always clearly expressive of well-defined political democracy, yet their general tenor is distinctly toward a broader base of political representation in government and a more adequate legal and judicial protection of all citizens equally before the law.

The most famous of these western protests was the popular uprising in North and South Carolina, in the two decades before the Revolution, known as the Regulator movement, which in its political aspects was an outburst against the heavy taxes, the irresponsible sheriffs, the extortionate fees of dishonest magistrates, and the scarcity of money in the western counties of the province. The frontiersmen of these counties had often demanded that these grievances be righted, but in vain, because they hadn't a sufficient number of representatives in the assembly to force it to act. They resorted to violence, at last, as an effort to force the provincial government to improve their situation. One of the ablest of their leaders was Herman Husband, a Quaker, who gave expression to many of the ideas that underlay their protests.

The Regulators argued their grievance against the assemblies on the grounds of their rights as Englishmen, just as the assemblies had been basing their grievances against the governors on the same rights: "for the King requires no money from His subjects but what they are made sensible what use it's for. . . ."[45] But "let us do nothing against the known established laws of our land — that we appear not as a faction endeavoring to subvert the laws, and overturn the system of our government. But let us take care to appear what we really are, free subjects by birth, endeavoring to recover our lost native rights, and to bring them down to the standard of law."[46]

The struggle of the Regulators was not against the governor or against the prerogative, but against the tyranny of the aristocrats of the seaboard, who controlled the assembly and society, and against the privilege of the established Anglican religion. This movement, like Bacon's rebellion a century earlier, was a protest against inequality and discrimination against the frontiers by the vested interests of the now conservative, even reactionary east. Implicit in the movement, as in nearly all the protests of the frontier, was the tendency to establish in law an equal level of political privilege and participation for all the

[45] *Colonial Records of North Carolina*, VII, 700.
[46] Ibid., VII, 90.

citizens. This democratic leveling was seen throughout the southern colonies in the attempts to upset or control the established Anglicanism; even the Anglican parishes themselves insisted on electing their own curates, to the dismay of the church officials.

This religious aspect of the murmurings of the western democracy is seen, too, in the "Parson's Cause." For the "Parson's Cause" and Patrick Henry's part in it were most significant, probably, because of the almost startling way in which they emphasize the closeness of the connection between economic, social, religious, and political convictions. Though the people who profited most financially from the "two-penny law" of 1758 were doubtless those tobacco-planters who in effect defrauded the clergy of a part of the income that was rightly due them as a result of the high price of tobacco — and it was these "gentlemen" who had passed the law in the first place — the members of the community where a particular case was tried, and the members of the jury, were likely to be mostly frontiersmen, members of the debtor class; anything that appeared to scale down the real value of their debts — and this seemed to have that effect on their debts to the clergy — met with their favor. Furthermore, most of these people were dissenters, and resented having to pay tithes to support the Anglican clergy, in whom they did not believe. Finally, the clergy were "gentlemen," members of the upper class; Henry was not a "gentleman," and he was able to appeal to the feeling of social distrust of one class toward another. Thus it appears that Henry's appeal was not only to constitutional theory, but also, apparently, to the impulses toward social leveling, the economic radicalism, and the religious independency of the frontiersmen and small farmers who made up the community in which this case was tried. This case was a milestone, not only as marking a colonial mood to reject the claim of the prerogative to the right to veto colonial legislation, but also because Henry's success and the acclaim that he received may properly be understood as an expression of the "democratic" or leveling tendencies of the frontier. Democracy in some of its ugliest, most primitive impulses, perhaps, yet a clear and unmistakable expression of the stirrings toward a reduction (in this case of a "negative" sort) of the power of the then vested interests in Virginia and in the Empire and toward an increase of the power of the common man.

The democratic characteristics of the frontiersmen and the sects frightened the aristocrats and the constitutionalists alike. To the conservatives, these were dangerous men, particularly the frontiersmen, and their democracy was a living threat to established society and government. Timothy Dwight, president of Yale, gave expression to this fear, in the years following the Revolution; but his was the same fear that the conservatives had felt thirty years earlier, and, if anything, more strongly then than when Dwight wrote :

> The class of pioneers cannot live in regular society. They are too idle, too talkative, too passionate, too prodigal, and too shiftless to acquire either property or character. They are impatient of the restraints of law, religion, and morality, and grumble about the taxes by which the Rulers, Ministers, and Schoolmasters are supported. . . . After exposing the injustice of the community in neglecting to invest persons of such superior merit in public offices, in many an eloquent harangue uttered by many a kitchen fire, in every blacksmith shop, in every corner of the streets, and finding their efforts vain, they become at length discouraged, and under the pressure of poverty, the fear of the goal, and consciousness of public contempt, leave their native places and betake themselves to the wilderness.[47]

The greatest voice of the frontier that democracy ever had in the years before the Revolution was Patrick Henry's. Yet even he did not find his voice for democracy until after the arrival of that crisis had crystallized political theory of all kinds. In the decade of the 1750's the embryonic ideals of democracy that were explicit in John Wise, implicit in the religious sects, and a matter of rough-and-ready reality in frontier practice were alive enough, but still waiting, as it were, to be born. It took the birth-pains of the Revolution to bring that great event about in the sublime words of the national statement of faith : "We hold these truths to be self-evident, that all men are created equal. . . ."

Science and scientific rationalism came at last to strengthen the ideal of equality. Men had been talking about natural law and natural rights in human affairs for a century, but that had been natural rights only for those who had vested interests in the community, in politics, and in religion. Now, at last, the natural law that Wise had preached was accepted at least in principle : that all men are created equal. There could be no democracy, in the nature of things, without an acceptance of the principle of equality. Yet, even so, the official birth of American democracy in the Declaration of Independence could not have taken place except as the natural culmination of a long period of gestation in the day-by-day experience of the common people.

THE NATURE OF THE BRITISH EMPIRE

The political thinking that culminated in the Tory-imperialist ideas of Kennedy, Hutchinson, and Boucher, in the assembly-autonomist ideas of Mayhew, Dulany, and Bland, and in the early democratic mur-

[47] Quoted in Frederick J. Turner : *The Significance of the Frontier in American History* (New York, 1920), pp. 251–2.

murings of Herman Husband and Patrick Henry, had also of necessity called up a great deal of thinking as to the fundamental nature of the British Empire. The English mercantilists had developed the idea of the self-sufficient Empire as an economic federation made up of interdependent sections; but they had never produced a corresponding political rationalization. Vaguely, of course, to the English imperialists, when they thought in political terms at all, the Empire appeared to them as a great, amorphous political mass held together by the royal prerogative and ruled over by the political nucleus made up of king, lords, and commons, plus the board of trade. William Pitt and Edmund Burke skirted the problem without penetrating it; it remained for a small group of Americans, the most outstanding of whom was Benjamin Franklin, to state the problem and a solution of it in fairly clear and systematic terms.

What was the British Empire politically, anyway? Was it a state, an empire, or an association of states? Was Britain an imperial mistress of the colonies, or their associate in a large unity? Nobody knew. But as Thomas Pownall warned Britain, there could be no real peace in the colonies after, say, 1754 until these questions were answered. And it was hardly probable — increasingly improbable, in fact — that the colonies would long remain contented in a position of political inferiority to Britain. Here, then, was a problem in political theory of the first magnitude, a problem that was pregnant with explosive potentialities for the future; for it underlay the whole future political growth of both the American colonies on the one side and the British Empire on the other.

This theoretical problem began to exercise the political thinkers of the colonies abundantly about the middle of the eighteenth century; and, as was so often the case, the theorizing was induced by a practical situation. For it was the presence of a dangerous brace of enemies upon the frontier and the threat of imminent war that forced the colonies to consider, first, the possibility of intercolonial union, and then, as the question of financing defense merged with the controversy over the prerogatives and imperial taxation, the grand problem of the nature of the Empire as a whole.

The first important expression of American interest in this problem is probably to be attributed to Dr. William Douglass, of Boston, who began publishing his historical survey of the colonies in 1747. In what he called "An Utopian Amusement," in Volume I of this work, Douglass advanced his idea thus:

The Colonies at this Time are arrived to a State of considerable Maturity, and the Conveniences and Inconveniences of the *Politia* or Polity of the several Colonies are now apparent; perhaps it would be for the Interest of the Nations of Great-Britain, and for the Ease of the Ministry or Managers at the Court of Great-Britain, to reduce them to some general Uniformity; referring to their several General Assemblies or Legislatures, the raising of Taxes and appropriating the same, with the Affairs relating to their different or Sundry Produces and Trade; these may be called their municipal Laws.[48]

Douglass proposed that there be set up a general or intercolonial council in London, to be made up of returned officials and others who knew the colonial situation well, which would have power to draw up a set of general regulations for the colonists, subject to the approval of Parliament. All the colonies would be made over into royal governments, with a uniform set of institutions for all of them, and all Christians, "Papists excepted," should enjoy religious liberty.

Douglass's idea as to the agency for co-ordinating the intercolonial interests of the "uniform" colonies seemed to center upon the proposed "general" council in London, and in Parliament. Whether the council would have been anything more than advisory, however, is not clear, although he does say that the Board of Trade would impose taxes upon the colonies to support their governments if they refused to do it themselves.

However that may be, another clear-cut proposal for an intercolonial union in America came from Archibald Kennedy, royal receiver-general for the province of New York. Kennedy was a Scotsman who about 1710 had come to New York as a young man and who, like his friend Cadwallader Colden, took an active part in that province's affairs throughout the middle decades of the century. In 1751 he wrote a pamphlet entitled *The Importance of Gaining the Friendship of the Indians to the British Interest,* in which he urged the necessity of a unified, intelligent policy toward the Indians in order to keep them from allying themselves with the French. He also suggested the need of some sort of colonial union for the more efficient conduct of colonial defense, and to the end of the pamphlet was appended the outline of a scheme for a colonial union prepared by Benjamin Franklin. In view of Franklin's later endorsement of a plan for a union to be created by an act of Parliament, it is of interest to find him writing, in 1751:

A voluntary Union entered into by the Colonies themselves, I think would be preferable to one impos'd by Parliament; for it would be perhaps not much more difficult to procure, and more easy to alter and improve, as Circumstances should require, and Experience direct. It would be a very strange Thing, if six Nations of ignorant Savages

---

[48] Douglass: *Summary, Historical and Political,* I, 242.

should be capable of forming a Scheme for such an Union, and be able to execute it in such a Manner, as that it has subsisted Ages, and appears indissoluble; and yet that a like Union should be impracticable for ten or a Dozen *English* Colonies, to whom it is more necessary, and must be more advantageous; and who cannot be supposed to want an equal Understanding of their Interests.[49]

The suggestions for a revision of Indian policy and for an intercolonial union had apparently been put together by Kennedy and approved by Franklin in the hope of influencing the conference on Indian affairs held at Albany in 1751, but they received little attention until the more famous intercolonial conference at the same place three years later. Whether the original suggestion came from Kennedy, as seems probable, or from Franklin is of little importance; the significant fact is that these two men, one in New York and the other in Philadelphia, collaborated on the proposal for colonial union that eventually reached the legislatures of most of the colonies. Early in 1751 Kennedy sent his ideas to Colden, who promptly embodied some of them in a report on Indian affairs to Governor George Clinton, in which he recommended, in view of the international importance of the problem, the consolidation of Indian affairs in all the colonies under the management of a single person. Three years later James Alexander passed on to Colden a new scheme for an intercolonial union for defensive purposes that had been worked out by Franklin. Colden expressed approval of the scheme, but wondered how the necessary money could be raised, whether by Parliament or by the colonies; he doubted, also, whether the colonies would authorize their delegates to the Albany Congress to discuss the matter. Colden did not attend the Albany Congress.

But if Franklin believed in "voluntary union" in 1751, he was apparently convinced in 1754 that union should be imposed upon the colonies by an act of Parliament, and he joined his colleagues at the Albany Congress of that year in preparing the celebrated plan for a union of the colonies on the continent that was based largely upon his ideas. This proposal called for an intercolonial union to be created by an act of Parliament, with a governor-general to be named by the crown and a grand council made up of delegates to be elected by the provincial assemblies.

Other plans for an intercolonial union had been submitted to the Albany Congress. Richard Peters submitted a plan that would have organized the colonies by sections: (1) New England, (2) New York

---

[49] Archibald Kennedy: *The Importance of Gaining and Preserving the Friendship of the Indians to the British Interest, Considered* (New York, 1751), pp. 28-9.

and New Jersey, (3) Virginia, Maryland, and Pennsylvania, and (4) North Carolina, South Carolina, and Georgia, each section to have its own "Committee of Union" to work with the others. Thomas Hutchinson also apparently submitted a plan that called for two districts, north and south. Governor William Shirley of Massachusetts had another idea (not submitted to the Albany Congress); but Shirley envisaged only an intercolonial council made up of the colonial governors and a few members selected from the appointed councils of the colonial legislatures; the power of this council would have been limited to questions of defense, and its expenses would have been paid directly by the British treasury, but covered eventually by taxation of the colonies by an act of Parliament.

Franklin's plan, which placed control of the proposed grand council and of finances in the hands of the colonial assemblies, was adopted by the Albany Congress apparently because it offered the best scheme for a united Anglo-American front in the face of the French and Indian enemy. The fact that this plan would have a stronger appeal to the colonial assemblies than the others may also have had some influence with its sponsors. In any case, Archibald Kennedy, arch-imperialist that he was, urged the colonial assemblies to accept the Albany Plan of Union in his pamphlet *Serious Considerations on the Present State of the Northern Colonies,* which was apparently written while the Albany Congress was in session.

The most significant aspect of the whole movement for an intercolonial union between the peace of Aix-la-Chapelle (1748) and the outbreak of hostilities in 1755 was the fact that so many leaders of public opinion were in favor of such a union. Most of the proponents of the idea, to be sure, were thinking in terms of a military union for defense purposes. But all of them saw the colonies as in fact bound together by the common problems inherent in actual circumstances, and their desire was to give those common interests and purposes a mechanism for concrete accomplishment. But the plan was rejected by all the colonial assemblies to which it was submitted, in most of them quickly and without a struggle. In those in which the proposal called forth comment, it appeared that it was regarded as involving too much of a sacrifice of the principles and the gains in provincial autonomy for which the colonial assemblies had been fighting for so long. In the first place, the assembly-party liberals objected to the imposition of any such supercolonial government by England, whether by Parliament or the crown; in the second, it was feared that the creation of a union involving the appointment of a grand governor-general by the crown must inevitably strengthen the prerogative; in the third place, the proposal to give the union power over western lands and Indian affairs seemed to threaten a curtailment of the individual colonies in those areas; finally, and most important of all, the proposal to give the grand council the power of imposing taxes and "general duties" upon the colonies for the support of the activities of the union seemed to be a direct curtailment of the most precious power the assemblies possessed: that of controlling provincial taxes and provincial finance. Such a curtailment, it was argued, must inevitably result in a reduction of the assemblies' power. As "Philolethes" put it for the opposition in Rhode Island: "The Instant it was established . . . [it would] revoke all His Majesty's Governors Commissions in North-America, and destroy every Charter, by erecting a Power above Law, over the several Legislatures." [50] This was the crux of the colonial opposition to the Albany Plan. The Massachusetts General Court, which debated the plan more fully, probably, than any other colonial assembly, rejected it for several reasons; but

> the great and prevailing reason urged against it was, that in its Operation, it would be subversive of the most valuable rights & Liberties of the several Colonies included in it, as a new Civil Government is thereby proposed to be establish'd over them with great & extraordinary power to be exercis'd in time of Peace, as well as War; such as those of making Laws to be of force in all the Colonies; building Forts and Ships of War, and purchasing Lands at discretion; and for these purposes raising monies from the several Colonies in such Sums and in such Manner as the President and Council shall think fit. These powers are in the Judgment of the two Houses inconsistent with the fundamental right of these Colonies, and would be destructive of our happy constitution. [51]

Even the Boston Town Meeting resolved, on January 17, 1755: "That the Gentlemen the Representatives of the Town be and hereby are Instructed to Use their utmost Endeavours to prevent the Plan now under Consideration of the General Court for an Union of the several Governments on the Continent taking effect — and they also Oppose any other Plan for an Union that may come under the Consideration of the said General Court, whereby they shall Apprehend the Liberties and Priviledges of the People are endangered." [52]

It is clearly evident that there was a widespread fear, in the assemblies and out of them, that the union proposed at Albany might lessen the power of the people and their representatives in the assemblies.

[50] Quoted in Lawrence H. Gipson: *The British Empire before the American Revolution* (6 vols., New York, 1936–46), V, 148.

[51] Quoted in *Commonwealth History of Massachusetts* (4 vols., New York, 1928), II, 461.

[52] Ibid., II, 463.

It was this fear, probably, that, more than anything else, prevented the acceptance of the plan. Thus this very rejection is a clear index to at least one aspect of the colonial political mind : it treasured "the Liberties and Priviledges" of the people's assemblies more than anything else ; and it would take no chance on losing them.

At the same time it should be noted that sectionalism played a part in leading the colonies to reject the proposed plan. The Massachusetts General Court was bluntly specific on this point when it stated that its reasons for rejecting the proposal were, among others, the "perpetuity of the propos'd Union ; [and] the great sway which the Southern Colonies (the Inhabitants whereof are but little disposed to and less acquainted with the affairs of war) would have in all the determinations of the Grand Council, &c." [53] Moreover, it is not without significance that the most vociferous opposition to the plan was chiefly in the smaller, seaboard colonies, which clearly feared the possibility that they might be overshadowed and overridden by the large, populous, and powerful provinces. Thus the intercolonial and intersectional distrusts that were to plague the development of the American nation for a century had already appeared in the American mind in 1754, and had already become significant as determinants of American history.

Franklin apparently saw the necessity for a creation of an American union by act of Parliament much as the founders of the Dominion of Canada saw it a century later. Such an act of Parliament would in effect be a sort of self-denying ordinance by which Parliament would voluntarily surrender much of its power, real or imagined, to a collateral American body like itself. Franklin was never very clear in his explanation why he favored this action ; he was probably wiser than he himself fully realized. Had he been able to get the plan past this first great hazard, he was convinced that the union would have an autonomy for continental affairs corresponding to that of the assemblies of Connecticut and Rhode Island for provincial affairs. Such an American government would have stood midway between the British crown on the one side and the autonomy-seeking provincial governments on the other. It is difficult to believe that it could have failed to place limitations upon both ; the assemblies, apparently, saw this more clearly than the agents of the crown, and promptly and decisively rejected the plan accordingly. Years later, after American independence had been won, Franklin said : "I am still of opinion, it would have been happy for both sides, if it had been adopted. The colonies so united would have been sufficiently strong to have defended them-

[53] Ibid., II, 461.

selves; there would then have been no need of troops from England; of course the subsequent pretext for taxing America, and the bloody contest it occasioned, would have been avoided. But such mistakes are not new; history is full of the errors of states and princes." [54]

As it turned out, the Albany Plan was no more seriously considered in England than it was in America. Shirley wrote home that it represented the opinions of the wisest men in the colonies but that, in his opinion, the prerogative would be weakened under the proposed plan. As a matter of fact, the Board of Trade had devised a plan of its own that was much more considerate of the feelings of the colonial assemblies than the Albany plan, in that it would have had them form some sort of union by their own voluntary action. Shortly after the Board of Trade's plan appeared to be unsatisfactory to the Privy Council, the Albany Plan was transmitted to it by the Board, but it was lost from sight, apparently, in the preparation for war.

Thus the rejection of the Albany Plan of Union must be understood chiefly as a part of the struggle of the American liberals of the assembly-autonomist movement for self-determination in provincial government; but it was also due in part to intercolonial and intersectional differences and distrusts that rested upon a century or more of intercolonial contests over boundaries, land, and trade. Actually, the proposal ran counter to the deepest trend in the thought and practice of the assemblies' struggle, the trend toward complete, particularistic, provincial autonomy for each separate colony, with the greatest possible degree of freedom from interference, either by the mother country, the other colonies, or a combination of them. On the other hand, the plan fitted with a fair degree of neatness into the political thinking of the Tory imperialists, since the proposed union would have been created by Parliamentary action, would have left the appointment of the governor-general and of military officials in the hands of the crown, and would have had the power of raising armies that might conceivably have been used to coerce the individual colonies. If it was feared by such crown agents as Shirley, it was because of the checks upon crown influence that were implicit in the powers given the representatives of the provincial assemblies in the grand council. Thus the whole controversy over the Albany Plan threw into a clear light the divisions of opinion in practical politics and the unfinished status of political theory, especially with regard to the relations between the colonies and the mother country and between the colonies and each other. Franklin himself saw the colonies almost hopelessly divided, and they were still so as late as 1760:

[54] Franklin: *Works* (Sparks ed.), I, 178.

Of this [supposition that the colonies may become dangerous to England], I own, I have not the least conception, when I consider that we have already *fourteen separate governments* on the maritime coast of the continent. . . . Those we now have are not only under different governors, but have different forms of government, different laws, different interests, and some of them different religious persuasions, and different manners. Their jealousy of each other is so great, that, however necessary a union of the colonies has long been, for their common defense and security against their enemies, and how sensible soever each colony has been of that necessity; yet they have never been able to effect such a union among themselves, nor even to agree in requesting the mother country to establish it for them.[55]

Thomas Pownall also remarked upon the differences between the colonies; but he warned the mother country to keep them that way, and never let them develop common interests:

It is essential to the preservation of the empire to keep them disconnected and independent of each other — they certainly are so at present; the different manner in which they are settled, the different modes under which they live, the different forms of charters, grants and frame of government they possess, the various principles of repulsion that they create, the different interests which they actuate, the religious interests by which they are actuated, the rivalship and jealousies which arrive from hence, and the impracticability, if not the impossibility of reconciling and accommodating these incompatible ideas and claims, will keep them for ever so. . . .[56]

The Albany Plan may perhaps be called the first in a series of steps that eventually led to the adoption of the Articles of Confederation of the United States of America; but after its rejection by the colonies and the mother country in 1754 and 1755 the idea of intercolonial union was, for the time being at least, thoroughly dead. And, as Franklin reported, it was still so in 1760. Yet that effort, and the problem it was designed to solve, had started men to thinking about the basic structure of the British Empire, and that problem was not dead; nor could it, ever again, even die.

It was in the course of the discussion of the Albany Plan for intercolonial union that Benjamin Franklin was led to formulate his first coherent theory of the British Empire and the logical and proper position of the colonies in it. For William Shirley, Governor of Massachusetts, who originally favored the general idea of a union, soon came to fear the Albany Plan as making for too liberal concessions to the "popular-government" propensities of the assemblies. He feared that

[55] Ibid., IV, 42.
[56] Pownall; *The Administration of the Colonies*, p. 37.

the proposed grand council, made up of representatives of provinces elected by the provincial assemblies, would seize power and control of the union much as the colonial assemblies were doing in the provincial governments. At the same time he had to come to believe that the only way effectively to support the military defense of the colonies must be by taxation imposed upon them by Parliament. He communicated his ideas to Franklin, who suddenly found himself in the position of having to defend the plan against one of its sponsors, in the name of the assemblies.

Franklin told Shirley that

excluding the people of the colonies from all share in the choice of the grand council will give extreme dissatisfaction; as well as the taxing them by act of Parliament, where they have no representation. It is very possible, that this general government might be as well and faithfully administered without the people, as with them; but where heavy burthens are to be laid upon them, it has been found useful to make it as much as possible their own act; for they bear better, when they have, some share in the direction; and when any public measures are generally grievous, or even distasteful, to the people, the wheels of government move more heavily.[57]

Franklin's discussion with Shirley drew out his own thinking relative to the nature of the Empire. For the question of taxation by a Parliament in which the colonies were not represented led Shirley to suggest that they be given representation in that body. Franklin's reply to this suggestion was a clear exposé of the difficulty of governing the colonies from outside, either by Parliament, made up of men living three thousand miles away, or by governors sent from England with little or no knowledge of the problems of the land to which they came. Government of the colonies, said Franklin, must be by Americans, or at least by a Parliament in which the Americans should have a voice. Certain taxes, the indirect taxes upon commerce imposed by Parliament, he said, were already paid by the Americans and without complaint; direct taxation, whether for defense or for any other purposes, would be paid by the Americans willingly only if imposed upon them by their own elected representatives. As for sending representatives of the colonies to Parliament, Franklin was ready to believe that

such a union [of the colonies with the mother country] would be very acceptable to the colonies, provided they had a reasonable number of representatives allowed them; and that all the old acts of Parliament restraining the trade or cramping the manufactures of the colonies be at the same time repealed, and the British subjects *on this side the*

[57] Franklin: *Works* (Sparks ed.), III, 57–8.

water put, in those respects, on the same footing with those in Great Britain, till the new Parliament, representing the whole, shall think it for the interest of the whole to reënact some or all of them. . . . I think too, that the government of the colonies by a Parliament, in which they are fairly represented, would be vastly more agreeable to the people, than the method lately attempted to be introduced by royal instruction, as well as more agreeable to the nature of an English constitution, and to English liberty.[58]

At this stage in his thinking about the Empire, Franklin was quite evidently thinking in terms of a simple organic whole. His belief was that adequate representation in Parliament might solve the problems, not only of the contest between the assemblies and the prerogative, but also of greater economic freedom for the colonies. As it was, the Britons in the colonies, under Parliamentary regulation of colonial commerce and manufactures, were being treated unfairly, since they had to suffer restrictions not suffered by the Britons in Britain; a common parliament for all of them, he thought, might have the very salutary effect — salutary, that is, from the Americans' point of view — of placing the Americans on a footing of equality with their fellow citizens in the mother country. If the Empire were organically one, it should be governed as one. This held true for economic life and military matters as well as for governments. As he put it then, "I should hope too, that by such a union, the people of Great Britain, and the people of the colonies, would learn to consider themselves, as not belonging to different communities with different interests, but to one community with one interest; which I imagine would contribute to strengthen the whole, and greatly lessen the danger of future separations."[59]

Franklin's voyage of 1757 to England, where he remained five years, apparently confirmed him, for the time being, in his intellectual faith in his concept of the British Empire as one community, one culture, one people, and his emotional attachment to it. He was inordinately proud of the cultural life that he found, and shared, in England, and he returned to America as more than ever a "British" nationalist. Already while in England he had written in 1760 his famous pamphlet on the desirability, for the Empire, of retaining Canada instead of Guadeloupe at the end of the war, in which he had said that, after all, the conquest of Canada was not for the colonies alone, but for the Empire as a whole : "Our North American colonies are to be considered as the *frontier of the British empire on that side.* The frontier of any dominion being attacked, it becomes not merely 'the cause' of the people immediately attacked, the inhabitants of that frontier, but properly 'the cause' of the whole body. . . . [The conquest of Canada] will not be

---

[58] Ibid., III, 65.   [59] Ibid., III, 65–6.

a conquest for *them,* nor gratify any vain ambition of theirs. It will be a conquest for the *whole;* and all our people will, in the increase of trade, and the ease of taxes, find the advantage of it." [60]

Franklin was still thinking in terms of one "whole" British Empire, and all his economic, sociological, and political thinking seemed to converge, in this pamphlet, in his concept of that pulsing, expanding, social and political organism. As he thought of it, he seemed to see the growing population of the Empire flowing over the crests of the mountains, taking up land and purchasing English manufactures, with a consequent expansion of imperial commerce. The Empire, he says, is one great economic unit, with each part producing commodities that the other parts need : America is an agrarian area ; and so long as the expanding American colonies have land, they will continue to depend upon England for their needed manufactured goods. Otherwise, as population becomes crowded and confined and poverty increases, they will turn to manufactures to compete with the mother country ; their interests will change, and the filial bond will be broken in the bitterness of economic competition.

Franklin was here writing as a "British" patriot, and he remained so until after his return to America. Far from encouraging any rupture of the Empire, he was convinced now, apparently even more than he had been in 1754, that the solution of America's ills lay, not in the direction of resistance to the mother country, but rather in a closer and closer assimilation of the colonies with the mother country in the greater organic empire.

But in the glow of his greater imperialism Franklin still left unanswered the question of the proper and logical role of the colonial governments in the greater organic empire. It was the tensions of the four or five years following his return to America in 1762 that were to force him finally to examine this question ; and the examination forced him to reverse himself and discard the concept of the monolithic Empire entirely.

He was back in England again in 1764, just in time to get caught in the Parliamentary program of colonial taxation that culminated in the Revenue Act of 1764 and the Stamp Act of 1765. Still under the spell, apparently, of his love of England and all things British, he at first saw nothing revolutionary or impractical in the proposed scheme for a stamp tax, although he thought it might be mildly unpopular. He even went so far as to suggest to George Grenville that the money be raised by the establishment in the colonies of an intercolonial loan office, or bank, that would issue an intercolonial currency and whose profits would be used for colonial defense instead of the money raised

[60] Ibid., IV, 20–1.

by taxation. But his suggestion got nowhere; the Stamp Act was passed, and Franklin apparently thought the Americans would resign themselves to it.

It was the unprecedented and extraordinarily unanimous outburst of resistance to the Grenville legislation among Americans of the assembly-autonomy party and its adherents that shook Franklin out of his complacence. And well it might; for not only did the assemblies themselves express their sentiments in no uncertain terms, but in 1765 and 1766 appeared the flood of pamphlets that marked the high tide of the American theory of legislative autonomy in the colonial period. Within a few months, even weeks, of each other, not only did the colonial assemblies voice, and in no uncertain terms, their conviction that, in matters of taxation at least, the colonial assemblies were clearly and by natural right autonomous, but such writers as Richard Bland arose to provide a basis in political theory for the American liberals' overt position. It was Bland's pamphlet, *An Inquiry into the Rights of the British Colonies,* that was the most revolutionary, for it was here that Bland, drawing both upon former theory and upon Virginian history, found, like Kennedy, that the colonies were bound only to the king, yet not as feudal fiefs, subject to the every caprice of the king, but rather as separate, new societies founded by the first settlers who had accepted him as their sovereign voluntarily in their charters or other agreements with him, and completely independent of the authority of Parliament.

Just how far Franklin was affected by the ideas of these American political thinkers would be difficult to say exactly. But he repeats, almost word for word, some of Bland's arguments; it is therefore easy to believe that he not only read Bland's pamphlet, but that, seeing the mind of America moving in the direction it was taking, he adopted the American attitude as his own and began to rationalize it. His first impulse was apparently to try to bridge the gap — to heal the wound in the body of his beloved empire. But he now had to ask himself the question: what, after all, was the logical and proper role of the colonial governments vis-à-vis the central government of the Empire? Were the elected colonial assemblies the true and sovereign representation of the British people in the colonies, or was Parliament? If they were, did Parliament have any power over them at all, and, if so, to what extent? As early as 1765 Franklin asked:

Are the children of English parents that are born in foreign parts of course subjects to our King? . . . And if they are not so naturally, what is it can make them so but their own consent? and if the first settlers then, that went over to America, had charters from the King, by which they and their posterity were to form assemblies, make laws,

&c. is it not a kind of compact by which their posterity agree to become his subjects upon those conditions? Now if these charters can be made void by an Act of Parliament, will that very Act destroy the Compact by which they became subjects? [61]

In 1766, in the margin of the *Protest against the Bill to Repeal the American Stamp Act, of Last Session,* an English pamphlet that represented the extreme reactionary position that Parliament had a right to legislate for the colonies in all matters, including taxation, Franklin wrote: "The Sovereignty of the Crown I understand. The Sov^y. of the British Legislature out of Britain, I do not understand." [62] And a little farther on, opposite the argument that the power of taxation extended to all the subjects of the British state, he wrote: "right; but we are different states. Subject to the King." [63] And on another pamphlet he wrote: "The People of G. Britain are Subjects of the King. G. B. is not a Sovereign. The Parliament has Power only *within the Realm.*" [64]

All this was in 1765 and 1766, and it is apparently the first time that Franklin had ever expressed the conviction that Parliament could not legislate for the colonies. It apparently marks a complete reversal of the position he held, certainly as late as 1760, that Parliament could legislate for the colonies, even to the point of imposing upon them an intercolonial union that he knew they would oppose. In his distinction between the power of Parliament "within the realm" — that is, in Great Britain — and its complete lack of authority over the British-American subjects of the crown "without the realm" he was taking a position that was for him completely new. It was a position taken by Bland; but Franklin clarified it.

Franklin was now moving clearly toward his own version of the idea of legislative autonomy for the colonies. Just a year or so later, in 1767, he wrote his old friend Lord Kames of his hope of preserving the union of the colonies with the mother country, but he clearly indicated that he was now thinking of them as separate states, attached to the Empire only by the common crown:

Parliament had no hand in their settlement, was never so much as consulted about their constitution, and took no kind of notice of them, till many years after they were established. . . . Thus all the colonies acknowledged the King as their sovereign; his governors there represent his person; laws are made by their Assemblies or little parliaments.

[61] Quoted in Verner W. Crane: *Benjamin Franklin, Englishman and American* (Baltimore, 1936), pp. 115–16.
[62] Quoted in ibid., p. 121.
[63] Quoted in ibid., p. 123.
[64] Quoted in ibid., p. 124.

. . . In this view, they seem so many separate little states, subject to the same prince. The sovereignty of the King is therefore easily understood. But nothing is more common here [in England] than the talk of *sovereignty* of Parliament, and the sovereignty of this nation over the colonies; a kind of sovereignty, the idea of which is not so clear, nor does it clearly appear on what foundation it is established. [65]

Franklin admitted the necessity for a central legislature of the Empire to regulate the Empire's commerce, and he felt sure his fellow-Americans would admit the same authority. But there that authority ended. And he warned his friend that the Americans must not be expected to submit to any extension of Parliament's authority to touch the internal concerns of the colonies, where their assemblies, or "little parliaments," were sovereign:

Upon the whole, I have lived so great a part of my life in Britain, and have formed so many friendships in it, that I love it, and sincerely wish it prosperity; and therefore wish to see that union, on which alone I think it can be secured and established. As to America, the advantages of such a union to her are not so apparent. She may suffer at present under the arbitrary power of this country [England]; she may suffer for a while in a separation from it; but these are temporary evils which she will outgrow. . . . In the mean time every act of oppression will sour their tempers, lessen greatly, if not annihilate, the profits of your commerce with them, and hasten their final revolt; for the seeds of liberty are universally found there, and nothing can eradicate them.[66]

He had just about arrived at his conclusion as to what the true nature of the Empire was, and where the true relationship between colonies and mother country ought to be. For early in the next year, in March 1768, Franklin wrote to his son, then Governor of New Jersey:

The more I have thought and read on the subject, the more I find myself confirmed in opinion, that no middle doctrine can be well maintained, I mean not clearly with intelligible arguments. Something might be made of either of the extremes; that Parliament has a power to make *all laws* for us, or that it has a power to make *no laws* for us; and I think the arguments for the latter more numerous and weighty, than those for the former. Supposing that doctrine established, the colonies would then be so many separate states, only subject to the same king, as England and Scotland were before the union.[67]

In 1770 Franklin expressed his completed idea of the federative empire again, and clearly, in a letter to Dr. Samuel Cooper of Boston:

[65] Franklin : *Works* (Sparks ed.), VII, 332–3.
[66] Ibid., VII, 334.
[67] Ibid., VII, 391–2.

That the colonies originally were constituted distinct states, and intended to be continued such, is clear to me from a thorough consideration of their original charters, and the whole conduct of the crown and nation toward them until the restoration. Since that period, the Parliament here [in England] has usurped an authority of making laws for them, which before it had not. . . . By our constitution [the king] is, with his plantation Parliaments, the sole legislator of his American subjects, and in that capacity is, and ought to be, free to exercise his own judgment, unrestrained and unlimited by his Parliament here. And our Parliaments have a right to grant him aid without the consent of This Parliament, a circumstance, which, by the way, begins to give it some jealousy.[68]

This, in brief, was the outline of a British commonwealth of nations. But Franklin knew that there was but little hope of having the idea find acceptance "while the nature of our present relation is so little understood on both sides of the water, and sentiments concerning it remain so widely different." The most significant thing about this is that Americans like Franklin — and Franklin was far from being alone — had arrived at a philosophy of the Empire that would have recognized colonial autonomy, if not actual sovereignty, within the commonwealth of states making up the British Empire. As for Franklin, his thinking had passed through three stages: at first he believed the problem of colonial autonomy could best be solved by an autonomous "voluntary union" of the colonies; when that failed, he turned to the thought of colonial representation in the British Parliament; completely disillusioned with that possibility, he then fell back upon the only position that seemed to him to provide guarantees for both the rights of the American English to self-government and their genuine loyalty to the crown as British subjects. To such a philosophical Tory as Thomas Hutchinson, Franklin's position was simply incomprehensible. He took Franklin to task for the evolution of Franklin's thought, which appeared to him to be nothing more than the mere shifting changes of expediency. The tragedy of Hutchinson's thought, and that of all those who saw things as he did, was that he and they simply could not conceive of a federative empire such as Franklin described; and Hutchinson was still insisting, as late as 1773, that the Empire was one simple state, one indivisible whole with one single government of king, lords, and commons, sitting in London to govern all Britons everywhere.

In any case, Franklin's theory is the culmination of American thought relative to the Empire in the colonial period: the embryonic concept of a British commonwealth of sovereign states. It was also the

[68] Ibid., VII, 466–79.

logical conclusion to the long struggle of the colonial assemblies for autonomy, although the Americans themselves as yet hardly realized it. Franklin admitted now that representation in an imperial parliament was impracticable, and that colonial government "by separate independent legislatures" was the only system flexible enough and adaptable enough to satisfy the legitimate political aspirations and ideals of all the diverse societies that made up the British Empire in America or even around the world.

Once this point in the development of the American political mind had been reached, it was but a short and easy step to the declaration of the first Continental Congress in 1774 :

> That the foundation of English liberty, and of all free government, is a right in the people to participate in their legislative council : and as the English colonists are not represented, and from their local and other circumstances, cannot properly be represented in the British Parliament, they are entitled to a free and exclusive power of legislation in their several provincial legislatures, where their right of representation can alone be preserved, in all cases of taxation and internal polity, subject only to the negative of their sovereign, in such manner as has been heretofore used and accustomed.[69]

The colonies were now agreed that the form of the Empire must be that of a federation of completely autonomous parts, leaving to the British Parliament only the power of legislation upon matters pertaining to intercourse between the parts of the Empire as a whole. This is essentially the idea advanced by Bland and developed by Franklin, and is the logical culmination of American thought as to the nature of the Empire. Even now, in 1774, the Americans thought of themselves as Britons, subjects of the British King, protesting in defense of their right to govern themselves. Their theory of the federative empire was not, therefore, to them, a new theory, but the clear statement of a principle that was old. It was the culmination of the evolution of a theory of the Empire that had been developing ever since the settlement of the first English colonies. Although they were not clearly conscious of the fact, their experience as emigrants, as settlers, and as architects of a new political structure in the wilderness had compelled the Americans to formulate their own new ideas as to the nature of the state and government generally and of the British Empire in particular. The new world had, indeed, made new ideas, in a new, American, mind.

[69] Morison, ed. : Sources and Documents, p. 120.

COLONIAL IDEAS ON INTERNATIONAL RELATIONS

In the course of the political struggles and other experiences that produced the political mind of the eighteenth-century Americans, there emerged certain fairly clear concepts of the relationship of the American colonies to the non-British members of the world community and some fairly well-defined ideas as to what those relationships ought to be. Naturally enough, these ideas had their beginnings in the actual experiences of the individual colonies; naturally enough, also, they tended to follow the lines of economic and political self-interest already observed.

The actual negotiations with other nations on international questions concerning the colonies were generally conducted for them by England. But there was much in the experience of the colonies themselves that stimulated them to develop ideas of their own as to what international policy should be. For from the beginning the colonies were called upon to negotiate directly with their neighbors, whether the Indians, the French in Acadia, the Dutch in New Netherland, or the Spanish in Florida. Furthermore, the colonies, throughout their history, negotiated with each other as quasi-independent states; and their experience reacted upon their thinking in the realm of international polity. Finally, and perhaps most important, practically all the colonies maintained permanent agencies to represent them in London; and their agents were in a very real sense "ambassadors of goodwill" from the colonies to the mother country. Incidentally, the mechanisms of control for these agencies, centering in the "committees of correspondence" of the colonial legislature, became in embryo the policy-forming agencies in the colonial constitution for matters pertaining to the colonies' external relations.

The earliest and most persistent matter in the realm of external relations to engage the attention of the colonists was foreign trade; and by 1660 Massachusetts, Virginia, Plymouth, and Connecticut had all made treaties with their French or Dutch neighbors for the provision and encouragement of the freedom of trade between them. But this freedom of commerce ran counter to the mercantile interests of England, and the series of Navigation Acts between 1651 and 1696 put a fairly effective bound to the colonial impulse to negotiate treaties of commerce directly. That these restrictions irked the colonists has already been seen; and the nullification of such of the Acts of Trade as the Molasses Act of 1733 demonstrated the probability that the external outlook of the Americans was bound to include the idea of freedom of international commerce. For, despite their early confused efforts to manipulate their own provincial commerce along mercantilist lines, the thinking of the Americans was in general moving toward the idea of freedom of commerce. It was no accident, therefore, that the desire of the colonies for freedom for commerce with foreign nations — or at least a *quid pro quo* — should have been linked to the Stamp Act controversy. Thus the question of foreign commerce becomes a part of the argument of Daniel Dulany:

> It is not contended that the colonies ought to be indulged in a general liberty of exporting and importing every thing in what manner they please, but, since they are hindered from making all the advantages they might do, and what advantage might they not make, if under no checks? they have a good plea against all vigour and severity, not absolutely necessary. . . .
>
> I confess that I am one of those who do not perceive the policy in laying difficulties and obstructions upon the gainful trade of the colonies with foreigners, or that it even makes any real difference to the *English* nation, whether the merchants who carry it on with commodities *Great-Britain* will not purchase, reside in *Philadelphia* . . . or *Liverpool,* when the balance gained by the *American* merchant in the pursuit of that trade centers in *Great Britain,* and is applied to the discharge of a debt contracted by the consumption of British manufactures in the colonies.[70]

Nor was it any less logical that the form of treaties devised by the Continental Congress in 1776 for its diplomatic representatives abroad should have contained not only clauses providing for freedom of international commerce in time of peace, but also a guarantee of the freedom of neutral commerce in time of war by a full acceptance of the principle that "free ships make free goods." Such an international objective was only the logical diplomatic counterpart of the free-trade economic doctrines held by Dulany, Franklin, and their contemporaries. How could it be otherwise when Franklin himself was one of the principal authors of this form treaty of 1776?

Another of the ideas of the Americans relative to external affairs grew out of the colonies' relationships to the wars of the European nations. The early settlers, particularly those in New England, rejoiced in their escape from the constant wars of Europe; and Francis Daniel Pastorius, leader of the German emigrants to Pennsylvania, could feelingly write that "After I had sufficiently seen the European provinces and countries, and the threatening movements of war, and had taken to heart the dire changes and disturbance of the Fatherland, I was impelled through a special guidance from the almighty, to go to

[70] Dulany: *Considerations on the Propriety of Imposing Taxes in the Colonies,* pp. 43, 46.

Pennsylvania." [71] This was the seed-germ of the American sentiment of isolationism : a feeling of escape ; of relief that a great and forbidding ocean lies between America and Europe to protect the new world from involvement in the passions and the tragedies of the old.

But it was more than a sentiment of escape. For this desire to avoid involvement in Europe's squabbles had led Massachusetts, as early as 1652, to proclaim its neutrality in the Anglo-Dutch war ; and in 1678 the French and English colonists in their respective zones on the island of St. Christopher had made a formal agreement, called the Treaty of Sandy's Point, to remain at peace as between themselves, even though their mother countries should go to war. This attitude of some of the colonists was even encouraged by the mother countries, and the idea of the separation of American international affairs from those of Europe was written into the Anglo-French Treaty of White-hall of 1686, only to be reversed in the English Declaration of War against France in 1689.

The idea of American isolation from European conflict had a steady growth in America. And in the middle of the eighteenth century, in the course of King George's War, there were many, particularly those whose pecuniary interests were involved, who simply ignored the fact that a war was going on. The merchants at Albany, for example, were notorious for the way in which they persisted in trading with the French in Canada during that war, directly in the face of all official efforts to prevent them from doing so.

At the same time there was a strong religious influence in the same direction that sprang from the pacifism of the Quakers and some of the German sects. For the Quakers, true to their principles, were unwilling either to participate in, or contribute to, war in any form or for any purpose. Their scruples against war were based upon their conviction that killing people, for whatever purpose, was contrary to the principles of divine love, and this conviction was given notable formal expression in the writings of Anthony Benezet. Practically, the situation was described at the time of the Anglo-Spanish War in 1740 by Israel Pemberton :

> as we are circumstanced here, People generally (and more particularly those of our Society) think it safest to stand still : And we are sorry to find, that some with you have been forward, in their Letters sent hither, to express themselves in a Manner quite contrary to the Profession we ever made . . . [and insinuate that the Quakers are "singular" in

[71] Quoted in J. Fred Rippy and Angie Debo : *The Historical Background of the American Policy of Isolation* (*Smith College Studies in History*, IX, Nos. 3 and 4, April, July, 1924), p. 71.

opposing warlike measures]. But tho' the Governor has been very urgent to bring the Assembly into these Things, they have hitherto avoided doing any Thing ; and have the Satisfaction to find, that their Conduct is much approved by the far greater Part, even of those, who do not refuse these Things on Principle, but as they believe they cannot be agreed to, without any Infringement of the fundamental Privileges we enjoy.[72]

The fact that Pemberton could refer to others who shared his isolationism on the basis of non-religious principles probably indicates with fair accuracy a wide prevalence of this feeling in the neighborhood of Philadelphia. This isolationism received a rude shock, however, when a Spanish privateer began to raid shipping in the very Delaware itself, and Franklin's pamphlet *Plain Truth* (1745) galvanized enough interest in the defense of Philadelphia to lead to the formation of a militia and the fortification of the city.

Yet the pacifism of the Quakers was not shaken by the persistence of war. On the contrary, it seemed to be the more justified. And Anthony Benezet, of New Jersey, the most outspoken American pacifist, could, in the midst of 1759, the *annis mirabilis* of British military success, proclaim that war was all wrong. For Christians know, he said,

> with the same certainty as they know their own existence, that human nature, left to itself, has no power but that of producing more evil. . . . They find war to be a sad consequence of the apostasy and fall of man ; when he was abandoned to the fury of his own lusts and passions, as the natural and penal effect of breaking loose from the Divine Government, and the fundamental law of which is LOVE. . . . But War, considered in itself, is the premeditated and determined destruction of human beings ; of creatures originally *"formed after the image of God,"* and whose preservation, for that reason, is secured by Heaven itself within the fences of this righteous law, That *"at the hand of every man's brother, the life of man shall be required."* [73]

It is probably true that the religious pacifism of the Quakers and some of the German sects, coupled with the feeling of "escape" of many of the immigrants to America, constituted one of the deep roots of the American feeling of isolationism. On the other hand, however, many Americans were apathetic toward the wars of the mother country simply because their own interests were not directly involved. And this "neutrality" or "isolationism" of a portion of the Americans toward

[72] "Copy of Part of a Letter from Israel Pemberton, and Son, of Philadelphia, to David Barclay, and Son, of London." A broadside, 1740.

[73] Anthony Benezet : *Thoughts on the Nature of War, and its Repugnancy to the Christian Life* (Philadelphia, 1766), pp. 3, 4, 6.

European wars highlights a sharp division in the American mind, again along the lines of self-interest. Yet while the merchants at Albany, for example, were clearly and stubbornly isolationist, Massachusetts, that same Massachusetts which had righteously proclaimed its isolationism a century earlier, was ardently for intervention in the war on the side of the mother country. It was Massachusetts, indeed, that, "with a little aid from England and the rest of New England," sent the amazingly successful expedition against the French fortress at Louisbourg on Cape Breton in 1745.

Generally speaking, the sentiment for intervention was promoted by the governors and the other agents of the crown in America; but it was ardently shared by those who had stakes in the colonial expansion westward, such as investments in western land, or in the northeast fisheries, or in the profits to be derived from privateering upon enemy commerce. Not that the interventionists were not sincere: they sincerely believed they were justified by the sins of the enemy, and particularly, at the mid-century, by the sins of France; and patriotism and religion were called into service to bolster their convictions. No sharp line was drawn between individual self-interest, American manifest destiny, British or imperial patriotism, and the necessary triumph of Anglo-American virtue and liberty over the fancied French malice and barbarianism; all these ideas were rolled together into the conviction that the American colonies should intervene in the conflict on the side of the mother country.

One of the most ardent and eloquent of the interventionists was Archibald Kennedy, of New York, who thought of himself as a sort of American Demosthenes rousing his people to the devilish designs of the enemy on the north:

> As *France* has hitherto, by the Means of *Great-Britain* chiefly, been prevented from enslaving the World and Mankind, they are become of Course our implacable and most inveterate Enemies, and of late every where our Competitors in Trade, and, as one of the Links of their grand System, Encroachers upon our Territories. . . .
>
> Thus by System they are become the Disturbers of the Peace of Mankind, and worse than a Pest, for there is no End of it to every contiguous Society; we are not the only Objects of their Resentment. . . .
>
> Our Case at present is neither more nor less than this, viz. That the *French* are now drawing a Line along the Borders of our Settlements in every Province, from the Mouth of *St. Lawrence*, to the Mouth of *Mississippi*, and building Forts to secure the most convenient Passes on the Lakes, that form the Communication; by which they will effectually cut off all Intercourse and Traffick, between us and the *Indians* inhabiting the inland Countries. . . . It therefore, I think behoveth

us at this time to exert our utmost Endeavours, by all the Means in our Power, to prevent so bad a Neighbourhood.[74]

Thus the roots of the American doctrine of isolationism go deep into the feeling of escape from the broils of Europe, the self-interest of groups of private individuals or entire colonies, and the convictions of religious groups opposed to war on any grounds; the countervailing sentiment for intervention, which probably represented the mood of the majority of Americans between 1748 and 1755, was a mixture of self-interest, nationalism, and the religious fervor of the anti-Catholic Protestant divines who preached the Anglo-French conflict as a sort of holy war against Catholic authoritarianism in both religion and politics. The colonies — the interventionist colonies, that is, who constituted the majority — were not dragged into the interimperial wars, but participated in them because they desired to do so. Those wars, and especially the Seven Years' War, fought in America from 1754 until 1763, were distinctly of the sort called "ideological," and the interventionists, at least, among the Americans supported them gladly.

The sentiment of isolationism probably represents more closely the true genius of the American colonial mind, once the French had been eliminated and the connection with the mother country finally broken, than the sentiment of interventionism, which as yet was closely identified in the memory of the Americans with the ideas of the Tory imperialists. For in its beginnings the American doctrine of isolationism was closely related to the American struggle for freedom: freedom for the colonies to manage their own affairs without external interference or "entanglements" of any kind, whether with mother country, other colonies, or foreign states. It has already been seen that the strong colonial drive toward self-direction defeated the Albany Plan of Union: the sentiment of interventionism in 1754, strong as it was, could not overcome the colonial "autonomy complex" even to the point of creating an international union. With the French menace removed, interventionism declined, and with the rising conflict with England the sentiment of isolationism took a new turn: isolationism was identified with the idea of self-government. And with independence John Adams could say, in 1776, in perfect confidence that he represented the mind of most Americans, that the young United States "should make no treaties of alliance with any European power . . . [but] should separate ourselves, as far and as long as possible, from all European politics and wars." [75]

American public opinion on the international situation, at least so

[74] Archibald Kennedy: *Serious Considerations on the Present State of the Affairs of the Northern Colonies* (New York, 1754), pp. 3–5.
[75] John Adams: *Works* (C. F. Adams, ed.), I, 201.

far as Anglo-French relations were involved, was fairly alive to the problems presented, and it was reflected in the newspapers, pamphlets, and correspondence of the years between 1750 and 1755. But opinion was divided. Generally speaking, the ardent Tory imperialists identified with the "court party" favored an aggressive military and diplomatic policy. Colden recommended the building of an armed vessel on Lake Ontario that would be more than a match for the sloops already there; Shirley, Kennedy, and others favored plans for an invasion of Canada. The more moderate wing of opinion, while prepared to make war, if necessary, for the maintenance of British claims in Acadia and on the Ohio, was not so ardently expansionist as the imperialists. Lewis Evans, for example, candidly admitted the right of the French to the land north of the St. Lawrence River and the Great Lakes, and was apparently willing to see this boundary established by negotiation. Which brought down upon his head the scathing denunciation of the imperialists, who called him a "traitor" for his honesty. Some of the provincial assemblies, most notable of which was that of Pennsylvania, held back from aggressive preparation for war; others, particularly that of Virginia, which had great stakes in the lands of the Ohio Valley, backed their imperialist governors with fairly ready support.

The imperialists carried the day; and their motivation was a mixture of self-interest, expansionism, interest in the Indian trade, nationalism, and religious bigotry. The moderates and the abstentionists were similarly moved by a mixture of motives : in many cases by self-interest, in some by fear of the military power of the large colonies, by a jealousy for their local prerogatives, amounting almost to a militant provincialism, or by genuine religious conviction. The significant thing is that the Americans, as never before, were coming alive to the problems of external relations.

Still another American concept having to do with external relations that had its genesis in the colonial experience was the belief in the pacific settlement of disputes. The idea and practice of peaceful settlement of disputes was not original with the Americans, of course, for the adjustment of claims and other international disputes by joint commission or by arbitration was already a long-established practice in European diplomacy at the time when the colonies were settled; and Hugo Grotius published his great work on *The Laws of War and Peace* shortly after the settlement of the earliest English colonies. The mode of peacefully adjusting difficulties with their foreign neighbors was adopted by the colonies very early in their history, notably in the negotiations of Massachusetts with the French in Acadia in 1644 and in the relations of the New England Confederation with the Dutch of New Amsterdam that culminated in the Treaty of Hartford of 1650. The principle was invoked in the missions sent by Massachusetts to Canada in 1723 and in Oglethorpe's Treaty of Frederica with Governor Sanchez of Florida in 1736. Meanwhile the British and French crowns had written the same principle into the Treaty of Whitehall of 1686, and arranged for joint commissions for the settlement of colonial boundary disputes, claims, and other matters in the Treaties of Ryswick (1697), of Utrecht (1713) and of Aix-la-Chapelle (1748); and the British and Spanish crowns had given lip-service to the principle in the Treaty of Seville (1729) and the Convention of the Pardo (1738). In actual practice, the efforts at peaceful settlement were seldom if ever successful, although joint commissions often met to make the effort, and an Anglo-French joint commission for the settlement of the disputes of those two nations, of which Governor Shirley of Massachusetts was a member, was meeting continuously almost throughout the interval of peace between 1748 and 1754.

The tender shoot of the ideal of peaceful settlement languished in the arid bitterness of international distrust and cynicism that characterized the international relations of the eighteenth century. Yet some there were who still believed, with the Quakers, that if men could only be taught to hearken to, and live by, the voice within, all international questions, even that of the Ohio Valley, might be settled peaceably according to the light of inspired reason. Some others there were, indeed, who hoped to find a natural law that they could apply to the rational settlement of international disputes; but these were few. Whatever the motive and however feeble its influence, the germ of the idea was present in the American mind of, say, 1750, and was very much alive.

The colonial agents of the American colonies in London were in a very real sense diplomatic representatives of the Americans "at the court of St. James's." And their century and a half of experience with these agencies gave birth to many ideas that were useful when the colonies were faced with the problem of formulating a foreign policy of their own after independence had been won. The most obvious duty of the colonial agents was to make every effort to secure and maintain the greatest possible degree of freedom from British interference for American commerce. Hardly less important, however, was the duty of the agents to present to the British authorities the case of the assemblies in their long struggle with the prerogative for legislative autonomy. The duties of the agents in connection with these American developments were, in a very real sense, those of diplomatic agents, and the instructions sent them by the committees directing their activities were, in effect, diplomatic instructions. Franklin, by his experience as agent for several colonies in England, was well trained for the delicate tasks awaiting him as the dean of all American diplomats in the era of independence. Furthermore, in their efforts to promote the interests of their colonies the agents gradually came to see that in a united front there is strength, and co-operation between them became increasingly customary between the time of the Molasses Act of 1733 and the Revolution.

What were the diplomatic principles evolved in this long experience of the colonial agencies? In general, they revolved about the trend toward the autonomy of the American legislatures. Thus, whether the agents were charged with securing the royal approval of an act of the provisional legislature, preventing action by the Board of Trade or Parliament running counter to the assembly's idea of what was good for the colony, or protesting against the arbitrary action of an unpopular governor, the work of the agent, as "diplomatic" representative of the colony — except, indeed, when he was the agent of the governor or the council or controlled by them — is to be linked closely with the struggle of the colonies for the right of self-government. As the colonies were growing toward the proclamation of their "sovereignty" as separate, self-governing states, the colonial agents were building up the principles and the practices upon the basis of which that sovereignty would one day be proclaimed to the world, the core idea of which was the principle of the right of self-determination. Jefferson only expressed the climax of a century of ideological evolution when he spoke of the British Parliament as "a body of men foreign to our constitution."

THE "SEEDS OF LIBERTY"

As Franklin said, the seeds of liberty were scattered abroad among the Americans, and were springing mightily into growth. Liberty, to them, meant the right to govern themselves: it was upon this theme that the political thinking of the vast majority of articulate Americans probably turned. For the great middle group of American moderates of the "liberal" assembly-autonomy faction this meant, at the time of its climactic development prior to the Revolution, the autonomy of the provincial government within a federative empire, and the supremacy of the legislature in that government. In some cases, if not in all, there was a clearly observable trend toward responsible cabinet government along English lines; such was the case, for example, in New York, where the leader for the executive in the legislature was already being called "the prime minister." The trend toward parliamentary responsibility was confused, it is true, by the efforts, based upon the expediencies of the struggle, of both the executive and the legislature to defend themselves against each other by the advocacy of "checks and balances" when it seemed to be to the advantage of one party or the other to do so. Yet the steady central drive toward autonomy and legislative supremacy is clear, both from the practice and from the theory of the assembly liberals.

For the conservative-minded, this sort of "liberty" seemed to be leading inevitably toward the destruction of the sacred element of the prerogative in the British constitution; the independence of the colonies; and the dissolution of the Empire. For them the British Empire was an indissoluble organic unity, and its head and soul were in England. And if their theory was valid, colonial autonomy was unthinkable and absurd. As well think of a hand or a finger as being autonomous and self-governing within the human body.

At the opposite extreme the radical political thinkers of the west were beginning to think in terms, not only of autonomy for the colonial legislatures, but also of a broader, more democratic base of representation in those assemblies and an even more clearly understood responsibility of the executive to them. But although the slow evolutionary movement of American political thought was generally toward this more progressive, more democratic ideology, as yet the Tory-imperialist protagonists of the prerogative were much less reprehensible than the "stinking republicans." The American political mind was moving, surely, toward democracy; but it was as yet far from having arrived at that way of thinking.

But if the drive for the autonomy of the provincial government and the supremacy of the legislature in it was working for complete self-government within the provinces, it was also leading the colonists slowly but surely toward the idea of the federative empire, in which each colony, each dominion, would be completely autonomous for its internal affairs and in which all the "dominions" or "states" would be bound together by a common allegiance to the British crown and in which the management of strictly intraimperial affairs and foreign relations would be left in the hands of the British government. Aside from the early, abortive suggestion that the colonies might be represented in a parliament of the unitary empire, which Franklin himself rejected after 1765, nobody, not even Franklin, ever developed the idea of the federative empire to the point of suggesting the collaboration of the colonies in the management of the Empire in anything like an "imperial conference" or an "imperial council." Something approximating the idea of "imperial preference" did appear, however, in the ideas of both Franklin and Daniel Dulany. With independence, the entire idea of the federative empire naturally disappeared. Immature as it was, this idea of the federative empire was the logical imperial counterpart to the internal provincial drive for political autonomy.

Similarly, if the mind of the Americans, at the stage in which it stood at the middle of the eighteenth century, was evolving toward provincial autonomy and the federative empire, it was also growing along lines of its own in its outlook upon international politics. The limited international free-tradism of the Americans, their irrepressible expansionism, their patriotism and "manifest destiny" proclivities, were prophetic of a later day; moreover, the isolationism and "escapism" of a large part of the Americans, when separated from their expansionism, was a clear derivative from the American environment and some of the American religions. Their increasingly active, effective, and mature relations with the mother country, particularly through their agencies there, followed along these same lines, and foreboded, whether within a federative empire or independent, a diplomatic relationship with Great Britain upon the footing of a status more nearly than ever approximating that of equality. Again, this awakening to the broad realities of the international community and the lines of American participation in it is to be seen as the international counterpart of the evolution of the colonies toward autonomous self-direction.

The colonies were, in fact, new societies in the world growing toward mature self-direction : their political thinking and the political self-respect accompanying maturity were growing with that growth.

If the American political mind appeared to be divided, it was really so only about the edges. The Tory imperialists represented reaction; the still inarticulate power of democracy represented black radicalism. Province distrusted province, and section felt coolly toward section; but chiefly in superficial things : on the great issue, the groundswell of self-direction, they were as one; indeed, they hardly realized as yet how nearly one they were.

Viewed in the long perspective of the history of political ideas, it is probably safe to say that the ideas with which the American conservatives justified their imperialistic position constituted a sort of tail-end of medieval feudalism in America. Kennedy's ideas, of course, were clearly so; but all the conservatives were under a sort of obsession that there was something sacrosanct and untouchable about the royal prerogative, even beyond all the justification for it that could be derived from Filmer, or even from any attempt to justify royal authority on the grounds of natural law in human society. There was, in other words, still a good deal of the late feudal concept of the divine right of kings in the theory of the prerogative; and in those who held this theory it was strongly tinged with emotion. Nor would it seem unreasonable to suppose that even this emotion was basically feudal — the emotional loyalty of a liege-man for his lord.

The American liberals, on the other hand, while they, too, felt the power of this psychological feudalism, were much more secular and much more modern in their political outlook. The basic idea that government derives from the people upward rather than from God downward is itself essentially secular. Far from admitting the divine right of the prerogative to intervene in legislation, the Americans were practically forced, by the logic of their position, to hold the king to be a secular agent, occupying his position only by right of a contract with the people. Far from being sovereign himself, the king was only the symbol of a sovereignty that existed, inherently and ultimately, in the people, and which, in delegating a part of itself to him, had actually created him. Thus, while the outward appearances of a feudal prerogative were retained, this was a complete break with feudal political theory; while it was not yet democracy, it was a long step toward democracy: for once the Americans had arrived at the conviction that their "state" and its sovereignty were derived from the people, the original founders of these new societies, democracy had to wait only upon a broader and more inclusive definition of "the people." The secularization of political thought was a long, slow process; though the Americans, by reason of their experience as builders of a new society, had invented a political theory that was more secular, more modern, and even more democratic than the theory of Lockian Whiggery in England, yet the process of the revolution in political ideas that produced the secular antithesis of feudalism, in 1750, was as yet incomplete, even in America. Even today there are still Americans who feel a sort of religious awe in the presence of a king.

The important thing is that this revolution was already so far advanced. Started in England, it had gone farther in America: it was here that the "seeds of liberty" had had — up to then — their smartest growth.

NOTE TO THE READER

It was never my intention to get enmeshed in the controversies of the American Revolution. The thinking that was crystallized in the debates of the ten or fifteen years prior to that event, however, was the final culmination of the political theorizing of the colonial period. It is as such that I present it here. Those pamphlets that I have selected are the coolest and the clearest, the considered thought of those men who, born before 1725, were already relatively old in the 1750's and 1760's, and ready in 1770 to surrender intellectual leadership to younger men.

The best writing on the Tory-imperialist side of political theory was done by Archibald Kennedy, William Smith, Jonathan Boucher, and Thomas Hutchinson. Thus Kennedy's *Essay on the Government of the Colonies* (New York, 1752) gives his feudal-fief idea, an idea that is still a little startling to Americans ; William Smith's *Brief State of the Province of Pennsylvania* (London, 1755) is full of a number of things, all interesting, presented from the Tory point of view ; Jonathan Boucher's *View of the Causes and Consequences of the American Revolution* (London, 1797) is a collection of his sermons, preached in the last few months before he fled Maryland for England ; *The Speeches of His Excellency Governor Hutchinson to the General Assembly of Massachusetts Bay* (Boston, 1773), which was published just before the Revolution, contains both Hutchinson's own excellent statement of his position and the assembly's statement of the American case. It was something of a tragedy that both sides were so completely unable to understand each other, and especially that Hutchinson was incapable, after all his experience, of understanding, not to say sympathizing with, the American idea.

For the American idea of the assembly liberals, Jonathan Mayhew's *Discourse Concerning Unlimited Submission* (Boston, 1750) is a striking statement of the nature of government and the right of revolution ; Daniel Dulany's *Considerations on the Propriety of Imposing Taxes in the British Colonies* (New York, 1765) is a statement of the emerging American idea at the time of the Stamp Act, although Richard Bland's *Letter to the Clergy of Virginia* (Williamsburg, 1760) goes rather far in that direction. Bland's *Inquiry into the Rights of the British Colonies* (Richmond, 1776) is the final statement of the American position, made just as war over the question was breaking. Franklin's statements are all fragmentary, and contained in letters or marginal notes.

Of genuinely democratic thinking in the eighteenth century there was little or none, except John Wise's *Vindication of the Government of New England Churches* and his *Churches' Quarrel Espoused,* both published before 1720 (in Boston).

Of the modern books, Verner W. Crane's *Benjamin Franklin, Englishman and American* (Baltimore, 1936), is a delightful and provocative series of essays, based largely upon hitherto unpublished Franklin materials. Volumes V and VI of Lawrence Gipson's *The British Empire before the American Revolution* are especially good on the Anglo-French conflict ; one of the best discussions of the Albany Plan of Union ever written is in Volume V.

CHAPTER VII

Of the Literary Expression
of Experience

"A theme more new, tho' not less noble, claims

"Our ev'ry thought on this auspicious day;

"The rising glory of this western world,

"Where now the dawning light of science spreads

"Her orient ray, and wake's the muse's song;

"Where freedom holds her sacred standard high,

"And commerce rolls her golden tides profuse

"Of elegance and ev'ry joy in life. . . ."

PHILIP FRENEAU.

ITERATURE is the expression, direct or indirect, of the living experience of the people who produce it. It is, as it were, the voice of a people. Its form may be a foreign form; but so long as it embodies a set of experiences, material or psychological, that no other people on earth could have had, it is native and peculiar to its producers and in that sense constitutes a "national" literature. In no other way is the mind of a people of a given time and place so broadly or so intimately "documented" as by its literature, conceived in the broadest possible sense.

It is in this sense that the Americans of the mid-eighteenth century may be said to have produced an American literature. The forms in which much of it was contained were foreign, and particularly English, since those forms seemed the most elegant. The Americans had not produced literary forms of their own; or, where they had, the new ones to many seemed too crude. Much of the matter, too, was foreign;

and there was little of this literature, or none of it, that achieved the qualities of the world's best. Yet where the writings of the Americans gave expression to experiences or reactions to them that were peculiarly American, the literature was essentially American. American literature, in the truest sense, thus germinated and grew in the soil of America; as American society and the American mind and American ideals became more definite and more mature, American literature expressed that growth and those ideals. There has always been an American literature, as long as there have been Americans who have thought and felt as Americans. American literature, whatever its strictly "literary" quality, is the documentation of the American mind and sensibility from the beginning.

The English and American Background

The English background from which the earliest Americans derived their literary heritage was Elizabethan and Puritan; and the first literary productions in America were created by English Elizabethans or English Puritans removed to Virginia or Massachusetts.

The fabulous Captain John Smith, for example, with his *History of Virginia*, was the perfect Elizabethan type of pithy, swashbuckling adventurer turned littérateur to describe the adventures of the Elizabethans in the southern colony, and the lusty poet Thomas Morton fathered the season of Elizabethan warmth on the frosty shores of Massachusetts Bay described in his *New English Canaan*. But Elizabeth was dead, and the rigorous winter of Puritan doctrine and Puritan literature was already creeping over England when the colony of Massachusetts Bay was founded; and the writings of the Puritan founding fathers John Winthrop, Nathaniel Ward, and Edward Johnson were full of the piety and the literary orderliness that was like unto the plan of God.

Back in England, Sir Francis Bacon, last of the great Elizabethans, had ceased writing his classical prose essays in 1626, in the sixth year of Plymouth and the nineteenth of Virginia, to be succeeded by John Selden, Thomas Hobbes, and John Milton in the age of seriousness. This prose, even at its best, was stiff, stilted, formal, and filled with classical references that only the educated could understand; generally, too, it had as its chief objective the advancement of a great moral principle or purpose. Even the great Milton himself found æsthetic delight in literary contortion and oblique classical reference.

But the age of rationalism that dawned in England shortly after the Restoration brought with it the simple, direct language of science; and literary style changed to follow the promptings of reason. Thus the advent of Samuel Pepys, John Dryden, John Locke, and William

Penn brought to literature a new directness and simplicity, with less of classical allusion. The Royal Society of London, the great emporium of scientific literature and ideas, deliberately set for itself the standard of rational simplicity, and ruled "to reject all the amplifications, digressions, and swellings of style : to return back to the primitive purity, and shortness, when men deliver'd so many things almost in an equal number of words. They have exacted from all their members, a close, naked natural way of speaking; positive expressions; clear senses; a native easiness; bringing all things as near the Mathematical plainness as they can." [1]

But it was not until Daniel Defoe, Jonathan Swift, Joseph Addison, and Richard Steele that the transition was made into the sprightly, gay, clear, simple, and direct prose of the *Spectator* and the *Tatler*. Gone was the complex, godly, purposefulness of a Milton or even a John Bunyan. English prose had become secular, this-worldly, ironical, gay.

A corresponding development was taking place in English poetry. The humanistic gaiety of the Elizabethans fell under a cloud, although kept alive by such irrepressible lyricists as Robert Herrick, and English poetry became, under the Puritan influence, ponderous, majestic, purposeful. Even Milton's *L'Allegro,* before it gets around to "Laughter holding both his sides," must derive the descent of the fair and free goddess Euphrosyne, or Mirth, from the classical Venus.

The greatest literary monument of Puritanism in England was, of course, John Milton's *Paradise Lost.* One of the world's greatest literary masterpieces, it is marked, aside from its sheer grandeur of concept and of expression, by its regularity, its orderliness, and its execution according to a plan. As is well known, this great epic poem recounts the entire story of the creation, the fall of man, and the redemption, as they were conceived by the Puritan theology. It was, in fact, the perfect literary expression of the Puritan's concept of the nature of the world and of man, of sin, and of God's plan for men. If Puritan literature was austere and disciplined in its æsthetic, consonantly with the Puritan theology from which it sprang, it was awful in its grandeur and the very majesty of its conception :

> *Of Mans First Disobedience, and the Fruit*
> *Of that Forbidden Tree, whose mortal taste*
> *Brought Death into the World, and all our woe,*
> *With loss of* Eden, *till one greater Man*
> *Restore us, and regain the blissful Seat,*
> *Sing Heav'nly Muse. . . .*

[1] Quoted in Thomas Sprat : *The History of the Royal Society of London* (London, 1722), p. 113.

That to the highth of this great Argument
I may assert Eternal Providence,
And justifie the wayes of God to men.[2]

This is not only great poetry; it is also a document that shows the closely knit unity of intellectual outlook that bound together Puritan social thought and religion with literature — as the literature of any age almost always does. Milton had favored religious freedom — for God's elect — and political freedom; but freedom, for him, as for all Puritans, had clearly defined limits. Milton puts this principle into the mouth of God:

I formed them free, and free they must remain,
Till they enthrall themselves. . . .[3]

Freedom existed within the rigidly prescribed plan; any deviation from the established order was an abuse of freedom and could only result in enslavement.

With the change of outlook that came with the Restoration, a new literary springtime dawned and a new poetry appeared, which, while gaily celebrating the passage of the Puritan shadow, also gave poetic expression to the new rationalism derived from the Newtonian science. Already with John Dryden the Newtonian universe begins to have poetic expression; and it reached full voice in poetry in Alexander Pope's *Essay on Man*:

Of Man, what see we but his station here,
From which to reason, or to which refer?
Through worlds unnumbered though the God be known,
'Tis ours to trace Him only in our own.
He, who through vast immensity can pierce,
See worlds on worlds compose our universe,
Observe how system into system runs,
What other planets circle other suns,
What varied being peoples ev'ry star,
May tell why Heav'n has made us as we are.[4]

Here was something of a revolution in literary thought: from the other-worldliness of Milton to the this-worldliness of Pope; from God's plan for men to the finding of God through men; from the acceptance of the scripture legends to the understanding of the universe by

[2] John Milton: *Milton's Complete Poems*, edited by Frank A. Patterson (New York, 1930), p. 160.

[3] Ibid. (*Paradise Lost*, III: 123–5), p. 198.

[4] Alexander Pope: *Pope's Essay on Man and Essay on Criticism*, edited by Joseph B. Seabury (New York, 1900), p. 18.

the penetration of nature herself with the sharp instrument of human reason. For from a baroque sort of other-worldliness, from godly purposefulness, literature had changed to the secular, gay, rationalism of the eighteenth century. And the progress of polite literature in America followed closely the course of the literary revolution in England.

The first serious attempts at English colonization in America, then, were made in the so-called Elizabethan era, the literary age of Raleigh, Shakespeare, Ben Jonson, and Bacon; and the Elizabethan literary tradition was planted in America by the earliest colonists. In Virginia, where it was planted by John Smith and his companions, it survived despite the mid-century influx of Puritans, and as the society of the Old Dominion and Maryland developed toward the status of sophisticated aristocracy, trends of literary expression followed the trends of literary change in England. There exist, indeed, all too few examples of literary production of seventeenth-century Virginia and Maryland. The chronicle of Bacon's Rebellion is probably the best, and its style is in the tradition, roughly, of the English secular baroque :

> And here who can do less than wonder at the muteable and impermenent deportments of that blinde Godes Fortune ; who, in the morning loades Man with disgraces, and ere night crownes him with honours : Sometimes depressing, and againe ellivateing, as her fickle humer is to smile or frowne, of which this Gent:mans [Nathaniel Bacon's] fate was a kinde of an Epittemey, in the severall vicissetudes and changes he was subjected to in a very few dayes. For in the morning, before his triall, he was, in his Enimies hopes, and his Friends feares, judged for to receive the Gurdian due to a Rebell (and such hee was proclamed to be) and ere night, crowned the Darling of the Peoples hopes and desires, as the only man fitt in Virginia, to put a stop unto the bloody ressalutions of the Heathen : And yet againe, as a fuller Manifestation of Fortune's inconstancye with in two or three days, the peoples hopes, and his desires, were both frusterated by the Governours refuseing to signe the promised Commission.[5]

This account is fairly complex in style, and does not escape the inevitable classical reference — in this case, to the goddess Fortune; yet, for all its quaint complexity, it is secular in tone and humanistic in its philosophic mood. Its tone is still essentially Elizabethan, as, indeed, was also the poem produced by "Bacon's Man" on the same occasion.

Not so, however, the literature of the Puritans. For the same chilly morality that closed the theaters in England, that same sober purposefulness and distrust of pleasure for its own sake that produced the ordered Puritan Commonwealth, controlled Puritan writing. For literature, as the Puritans of old and New England saw it, must be pur-

[5] *Proceedings of the Massachusetts Historical Society, 1866–1867,* pp. 305–6.

poseful, pious, utilitarian; either justifying the ways of God to men or improving the ways of men before God. There was no place in Puritan writings for literature justified solely for its quality of giving pleasure. Any effort to give pleasure for pleasure's sake alone would have run counter to every canon of the Puritan way of life. The only legitimate objective of literature was the conversion, or the conviction, of one's hearer or reader. Life was a serious business; literature, like anything else, was justified only if it served the grandly serious purposes of God with man.

Even at that it was wordy, difficult, and logically overorganized. Increase Mather, of the second generation, furnishes a fairly good, typical example of Puritan prose :

SLEEPING AT SERMONS

Instr. 1. *We may here take notice that the nature of man is wofully corrupted and depraved,* else they would not be so apt to sleep when the precious Truths of God are dispensed in his Name, Yea, and men are more apt to sleep then, than at another time. Some woful Creatures, have been so wicked as to profess they have gone to hear Sermons on purpose, that so they might sleep, finding themselves at such times much disposed that way . . . when Paul was alive, there was not a better Preacher upon the Earth than he . . . but notwithstanding *Pauls* being so excellent a preacher, there were some that could sit and sleep under his Ministry. . . . When soul-awakening Sermons are Preached, enough to make rocks to rend and to bleed; when the word falls down from Heaven like Thunder, the voice of the Lord therein being very powerful and full of Majesty, able to break the Cedars of *Lebanon,* and to make the wilderness to shake; yet some will sit and sleep under it : such is the woful corruption and desperate hardness of the hearts of the Children of men.[6]

Nor was Increase Mather joking. He spoke in deadly earnest always, about small things as well as large. His object was practical; nothing was justified that had no practical result in the promotion of godliness in the lives of men. Not even poetry; not even music; not even art. The poetry of the Puritans, like their music and their art, was designed to the same end. Some of their cultural products were fine, as will be demonstrated; but there was no room in Puritan cultural life for æsthetic pleasure for pleasure's own sake. If there was pleasure in it, it must be Godly pleasure.

This is not at all to say, however, that the Puritans had no genuine literary impulses. On the contrary, the same deep sense of the power and majesty of God in the world that gave birth to *Paradise Lost*

[6] Miller and Johnson : *The Puritans,* pp. 348–9.

moved the Puritans in the New World; if the quality of their product was less high, it was not because the impulse to worship God in beautiful literature was less strong, but simply because they were more humble instruments of expression. The moving impulse was the same.

Thus the Puritan writers in America, trained as they were in the scholastic tradition, nevertheless knew very well the effectiveness of a style that would appeal to the æsthetic sensibilities of their audience as well as to its reason. As a result, they consciously studied the effects of style, and in this conscious striving for a more or less preconceived intellectual and emotional effect they, too, fell into the tradition of the baroque. Cotton Mather, for example, himself a third-generation American, while fully conscious of a trend toward the plain style and fully able to use it, deliberately avoided it in many of his books, partly because that old style gave him a chance to display his erudition, and partly simply because he liked it — as he himself says in the introduction to his *Magnalia Christi Americana*:

> I cannot say whether the style wherein this Church-History is written, will please the modern critics : but if I seem to have used . . . a simple, submiss, humble style, 'tis the same that Eusebius affirms to have been used by Hegesippus, who, as far as we understand, was the first author (after Luke) that ever composed an entire body of Ecclesiastical History, which he divided into five books. . . . Whereas others, it may be, will reckon the *stlye* embellished with too much of *ornament*, by the multiplied references to other and former concerns, closely couched, for the observation of the attentive, in almost every paragraph; but I must confess, that I am of his mind who said, Sicuti sal modici cibis aspersus Condit, et gratiam saporis addit, ita si paulum antiquitatis admiscueris, Oratio sit venustior [as a lttle salt seasons food, and increases its relish, so a spice of antiquity heightens the charm of style]. And I have seldom seen that way of writing faulted [criticized], but by those who, for a certain odd reason, sometimes find fault that "the grapes are not ripe." [7]

This style of writing is almost impossible for the modern reader to follow. It is not only difficult to read; it also displays a self-satisfied pride in one's aristocratic learning that is foreign to the mood of later writers — a new mood, indeed, which was developing at the same time as that when Cotton Mather was writing, and of which he was fully conscious.

For some of the Puritan preachers realized their effectiveness was in the last analysis decreased by a style that was too complex for their frontier audiences to understand. Puritanism itself, indeed, was a re-

---

[7] Cotton Mather : *Magnalia Christi Americana* (2 vols., Boston, 1855), I, 31.

volt against ostentation and sensual pleasure, even when that was rolling high-sounding words under the tongue; in their effort to be more direct, more simple, and more honest in their literary style, they were but applying in literature their condemnation of ritualism and their belief in the essential and ultimate directness of the relationship between the individual and his God. Their reaction against the baroque religious literature of the Anglicans was of a piece with their revolt against Anglican ecclesiasticism. Thus even Puritan literature, at the turn of the century, was beginning to use a more simplified style; and its efforts at literary simplicity constituted a sort of literary revolt against the English baroque, a sort of literary counterpart of the Puritan secession from Anglicanism.

The prose epic of Puritan New England was neither ecclesiastical history for the erudite nor sermons for sleepers in church, but the narrative of Mary Rowlandson's captivity among the Indians. For in this moving description of her suffering, written in simple, direct, and un-adorned style, Mrs. Rowlandson, housewife, never loses her great faith in the goodness of God or her sense of utter dependence upon him. Never was the Puritan outlook upon life more clearly embodied in a literary narrative; never, also, does the ultimate resting of the Puritan ideal upon God's beauty more clearly shine through the Puritan's prose:

At length [the Indians] came and beset our house, and quickly it was the dolefulest day that ever mine eyes saw. The house stood upon the edge of a hill; some of the Indians got behind the hill, others into the barn, and others behind any thing that would shelter them; from all which places they shot against the house, so that the bullets seemed to fly like hail, and quickly they wounded one man among us, then another, and then a third. . . . Now is the dreadful hour come that I have often heard of in time of the war, as it was in the case of others, but now mine eyes see it. Some in our house were fighting for their lives, others wallowing in blood, the house on fire over our heads, and the bloody heathen ready to knock us on the head if we stirred out. Now might we hear mothers and children crying out for themselves and one another, *Lord, what shall we do!* Then I took my children, and one of my sisters hers to go forth and leave the house, but as soon as we came to the door and appeared, the Indians shot so thick that the bullets rattled against the house as if one had taken a handful of stones and threw them, so that we were forced to give back. We had six stout dogs belonging to our garrison, but none of them would stir, though at another time if an Indian had come to the door, they were ready to fly upon him and tear him down. The Lord hereby would make us the more to acknowledge his hand, and to see that our help is always in him. But out we must go, the fire increasing, and coming along behind us roaring, and the Indians gaping before us with their guns, spears, and hatchets to devour us. . . . The bullets flying thick, one went through my side, and the same, as would seem, through the bowels and hand of my poor child in my arms. . . .[8]

Great, indeed, and beautiful, was the faith of this Puritan woman; and moving, indeed, is the simple narrative of her woes. It is no wonder at all that in the eighteenth century, when novels, for Americans, practically did not exist, this first-hand relation of sharp adventure, bitter suffering, and deeper faith should have passed through so many editions. Needless to say, too, this was the germ of a literature that was alive; for it was of the very core and fiber of the American experience in the forest and on the soil of America.

Mary Rowlandson's narrative is an impressive documentation of the heights to which the sincere ordinary Puritan man or woman could rise in the completeness of his trust in and dependence upon God and his will. Yet this relation is in a new tradition; it is the beginning, all unbeknown to itself, of a new literature; for it is the expression, in the direct and honest language of literary realism, of a profound human experience, an experience that could have occurred, in its own exact terms, nowhere else in the world. It was rooted in the soil and shadows of the American wilderness; and it embodied in literary form the genuine reactions of a human being who brought her old inherited faith to bear upon the peculiar conditions of the new world; the literary expression of this combination of subjective and objective experience is something that was distinctly and genuinely American.

The same general observations hold true for poetry. The Puritan century in America had its own mind, its own forms to express the Puritan's awe of God and his sense of utter dependence upon the divine will. Similarly, his sensibility, his æsthetic reaction to his world, was framed in this sense of awe and dependence and was thoroughly instinct with it. Thus Anne Bradstreet's poems, while they do not always treat of religious themes, almost invariably place the feelings in a religious — a Puritan — setting. The poem on her husband's departure for England (1657) is typical:

> *Into the everlasting Armes*
> *Of mercy I commend*
> *Thy servant, Lord. Keep and preserve*
> *My husband, my dear friend. . . .*

[8] John Frost, ed. : *Frost's Pictorial History of Indian Wars and Captivities* (New York, 1873), Part II, pp. 21–5.

Lord, be Thou Pilott to the ship,
And send them prosperous gailes ;
In storms and sickness, Lord, preserve
Thy Goodness never failes. . . .

Lord, let my eyes see once Again
Him whom Thou gavest me,
That wee together may sing Praise
For ever unto Thee.[9]

Anne was reared in the tradition of the Puritan baroque ; her poems are often, therefore, labored and wordy, taking their subject matter out of books, rather than nature, and filled with classical references. Yet she, an Englishwoman born, adapted herself to the American scene, and she reached her best when she turned to nature as her subject matter, and to clear, direct, and simple language as her idiom. Her "Contemplations" is probably her best poem ; in it she does not escape completely the labored wordiness and classical reference of the more ambitious poems, but she moves more clearly — and more enjoyably — toward a simple and direct expression. Anne Bradstreet never achieved the status of a great poet. Good Puritan that she was, she did, nevertheless, have a sensibility to the beautiful and the subtle ; and though constrained, perhaps, by the Puritan frame of mind that permitted nothing not useful to the purposes of God, her poems show the flights of sensibility and of fancy that were possible within the Puritan framework.

Michael Wigglesworth, who came to America as a child, was the popular poet *par excellence* of Puritan New England. His poetic genius is to be measured by his power of imagery ; but his significance lies chiefly in the popularity of his poem "The Day of Doom," an exposition in verse of the Calvinist doctrine. For the very popularity of his doggerel attests its validity as an expression of the poetic mind — such as it was — of the Puritan generation, just as Increase Mather expressed the current taste for literary prose. This is the sort of thing the Puritan population of New England seems to have liked as poetry :

THE DAY OF DOOM

Reader, I am a fool
And have adventurèd
To play the fool this once for Christ,
The more his fame to spread. . . .

9 Anne Bradstreet : *The Works of Anne Bradstreet,* edited by John H. Ellis (Charlestown, 1867), pp. 32–4.

I

Still was the night, serene and bright,
*   when all Men sleeping lay ;*
Calm was the season, and carnal reason
*   thought so 'twould last for aye.*
"Soul, take thine ease, let sorrow cease,
*   much good thou hast in store."*
This was their Song, their Cups among,
*   the evening before.*

CCXXII.

Oh blessed state of the Renate !
*   Oh wond'rous happiness,*
To which they're brought beyond what thought
*   can reach or words express !*
Grief's watercourse and sorrow's source
*   are turned to joyful streams ;*
Their old distress and heaviness
*   are vanished like dreams.*

CCXXIV.

For there the Saints are perfect Saints,
*   and holy ones indeed ;*
For all the sin that dwelt within
*   their mortal bodies freed ;*
Made Kings and Priests to God through Christ's
*   dear Love's transcendency,*
There to remain and there to reign
*   with him Eternally.*[10]

The first native-born American poet was Benjamin Tompson, Puritan schoolmaster, of Boston and Charlestown, who was graduated from Harvard in 1662. Tompson wrote in the Puritan baroque, and his poems are literally studded with classical allusions and twisted by rhetorical convolutions.

In seventy five the Critick *of our years*
Commenced our way with Phillip and his peers,
Wither the sun in Leo *had inspir'd*
A feav'rich heat, and Pagan *spirits fir'd ?*
Whither some Romish *Agent hacht the plot ?*
Or whither themselves ? appeareth not. . . .

But doleful shrieks of captives summon forth
Our walking castles, men of noted worth,
Made all of life, each Captain was a Man,

[10] Michael Wigglesworth : *The Day of Doom* (New York, 1867), pp. 13, 21, 84–5.

His name to strong to stand on waterish verse :
Due praise I leave to some poetic hand
Whose pen and witts are better at command.
Methinks I see the Trojan-horse *burst ope,*
And such rush forth as might with giants cope :
These first the native treachery felt, too fierce
For any but an eye-witness to rehearse. . . .[11]

Tompson was a voice of his generation ; completely Puritan in mind and outlook. In his rhyming about the American scene, nevertheless, in his satire in the name of sincerity, and in his approaches to humor, he gets closer than his predecessors to the true genius of the American way in poetry.

Puritan New England did produce one real poet, in the person of Edward Taylor, pastor of the church in the frontier village of West-field, in Massachusetts. He, too, wrote in the style of the Puritan baroque ; but he mastered it so well as to make that uncongenial style beautiful, even to modern ears. Taylor's greatest significance lies in the fact that nowhere, probably, in all the literature of American Puritanism, does the beautiful side of the Puritan mind so clearly appear. He was born in England, and came to Massachusetts in 1668 ; he attended Harvard, where he graduated in 1671, and then went to Westfield, where he served as pastor for fifty-eight years. His life was quiet, though not untouched by sorrow ; his poetry was written as the quiet outpouring of his sublime, unquestioning faith in the beauty and goodness of God. For example :

MEDITATION ONE

What Love is this of thine, that Cannot bee
  In thine Infinity, O Lord, Confinde,
Unless it in thy very Person see
  Infinity and Finity Conjoyn'd ?
  What ! hath thy Godhead, as not satisfi'de,
  Marri'de our Manhood, making it its Bride ?

Oh, Matchless Love ! Filling Heaven to the brim !
  O'rerunning it : all running o're beside
This World ! Nay, Overflowing Hell, wherein
  For thine Elect, there rose a mighty Tide !
  That there our Veans might through thy Person bleed,
  To quench those flames, that else would on us feed.

Oh ! that thy love might overflow my Heart !
  To fire the same with Love : for Love I would.

[11] "New England's Crisis," in Howard J. Hall, ed. : *Benjamin Tompson 1642–1714, First Native-born Poet of America* (New York, 1924), pp. 53–4.

But oh! my streight'ned Breast! my Lifeless Sparke!
My Fireless Flame! What Chilly Love, and Cold?
In measure small! In Manner Chilly! See!
Lord, blow the Coal: Thy Love Enflame in mee.[12]

In a way Taylor's poems are so purely contemplative as to seem remote from the reality of the frontier about him. His meditations dwell upon the beauties of wedlock, children, and the shock of misfortune and death, universal experiences and emotions that might have been felt and described by a deeply pious and sensitive man almost anywhere. It was as though he rose completely out of the daily realities of frontier life. If this poetry is the product of the frontier at all, it is such only as the escape of Puritan piety from it. In this sense it seems almost outside the American tradition: but in its deep religious feeling, in its idealistic aspiration, and in its sense of utter dependence upon the goodness of God, it is thoroughly Puritan and an integral part of the Puritan experience in America. Even so, he was a poetic voice of pure Puritanism, singing at a moment when Puritanism in its original form was losing its hold upon the people and when the more prosaic voices of rationalism were increasingly more widely heard in the land.

Out of seventeenth-century Virginia there has survived only one poem. This was "Bacon's Epitaph," said to have been made "by his Man." Whether "his Man" was a servant or a knightly retainer in the feudal sense is not clear; but the poem itself is certainly one of the finest written in America before 1700, and shows poetic qualities excelled, probably, only by those of the Puritan Edward Taylor. In form it follows the Miltonic iambic pentameter, with similar long, involved constructions, studded with classical allusions. Yet it embodies a deep emotional experience; and despite its intricate form and antique spelling, it is an eloquent plea for the incipient cause of freedom that Bacon represented:

Death why so crewill! What no other way
To manifest thy splleene, but thus to slay
Our hope of safety; liberty, our all
Which, through thy tyranny, with him must fall
To its late caoss? . . .
                    Now wee must complaine
Since thou, in him, Lost more than thousand slane
Whose lives and safetys did so much depend
On him there lif, with him there lives must end.[13]

[12] Edward Taylor: *The Poetical Works of Edward Taylor*, edited by Thomas H. Johnson (New York, 1939), p. 123. By permission of Princeton University Press.
[13] Peter Force, ed.: *Tracts and Other Papers, Relating principally to the Origin, Settlement, and Progress of the Colonies in North America* (4 vols., Washington, 1836–46), I, No. XI, pp. 29–30.

The literature of the seventeenth century in America, then, was dominated by the baroque form. But its mood in Virginia was less serious, less other-worldly, more humanistic, while its mood in New England was pious, purposeful, devoted, in its highest reaches, to portraying the ineffable beauty of God. Yet the rigidity and the complexity of the baroque, whether the courtly baroque of the Stuart courtiers or the Miltonic baroque of the Puritan revolt, was already beginning to soften under the influence of the new world experience : the sincere dislike of the Puritans for ostentation and sensual pleasure, as well as the necessary frontier emphasis upon the practical and the utilitarian, unquestionably made for more directness and simplicity of style; but the greatest generative force at work upon literature was probably the profoundly humanizing influence of the experience of the Americans on the frontier along the edge of the wilderness, whether in the outpouring of the emotional and spiritual movements of Mary Rowlandson in her travail, in the quiet contemplative faith of the frontier parson expressed in the poems of Edward Taylor, or in the lament of "Bacon's Man" at the death of that great frontier hero. Thus, even while Cotton Mather was indulging himself in the enjoyment of his own literary complexities, the germ of a genuine literary experience among the Americans had come into being, the first beginnings of a literature whose emotional generative power and whose content, if not its form, were strictly and deeply American.

IMITATION AND CREATIVENESS IN AMERICA

The turn of the century that saw the flowering of Addison and Steele in England saw a corresponding change in the literary mind in America. For although America was somewhat slower than England to shed its Puritan outlook — if it ever did — with a consequent persistence of the Puritan influence in literature, American literary expression in general, whether in the north, the middle, or south, felt just as clearly the rationalistic impact upon literature that was derived from Newtonian science. But it also felt a new and earthy influence that England could not feel, in the profound impact upon literature that was derived from the American frontier. For it was this element in the American experience that was to give to American literature its characteristic content, if not its form, to make it something new and different.

The American imitators : the simple prose style

The transition in the development of American literature that derived from the advance of secularism and rationalism made itself felt first in the adoption of a new prose style. For Cotton Mather had been right about one thing: there were, indeed, "others" — many others, from that day to this — who found his style unbearable. One such critic was Benjamin Franklin; another was Mather Byles, whose little essay on "Bombastic and Grubstreet Style" not only expressed the true trend of eighteenth-century prose style, but actually poked fun at the labored baroque:

> Authors of this Kind may be divided into two Classes, generally known under the Denomination of the *Bombastick* and the *Grubstreet*. The latter of these Characters is easily attained, provided a Man can but keep himself from thinking, and yet so contrive Matters, as to let his Pen run along unmolested over a Sheet of White Paper, and drop a convenient quantity of Words, at proper Intervals on it. . . . [14]

This satirical essay marks an important moment in American literary history; for besides making fun of such labored writers as Cotton Mather, it injects a deliberate and self-conscious effort at humor into literature. Most important of all, it marks a deliberate turning away from the "grubstreet" and the "bombastic" style to a prose style that has for its ideal simplicity, directness, and literary integrity.

The most obvious and the best-known example of the conscious effort of the Americans to achieve a clearer, more readable style was Benjamin Franklin, who early in life determined to discard the florid, difficult style of writers like Mather and deliberately patterned his own prose style after that of the English writers of the period of Addison and Steele. As he described his effort many years later:

> About this time, I met with an odd volume of the *Spectator*. It was the third. I had never before seen any of them. I bought it, read it over and over, and was much delighted with it. I thought the writing excellent, and wished it possible, to imitate it. With that view, I took some of the papers, and making short hints of the sentiments in each sentence, laid them by a few days, and then, without looking at the book, tried to complete the papers again, by expressing each hinted sentiment at length, and as fully as it had been expressed before, in any suitable words that should occur to me. . . . By comparing my work afterwards with the original, I discovered my faults and amended them; but I sometimes had the pleasure to fancy, that, in certain particulars of small consequence, I had been fortunate enough to improve the method or the language, and this encouraged me to think, that I might in time come to be a tolerable English writer; of which I was extremely ambitious.[15]

Franklin was probably more methodical and more determined to achieve a clear style than most American writers; but his desire was

---

[14] Miller and Johnson : *The Puritans*, p. 690.
[15] Franklin : *Works* (Sparks ed.), I, 18–19.

typical. But not only was prose-writing in America becoming more simple, more direct; it was also becoming secular, concerned with non-religious affairs. Further, essays were being written for enjoyment, without any particular effort to reform anybody.

A simpler prose style was also being consciously produced by the great sermon-writers, Mather Byles, Jonathan Mayhew, and Charles Chauncy. Said Byles, the preacher "must study an easy style, expressive diction, and tuneful cadences. . . . Rattling periods, uncouth jargon, affected phrases, and finical jingles — let them be condemned; let them be hissed from the desk and blotted from the page." [16]

So strongly did Chauncy feel on the subject of the florid, oratorical style, indeed, that he was said to have exclaimed that he prayed that he might never be an orator, upon which one of his parishioners was said to have remarked that his prayer had most assuredly been granted. [17]

The sermons of the clergy, indeed, wherever they were, constituted a large part of the literature consumed by the American reading public at the middle of the eighteenth century. The people who read Chauncy and Mayhew were the educated elite. Those who read the writings of such religious leaders as Thomas Clap and Jonathan Edwards were the conservatives in religion, usually members of the middle class and often enough solid, respectable members of the assembly-party in politics. These were not the great political thinkers and leaders, but rather the rank-and-file Americans whose chief political interests centered on the protection of their rights as Englishmen in the business of self-taxation. Among the religious writers of this conservative school, Jonathan Edwards certainly stood head and shoulders above the rest. Edwards' style is usually stiff and formal, and difficult for the modern reader to enjoy. Yet it suited the conservative literary tastes of his readers; and when he was writing for himself, in a mood of relaxation, he was one of the greatest masters of English prose in the colonies. Consider, for example, the simple directness of the following passage on the beauty of God from his "Personal Narrative":

> Since I came to Northampton, I have often had sweet complacency in God, in views of his glorious perfections, and of the excellency of Jesus Christ. God has appeared to me a glorious and lovely Being, chiefly on account of his holiness. The holiness of God has always appeared to me the most lovely of all his attributes. The doctrines of God's absolute sovereignty, and free grace, in showing mercy to whom he would show mercy; and man's absolute dependence upon the operations of

---

[16] Quoted in Moses C. Tyler: *History of American Literature 1607–1676, 1676–1765* (2 vols. in one, New York, 1878), II, 195.

[17] Evert A. Duyckinck and George L. Duyckinck: *Cyclopedia of American Literature* (2 vols., New York, 1856), I, 95.

God's Holy Spirit, have very often appeared to me as sweet and glorious doctrines. These doctrines have been much my delight. God's sovereignty has ever appeared to me a great part of his glory. It has often been my delight to approach God, and adore him as a sovereign God, and ask sovereign mercy of him.[18]

On the other hand, the readers of the sermons of the revivalists, Whitefield, Tennet, or Davenport, were the poor and the uneducated. The great appeal of these revivalists was to the emotions and the sense of individual worth; and, by and large, their literary style was just about as flamboyant as their oratorical delivery. Literary taste tended to follow, if somewhat erratically, economic, social, political, and religious status and outlook.

For most Americans of a literary turn of mind the development of the new style was in large measure the result of deliberate effort. If it was copied from England, that was because the English prose of the homeland was, for the American writers, the best. Franklin's own style was deliberately copied; and he liked the new style so well that he went even farther and suggested that the entire Bible be revised to bring it into accord with the "modern" literary taste. Meanwhile, the Addisonian prose was finding its way into the southern colonies through the writings of those Virginians and Carolinians who had actually been in England as well as through English books. The most striking example of this was William Byrd, who had actually been educated in the England of King William and Queen Anne. He had written a number of polite and witty essays in London, and he continued his writings after he came back to Virginia to stay, although the best of what he wrote was not published until many years later. Here is a passage from his *History of the Dividing Line:*

> The Sabbath happen'd very opportunely to give some ease to our jaded People, who rested religiously from every work, but that of cooking the Kettle. We observed very few corn-fields in our Walks, and those very small, which seem'd the Stranger to us, because we could see no other Tokens of Husbandry or improvement. But, upon further Inquiry, we were given to understand People only made Corn for themselves and not for their Stocks, which know very well how to get their own Living. . . .
>
> Some, who pique themselves more upon Industry than their Neighbours, will, now and then, in compliment to their Cattle, cut down a Tree whose limbs are loaden with the Moss aforemention'd. The trouble wou'd be too great to Climb the Tree in order to gather this Provender, but the Shortest way (which in this Country is always counted the best) is to fell it, just like the Lazy Indians, who do the same by

18 Edwards: *Works* (Hickman ed.), I, lxxxviii–lxxxix.

such Trees as bear fruit, and so make one Harvest for all. By this bad Husbandry Milk is so Scarce, in the Winter Season, that were a Big-belly'd Woman to long for it, She would lose her Longing. And, in truth, I believe this is often the Case, and at the same time a very good reason why so many People in this Province are markt with a Custard Complexion. . . .[19]

The simplification of prose at the hands of American writers and the secularization of literary interest is also to be observed in the flood of travel literature produced in the middle decades of the eighteenth century. Most of this descriptive writing was produced by "foreigners," for the benefit of foreign audiences. Such, for example, were the descriptions by Andrew Burnaby, Peter Kalm, and Janet Schaw. A considerable body of travel literature was produced by Americans, however, for the benefit of Americans; and its extensive market was indicative of the stirring of a "national" consciousness that expressed itself in an interest in regions and provinces of America other than one's own. Both the secularization of interest and the popularity of travel literature are exemplified in the journal of Dr. Alexander Hamilton, of Annapolis, who wrote in his *Itinerarium* a popular description of his journey from Maryland to New Hampshire about mid-century; in that of Philip Fithian, who went to Virginia as tutor for the Carter children in the decade just prior to the American Revolution; and, especially, in such frontier travel-narratives as John Bartram's *Observations. . . in his travels from Pennsylvania to Lake Ontario*, published in 1751, and the *Journal of Christian Frederick Post in his Journey from Philadelphia to the Ohio*, published in 1759. There is a fairly sharp distinction between the polite travel-journals of the educated elite, however, and the descriptions of the frontier and Indian country written by humbler men; and while both sorts were widely read, the latter were probably closer to a true literary expression of the Americans than the former, and will be considered separately.

The American prose-writers were now covering the whole intellectual world. Without mentioning the numerous essays being written in other fields, account should be taken of the appearance of essays of a purely literary sort, such as are to be found scattered through all the colonial newspapers of the mid-century. Even fiction was making its appearance in the moral fables of the time; and the first novel by an American, *The Adventures of Alonso*, by Thomas Atwood Gibbes, of Warburton, Maryland, was published in 1775, precisely at the end of the colonial period. But this was the age of the essay; every man was an essayist, indeed, for every educated man was a prolific letter-writer,

[19] William Byrd: *The Writings of William Byrd of Westover in Virginia, Esqr.*, edited by John Spencer Bassett (New York, 1901), pp. 44–6.

and many letters were in effect essays : long and well composed, some-times erudite, almost always interesting, and possessed of a certain literary polish. Numberless examples might be cited ; here is one by that sprightly southern genius, Eliza Pinckney, written to the Honorable Charles Pinckney, her future husband :

SIR

The penance you have enjoyned is equal to an Egyptian task for I take it to be full as hard for me to repeat Dr. Parnel's Hermit to you having never read it more than twice, as it was to them to make bricks without straw ; but if you will be so good to lend me the book I'll promise to repeat it to you some time in Sept. next which is the soonest I can promise myself the pleasure of waiting on Mrs. P. [Charles Pinckney's mother]. We are much obliged to Mr. Dart for the mocking birds, my papa will be very much pleased with them ; to secure them from their mortal foe the catt I have put them in my own closet where they afford me a thousand useful reflections ; here the nigard that eats his morsel alone, and the mean suspicious wretch whose bolted door near [ne'er] moved in pity to the wandering poor, may learn a lesson of hospitality from the birds of the air. The little chirpers have drawn to the window an old bird that has a nest in a tree in the garden with 3 young ones in it. These 6 imploy her morning in providing for and feeding them. I was one day siting in the room viewing them perched, and as I suposed expecting their warbling Benefactress, when she came to the window, from whence I imagined the sight of me must soon fright her, (it was impossible for me to move,) but even that could not prevent her generous purpose to the little strangers, but she flew close by me and perching on the cage drop'd in what her bounty had before provided : This thing pleased me more than you can imagine . . . but in this case there was nothing extraordinary for it was very common to hang a cage of young mocking birds in the garden to be raised by the old one, if there was one near, but this I was a stranger to.

I see you smile while you have been reading this to Mrs. Pinckney, and she replys, the dear girl forgot she was not writing to little Polly when she indulged her descriptive vein, and that the subject of her birds is too triffling a one to engage your attention. Be it so, but 'tis your own fault, you will have me write, and as my ideas are triffling my subject must be conformable to them.[20]

This was the age, too, of the autobiography and the journal. Many of the intellectual leaders of the eighteenth century wrote journals or autobiographies. Franklin's famous *Autobiography* is only the best-known of dozens of similar literary products. One of the most charming of these, and probably, after Franklin's, the greatest from a literary

[20] Eliza Lucas : *Journal and Letters*, pp. 11–12. Eliza's abbreviations in this letter have been put in modern form.

point of view, is the *Journal* of John Woolman, "the Quaker saint." For Woolman, a deeply consecrated, sensitive man, was a master of the simple, humble, and quaint style of the Quakers, and put into a prose that is often moving the religious feelings and the experiences of a very considerable body of the Americans of his generation. For example :

> Some glances of Real beauty is perceivable in their faces, who dwell in true meekness. Some tincture of true Harmony in the sound of that voice to which Divine Love gives utterance, & Some appearance of right order in their temper and Conduct, whose passions are fully regulated, yet all these do not fully show forth that inward life to such who have not felt it ; but this white stone and new name is known rightly to such only who have it. . . .
> Remember, O my soul ! that the Prince of Peace is thy Lord : that he communicates his pure wisdom to his Family. That they, living in perfect Simplicity, may give no just cause of offence to any Creature, but may walk as he walked.[21]

Woolman's way of writing presents a sharp contrast to that, say, of Franklin. For whereas Franklin consciously fashioned his style in the newer, more direct and honest style of the best English prose-writers of his time, Woolman strove for simplicity and sincerity because it was his nature to be so himself. His style, therefore, is direct expression of himself, of his own inner life, his own personal experience, as well as of the mood of all sincere Quakers. The difference is slight, perhaps, but it is the difference between a borrowed style and one that is inherently native and sincere.

That is not to say, however, that Franklin's writing, which clothed an American experience in an English literary style, was not sincere. For Franklin, probably at once the most natural and the most typical of eighteenth-century Americans, wrote American prose at its best. He, more nearly, perhaps, than any other writer, represented the literary synthesis of English inheritance with the American experience that was most typically American. Nor was he unconscious of the growth of a new literature out of the new experience, or of the growing emotional impetus of an American patriotism in it. Among the many examples of his writing that might be given, the following is perhaps most expressive of his almost apologetic consciousness of a cultural divergence between the mother country and the colonies growing out of their diverging histories :

> Of all the enviable things England has, I envy it most its people. Why should that petty Island, which, compared to America, is but like a

21 John Woolman : *Journal and Essays* (Gummere ed.), pp. 157, 270.

stepping-stone in a brook, scarce enough of it above water to keep one's shoes dry; why, I say, should that little Island enjoy, in almost every neighborhood, more sensible, virtuous, and elegant minds, than we can collect in ranging a hundred leagues of our vast forests? But it is said the Arts delight to travel westward. . . . After the first cares for the necessities of life are over, we shall come to think of the embellishments. Already, some of our young geniuses begin to lisp attempts at painting, poetry, and music. We have a young painter now studying at Rome. Some specimens of our poetry I send you, which, if Dr. Hawkesworth's fine taste cannot approve, his good heart will at least excuse.[22]

That a taste for literary enjoyment was developing in the colonies by the middle of the eighteenth century is indicated by the fact that, aside from the popular consumption of newspapers, pamphlets, and almanacs, numerous efforts were made to launch literary magazines as business enterprises. That all of them published before the Revolution failed, without exception, seems to be sufficient evidence that American literary taste was not quite sufficiently developed or sufficiently widespread, for one reason or another, to support them. Yet the fact that there were so many of them is equally indicative of the existence of a genuine impulse of literary interest. The literary entrepreneurs were convinced, in their own minds, that there was a market for their product if they could only catch the market's eye. It was an intercolonial market, however; nearly all the magazines appealed to the interest of "all the British colonies," and this appeal is itself indicative of a belief, at least, that "all the British colonies" had developed a common literary interest and taste. The most important of these literary journals, by far, was the *American Magazine* of Philadephia, which was edited by William Smith, the distinguished provost of the College of Philadelphia. Of which, more later.

COLONIAL SELF-CONSCIOUSNESS: AMERICAN WRITERS OF HISTORY

One of the most interesting and significant literary developments in the colonies in the middle of the eighteenth century was the appearance of a series of histories of the colonies, one of which was a history of the British settlements in America as a whole. This burgeoning interest in the history of the colonies themselves was significant, for it illustrated and expressed several of the major tendencies then developing in the American mind. In the first place, this serious history-writing indicated the secular trend in literary thought. A century earlier these historians might well have been ministers of the gospel; and it is

[22] Franklin: *Works* (Sparks ed.), VII, 246.

probably safe to say that, even had they written history instead of sermons, their histories would have had a strongly religious flavor, as did, indeed, the seventeenth-century chronicles of William Bradford, Edward Johnson, and John Winthrop. Even Cotton Mather said of his task in the *Magnalia Christi Americana*, that "I write the Wonders of the Christian Religion, flying from the depravations of *Europe*, to the *American Strand*; and, assisted by the Holy Author of that Religion, I do with all conscience of Truth, required therein by Him, who is the Truth, itself, report the wonderful displays of His infinite Power, Wisdom, Goodness, and Faithfulness, wherewith His Divine Providence hath irradiated an Indian Wilderness." [23]

Needless to point out that Mather's mood, as well as his style, was still that of the "old Puritans." His whole point of view was religious : he was still convinced that God had had a clear and definite purpose in leading his forebears into the American wilderness. The striking fact is that even these writers who saw human history as the record of the unfolding of God's plan saw in themselves the objects of God's peculiar interest and their land as one enjoying a large measure of God's special favor and attention as the scene for the working out of God's special purposes in the world. These early writers were extremely self-conscious ; but their self-consciousness was of an extremely religious sort that fitted itself neatly into the rest of their thinking about what they understood to be the over-all plan of God. As the eighteenth century came on, the self-consciousness continued, but its overwhelmingly religious orientation was sloughed off, and American historical writing became more secular in tone, more humanistic in content, and more nationalistic, rather than religious, in mood.

Thus even the Reverend Thomas Prince, Cotton Mather's younger contemporary, although deeply religious, wrote in a vein that was essentially secular. Prince's *Chronological History of New England* and *Annals of New England*, indeed, were probably motivated more by patriotism than by religion, although in him the two faiths were as one. As he says in his preface, "Next to the sacred History, and that of the Reformation, I was from my early Youth instructed in the History of this country. . . . Yet still I long'd to see all these things disposed in the Order of Time wherein they happened, together with the Rise and Progress of the several Towns, Churches, Counties, Colonies, and Provinces throughout this Country." [24] Bradford, Dudley, and Johnson had written on various aspects of the experience of his people ; it was his desire to put all that into proper chronological

[23] Cotton Mather : *Magnalia Christi Americana*, p. 25.
[24] Thomas Prince : *A Chronological History of New England in the Form of Annals* (Boston, 1736), p. i.

order. But he did it with critical and methodical eye. As he himself stated his ideal, worthy of a later day :

> It is the *orderly Succession* of these Transactions and Events [the history of the Fathers of these Plantations], as they precisely fell out in Time, too much neglected by our Historians, that for some years past I have taken the greatest Pains to search and find, even vastly more than in composing, and which thro' a world of Difficulty and much Expence, I here present You : not in the specious Form of a *proper History*, which admits of artificial Ornaments and Description to raise the Imagination and Affections of the Reader ; but of a *closer* and naked Register, comprizing only *Facts* in a *Chronological Epitome*, to enlighten the Understanding : some what like the Form of *Usher's* Annals, which a competent Historian may easily fill up and beautifie.[25]

Prince wrote with a devotion to accuracy and truth that was hardly equaled again for a century ; in his devotion to truth, however, he reserved his own interpretation and feeling so rigorously that his style is generally dull, without being ugly. Now and again, however, his self-imposed restraint slips a little and there becomes visible a spark of that love of his land and its people that mark him as one of the earliest American nationalists. Prince fell in with the Great Awakening, which he considered a manifestation of the spirit of God, and his historical instincts led him to edit and publish for a couple of years, in 1743 and 1744, a weekly periodical devoted to recording the events in that great religious movement, which he called *The Christian History*. About a decade later he began a continuance of his *History of New England in the Form of Annals*.

Prince's work is significant less as fine literature than as a literary expression of a growing cultural self-consciousness among the Americans. He stood clearly in the line with Mather and Edward Johnson in his belief that the settlement of America was peculiarly and specifically sanctioned, if not directly inspired, by God ; and his history, like Mather's, implies, at least, that the people of New England were therefore in a very real sense God's chosen people. Jonathan Edwards wrote in much the same tradition ; but his *History of the Work of Redemption*, originally written as a series of sermons, took the whole of civilization as his field and saw in the appearance of New England only one grand chapter in the continuing unfolding of God's plan : "The work of redemption," he wrote, "is a work that God carries on from the fall of man to the end of the world." [26] Edwards thought of the history of the world up to his time as falling into three periods : the

[25] Ibid., pp. 3–4.
[26] Jonathan Edwards : *The History of the Work of Redemption* (Edinburgh, 1782), p. 9.

first, from the fall of man to the incarnation of Christ; the second, the period of Christ's career on the earth; the third, now in the mid-course, the period from Christ's death until the end of the world. Of all the colonial historians and pseudo-historians, Edwards was the one whose concept of human history was most universal in scope. Its great significance, however, lies in its character as an expression of the "divine plan" theory of history at the moment when most historians were becoming more secular in outlook and more humanistic or nationalistic in their interpretations.

Of a more scholarly sort than any history preceding it was Thomas Hutchinson's *History of the Colony and Province of Massachusetts Bay*, which was probably the best history, as history, written in the colonies before the Revolution. Wise, serious-minded Thomas Hutchinson, moved by the sense of the differentness of America and its novelty in the history of the world, expressed his reasons for undertaking his study thus, in the preface of the collection of documents published to accompany his *History*:

> The natural increase of people upon the British continent of North-America is so great as to make it highly probable that in a few generations more a mighty Empire will be formed there.
> The rise and progress of the several Colonies, of which this Empire will be constituted, will be subjects of entertainment for speculative and ingenious minds in distant ages.
> He who rescues from oblivion interesting historical facts is beneficial to posterity as well as to his contemporaries, and the prospect thereof to a benevolent mind causes the employment to be agreeable and pleasant which otherwise would be irksome and painful.[27]

Hutchinson was a deeply religious man; but the tone of his historiography was naturalistic, humanistic, secular, and rationalistic; most of all, it is imbued with a quiet sense of the future development and greatness of his people. He wrote in a clear and forceful prose, and his general historical mood was one that interpreted the course of history in terms of the individual characters who made it.

A similar, if more secular, provincial self-consciousness had begun early to stir the south; and Robert Beverley of Virginia ranks with Cotton Mather of New England as being among the first American historians to manifest it. Beverley, however, whose *History of Virginia* was published in London in 1705, was already a secular historian when Mather was writing the wonders of Christ in America; his history, though it is hardly more than the personal memoirs of Bever-

---

[27] Thomas Hutchinson, ed.: *A Collection of Original Papers Relative to the History of the Colony of Massachusetts Bay* (2 vols., Boston, 1769), I, preface, p. i.

ley himself, is clearly rooted in the experience of the Virginians and in the soil of Virginia.

A much more respectable job of history-writing was performed by William Stith, one-time president of William and Mary College. Stith's *History of the First Discovery and Settlement of Virginia* was based upon the original documents of the Virginia Company and was relatively accurate. But Stith had no sense of what to leave out, with the consequence that his book is too detailed for pleasure and never got beyond the story of the end of the company period in Virginia history.

Of all the historical or quasi-historical literature produced in America in the eighteenth century, the most delightful, probably, is that which came from the pen of William Byrd of Virginia, who died in 1744. For their gaiety, wit, sparkle, grace, and generally amusing qualities, these writings stand alone in American eighteenth-century literature. For Byrd was able to a degree unequaled by any other American of his time except Franklin to express in the graceful forms of the best English prose of the age of Addison and Steele a genuine and sincere American experience.

The most notable of Byrd's writing is his *History of the Dividing Line*, which he seems to have prepared for publication, but which was not actually published until 1841. This is a narrative of the running of the boundary line between Virginia and North Carolina in 1728; his *Progress to the Mines* and *A Journey to the Land of Eden* are journals of similar frontier experiences. These writings are rather journals than genuine histories, however, and Byrd should probably be regarded as a journal-writer and diarist rather than as a historian. Whatever they be called, however, these writings constitute some of the finest prose writing produced in colonial America.

Byrd prefaces his *History* with an account of the development of Virginia, from which "the other British Colonies on the Main have, one after the other, been carved." The first permanent settlement at Jamestown, he says, was made by "about an Hundred men, most of them Riprobates of good Familys," who "like true Englishmen . . . built a church that cost no more than Fifty Pounds, and a Tavern that cost Five hundred." [28] In his history Byrd relates the adventures of the commission of surveyors, with copious comments upon the condition of the frontier and the frontiersmen living there. Byrd was himself probably the wealthiest man in Virginia, and a complete Virginia aristocrat; his witty descriptions of the frontier are at once literature and historical documentation; and they also furnish unintended glimpses into the Virginian aristocratic mind:

[28] Byrd : *Writings* (Bassett ed.), pp. 6, 8.

Tis hardly credible how little the Bordering inhabitants were acquainted [with] this mighty Swamp [the Great Dismal Swamp], notwithstanding they had liv'd their whole lives within Smell of it. Yet, as
great Strangers as they were to it, they pretended to be very exact in
their Account of its Demensions, and were positive it could not be
above 7 or 8 Miles wide, but knew no more of the Matter than Star-
gazers know of the Distance of the Fixt Stars. At the Same time, they
were Simple enough to amuse our Men with Idle Stories of the Lyons,
Panthers, and Alligators, they were like to encounter in that dreadful
Place.[29]

Byrd's interest in history was hardly a philosophical one; he derived his great enjoyment in it, apparently, from satisfying his impulses
to literary creation and from describing the genuinely interesting and
amusing situations that he saw. His interest, therefore, was chiefly
literary in character.

This was not the case with other colonial historians, however. William Smith, Jr., for example, wrote a very respectable and readable *History of New York,* published in London in 1757; but he was
motivated, at least in part, by the desire to justify the New York Assembly in its struggle against the prerogative, and his book is unfortunately marred by his inability to resist the temptation to use his
book as a sounding-board for his antipathies toward his political
enemies. Yet Smith, too, is moved by the budding love of country
and provincial pride that are to be observed in nearly all the colonial historians, and the desire to inform the rest of the world about
America:

Whoever considers the number and extent of the British colonies,
on this continent; their climates, soil, ports, rivers, riches, and numberless advantages, must be convinced of their vast importance to Great
Britain; and be at a loss to account for the ignorance concerning them,
which prevails in those kingdoms, whence their inhabitants originally
sprang. . . . But the main body of the people [of England] conceive
of these plantations, under the idea of wild, boundless, inhospitable,
uncultivated desarts; and hence the punishment of a transportation
hither, in the judgment of most, is thought not much less severe, than
an infamous death. . . .
When I began to frame this digest, it was only intended for private
use; and the motives which now induce me to publish it, are the
gratification of the present thirst in Great Britain after American in-
telligences; contributing, as far as this province is concerned, to an
accurate history of the British empire in this quarter of the world; and
the prospect of doing some small service to my country, by laying be-

[29] Byrd: *History of the Dividing Line and Other Tracts,* I, 36–7.

fore the publick a summary account of its first rise and present state. . . .[30]

Smith's motives and intentions were good; it is a pity his execution wasn't better. Yet this work is a significant product, if only because it is a solid testimonial of the increasing self-consciousness of the Americans relative to themselves.

Still another history illustrating the American provincial development was *An Historical Review of the Constitution and Government of Pennsylvania*, probably written by Richard Jackson in London under Benjamin Franklin's direction and published there in 1759. This stout tome, written to justify the Pennsylvania Assembly in its struggle against the proprietary interest, is biased and one-sided, but it is essentially accurate and heavily documented. It was successful in that it was apparently quite widely read, in both England and America; but its greatest significance, whether as literature or as propaganda, probably resides in the fact that it was another expression of the growing self-consciousness of the Americans in their growth and their struggle to manage their own affairs. Thus was the literature of propaganda inseparably linked to the political struggle and the developing American political mind.

Thus the religious-minded, like Prince, were producing their histories, and the local historians were producing histories of their provinces. But the history that most significantly reflected the mind of mid-century America was probably that of Dr. William Douglass of Boston. This was by far the most remarkable of them all, for not only was it thoroughly secular in outlook and built upon a genuine effort to get the facts, even if they were sometimes badly used — but — and this was its most remarkable feature — it set out to be a history of all the colonies taken as a whole. It was never completed; but it was the first effort to present the American colonies as a unity; and though its completion was prevented by the death of its author, it must be considered as a literary expression of the same intercolonial mood that was beginning to see the necessity for a union of all the continental colonies for the purposes of defense and the promotion of "continental" or "national" interest. This book, entitled *A Summary, Historical and Political, of the British Settlements in North America*, appeared in small parts between 1747 and 1752, and was then published at Boston in two volumes in 1755.

Douglass, as historian, was impatient of dull chronicles and relations of fact. He was remarkably modern in his determination to

---

[30] William Smith : *History of New York* (Albany, 1814), preface, pp. ix, xiii, xiv.

take "every thing" as his province; but he was also willing to use a little "salt" now and then to make his history interesting. His objective and his method he described as follows :

> The author, after thirty years residence in these colonies, and correspondence with some inquisitive gentlemen of the several governments, does generously offer to the publick, the following collection . . . without any mercenary, sordid, scribbling view of profit, or ostentation of more knowledge in these things than some of his neighbours, but to contribute toward a solid certain foundation for the histories of these countries in time to come. . . .
>
> Descriptions and bare relations, although accurate and instructive, to many readers are insipid and tedious; therefore a little seasoning is sometimes used; where a *mica salis* occurs, may it not be disagreeable, it is not designed with any malicious invidious view. For the same reason a small digression, but not impertinent to the subject, is now and then made use of; as also some short illustrations.[31]

But Douglass was too impatient to achieve the methodical accuracy of either Prince or Hutchinson; on the other hand, the breadth of his concept of the colonies as a whole surpasses those of the provincial historians, and his imagination and his style are both of a kind to be more successful in holding the reader's interest. His plan was to divide his work into two parts, the first a general discussion of the colonies as a whole and their common problems, the second to be devoted to individual colonies. It was Part II which was left uncompleted.

The appearance of this book was a literary event of considerable importance to the young America. For it not only provided a notable contribution to American writing; it also took cognizance of a new idea and a new loyalty, the loyalty to "America," and by its publication it gave considerable impetus to the further development of that generalized concept. It is this, perhaps, more than anything else, that makes this Scotsman significant as a historian of his adopted land. But he is far from standing alone; it is no accident that his book and his mood find expression at the same moment when Benjamin Franklin, William Shirley, and others were preparing the effort actually to unite the colonies that saw the light at the Albany conference of 1754. This book, indeed, contained one of the first proposals of the period for some sort of centralized administration of the colonies for better defense and the promotion of "continental" or "American" interest. Douglass was verbose, combative, and patriotic, especially where the neighboring French were concerned.

Another historian, of a different sort, was Cadwallader Colden,

[31] Douglass : *Summary, Historical and Political,* I, 1.

who wrote and published an elaborate and readable *History of the Five Indian Nations of Canada*, or the Iroquois. Colden carefully collected a mass of material on the Indians that, though recent ethnological study has modified much of it, is still useful and interesting. It should perhaps be called anthropology rather than history, for it shows clearly the influence of the anthropological interests of the eighteenth-century scientific outlook, and it is especially valuable as a description of the Indians as they were in his own time. The parts dealing with the developments of his own lifetime, in which he himself participated, have a considerable historical value for an understanding of the relations of New York and the British generally with the Iroquois. As literature it hardly merits the name of belles-lettres, but Colden had a very adequate control of the language, and his book is written in a good, clear, direct, and unaffected prose style. For example:

> The Five Nations think themselves by Nature superior to the rest of mankind, and call themselves Ongue-honwe; that is, Men surpassing all others. This Opinion, which they take Care to cultivate into their Children, gives them that Courage, which has been so terrible to all the Nations of North America; and they have taken such Care to impress the same Opinion on all their Neighbours, that they, on all Occasions, yield the most submissive Obedience to them. I have been told by old Men in New England who remembered the Time when the Mohawks made War on their Indians, that as soon as a single Mohawk was discover'd in the Country, their Indians raised a Cry from Hill to Hill, A Mohawk! A Mohawk! upon which they all fled like sheep before Wolves, without attempting to make the least Resistance, whatever Odds were on their Side.[32]

All the histories thus far noted were written by and for the intellectual classes, especially that group of Americans who were feeling the new sense of American destiny — that is to say, the middle-class American liberals in politics, economics, and religion. Most of them showed the bias of their authors, while revealing the awakening interest in America and its problems; one of them, the *Historical Review of the Constitution and Government of Pennsylvania*, was deliberately composed as propaganda for the promotion of a cause. This was true, too, of the only deliberately written history of any part of the frontier experience, Herman Husbands's *A Fan for Fanning* (Boston, 1771), which, while a history of the Regulator movement,

[32] Calwallader Colden: *The History of the Five Indian Nations of Canada* (2 vols., New York, 1904), V, xvii–xviii.

is also a plea for a recognition of the justice of the Regulators' cause. As a plea to the people of the seaboard for a more equitable and democratic management of affairs in the western counties, it was the only bit of historical writing — indeed, one of the few literary products of any sort — to emanate from the frontier itself.

These colonial histories were the products of an emerging and widespread sense of the importance of the colonies in the world, an interest in themselves, and a faith that their importance in the future was to be greater still. This sense of American destiny, in one form or another, was expressed by nearly all the colonial historians; at the same time it was reflected in the historical articles in the newpapers, and practically all the literary magazines launched in Anglo-America during the colonial period are quite explicit as to two things : their interest is intercolonial, and they aim to serve as a medium of literary exchange for all the colonies ; and they all contain historical summaries of events that consciously cater at once to the historical interests of their audience and the future historians of their time. In general, it may be said that the history written in America in the age of Hume and Robertson and Gibbon in England is, everything considered, one of the best secular literary products of the eighteenth-century American mind. It is secular in tone and in subject matter ; more important still, it rests upon the American experience and springs from a self-consciousness about America, a love for the land, and a respect for the epic struggle that carved these provinces out of the wilderness. Very little American prose of the eighteenth century even approached the quality of belles-lettres, but there are passages in Prince, in Hutchinson, in Colden, and even in Smith that get about as close to that distinction as any other American writing of that time. Its distinction lies not in its style, however; it lies rather in the fact that it is the literary expression of a growing realization that this is America, a country and a people in its own right.

THE THEATER

The literature of the theater in colonial America was almost wholly a borrowed one. To all intents and purposes the theater was not allowed to exist in New England, although plays were sometimes given as literary exercises by students or by private individuals who succeeded in hoodwinking the authorities. In the more urbane south, however, an active theater did exist, if somewhat irregularly, in Charleston and Williamsburg from near the beginning of the eighteenth century. New York was enjoying plays by the third decade of the century, and Annapolis and Philadelphia managed to see a few once in a while after about 1750. In Philadelphia, however, sentiment against the theater was still strong.

By the middle of the eighteenth century, in any case, a theater of sorts had appeared in all the colonies from New York southward, despite the fact that in all the colonies except Maryland and Virginia theater plays were prohibited by law.

The plays given in the colonies included Shakespeare's *Merchant of Venice* and *King Richard IV,* Congreve's *Love for Love,* Dryden's *Spanish Friar,* Gay's *Beggar's Opera,* Lillo's *George Barnwell,* Otway's *The Orphan,* and, later, Goldsmith's *She Stoops to Conquer.* There were no plays written in America until Thomas Godfrey, Jr.'s *The Prince of Parthia,* written in 1759, although there were numerous student farces written at the colleges. But even Godfrey's play was largely foreign to America, in form, plot, and mood.

The actors were generally Englishmen, members of traveling companies, such as those of Lewis Hallam, father and son, and of David Douglass, all of whom made extensive tours of the theater-minded cities. As for the patrons, they were in general the wealthy patrons of the arts, although journeymen and shopkeepers did attend. It would of course be a mistake to assume too sharp a class distinction with regard to the theater; yet it flourished only in the centers of wealth and aristocracy, and its chief patrons were of that social class. It was almost exclusively a prerogative of the rich; and it was almost exclusively an element of cultural life imported from England.

AMERICAN WIT AND HUMOR

One of the most striking characteristics of the American mind has always been the American sense of humor. The emergence of a genuine American outlook, in fact, can be located chronologically and with striking coincidence at the time of the first expressions of the peculiarly American style of humor; these expressions began to appear about the middle of the first half of the eighteenth century.

The American instinct for the comical nature of things, as it began to find its voice, expressed itself in various forms. In New England it was somewhat heavy and full of effort; how could it have been otherwise, considering the weight of a century of Puritan seriousness that it had to overcome? As early as about 1720, when Jeremiah Dummer was colonial agent for Massachusetts in England, he gave a humorous turn to his defense of the New England charters. It is objected, says he, that the colonies will grow great and throw off dependence on England and declare themselves a free state. But this is unthinkable; "So that I may say without being ludicrous, that it would not be more absurd to place two of His Majesty's Beef-Eaters [Yeomen of the

Guard] to watch an infant in the Cradle that it don't rise and cut its Father's throat, than to guard these weak Infant Colonies to prevent their shaking off the *British* yoke." [33]

But it was the Reverend Mather Byles, poet and critic, and Joseph Green, poet, who became the most noted New England wits of this period. For with Byles, to begin with, humorous utterance was consciously studied and contrived; he was reported to have had a dozen joke-books in his library when he died. But his humor was effective. His humorous essay on prose style has already been described; his other efforts included parodies of his own hymns, and puns. Especially puns, for Byles was a famous punster. His nephew, Jeremy Belknap, quoted him as saying on the occasion of one of Belknap's visits to his "punning uncle": "you must excuse my not getting up to receive you, cousin; for I am not one of the *rising* generation." [34] At another time, entering a room where a group of men were in conversation about the smallpox, he was reported to have said: "Pox take em," an atrocious pun on the Latin words *pax tecum* (peace be with you); and during the Revolution, when he was under arrest as a Tory, he was said to have indicated his guard to a visitor with the remark: "he is my observ-a-tory."

Byles once went to Maine with Governor Belcher on the occasion of some dealings with the Indians. They went to sea and, finding themselves without a hymnal, the poet-parson composed a hymn, which ran thus:

> *Great God! Thy works our wonder raise,*
> *To thee our swelling notes belong;*
> *While skies and winds and rocks and sea*
> *Around shall echo to our song.*

> *Thy power produced this mighty frame,*
> *Aloud to thee the tempests roar;*
> *Or safer breezes tune Thy name*
> *Gently along the shelly shore.*

> *Round Thee the scaly nation roves,*
> *Thy opening hand their joys bestow;*
> *Through all the blushing coral groves,*
> *These silent gay retreats below. . . .*[35]

Byles's friend and rival poet Joseph Green, hearing of it, took it as an excuse for the following parody:

[33] Hart, ed.: *American History Told by Contemporaries*, II, 136.
[34] *Colls. Mass. Hist. Soc.*, 5th Ser., IV, 285.
[35] Ibid., 5th Ser., II, 70. Byles's "muse" was his cat.

THE 151ST PSALM

With vast amazement we survey
The wonders of the deep
Where mackrel swim, and porpoise play,
And crabs and lobsters creep. . . .

From raging winds and tempest free,
So smooth that, as you pass,
The shining surface seems to be
A piece of Bristol glass.

But when the winds Tempestuous rise,
And foaming billows swell,
The vessel mounts above the skies,
Then lower sinks than hell.

Our brains the tottering motion feel,
And quickly we become
Giddy as new-dropt calves, and reel
Like Indians drunk with rum.

What praises then are due that we
Thus far have safely got,
Amariscoggin *tribe to see,*
And tribe of Penobscot.[36]

Whereupon Byles, not to be outdone, wrote his own parody:

In Byles' hymn an oversight
Greene spy'd one evening o'er his junk;
Alas! why did not Byles indite
A song to sing when folks are drunk. . . .

What vast amazement we survey
The Can so broad, so deep,
Where Punch succeeds the strong Sangree,
To both delightful Flip.[37]

It seems hardly necessary to suggest that such an exchange could never have taken place between two of the Puritan leaders of the days of Cotton and Winthrop. The mere fact that such things could even be thought, to say nothing of their being printed, is evidence enough that even Puritan New England had gone a long, long way toward a humanization of its outlook on life, as well as literature.

Joseph Green, Byle's opponent in this exchange, was, if anything, a more genuine wit than Byles. A businessman, he was also one of the

---

[36] Ibid., 5th Ser., II, 73.   [37] Ibid., 5th Ser., II, 73.

lesser of the lesser American poets as well as a wit; and he took great delight in satirizing his contemporaries. Thus when Byle's cat, which was said to have sat in his lap as he worked, died, Green wrote a satirical lament, which ran in part as follows:

> *Oppress'd with grief, in heavy strains I mourn*
> *The partner of my studies from me torn.*
> *How shall I sing? What numbers shall I chuse?*
> *For in my fav'rite cat I've lost my muse.*[38]

Green's most important satire was his *Entertainment for a Winter's Evening*, in which he poked satirical fun at a Masonic celebration, including even the sermon and the subsequent retirement of the entire body of celebrants to a near-by tavern. Even when at his best, however, Green's wit, like that of Byles, seems a little forced and unable completely to divest itself of a sort of subconscious soberness.

But to William Byrd, already a very old man in 1740, humorous comments on everything and everybody were just about as irrepressible as life itself, and as natural as drawing breath. His sense of humor was obviously native to him; but it had been anything but stifled by his student days in the England of Mr. Pickwick, and he had already composed some humorous writings while there. In the last three decades of his life, which were spent in America, Byrd's humor cropped out in everything he wrote. In the *History of the Dividing Line*, for example, there is a humorous remark, or two or three, on nearly every page. Such as this, for example:

> While we continued here [at Coratuck Inlet], we were told that on the South Shore, not far from the Inlet, dwelt a Marooner, that Modestly call'd himself a Hermit, tho' he forfeited that Name by Suffering a wanton female to cohabit with Him.
>
> His Habitation was a Bower, cover'd with Bark after the Indian Fashion, which in that mild Situation protected him pretty well from the Weather. Like the Ravens, he neither plow'd nor sow'd but Subsisted chiefly upon Oysters, which his Handmaid made a Shift to gather from the Adjacent Rocks. Sometimes, too, for a change of Dyet, he sent her to drive up the Neighbour's Cows, to moisten their mouth with a little Milk. But as for raiment, he depended mostly upon his Length of Beard, and She upon her Length of Hair, part of which she brought decently forward, and the rest dangled behind quite down to her Rump, like one of Herodotus's East Indian Pigmies.[39]

Byrd's *Progress to the Mines* (1732) was sprinkled with remarks like these: "I had the Grief to find them both [his mills] stand as still

[38] Duyckinck: *Cyclopedia of American Literature*, I, 122.
[39] Byrd: *History of the Dividing Line and Other Tracts*, I, 26.

for the want of Water, as a dead Woman's Tongue, for want of Breath"[40] ; "At [nine] we met over a Pot of Coffee, which was not quite strong enough to give us the Palsy."[41] Or the following anecdote : "I got about seven a'clock to Colonel Harry Willis's, a little moisten'd with the Rain ; but a Glass of good Wine kept my Pores open, and prevented all Rheums and Defluxions for that time. I was oblg'd to rise Early here, that I might not starve my Landlord, whose constitution requires him to swallow a Beef-Steak before the Sun blesses the World with its genial Rays. However, he was so complaisant as to bear the gnawing of his Stomach, till 8 o'clock for my sake."[42]

Eliza Lucas was another letter-writer whose good humor was practically irrepressible. To her brother she wrote, in 1742 : "I began in haste and have observed no method or I should have told you before I came to Summer, that we have a most charming Spring in this Country especially for those who travel through the Country for the Scent of the growing Myrtle and yellow Jessamine with which the woods abound is delightful."[43] At another time, writing to her friend Miss Bartlett, Eliza related how she was inspired "with the spirit of rhyming and produced the 3 following lines while I was lacing my stays :"

> *Sing on thou mimick of the feathered kind*
> *And let the rational a lesson learn from thee*
> *to mimick (not defects) but harmony.*

To which she then added : "If you let any mortal besides yourself see this exquisite piece of poetry you shall never have a line more than this specimen and how great will be your loss you who have seen the above may judge."[44]

Humor, indeed, was even finding its way into serious literature of propaganda and controversy, to say nothing of the light forms of literature. Archibald Kennedy was particularly felicitous in the use of humorous anecdotes, and Daniel Dulany, in the midst of his weighty discussion of the propriety of taxing the colonies without their consent, could stop to write that the argument against the claims of the colonies "puts me in mind of the ingenuity of the female discutent, who used to silence debate, by crying out, *God bless the king, and what have you to say to that ?*"[45]

At the same time, too, the literary magazines that were launched in

[40] Ibid., II, 60.
[41] Ibid., II, 60.
[42] Ibid., II, 71.
[43] Eliza Lucas : *Journal and Letters*, p. 18.
[44] Ibid., p. 11.
[45] Dulany : *Considerations on the Propriety of Imposing Taxes in the American Colonies*, p. 42 fn.

the middle decades of the century recognized the place of humor in the American scheme of things. The *American Magazine*, published in Boston from 1743 to 1745, was conscious of the therapeutic value of a little levity now and then, and even published an essay on the subject, which, however, turned out to be hardly more than a moral essay on the desirability of hiding our vices and cultivating a pleasant demeanor. But it did a little better in its poetry, and occasionally broke the glaze of life's seriousness by verses that, if not light in themselves, were at least light in their intentions. Here's part of one of these:

A RIDDLE FOR THE LADIES

To you fair maidens, I address;
Sent to adorn your Life:
And she who first my name can guess,
Shall first be made a wife. . . .[46]

To which, in the October number there appeared "An Answer to the Riddle for the Ladies."

The later *American Magazine* of Philadelphia, sponsored by William Smith, did a great deal better. It might almost be said that the twelve years that elapsed between the last issue of the Boston *American Magazine* and the first number of Smith's publication were a period in which the American sense of humor enjoyed a great and rapid growth; perhaps, again, the difference was due to the fact that the people of Philadelphia — the Quakers excepted — found natural laughter as much easier than the residents of Boston as the gay cavaliers of the south found it easier than the more somber ones of Philadelphia. Be that as it may, Smith's *American Magazine* contained a continuous series of humorous essays perpetrated by one "Timothy Timbertoe," whose early efforts were directed to that eternally sure-fire laugh-getter, feminine attire. For it appeared to Mr. Timbertoe that women were wearing less and less. They had left off wearing caps in the evening, and — to save money, of course — they were now wearing as little as possible on their bosoms:

And tho' some people are malicious enough to insinuate, that this is done to *cool their own* and *inflame* the breasts of *others*, yet I am far from entertaining any such injurious opinion of my fair country-women. . . .

As this seems a fair challenge to the *other* sex, I expect every day to see the *Gentlemen* begin to *strip;* and doubt not but the spirit of emulation will at least bring us to the primitive happy state of *innocence*, and a *Fig-leaf. . . .*[47]

[46] *American Magazine*, I (September 1743), p. 34.
[47] *American Magazine and Monthly Chronicle*, I, No. 2 (November 1757), pp. 125–6.

The almanacs, too, were full of the homely, broad, and utilitarian humor of the common people. Nathaniel Ames's *Astronomical Diary*, for example, was studded with witty sayings such as the following :

> *Now freezing cold*
> *Which makes old Maids to fret and scold.*[48]
>
> *Politicians, Projectors, Directors*
> *Dictators and Detractors,*
> *How many there be ?*
> *But how fruitless are most,*
> *You may easily see.*[49]
>
> *An honest Friend is good Company,*
> *but a good Conscience is the best Guest.*[50]
> *More die by Gluttony, than perish by the Sword.*[51]

But if Ames was the better poet, Franklin was the better humorist. Franklin, indeed, was undoubtedly the most widely read and best-liked humorist in the colonies ; and his mirthful *Poor Richard* made its first appearance in 1733, at the very instant, as it were, when the new-born American humor was just opening its eyes upon the American scene. Very often Franklin's humor had a utilitarian twist, and took the form of wise sayings, such as the following :

> *Different Sects like different clocks,*
> *may be all near the matter, tho*
> *they don't quite agree.*[52]
> *All would live long, but none would be old.*[53]
> *Mankind are very odd Creatures : One*
> *Half censure what they practice, the*
> *other half practice what they censure ;*
> *The rest always say and do as they ought.*[54]
> *It is ill Jesting with the Joiner's tools,*
> *worse with the Doctor's.*[55]
> *Hold your Council before Dinner ; the*
> *full Belly hates Thinking as well as*
> *Acting.*[56]
> *Never spare the parson's wine, nor the baker's*
> *pudding.*[57]
> *The Way to see by Faith is to shut the Eye of*
> *Reason.*[58]

[48] *Astronomical Diary*, 1750.
[49] Ibid., 1753.
[50] Ibid., 1753.
[51] Ibid., 1754.
[52] *Poor Richard Improved*, 1749.
[53] Ibid.
[54] *Poor Richard Improved*, 1752.
[55] Ibid.
[56] Ibid.
[57] Ibid.
[58] Ibid.

On the occasion of *Poor Richard's* twentieth anniversary, Franklin poked fun at his readers in the following preface :

> I am particularly pleas'd to understand that my *Predictions of the weather* give such general Satisfaction ; and indeed, such Care is taken in the Calculations, on which those Predictions are founded, that I could almost venture to say, there's not a single One of them, promising *Snow, Rain, Hail, Heat, Frost, Fogs, Wind,* or *Thunder,* but what comes to pass *punctually* and *precisely* on the very Day, in some place or other on this little *diminutive* Globe of ours . . . I say on this Globe ; for tho' in other Matters I confine the Usefulness of my *Ephemeris* to the *Northern Colonies,* yet in that important Matter of the Weather, which is of such *general Concern,* I would have it more extensively useful, and therefore take in both Hemispheres, and all Latitudes from *Hudson* Bay to Cape Horn.[59]

Franklin's humor was often pretty broad, more or less deliberately, to suit his audience. An instance is the story he inserted in his *Pennsylvania Gazette* about the man down in Bucks County who had had the pewter buttons melted off his trousers by lightning, to which he added the editorial comment that "Tis well nothing else thereabouts was made of pewter."

Franklin often indulged his sense of humor in verses ; for example, this one, from *Poor Richard* :

EPITAPH ON ANOTHER CLERGYMAN

> *Here lies, who need not here be nam'd,*
> *For Theologic Knowledge fam'd ;*
> *Who all the Bible had by rote,*
> *With all the Comments Calvin wrote ;*
> *Parsons and Jesuits could confute,*
> *Talk Infidels and Quakers mute,*
> *To every Heretick a Foe ;*
> *Was he an honest Man? . . . So so.*[60]

Or letters to the editor such as this :

> I am about courting a girl I have had but little acquaintance with. How shall I come to a knowledge of her faults, and whether she has the virtues I imagine she has ?
>
> Answer. Commend her among her female acquaintances.[61]

Franklin's humor probably reached its highest quality in his fables, moral essays, and dialogues. His famous "Dialogue with the Gout" is well known ; others were "An Arabian Tale," "A Petition to the Left

---

[59] *Poor Richard Improved,* 1753.
[60] *Poor Richard Improved,* 1755.
[61] Franklin : *Works* (Sparks ed.), II, 550.

Hand," "The Handsome and the deformed Leg," and so on. Similarly, Franklin was a master of that typical American phenomenon, the "tall tale," and he delighted to mystify his English friends and heap a disguised satire upon his critics with little yarns like the following:

> Dear Sir, do not let us suffer ourselves to be assured with such groundless objections [to American manufactures]. The very tails of the American sheep are so laden with wool, that each has a little cart or wagon on four wheels, to support and keep it from trailing on the ground. Would they caulk their ships, would they even litter their horses with wool, if it were not both plenty and cheap? . . .
>
> And yet all this is as certainly true, as the account said to be from Quebec, in all the papers of last week, that the inhabitants of Canada are making preparations for a cod and whale fishery this "summer in the upper Lakes." Ignorant people may object, that the upper Lakes are fresh, and that cod and whales are salt water fish; but let them know, Sir, that cod, like other fish when attacked by their enemies, fly into any water where they can be safest; that whales, when they have a mind to eat cod, pursue them wherever they fly; and that the grand leap of the whale in the chase up the Falls of Niagara is esteemed, by all who have seen it, as one of the finest spectacles in nature.[62]

These American "tall tales" were a far cry from both the labored humorous essays of Byles and Green in New England and the graceful, aristocratic witticisms of Byrd in Virginia. If the New England wits were frustrated by the shadow of Puitanism and the southern wits like Byrd and Eliza Lucas were out of touch with the commoners, Franklin and Ames were the very voice of the farmer and the frontiersman and the tradesman. It seems fairly safe to say, again in very general terms, that literary humor tended to follow the lines of differentiation laid down in the other forms of literature, or, for that matter, in all the other facets of thought.

The Literature of the Common Man

The newspapers

It was almost inevitable that with the secularization of life and thought and literature there should appear a secular organ to publish to the world the more evanescent creations of the colonial literary mind. This organ did appear, in due season (shortly after 1700), in the form of the American newspaper. The idea was borrowed from England, and the form of the newspaper was, in general, the English form.

---

[62] Ibid., VII, 289, 290.

At first, and for a long time thereafter, the news-matter of colonial newspapers was drawn chiefly from abroad; and foreign news was supplemented by stuffy legal and governmental matters emanating from the provincial state-house. Benjamin Franklin changed all that, or tried to, when as a boy working for his brother James he began to liven up the *New England Courant* by his anonymous "Essays of Silence Dogood." To be sure, Silence Dogood borrowed her ideas, language, and style from the *Spectator*. But the situations and the personalities discussed are those of Boston, in Massachusetts; nothing could be more convincing of the vitality and the literary validity of these little essays than the storm of bitter protest that they aroused, such a storm as finally to force the *Courant* forever to stop its press.

By the middle of the eighteenth century nearly every colony had at least one newspaper, and they all had them by the Revolution. Every important city had its newspaper, or its newspapers, and it seems reasonable to suppose that most of the literate persons in the city read the papers, at least occasionally. But the circulation of a paper was not limited to the city; the improvement of the postal service, especially after Franklin took charge of it in 1753, made it possible to send the newspapers by mail from one end of the colonies to the other. It would be difficult to estimate the proportion of the total population of the colonies that read the newspapers, but in all probability it was still relatively small; it also seems probable that, among the classes of the people, it was the fairly well-to-do and the fairly well-educated who did most of the reading. Yet the newspaper almost certainly reached a wider audience than any other form of printed matter except the almanac, and it therefore must be regarded as catering to a much broader literary taste than the writings of the poets and the essayists, or even the sermon-writers.

The contents of the newpapers were probably indicative of the literary tastes of the readers. Much of the space was filled up with news from abroad, received directly or copied from other colonial papers. In addition to news-letters, there were also essays by distinguished Europeans, such, for example, as David Hume's essay on "The Liberty of the Press," printed in the *South Carolina Gazette and Country Journal* of December 31, 1765. But American essayists contributed also, and the papers of the colonies in the 1750's contained a surprisingly large number of essays on politics, religion, and science. As this was a moment of awakening patriotism, both "British" and "American," a considerable number of these were patriotic in tone.

Finally, the newpapers were receptacles for native poetry. Nearly all of them were studded with poems published at the request of the authors. Most of that poetry was trash and was significant only be-

cause it marked a conscious effort to produce examples of art-litera-
ture and because practically any ambitious poet could see himself
in print just for the asking. Some of it, however, shows sparks of fire,
although in none do the sparks burn very brightly.

Some of this verse is written in sheer fun; some, too, combines fun
with utilitarian ends, as in the following poetic advertisement for a
runaway servant:

> *A Thomas Clemson ran away*
> *One evening on a Saturday*
> *That sixth and twentieth day of July*
> *Of that I am informed truly.*
> *A man, one Joseph Willard called*
> *His hair is brown, he is not bald.*
> *His hat it is of ancient date*
> *Which keeps the weather from his pate.*[63]

It was one of the significant marks of the developing American
mind that the press in America was relatively free. The famous Zenger
trial had been a great milestone on the road to freedom of the press,
but a good many other milestones had to be passed before the colonial
papers could consider themselves safely beyond the crevasses and
obstacles of colonial politics and prejudice. Yet the sentiment for freedom of the press was growing, and had been accepted in principle
everywhere. And Poor Richard probably represented the feelings of
many, if not most, Americans when he moralized in verse that

> *While free from Force the Press remains,*
> *Virtue and Freedom chear our Plains,*
> *And Learning Largesses bestows,*
> *And keep unlicens'd open House. . . .*
>
> *This Muse of Arts, and Freedom's Fence,*
> *To chain, is Treason against Sense:*
> *And Liberty, thy thousand Tongues*
> *None silence who design no Wrongs;*
> *For those who use the Gag's Restraint,*
> *First Rob, before they stop Complaint.*[64]

Thus the advent and the growth of newpapers in the eighteenth
century was no mere literary event. It gave the common people both
a constant supply of reading-matter and a sounding-board for their
own literary expression. But it also accelerated the process of secularization going on in the American mind and furnished another area,
along with those of science and education, for the battles — and the
victories — of intellectual freedom.

[63] *Pennsylvania Gazette*, October 15–22, 1745.
[64] *Poor Richard Improved*, 1757.

The almanac

The most widely read single literary product in the colonies was unquestionably the almanac. This intellectual phenomenon was not peculiar to America, nor did it originate here; yet it became a peculiarly American product, peculiarly suited to the intellectual needs of the Americans.

The literature of the common man: the literary content of the almanac. (a) Poor Richard's Almanack, 1749; *(b)* Ames' Astronomical Diary, 1748.

The almanacs were not only, or even primarily, literary in nature. The first almanacs were published in 1639 at Harvard, as a sort of calendar and potpourri of scientific and pseudo-scientific information. But by 1750 dozens of them were being published in the colonies, and they contained reading-matter of sorts for every day in the year. The most famous of these almanacs were those of Nathaniel Ames, of Boston, called *An Astronomical Diary*, and of Benjamin Franklin, in Philadelphia, called *Poor Richard*, later *Poor Richard Improved*.

The formats of the almanacs, from year to year, were not always alike; but generally each year's edition would open with an introduction or preface of some amusing sort, and this introduction would be followed by the twelve pages devoted to the twelve months in the year. On each of these pages was a calendar of the month, introduced generally by some appropriate poem; and the extra spaces would be filled by useful or witty sayings or by notes of a scientific or pseudo-scientific nature — anything from estimates of the circumference of the earth to the best use of manure and how to dose one's horse or oneself in case of illness. The final page or pages (to make the usual total of sixteen) would be occupied by serious essays or humorous poems. The calendars contained not only the days of the month, but also signs indicating the astrological combinations, the fluctuations of the tides, the phases of the moon, and predictions as to the weather for the entire year.

A good many examples of the literary content of the almanacs have already been given, either as examples of American humor or as articles of scientific interest. Perhaps it may suffice here merely to give one example of the almanac's prose style, Franklin's preface to *Poor Richard Improved* for 1756, in which he explains in his own words his ideal:

> I suppose my Almanack may be worth the Money thou hast paid for it, hadst thou no other Advantage from it, than to find the Day of the Month, the remarkable Days, the Changes of the Moon, the Sun and Moon's rising and Setting, and to foreknow the Tides and the Weather; these, with other Astronomical Curiosities, I have yearly and constantly prepared for thy Use and Entertainment, during now two Revolutions of the Planet Jupiter. But I hope this is not all the Advantage thou hast reaped; for with a View to the Improvement of thy Mind and thy Estate, I have constantly interspers'd in every little Vacancy, Moral Hints, Wise Sayings, and Maxims of Thrift, tending to impress the Benefits arising from Honesty, Sobriety, Industry and Frugality; which if thou hast duly observed, it is highly probable thou art wiser and richer many fold more than the Pence my Labours have cost thee. Howbeit, I shall not therefore raise my Price because Thou art better able to pay; but being thankful for past Favours, shall endeavour to make my little Book more worthy thy Regard, by adding to those Recipes which were intended for the Cure of the Mind, some valuable Ones regarding the Health of the Body. They are recommended by the Skilful, and by successful Practice. I wish a Blessing may attend the Use of them, and to thee all Happiness.[65]

As for poetry, the poems of Nathaniel Ames in the *Astronomical Diary*, as has been said, were probably better, on the average, than those of Franklin in *Poor Richard*. Here's one of Ames's creations:

[65] Ibid., 1756.

JULY

'Tis now the Shepherds shun the noon Day Heat,
And lowing Herds to murmuring Brooks retreat;
And sultry Syrius *burns the thirsty Plains,*
And Choler *in each Constitution reigns.*[66]

It would be difficult to estimate with any real exactness the literary importance of the almanacs. Certainly the literary quality of their contents was low, judged by any standard even remotely related to that of belles-lettres. But they were printed and sold by the thousand, and they brought their literary content, such as it was, to thousands of people who would probably never have read anything else. Since their tone and style were decisively secular, they played an important role, like that of the newspapers, of at once spreading and catering to the increasingly secular mood of the Americans. The literary taste to which they catered was apparently that of the common people, particularly the farmers; and while they did not distribute a very high quality of literature, it is probably safe to say that they had a considerable effect in the cultivation of some sort of a literary interest and culture in their readers. Their importance, therefore, may probably be said to have lain chiefly in their role as popular disseminators of literature, the secularization of literary outlook, and the fostering of literary interests among the people.

THE LITERATURE OF THE FRONTIER

The frontier as a producer of literature of its own was practically inarticulate; the only frontier conflict to stir men's souls enough to produce poetry of any sort was apparently that which caused the Regulater riots in North Carolina. That movement did produce some partisan songs, written by Rednap Howell, a schoolteacher from New Jersey. As poetry these songs do not rank very high; but they do show the mentality of the Regulators and how poetry is often the literary expression of the emotions generated by human conflict. Most of these songs are humorous and satirical and seem calculated to promote the morale of singer and hearer. Here is one satirizing Edmund Fanning, one of the agents of the westerners' misery:

When Fanning first to Orange came
He looked both pale and wan,
An old patched coat upon his back,
An old mare he rode on.

[66] Ames's *Astronomical Diary*, 1747.

Both man and mare were worth five pounds,
As I've been often told,
But by his civil robberies
He's laced his coat with gold.[67]

The democratic forces at work in American society were as yet almost entirely without a literary voice. The clearest expression of democratic stirring on the frontier, about mid-century, was probably in the religious manifestations connected with the Great Awakening; the nearest approximation of a literature of this movement is therefore made up of the hymns that were sung in the frontier and "New Light" churches, many of which were actually inherited from their Calvinist predecessors. The Great Awakening was a period of much hymn-singing, and a good many hymns were actually written, if only to be set to old tunes, in the course of that revival. Some of the new religious verses were set to old folk-tunes that were originally secular, for the sake of giving them greater liveliness. Thus the subjective individualism of the Great Awakening found its way into literary expression in the hymn "Poor Wayfaring Stranger":

I'm just a poor wayfaring stranger
A-traveling through this world of woe,
But there's no sickness, toil, nor danger
In that bright world to which I go.
I'm going there to meet my father,
I'm going there no more to roam,
I'm just a-going over Jordan,
I'm just a-going over home.[68]

More interesting to the ordinary readers of the colonies than the political propaganda of the western reformers or the hymns of the redeemed were the descriptions of the land beyond the frontier by the travelers who had been there. For the mid-century was a period of active social expansion westward, and there were few men in the colonies who had no interest, either financial or personal, in the great western *el dorado*; it was also a moment of tension between the rival empires of France and England. Most loyal Americans, prompted by their distrust of what they sincerely believed to be "gallic perfidy" and their active belief and fear that the French had intentions of seizing the western lands and even, it might be, swooping down upon the older colonies themselves, felt a vital, burning concern in everything that

[67] Quoted in John S. Bassett: "The Regulators of North Carolina (1765–1771)," *Annual Report of the American Historical Association, 1894*, p. 157 fn.

[68] Quoted in John A. Lomax and Alan Lomax: *Our Singing Country* (New York, 1941), p. 37.

touched either the western settlers, the Indians, or the French. The interest in the lands along the frontier and beyond was white-hot, in both America and England, and readers seized upon any first-hand description of the back-country, especially if it was written in an attractive and interesting literary style.

Such a book was John Bartram's *Observations . . . made by Mr. John Bartram in his Travels . . . to . . . Lake Ontario.* Not that John Bartram's style was ever of a very high literary quality; it is clear, direct, and honest, and nothing more. The characteristic of the book that gave it its genuine and widespread appeal to the public was its personal first-hand description of the country through which he journeyed with Conrad Weiser, the Indian agent, to Oswego, and, most of all, his intimate description of the life and customs of the Indians, those uncivilized, savage middlemen of the American forests upon whom the ultimate destiny of the entire continent might depend. Bartram's narrative was certainly interesting reading. For example, consider this relation of his stop at Shomokin, a traders' town :

> I quartered in a trader's cabbin, and about midnight the *Indians* came and called up him and his squaw, who lay in a separate part where the goods were deposited, whether together or no I did not ask. She sold the *Indians* rum, with which being quickly intoxicated, men and women began first to sing and then dance round the fire ; then the women would run out to other cabins and soon return, leaving the men singing and dancing the war dance, which continued all the next day. An *Englishman* when very drunk will fall fast asleep for the most part, but an *Indian,* when merry, falls to dancing, running, and shouting, which violent action probably may disperse the fumes of the liquor, that had he sat still or remained quiet, might have made him drowsy, and which is even carries [*sic*] off by continued agitation. . . .
>
> As soon as we alighted they shewed us where to lay our baggage, and then brought us a bowl of boiled squashes cold ; this I then thought poor entertainment, but before I came back I had learnt not to despise good *Indian* food. This hospitality is agreeable to the honest simplicity of antient times, and is so punctually adhered to, that not only what is already dressed is immediately set before a traveller, but the most pressing business is postponed to prepare the best they can get for him, keeping it as a maxim that he must always be hungry, of this we found the good effects in the flesh and bread they got ready for us.[69]

Another of these descriptive narratives of the west was the journal of Christian Frederick Post, another negotiator with the Indians, whose work was very effective in preserving peace with the Indians of the

---

[69] John Bartram : *Observations . . . Made by Mr. John Bartram in His Travels from Pennsylvania to . . . Lake Ontario . . .* (London, 1751), pp. 15–16.

Ohio Valley after 1758. Of a somewhat higher literary quality than Bartram's *Observations*, it also had great interest for its readers in its descriptions of the Indians. For example :

> There is not a prouder, or more high-minded People in themselves than the Indians. They think themselves the wisest and prudentest Men in the World, and look upon all the Rest of Mankind as Fools if they do not consent to their Way of thinking. They think themselves to be the strongest People in the World ; and that they can over-power both the *French* and English when they please. The white People are in their Eyes nothing at all. They say that through their conjuring Craft they can do what they please, and nothing can withstand them. . . .
>
> The *Indians* are a People full of Jealousy, and will not easily trust any Body, and they are very easily affronted and brought into Jealousy ; then afterwards they will have nothing at all to do with those they suspect; and it is not brought so easy out of their Minds; they keep it to their Graves, and leave the Seed of it in their Children and Grand-Children's Minds. . . .[70]

These relations of travel and experiences among the savages were not high literature, but they were extremely interesting, and they had a gripping quality for the colonial readers that sprang from the realization that these were conditions just outside their own front doors, as it were, which might at any moment have some violent or dramatic effect upon their own fortunes. These narratives represented, in other words, over and beyond the mere enjoyment of interesting adventure, a vital and profound experience that was fearfully close to them and big with possible consequences for them. This was literature in the most penetrating sense, for it was the sincere record of one of the most profound experiences of a whole people.

But the most poignant and gripping form of the frontier literature was that which was made up of the accounts of the captivities of white people by the Indians. For all along the frontier the whites were constantly falling into the hands of the savages ; some of them perished ; some returned to tell the tale. Children, when captured, were often adopted into the Indian tribes to be raised as Indians ; and, once having made the transition, they refused to return to the people and the civilization of their parents. This almost eternal conflict, the constant, unstable, and frightening contact of two widely different races and cultures involved in the slow, ineluctable process of driving the Indians farther and farther back into the continental wilderness, was one of the most profound themes in the American story ; and it lay

[70] "The Journal of Christian Frederick Post," in Charles Thomson : *Enquiry into the Causes of the Alienation of the Delaware and Shawnee Indians . . .* (London, 1759), p. 169.

close to the heart of the colonial experience in the founding of a new culture. Naturally enough, it was this living experience that had the widest and most profound hold upon the minds of the Americans. It was no accident that narratives of Indian captivities, from Mrs. Rowlandson's onward, ran through edition after edition; it would probably be no exaggeration to guess that, next to the almanacs, more books of this type were read, and by more people, than any other printed or circulated in the colonies. They were written by amateurs, just as the "primitive" American paintings were painted by amateurs. But they were written in a straightforward, clear, and sincere style that every layman could understand; more important still, they recorded an experience that almost every American could feel — and that nobody else in the world could, at least in the same way.

This experience of the American settlers was repeated over and over again. Such was the narrative of the captivity of Mrs. Elizabeth Hanson, in 1724, published under the title *God's Mercy Surmounting Man's Cruelty*. Another was the narrative of Peter Williamson, of Pennsylvania, captured in 1754 :

> The place pleasing me well, I settled on it. My money I expended in buying stock, household furniture, and implements for out-of-door work ; and being happy in a good wife, my felicity was complete : but in 1754 the Indians, who had for a long time before ravaged and destroyed other parts of America unmolested, began now to be very troublesome on the frontiers of our province, where they generally appeared in small skulking parties, committing great devastations.
>
> Terrible and shocking to human nature were the barbarities daily committed by these savages! Scarce did a day pass but some unhappy family or other fell victims to savage cruelty. Terrible indeed, it proved to me, as well as to many others. I, that was now happy in an easy state of life, blessed with an affectionate and tender wife, became on a sudden one of the most unhappy of mankind : scarce can I sustain the shock which forever recurs on recollecting the fatal second of October, 1754. My wife that day went from home, to visit some of her relations : as I staid up later than usual, expecting her return, none being in the house besides myself, how great was my surprise and terror, when at about eleven o'clock at night, I heard the dismal warwhoop of the savages, and found that my house was beset by them. I flew to my chamber window, and perceived them to be twelve in number. Having my gun loaded, I threatened them with death if they did not retire. But how vain and fruitless are the efforts of one man against the united force of so many blood-thirsty monsters! One of them that could speak English threatened me in return, "that if I did not come out they would burn me alive," adding, however, "that if I would come out and surrender myself prisoner they would not kill

me." In such deplorable circumstances, I chose to rely on their promises, rather than meet death by rejecting them ; and accordingly went out of the house, with my gun in my hand, not knowing that I had it. Immediately on my approach they rushed on me like tigers, and instantly disarmed me. Having me thus in their power, they bound me to a tree, went into the house, plundered it of everything they could carry off, and then set fire to it, and consumed what was left before my eyes. Not satisfied with this, they set fire to my barn and stable, and outhouses, wherein were about two hundred bushels of wheat, six cows, four horses, and five sheep, all which were consumed to ashes.

Having thus finished the execrable business about which they came, one of the monsters came to me with a tomahawk and threatened me with the worst of deaths if I would not go with them. This I agreed to, and then they untied me, and gave me a load to carry, under which I travelled all that night, full of the most terrible apprehensions, lest my unhappy wife should likewise have fallen into their cruel power. At daybreak my infernal masters ordered me to lay down my load, when, tying my hands again round a tree, they forced the blood out at my fingers' ends. And then kindling a fire near the tree to which I was bound, the most dreadful agonies seized me, concluding I was going to be made a sacrifice to their barbarity. The fire being made, they for some time danced around me after their manner, whooping, hollowing and shrieking in a frightful manner. Being satisfied with this sort of mirth, they proceeded in another manner : taking the burning coals, and sticks flaming with fire at the ends, holding them to my face, head, hands, and feet, and at the same time threatening to burn me entirely if I cried out. Thus tortured as I was, almost to death, I suffered their brutalities, without being allowed to vent my anguish otherwise than by shedding silent tears ; and these being observed, they took fresh coals and applied them near my eyes, telling me my face was wet, and that they would dry it for me, which indeed they cruelly did. How I underwent these tortures has been a matter of wonder to me, but God enabled me to wait with more than common patience for the deliverance I daily prayed for. . . .

Here I began to meditate an escape, and though I knew the country round extremely well, yet I was very cautious of giving the least suspicion of any such intention. However, the third day after the grand body left, my companions thought proper to traverse the mountains in search of game for their subsistence, leaving me bound in such a manner that I could not escape. At night, when they returned, having unbound me, we all sat down together to supper on what they had killed, and soon after (being greatly fatigued with their day's excursion) they composed themselves to rest, as usual. I now tried various ways to try whether it was a scheme to prove my intentions or not ; but after making a noise and walking about, sometimes touching them with my feet, I found there was no fallacy. Then, I resolved, if possible, to get one of their guns, and, if discovered, to die in my defence, rather than be taken. For the purpose I made various efforts to get one from under their heads, (where they always secured them,) but in vain. Disappointed in this, I began to despair of carrying my design into execution; yet, after a little recollection, and trusting myself to the divine protection, I set forwards, naked and defenceless as I was. Such was my terror, however, that in going from them I halted, and paused every four or five yards, looking fearfully towards the spot where I had left them, lest they should awake and miss me; but when I was two hundred yards from them, I mended my pace, and made as much haste as I possibly could to the foot of the mountains; when, on a sudden I was struck with the greatest terror at hearing the wood cry, as it is called which the savages I had left were making upon missing their charge. The more my terror increased, the faster I pushed on, and scarce knowing where I trod, drove myself through the woods with the utmost precipitation, sometimes falling and bruising myself, cutting my feet and legs against the stones in a miserable manner. But faint and maimed as I was, I continued my flight till daybreak, when, without having anything to sustain nature but a little corn left, I crept into a hollow tree, where I lay very snug, and returned my prayers and thanks to the divine Being that had thus far favored my escape. But my repose was in a few hours destroyed at hearing the voices of the savages near the place where I was hid, threatening and talking how they would use me if they got me again. However, they at last left the spot where I heard them, and I remained in my apartment all that day without further molestation.[71]

It is no wonder these narratives gripped the very souls of the Americans. For this was a life-and-death experience that could happen to any of them; there were few Americans, in fact, who did not either know someone who had been captured or someone else who did. The tone had changed, somewhat, to be sure: the mood of this is far more secular than that of Mrs. Rowlandson's narrative; and Peter Williamson, while still devoutly religious, nevertheless effected his own escape and return to civilization, showing almost none of that sense of utter dependency that was so characteristic of the Puritan way. It would be easy to exaggerate these differences; but it is safe to say at least that Williamson's tale certainly reflected the relatively more secular mood of his own time. The important thing, however, is the fact that this and similar narratives are the literary expression of an essentially American experience. Compared with the sermons that constituted the chief item of literary diet for an earlier generation, these narratives of eighteenth-century life were vital and stimulating fare indeed. Sooner or later the genuine experiences related here would find belles-lettres expression in the hands of a literary master. Eventually such a master was to ap-

[71] John Frost, ed: *Indian Wars of the United States* (2 vols. in one, New York, 1856), pp. 148–55.

pear in the person of James Fenimore Cooper, who is not without reason called one of the fathers of American letters.

IMITATION AND CREATIVENESS IN POETRY

While American prose writing was developing from the seventeenth-century baroque into the prose of eighteenth-century rationalism and naturalism, poetry was passing through a similar evolution. For the change of the poetic mood from that of Edward Taylor to that of Philip Freneau was in itself a minor intellectual revolution. And in the early development of poetry in the eighteenth century may be seen the same two currents of conscious imitation of English forms and the slow discovery, realization, and expression of the native experience that was taking place in the evolution of American prose.

Edward Taylor lived on in Westfield until 1729, and perhaps knew Jonathan Edwards, the young pastor of the church in the near-by town of Northampton. But he represented an epoch in American literary history that was gone before he died. For the eighteenth-century secularization of life and ideas had already begun, and some poetry had already been written to mark the change. The new poetry was of two kinds : one, crude, rough, direct, honest, and a native commentary on the American scene, couched in an American idiom ; the other, more consciously stylized, more refined, deliberately copied after English models, gave literary expression to the American experience, to be sure, but did it in an idiom that was borrowed from abroad and in a manner that betrayed a mood of provincialism and the sense of colonial inferiority. The same consciousness of colonial crudeness that led Benjamin Franklin deliberately to copy the prose style of the *Spectator* led the American poets to copy their poetic forms from Dryden, Pope, Blackman, Thomas, and Young.

Thus in the year in which Benjamin Tompson died there appeared in New England a volume of essays and verse entitled *Select Essays, with some few miscellaneous copies of Verses drawn by Ingenious Hands,*[72] probably written by young men in the new, eighteenth-century Harvard, which marks the turning-point to the secular mood of the new century. This little collection, however, is even more a copy of English poems of the age of Dryden and Pope than the essays of the young Franklin were of the writings of Addison and Steele.

This conscious copying of English models is typical of much of the poetry written in America in the eighteenth century. The Reverend Mather Byles, pastor of the Hollis Street Church in Boston, was perhaps the outstanding exponent of this mood in New England. He was an ardent admirer and friend of Pope, and his poems are frankly

[72] Boston, 1714.

copies that reveal a mood of admiration for Pope and all things English that was to make him a Tory in the political crisis in the Empire that was to come. In 1744 Byles published a little volume of poems entitled *Poems on Several Occasions*. The publication of this booklet was regarded by his American contemporaries as a literary event, and he was promptly dubbed the American Pope and the American Homer all in one. His poems, however, do not measure up to this encomium. Byles does, in his more serious efforts, betray a certain sensibility and literary mind. But he was no Homer, despite the fact that his own opinion of his poetic talents was pretty high. Here is an example of the work of this self-appointed New England poet laureate :

TO HIS EXCELLENCY GOVERNOUR BELCHER, ON THE DEATH OF HIS LADY

Belcher, once more permit the Muse you lov'd,
By honour, and by sacred Friendship mov'd,
Wak'd by your woe, her numbers to prolong,
And pay her tribute in a Funeral song. . . .

Ah! what avail the sable velvet spread,
And golden ornaments amidst the dead?
No beam smiles there, no eye can there discern
The vulgar coffin from the marble urn :
The costly honours, preaching, seem to say,
Magnificence must mingle with the clay.

Learn here, ye fair, the frailty of your face,
Ravished by death, or nature's slow decays : •
Ye Great, must so resign your transient pow'r,
Heroes of dust, and monarchs of an hour!
So much each pleasing air, each gentle fire,
And all that's soft, and all that's sweet expire. . . .[73]

Byles was at his best in his religious poems and hymns, in which he expressed a religious fervor that was sometimes almost erotic :

THE ALTOGETHER LOVELY

Oft has thy Name employ'd my Muse,
Thou Lord of all above :
Oft has my song to thee arose,
My Song, inspir'd by Love. . . .

Each Feature o'er thee is a Charm,
And ev'ry Limb a Grace ;
Divinely beauteous all thy Form,
Divinely fair thy Face. . . .

[73] Mather Byles : *Poems on Several Occasions* (Boston, 1744 ; facsimile reproduction, New York, 1940), pp. 76–7.

Those bleeding Hands which on the Cross
Were stretch'd for my Caress:
In the dear Thought my Life I loose —
Was ever Love like this! . . .

Conspiring Love, conspiring Charms,
Confess thee all my Joy:
Come heavn'ly Fair, come to my Arms,
And all my Pow'rs employ.[74]

This is strangely reminiscent of the religious eroticism of some of the medieval mystics; but it is not unlike the far superior poetry of Edward Taylor in its disciplined emotionalism. Yet it is more relaxed and somewhat more informal in its attitude toward the relationship between God and man. Similarly, Byles, although relatively orthodox in his religious views as compared with, say, Charles Chauncy or Jonathan Mayhew, and relatively Wigglesworthian in his theological poetry, was also conscious of the scientific rationalism that was flowing about him and could not remain unaffected by it:

ETERNITY

Before this System own'd the central Sun;
Or Earth its race about its Orbit run,
When Light ne'er dawn'd, nor Form display'd its Face,
But shapeless Matter fill'd th' unmeasur'd Space,
E'er Chaos self with jarring Discords rung
Or the rude Elements were together flung;
Then, then, Eternity, thy Pow'r was known,
Then didst thou sit on thy unshaken throne,
Thy Scepter flourish'd near to decay;
Immensity *the Kingdom of thy Sway.*[75]

Mather Byles wrote poems on comets and on earthquakes; he did not question very seriously the scientific explanation of them, but he was still under the conviction that they were signs from God to man, of God's anger, or of some other divine mood. Perhaps his popularity as a poet arose in part from his rational orthodoxy; certainly his popularity is an index to his success as an exponent of a part, at least, of the American mind.

The self-conscious Americans were represented in New York by William Livingston, who published his *Philosophic Solitude* in 1747. This poem, written in the almost universal rhymed couplets, is a panegyric on the rural life. It begins:

---

[74] Ibid., pp. 10–12.   [75] Ibid., pp. 106–7.

Let ardent heroes seek renown in arms,
Pant after fame, and rush to war's alarms;
To shining palaces, let fools resort,
And dunces cringe to be esteem'd at court —
Mine be the pleasures of a rural life,
From noise remote, and ignorant of strife;
Far from the painted belle, and white glov'd beau,
The lawless masquerade, and midnight show.
From ladies, lap dogs, courtiers, garters, stars,
Tops, fiddlers, tyrants, emperors, and czars.[76]

The poet relates the pleasant pastimes to be enjoyed in his retreat, and names the books he would read : Milton, Dryden, Pope, Locke, and the ancients. At other times,

Oft' wou'd I wander thro' the dewey field,
Where clust'ring roses balmy fragrance yield;
Or in lone grotto, for contemplation made,
Converse with angels, and the mighty dead:
For all around unnumber'd spirits fly,
Waft on the breeze, or walk the liquid sky. . . .[77]

This verse is pleasant enough, and doubtless mirrors the intellectual tastes of Livingston and many of his contemporaries. But it has little depth, little of any experience that is moving enough to justify the poet's writing about it. He is a little happier, however, in his other published poem, *America*, in which he expresses what appears to be a genuine patriotic emotion. This poem, published in 1770, is one of many published in the two decades preceding the Revolution which mark the maturing of the new and flowering consciousness of an American tradition and nationality :

From sylvan shades, cool bowers and fragrant gales,
Green hills and murm'ring Streams and flowery vales,
My soul ascends of nobler themes to sing;
America shall wake the sounding string.
Accept, my native Land, these humble lays,
This grateful song, a tribute to thy praise. . . .

Hail Land of light and joy! thy power shall grow
Far as the seas, which round thy regions flow;
Through earth's wide realms thy glory shall extend,
And savage nations at thy scepter bend. . . .[78]

[76] William Livingston : *Philosophic Solitude, Or, The Choice of a Rural Life* (New York, 1747 ; reprint, 1762), p. 15.
[77] Ibid., p. 31.
[78] William Livingston : *America, Or, a Poem on the Settlement of the British Colonies* (New Haven, 1770), p. 7.

A fellow New Yorker of Livingston's was William Smith, who had come to the colony as a tutor. Smith was to make a career for himself as an educator and as a patron of literature and the fine arts; but he was also an ardent student of poetry and a poet of some slight ability in his own right. Of his own poetry the following stanza from his *Poem on Visiting the Academy of Philadelphia, June, 1753*, which expresses his educational ideal, is perhaps a fair sample:

> *To follow Nature, and her Source adore;*
> *To raise the Being, and its End explore;*
> *To center every Aim in Common Weal;*
> *In publick Deeds to spend all private Zeal;*
> *With social Toils, in every Street, to glow;*
> *In every House, with well-earn'd Wealth to flow;*
> *To plant each Virtue in their Childrens Hearts;*
> *And grace their Infant Land with polish'd Arts;*
> *If this, O Muse, can win a People Praise,*
> *Thy honest Plaudit give, in hasty Lays.*[79]

Obviously Smith's verse followed closely the English pattern. His significance, however, is after all not that of a poet, but that of a patron of poetry; for after he became provost of the Philadelphia College he developed an ardent desire to promote literature and the arts in the colonies, and became one of the distinguished leaders of an inter-colonial cultural movement that had its center in Philadelphia. Of which more later.

The purely imitative school of American poetry reached its highest and best development, probably, in John Trumbull, Timothy Dwight, and Joel Barlow, all of Connecticut, who flourished in the period of the American Revolution. In them eighteenth-century satire, in its American form, gives expression to the American impulse to cultural maturity, the growing Revolutionary antipathy for England, and the budding native American wit. Trumbull published *The Progress of Dulness* in 1772 as a satire on the educational system, or lack of it, underscoring the eighteenth-century secularization of life and thought by its gibes at the ignorance of the clergy. *M'Fingal*, Trumbull's most important work, is a long Whig satire that belongs in the mood of the Revolutionary generation. Dwight's *Greenfield Hill*, on the other hand, is a descriptive piece that, similarly inspired by patriotism, starts as description of the American scene and ends as morality. These "Connecticut wits," so called, moved by the emotions of patriotism engendered by the Revolution, mark the culmination of the uses of styles borrowed from England to express American feelings; but they belong more properly in

[79] William Smith: *A Poem on Visiting the Academy of Philadelphia* (Philadelphia, 1753), p. 5.

the transition in poetic moods and forms that led, through independence, to the "flowering of New England" in the early nineteenth century.

Meanwhile, however, the appearance of a sense of intercolonial or continental cultural bonds had begun to make itself manifest shortly after 1740, when a number of men conceived the idea of publishing magazines, or literary repositories, "for all the colonies." Of this sort were William Bradford's *American Magazine* and Franklin's *General Magazine,* both launched in Philadelphia in 1741, only to flounder immediately. The *American Magazine and Historical Chronicle,* published at Boston, which ran through two volumes in 1744 and 1745, was a highly ambitious project, and contained, besides historical summaries and prose essays such as Byles's essay on style, copies of poems written in England, others from the newspapers of Virginia and Pennsylvania, and some composed by its own New England poets. A much more ambitious project, however, was the magazine launched in Philadelphia in 1757, in the midst of the Seven Years' War, by Provost William Smith, known, again, as the *American Magazine and Monthly Chronicle for the British Colonies.* This magazine was the organ of expression for a remarkable group of young men whom Smith had gathered about him, and is the more notable because it was one of the most striking manifestations of the awakening American and intercolonial cultural self-consciousness. The nature of its ideal and of its objectives was explained by Smith himself in the preface to the first issue :

> It has long been matter of just complaint, among some of the best friends of our national commerce and safety, that the important concerns of these *Colonies* were but little studied and less understood in the mother-country, even by many of those, who have sustained the highest offices of trust and dignity in it. But such is the nature of human affairs, that events, in themselves otherwise the most unprosperous and the least to be desired, are sometimes attended with real and unexpected good.
>
> This has, in some degree, been the case of the present war in *America.* For tho' we have not much else to boast from it, yet it has been productive of one truly desirable effect. It has rendered this country, at length, the object of a very general attention, and it seems now become as much the mode, among those who would be useful or conspicuous in the state, to seek an acquaintance with the affairs of these colonies, their constitutions, interests and commerce, as it had been before to look upon such matters as things of inferior or secondary consideration. . . .
>
> It is evident, then, that an undertaking calculated to give persons at a distance a just idea of the public state of these *American* colonies,

or to give one colony an idea of the public state of another, must be something executed on a different plan from common gazettes, and which will by no means interfere with their design, nor limit them in their circulation and use. . . .[80]

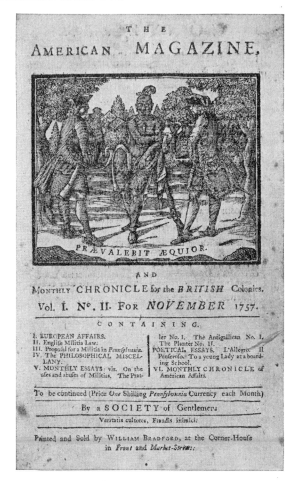

The effort to create an "American" literature: title page of The American Magazine *(Philadelphia, 1757).*

Smith was definitely committed to the purpose of presenting the culture of the colonies to the mother country and to each other. He promised to publish nothing that might "weaken us as a nation" or be of benefit to the enemy. "But, on the other hand, we shall think it our duty to give our readers such an authentic account of every thing re-

[80] *The American Magazine and Monthly Chronicle for the British Colonies* (Philadelphia, 1758), I, No. 1, October 1757, pp. 3–4.

lating to their own happiness and safety, as a *free people* have a right to expect; and, as we are independent in our situation, no power whatsoever shall either awe or influence us, in the discharge of so essential a part of our engagement with the public." [81]

This remarkable magazine, within the framework of a set of loyalties that were both British and colonial, was thoroughly self-conscious, thoroughly self-assured, and thoroughly British-American. It contained articles on European, English, and international affairs, a philosophical (scientific) miscellany, essays on various subjects, including monthly "columns" by "The Hermit," "The Antigallican," "The Planter," and others, a running history of the conflict between England and France, and notes and reviews of current books. In all this the magazine was probably a fairly dependable mirror of the active intellectual interests of the more sophisticated Americans of the 1750's. But its most notable content was its monthly section devoted to poetry, in which the patron editor took a peculiar and personal interest. This section included contemporary poems from all over the western world, including some by the great Prussian poet despot himself, Frederick II. Most of the poems, however, were either from poets in other American colonies or by Smith's own disciples. Thus the issue of the *American Magazine* for March 1758 contained a "Poem on the Mention of Letters and the Art of Printing" by "a gentleman of Maryland" who was a friend of Alexander Pope; the June issue contained a poem in Latin by John Beveridge, with a translation by the Reverend Jonathan Mayhew of Boston; the July issue contained some poems "from an ingenious clergyman" of Virginia; in August appeared a poem by the Reverend James Sterling, of Kent, Maryland. The editor was making a conscious effort to give his magazine an intercolonial character, and he was succeeding. It is a pity that his involvement in Pennsylvania politics, which landed him in jail, forced the suspension of his publication.

But the most remarkable and significant content of Smith's *American Magazine* was a series of poems by Smith's own students, all members of that remarkable group of young writers and artists who were making Philadelphia the outstanding cultural center of the colonies. Smith himself was a great Anglophile, and he coached his disciples in the English style of the classical revival. These poems, none of which achieves great distinction, therefore show the English influence, although they are not without flashes of a genuine native genius. Here is part of a poem by Francis Hopkinson, whom the editor proudly notes as "a young Gentleman of 17, on his beginning to learn the Harpsichord":

[81] Ibid., I, No. 1, p. 5.

ODE ON MUSIC

Harke! hark! the sweet vibrating lyre
Sets my attentive soul on fire;
Thro' all my veins what pleasures thrill,
Whilst the loud trebble warbles shrill,
And the more slow and solemn base
To charms give charms, and grace to grace. . . .[82]

And from another by Hopkinson, a long poem in fourteen stanzas:

L'ALLEGRO

Hence Melancholy, Care *and* Sorrow!
My heart defers you 'till tomorrow,
I have no room within my breast
For any dull, cold, lifeless guest.
Hence vanish quickly from my sight,
and sink to cells of solid night.[83]

Hopkinson's work, despite the incubus of his classical training and the English form, tended to be lighthearted and gay. His "Ode to the Morning," for example:

Arise! and see the morning sun
Dispel the shades of night;
His rays waft comfort to the soul,
And gladness to the sight.[84]

Another member of this constellation of boy poets who showed considerable promise was Thomas Godfrey, Jr. whose poem "The Invitation," a dialogue in classical form between Damon and Sylvia, was published in the January issue of the *American Magazine.* In August 1758 appeared his "Pindaric Ode on Friendship." Godfrey's poetical drama, *The Prince of Parthia,* probably the first such drama written by a native American, was published in 1759. There is little that is American in it, for it is classical in form, content, and mood. This poem shows genuine poetic ability, however, and his less well-known fantasy "The Court of Fancy," copied from Chaucer's "House of Fame," shows, with more originality than his other poems, the influence both of English style, American Puritanism, and the age of reason. For the poem ends:

"Just Heaven," I cried, "Oh! give me to restrain
Imagination with a steady rein!
Though yet she leads through Pleasure's flowery ways

[82] Ibid., I, No. 1, p. 44.
[83] Ibid., I, No. 2 (November 1757), pp. 84 ff.
[84] Ibid., I, No. 4 (January 1758), p. 187.

In Errors thorny path she sometimes strays.
Let me my hours with solid judgment spend,
Nor to Delusion's airy dreams attend;
By Reason guided, we shall only know
Those heavenly joys which Fancy can bestow!" [85]

Godfrey showed real promise as a poet, if he had ever been able to free himself from the strait-jacket of English classicism imposed upon him by his teacher. Unhappily, he died in North Carolina in 1763, and his gifts were lost to the young school of American letters.

The third of the remarkable boy poets was Nathaniel Evans, whose quite respectable poetic impulse was stifled by classicism, and who also died young. Evans was caught in the youthful impulse of the group about him to bring his native Pennsylvania into the great cultural world, so he attempted to do it by writing a poem along classical lines called "Daphnis and Menaleas" (1758):

Shall fam'd Arcadia own the tuneful choir,
And fair Sicilia boast the matchless lyre?
Shall Gallia's groves resound with heav'nly lays,
And Albion's poets claim immortal bays?
And this new world ne'er feel the muse's fire;
No beauties charm us, or no deeds inspire?
O Pennsylvania! Shall no son of thine
Glow with the raptures of the sacred nine? . . .

Fir'd with the thought, I court the Sylvan muse,
Her magic influence o'er me to diffuse;
Whilst I aspire to wake the rural reed
And sing of swains, whose snowy lamkins feed
On Schuylkill's banks, with shady walnuts crown'd,
And bid the vales with music melt around. [86]

Evans expressed his patriotism in panegyric elegies and odes written to such people as "Theophilus Grew, A.M., Professor of Mathematics in the College of Philadelphia," General James Wolfe, killed at the Battle of Quebec, and his friend Thomas Godfrey. But all his poems were in classical form and mood, full of classical references, and almost empty of genuine feeling. The task that Evans and his tutor and his friends had set themselves, indeed, was well-nigh impossible. For they were trying to force a new and potent American wine into a classical bottle that was old and brittle long before it even arrived in England. American poetry was not to achieve a status of maturity until it freed

---

[85] William B. Otis: *American Verse, 1625–1807* (New York, 1909), p. 181.
[86] Nathaniel Evans: *Poems and Writings on Various Subjects* (Philadelphia, 1772), pp. 1–2.

itself from its slavish submission to the strait-jacket of English forms and moods that were uncongenial to its own native genius.

Meanwhile, the brittle, rigid forms of English doggerel were reaching down among the people. For the newspapers had become the emporiums of poetry drawn from all over the western world. Whenever news was scarce, the editor could insert a poem; and almost any amateur who fancied himself an unknown Pope could be almost sure of having his verses printed by the local gazette. Thus the newspapers had begun to serve a very useful purpose, both in promoting an interest in poetry by publishing it and by providing a poetry forum in which the amateur could have his say. Most of this newspaper poetry, needless to say, is pretty bad. Some, however, is bearable, especially when it is made a vehicle for the expression of humor. Here are some lines, for example, that were part of a poem in the *Maryland Gazette* :

THE PLANTS, THE HORSE, AND OTHER BEASTS
A Fable

The man, who seeks to win the Fair,
(So Custom Says) must Truth forbear;
Must fawn and flatter, cringe and lie,
And raise the Goddess to the Sky;
For Truth is hateful to her Ear,
A Rudeness, which she cannot bear : —
A Rudeness! — Yes. — I speak my Thoughts;
For Truth upbraids her with her Faults.

How wretched, Chloe, then am I,
Who love you, and yet cannot lie;
And still, to make you less my Friend,
I strive your Errors to Amend. . . .

Trust not, my Girl, with greater Ease,
Your Taste for Flatt'ry I could please,
And Similies in each dull Line
Like Glow-worms in the Dark should shine.
What if I say your Lips disclose
The Freshness of the opening Rose?
Or that your cheeks are Beds of Flow'rs,
Enripen'd by refreshing Show'rs?
Yet certain as these Flow'rs shall fade,
Time ev'ry beauty will invade.[87]

The significance of this newspaper verse is not that it is particularly good, but lies in the fact that so many people were writing poetry and that it was so easy to get a hearing. It was probably no accident that,

[87] *Maryland Gazette*, April 23, 1752.

with such a widespread public interest in poetry, there should have emerged so many American poets in the 1750's and '60's. Moreover, the poetry written by Byles, Livingston, Smith and his circle, and the Connecticut poets was written chiefly for the erudite, the educated and sophisticated wealthy. But there was another stream of verse — one dares not call it poetry — that was largely anonymous and that sprang from a group of writers who were obviously closer to the people and to the American soil. These, the people's poets, were the writers in the almanacs and the newspapers.

For example, in Nathaniel Ames's almanac for the year 1747 appears the following whimsical and patriotic salute to the year:

> *Above Five Thousand Times the glorious Sun*
> *His annual Circuit round the Skies has run.*
> *Since this our World, and all things in't begun.*
> *Strange Revolutions in this Time have been;*
> *Strange things indeed has the last century seen,*
> *King Charles dethron'd, surprizing Cromwell Reign,*
> *Hanover's House established on the Throne,*
> *The Nation that illustrious Offspring own.*
> *The last Year saw a grand rebellious Rout,*
> *And glorious William root those Rebels out.*
> *The Year to come shall wondrous Things behold,*
> *But what? To me the Stars have not foretold.*[88]

Franklin made up in quantity what he missed in quality and became, in terms of prolixity at least, the most productive poet in America. Here are a few samples of poetry that appeared in *Poor Richard's Almanack*:

Of a religious nature:

> *First, Let the Fear of Him who form'd thy Frame,*
> *Whose Hand sustain'd thee e'er thou hadst a Name,*
> *Who brought thee into Birth, with Pow'r of Thought*
> *Receptive of immortal Good, he wrought*
> *Deep in thy Soul. His, not thy own, thou art;*
> *To him resign the Empire of thy Heart.*
> *His Will, thy Law; His Service, thy Employ,*
> *His Frown, thy Dread, his Smile be all thy Joy.*[89]

Scientific:

> *Astronomy, hail, Science heavenly born!*
> *Thy Schemes, the Life assist, the Mind adorn.*
> *To changing Seasons give determin'd Space,*
> *And fix to Hours and Years their measur'd Race.*

---

[88] Ames's *Astronomical Diary*, 1747. [89] *Poor Richard Improved*, 1749.

The paint'ng Dial, on whose figur'd Plane,
Of Times still Flight we Notices obtain;
The Pendulum, dividing lesser Parts,
Their Rise acquire from thy inventive Arts.

Cassini next, and Huygens, like renown'd,
The moons and wondrous Ring of Saturn found
Sagacious Kepler, still advancing saw
The elliptic motion, Natures plainest Law,
That Universal acts thro' every Part,
This laid the Basis of Newtonian Art.
Newton! vast mind! whose piercing Pow'rs apply'd
The secret Cause of Motion first decry'd,
Found Gravitation was the primal Spring
That wheel'd the Planets round their central King.[90]

Science in religion :

Ere the Foundations of the World were laid,
Ere Kindling Light th'Almighty Word obey'd,
Thou wert; and when the subterranean Flame,
Shall burst its Prison, and devour this Frame,
From angry Heav'n where the keen Lightning flies,
When fervent Heat dissolves the melting Skies,
Thou still shalt be; still as thou wert before,
And know no Change when Time shall be no more.[91]

Nathaniel Ames and Benjamin Franklin were of course both familiar with contemporary English literature and imitated it, as the rhymed
couplets will show. But the subject matter of the almanac versifiers
was subject matter familiar to, and, generally close to, the American
farmer. They were writing for him, and they had to appeal to him by
stirring in him emotions derived from his own experiences, whether
his loyalty to his king, his local patriotism, or his joy in his land and
the woods about him. And their poems clearly show the way in which
science, religion, patriotism, and literature came together to express
the common experience; the poetry of the almanacs was distinctly the
poetry of the common man.

The arty, self-conscious poetic expression of the Americans, such as
it was in the 1750's, was rigidly bound by the canons of English poetry :
rhymed couplets and classical erudition were as indispensable to poetry
as balanced mass and classical decorative features were to the Georgian
house. Poetry, it seems, simply could not be written without them. Yet
even within these forms there already could be heard the stirrings of an
American feeling that was to express itself first in the terms of a nascent

[90] *Poor Richard Improved,* 1756.   [91] *Poor Richard Improved,* 1751.

patriotism. For the wars with the French had already inspired a considerable quantity of patriotic verse, and the events of the Seven Years' War were to give occasion for much more. Of these patriotic poets, John Maylem, of Newport, was probably most worthy of note. Little is known of him except that he served in two of the campaigns of the war; the few of his poems that have survived show him to have been a man of penetrating cynicism and vigorous personal and patriotic hate. He wrote "The Conquest of Beausejour" in 1755 at the age of fifteen; three years later he published *Gallic Perfidy* and *The Conquest of Louisbourg*. These poems, the product of the war psychology, are strongly nationalistic and filled with the British imperialist's hatred of the French. Here are some lines from *Gallic Perfidy*, which was probably inspired by the Indian massacre of prisoners following the fall of Fort William Henry, on Lake George, which Maylem probably saw with his own eyes :

> *Amazing Perfidy! . . .*
> *Ye Power of Fury lend*
> *Some mighty Phrensy to enrage my Breast*
> *With solemn Song, beyond all Nature's Strain! . . .*
>
> *O Chief in War! of all (young) Albion's Force,*
> *Invest me only with sufficient Power;*
> *I (yet a boy) will play the Man, and chase*
> *The wily Savage from his secret Haunts:*
> *Not Alpine Mounts shall thwart my rapid Course;*
> *I'll scale the Craggs, then, with impetuous Speed,*
> *Rush down the Steep, and scow'r along the Vale;*
> *Then on the Sea-Shore halt; and last, explore*
> *The green Meanders of eternal Wood!* [92]

While he was in Halifax in connection with the campaign against Louisbourg, Maylem seems to have developed an intense dislike of the place, which appears in the following lines :

> *Oh Halifax! the worst of God's creation*
> *Possesst of the worst scoundrels of Each nation*
> *Whores, rogues & thieves the dregs and skum of vice*
> *bred up to villany, theft, Rags and Lice*
> *proud upstarts here tho starved from whence they come*
> *just such a scoundrel pack first peopled Rome*
> *Send them to hell & then they'll be at home.* [93]

[92] Quoted in Lawrence C. Wroth : "John Maylem : Poet and Warrior," *Publications of the Colonial Society of Massachusetts* (Vol. XXXIX, 87–120), pp. 100–1.

[93] Quoted in ibid., XXXIX, 104.

Maylem also wrote a long satirical poem on Jonathan Bird, called "The Birdiad," that was patterned after a similar poem by Joseph Green. He was nothing if not intense in his feelings, even though he expressed them in the usual stiff English rhymed couplets, and his verse probably carries more conviction than any other, with the possible exception of that of Thomas Godfrey, Jr., produced by a native American before 1760.

A genuine and convincing American poetry was close at hand, however, and the signs of it were already to be seen. Benjamin Franklin, one of the most voluminous if not one of the most exciting of American verse-writers, realized the banal monotony of the inescapable rhymed couplets of his day; and what may have been the best poem he ever wrote was an epitaph to Mungo, a pet squirrel, written in what he called "the monumental style and measure, which, being neither prose nor verse, is perhaps the properest for grief; since to use common language would look as if we were not affected, and to make rhymes would seem trifling in sorrow." Surprisingly enough, Franklin in this apology came closer than any other colonial to a true statement of the sincere mood of modern American free verse; and the little poem that he wrote affords a genuine relief from the unbroken monotony of most of the verse of its time:

EPITAPH

Happy wert thou, hadst thou known
Thy own felicity.
Remote from the fierce bald eagle
Tyrant of thy native woods,
Thou hadst naught of fear from his pining talons,
Nor from the murdering fun
Of the thoughtless sportsman.
Safe in thy wired castle,
Grimalkin never could annoy thee. . . .

Learn hence,
Ye who blindly seek more liberty,
Whether subjects, sons, squirrels or daughters,
That apparent restraint may be real protection,
Yielding peace and plenty
With Security.[94]

To which Franklin added the comment: "You see, my dear Miss, how much more decent and proper this broken style is, than if we were to say, by way of epitaph, —

[94] Franklin: *Works* (Sparks ed.), II, 170–1.

> *Here Skugg*
> *Lies snug,*
> *As a bug*
> *In a rug."* [95]

It is probably significant that he felt the impulse to break free from the rigid artificiality of the universal verse form and express his feelings in something freer and more sincere.

The man who was to provide the culmination of the development of American poetry in the colonial period was Philip Freneau, of Philadelphia. Freneau, like the artist Charles W. Peale, really flourished in the great republican era of the American Revolution, and just as Peale became the great exponent of the Revolution in painting, so Freneau became its greatest exponent in poetry. But Freneau's genius, like that of Peale, was already well developed by 1770, and his "Poem on the Rising Glory of America," delivered at the Princeton commencement in 1771, probably marked the highest point reached by native American poetry in the colonial period. This poem, although its appearance as a dialogue in classical form is forbidding, is, first of all, unrhymed; more important, however, it embodies a genuine patriotic emotion; furthermore, it is written with real gracefulness and art. It becomes, therefore, at once the best American poem of the period and the most compelling expression of the new, almost universal sense of American destiny :

> *A Theme more new, tho' not less noble, claims*
> *Our ev'ry thought on this auspicious day;*
> *The rising glory of this western world,*
> *Where now the dawning light of science spreads*
> *Her orient ray, and wakes the muse's song;*
> *Where freedom holds her sacred standard high,*
> *And commerce rolls her golden tides profuse*
> *Of elegance and ev'ry joy of life. . . .*[96]

The poet reviews the history of America and pays tribute to the cities, especially Philadelphia. But then :

> *Nor these alone, America, thy sons*
> *In the short circle of a hundred years*
> *Have rais'd with toil along thy shady shores,*
> *On lake and bay and navigable stream,*
> *From Cape Breton to Pensacola south,*

[95] Ibid., II, 171.
[96] Philip Freneau : *A Poem on the Rising Glory of America* (Philadelphia, 1772), p. 4.

Unnumber'd towns and villages arise,
By commerce nurs'd these embrio marts of trade
May yet awake the envy and obscure
The noblest cities of the eastern world;
For commerce is the mighty reservoir
From whence all nations draw the streams of gain.
'Tis commerce joins dissever'd worlds in one,
Confines old Ocean to more narrow bounds;
Outbraves his storms, and peoples half his world. . . .

To mighty nations shall the people grow
Which cultivate the banks of many a flood,
In chrystal currents poured from the hills
Apalachia nam'd, to lave the sand
of Carolina, Georgia, and the plains
Stretch'd out from thence far to the burning Line,
St. Johns or Clarendon or Albemarle. . . .

And here fair freedom shall forever reign.
I see a train, a glorious train appear,
Of Patriots plac'd in equal fame with those
Who nobly fell for Athens or for Rome. . . .[97]

This is not to be numbered among the world's great poems, but it is probably the most satisfactory piece of poetry produced in colonial America after the Puritan age and Edward Taylor; and it certainly provides a most welcome relief from the arid wastes of rhymed couplets that covered the colonies through all the decades before it. But it is not only acceptable poetry; it is a remarkable epitome or documentation of the American colonial mind. For the Americans were beginning to be deeply conscious of their own traditions, within the broad cultural pattern of the British Empire, without the slightest thought of political independence from England. Their commerce, their cities, their political struggles and their struggle with the wilderness, their strong religious convictions and their freedom — most of all, their freedom — to this, all this, Freneau had given eloquent voice. Poetry had become a literary expression of the economic and political moods of Franklin, the scientific moods of John Winthrop, or the religious moods of Charles Chauncy and Jonathan Mayhew. In the fullness of time Anglo-America had at last produced a poet.

The Indian Treaty as Literature

The contact of the sophisticated culture of the white man with the primitive culture of the Indians was productive of another literary

[97] Ibid., pp. 17, 22–3, 26–7.

phenomenon that had an important place in the literary and political life of the Americans. This was the Indian treaty, or rather the speeches made in the course of important negotiations with the Indian chieftains. For the speeches made at these meetings, whether by the white men or the Indians themselves, were couched in the picturesque, imaginative language of the aborigines, and surrounded by all the supporting ceremonial of primitive savages who had no written language. Thus when a leader, white or Indian, made a speech, he usually marked it in the memory of his hearers by presenting them with a string or belt of wampum, or a pipe, or some other gift if it were a matter of peace, or a tomahawk if it were a request for war against a common enemy.

The language of these speeches was highly figurative and full of quaint allegorical reference, and quite often reached a height of intensity of mood and expression that made it genuine poetry of a high order. As there were no prescribed forms, of course, this expression was perfectly free: the speaker followed his mood without any inhibitions. The result was something that approximated poetic prose or, perhaps better still, very free, unrhymed poetry.

The political literature of the eighteenth century is full of these speeches, and many people recognized in them a certain literary value, Franklin among them. Colden gave the texts of many, and the journals of Indian agents, like Sir William Johnson and Conrad Weiser, contain many of them. Several Indian speeches are reproduced in the journal of Christian Frederick Post, of which, allowing for defects of interpretation and recording, the following speech of the Cayuga chief Petrimontonka in 1758 to the tribes that had been helping the French in the war against the English is a fairly good example:

> Cousins, hear what I have to say; I see you are sorry and the tears stand in your Eyes. I would open your Ears and clear your Eyes from Tears, so that you may see and hear what your Unkles the six Nations have to say, we have established a Friendship with your Brethren the *English*. We see that you are all over bloody on your Body; I clean the Heart from the Dust, and your Eyes from the Tears, and your Bodies from the Blood, that you may hear and see your Brethren the English, and appear clean to them, and that you may speak from the Heart with them. . . .

Four strings [of wampum].[98]

Next day King Beaver replied to the Cayuga chief as follows:

> My Unkles . . . I thank you that you took so much Notice of your Cousins, and that you have wiped the Tears from our Eyes, and

[98] Christian Frederick Post: *The Second Journal of Christian Frederick Post* (London, 1759), p. 43.

cleaned our Bodies from the Blood ; when you spoke to me I saw myself all over bloody, and since you cleaned me, I feel myself quite pleasant through my whole Body, and I can see the Sun shine clear over us.

Four strings.

Then he continued :

As you took so much Pains and came a great way through the Bushes, I by this String clean you from the Sweat, and clean the Dust out of your Throat, so that you may speak what you have to say from your Brethren the *English,* and our Unkles the six Nations to your Cousins, I am ready to hear. . . .[99]

To which Petrimontonka replied :

We had almost slipped and dropt the Chain of Friendship with our Brethren the *English ;* now we let you know that we have renewed the Peace and Friendship with our Brethren the *English,* and we have made a new Agreement with them. . . . We desire you would lay hold of the Covenant we have made with our Brethren the *English,* and be strong. We likewise take the Tomahawk out of your Hands, that you received from the white People's ; let them use it among themselves ; it is theres, and they are of one Colour ; let them fight with one another, and do you be still and quiet in kushkushking.[100]

The contacts of the white race with the Indian in the North American wilderness, sometimes friendly, often warlike, but always deeply and instinctively antagonistic, could not but affect the literary impulses and modes of the growing American mind. Whether expressed in the narrative prose of descriptions of Indian captivities or in the more picturesque and often poetic translations of the idiom of the natives themselves, the experiences represented by this literature are probably the most profound, next only to the conquest of the land itself, in the early history of the American people. Nor could precisely this same racial conflict have taken place anywhere else in the world. This part of the American experience was unique, and its influence upon the spirit of American letters was profound ; if the Indian mind and sense of poetry had no more direct influence upon American literature than it did, it is because so deep a gulf was fixed between the white man's mentality and the Indian's. But the experience itself, the epic struggle by which the white man drove the Indian westward before him, profoundly influenced both the white man's character and the matter and the mood of his writing.

[99] Ibid., p. 44.　　　　　　　　　　　[100] Ibid., p. 45.

THE LITERATURE OF A FREE BRITISH PEOPLE

Literary expressions among the Americans, then, covered wide ranges of tastes and of mood. Among the conservatives, whether of economics or of politics or of society, literary taste was likely to prefer the style and the actual writings of England; and bookstores and libraries were full of books written in England. Writers in this mood deliberately copied the English style and distrusted and disdained the work of the native Americans. These were the copiers; as might have been expected, they were to be found chiefly, though not exclusively, among the aristocrats and the Anglophiles who some day would become the American Tories. Of such were Byrd of Virginia and Byles of Massachusetts.

But the Americans were becoming culturally self-conscious; and while they never quite freed their polite literature from the limiting influence of English forms, they were beginning to produce a literature that was their own. William Smith, himself an Anglophile and a political conservative, deliberately encouraged the production of an American literature. He taught his protégés the English forms and moods, unfortunately, but he gave a great impetus to a burst of literary creativeness that may even be called the beginning of a national literature. For, despite its English form and mood, the writings produced by Hopkinson, Evans, Freneau, and even Godfrey were fervently American in motivation and contained more than one spark of inspiration drawn from experience that was their American own.

The unfolding American cultural self-consciousness was to be seen very clearly in the vogue of history-writing that swept through the colonies between 1725 and 1765. The Americans were now definitely interested in themselves; and if Thomas Prince's history, or Thomas Hutchinson's, was tempered and restrained by the Puritan drive for accuracy, order, and truth, the urbanity of William Byrd's histories was strictly consonant with his intellectual and social environment. Similarly, the provincial histories of Pennsylvania and New York were clear-cut products of the struggle of the American middle class for the control of political power. But the most significant product of the American self-consciousness in the realm of history was the *Summary* of William Douglass, which for the first time saw all the colonies as one.

This cultural self-consciousness of the Americans and their deliberate effort at creativeness and cultural autonomy were in general a phenomenon of the American middle class, the class that stood for assembly dominance and provincial autonomy in politics. But the literature of the frontiers, the French, and the Indians, the experiences not only of the present frontiersmen but the frontiersmen who were also the grandfathers of the present bourgeois and aristocrat, was the literature of a profound experience that was common, at first or second hand, to practically everybody in America. And if, as literature, these narratives, journals, and speeches had a powerful grip on the minds and imaginations of practically everybody, it was because this was the literature of an epic common experience. Despite superficial differences in the thinking of various groups among the population, this experience and its literature were common to all, the basis of a common tradition. Literature, a true, native, American literature, was generated by the experience of the Americans on the soil and in the forests of America. It was this experience, and the common tradition represented by its literature, which, more than anything else except the epic conquest of the land itself, bound them together and had made them, now, at last, a single people.

NOTE TO THE READER

The Americans of the eighteenth century wrote much. The corpus of American literature from that period, therefore, if everything is included, is large, and individual items are not too difficult to find. Thus the sermons of such people as Jonathan Mayhew, Charles Chauncy, Samuel Davies, Jonathan Edwards, Samuel Quincy, and George Whitefield are relatively available; and these sermons bulked large in the sum total of literary production.

Among the autobiographies, that of Benjamin Franklin is by far the most interesting and the most famous; it has been printed in many editions separately, and it may be found in any collection of Franklin's writing. The *Journal* of John Woolman is well worth reading, as is also the autobiography of Samuel Johnson, most easily available in the Schneider edition of his *Career and Writings*, Volume I.

For personal letters of a charming, quasi-literary sort, the papers of Eliza Lucas [Pinckney], published as *The Journal and Letters of Eliza Lucas*, edited by Harriott P. Holbrook (Wormsloe, Ga., 1850) are delightful; the *Papers of Cadwallader Colden*, already mentioned, sometimes have a literary flair, although concerned almost exclusively with science, politics, Indian relations, and philosophy.

Of the histories written by Americans, four are of outstanding interest. William Byrd's *History of the Dividing Line*, in *The Writings of "Colonel William Byrd, of Westover in Virgina, Esqr."*, edited by J. S. Bassett (New York, 1901), is a charming, witty, and entertaining description of frontier society rather than a history, but thoroughly worth reading. William Smith's *History of the Province of New York* (London, 1757) is a political history of that province, somewhat marred by the author's bias. Thomas Hutchinson's *History of the Colony and Province of Massachusetts Bay,* edited by Lawrence S. Mayo (3 vols., Cambridge, 1936), is a surprisingly able and objective historical narrative. But, above all, William Douglass's *Summary, Historical and Political . . . of the British Settlements in North America* (2 vols., Boston, 1749–52), is the most interesting and the most significant of all the histories written in America. It is not so trustworthy as it might be ; much less so, indeed, than Hutchinson's *History;* but both the concept of the colonies as a whole and Douglass's pithy style make this a significant book.

There is no real study of early American wit, so far as I know, and no single place where it can be found. The most interesting way to find it is to get hold of copies of Ames's, Franklin's, Hutchins's, or some other almanac and read it in its natural setting. The writings of William Byrd, too, are full of it.

Colonial newspapers can be found in the large eastern libraries, but they are somewhat disappointing to a twentieth-century reader. They are interesting, however, as repositories of foreign news, essays on many topics, and bad poetry. The almanacs are much more fun.

For the frontier literature, John Bartram's *Observations . . . Made by Mr. John Bartram in His Travels from Pennsylvania to . . . Lake Ontario* (London, 1751) is one of the most fascinating examples. The journals of Christian Frederick Post are also highly worth reading ; the first of these was printed with Charles Thompson's *Enquiry into the Causes of the Alienation of the Delaware and Shawnee Indians* (London, 1759), and the second was published separately as *The Second Journal of Christian Frederick Post* (London, 1759). Cadwallader Colden's *History of the Five Indian Nations of Canada* (2 vols., New York, 1747), also, really belongs with this frontier literature, and was read widely both in England and in America. Colden's book also contains the texts of a number of Indian speeches, which are notable for their literary flavor.

Of the general books, the most satisfying, probably, is still Moses Coit Tyler's *History of American Literature, 1607–1765* (2 vols. in one, New York, 1881).

CHAPTER VIII

Of the American Spirit in Painting and in Architecture

PAINTING

THE EUROPEAN INHERITANCE

 RT is the expression of man's æsthetic reaction to the universe in which he lives. This æsthetic reaction, however, is bound very closely, psychologically speaking, to religion and philosophy, which are attempts to explain, emotionally or rationally, that same universe and man's place in it. In its broadest sense, art includes literature and music and, indeed, every conscious effort that human beings make to give expression to the beauty they find in nature or in themselves and their reactions to it. And although there occasionally occur *objets d'art* that attempt to express pure beauty for its own sake, historically art has generally had some functional significance. There have been many instances, among primitive peoples, of arts that had a magical function — a power, that is, that the *objet d'art* was thought to give its possessor in the struggle for existence, like the picture of the buffalo pierced by an arrow that was thought to give to the human hunter a greater power over the beast, or the statue of a woman with many breasts that was thought to give its possessor some vague power over the fertility of the soil or the production of human offspring. Among more sophisticated societies, however, the magical function of art has largely, but not entirely, disappeared. Yet the uses to which art is put, and its styles, reveal fairly

[428]

clearly the mind of the civilization that produces it, in so far as that social mind expresses itself through the mind of any individual artist. It would have been unthinkable, for example, for the Puritan artist to portray the figure of a nude woman; it was, on the other hand, clearly the function of art for the Puritan to portray the persons of godly individuals in such a way as to turn the beholder's thoughts to the noble purposes of God. Similarly, other aspects of thought, such as social and political ideals, cultural moods, or the brute struggle for existence, may often, if not always, be documented by the works of art produced by any given culture.

This was very largely true in colonial America, where the native moods in art were strongly functional — carrying great emphasis, that is, upon use — but where the more sophisticated mood was one of colonialism, or cultural inferiority, that resulted in a deliberate borrowing from Europe, and particularly England, of art forms that were in large measure essentially foreign to America. These two modes, or tastes, in painting and architecture developed in colonial America along parallel lines, very much as in literature.

The period in which the English colonies in America were first founded was the period that is called, in the history of art, the age of the baroque. This epoch is said to have begun with Michelangelo, and it included, in the countries of western Europe, such widely different painters as El Greco and Velasquez in Spain, and LeBrun in France, Rembrandt and Rubens in the Low Countries, and Van Dyke, Lely, and Kneller in England. The baroque mood in art was not confined to painting, however; it is to be seen in architecture, sculpture, the household arts, and dress as well. In general, the baroque style was one marked by a conscious effort for effect, superlative technique, sensuousness, exaggeration, and over-ornamentation. In England this new style, which really flourished after the Puritans had had their day, represented a revolution in æsthetic temper from that of the age of Elizabeth. For the art of the Elizabethan Renaissance, derived from medieval English art, was plain and severe; whereas the mood introduced by Van Dyke and continued through Lely and Kneller to Gainsborough and Reynolds was a mood of indulgence, of sensual pleasure, of studied efforts to make the painting please both the sitter and the beholder, even if at the cost of the literal truth.

The painting of Holland, which was the source of inspiration for such painting as there was in New Netherland, was the school of which Rembrandt was the dominant exponent; and one, at least, of the painters of New Amsterdam was said to have studied under the great Rembrandt himself.

Puritanism itself was in some ways a violent and severe reaction against the baroque, for whereas the baroque appealed through the emotions and the senses, the Puritans, even when appealing to the soul, distrusted the senses; that is to say, they ruled out every appeal to the senses that was in the last analysis an appeal to pleasure. Art, like music and literature, must be disciplined and vigorously self-controlled, confining itself strictly to the promotion of the purpose of God with men. It was beautiful only in so far as it somehow reflected the beauty of God. If the Puritans ruled the organ out of the church because it tended to divert men's minds from the pious sense of the psalms they sang, they ruled all soft, sensuous, or decorative features out of their painting for the same reason.

The style of art most favored by the Puritans in England seems to have derived in part from the flat drawing inherited from medieval England and the age of Elizabeth, and in part from the Dutch realism of their Calvinistic brethren in Holland. Queen Elizabeth herself is said to have expressed this mood of plain, flat representation when she demanded of Nicholas Hilliard that he paint her portrait "in the open alley of a goodly garden where no tree was near nor any shadow at all." [1] This preference for plainness, which with Elizabeth was probably due chiefly to her inbred æsthetic taste, was carried a good deal farther by the English Puritans, who found their favorite artist in Robert Walker, who "hated 'ornamentation' as much as Van Dyck's followers relished it." [2] For the Puritans hated the softness, the luxury, and the sensuousness of the court of Charles I as abominations in the eyes of God and as complete and sinful perversions of the divine purpose with men. Even the painting of a portrait was a mere vanity to some of the stricter Puritans; and to paint genre subjects or landscapes would have been a useless and therefore vicious waste of time, if not definitely sinful.

Not that this Puritan rigor represented the mood of all the Puritans, in either England or America; for, try as they might, the extremists could not stifle the natural search for, or expression of, beauty. This is shown quite clearly, for example, by the early New England silversmiths. Yet this mood of vigorous, disciplined plainness had its effect, even there; and the silver produced in America shows a tendency toward a plainer, simpler style while the grotesquely oramental products of the baroque silversmiths were reproducing the sensuousness of a Rubens in the round.

Thus the paintings that emanate from Puritan New England are severely plain, severely religious, severely moral. They are confined to

[1] Quoted in Oskar Hagen : *The Birth of the American Tradition in Art* (New York, 1940), p. 8.
[2] Ibid., p. 12.

portraiture, generally of godly persons; for a good likeness of a godly person, especially if one's ancestor, could not fail to be a constant reminder of the subject's godly life, and to teach by constant example the beauty of the character that rests in the beauty of God.

The earliest native American painters were probably the "limners" who got their start painting houses, carriages, and signs. In a day when houses were not numbered, indeed, the making of these signs was an important business and constituted an art in itself; the making of a

The sign-painter's art: (a) England and (b) America on the sign-board of Arah Phelps' Inn, Colebrook, Connecticut.
[By courtesy of the Library of Congress]

sign for a tavern that identified itself as "at the sign of the dragon" or "at the sign of the coach and four" presented to the imaginative painter an opportunity for æsthetic expression that the painting of mere houses or carriages could never offer. The Puritan distrust of display and sensual pleasure probably operated in him and upon him to effect a certain reserve in the expression of his imagination; yet within the framework of Puritan utilitarianism and purposefulness his product might become a genuine *objet d'art.*

Presently the limners began to paint likenesses of living people. Their Puritan outlook restricted them to godly subjects, and this, coupled with their lack of a technique for modeling and perspective, made their paintings excessively flat. Their knowledge of pigments was apparently limited to what they could invent for themselves, and their theories of composition and color were necessarily those of the untutored amateur. Finally, possibly because of a conscious effort at realism, possibly just because they did not know better, these early painters were excessively interested in realistic detail and apparently saw no reason why they should sacrifice detail in the interest of the whole.

Toward the end of the seventeenth century certain names begin to appear, notably those of John Foster, the engraver of a print of the Reverend Richard Mather, Joseph Allen, a painter, and Thomas Smith, who was active in the 1690's. And as the American interest in portraiture advanced, it developed an improved skill in drawing and a better sense of perspective, while preserving the dignity and the devotion to reality that characterized the primitives. The turn of the century, particularly in New England, was a period of transition to the generations of Smibert and Copley.

Another of the earliest native American painters and one of the

The American primitives: portrait of John Davenport painted by an anonymous artist in 1670.

[By courtesy of the Yale University Art Gallery]

first to sign their work, apparently, was Jeremiah Dummer. Dummer was a silversmith by trade, and was presumably familiar with some English painting. Yet he could hardly be called anything more than an amateur painter, and his work is more direct and factual, flatter and more simple — in short, more primitive and, probably, more "American" — than any contemporary English painting, even among the Puritans.

There is little evidence to show exactly what the artistic tastes of the early Virginians was; but it is certain that as the tobacco aristocrats began to emerge in Virginia society toward the end of the seventeenth century, they began to have their portraits painted by artists in Eng-

land, and at that time the predominant school was that of Van Dyck
and Lely. It would seem reasonable to suppose, therefore, that the
earliest Virginians probably brought with them paintings of that school,
and that the incoming Puritans, if they brought any paintings, imported
the sort that was prevalent in New England. Later importations into
Virginia certainly show a taste for the English baroque of the Restoration; and later development in the southern colonies was clearly in

*The earliest American school of painting: Thomas Smith, self-
portrait.*

[By courtesy of the American Antiquarian Society]

that tradition, and presented an urbanity that was in fairly sharp contrast with the plain style of the north — a contrast that corresponds to
those similarly presented in literature and architecture.

New Amsterdam, meanwhile, actually had some resident painters,
such as Jacobus Gerritson Strycker, who came to New Amsterdam in
1651, and Evert Duyckinck, who had come over in 1638 and founded
a noted family of New York painters, the best of whom was probably
Gerret Duyckinck. These early Dutch painters came directly out of
the Dutch school, and it was Strycker, for example, who has been
thought to have studied with Rembrandt. The painting of Dutch New
Amsterdam was thus obviously in the tradition of Dutch realism that
was akin to the Puritan plainness; it is probable, also, that some of
these Dutch painters of New York may have influenced the work of the
rising generation of American primitives in New England.

It may be concluded, then, that the European inheritance in painting received by the earliest colonies in America was of three slightly distinguished patterns : English Puritan in New England, Dutch realist in New Amsterdam, and the Van Dyck and Lely baroque in Virginia. But the effect of local intellectual and religious moods, coupled with that of the primitive conditions of the local environment, seems to have been to produce an even greater plainness, directness, and realism than was to be seen in the art of the heritage. In the colonies founded after the Restoration — that is, after 1660 — the imported style was already the style of Restoration and eighteenth-century England, particularly that of Kneller and Richardson.

COLONIAL ARISTOCRATS AND CULTURAL PROVINCIALISM

As the seventeenth century wore into the eighteenth, and as the merchants of the cities and the great planters of the plantation colonies continued to amass wealth and to develop a taste for the refinements of life, the self-conscious interest in painting developed rapidly; and as those self-conscious provincial culture-seekers turned to England for books, dress, furniture, and ideas, they also looked to the mother country for paintings and painters. Responding to this mood, a number of English painters saw fit to journey to America in the first half of the eighteenth century, and they were welcomed here with open arms by the new, culturally self-conscious American aristocracy.

One of the earliest of these overseas artists was Henrietta Johnson, who went to Charleston just at the beginning of the eighteenth century and made pretty, graceful pastels of the budding Carolina aristocracy until her death in 1728. She was followed there by Jeremiah Theus, a Swiss, who arrived in Charleston about 1735 and advertised himself as one who would paint portraits, landscapes, and coats of arms on carriages, and would teach his art to those interested in painting. In the course of a long life he painted portraits of most of the outstanding South Carolinians of that period.

Theus was not very expert in his art, with the result that his paintings are stiff and unnatural. He painted in the school of flattery and, like Charles Bridges in Virginia, sought to please his feminine sitters by making them pretty rather than presenting them as they really were. His portraits of men were more successful, but still show his effort to flatter their egos by tricks of decoration and by making them appear "superior." As he grew older and more mature, his work became more stylized and probably reflected fairly clearly the artistic taste and ideas of his aristocratic sitters.

By the middle of the century a considerable number of lesser artists had come to Charleston, and by 1770 there was a large group of them. Most of them came from England; naturally, the English school of artistic taste predominated among them; at least one of these young men had been a pupil of the great Sir Joshua Reynolds. Painting in Charleston fell even more into the school of baroque "artiness" than Theus had been; for in Charleston, despite the strong Huguenot and

American painting: the English and aristocratic mood in South Carolina: portrait of Mrs. Gabriel Manigault by Jeremiah Theus.
[By courtesy of the Metropolitan Museum of Art, New York]

West Indies influences, the mood of imitation of things English was becoming, at the mid-century, increasingly strong.

This imitative mood was paralleled, if not surpassed in intensity, among the aristocrats of North Carolina and Virginia, where Charles Bridges was regarded — after Kneller back in England — as the most satisfactory painter of aristocracy. It was he of whom the aging William Byrd wrote : "tho' he has not the master hand of a Lilly or Kneller, yet had he lived so long ago as when places were given to the most deserving he might have pretended to be Sergeant Painter of Virginia." [3]

[3] Quoted in Alan Burroughs : *Limners and Likenesses* (Cambridge, 1936), p. 32.

Bridges knew all the tricks ; he followed Kneller's style closely, and took care to pose his sitters and paint their backgrounds in such a way as to confirm the convictions of their own superiority. As Oskar Hagan says, he would have fitted exactly Hogarth's cynical remark that "phiz mongers, if they have silks and satins and velvets to dress their laymen,

American painting : the English and aristocratic mood in Virginia : portrait of Mrs. Maria Taylor Byrd by Charles Bridges.

[By courtesy of the Metropolitan Museum of Art, New York]

can carry on a very profitable manufactury without a ray of genius." [4] But Bridges was not entirely without genius. He flattered his women, as did Theus, by painting them all prettily alike ; but he was more successful — also like Theus — in his portraits of men, where he shows the ability to catch character despite his determination to make them look well.

Another visitor to the colonies who worked in the south was John Wollaston, who first established himself in the middle colonies about 1751 and then moved into the south, where his style was apparently

[4] Quoted in Hagen, op. cit., p. 63.

more appreciated. Wollaston was not a particularly skillful painter, but he earnestly sought to please, and his portraits, full of self-conscious effort as they are, are not without a flair for character, and are quite agreeable.

What the people of the south who could afford to have their por-

American painting: the English and aristocratic mood in New York: portrait of Mrs. William Walton by John Wollaston.
[By courtesy of the New York Historical Society, New York City]

traits painted desired above all was to be presented as superior beings. Their position in economic life and society, their outlook on life, their whole philosophy — with a few exceptions, to be sure — convinced them that they were superior; that it was in the natural order of things that they should occupy the position of social and intellectual leadership that they did, and that their portraits should show it. This, to them, was reality; it was probably inevitable that their æsthetic creations should document this frame of mind.

The most distinguished artist to come to America from England in the first half of the eighteenth century was John Smibert. Smibert came to New England with Bishop Berkeley, probably with the idea of assisting him in setting up an American university; but when that project failed, he went to Boston, where he settled. He had studied painting in London and had then gone to Italy, where he acquired the techniques and the tastes of the Italo-English baroque. When he got to America, however, he encountered the already developed American taste of simplicity, directness, and honesty, and he modified his own style somewhat to suit the tastes of his patrons. The result of this modification was

The English artistic tradition in New England: "Bishop George Berkeley and His Entourage," by John Smibert.
[By courtesy of the Yale University Art Gallery]

a style that used some of the techniques and the mannerisms of the English but strove to portray the characters of his sitters honestly and candidly. He did not completely succeed; the force of his training was too strong upon him. Thus his work probably should not be regarded as belonging to the native American tradition; yet the refinements of his style contributed a good deal to the development of that tradition through his apparent influence, direct and indirect, upon Peter Pelham and John Singleton Copley.

The modification of Smibert's style after he came to America was probably an indication of the artistic tastes of his New England sitters; and that taste stood in sharp contrast, in some respects, to the taste of the southerners. For if the great desideratum in art for the southerners was to be shown as superior beings, that of the New Englanders was to be shown as sober, intelligent, respectable citizens of distinction. It was much easier, apparently, for the New England merchant to face the facts of his own plainness if the artist showed his character to be that of a real live person of ability. This frame of mind may be presumed to have stemmed from the Puritan ideal of soberness, frugality, and self-control; but, however that may be, the result upon art was clearly in the direction of a greater realism. This realism was close to the native genius of America in art. There were some, however, even in New England, who deliberately looked to England for inspiration and instruction and liked their paintings in the English style. The paintings of Smibert seem to have catered to this taste, and even Robert Feke, greatest of the native Americans before Copley, showed moments when he felt like covering his native realism with the veneer of the English baroque. It was these two streams, native realism and the studied technique of the English style, that came together with such brilliant success in Copley.

As for Smibert, his best-known painting is probably his picture of Bishop Berkeley and his family. This picture is direct and honest, but it is stiff and artificial in the "artiness" with which Smibert posed the persons in the picture and the obvious striving for effect.

Smibert's greatest significance, probably, lies in the fact that he came to America and did his work here just at the moment when the American artistic mind was becoming conscious of itself and its interests. He clearly impressed the æsthetically-minded of New England and inspired such expressions of the awakening American artistic mood as the following :

> Ages our Land a barb'rous Desert stood,
> And Savage Nations howl'd in every Wood;
> No laurel'd Art o'er the rude Region smil'd,
> Nor blest Religion dawn'd amidst the Wild;
> Dullness and Tyranny, confederate, reign'd,
> And Ignorance her gloomy State maintain'd.

> An hundred Journeys now the Earth has run
> In annual circles round the central Sun,
> Since the first Ship th'unpolished Letters bore
> Thro' the wide ocean, to the barb'rous shore. . . .

> Each year succeeding the rude Rust devours,
> And softer Arts lead on the following Hours;
> The tuneful nine begin to touch the Lyre,

And flowing Pencils light the living Fire.
In the fair Page new Beauties learn to shine,
The Thoughts to brighten, and the Stile refine;
Till the great year the finish'd Period brought,
A Smibert *painted and a [Byles?] wrote,*

Thy Fame, O Smibert, shall the Muse rehearse,
And sing her Sister-Art in softer Verse. . . .[5]

The anonymous writer of this poem (*c.* 1730) listed Smibert's paintings : copies of Van Dycks and Rubenses, pictures of Roman ruins, and landscapes, as well as portraits of the leading men and women of New England. It would be difficult to estimate the influence that Smibert had upon the new generation of native American artists; that he did have a great influence upon such men as Feke and Copley, at least, seems certain.

Another Englishman who came to this country to paint was Joseph Blackburn, who apparently worked in New York for a while before he went to Boston and Portsmouth. Little is known of Blackburn's antecedents, but those of his works that have been identified show him to have been of the English school, with a special flair for painting textiles, as well as for decorating his portraits with lambs, shepherds' crooks, and ornamental draperies. While Blackburn's work resembled Copley's, he did not have Copley's instinct for character-study; on the other hand, it was almost certainly from Blackburn that Copley learned his phenomenal skill at painting silks and satins. Blackburn was one of the best and most typical of the English school of painters to come to America; and, of all of them, he probably was the one who modified his style to suit the American taste the least.

Another foreign painter to come to America was Gustavus Hesselius, who arrived in Delaware about the year 1720. Hesselius had learned to paint in Sweden, and may have studied a little in England; but he stands apart from the other foreigners by reason of the fact that, whatever had been his training, he fell quickly and wholeheartedly into the American tradition of stark, direct realism; his paintings, therefore, belong distinctly in that school and that tradition.

There were a good many other imported artists, who brought with them the English or other foreign tradition; but they were hardly important. The significant thing was that their appeal was primarily to an artistic taste that expressed the American "colonialism" that has already been observed in literature and religion.

Needless to say, a taste for fine painting was a prerogative of the

[5] Quoted in Henry W. Foote : "Mr. Smibert Shows his Pictures, March, 1730," in the *New England Quarterly*, VIII, 19–21.

rich, and the self-conscious copying of English styles and painters was peculiar to the type of American whose loyalties turned most strongly to England. This was the art, in other words, of the Tory-imperialist class, who looked upon themselves as the best in Anglo-American society and upon the culture of England as the highest and best in the Empire. Thus taste in things artistic was consonant with the other facets of the aristocratic mind.

Adaptation to American plain taste in painting: portrait of James Logan by Gustavus Hesselius.

[By courtesy of the Historical Society of Pennsylvania]

MIDDLE-CLASS AMERICAN REALISM

The first native painter of genuine talent to appear in America was Robert Feke, of Newport. Feke was probably, in the main, self-taught; but he almost certainly saw Smibert's work, and he seems to have made a voyage to England about 1746, in the course of which he probably saw, and was influenced by, the works of the English school. Feke's earliest known work is a self-portrait, made perhaps as early as 1725; but his best-known painting, and one of the most typical of his style, is of the family of Isaac Royal, made at Boston in 1741. This painting, when compared with Smibert's picture of the Berkeley family, shows a greater bluntness and less striving for effect than Smibert's work, and perhaps represents more accurately than any other painting made in America before 1750 the artistic taste of the men and women of New England's middle class.

Feke had great skill as a draftsman, and a fine sense of color; but, aside from a few paintings made after 1746, all his work shows a deter-

American realism: "Isaac Royall and Family," by Robert Feke.
[By courtesy of the Fogg Museum of Art, Harvard University]

mination to portray character realistically and honestly, with a minimum of studied posing or decoration for effect. It is this that places him squarely in the American tradition.

Dr. Alexander Hamilton of Maryland visited Newport in 1744 and met Feke, whom he described as follows: "[Dr. Moffatt] carried me to one Feake, a painter, the mose extraordinary genius, ever I knew, for he does pictures tolerably well by the force of genius, having never had any teaching. . . . This man had exactly the phiz of a painter, having a long pale face, sharp nose, large eyes, — with which he looked upon you steadfastly, — long curled black hair, a delicate white hand, and long fingers."[6]

Feke disappeared from the world of art shortly after 1750, leaving

[6] Alexander Hamilton: *Itinerarium*, edited by Albert B. Hart (St. Louis, 1907), p. 123.

behind him the finest and the most typically American paintings made up to that year. His work showed a higher degree of skill and technique than any other American artist had yet achieved; at the same time, with few exceptions, his paintings show the devotion to the undistorted truth that had distinguished and was to distinguish American painting from the primitives onward. If Feke and Copley and Charles Willson Peale showed the refining influence of the English way of painting, it was never at the sacrifice of that essential realism which expressed itself in the search for genuine character and personality.

In New York the tradition of Dutch realism continued into the eighteenth century with Gerret and Gerardus Duyckinck. But even these Dutch painters found it advisable to paint in a flatter, simpler, more naïve style than their ancestors. This may have been in part also because of lack of skill and imagination; probably, however, it was at least in part a response to the tastes of their patrons.

The most striking fact in the paintings of the first decades of the eighteenth century is thus its directness, realism, honesty, and relative simplicity. Even in the south, where there was already a more conscious copying of English style, this realism was becoming a part of the American taste. The Americans, as yet, were demanding a painting that was elementary, that they could easily understand, and that had a supreme regard for the truth, the truth that the layman could recognize. This probably may be taken as the true genesis of a genuine American taste in painting.

In any case, the American plain style is nowhere to be seen more starkly than in the work of Joseph Badger, of Boston. Certainly he was not as skillful a draftsman and painter as his neighbor Feke. But whether his naïve bluntness was the result of lack of skill and artistic sensitiveness or of conscious design, his paintings are painfully honest; and the remark is probably justified that if Smibert painted for the New England aristocracy and Feke for the wealthy but more modest and sober bourgeoisie, Badger painted for those who had lost none of their Puritan severity, in favor of either intellectual or emotional indulgence. It would be easy, if a bit daring, to see in Badger the painter *par excellence* of the Calvinistic religious reactionaries. He certainly was one of the truly American painters of the middle of the eighteenth century. He painted, apparently deliberately, in the manner of the primitives, presumably because it seemed to him more honest, more sincere. Badger thus has a significant place in the development of the American tradition in painting in his own right; but he is also of very great importance by reason of his apparent influence upon the young Copley.

John Singleton Copley was undoubtedly one the two finest painters produced in America prior to the American Revolution. He was born in 1738, and was thus only seventeen when the Seven Years' War began; yet he was already painting, and was shortly to have one of his paintings exhibited in London.

American realism: portrait of Mrs. John Edwards by Joseph Badger.

[By courtesy of the Boston Museum of Fine Arts]

Copley was the stepson of Peter Pelham, the engraver, who probably helped the youngster to learn to draw. But the greatest influence in his work was probably that of Joseph Badger, who imparted to him, above all things, his sincerity. Yet Copley improved upon his master and gradually achieved both a much greater refinement of style and a more perfect — because less crude — portrayal of reality. Under the tutelage of Joseph Blackburn, whose influence over him was second

only to that of Badger, Copley began to use some of the graceful artificialities of background that marked eighteenth-century portraiture,
such as columns, draped curtains, statues, and the like. Yet he was not
willing to sacrifice realism for grace; and he unconsciously described

*American realism: portrait of William Welsteed by John S.
Copley.*

[By courtesy of the Massachusetts Historical Society]

the artistic task of his contemporaries when he wrote that close resemblance of a portrait to its subject was "a main part of the excellency of a
portrait in the opinion of our New England Conoseurs." As he grew,
Copley became, if anything, more realistic, at least until he departed
for England, where he fell completely under the spell of the then current English style.

Copley's early pictures, made while still a boy, were crude. His portrait of the Reverend William Welsteed, for example, painted in 1753,
while it shows great skill in catching the secret of character, yet is as
crude as one of Badger's pictures. On the other hand, after he had
learned from Blackburn the secret of painting silks and satins and the
fact that beautiful clothes need not necessarily destroy the essential
reality of the sitter's character, his paintings took on more and more of

the sophisticated English style without sacrificing his great genius for the depicting of personality. And he added to the decorative qualities of his pictures an ease and naturalness of posture that were his own ; similarly, too, among the decorative features of his paintings there be-

American realism: portrait of Mr. and Mrs. Thomas Mifflin by John S. Copley.

[By courtesy of the Historical Society of Pennsylvania]

gan to appear, instead of classic column and antique drapery, features of the American scene, such as the birch tree, the huntsman's rifle, and the powder pouch that appear in the portrait of Jacob Fowle.

His portraits of Mrs. Nathaniel Appleton, of Mrs. Thomas Hooper, and of Governor and Mrs. Mifflin show Copley at his very best, with great skill in molding, in perspective, in the portrayal of textures and figures, and all marked by a penetrating realism in the depicting of character that was excelled, if at all in the colonial period, only by Charles Willson Peale.

Copley's work probably reached its highest peak of greatness in the 1770's; certainly that was his best so far as strictly American painting is concerned. For at this point in his career he had perfected his technique for painting beautiful textures, objects, and persons; but he had not yet lost the essential realism and honesty that made him one of the greatest of the colonial founders of the American tradition. In him the two streams in American painting seemed to merge; an American realism was refined by English sophistication, but the essential quality was realism. As he wrote to Benjamin West in 1776:

> Your c[a]utioning me against doing anything from fancy I take very kind, being sensable of the necessity of attending to Nature as the fountain head of all perfection, and the works of the great Masters as so many guides that lead to the more perfect imitation of her, pointing out to us in what she is to be coppied and where we should deviate from her. In this Country as You rightly observe there is no examples of Art, except what is to [be] met with in a few prints indiferently exicuted, from which it is not possable to learn much, and must greatly inhance the Value of free and unreserved Criticism made with judgment and Candor.[7]

Throughout his American years Copley insisted that true painting was the reproduction of the genuine, natural features and personality of the sitter. His style matured, after 1765, in modeling, in color, in composition, and in the smooth portrayal of textiles; but he never departed, before he went to England, from his strict canons of realism and honesty. When he went to England he changed — he adapted himself to that baroque old world as Smibert and Hesselius had adapted themselves to the more primitive directness and integrity of the new.

Yet Copley could not but feel the tug of the English influence, as Benjamin West and others had already felt it. And it was at this moment in 1766, apparently, that Copley's faith in his own American tradition and native genius, of which he was one of the highest exponents, wavered, and he began that process of thought that was to lead him into the ranks of the Americans who looked to England as the source of all things cultured and refined, and eventually out of America into England itself, where he lost his character as the greatest American realist and moved into the ranks of the baroque artistic descendants of Van Dyck and Lely. That was a mild tragedy both for him and for the American artistic tradition.

Meanwhile there was taking place in Philadelphia a cultural development that was as remarkable as it was unique. For William Smith,

---

[7] *Letters and Papers of John Singleton Copley and Henry Pelham, 1739–1776* (*Massachusetts Historical Society Collections*, Vol. LXXI), p. 51.

patron of literature, was also a patron of the arts, and he gathered about him several young painters, the best-known of whom was Benjamin West, whom he encouraged to launch out on their own in the field of painting. Philadelphia itself, in fact, was becoming a center of the arts. For this was the period when Gustavus Hesselius, James Claypoole, and William Williams, among the older artists, were at work, and their activities were supplemented by visits by Robert Feke and John Wollaston. All these artists except Feke were foreign-born; but they had adapted their styles, in one degree or another, to the taste of their patrons for plain and honest likenesses. The college, too, was committed to instruction in painting, and courses were apparently given by a German named Creamer. Henry Bembridge was one of those who took this course, as was also William Bartram, naturalist son of a naturalist father.

Under the tutelage and inspiration of these older men there had sprung into existence a notable group of youngsters, some of whom were still in their teens, who were beginning to produce a body of paintings that constituted a definite nucleus for a future American school. Unfortunately for the American tradition, William Smith was an Anglophile, an Anglican Tory aristocrat, and the other Philadelphia patrons of this American florescence shared his belief in the superiority of the English tradition. Their influence, therefore, while it gave a great impetus to the birth of an American cultural self-consciousness, tended to force the budding American culture into forms that were too rigidly English and therefore too foreign to the native American impulse. The net result was that much of the young American talent was misdirected into channels of expression foreign to it, with effects that were consequently stifling and restrictive rather than encouraging to natural growth.

Of the young artists who began, as Franklin said, to "lisp" their art in the Philadelphia florescence, Matthew Pratt, Claypoole's apprentice, was fairly well established by 1758. Pratt presently went to England to study under another one-time member of the group, Benjamin West. But he returned to Philadelphia in 1768, with a somewhat more sophisticated style, but without having lost completely his instinctively candid American touch. Henry Bembridge, who presently went to Italy and London to study, also returned to America, where he finally settled in Charleston among the group of painters in the English style that was flourishing there. Still another member of this remarkable group of youngsters was Francis Hopkinson, who, besides being a musician, was also an amateur artist, devoted particularly to work with pastels.

The most famous of the Philadelphia boy artists was Benjamin

West. West had been born in 1738 on a farm not far from Philadelphia ; and legend has it that he showed a genius for drawing at the age of six. Legend also has it that he learned how to mix pigments from the Indians and cut off most of the hairs of his father's cat for brushes. When he came to Philadelphia he studied under William Williams

American realism: portrait of Mrs. William Digges by Benjamin West.

[By courtesy of Mrs. Jerome M. Graham and the Corcoran Gallery of Art]

and tutored under the supervision and patronage of William Smith. West doubtless saw the work of Williams, Hesselius, and Wollaston, and probably received inspiration from them. He was himself established professionally by 1756, at the age of eighteen, and was recognized as a man of genius — "the Raphael of America." The deep impression that he made on his contemporaries was exemplified by William Hick's poem "Upon Seeing the Portrait of Miss xx— by Mr. West," published in the *American Magazine* for 1758 :

> *Since Guido's skilful hand, with mimic art,*
> *Cou'd form and animate so sweet a face,*
> *Can nature still superior charms impart,*
> *Or warmest fancy add a single grace?* . . .

The easy attitude, the graceful dress,
The soft expression or the perfect whole,
Both Guido's judgment and his skill confess,
Informing canvas with a living soul. . . .[8]

With regard to which occurrences the editor patron, William Smith, could not restrain himself from the following proud comment: "The first [poem], upon one of Mr. West's Portraits, we communicate with particular pleasure, when we consider that the lady who sat, the painter who guided the pencil, and the poet who so well describes the whole, are all natives of this place, and very young."[9]

Unfortunately for American painting, and possibly for West himself, the group of art patrons into whose hands West fell belonged to that wing of the Americans who distrusted their own native cultural instincts and felt that the source of true culture was the mother country, which had been drawing its own inspirations in painting from Italy. It thus fell out that West was sent to Italy to study, and made his way to England, where he lost his sure instinct for expressing native American realism along with his crude habits. From that time on he was neither really an American artist nor one who ever realized the promise of his youth.

The man who, above all others, was to carry forward the American tradition in painting that emerged in the 1750's was Charles Willson Peale, who had a revelation of the possibilities of painting when he came up to Philadelphia from Maryland in 1762. Peale, too, went to England in 1766, but his instinctive loyalty to his native culture brought him back in short order, after which he became, more than anyone else except the young Copley, the painter of eighteenth-century America.

Peale had been born in Maryland and at an early age had been apprenticed to a saddler. He had tried his hand at many things, however, and, endowed as he was with a supreme self-confidence, apparently having seen a few paintings and believing there was nothing esoteric about it, he decided to try his hand at it. Much of his time was spent evading his creditors; but after his return from England he entered into the life of Maryland and the mood of republican revolt to become the greatest painter of the Revolution. Prior to that great crisis he had turned out a number of notable works, the best-known of which was his group painting of the Peale family (frontispiece of this book).

Peale's work is marked by a certain delightful rustic quality; but it is hardly naïve. For his draftsmanship, his color, his design, and his

---

[8] *American Magazine,* I, No. 5 (February 1758), p. 238.
[9] Ibid., I, No. 5, p. 237.

modeling are all of a very high order. His greatest genius lay in his ability to penetrate and depict character ; in this he was Copley's only rival. In sharp contrast to Copley, however, a contrast as sharp as that between the urbane south and the sober-sided north, was the gaity and *joie de vivre* of Peale's personalities. He felt a fierce fidelity to the truth in what he painted, but he painted the truth gaily — with a freedom

American realism : portrait of Benjamin Franklin by Charles Willson Peale.

[By courtesy of the Historical Society of Pennsylvania]

from Puritanical inhibitions or stuffy respectability that made him, if anything, more truly expressive of the American spirit than Copley himself.

Colonial painting reached its clear apogee in those two genuinely great American realists, who were to American painting what Philip Freneau was to American writing. Painting was thus in a stage of development comparable to that of literature. There was unquestionably a native tradition already established, which had found expression in Thomas Smith, Dummer, Duyckinck, the modified Smibert, and Hesselius, and had produced its best native artists in Feke, Copley, Pratt, the young West, and Peale. But it had to contend with the provincialism, the "copying" attitude, of those Americans who distrusted their own native artistic instincts. Thus the artistic mind of the Americans was divided, as its literary, religious, social, and political minds were divided, into the copiers, the Tory imperialists, on the one side, and, on the other, those who found in the first young and tentative exponents

Commercial art: woodcuts from advertisements in the Pennsylvania Gazette.

of a native tradition the expression of feelings that were most nearly their own. These were in general the people of the middle class; needless to say, the nativists in art, the patrons, that is, who understood and promoted the native tradition as against the imported artificial English ways, were, generally speaking, the same people who favored an increasing measure of colonial autonomy, whether in economics, politics, society, or culture.

The Art of the Common Man

Oil painting was exclusively a prerogative of the wealthy, whether aristocratic baroque or middle-class realism. But the more humble folk of the cities and the farms were not without their art, too. And of this there were several classes.

The first of these was the woodcuts that appeared in newspaper advertisements. These were crude, and might represent the figure of a ship, or a slave, or a house for sale; but many of them were skillfully executed and possessed an inherent charm of their own. On the other hand, the bookshops sold prints made from engravings of famous paintings or the portraits of famous men, or views of cities and ships, city plans, and maps. The engraving of such an extensive map as Lewis Evans's map of the middle colonies, for example, required great skill and artistry. In Philadelphia, too, young William Bartram, studying at the academy, was already producing excellent engravings of the flora and fauna about which he had received his first instruction from his famous father. Bartram had probably seen Mark Catesby's engravings; his own were probably superior to those of the older English naturalist. William Bartram became a famous naturalist in his own right and carried on the work his father began; as an American and as an artist, and

Popular art : the Engravers : mezzotint of Cotton Mather by Peter Pelham.

[By courtesy of the Smithsonian Institution]

with a good formal education, he was able to produce engravings that apparently show a truer sense of the American phenomena and the American scene than either Catesby or his father were able to achieve.

Henry Pelham, Copley's stepfather, was an engraver. So was Pierre Eugène du Scimitière, who opened a print and curio shop in Philadelphia about 1765. Many of the engravers were anonymous, however. The best of the colonial engravers was doubtless Paul Revere, who made prints and cartoons, and made the engraved plates for music, as in Josiah Flagg's *Collection of the Best Psalm Tunes*, which was printed in 1764.

Still another graphic form that reached the status of an art was the popular silhouette. Many people who could not afford oil paintings had silhouettes made instead; those who could afford both were likely to have collections of silhouettes as well as of paintings. This unostentatious form of art was very popular with the Quakers. All the cutters of silhouettes remain unknown.

But the most popular development among these cheaper and more popular forms of the graphic arts was the appearance of the cartoon.

Popular art : the silhouette : silhouette of George Morgan of Philadelphia, artist unknown.

This form was not exactly new, of course, and was already being popularized by such artists as Hogarth and Gilbray in England. But its appearance in America was induced by peculiarly American conditions, and it proved to be admirably adapted to the expression of the American sense of humor, parallel to which, indeed, the cartoon developed.

The first cartoon printed in America is generally agreed to have been the one in Franklin's *Plain Truth*, published in 1747.

This cartoon, published by Franklin with the obvious intent of pointing a moral, was printed at the time when Philadelphia lay open to attack by enemies at sea. It showed a team bogged in the mire, with the driver praying to Zeus for help; Zeus, sitting on his cloud, did nothing; and the obvious moral was that "God helps those who help themselves," the suggestion being, of course — and this was an indirect comment on Quaker pacifism – that God would protect Philadelphia from the Spaniards or other enemies only if Philadelphia put itself into a condition to protect itself. Whether Franklin himself engraved this cartoon is not quite certain, but it is generally attributed to him.

Also attributed to Franklin was the famous snake device, published on the eve of the Albany Congress, which showed a snake broken to

Popular art: the cartoon (woodcut): "God Helps Those Who Help Themselves," in Benjamin Franklin: Plain Truth (*Philadelphia, 1747*).

pieces – following an old popular superstition that there were snakes of a sort that broke into pieces when in danger and then rejoined all the pieces at a convenient time – with the legend "Join or Die." The moral is obvious; Franklin was using the cartoon again to comment upon public affairs and to give emphasis to his own point of view. The "Join or Die" device was printed in the *Pennsylvania Gazette*, May 9, 1754, in the same column with an editorial relating seizure, by the French, of the forks of the Ohio, and lamenting the danger the English colonies were in because they were disunited, while the French were under a single unified command.

These earliest cartoons were the direct outgrowth of current public issues and were commentaries upon them. The objective character of the cartoon soon disappeared when it became a powerful agent for partisan campaigning in the Pennsylvania election of 1764 and the Stamp Act controversy that followed it. In Pennsylvania the cartoon was used by all factions, but the cleverest cartoonist, as well as the most vicious, was David Dove, a Quaker schoolmaster who enlisted his talents in the service of the Quaker party. When the Stamp Act controversy broke, Paul Revere, in Boston, made a number of cartoons, the most famous of which was "The Tree of Liberty." Franklin entered the lists again, too, with his cartoon of Britannia dismembered — by the unjust actions of the British ministry.

Popular art: woodcuts in the almanacs. From Poor Richard's Almanack, 1750.

The engraved prints and the newly appeared cartoon obviously enjoyed a far wider audience than the oil paintings made for the wealthy. But there was one other form of art that reached a wider audience still : the little illustrations printed in the almanacs, whether to illustrate an astronomical problem, astrological charts, or the varying activities of the months of the year. These illustrations, made by woodcuts to decorate and illustrate each separate month, generally depicted the typical tasks, the sport, or extraordinary happenings of the month, and bear a remarkable resemblance to the comparable illustrations in the old medieval books of hours.

Thus the common people had their art, too ; and if they enjoyed most the crude woodcuts of the almanacs, it was because the subjects were experiences that they knew and understood.

At the same time, too, the Indian and the frontier were beginning to appear in American painting. Hesselius, for example, interested himself in the portrayal of Indians, with genuine success.

The frontier experience in American painting: portrait of Tish-cohan by Gustavus Hesselius.

[By courtesy of the Historical Society of Pennsylvania]

CONCLUSION

The graphic arts in America, then, followed, as did literature, the general pattern of American culture. It would probably be a distortion of the truth to say that the aristocrats always chose the baroque, aristocratic forms of painting, or that the bourgeois middle class always insisted upon an honest, realistic portrait, or that the common people either knew well all the forms of art at their disposal or enjoyed all of them. But it is apparently none the less true that while the gradations were gradual, the distinctions here made are basically sound. Thus a portrait by Bridges placed alongside another by Badger and another by Feke or Copley seems to document the differences in taste represented as being unquestionably real. By the same token, while the engraved prints were probably most popular with the fairly well educated, it seems also probably true that the cartoon and the woodcuts in the almanacs appealed chiefly to a wide and popular and relatively unenlightened audience and point of view, and document a difference in social class and intellectual status as well as a different æsthetic outlook. Artistic taste and expression apparently followed the social pattern as the social pattern followed the economic. And it would perhaps not be too much to say that, of all the art forms then current, it was the cartoon and the woodcut that most nearly represented the stirring forces of democracy.

But American society was not dominated by its democratic elements, any more than American æsthetic taste was dominated, as yet, by the cartoon. American society was predominantly middle-class, if the farmers as well as the merchants be considered middle-class. And while the aristocracy was powerful on the right and democracy was just beginning to stir on the left, it was this middle class that held the keys to the future of America for many decades to come. And it was the taste of this class that most nearly represented the taste of the body of artistically articulate Americans. This taste was for realism, for truth, for the representation of nature as she is : beautifully done, to be sure, and admitting the expression of the individual instincts and reactions peculiar to the artist, but never sacrificing the essential, visible reality of the subject in the interest either of subjectivism in the artist or of personal vanity in the sitter.

What was the source of this demand for the realistic imitation of nature ? It was strongest in New England, but it had a great exponent in Charles Willson Peale in the south, as well as in others all over the colonies. Even the imitators of the English baroque showed its impress on occasion, so it must be regarded as existing, if in varying strength, in all the colonies. Unquestionably the Puritan heritage in the form of a demand for sober reality and a rejection of any embellishments that might be suspected of pleasantly indulging the senses must be considered one of the sources. At the same time, however, the frontier experience, which was itself severe and exacting, surely contributed its feeling of discomfort in the presence of luxury and ostentation to the demand for rigorous honesty, even to the point of crudeness, in its art. If, then, the heritage of ideas and the formative influence of the frontier struggle may both be included in the "experience" of the Americans, it may be concluded that the æsthetic tradition, precisely like the native American literary tradition, was derived from or generated by the American experience. If the taste of the aristocrats was other, it was because their experience was other ; and if the taste of the democratic forces demanded something simpler, easier to understand, and closer to the soil, it was because their living experience upon that very soil had made it so.

Finally, it seems clear that the peculiarly American pattern of creativeness in painting stood in a position relative to the pattern of British painting in general comparable to that of literature. For it was a new and native American mood derived from the American experience; a mood, as it were, expressive of the peculiarly American outlook on life and experience, but within the broad lines of "British" culture and the outlook on life of "Britishers" everywhere.

NOTE TO THE READER

The best way to observe the moods of the early American painters is to look at their paintings. That is difficult, because the paintings are scattered and difficult to find, although most of the great eastern art museums have sizable collections of them. The clearest way to see the contrast between the mood of American realism and the English soft style is to put a typical English picture alongside a typical American picture. Like this:

The contrast between English and American styles in painting:

(a) portrait of the Duchess of Portsmouth by Peter Lely.
[By courtesy of the Frick Art Reference Library]

(b) portrait of Mrs. William Peters by Robert Feke.
[By courtesy of the Historical Society of Pennsylvania]

One of the most interesting contemporary collections of engravings of American scenes in the eighteenth century is a book called *Scenographia Americana*, published in London in 1768. The engravings in the book are from drawings of scenes in America made by artists, mostly English, who were attached to the English armies in America during the Seven Years' War and after. The art, as art, is thus English and not American; but the subject matter is the American scene as observed through English eyes, and is interesting as an artist's conception of what America was like.

Of the modern books on early American painting, Alan Burroughs's *Limners and Likenesses* (Cambridge, 1936), and Oskar Hagen's *The Birth of the American Tradition in Art* (New York, 1940), are outstandingly the best. These authorities differ quite widely, however, as to the origin and the nature of the true American tradition in art, and even, in some cases, as to which painters do represent it and which do not. The conclusions I have presented in this chapter are my own; since the authorities disagree, every observer may be expected to form his own judgment.

THE AMERICAN SPIRIT IN ARCHITECTURE

SEVENTEENTH-CENTURY ARCHITECTURE IN ENGLAND AND AMERICA

While all the arts may be said to be functional, architecture may perhaps be said to be the most functional of all. It is so functional, indeed, that there often occur moments in the history of architecture when it ceases to be an art at all. Thus the original huts of the first-comers to Plymouth or Virginia had little appeal for the æsthetic sensibilities; nor were they intended to have. Their purpose was simply to protect their inhabitants from the weather and the other destructive forces in their new enviroment, and the settlers built the sort of shelter that could be erected most effectively and most efficiently, with the tools they had, in the time at their disposal. It was not long, however, before the first-comers to America began to build real houses, and to embellish them with architectural features calculated to lend them beauty and to satisfy the æsthetic sensibilities of their owners. Naturally enough, the first houses built by Englishmen in America followed the patterns with which those Englishmen were familiar. But the adaptation of that old English style to frontier conditions, to the ideas of the Americans themselves, and to the new styles imported from Europe developed eventually a style of architecture that was essentially the Americans' own.

During the Tudor period English architectural styles emerged from the medieval heaviness that hung upon the fortified house and entered a new era of relative lightness and gaiety corresponding with the society of the Tudor monarchy. The battlemented parapets and fortified gateways hung on, to be sure; but they had lost their functional validity and stayed only as ornament. The number of chimneys increased as the habit of heating houses spread, and the medieval great hall, while functionally less important than before, became much more beautiful by reason of the carving and other decorative features that adorned it. As wealth and luxury increased, the number of rooms increased, and with the rooms, the leaded windows.

During the reign of Elizabeth the influences of the Italian Renaissance began to be felt in England, and the Tudor style gradually gave place to the Elizabethan. Few churches were built, and Elizabethan architecture remained largely secular, concerned chiefly with dwellings and business houses. The period of Elizabeth was in fact a transitional period, in which the irregularity of the sprawling floor plan was retained, with high gables, towers, grouped chimneys, leaded windows, and second-story overhang, while classical decoration was beginning to appear in the form of Greco-Roman columns, pediments, and quoins.

The Elizabethan passed into the Jacobean, and Greco-Roman regularity of plan replaced Elizabethan irregularity, with an increasing number of columns, triangular pediments, and horizontal lines. It was the transitional architecture of Elizabethan England that the first settlers took with them to America.

But as the seventeenth century wore on in England, past the Puritan republic and into the reigns of the later Stuarts, the classical influence went on apace, to reach its climax in the work of Inigo Jones and Sir Christopher Wren. Between them, Jones and Wren brought about an abrupt completion of the transition to the Renaissance style in England — a change that amounted almost to an architectural revolution, a revolution that carried right across the Atlantic to America. Already when Jones was born in 1573, in the midst of the reign of the great Elizabeth, the classical style had appeared in England along with other Renaissance influences. But it was Jones who established it firmly, in a series of great public buildings such as the so-called Banqueting House, built in 1619, one year before the settlement of Plymouth. This building was erected upon a rectangular plan, and its two stories are marked by long rows of identical rectangular windows, which in the lower story are surmounted by alternating triangular and arched pediments. Between the windows stand columns and pilasters, and around the top of the building below the cornice runs a garland frieze; the whole is topped by a balustrade, and the roof is almost flat.

Jones died in 1652, but the importation of Renaissance styles into

English architecture was continued by Sir Christopher Wren, who seems to have got a good deal of his inspiration from the Renaissance styles so popular at the court of Louis XIV. Wren's greatest masterpiece was St. Paul's Cathedral, in London, which was built upon a

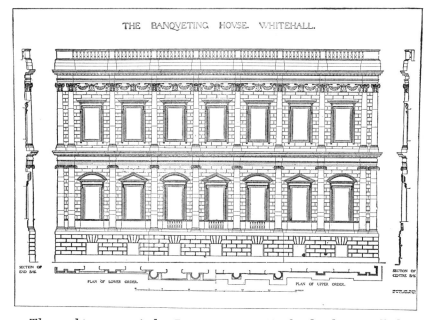

The architecture of the Renaissance in England: the so-called "Banqueting House" in London; Inigo Jones, architect.
[By courtesy of the Library of Congress]

basically medieval plan of a cross in a Greco-Roman style. But that is as far as the medieval influence goes. For from the outside this great church appears to be of two stories, with one set of columns and pediments imposed upon another; over the transept is a Roman dome, but at the front of the building are two towers, or spires, achieved by setting two or three small Greek shrines upon one another.

But Wren was much more successful in his combination of medieval, Renaissance, and occasional Dutch elements in his small churches, in which the medieval spire persisted, although he could not resist the temptation to elaborate even his spires with rows of classical columns. The ideas of Jones and Wren and their followers deeply affected domestic architecture, also. Starting with the brickwork style imported from Holland, Wren practically created a style of his own by applying to his houses certain classical elements of ornamentation, paying great attention to the nice problems of balance and proportion. This new style became the basic pattern in English architecture of the eighteenth century, called the Georgian, and this style was copied, often to the least detail, by many of the English colonists in America. Those, that is, who could afford it.

The architecture of the Renaissance in England : St. Mary-le-Bow Church ; Sir Christopher Wren, architect.
[By courtesy of the Library of Congress]

As the Georgian style emerged, it increasingly followed the basic rectangular plan, while developing the use of classical decorative elements. This style, which flourished in England in the first half of the eighteenth century, is thus to be described as a style which built upon a basically rectangular plan, with balanced masses arranged along horizontal lines, rows of identical windows with pediments, generally triangular, and hipped roofs, surmounted by balustrades; it made much use of fluted pilasters as frames for doorways, triangular, arched, or broken pediments over the doorways, quoins at the corners, and cornices marked by evenly spaced modillions, with, on occasion, friezes with trigliphs and decorative metopes. In the interior, the classical motif persisted, with pilasters and pediments and cornices, particularly in mantels and main doorways. The typical Georgian building was thus likely to be a rectangular, boxlike mass with hipped roofs, even in the churches; still, the most beautiful Georgian churches were those which succeeded in breaking the monotonous rectangularity of the body of the building by a graceful, slender spire, which derived, in a direct line, from the spires of the medieval cathedrals.

Such was the style of the Renaissance in England, founded by Jones and Wren, and planted in America by the plan of Wren himself for the College of William and Mary. But William and Mary was built almost a century after Jamestown; and it was a far cry from the architecture of the Elizabethan and Jacobean Englishmen who founded the English colonies. Their architecture, like their religion and their economics, was at first simply what they had brought with them from England.

The first habitations of the Englishmen who settled on the shores of America were of the rudest, most primitive type — the sort of mud and stick hut that was used by the most humble and primitive classes in rural England. In Massachusetts it was a sort of hole in the ground with the excavated dirt used for walls and roof. As Edward Johnson described the process, the people "burrow themselves in the Earth for their first shelter under some Hill Side, casting the Earth aloft upon Timber; they make a Smoaky fire against the Earth at its highest side. . . . Yet in these poor *Wigwames* (they sing Psalms pray, and prase their God) till they can provide them houses." [10]

In Virginia the first settlers lived in tents or built mud and stick huts; even their church was such a structure: "In foule weather we shifted into an old rotten tent; for we had few better. . . . This was our Church, till we built a homely thing, like a barne, set upon Crotchets, covered with rafts, sedge, and earth, so was also the walls: The best part of our houses [were] of the like curiosity; but the most part farre much worse workmanship, that could neither well defend wind nor raine." [11]

As soon as they could, however, the colonists began to build frame houses and churches. And these first real houses and meeting-houses in colonial America were naturally built upon an Elizabethan pattern. But the life of the first generation was strongly communal, and its houses and churches may be properly understood only in their social setting. Thus the most obvious feature of the New England village was

[10] Quoted in Fiske Kimball: *Domestic Architecture of the American Colonies and of the Early Republic* (New York, 1922), p. 5.
[11] Quoted in ibid., p. 4.

its common, whether small and square or long and narrow, along a road or river. For the common was the center of the community, and the houses, the church, and eventually the school were built around it, facing upon it.

Generally speaking, the New England village was built according to a plan. The Puritan obsession with order led to organization: a place for everything, and everything in its place. If economic life and social life and politics were made to conform to what was regarded as the

Elizabethan architecture in New England: the John Beford House, Kingston, Massachusetts.
[By courtesy of the Library of Congress]

plan of God, so also were the town and its buildings, the visible materialization of the planned social unit. The more ambitious buildings of these growing New England towns were of the Elizabethan style, with steep roofs, sharp gables, leaded windows when they could afford glass, and second-story overhang. But the Puritan leaders distrusted ostentation. These houses were simple — generally, severely simple — and showed plainly the influence of the Puritan ideal. For it was not only the practical needs that determined architectural styles. Ideas, too, played their part; and the leaders kept an eagle eye upon those who might succumb to the temptation to build beautifully just for the sake of enjoying beauty. Thus Governor John Winthrop felt himself called upon to question Thomas Dudley about the richness of his dwelling: "The governor having formerly told him, that he did not well to bestow such care about wainscotting and adorning his house, in the beginning of a plantation . . . his answer now was, that it was for the

warmth of his house, and the charge was but little, being that clap-
boards nailed to the wall in the form of wainscot." [12]

In Virginia, social life differed from that of New England, and
architectural styles varied with society. At first the town of Jamestown
was not unlike the towns of New England. But economic life developed
into a plantation system of production, and the communal life of James-

Jacobean architecture in Virginia : "Bacon's Castle," Surry County.
[By courtesy of the Library of Congress]

town gave place to a social dispersion in which the basic unit of society was the plantation group centered in the person of the capitalist
planter. Economic and social individualism replaced the communal
idea. And as the forms of society and social organization changed, the
forms of architecture changed with them; as the aristocracy began to
emerge, toward the end of the seventeenth century, this social dispersion and individualism began to manifest itself in the substantial mansions built on the plantations. These mansions, each one standing alone
on its plantation, were miles from one another; but they were the cen-

[12] John Winthrop : *Winthrop's Journal, "History of New England" 1630–
1649,* edited by James K. Hosmer (2 vols., New York, 1908), I, 77.

ters of the social life of the planters, who, in their desire to get the finest possible, turned to England for plans, furniture, and ornamentation.

Thus the great house known as Bacon's castle, built about 1670, was a mansion built in the best Jacobean style of its day. It was built of brick, set in English bond (alternating courses of brick ends and sides), grouped chimneys, and Flemish gable-ends. It was certainly a very

The perseverance of the Gothic influence in Virginia church architecture: St. Luke's Church, Isle of Wight County.
[By courtesy of the Library of Congress]

pretentious house for a remote colony, but it was expressive of the desire of the emerging Virginia aristocracy to vindicate their social and intellectual position by imitating the best of the current styles in England.

The churches of Virginia, however, remained essentially Gothic. This was true of St. Luke's Church, near Smithfield, for example, which, built of brick in Flemish bond, had pointed windows, stepped gable-end, and buttresses.

In New Amsterdam, too, the first and second generations of Dutchmen copied the styles of old Amsterdam, and since the crowded conditions of old Amsterdam had induced the narrow Dutch front with the terraced gable-end, the unimaginative Dutch burghers reproduced the narrow building in New Amsterdam, even though in that day, strange as it may seem, empty space on Manhattan Island was plentiful. These Dutchmen, just like their English neighbors, simply reproduced the forms they knew.

In the country, however, the Dutch and Flemish settlers were willing to spread out a little more; after all, it was that way in the rural farming areas back home, even in Holland. There they reproduced the Flemish gambrel-roofed farmhouses and great Flemish barns.

In Charleston, founded in 1680, the early influx of Frenchmen and of immigrants from the West Indies gave a strong French and West Indian flavor to architectural style. This seems to account, for example, for the popularity of ornamental ironwork in decoration and the use of stucco for exterior house-covering. Here, too, the pattern repeated itself : the settlers reproduced what they knew. But since they came from different areas of culture, the imported styles of architecture were different from each other, and had to become assimilated to each other as well as to the new Georgian style before the Charleston synthesis could appear.

In Philadelphia, on the other hand, the earliest buildings, built as the century turned, were already showing the influence of the English Renaissance, and the regional adaptation to the most plentiful native material, brick, produced some of the earliest American examples of the style that was later to be called American Georgian. Yet as the Germans began to pour into Pennsylvania, they, too, built the sort of houses to which they were accustomed, and German half-timbered houses and great German barns appeared within a few miles of the germinating Philadelphia Georgian.

The architecture in the English colonies in the seventeenth century, then, had little or no unity of style. On the contrary, in the last quarter of the century the architecture of each region differed sharply from that of every other region, according to the architectural styles inherited from the mother country from which the settlers in each had emanated. Thus the architecture of New England was still predominantly Elizabethan-Jacobean ; the architecture of New York was still predominantly Dutch ; that of Pennsylvania was already showing the influence of the English Renaissance while alongside this English style stood the imported styles of the Germans ; in Virginia the grand style was the Restoration-Jacobean, while in South Carolina architecture seems to have been characterized by its West Indian elements. As yet, in 1700, American architecture had no architectural style that was in any way its own.

THE DEVELOPMENT OF ARCHITECTURAL STYLE IN AMERICA

The seventeenth-century Americans, then, had built in the architectural styles they had brought with them. There had been little modification of the old styles in the first generation, but the settlers were faced with certain influences in the new world that induced them to modify their styles, and these modifications were already becoming apparent before the seventeenth century ended. As adaptation progressed, it followed the dictates of regional conditions, with the result that in Charleston architectural style tended to become an amalgamation of French and English styles; in Virginia the new and self-conscious gentry deliberately followed the English turn from Gothic and Jacobean to the supposedly superior styles of the English Renaissance. New England, too, felt the influence of the English Renaissance, but there the modification was notable for the simplification of architectural styles under the impact of frontier conditions and Puritan ideals, while in New York and New Jersey there began to take place an assimilation of Dutch and English styles to parallel the similar amalgamation of English and German styles that would eventually take place in Pennsylvania and Delaware.

Thus the turn of the century saw transition already under way; and as wealth and luxury accumulated in the cities and on the plantations, the increasing refinements of life found expression in the building of fine houses and churches in the new styles at the same time that the wealthy were beginning to perpetuate themselves in fine portraits. The direction that the development of American architecture took was also in part determined, as was that of painting, by the pattern of economic and social ideas and ideals. At the same time, in architecture as in polite literature an important, almost decisive influence was that exercised upon American building plans by the current English fashion, in this case initiated by Jones and Wren and developed by their successors.

The conscious importation of architectural styles was marked by the immigration to the colonies of a number of English architects, such as Richard Munday of Newport and Samuel Rhodes of Philadelphia. But it was nowhere so visible as in the number of English books on architecture that were sold and read in America. For professional architects were not everywhere considered necessary. The wealthy planter took a great artistic pride in designing and supervising the construction of his home; every planter was his own architect. At the same time the American carpenters were highly skilled; and why engage an architect when the local carpenter could buy a book containing plans drawn by the great English architects, Abraham Swan or James Gibbs, or even the great Inigo Jones himself? For Gibbs's *Book of Architecture,* published in London in 1728, was immediately available to American builders, as was *The Designs of Inigo Jones,* collected by William Kent and published in London in 1727. Isaac Ware published another set of Jones plans as *Designs of Inigo Jones and Others* in London in 1743. Abraham Swan's book, *The British Architect,* was published in 1745, and was so popular in the colonies that it was reprinted here on the eve of the American Revolution. It was architecture, probably, more than any other aspect of American cultural activity, that was most consciously affected by deliberate copying of English patterns; yet even this deliberate copying had to submit to certain modifications that were forced upon the builders of the new American structures by the conditions presented by the available supplies of materials, labor, the climate, or their own developing ideas of beauty.

The English renaissance in American architecture: The Governor's Palace (restored), Williamsburg.
[By courtesy of the Library of Congress]

Public buildings and churches

The fifty years between 1725 and the beginning of the American Revolution constituted a period of widespread building, despite the fact that in that period two wars were fought along the American frontier. The interest in building extended to public buildings, churches, and houses, and this cultural development should properly be considered as a part of the same emerging cultural and political self-consciousness that gave rise to a young American school of painters and writers, on the one hand, and a somewhat bumptious, adolescent nationalism on the other. Naturally enough, when the Americans sought to express their public spirit in brick and stone and lumber, they turned, as they did in literature, to the models available to them in England.

Not that the public buildings erected in this period were always slavish copies : far from it; they were adapted to the climate, the most available materials, and the tastes of the builders, which varied sharply from one section to another. In general, however, they followed fairly closely the English style.

The English renaissance in American architecture : Faneuil Hall, Boston, as rebuilt after the fire of 1763.
[From the *Massachusetts Magazine*, March 1789]

One of the earliest and most ambitious public building projects was the one involved when it was decided to move the capital of Virginia away from Jamestown and to build a completely new capital city at Williamsburg, where the College of William and Mary and the Bruton Parish Church were already located. Both these buildings already showed the influence of the changing style. Bruton Church, built in 1683, showed the new influence but little; but the college building was said to have been built upon plans prepared by Sir Christopher Wren, and there was little in it of any surviving traces of the Jacobean or Tudor styles. On the contrary, this building was a typical English Renaissance product, with balanced mass and long, horizontal rows of equal-sized windows, dormers, hipped roof, and certain classical elements such as fluted pilasters with classical capitals, or triangular pediments above doors and windows.

When the new buildings for the seat of government were erected, they followed the Renaissance style without completely surrendering all the antique English elements. Thus the steeple and the rounded, towerlike ends of the wings of the Capitol derive from an earlier time in Holland and England; but the balanced mass, the Flemish bond in the brickwork, the horizontal lines, and the classical decorative elements place these buildings in the Renaissance style. This is especially true of the Governor's Palace, which was built on the rectangular plan,

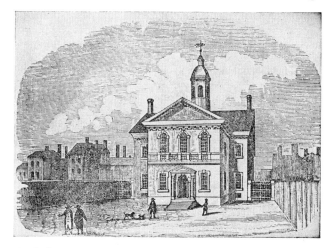

The English renaissance in American architecture: Carpenters' Hall, Philadelphia.

[By courtesy of the Library of Congress]

with classical ornamentation, hip roofs surmounted by a balustrade, dormer windows, and cupola.

The buildings at Williamsburg probably had a considerable influence upon the developing Georgian style of the homes of the Virginia aristocrats, of which more later. Suffice it to say here that the fine buildings in Virginia's provincial capital, which did not take their final form until about 1750, both set the pace for public buildings in all the colonies and expressed the growing feeling of self-importance in the colony itself.

After about 1740 all the colonies began to make conscious efforts to erect imposing public buildings. This impulse was not confined to the officials, however, for public-spirited citizens on several occasions took matters into their own hands and erected the buildings with little governmental help, if any. Such was the case with Peter Faneuil, who built his famous market and meeting-hall in Boston, with John Smibert as architect, about 1741, and then presented it to the city. This building, a great rectangular structure, was built in the Georgian mode, with balanced mass, long rows of pedimented windows, pilasters, hipped roof, and cupola.

Another fine building erected by private funds was the Pennsylvania Hospital, built in 1755. This building was a very good example of the Georgian style, of brick construction on a rectangular plan, with pedimented windows, classical pilasters, and cupola.

Carpenters' Hall, built as a meeting-place by the carpenters' guild

The mingling of Gothic and Renaissance styles in church architecture: Bruton Parish Church, Williamsburg.

[By courtesy of the Library of Congress]

in Philadelphia, was another of these distinguished public or semi-public buildings erected, about 1728, under private auspices.

It was in the Pennsylvania provincial capitol building, erected about 1770, just a few blocks from Carpenters' Hall, and a beautiful example of American Georgian architecture, that the Declaration of Independence was signed in July 1776.

The colony of Rhode Island built its Colony House in 1739, on a typical Georgian plan; other public buildings erected in this period, and all in the same general style, were Governor Tryon's palace at New Bern, in North Carolina, the so-called "state-house" at Annapolis, the Massachusetts Bay Colony House, built in 1748, and many others.

The Massachusetts Colony House, now known as the "Old State House," if a little less consistently "Georgian," was probably more successful, architecturally, than Faneuil Hall. Built upon the rectangular plan, its gable-ends show Jacobean influence rather than a strict Georgian mood. At the same time it has the balanced mass, horizontal lines,

Georgian church architecture: the Pohick Church, Fairfax County, Virginia.

[By courtesy of the Library of Congress]

and classical decoration — pilasters, pediments, balustrade, and cupola — of the Georgian.

During this same period, while American public spirit was materializing itself in imposing public buildings, the same self-consciousness of cultural maturity was expressing itself in the numerous churches built to meet the spiritual needs of the rapidly expanding population. These churches, built between 1725 and 1775, were almost without exception monuments of genuine beauty. Nearly all of them fell into a single general style; but they varied from region to region, and from colony to colony. Those in the south were of brick; and, as befitted the society of Anglicans, their interiors contained choir-stalls and canopied pulpits, and were not averse to the softening and beautifying influences of colored glass, silverware, religious images and pictures. The Gothic tradition in architecture persisted in Virginia, in fact, and Virginia churches tended to be less Georgian and more Gothic than those of New England, which followed the Wren tradition more closely. Thus the Bruton Parish Church, in Williamsburg, which, though completed before 1715, was remodeled in 1751, was basically Gothic, with nave, choir, and steep roof in the Gothic style. It had no buttresses, however, the cornices were relatively plain, and the tops of the windows were rounded — features that were neither purely Gothic nor yet completely Georgian.

Georgian church architecture : Holden Chapel, Harvard University.

[By courtesy of the Library of Congress]

Other examples of this "Virginia Gothic" were to be found throughout the tidewater areas of the south. There were exceptions, however ; and the church at Pohick, Virginia, was almost purely Georgian in concept and style. Another beautiful example of the Georgian style in church architecture was Holden Chapel, at Harvard University.

Northward from Virginia the church styles remained more purely Georgian, although most of them followed the Wren-Gibbs tradition of retaining the medieval spire. St. Paul's Chapel, in New York, built in 1764, was a good example until it was made over into a Greek temple, complete with columns but still retaining its Wren-style medieval steeple, added after the Revolution. A better example of the mingling of Renaissance and Gothic elements, perhaps, is the First Church of Christ, at Wethersfield, Connecticut.

The beautiful white steepled churches of New England were mostly of wood. But the Puritan influence persisted in them, in their plainness and their simplicity ; the same frame of mind that gave birth to sober New England realism in painting also produced the severely chaste interiors of the New England churches, which were much more severe, indeed, than the comparable churches of Mother England. There was no place for choir or organ; the windows were plain, and the benches were hard and uncomfortable, as befitted the men who felt it really necessary to stay awake and keep one's mind on the sermon.

The mingling of Gothic and Renaissance elements in New England architecture: the First Church of Christ, Wethersfield, Connecticut.

[By courtesy of the Library of Congress]

It would be a mistake, nevertheless, to suppose that these lovely churches of the wealthy represented the only American expression of the æsthetic impulse in religious architecture. The Germans had their own peculiar types of church architecture, and the Quakers had their own simple and unadorned meeting-houses to correspond with their simplicity in dress and their dislike of ostentation.

After the Great Awakening, too, a host of barnlike churches sprang up in the rural areas to house the "new light" worshippers, and some of them were not without a naïve, primitive charm. But if they were plain and often ugly, it was only partly because their congregations were too poor to build finer ones; for it was also partly because those people were, for the most part, humble souls of little æsthetic instruction, as also, probably, because these simple, bare houses of worship seemed

Quaker simplicity in church architecture: Quaker Meeting House at Catawissa, Pennsylvania.

[By courtesy of the Library of Congress]

to those humble folk to be purer and closer to the heart of God than the relatively lush, beautiful churches of the worldly aristocracy that could not, with their beauty, but divert a man's mind from the business he had with God. It was thus only in part accidental that the frontier churches were unlovely and stern; they were so, too, because they were only thus appropriate to the frontiersman's stern, hard way of life: he would not have felt at home in any other.

In fact, it may be stated in general that the American churches everywhere, built of brick or wood or occasionally of stone, were of somewhat lighter construction than their English models, and simpler and plainer in their design and decoration. This may have been due, in part at least, to the relative poverty of the Americans or to the fact that they were less sophisticated in their knowledge of architecture than their English brethren and less skillful as craftsmen; but it is probably safe to say also that the American taste was inherently plainer; that the Americans would not have built more elaborate and stylized churches — or other buildings, either, for that matter — even granted that they knew how. For the Puritan and frontier influences were still strong within them; they simply did not like too much ostentation and display in their buildings, any more than they did in their paintings.

HOMES OF THE ARISTOCRATS:
THE "AMERICAN GEORGIAN"

For the wealthy Americans who could build fine houses, the one almost universally accepted style was the English Georgian; and

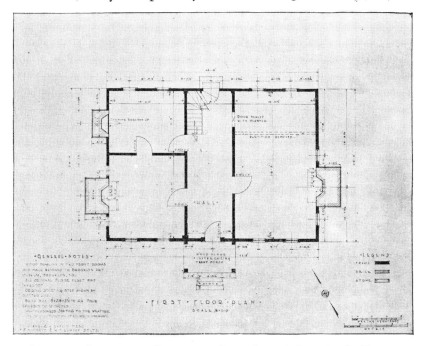

Georgian domestic architecture: floor plan of the Cupola House, Edenton, North Carolina.

[By courtesy of the Library of Congress]

house-builders, whether the southern planter who delighted in being his own architect or the "carpenters" of the cities who built houses under contract, imported English books of plans and instructions to go by. In general, the Georgian house was one built upon a strictly rectangular plan, of two or three stories, with an exterior marked by orderly arrangements of windows, dormers, and horizontal lines in roof and story-levels. Its decorative features were unfailingly classical, with triangular or arched pediments, Greco-Roman pilasters and capitals, modillioned cornices and quoins in the corners of the house. All these elements of plan and decoration were brought from England, chiefly in the architects' and carpenters' handbooks. But the Georgian houses built in America differed from their prototypes in some details, and the houses of the same type built in the different sections differed considerably from one another. Sometimes these differences were due to the availability of materials, sometimes to the influence of the style of architecture that dominated in the locality in the preceding generations, and sometimes, probably most important of all, to the influence of the intellectual and artistic outlook of the society of the area concerned —

Georgian domestic architecture in New England: the Sheldon house, Litchfield, Connecticut.

[By courtesy of the Library of Congress]

such, for example, as distinguished Puritanical New England from the gay sophisticated cavalier society of Virginia and Carolina.

The New England houses were generally built of wood; there was, indeed, an active prejudice against the use of brick in New England, since brick was regarded as being unhealthful. Generally speaking, also, these houses were plainer and less ostentatious than those, say, of Virginia or Maryland or South Carolina. The plentifulness of wood made also for the extensive use of fine wood paneling in the interiors — a usage that, if not peculiar to New England, was apparently more common there than elsewhere. The Georgian houses of the southern colonies were most often of brick, although stucco was popular in Charleston and the use of wood was more general in North Carolina. The southern houses were also larger and more elaborate, with more extensive and intricate decoration, particularly in the interiors, than the houses of New England. In Pennsylvania, New Jersey, Delaware, and New York, brick, stone, and wood were used, with brick and stone predominating, particularly in Pennsylvania and Delaware. These houses, too, were aristocratic and showy, consciously striving to be impressive — and successful in it. The houses of the Pennsylvania aristocrats, in fact, presented a sharp contrast to those of their more humble neighbors, the conservative Quakers and the German sectaries. In Charleston

Georgian domestic architecture in Virginia: Westover, the home of William Byrd.

[By courtesy of the Library of Congress]

Georgian domestic architecture in the middle colonies: the Johnson house, Germantown, Pennsylvania.

[By courtesy of the Library of Congress]

the advent of the Georgian produced a unique synthesis of the older elements with the new, and an adaptation of the new style to the older Charleston custom of building the house with its side, rather than its front, to the street.

Georgian domestic architecture in South Carolina: the house at 46 Tradd Street, Charleston.

[By courtesy of the Library of Congress]

THE HOUSES OF THE MIDDLE CLASS: THE AMERICAN COTTAGE

The great Georgian houses of the colonial aristocrats were the most striking and impressive type of domestic architecture built in the British colonies; but they were not the most characteristically American. For with all their slight modifications of detail in the direction of simplicity and plainness, these houses were still fairly deliberate copies of the Georgian houses of England. They were not for the poor, the farmer, or the frontiersman. They were not even for the middle class, in the last analysis; and this great middle group of Americans had to be content with something less ambitious, less expensive to build and to maintain. The result was the American frame cottage, which, while less pretentious than the mansion, had a distinct beauty and charm of its own. Indeed, it is probably true that the American cottage was a much more distinctively American type of architecture than any other; it was certainly more American than the adapted Georgian.

The American cottage, of course, had a very diverse ancestry in Europe. For it drew from an English background in New England;

from a Dutch-Flemish background in New York and New Jersey; from a German background in Pennsylvania and Delaware; the heritage was English again in Maryland, Virginia, and North Carolina; and the background of France and the West Indies, as well as England, showed the strongest influence in South Carolina. It was not at all the creation or the adaptation of some great architect like a Jones or a Wren or a Gibbs, but a product of the eclectic combination and adap-

The American cottage in New England: the Cape Cod type of cottage: the Joseph Atwood house, Chatham, Massachusetts.
[By courtesy of the Library of Congress]

tation of ideas from all the imported forms. It paid little attention to the basic rectangular plan, or any other, although the rectangular form for the body of the house was more popular than others simply because it was easier to build and to expand. Generally of wood, the cottage followed no precise plan for roof or chimney or porch, but adapted these elements, or discarded them altogether, according to their functional value in the environment where they were built.

The cottage in old England had been the residence of the poor and the less well-to-do for centuries. In the seventeenth century most English cottages were built of "cob," a sort of mud or plaster supported by a timber frame. A few were of stone, and a very few were beginning to use clapboard. They had broad, low, or moderately high roofs, generally thatched, with wide eaves overhanging the walls, and a few had low dormers with flat sloping roofs. Most of the chimneys were inside the house, although some of the more pretentious cottages had the chimneys outside. As time wore on, clapboard, some of it imported from America, became more popular, and shingles or slate began to replace the older thatched roofs, while shingles or shakes began to be used as outside covering for the walls.

The earliest houses of the English settlers in America were the rudest mud huts, but it was not long before they began to build timber-and-plaster houses, or frame buildings with clapboard or shingle exterior on the English model. As lumber was plentiful in New England, it was easy for the New Englanders to build of wood, and frame cot-

The American cottage in New Jersey: the Lydecker house, Englewood.

[By courtesy of the Library of Congress]

tages became far more numerous in New England than in old England. These New England cottages, too, tended to follow the English style of house with chimneys inside, for the sake of economy and warmth, and without a porch: there was little use for porches in that climate.

In the middle colonies, also, many cottages were built of lumber; but many, also, were built of stone; and there was much more use of porches and the gambrel roof, elements that were brought, presumably, from Flanders. Half-timber or timber-and-plaster construction was brought into Pennsylvania by the Germans and was used much in the cottages of the poor and the middle class. Farther south, cottages were almost uniformly of wood, and porches were particularly popular, as befitted a warm climate; but the cottages of Virginia, Maryland, and North Carolina tended to show the tall, outside chimneys that seem to have derived from Jacobean England. The cottages of South Carolina, again as suited a warm climate, were raised off the ground and displayed extensive porches for protection from the heat.

In general, these cottages were the residences of the less well-to-do farmers and shopkeepers, and may be said to have been the typical architecture of the middle class. As this type of house developed, it tended to amalgamate all the foreign influences, as well as the characteristically American elements. Thus most of the American cottages were generally of frame construction, of one or one and one half stories, with porches, which were rare in New England but were more numerous as one traveled southward and tended to be wider in the southern

The American cottage in South Carolina: Snee Farm, Mount Pleasant.

[By courtesy of the Library of Congress]

colonies. They had relatively tall chimneys, and often were built with gambrel roofs, especially in the north, and dormer windows with triangular pediments and horizontal ridge roofs. They were simpler than their European prototypes, were generally built upon a basically rectangular pattern, were of much lighter construction, and had more and larger windows. It probably would not be too much to say that the most distinctive American creation in architecture in the eighteenth century was the style represented by these cottages. For it seems quite evident that this style clearly existed nowhere else in the world. They were eclectic in their designs, to be sure, but they used the combination of elements in such a way as to create a new, American type of house. They could also be large, on occasion, and even mildly elaborate in their decoration. But they are always and everywhere in sharp contrast, both in style and in mood, to the great Georgian mansions of the rich. In their very diversity, their freedom from any fixed or preconceived or borrowed style, they were more typically American. In its simple, refined, and modest elegance the American cottage was the architectural counterpart of the American taste in painting : the spirit that produced the one was the same that produced the other.

The houses of the poor and of the frontier

The homes of the pioneers on the frontier were of a still more primitive type. Often enough they reproduced the dugouts of the earliest

Frontier architecture : the log cabin : Lower Swedish log cabin near Darby, Pennsylvania.
[By courtesy of the Library of Congress]

English settlers. But by this time the practicability of the log cabin, apparently first brought to the shores of the Delaware River from Sweden about the middle of the seventeenth century, had become known in all the colonies and had become the prevailing frontier type of house. These cabins were simple in the extreme. Generally first built as a single rectangular room, the logs were laid upon each other whole, with or without the bark removed, and with the ends mortised or dovetailed together. At times not even this amount of fitting was done, and in these cases the intervening spaces were filled with mud and straw. Where speed was no object, logs would be squared and evened off to fit the logs snugly together, after which the chinks were carefully filled with clay or straw or both. There was usually but one door, at the middle of one of the long sides of the cabin, and this might be closed only by a single skin or blanket. It was customary to build a fireplace in one end of the cabin, usually of stone, with the bulk of the construction, including the chimney, outside the house. The chimney was generally built of sticks and clay, although this flimsy construction might be replaced by stone because of the risk of fire or the desire for greater permanence. The floor of the cabin was generally the ground upon which it was built; but presently floors of hewn boards were added, or the ground was covered with skins. The roof might be thatched, but by the eighteenth century board roofs were more general.

The rule of the frontier cabin was thus simplicity of construction and functional validity above all things. For it must be built quickly and economically. These people had no money or time to invest in privacy or decoration; nor would they have invested in these things, probably, had they been able. For they had a tendency to scorn all such signs of softness and effeminacy. Nevertheless, the one-room log cabin presently began to bulge with lean-tos to provide separate kitchen or storage or sleeping room, and to sport an attic, which was in effect a separate room for the children or for the storage of other less lively impedimenta. As in the frontier churches, the simplicity, the barrenness, and the concentrated utilitarian efficiency of the frontier house was probably, at least in part, as much a matter of taste and inclination as of necessity.

The cabins occupied by the Negro slaves on the southern plantations were of the simplest possible construction. Usually of one room, they were built of logs, of clapboard, or of brick, whichever was cheaper. They hardly represented an artistic taste of the Negroes; while they did apparently run to an architectural type, and did take on a certain picturesqueness with age, it was a type derived from the motives of functional economy in the minds of the plantation-owners rather than from any impulse to æsthetic expression.

CONCLUSION: THE AMERICAN SPIRIT IN ARCHITECTURE

The wave of building that took place in the British-American colonies in the middle decades of the eighteenth century was an expression of certain American conditions and moods. The conditions were these: in the cities and on the plantations enough wealth had accumulated to make it possible for the urban and plantation aristocracies that had been pushed up by that same wealth to indulge their taste for cultural enjoyment. At the same time, the rapid expansion of the population compelled a rapid expansion of housing facilities and so improved the economic status of the already settled farmers on the land and the small shopkeepers in the towns as to make it possible for them, too, to have homes of a comfortable, even moderately luxurious sort. But the newcomers, forced out to the frontiers, had to be content with the most simple and functionally efficient type of house or church that they could invent.

The mood of the aristocrat was one of conscious borrowing. In his desire to get the best, he naturally turned to the mother country and brought to America the best that she had to offer, and that he could afford. The result, after some slight adaptation, was the American Georgian. The mood of the farmer and the shopkeeper was dominated, on the other hand, by the ideal of utility, and in building his house he sacrificed academic style and form to comfort and practicability, taking for his purpose any element of any style that happened to suit it, without, however, too great a sacrifice of elegance. In doing so, he produced the American cottage and an architectural style that may safely be called American. The mood of the frontiersman was almost completely utilitarian; it was not until he had achieved a certain economic security that he could afford a cottage, or even develop a taste for it.

The styles of architecture to be observed in colonial America thus indicated the moods of the builders; and in every case the mood arose directly from the builder's experience. The relatively easy accumulation of wealth, on the one hand, permitted, even suggested, the aristocratic, ostentatious great house. The achievement of economic and social competence by the middle class as a result of industry, thrift, and frugality, on the other hand, seems to have sprung from habits of mind that would accept utility, modest comfort, and chaste elegance as the standards of excellence most to be preferred in one's house. The taste of the frontiersman for utility and plainness was doubtless a psychological product of harsh necessity; but it was unquestionably a taste, none the less, the source of which is not entirely clear but may have been both practical experience and the taste for plainness in the religious traditions of Calvinism and the pietists. Be that as it may, it seems safe to say that the true American spirit in architecture expressed itself in its preference for the plain and simple forms of elegance.

The American style of architecture was thus not clearly self-conscious in the colonial period. As in literature and painting, the Americans who were genuinely self-conscious about their architecture were those who wished to mold American architecture in English forms. These Americans, it is true, from patriotic motives were consciously striving to produce great artistic creations in Anglo-America as the cultural province of the British Empire that could look forward to the most glowing future; but this was talent that was essentially misdirected. The true genius of America in architecture, as in painting, lay in the direction of simple, direct naturalism and integrity. In so far as American architecture was self-conscious at all, its ideal was to develop its own subdivision of the Georgian, or imperial, style. When the colonies declared their complete cultural independence of the mother country they turned away from England as the source of their inspiration and,

Social status and architectural style : (a) mansion : the Chase house, Annapolis ; (b) cottage : the Myers house, Bethel, N.C. ; (c) cabin : clapboard cabin near Cross, S.C.

[By courtesy of the Library of Congress]

like the ardent republicans they were, found it in the architecture of republican Greece and Rome. It was still to be a long time before America discovered its own genius for architecture, either formal or informal. Yet there it was, just as in literature, in painting, or in political thought : the true American spirit in architecture was that which most nearly expressed the living experience of the great mass of Americans rooted in the American soil.

NOTE TO THE READER

The architectural documentation of the American mind of the eighteenth century is to be read, as in the case of painting, most clearly in the actual edifices erected by the Americans themselves. Taste and wealth went together ; thus taste in architecture was an index of wealth and social position. Not entirely, however ; for climate, terrain, and social milieu had much to do with it.

The finest collection of contemporary plans and drawings of forts, buildings, ports, ships, and the like is I. N. Phelps Stokes : *The Iconography of Manhattan Island* (6 vols., New York, 1915), and especially, for the colonial period, Volume I.

Many books and photographic studies have been prepared on the subject of early American architecture ; one of the finest collections of photographs is that of the Historic Buildings Survey of the Library of Congress. The most satisfactory book on the subject, probably, is Fiske Kimball's *American Domestic Architecture of the American Colonies and of the Early Republic* (New York, 1922). Unfortunately, Kimball completely overlooked the evolution of the American frame cottage.

Thomas J. Wertenbaker's three delightful volumes on the *Founding of American Civilization* have much to say about early American architecture and contain many photographs and drawings. These volumes are especially valuable for the way in which they place architecture in its sociological and intellectual setting.

CHAPTER IX

Of Music, and of America Singing

"The Catechism which Wicked men teach their Children is to Dance

"and to Sing."

INCREASE MATHER.

"Three roguish chaps

"Fell into mishaps,

"Because they could not sing."

EIGHTEENTH-CENTURY FOLK-SONG.

USIC, like the other arts, exists less as an entity apart than as a reflection of the history and culture from which it is derived. Each cultural epoch has produced its own distinctive musical expression, isolated selections of which have seldom been significant in themselves, but which, taken together, have formed both a revelation of a given historical span and an inextricable accompaniment to it. All history has been enacted to a musical background; and to recall a segment of history without this background is to deal in a conception as lacking in suggestive color as a motion picture deprived of a musical score.

The music of seventeenth- and eighteenth-century America followed roughly the same stratification according to social class as the other manifestations of the colonial mind. And the music of each social class expressed the spirit of those who performed and listened to it. If it had not, they would neither have performed nor have listened to it.

MUSIC OF THE ENGLISH BAROQUE

William Byrd and Orlando Gibbons, the greatest of the Elizabethan madrigal-composers, were still living when the *Mayflower* sailed; but so far as is known, nobody sang madrigals in colonial America. What the first settlers of the English colonies sang were Elizabethan folk-songs and Calvinist psalm tunes. When more arty music materialized, it was in a tradition that did not antedate the baroque.

[490]

As a matter of fact, though the colonies began to be settled at the very opening of the baroque, America (understandably) missed more than a century of it in art music. Perhaps it is because of this gap in tradition that art music, when it was transplanted to American soil, needed some of the artificial care of an exotic plant.

Opera

In operatic music, specifically, America missed every baroque development prior to the phenomenon known as ballad-opera. But a consideration of the antecedents of opera in America must begin with the earlier phenomenon of Italian opera and George Frideric Handel.

Handel, a German, decisively established Italian opera in England in 1711 with his enormously successful *Rinaldo*, and for seventeen years thereafter Italian opera held a hardly challenged hegemony over the English stage. Handel settled permanently in England and became a naturalized citizen. When he was buried in Westminster Abbey in 1759, he had left a deeper impress on English music than any other composer ever has. Together with Bach, he was the culmination of the baroque.

Italian opera in Handel's day was in the decadent era of the so-called Neapolitan school, featuring the "celestial whine" of male sopranos and male altos (*castrati*). It was struck a death-blow in England by the appearance in 1728 of *The Beggar's Opera*, the first of the ballad-operas, a potpourri of street, folk, and popular tunes of the day reworded and strung together with coarse, spoken dialogue, in English. John Gay, its author, was included in Samuel Johnson's *Lives of the English Poets;* the Prussian violinist-composer Dr. Johann Pepusch adapted its sixty-nine airs. In its realism and satire it was the theatrical counterpart of the paintings of Hogarth, whose *Harlot's Progress* was done in 1730–1. The complex of social circumstances that gave rise to art types like *The Harlot* and *The Beggar* did not exactly exist in America, where ballad-opera was likely to be viewed therefore in a sightly different light.

The Beggar and its imitations finally drove Handel (about 1740) to forsake opera for concentration on oratorio, in which he concerned himself with religious texts — in English — and emphasized choruses as well as solos. In spite of the diverse national elements that his genius coalesced in these choruses, they were written in a way that built on the Elizabethan and Restoration choral tradition. Though religious in theme, the oratorios still were conceived for a Covent Garden audience rather·than a cathedral congregation, and were at first a substitute for opera during the Lenten season. They were sung by a chorus hardly larger than the little orchestra, choir boys taking the soprano and alto in lieu of women. Between acts Handel sometimes played an organ concerto.

Meanwhile the original ballad-opera craze had waned. But Thomas Augustine Arne with his *Love in a Village* in 1762 established a new kind of ballad-opera, more for singers than for actors, in which the tunes were largely original. Arne, who in 1773 reputedly first used women in an oratorio chorus, was the composer of the patriotic song *Rule, Britannia,* and his settings of Shakespeare lyrics such as *Under the Greenwood Tree* were standard art-songs of the latter eighteenth century.

From *Love in a Village* to the end of the century English ballad-opera closely resembled French and Italian comic opera. In fact, Rousseau's *Le Devin du village* and Pergolesi's *La Serva Padrona* had been known in London since the 1750's. Serious Italian opera, however, continued to fare with but mediocre success until the next century. Even the operatic masterworks of Gluck and Mozart were virtually unknown in England in the eighteenth century.

Instrumental music

From Elizabethan times to the age of Handel the most important instrument to cultured Englishmen was the virginal (spinet), a small, relatively simple, harpsichord. The music played on it consisted conspicuously of dance forms, of which a typical selection was Byrd's arrangement of *Sellinger's Round.* The diarist Samuel Pepys makes mention of the special care of Londoners during the Great Fire to save their virginals.

Englishmen also liked lutes, to which they sang their quaint ayres that were closely patterned after folk-songs. But both lutes and virginals were outmoded in the invasion of Italian opera ; for the foundation of the opera orchestra was the more complex and brilliant "grand" harpsichord.

Concurrently with opera the Italians had been perfecting the violin family of instruments, which they had incorporated also into the opera orchestra. With the Restoration, Charles II brought the violin tradition from the Continent and installed a royal band of twenty-four violinists. But it was the violin vogue established through the popularity of Italian opera that, again, effectively displaced the old chests of viols in England.

The average baroque orchestra of the eighteenth century numbered approximately fifteen players and in instrumentation varied according to local situations. Its strangest aspects to modern ears would be, first, the little "Bach trumpet" piping blithely away like a reed instrument ; second, the strumming-tinkling of the harpsichord ; and third, the prominence of oboes and bassoons in relation to strings. Whereas the ratio today is something like one oboe to twenty or thirty violins, the ratio then was one to two or three, or even one to one; and since oboes were much less perfect instruments in those days, they played notoriously out of tune.

With Haydn, Stamitz, C. P. E. Bach and his brother Johann Christian, came the standard rococo (classical) orchestra and the rococo sonata principle, which was based on the contrast of themes and keys in composition. Of these representative men, Johann Christian (the "London") Bach actually lived in England, and held little Mozart on his knee to play clavier duets when the child prodigy was in London in 1766.

Bach's father, Johann Sebastian Bach, whose extraordinary baroque compositions today eclipse the rococo production of his sons, was known to the eighteenth-century English, in so far as he was known to them at all, only as a very competent provincial organist and the father of his more famous sons.

Concerts

The taverns or "Musick Houses" of latter seventeenth-century England hired scraping fiddlers and grating oboists to entertain their patrons with *Sellinger's Round, Greensleeves,* and similar familiar tunes. During the same period clubs of amateurs met to perform chamber music and imbibe ale and tobacco. Even when actual concerts were under way in 1672, they retained the attractions of smoking and drinking, and all through the first half of the eighteenth century (when the annual consumption in England of gin alone reached eleven million gallons) a large proportion of concerts was still held in taverns. They were also held at schools, theaters, ballrooms, private houses, and elsewhere, and were remarkably numerous. They were sometimes given in conjunction with a public breakfast and at other times with activities like horse vaulting. A certain harpsichordist was known to play several of her numbers with her feet, and concerts in 1746 featured the future opera-reformer Gluck playing tuned drinking-glasses.

In 1732 the Vauxhall Gardens summer concerts opened in London, at which patrons could listen to concert music all during the afternoon and evening, promenade in the park, drink liquor, and be entertained by such extra-musical fare as fireworks, a menagerie, and tight-rope walking. The music itself was an indiscriminate mixture of instrumental numbers, singing, and dancing.

Concerts, whether held in parks or taverns, contained, in spite of the diversity of their programs, some of the best music then known. Haydn himself was a guest conductor in London in the 1790's and thought the music even at Vauxhall Gardens to be "fairly good." The principal point, regardless of the prevailing taste, is that to an unusual extent art music of that age in England was an unpretentious and natural part of everyday urban life, and was genuinely enjoyed as an artistic expression of, or reaction to, that life. In America, for a long while, the same concert music had to be fairly deliberately intruded into a culture that had not helped to create it.

Church music

On the other hand, not only was there no gap in church musical tradition between the time of colonial settlement and the emergence of American self-consciousness, but the tradition itself stemmed all the way from the Reformation.

The Reformation was, in a sense, a part of the middle-class revolution against feudalism, and Protestant church music is, in that sense, the music of the middle class. The ideology of the movement tended in the direction of republicanism. The music of the movement — Protestant psalms and hymns — was sung by all of the people of a congregation — a democratic turn in itself — and was, in contrast to the unmeasured chants that preceded it, an epitome of defiance and resurgence and a will to liberty. The American colonies were settled principally by men of the middle class, and long before the American Revolution they sang the revolutionary music of the Reformation.

The Moravians, Swedes, and many of the Germans who settled in America were heirs of the Lutheran musical tradition, which had evolved a body of hymns (chorales) like *Ein' feste Burg ist unser Gott* (*A mighty fortress is our God*), and which freely employed choirs and, when possible, organs. This was a much less inhibited tradition than that of Calvinism; for Calvin was a literalist who distrusted choirs, instruments, and music in general as "popish" distractions from the sacred texts that were sung and accompanied. He would not have the merely religious poetry of hymns, but only psalms straight from the Scriptures, translated as accurately as possible into metrical stanzas. The Pilgrims and Puritans, Presbyterians, French Huguenots, the Reformed Dutch, Germans, and Swiss, and some other sects of early America were heirs of the Calvinist tradition. Roman Catholics represented the third (and oldest) church musical tradition in the colonies; while Anglican music, like Anglican dogma and ritual, was partly Catholic and partly Calvinist in descent. It was Calvinist in that Anglican lay singing consisted of psalmody. For early America the psalmody was the more important, because only very late in colonial times was any other Anglican music regularly performed.

Except, then, for some of the non-English-speaking minority groups, and Catholics and Quakers, Calvinist psalm-singing was the prevailing church music in America until the second quarter of the eighteenth century, when hymns began to complement psalms.

The French Huguenots in America sang directly from the original Reformed Church psalmbook, the French Genevan Psalter. Calvin himself and a number of distinguished French poets and musicians had collaborated from time to time in adapting the psalms and setting them to arrangements of French folk-songs. The first complete edition of 1562 included one hundred and twenty-five harmonized tunes. The Reformed Dutch and Reformed Germans in America also used the Genevan Psalter, as translated into their respective languages. At the first church organized in New Amsterdam (1628) the French and Dutch joined, each in their own language, in singing the Genevan Psalter tunes.

The Anglicans in America, and the Puritans except at Salem, sang from Sternhold and Hopkins's *Whole Booke of Psalmes*, which was a kind of second-rate Genevan Psalter, the first edition of 1652 containing just the melodies of only forty-two tunes. It went through more than six hundred editions and was the standard English psalter until 1696, when it was partially superseded. The reason the English took their church musical cue from Geneva is that when the Protestant exiles from the persecutions of Mary Tudor were permeated with Calvinism in Switzerland, they also fell into Calvinist psalm-singing and succeeded in having it officially adopted the very next year after their return (1559). Lutheran hymnody, so far as it had taken hold at all, was dropped completely by the English for a hundred and seventy-five years — until the Wesley translations.

The first more-than-incidental competitor to Sternhold and Hopkins in England was Ainsworth's *Book of Psalmes*, prepared in 1612 for the English Separatists in Holland by one of their group, a Cambridge-educated Hebrew scholar, Henry Ainsworth. It contained thirty-nine melodies (not counting duplicates) in diamond-shaped notes and without bar lines, in the custom of the time. Because it employed a variety of meters, it was a less monotonous psalter musically than Sternhold and Hopkins. About half the tunes were taken from Sternhold and Hopkins, the other half from longer French and Dutch tunes, among them *Toulon*. This Ainsworth Psalter was the one used by the Salem Puritans and the Plymouth colony Pilgrims. Longfellow correctly has Priscilla singing from it in *The Courtship of Miles Standish*. The Presbyterians of New York and southward in the eighteenth century used Rous's Psalter (1643, revised 1647) and Barton's (1644), which were improved versions of Sternhold and Hopkins, but which could not dislodge the traditional book — although the *Scottish Psalter* of 1650 was based largely on Rous.

Toward the middle of the seventeenth century the great English authors from Spenser to Milton had stamped their influence on English letters since Sternhold and Hopkins had written their psalm adaptations. The demand now for better verse, as well as for more accurate translations, culminated in the *Scottish Psalter* of 1650, *The Bay Psalm Book* of 1640 in America, and Tate and Brady's *New Version of the Psalms* in England in 1696.

The Irishmen Nahum Tate and Nicholas Brady were poet laureate and court chaplain respectively under William III. Their *New Version* was a modernization of the psalms in the direction of hymns. In fact, a supplement in 1700 contained a small selection of hymns, which were used, with rare exceptions, only in private home singing; and the edition of 1708 contained both a few more supplemental hymns and many new psalm tunes, including *Hanover* and *St. Anne*.

The Church of England sang both from Sternhold and Hopkins (the "Old Version") and from the *New Version* until it finally adopted hymnody in the nineteenth century. The Nonconformists by and large clung to the Old Version until they adopted Watts's hymnbooks around the middle of the eighteenth century.

At first the English had taken up psalm-singing with the same zeal that the Lutherans had taken up hymn-singing, as a new democratic religious expression. Toward 1700, however, when the spiritual force of the Reformation was somewhat spent, psalmody fell to an incredible degeneracy, which was relieved only with hymnody and the Great Awakening.

Hymns — at first short paraphrases of psalms — began to be written as a relief from the wearisome psalm renderings, though they conflicted with the entrenched desire of a literal translation of "God's word." The traditional father of English hymnody is Isaac Watts, the outstanding Nonconformist theologian of his day. He brought out his *Hymns* in 1707 and his *Psalms*, which actually were hymnic versions of psalms, in 1717. Among the Watts hymns that are still sung is *O God, our help in ages past* to the Croft tune *St. Anne*. (William Croft was a Westminster Abbey organist.) Watts's *Psalms* and *Hymns* were adopted, though at varying degrees of rapidity, by the Independents and by the evangelical Nonconformists generally.

A much more dynamic impetus to hymnody was in connection with the founding of Methodism by John Wesley, who went with his brother Charles to the newly founded colony of Georgia as an Anglican missionary in 1735. On their voyage there, the hymn-singing of twenty-six

Moravians aboard so impressed John that he began studying German and translating their hymns. In 1737 at Charleston he compiled a hymnbook, and in the same year was arraigned by the grand jury at Savannah, among other things for introducing unauthorized psalms and hymns into the Anglican church services. This helped hasten his return to England, where he shortly brought out a second hymnbook, the selections written in large part to German tunes. It was 1761 before he published his first hymnal with music (melodies only), nearly one third of which were in the minor mode. Charles Wesley, the more prolific poet of the two brothers, produced over six thousand hymns, including *Hark! the herald angels sing* (though the present-day musical setting of it is Mendelssohn's).

The return of lusty congregational singing with Methodism was a vocalization of that groundswell of the lower and lower-middle classes for emotionalism and individualism that is known as the Great Awakening. Although hymns were in time incorporated into the music of the more conservative sects, it was Methodists and Baptists on the American frontier with a further radical development, folk-hymnody, who maintained this original lower-class connotation of hymn-singing.

On the other hand, Anglicanism had come more and more to be the religion of the English aristocracy; with few exceptions, hymns were not admitted into Anglican services in the eighteenth century. Also, the only cultivation among English Protestants of aristocratic — or art — music that was religious was in the royally patronized and other wealthy Anglican churches, where it co-existed with psalm-singing.

The highly developed Anglican art music of the age of Byrd and Gibbons had been terminated by the Commonwealth. With the Restoration, which meant also a restoration of choirs and organs that the Puritans had silenced, came the Anglican chant and a return to antiphons and anthems, albeit of a new, baroque type. Beginning in the second quarter of the eighteenth century, composers of anthems and Anglican services reflected the spell of Handel oratorio, whereunder they more or less remained for the balance of the century. But the standard Anglican art music even through most of the nineteenth century was the three-volume *Cathedral Music,* compiled about 1770 by the estimable Chapel Royal organist, William Boyce, who included most notably Elizabethan anthems by Byrd and Gibbons and Restoration anthems by the great genius Henry Purcell.

Thus Anglo-American church music of the seventeenth and eighteenth centuries showed a rough, class alignment, with Anglican art music at one extreme and American frontier folk-hymnody at the other. The original middle-class, literal psalmody of Calvin persisted through the whole time, but from it, in due course, developed a more literary and modern psalmody, and that in turn paved the way to brief paraphrases of psalms, or hymns, such as Watts's.

None of these three developments, which continued side by side, quite met the need of the new lower-class upsurge that, beginning with the translated Lutheran hymns of the Methodists, was expressed in enthusiastic evangelical singing. The hymns of Watts might be considered the middle ground of mid-eighteenth-century church music. In the evangelical singing they were merged with the proletarian hymns of Wesley, just as the more staid sects, in their singing, merged Watts's hymns and the conservative psalms. Folk-hymnody was the logical end-product of the evangelical tendency.

Music in Early America

Such, in briefest outline, is the background of early American music except for folk and popular music, which may be introduced without these preliminaries. For the most part, the course of baroque and rococo music in America paralleled that of England, but there was also a divergent American development occasioned by the same New World influences that forced modifications on every other cultural field. In the decade before the American Revolution the British colonies were reproducing and imitating English music, but also, especially in the works of Billings and the frontier folk, they were producing music that could be called their own.

Regardless of where or by whom produced, the music in America, as with literature and architecture, tended to appear in distinct categorical forms according to the social, economic, and intellectual status of its patrons.

American church music

Seventy-two years after the landing of Columbus, Protestant psalmody was introduced in America, in the Huguenot settlements on the coast of Florida and South Carolina; and Indians of the vicinity are said to have sung psalms long after the settlements were wiped out by Spaniards. English psalmody, from Sternhold and Hopkins, arrived in America in 1579 when Sir Francis Drake stopped five weeks in California for ship repairs on his voyage around the world. Though no specific reference to either singing or psalmbooks is made in the documents on Jamestown, the church services there must certainly have included psalm-singing, also from Sternhold and Hopkins. And thenceforth, through the seventeenth and early eighteenth centuries, as has already been seen, Calvinist psalmody prevailed in the churches of British America.

The psalmody was unaccompanied and the tunes sung largely from memory; but the day of lay proficiency in part-singing was not yet done, and it may be presumed that until the mid-seventeenth century American psalmody was still of a high order. The custom was to sing the psalms in strict succession, two or three per Sunday, so that all one hundred fifty might be gone through in the course of a year. Whereas the English generally sat to sing and stood to pray, the Americans stood for both — which often was an interminable time in either exercise.

As in England, there grew in America a desire for a closer and less crude translation of the psalms than that of Sternhold and Hopkins, and in 1640 a committee of Puritan preachers brought out what soon came to be known as *The Bay Psalm Book* because nearly every congregation of the Massachusetts Bay colony adopted it without hesitation. (Salem, the notable exception, voted to use *The Bay Psalm Book* along with Ainsworth in 1667, and even Plymouth gave in finally, in 1692.) In the revised edition of 1651 *The Bay Psalm Book* was adopted throughout New England and as far south as Philadelphia. It went, in all, through twenty-seven editions in America, the last in 1762, and at least twenty in England.

So far as is known, the first eight editions had no music. The ninth (1698) is the first surviving book with music printed in the colonies. Its thirteen tunes were inserted at the back, and had been copied, with mistakes, in the characteristic diamond-shaped notes and two-part harmony, and without bars except at the end of the line.

The tunes were the bulk of those most sung in colony churches before the advent of hymnody. They were *Oxford, Litchfield, Low-Dutch, York, Windsor, Cambridge, St. David's, Martyrs, Hackney, 119th Psalm Tune, 100th Psalm Tune* (the *Doxology*), *115th Psalm Tune*, and *148th Psalm Tune.*

YORK [1]

Sure God is good to Is-ra-el, | Ev'n to the clean in heart; etc.

Later editions included additional tunes, and the arrangements were in three parts — cantus, or tenor, taking the melody; medius, or female voices; and bass.

[1] William Arms Fisher, ed: *Yᵉ Olde New-England Psalm-tunes 1620–1820* (Boston: Oliver Ditson Co.; 1930), p. 3. By permission of the publisher.

The Massachusetts Bay authors did achieve a more literal versifi-
cation of the psalms, but not a more singable one. The first stanza of the

*Church music in New England: (a) title page and (b) a page of
tunes from the Bay Psalm Book, edition of 1742 (Boston).*

Doxology, for example, is given below in the version of Sternhold and
Hopkins and in the version of *The Bay Psalm Book:*

Sternhold and Hopkins	Bay Psalm Book
All people that on earth doe dwell, sing to the Lord with cheereful voice :	*Make yee a joyfull sounding noyse unto Iehovah, all the earth :*
Him serue with feare, his praise forth tell :	*Serve yee Iehovah with gladness : before his presence come with mirth.*[3]
come ye before him and reioyce.[2]	

Meanwhile, American church singing had been deteriorating just
as it had in England. With a waned enthusiasm in glorifying God as

[2] *The Whole Booke of Psalmes,* Collected into English Meeter by Thomas
Sternhold, Iohn Hopkins, and others (London, 1623), p. 299.

[3] *The Bay Psalm Book,* Being a *Facsimile* Reprint of the First Edition (New
York, 1903). The words "Praise God from whom all blessings flow" come from
the final stanza of an Evening Hymn of Bishop Thomas Ken's, written at the end
of the seventeenth century for the Anglican scholars at Winchester College,
England.

perhaps the underlying factor, and waning literacy as another, congregational memories for melodies grew dim, and ability to read the metrical Scriptures sometimes disappeared without a trace. During the drudging church-going of the last quarter of the seventeenth century, a half-dozen tunes or less were used for all the psalms, and they were undevoutly decorated with grace-notes until hardly recognizable. The recourse to "deaconing," or "lining out," which churches in England had been unable to avoid, followed from necessity, first at the Plymouth church in 1681. A clerk or deacon would intone one line of a psalm at a time (later two lines), to be repeated cacophonously by the congregation at large.

The deacons themselves, like the "clarks" in England, were not very successful at remembering the tunes they set. Even Samuel Sewell, the venerable judge of Massachusetts, recorded his embarrassment on at least three occasions:

> Mr. Willard . . . spake to me to set the Tune; I intended Windsor and fell into High-Dutch, and then essaying to set another tune went into a key much too high. . . . [December 28, 1705.]

> I try'd to set Low-Dutch Tune and fail'd. Try'd again and fell into the Tune of 119th Psalm. [July 5, 1713.]

> In the morning I set York Tune, and in the 2d going over the Gallery carried it irresistibly to St. David's, which discouraged me very much. . . . [February 2, 1718.] [4]

And church singing had become so draggy that a Puritan preacher, Thomas Walter, was able to say: "I myself have twice in one note paused to take breath." [5] Cotten Mather, who in 1718 wrote a pedantic psalmbook in blank verse entitled *Psalterium Americanum*, described the singing of some congregations as "an odd noise." [6]

Mather and Walter were but two of a large number of Puritan divines who agitated for reformed church singing and precipitated a controversy that raged from, say, 1710 to the virtual overthrow of deaconing around the time of the Revolution and later. "Our fathers never learned to sing by note, and they are got to heaven without it," [7] was a typical New England argument against reform; and the old farmers hated to give up their extemporaneous internote elaborations of the

---

[4] Quoted in Percy A. Scholes : *The Puritans and Music in England and New England* (London, 1934), pp. 262–3.

[5] Quoted in J. Spencer Curwen : *Studies in Worship-Music* (London, 1880), p. 59.

[6] Quoted in ibid., p. 60.

[7] Quoted in John Atlee Kouwenhoven : "Some Unfamiliar Aspects of Singing in New England, 1620–1810," in the *New England Quarterly*, VI, 576.

tunes. "I have great jealousy," said a writer in the *New England Chron-icle* in 1723, "that if we once begin to sing by note, the next thing will be to pray by rote, and then comes popery."[8] The transition to better psalmody was fraught with many serious complications. In Wilbraham, Massachusetts, where, according to its early records, the clapping of time in church caused a great disturbance, a committee of ten was appointed to consider "the broken state of this town with regard to singing."[9]

The "new way" of psalm-singing—that is, by note—penetrated Virginia late in 1710, where an indication of the resultant dissension is given by the wealthy Westover planter William Byrd. "In the afternoon my wife and I had a quarrel about learning to sing Psalms in which she was wholly in the wrong. . . ." But a week later in their church pew, he says, "We began to give in to the new way of singing Psalms."[10]

The thirteen tunes of the 1698 edition of *The Bay Psalm Book* were the first perceptible stimulus of the movement back to singing by note. Outright instruction began in 1712 when the Reverend John Tufts, a Harvard graduate and one of the first organizers of singing schools, published a crude pamphlet entitled *An Introduction to the Singing of Psalm Tunes,* which contained twenty-eight melodies in three-part harmony, the notes indicated by initials (for fa, so, la, mi) on a staff, and their length by punctuation marks. Better textbooks came in time, one of the earliest and most popular being Walter's *Grounds and Rules of Musick* (1721), which was printed by Benjamin Franklin's brother James and was the first music printed in America containing bar lines.

The fa-so-la system, often with "buckwheat" or shaped notes to in-dicate pitch, was the rigorous but successful method by which eager aspirants were taught to sing on key without accompaniment. Singing schools mushroomed, and with them the singing-master profession; while psalm collections flooded the market to meet the demand for books. Then, as in England, the young products of the singing schools formed into choirs and began otherwise to take church musical matters into their own hands. Lining out was all but dead — in the towns — by 1779, when at Worcester, Massachusetts, the young singers drowned out their die-hard deacon. Symbolic of the passing of an era, he seized his hat and retired from the meeting-house in tears.

The church-singing renascence coincided with the emergence of colonial cultural self-consciousness. For instance, the Boston publisher, concert manager, and leader of the city militia band, Josiah Flagg, com-

[8] Quoted in Curwen, op. cit., p. 60.
[9] Quoted in Hazel G. Kinscella: *History Sings* (Lincoln, Nebraska, etc., 1940), p. 39.
[10] *The Secret Diary of William Byrd of Westover 1709–1712,* edited by Louis B. Wright and Marion Tinling (Richmond, 1941), pp. 272, 276.

piled in 1764 *A Collection of the Best Psalm Tunes* (the music engraved by Paul Revere), in which he apologizes that although he is indebted to the other side of the Atlantic for the tunes, "the Paper on which they are printed, is the Manufacture of our own Country."[11]

American self-consciousness in church music: (a) title page of Josiah Flagg's A Collection of the Best Psalm Tunes (Boston, 1764; engraved by Paul Revere), and (b) Flagg's patriotic preface to the collection.

This nationalist trend helped spur the popularity of the lusty "Musical Tanner" William Billings, the first American to make music his profession, composer of more than three hundred compositions, and the foremost exponent of the English fugal-tune vogue. Because his "fuguing-tunes" were in such individualistic contrast to the Handel-in-

[11] Josiah Flagg: *A Collection of the Best Psalm Tunes* (Boston, 1764), preface.

spired English variety, Billings has sometimes been called the inventor of the form. In his *Continental Harmony* he claimed for fuguing-tunes that they had

> more than twenty times the power of the old slow tunes, each part straining for the mastery and victory. The audience entertained and delighted, their minds surpassingly agitated and extremely fluctuated. . . . O ecstatis ! Rush on, you sons of harmony.[12]

In dismissing his lack of grounding in musical theory he said : "*Nature is the best Dictator,*" and "I don't think myself confined to any rules for composition laid down by any that went before me."[13] What he wrote, despite its crudities, was cheerful and virile. And anthems such as *The Lord is Risen Indeed*, since they could not be lined out, had the same decisive effect in overthrowing deaconing that fugal anthems in England had.

THE LORD IS RISEN INDEED[14]

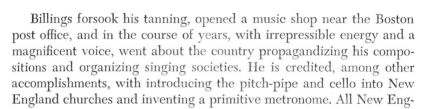

Billings forsook his tanning, opened a music shop near the Boston post office, and in the course of years, with irrepressible energy and a magnificent voice, went about the country propagandizing his compositions and organizing singing societies. He is credited, among other accomplishments, with introducing the pitch-pipe and cello into New England churches and inventing a primitive metronome. All New Eng-

[12] Quoted in Edwin Hall Pierce : "The Rise and Fall of the 'Fugue tune' in America," in the *Musical Quarterly*, XVI, 221.

[13] Quoted in Raymond Morin : "William Billings, Pioneer in American Music," in the *New England Quarterly*, XIV, 31–2.

[14] Quoted in Fisher, op. cit., p. 18, from William Billings's *Supplement to Suffolk Harmony* (1786). By permission of the publisher.

land was familiar with his fuguing-tunes by the time of the Revolution, when they spread as well through the south and were accepted there with equal fascination. His masterpiece, *Chester*, which he composed in 1770, had become a well-known sacred song when he reset patriotic words to it in 1778. In this version it rapidly became, throughout the states, the war hymn of the Revolution.

Nationalism in American music: "Chester" from William Billings: The Singing Master's Assistant.

This illustration of *Chester* is rearranged in a readable way on the next page.

William Bentley, a Salem preacher who knew Billings, wrote in 1800, two days after the composer's death, a soundly judged and somewhat wistful memorial:

> This self taught man thirty years ago had the direction of all the music of our Churches. His Reuben, as he whimsically called it, with all its great imperfections, had great fame and he may justly be considered as the father of our new England music. Many who have imitated have excelled him, but none of them had better original powers. His late attemps & without a proper education were the true cause of his inferior excellence. He taught the Singers at the Brattle street Church in 1778 with great approbation & his fame was great in the Churches. He was a singular man, of moderate size, short of one leg, with one eye, without any address, & with an uncommon negligence of person. Still he spake & sung & thought as a man above the common abilities. He died poor & neglected & perhaps did too much neglect himself.[15]

[15] *The Diary of William Bentley* (4 vols., Salem, Mass., 1907), II, 350–1.

Musicians may dimiss the works of Billings with an indulgent smile, but the historian cannot. For even the severe limitations of Billings's training and of American precedent in composition could not hold back a bursting bourgeois vitality, with which his strains are charged. Here

Let ty - rants shake their i———— ron rod,

And slav'ry clank her gall———— ing chains.

We fear them not, We—— trust———— in God,

New—— Eng-land's God———— for - ev———— 'er reigns.

in this awkward, medieval-sounding music, written during the fervor of war and imminent war, is the unrestrainable and resilient spirit that waged a victorious Revolution.

Following the Revolutionary heyday of Billings, the expanding number of American sacred composers either reacted back to the slow psalm pace or fugued to high heaven; and, as in England, it was the reactionary element that won out. By chance, this tendency was contemporaneous with the conservative reaction that produced the Constitution, and also with the predilection in the other arts for unadorned simplicity. Billings's fuguing-tunes gradually disappeared from song-books, as the simpler and more "correct" hymns of Watts and later Wesley and others took firmer hold.

Of the early American hymn-writers, one of the most acceptable to his time was a graduate of Rhode Island College, Andrew Law, who is believed to be the first composer in America to place the melody in the soprano. The first American, however, to produce a hymn that has been used continuously from his own time to the present was Oliver Holden, a Baptist carpenter turned singing-teacher, and an emigrant from Massachusetts who became a representative in the South Carolina legislature. He composed his tunes on a little pipe organ and harmonized them in the traditional manner of melody in the alto. His still-sung composition, dating from 1793, is the familiar setting of the poem *All Hail the Power of Jesus' Name*, which he called *Coronation*.

With the spread of hymnody in the last half of the eighteenth century, *The Bay Psalm Book* went out. The Puritans, even before the Revolution, were beginning generally to prefer the *Psalms* and *Hymns* of Watts over all other hymnbooks. The Anglicans clung to Sternhold and Hopkins or Tate and Brady long after the Revolution; while the Presbyterians split into "Old Side" and "New Side" over the singing issue : the Old Side kept the psalmody of Barton or Rous, and the New Side, to whom the ancient psalms had become "more and more flat, dull, insipid and undevotional," [16] turned to Watts or Tate and Brady. The Reformed Presbyterians, like the Quakers, did not countenance music in worship at all.

The controversy attending the introduction of musical instruments into church was coincidental with that over the introduction of hymnody. Cellos, which were making their entry into New England churches about the time of the Revolution, were greeted with such opposition that meeting-houses were called "catgut churches" or "anti-catgut churches" according as they accepted or rejected the instrument.

The cello (or bass viol, as it was then called) was followed by the flute, an inexpensive and very popular instrument in the eighteenth century, and later by the oboe, clarinet, and trombone. Even violins, which had been inseparably associated with tavern and dance-hall revelry, were finally accepted, suspiciously. Poorly heated churches made constant tuning of such instruments as were used — or their out-of-tune playing — a rather unreligious racket.

Organs, as well as an assortment of band instruments, had made their appearance in many market towns throughout England by 1770.

---

[16] Quoted in Henry Wilder Foote : *Three Centuries of American Hymnody* (Cambridge, Mass., 1940), pp. 152–3, from an undated manuscript journal of the trustees of the Presbyterian Church in New York.

A London teacher of psalmody was recommending organs in 1765 as "very convenient to drown the hideous cries of the people." [17] In America various sects in rare instances used organs early in the eighteenth century, among them German pietists in Pennsylvania, Reformed Dutch in New York, and Anglicans in Boston. But by and large it was near 1820 before the obstruction of cost and prejudice was sufficiently overcome for organs to begin to be widely installed. Their irresistible arrival — hand in hand with the general secularization of life in the eighteenth century — helped split the Puritan denomination in two. The orthodox (Congregational) branch (that whose collapse is commemorated by Holmes's *One-Hoss Shay*) subbornly rejected the innovation, while the liberal branch that tended toward Unitarianism just as resolutely adopted it.

There are said to have been fewer than twenty church organs in all New England in 1800, and the number for the rest of the country was probably less than that. The Puritans were by no means alone in their anti-organ prejudice, which was shared by practically every English dissenter sect. Anglicans, who had no such tradition, were the first of the English-speaking churchmen to introduce organs generally; which fact was forecast as early as 1713 by the famous probation of the Brattle organ. A wealthy Bostonian, Thomas Brattle, in 1711 imported for private use (which the Puritans approved) the first organ seen in New England, and at his death beqeathed it to the relatively enlightened Brattle Street Church. But the Puritan congregation refused it, so it went to the Anglican King's Chapel.

The Catholic congregations did not sing psalms or hymns, but their choirs and priests were trained in Gregorian chanting, which John Adams described in his diary as "exquisitely soft and sweet" when he attended St. Joseph's in Philadelphia in October 1774. "The scenery and the music are so calculated to take in mankind," he said, "that I wonder the Reformation ever succeeded." [18] In August 1774 the "old way" singing at a Presbyterian meeting-house in New York impressed Adams as "all the drawling, quavering discord in the world," [19] but later in the same month that he attended St. Joseph's, he referred to the singing at St. George's, a Methodist church in Philadelphia, as "very sweet and soft indeed; the finest music I have heard in any society, except the Moravians, and once at a church with the organ." [20]

The Moravians Adams mentioned were the same amazing group that moved Wesley to translate their hymns nearly twenty years before,

[17] Quoted in Curwen, op. cit., p. 10.
[18] Charles Francis Adams, ed. : *The Works of John Adams* (10 vols., Boston, 1850), II, 385.
[19] Ibid., 348.
[20] Ibid., 401.

and who migrated to Bethlehem, Pennsylvania, from Savannah via Philadelphia. They remained in constant touch with musical developments in Europe, maintained highly trained choirs and organists, and produced numerous original works. Among the latter were hymns prompted by American inland geography — for instance, those written in 1742 by the Moravian leader-bishop Count Zinzendorf, one describing the scene in Sickihillehocken, near Philadelphia, and another the Wyoming Valley in Pennsylvania, opening : *"Dort in der Fläche Wajomik."* Benjamin Franklin attended services at Bethlehem in 1756 and revealed mild astonishment in a letter to his wife that he "heard very fine music in the church — flutes, oboes, French horns and trumpets accompanied the organ."[21]

Probably no sect was so cosmopolitan as the Moravians. On the occasion of a "love feast" in 1745, for example, the German hymn *In dulci jubilo* was sung simultaneously in thirteen languages to instrumental accompaniment. Of all the customs at Bethlehem, however, the most distinctive was the use of trombone quartets from 1754 on ; for the trombone was considered a symbol of the "last trumpet" of the Bible, and on special holidays or at the death of a citizen the quartet intoned from the church belfry the chorale *A pilgrim us preceding*, which elsewhere became widely known by the German words translated *O sacred head now wounded.*

ANNOUNCEMENT OF DEATH[22]

Fifty miles west of Philadephia was the anomalous Ephrata Cloister, founded by German Dunkers in 1720, where women turned out handwritten and illuminated hymnbooks as in medieval monasteries, and where there was high-quality singing and hymn-writing, and compositions in imitation of the Æolian harp, in which a two- to seven-part choir sang in falsetto. This last was according to a system of harmony and vocal arrangement invented by Ephrata's leading light, Conrad Beissel, who trained the Cloister Sisters to celebrate the sunset and the

[21] Quoted in Virginia Larkin Redway : "Handel in Colonial and Post-Colonial America," in the *Musical Quarterly*, XXI, 200.

[22] Pennsylvania Society of the Colonial Dames of America : *Church Music and Musical Life in Pennsylvania in the Eighteenth Century* (3 vols., Philadelphia, 1926, 1927, 1938), II, 188.

midnight with it, and composed mystic hymns like *The Song of the Solitary and Deserted Turtle Dove.*

The most important church of the Lutheran Swedes was the Gloria

The music of the immigrant: two pages from the illuminated manuscript choral book of the Ephrata Cloister.
[By courtesy of the Library of Congress]

Dei, which is still standing in what is now Philadelphia. Its ministers were missionaries sent from Sweden, and its hymnbooks sent as gifts by the King. Services were held in Swedish, German, and English, though without organ.

These several, and similar, minority groups, while they by and large upheld superior church-musical standards, were isolated islands in the enveloping Anglo-Saxon culture. Their traditions apparently did not permeate far beyond the settlement limits and had no appreciable influence on the main currents of musical culture in this country.

Neither did Indian music, which the English only scorned, as did John Winthrop, Governor of Massachusetts, when he remarked that the "Indians sang themselves asleep with barbarous singing." [23] On the other hand, in every known case in which Indians were brought in contact with European psalms and hymns, they liked and sang them. The first instances were the sixteenth-century Huguenot singing on the east coast and the Anglican psalm-singing of Sir Francis Drake's men on the west coast. In 1661 John Eliot, the Cambridge-educated missionary who had translated the Bible into the Algonquin language for the Indians of Massachusetts, versified the psalms for them also. More decided missionary efforts were made a century later in Pennsylvania by the Moravians, who published their first hymnbook in the Delaware language in 1763.

The distinctively American development in church music turned out to be the folk-hymnody which sprang from the Great Awakening and the frontier. This was especially true after the east settled down to a scrupulous conformity to European "correct" hymn-writing.

The music of the Great Awakening was much more conservative at the beginning than it was after the movement had run its course awhile on the frontier. When, for instance, George Whitefield made his celebrated preaching tour through the colonies in 1739–41, he carried the *Hymns* and *Psalms* of Watts and the *Hymns and Sacred Poems* of the Wesleys. Jonathan Edwards had encouraged singing at Northampton from 1734, and by 1742 his congregation was so attached to the hymns of Watts that he had difficulty in reinstituting the old psalms on a fifty-fifty compromise. Although congregations such as that of Edwards sang wholeheartedly, the hymns and psalms were still lined out, two lines at a time, and the tempo may be described as stately.

Slow psalms and slow hymns could nowise satisfy the emotional zeal of the back-country folk, who resorted to their basic treasury of fiddle tunes and ballad tunes, set their own crude religious verse to them, added choruses and hallelujahs, and opened wide their mouths and sang.

Their grouping was principally Baptist and Methodist, augmented early in the nineteenth century by an increasing number of the Christian denomination. The Baptists, in the midst of their persecutions in

[23] Quoted in Roy Lamson, Jr. : "English Broadside Ballad Tunes of the 16th and 17th Centuries," *Papers Read at the International Congress of Musicology Held at New York Sep. 11th to 16th, 1939* (Richmond, 1944), p. 119.

England, had alternately banned and admitted music in worship. "Why not sing our sermons if words gain in force by being set to music ?" [24] a leader of the General Baptists, Gilbert Boyce, had ranted in opposition to singing. But the controversy was virtually resolved by the time Baptists arrived in America in substantial numbers, and in England they even discarded lining out late in the eighteenth century. (As late as 1844 the Methodist Conference condemned the innovation of singing a whole verse at a time as being unfair especially to the worshippers of the poorer classes.)

Baptists in America no doubt used *The Bay Psalm Book* until, in 1740 in Boston, they changed to Tate and Brady and later, in some places, to Watts. But during the time that singing schools were effecting a reform of church singing, the Baptists of the hinterland were turning to the new popular religious music, known variously as camp-meeting songs, folk-hymns, or spirituals. The words of these hymns were cheerless, dealing mainly with death and divine vengeance; to wit:

> *Remember, sinful youth, you must die, you must die,*
> *Remember sinful youth, you must die.*[25]

But they were sung from the lyric sheets or tuneless books, or from nothing at all, to melodies often gay and even triumphant — any folk-melody that struck a rhymer's fancy, including *Barbara Allen, Greensleeves*, and *Turkey in the Straw*. The rhymers were in many cases the barely literate circuit preachers themselves, who led their own singing. In their hands, lining out veered to a solo-and-chorus form, which itself was a step in the direction of freedom from established criteria. The body of Baptist folk-hymnody was taking shape around 1770, at the very time that America in other spheres was discovering its nationality.

A similar tendency to folk-music was observable among the Methodists, though it was suppressed by the injunction of Wesley to "sing no hymns of your own composing" [26] and by that of their American leaders to respect the authority of the conference and purchase no hymnbooks but those signed by the bishops. The aim of the Methodist leadership was to maintain high standards of hymnody. And the Methodists of the tidewater did largely sing from Wesley hymnbooks; but the Methodists of the piedmont irresistibly followed the call of the frontier and the Baptist folk-hymn lead.

The earliest folk-hymnody and folk-hymnbooks were products of rural New England. The singing schools, however, brought in stand-

[24] Quoted in Curwen, op. cit., p. 56.
[25] Quoted in Foote, op. cit., p. 175.
[26] Quoted in George Pullen Jackson : *White and Negro Spirituals* (New York, 1943), p. 55.

ards of art hymns and hymn-singing that prevented an entrenchment of folk-hymnody there. Folk-hymns, too, were best adapted to out-of-door services, for which southern weather was more conducive, as well as the lack of New England's communal life in the southern west and the consequent eager welcome of any kind of social gatherings. So while losing ground in the north, folk-hymnody spread to the south and became a southern institution. It survives today chiefly among the Primitive Baptists of the south, though also in isolated areas elsewhere, such as in New Jersey. Billings's fuguing-tunes also spread southward, from rural New England singing schools; and hymns of the fuguing type too are still sung in the upland south.

The folk-hymn tradition was about thirty years old when the first camp meetings were held, in the summer of 1799, in Kentucky. In the next eight years they were being held over the whole country, and mass emotional excitement in them, as in gatherings of the Great Awakening for decades past, was so great that the unrestrained singing was not only accompanied with the familiar shouts and hand-clapping, but with country-dance routines, rolling on the ground, shrieks and wailing, and simulations of epileptic fits.

The camp-meeting custom was exported to England, where the Primitive Methodists were organized in 1812. After that, American camp-meeting songs were sung in revival circles throughout the British Isles up to about 1870.

Camp-meeting songs, or white spirituals, were predecessors of Negro spirituals, which were a nineteenth-century development. The Anglican planters had been reluctant to permit their slaves a common organization, even that of a church. So the militant missionizing of the Baptists and Methodists was the first large-scale introduction of Christian music as well as Christian dogma among American Negroes. And from the white spirituals, which were part and parcel of this missionizing, the colored converts adapted their own similar body of religious song. Since the Negroes became acquainted first with the old psalms and hymns, before the missionaries were singing folk-hymns, those too were incorporated somewhat into the Negro musical tradition. The draggy, lined-out singing of that time was the probable partial origin of Negro "surge" songs, which embedded a white hymn melody beyond recognition in elaborate modal ornamentation.

Negroes, naturally, were singing in America before they ever learned white melodies. What their singing was like may be surmised from the Cherokee Indian music of the southeast, which differs from other Indian music for having been influenced by contact and intermixture with African music.

It can be shown that, thematically, in every case, Negro spirituals are adapted versions of white spirituals. It can also be shown that white folk-hymnody reinforced a pre-existing African folk-type. For instance, the music of all Negro Africa is dominated by the prevalence of the solo-chorus technique — a technique very rare among Indians, except those of the southeast, who acquired it from Negroes before the advent of white folk-hymnody. The calls and shouts characteristic of white hymnody were also characteristic of African folk-singing. So the Negroes evidently incorporated the more highly developed white tunes into their own independently developed folk-musical forms. When secular Negro folk-music has been as thoroughly investigated as the religious, this may become even more evident.[27]

The proselytizing white hymnody did not penetrate to the Negroes of New Orleans, the first of whom were not landed in Louisiana until 1712, and who already by 1725 sufficiently outnumbered the white population to prevent white influence of any kind from greatly suppressing their African heritage. This heritage in music did, however, merge with French secular folk-music. That its indigenous African character persisted in some strength is evidenced by the long-later manifestation of it — as combined with other influences — in jazz.

White spirituals — the folk-hymns of the frontier — started with old English tunes and English religious ideas, but they were not an English end-product. They were a new cultural contribution, which was American. And some of them, such as *Poor Wayfaring Stranger*, are unexcelled expressions of devout and humble feeling.

POOR WAYFARING STRANGER [28]

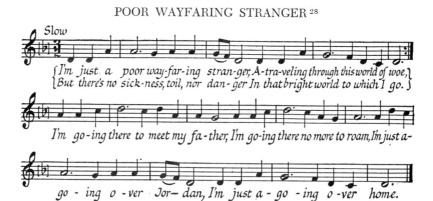

[I'm just a poor way-far-ing stran-ger, A-tra-veling through this world of woe,]
[But there's no sick-ness, toil, nor dan-ger In that bright world to which I go.]

I'm go-ing there to meet my fa-ther, I'm go-ing there no more to roam, I'm just a-

go - ing o -ver Jor- dan, I'm just a - go -ing o -ver home.

[27] Cf. George Herzog : "African Influences in North American Indian Music," *Papers Read at the International Congress of Musicology*, op. cit., and Jackson, op. cit.

[28] John A. Lomax and Alan Lomax : *Our Singing Country* (New York : The Macmillan Company ; 1941), p. 37. By permission of John Lomax.

To get into the spirit of folk-hymnody is to perceive something of the force of what gave it rise. For folk-hymnody was the music of the westward movement of the eighteenth century. It was a crusading music, though not actually articulate as such. It betokened the toilsome but triumphant conquest of the wilderness, and its zeal, together with the vigor of secular folk-dances, attested the vitality behind the purpose.

Art music in eighteenth-century America

Cultural sophistication is at bottom urban, and the great majority of America's early settlers came not from urban centers but from farms and small towns. To them art music was a luxury, entirely inappropriate while the bare business of subsistence occupied so much of their time. Any notions to the contrary were further discouraged by the limitations and expensiveness of shipping-space for the necessary instruments.

Entering the eighteenth century, however, America enjoyed an expanding, if modest, prosperity; and with better shipping-accommodations also, more than a select few were able to acquire the materials for serious music study. One indication is a music-shop advertisement that appeared in the *Boston News-Letter* in April 1716 giving notice of the receipt from London of flageolets, flutes, oboes, bass viols, and violins, and reiterating a previous announcement of a stringing-tuning service for virginals and spinets. From about 1720 to the Revolution, professional musicians, instrument-makers, music dealers and music-publishers increased steadily in number. Their business growth was proportionate to the growth of cities, and the musical capitals were six : Boston, New York, Philadelphia, Williamsburg, Charleston, and (after the Revolution) Baltimore, which edged out the earlier bid of Annapolis.

Although there were, to be sure, individual differences in the art-musical life of these cities, its basic similarity was the more remarkable feature. The similarity bespoke an interrelationship arising from self-conscious imitation of the mother country.

Quite apart from this development, in an incredible cultural isolation, was Bethlehem, Pennsylvania, which was unique in secular as well as religious music. Here the Moravians early established orchestras, string quartets, and choral groups, and were the first to perform in America such works as Haydn's *The Creation* and *The Seasons*. They also fostered customs like marching to harvest playing band music and, from 1744 on, nightly serenading by the young men of the town, who, incidentally, serenaded Washington when he passed through Bethlehem in 1782.

In the seaboard cities the cultivation of art music, rather less admirable than in the towns of German background, fell into three broad categories : concerts, opera, and oratorio, which last was presented in the form of church concerts. Of these three categories, secular concerts had the closest aristocratic connections. The first concert patrons were wealthy merchants and planters and the dignitaries of colonial government, or coteries of musical dilettantes. Oftener than not, the sponsors were "Tory" Anglicans, and concerts were customarily held in conjunction with the grand balls and salon parties of high society. As a rule, only the wealthy subscribers and their guests were admitted to a concert. Even when subscription concerts shortly after the Revolution became public "city concerts" in name, they remained more or less exclusive aristocratic functions in fact.

Pre-Revolutionary concerts were almost entirely of the English chamber variety — solo sonatas and suites, duos, trios, quartets ; some vocal compositions, and some for small orchestral ensembles. With little question, the composers whose works were often played were those whose works were also often played in London, particularly Corelli, Vivaldi, Domenico Scarlatti, Purcell, and Handel. A typical selection would have been Handel's Fifth Clavier Suite with its *Harmonious Blacksmith* air, played on a harpsichord or, especially in post-Revolutionary concerts, occasionally on a piano ; for pianos were being manufactured in Philadelphia as early as 1775, and had begun to be imported in America even before that.

HARMONIOUS BLACKSMITH AIR [29]

The Revolution of course brought a practical cessation of concerts, except in those cities occupied for a longer or shorter time by the British, where musical redcoat officers, with the help of army band musicians and Tory ladies, organized musical parties, which included concerts of the same general type that those cities had known before. Generals Howe, Clinton, and Burgoyne merely substituted for the former civilian sponsors, so that the caste character of concerts was unaltered. The cities in point were New York in particular, which was

[29] Louis Oesterle, ed. : *The Golden Treasury of Piano-Music* (3 vols., New York, 1904), III, 137.

British-occupied from 1776 to 1783, Boston, and Philadelphia. The other notorious Tory center, Charleston, happened to be occupied by the British so late in the war that bitter military seriousness prevented anything further than a few routs (big evening parties), dinners, and balls which did not nearly equal the earlier festive occasions in the other three cities.

The available programs from post-Revolutionary concerts show the same predominance of Handel, Haydn, Pleyel, and Stamitz that contemporaneous London programs show. Less frequently performed were works of Grétry, Mozart, Corelli, Daveaux, Cimarosa, Gluck, and the younger Bachs.[30] After 1790, especially in the south, American concert programs contained a substantially larger percentage of French works than did English programs because of the talented refugees from the revolutions in France and Santo Domingo who quickly augmented the personnel of American orchestras.

Until the influx of these French musicians, the programs of each city featured compositions of local composers about as often as they did those of the most popular European masters. Some of these local favorites were native Americans, some English immigrants. The latter were by and large second-rate musicians unable to find adequate employment in England who, in America, associated themselves mainly with the theater and ballad-opera, directing from the pit and writing patriotic pastiches and marches; or they turned (or remained) organists. Alexander Reinagle, Benjamin Carr, James Hewitt, and William Selby were perhaps the best-known of these Englishmen. William Brown of Philadelphia is an example of the native composer; in 1787 he published three rondos for piano or harpsichord.

The aristocratic French refugees, because of their superior training, outclassed the local American musicians, and as the latter's efforts were dispensed with, American concert life took on a degree of French rococo elegance, although, to be sure, it was still in the main the British lead that concerts attempted to follow.

From the Revolution to the French incursion, and even afterward, American concert orchestras consisted in large part, as might be expected, of German-born residents of the American cities. And the American orchestras, which divided their appearances between concert rooms and the theater, were probably on a par with orchestras of English cities, excepting London.

Nearly a decade before the Revolution, American orchestras were adopting the Vauxhall Gardens custom of London; in the extended post-Revolutionary democratization, concert programs carried even

[30] Cf. O. G. Sonneck : *Early Concert-Life in America, 1731–1800* (Leipzig. 1907).

farther the popularizing, diversifying trend of England; and toward the end of the century the concert season shifted from winter to summer.

Following European practice, the first movement of a symphony or a sinfonia was ordinarily played separately as an overture, and other movements might be sandwiched in later on among chamber works, dance music, refreshments, and vocal solos. As soloists, famous prima donnas began to be imported in the decade of the 1790's. Both they and local soloists sang arias from Italian opera (Piccini's, for example) and from oratorio, especially "Comfort ye my people" and "I know that my Redeemer liveth," from the *Messiah,* and polished British ballads such as those of Arne. The favorite bravura song of concert singers after the Revolution was *The Soldier Tired of War's Alarms* by Arne, first published in America in 1789.

Ballad-opera, which was almost the sole operatic fare of early America, had the earmarks of the popular theater of the day, including the sprinkling of street tunes of each production and the catering to theatrical vulgarity. Still, the opera was an event for the aristocracy, which sat in boxes in formal attire.

The Beggar's Opera reached New York in 1750, after that type of ballad-opera had gone out of style in England; imitations of *The Beggar* were heard in America thirteen years earlier than *The Beggar* itself. Ballad-opera production in America was the virtual monopoly of the London Company of Comedians, which began its American career in Williamsburg late in 1752 under the management of William Hallam, a British capitalist, and was reorganized in subsequent years as the American Company and later the Old American Company.

Upon the resolution of Congress in 1774 to discourage "every species of extravagance and dissipation" to meet the straitened times, Hallam's company withdrew to the West Indies for the duration. But as the British and Tories kept concerts alive where they were in control, so they also, and to a greater extent, organized play and ballad-opera performances. In addition, neutral southern troupes, particularly the Baltimore Company, operated along the seaboard to New York without interference from either belligerent.

Within two or three years following the war the Old American Company re-established a year-round circuit, with concentration on New York and Philadelphia, giving as many as three performances a week from an operatic repertory that, though subordinate to straight plays, included between fifty and sixty works, a number of them American.[31]

[31] Cf. Sonneck : *Early Opera in America* (New York, 1915).

Although much of its satire was lost on American audiences, *The Beggar's Opera* during the whole generation before the Revolution was the most reliable single offering, and after the war for the balance of the century still held a respectable rank in the repertory. Some idea of its appeal may be got from an attractive sequence, *Before the barn-door crowing*, to an old English air, *All in a Misty Morning*, which was followed by a sprightly dance of the female chorus.

BEFORE THE BARN-DOOR CROWING

Arne's *Love in a Village* was also long-lived in America, with an imposing list of performances from 1766 through 1799; though it was

only one of a large fund of favorites. *The Duenna* (1775), which was the most popular opera in England in the eighteenth century since *The Beggar,* was at least fairly well known in America. Its author was Richard Sheridan (*The Rivals, School for Scandal*), and the composer-compiler of the music was his father-in-law, Thomas Linley. In America the most successful opera after *The Beggar* was *The Poor Soldier* (1783), composed by William Shield of the Covent Garden Theater, to a libretto by an Irishman, John O'Keefe. Season after season in America it achieved the unprecedented regular run of eighteen nights — a popularity that was partly accountable by Thomas Wignell, one of the leading actors of the day, who played the chief character, Darby. Often the opera was acted at President Washington's desire when he visited the John Street Theater in New York.

Sheridan's *Duenna,* about the ingénues befooling their lovers, was too much sophisticated tomfoolery for thorough American appreciation, while Shield's *Poor Soldier* was perhaps too unsophisticated for catch-all English appreciation. Featuring a couple of unkempt characters, Patrick and Darby, speaking and singing Irish brogue, *The Poor Soldier* was much the more comprehensible to the American cultural orientation.

French players, on their own or incorporated into American companies, brought various French and Italian light operas (including *Le Devin du village* and *La Serva Padrona*) to the American stage during the decade of the 1790's. Their nominal headquarters was New Orleans, which, though a lively place, could not yet claim cultural pre-eminence, because its population was only ten thousand, more than half of whom were Negro slaves.

Probably the earliest and best American imitation of *The Beggar* was *The Disappointment* (1767) by an unidentified Andrew Barton. It was withheld from performance because of "personal reflections," but was reissued later in the century in an inferior expanded version. The characters have names like Rattletrap and Washball, and the plot involves men duped to search for hidden treasure — a satire on Philadelphians who were at that time seeking the treasure of the pirate Blackbeard. The original version contains the first known reference in American literature to *Yankee Doodle,* to which tune one of the dupes sings:

> *O! how joyful shall I be*
> *When I get de money,*
> *I will bring it all to dee;*
> *O! my diddling honey!* [33]

[33] Quoted in Sonneck: *Miscellaneous Studies in the History of Music* (N.Y., 1921), p. 30.

Little serious attempt was made to alter the British institution of ballad-opera by composers in America until 1794, when the orchestra leader James Hewitt set a libretto, *Tammany*, about the Indian chief and a villain from Columbus's band and attempted to utilize Cherokee Indian themes.

American titles like *The Sicilian Romance, Slaves in Algiers, The Archers* (William Tell), and *Ariadne Abandoned* began to make way in the final years of the century for titles such as *The Fourth of July* and *The Launch; or, Huzza for the Constitution!* — the latter by the French immigrant, Victor Pelissier, who had been trained at the Paris Conservatoire. Glorified masques were also appearing, such as *Americana and Elutheria* and the *Apotheosis of Franklin*.

In Boston, Philadelphia, and even New York, prejudice against the theater, dancing, and other aspects of musical life required many decades to wear down sufficiently for unconfined musical cultivation. And although the first concert on record in America was presented at Boston (under the auspices of Anglicans, in 1731), musical refinement first flourished in the more worldly south, which was comparatively free of retarding religious prejudices.

Charleston, proportionately perhaps the gayest and richest city in America, had a concert, in the Council Chamber, a year later than the first known Boston concert, and, like later concerts there and at the Queenstreet Theater, it was followed by a ball. In 1733 Charleston had the first American song recital, and in 1735 the first performance in America of a ballad-opera, which was *Flora*, one of the imitations of *The Beggar's Opera*.

Between 1735 and 1760 Charleston concerts seem practically to have died out, in favor of ballad-opera and, even more, the numerous balls and dancing assemblies given by socialites and dancing masters. (Dancing masters in the colonies were often also fencing teachers.) However, the Cecilia Society, founded in 1762, not only took Charleston aristocratic music in hand and reinstituted concerts, but advertised in Boston, Philadelphia, and New York for musicians.

Josiah Quincy, the sensitive, tuberculous Boston patriot, in his *Journal of a Voyage to South Carolina*, recounts his impressions of a Charleston concert of March 1773 and, perhaps unconsciously, reveals the social-caste significance of such occasions :

> The concert-house is a large, inelegant building, situated down a yard. . . . The music was good — the two base viols and French horns were grand. One Abercrombie, a Frenchman just arrived, played the first violin, and a solo incomparably better than any one I ever heard. He cannot speak a word of English, and has a salary of five hundred

guineas a year from the St. Cecelia Society. There were upwards of two hundred and fifty ladies present, and it was called no great number. In loftiness of headdress, these ladies stoop to the daughters of the north, — in richness of dress, surpass them. In taciturnity during the performances, greatly before our [New England] ladies ; in noise and flirtation after the music is over, pretty much on a par. . . . The gentlemen, many of them dressed with richness and elegance, uncommon with us : many with swords on. We had two macaronis present, just arrived from London.[34]

Charleston took up the open-air concerts of Vauxhall Gardens in 1767, serving tea and coffee ; fireworks, magicians, and tight-rope walkers turned these fetes, also, in the direction of vaudeville. The gravitation of well-to-do French Huguenots to Charleston had already given the city a French touch when the refugee French of the 1790's made Charleston musical life very nearly predominantly French. In 1794, in fact, the Vauxhall Gardens fashion was styled explicitly as "after the Parisian manner." [35]

In Virginia a chief aristocratic feature was the chamber concerts in the ballroom of the Governor's palace at Williamsburg, which were scrupulously copied after the precedent of similar functions in England. All told, in fact, Williamsburg musical life reflected the express desire of the inhabitants to "live in the same neat Manner, dress after the same Modes, and behave themselves exactly as the Gentry in London." [36]

More significant than the concerts, and opera at the Play House, were the grand balls in the palace ballroom and in the Apollo Room of Raleigh Tavern, the famous Williamsburg inn. A dignified minuet opened each ball, followed by lively cotillions and Virginia reels, which were interspersed with the formal gavotte. This was in keeping with the British custom, wherein formal dances were alternated with country dances. The American ball always ended with a Virginia reel, especially to *Roger de Coverley*, an English tune in $\frac{9}{8}$ time first printed in 1685.

The planter William Byrd, whose diary so often contains the entry : "Then I danced my dance," tells of a dinner in Williamsburg in 1711 at the Governor's home where Byrd was the moving spirit in rounding up a couple of fiddlers, sending them and candles ahead to the Capitol and holding a ball there until midnight. Through the decades he never

---

[34] Quoted in Sonneck : *Early Opera in America*, pp. 51–2.

[35] Quoted in Irving Schwerké : "The French in Early Musical Life in America," *Légion d'Honneur*, III, 110.

[36] Quoted in program notes for the harpischord and violin concerts of October 10–15, 1938, which were part of the painstaking modern reconstruction of colonial Williamsburg.

lost his enthusiasm for dancing. In an April entry of 1741 he can still confess : "At night the women got me to quadrille." [37]

It was as an indispensable ornament to prove their high breeding that the patrician southerners provided instruction in dancing and playing for their children, sometimes importing tutors from abroad. They designated it "dance day" when a dancing master would give lessons at a plantation home and the young people of neighboring estates would come to share them. The extent of this musical cultivation is revealed in a letter (of 1774) of Philip Fithian, a Princeton graduate just arrived at a plantation in Westmoreland County, Virginia to tutor the children of the wealthy Robert Carter family :

> Mr. Carter is practicing this evening on the guitar. He has here at home a harpsichord, forte-piano, harmonica [musical glasses], guitar, violin, and German flutes ; and at Williamsburg, he has a good pipe organ. Mr. Christian, in the dancing room, teaches the children country-dances and minuets. There a number of young persons are moving easily about to the sound of well-performed music, and with perfect regularity. Again in the evening, when candles are lighted, they repair to the drawing room. First, each couple dances a minuet, then all join, as before, in the country dances. The eldest daughter plays well on keyed instruments.[38]

Accomplished ladies of the colonial south could play the spinet, harpsichord, or guitar. Still in the drawing-room at Mount Vernon is the thousand-dollar harpsichord Washington bought for his adopted daughter, Nellie Custis. But it was considered unladylike for girls to learn the violin or flute, which two instruments were among the distinguishing paraphernalia of southern gentlemen. Patrick Henry was said to be the worst violinist in Virginia next to Thomas Jefferson. Jefferson used to rise at five in the morning to practice and was an eager purchaser of the latest minuets.

There was another type of Virginian violinist, most graphically described by the British captain Thomas Anbury, who was captured at Saratoga and hospitably interned near Charlottesville. Anbury depicts the "gentleman" who, between rides round his plantation, spent his day sitting on the porch floor scraping at a fiddle and drinking peach brandy, while his illegitimate mulatto children ran about the yard.

[37] *Another Secret Diary of William Byrd of Westover, 1739–1741, With Letters & Literary Exercises 1696–1726,* edited by Maude H. Woodfin, decoded by Marion Tinling (Richmond, 1942), p. 149.

[38] Quoted in Kinscella, op. cit., p. 56. "German" flutes were the modern transverse instruments, as distinguished from the now obsolete "beak" flutes, which were blown at one end. Fithian, after a year with the Carters, became a Presbyterian minister, married in 1775, and died as a Revolutionary soldier in 1776.

In Philadelphia it would have been difficult to escape the pervasive influence of the renowned author of ballad verses, publisher of music, and patron of the arts, Benjamin Franklin. It was he who perfected Gluck's drinking-glasses into that curious instrument the harmonica, a set of revolving glass bands arranged as a xylophone and played by

Early American composers: portrait of Francis Hopkinson by Robert Edge Pine.

[By courtesy of the Historical Society of Pennsylvania]

rubbing the moistened fingertips over them. He gave frequent recitals on the instrument in his home; it was also featured in chamber concerts in the other major American cities; and for a long while it was a fad in Europe, for which even Beethoven composed pieces. Among his other musical activities, Franklin composed at least one string quartet. In fact, there is probably nothing he did not do at least once.

The center of Philadelphia musical culture, before the Revolution more conspicuously, was a distinguished group of amateurs including the violinist Governor John Penn, grandson of the founder of Pennsylvania. This group met for sessions of chamber music in the home of Francis Hopkinson, who had begun his artistic career under the encouragement of William Smith, provost of the Philadelphia Academy, and owned probably the most complete musical library in America. Hopkinson, who directed the ensemble from the harpsichord, was a signer of the Declaration of Independence, designer of the American flag (1777), judge of the admiralty for Pennsylvania, a poet and inventor, a painter pupil of Benjamin West, the successor of his English music teacher as organist of Christ Church, versifier of the psalms for the New York Reformed Dutch, and the quintessence of the charming colonial dilettante. John Adams described him in a letter to his wife:

> He is one of your pretty, little, curious, ingenious men. His head is not bigger than a large apple. . . . I have not met with anything in natural history more amusing and entertaining than his personal appearance — yet he is genteel and well bred and is very social.[39]

Hopkinson was the first native American composer, preceding even Billings by about a decade. A song he wrote in 1759, when he was twenty-two, is the earliest surviving secular composition from the colonial period. It was a setting of Thomas Parnell's *Love and Innocence* which he entitled *My Days Have Been So Wondrous Free* and patterned after the European fashion of polished, romanticized pastorals. Also in the European fashion, he indicated only the melody and bass, leaving the performer to fill in the harmony as he played.

MY DAYS HAVE BEEN SO WONDROUS FREE [40]

[39] Charles Francis Adams, ed.: *Letters of John Adams, Addressed to His Wife* (2 vols., Boston, 1841), I, 157.

[40] John Tasker Howard: *Our American Music* (New York: Thomas Y. Crowell Co.; 1929), p. 38. By permission of the publisher.

Hopkinson's songs were known only to a small circle, since they were not published until the twentieth century. In 1789 he sent copies of a group of eight to his friends Washington and Jefferson. Washington replied from Mount Vernon :

> I can neither sing one of the songs, nor raise a single note on any instrument. . . . But I have, however, one argument which will prevail with persons of true taste (at least in America) — I can tell them that *it is the production of Mr. Hopkinson.*[41]

Jefferson replied from Paris, referring specifically to the last of the eight selections :

> . . . while my elder daughter was playing it on the harpischord, I happened to look toward the fire & saw the younger one all in tears. I asked her if she was sick ? She said "no ; but the tune was so mournful."[42]

Jefferson, in other letters, was enthusiastic about Hopkinson's invention for improved quilling of the harpsichord, which was prevented from universal adoption because the piano superseded the harpsichord in a matter of years.

Hopkinson's most ambitious creative undertaking was *The Temple of Minerva*, a semi-operatic allergory in two scenes, performed in the presence of the French minister and the Washingtons in 1781. It was in line with the blatant postwar patriotism of musical and theatrical creativity. The goddess Minerva and her high priest, together with the Genius of America and the Genius of France, unite in laudation of the French-American alliance and of Washington. The music has not survived.

Opera in Philadelphia, in spite of the governorship of the musical Penn, had only slightly less opposition than straight drama. Yet, both before the war and after, the biggest success of ballad-opera companies was usually in Philadelphia. Opposition to them took the typical tone of a card addressed to the *Pennsylvania Gazette* in 1773 over the signature of Philadelphus : "It is a matter of real sorrow and distress to many sober inhabitants of different denominations to hear of the return of those strolling Comedians, who are travelling thro' America propagating vice and immorality."[43] After the war the opposition took its stand behind the anti-theater law of 1778, which was not repealed until 1789. As the founder of English opera, Davenant, had got round the Puritan theatrical prohibition in England by using the word "opera,"

---

[41] Sonneck : *Francis Hopkinson* (Washington, D.C., 1905), p. 114.
[42] Quoted in ibid., p. 115.
[43] Quoted in Sonneck : *Early Opera in America*, p. 49.

so now the American Company smuggled in opera by using the word "lecture" and "pantomime."

The first performance of *The Poor Soldier* in Philadelphia was as a puppet show (1787) on the third floor of a downtown building, the voices being those of players of the newly opened Southwark Theater. Since by the time of the Constitutional Convention it was established that musical entertainments had not quite the stigma of spoken drama, the Southwark Theater was called an opera house, probably the first building so called in America.

Over the objections of the clergy in New York, ballad-opera was successfully reinstituted there after the war; in fact, it did not have to be called "lectures" after a short while. And when New York became the seat of the national government, in 1789, the presence of the theater-going President helped cause business to boom at the reopened John Street Theater of the Old American Company.

The enlarged postwar concerts in New York were presented at the City Tavern and Corre's Hotel. Open-air concerts had been known as early as 1765, between selections featuring fireworks, wine, alamode beef, tarts and cakes. Toward the close of the century there were no less than three New York Vauxhall Gardens, at one of which the chief attraction was ice cream.

That earlier-mentioned first known concert in America, a "Concert of Music on Sundry Instruments," was presented in 1731 by the versatile Peter Pelham, at his "great Room" in Boston. Pelham was an engraver, dancing master, boarding-school keeper, and tobacco dealer. From the following year until 1744, Boston concerts were customarily held in the Concert Room in Wing's Lane near the Town Dock. From 1744 Faneuil Hall was the accepted place, and from 1755 the Concert Hall in Queenstreet, where also a William Turner taught "the polite arts of dancing and fencing in the newest and most approved method." [44]

Boston's anti-theater blue law of 1750 does not appear to have been relaxed until 1793; but though the attorney general raided a Boston opera performance in 1792, opera there was never entirely suppressed. Also, although the Puritans of Boston in general continued to harbor reservations toward fine music, and were still so musically unsophisticated in 1790 as to prefer Billings to Handel, an admixture of Anglicans kept concerts extant.

Artistic development does not usually thrive in compartments. For instance, when the Puritans disapproved of instruments in church, their

[44] Quoted in Carl E. Lindstrom : "William Billings and His Times," in the *Musical Quarterly*, XXV, 489.

cultivation of instrumental music outside of church was anything but stimulated. The Puritan attitude was not directed against music so much as it was in part an inevitable carry-over of other repressions of mind. Yet the propensity of American art at this time was toward plainness to the point of severity, and it could be that finished art music did not appeal to Puritan taste, in so far as that taste was receptive to other than literary art forms.

Nowhere, in any case, is the Anglican-aristocrat-Tory alignment against Puritan-bourgeois-Whig more clearly drawn than in pre-Revolutionary and Revolutionary Boston music. Billings, self-taught champion of the militant middle class and renowned among the body of Puritans, taught his fuguing-tunes to the religious-minded youth (though not merely Puritan youth, and not without Anglican encouragement). On the other hand, William Selby, organist of King's Chapel and an Anglican from England, managed the elite Boston concerts of European masters for high society. Concert tickets were sold at the British Coffee House. The British soldiers were of course at home among the Anglicans — or at any rate more at home than among the Puritans, whom they often shocked with their worldly ways. And not only did the redcoat bandsmen sometimes furnish talent for the concert orchestra, but imperial soldiers attended the concerts. For instance, Lieutenant John Barker "of the King's own regiment" noted in his diary for November 21, 1774 that he "Went this eveng. to the Concert and heard the most miserable of all female Singers. . . ."[45]

The various singing societies of the colonial cities were concerned almost solely with religious music — anthems and oratorio — and their concerts were church functions. Only on rare occasions did they participate in secular celebrations, as when a Boston singing society welcomed Washington on his arrival at the triumphal arch in October 1789 with an ode written to the march from Handel's *Judas Maccabæus*.

Probably the biggest event for American singing societies in the eighteenth century was their effort in 1786 in the several cities to imitate the Handel Commemoration Festival of 1784 at Westminster Abbey in which on two successive days a chorus of two hundred and seventy-five and an orchestra of two hundred and fifty presented a concert of Handel's compositions. The nearest American approach to this festival in size was the concert at the Reformed German Church in Philadelphia, where two hundred and thirty voices and fifty instruments performed anthems of American composers, including William Billings, and ended with the Hallelujah Chorus. Two thousand tickets were sold, the proceeds from which went to charity.

[45] Quoted in ibid., XXV, 491

In New York, at the Assembly Room on Broadway, Alexander Reinagle, the pianist and ballad-opera composer from Portsmouth, England, presented a "Grand Concert" which included a violin concerto, a piano sonata, and the first movement of three Haydn symphonies, and in the second part, solo vocal selections from Handel's *Messiah* and *Samson*, a duet, a song, and a Piccini opera aria in Italian.

In Boston the festival imitation took the form of a great church service conducted at Chapel Church by our friend William Selby, leader of the Boston Musical Society who had been organist of St. Sepulchre's in London. The choir sang selections from the *Messiah* and one from *Samson*, and at the organ, among other works, Selby played one of his own organ concertos and concluded with a Bach sinfonia. The proceeds went to prisoners.

The first time Americans heard the *Messiah* (which was earlier than the European continent heard it) was the occasion when William Tuckey, who had been vicar choral at the cathedral of Bristol, presented seventeen numbers of the oratorio at Mr. Burns's Room in New York in 1770. The singing was preceded by instrumental selections, including a French horn concerto. The concert began at six p.m., with a price of eight shillings a ticket.

In spite of the idolization of Handel, Benjamin Franklin, who was not quite accepted in elite social circles, typified the American bourgeois repugnance to the artificialities of oratorio and Italian opera. Although acknowledging Handel's greatness, he had little use for that master's disregard of language. In a letter from London to his brother Peter, he noted that a typical song from *Judas Maccabæus* included the following defects and improprieties of common speech : wrong placing the accent, drawling, stuttering, unintelligibleness, tautology, and screaming without cause.

> The fine singer, in the present mode [he said], stifles all the hard consonants, and polishes away all the rougher parts of words that serve to distinguish them from each other, so that you hear nothing but an admirable pipe, and understand no more of the song than you would from its tune, played on any other instrument.[46]

The art-musical activity of the cities of eighteenth-century America was not much below English standards, and well exceeded similar activity in cities of comparable size in America today. Yet it was extremely limited in its place in eighteenth-century American culture as a whole. An English musician, John Owen Jacobi, though he played the organ at Trinity Church, Newport, the most magnificent organ in America at

[46] Quoted in Elie Siegmeister, ed. : *The Music Lover's Handbook* (New York, 1943), pp. 668–71.

the time, wrote to a friend in England what musicians were to say in
one way or another in much of America ever afterward :

> The want of instruments, together with the Niggardliness of the people
> in this Place, and their not having a taste for Musick, render it im-
> possible for anyone of my profession to get a competent maintenance
> here and the Feuds and Animosities are so great concerning their Gov-
> ernment that a Man can take but little Satisfaction in being among
> them, so that it is no better than burying oneself alive.[47]

Popular music

Dancing, sleighing, and serenading were among the major convivi-
alities involving popular music ; for until the Revolution, when it took
on more profound implications, popular music was, generally speaking,
the social music of youth, mostly the youth of the towns and cities. But
from the very first, their gaiety felt the restraints that the aged would
impose. In 1625 (before he left England) the Reverend John Cotton
pronounced in regard to dancing that he did not object to certain types
of religious dancing and dancing to the praise of conquerors, as were
found in the Old Testament. "Only lascivious dancing to wanton ditties, and in amorous gestures and wanton dalliances, especially after
great feasts, I would bear witness against, as a great flabella libidinis." [48]

This more or less official Puritan attitude was outraged just two
years later by the colonists at Merriemount in their renowned celebration of May Day. Which must have been a flabella libidinis to end all
flabella libidinises, according to the description of William Bradford,
Governor of Plymouth : "They allso set up a May-pole, drinking and
dancing aboute it many days togeather, inviting the Indean women, for
their consorts, dancing and frisking togither . . . and worse practices." [49] As they danced hand in hand round the maypole, they sang
a Renaissance refrain :

> Drinke and be merry, merry, merry, boyes,
> Let all your delight be in Hymens ioyes. . . .[50]

The Merriemount maypole was by no means the first maypole in
America, nor the last, Puritanism notwithstanding. In England before
the Commonwealth, it was the custom on May first to make merry all
day long, build bonfires in the streets, and attend stage plays and ban-

---

[47] Quoted in Harold Milligan : "Pioneers in American Music," in the *American Scholar*, III, 229.

[48] *Collections of the Massachusetts Historical Society*, second series, X, 184.

[49] William Bradford : *History of Plymouth Plantation 1620–1647* (2 vols.,
Boston, 1912), II, 48.

[50] Thomas Morton : *The New English Canaan*, edited by Charles Francis
Adams, Jr., Prince Society series (Boston, 1883), p. 279.

quets. To Puritans this bordered on pagan idolatry, but Charles II revived and encouraged it. Until 1686, when Sir Edmund Andros was sent to Massachusetts as that colony's first royal Governor, Massachusetts did not even observe the "popish" holiday of Christmas. With Andros, not only was Anglicanism brought in, and the Anglican observance of Christmas, but, to the horror of the good burghers, a maypole was set up on the Boston Common.

The problem of dancing was not confined, however, to the maypole type once a year, as the conscientious theocrats were well aware. In 1684 Increase Mather published his famous essay, *An Arrow against Profane and Promiscuous Dancing*.

> Concerning the Controversy about Dancing [he said], the Question is not, whether all Dancing be in it self sinful. . . . But our question is concerning *Gynecandrical Dancing*, or that which is commonly called *Mixt* or *Promiscuous Dancing*, viz. of Men and Women . . . together.

This type, he says, cannot be tolerated in New England without great sin ; for "It has been proved that such a practice is a *Scandalous Immorality. . . .*" [51]

Gynecandrical dancing gained ground, and the once-a-fortnight dancing assembly, even if supported mainly by non-Puritans, thrived in the early eighteenth century, as a counterpart of the singing-school movement. The predilection for dancing in the southern colonies, which has already been discussed, was not confined to the formal balls of the influential. By 1755 one John Kello could write from Virginia to a friend in London : "Dancing is the chief diversion here." [52]

By then, however, dancing was common throughout the colonies, and often went with other festivities, like sleigh parties. Alexander Mackraby, an unmarried visitor from England, described such a sleigh party of January 1769 in Philadelphia. "Seven sleighs with two ladies and two men in each, preceded by fiddlers on horseback," set out over the snow, he said, to a public house a few miles out, "where we danced, sung, and romped and eat and drank, and kicked away care from morning till night, and finished our frolic in two or three side-boxes at the play." [53]

Mackraby was also informative about colonial serenading. In March 1768 he wrote to his sister from "this confounded Quaker town" that

---

[51] Perry Miller and Thomas H. Johnson : *The Puritans* (New York, 1938), pp. 411–12.

[52] Quoted in Fisher : *The Music That Washington Knew* (Boston, 1931), p. xxi.

[53] "Philadelphia Society before the Revolution. Extracts from Letters of Alexander Mackraby to Sir Philip Francis," *Pennsylvania Magazine of History and Biography*, XI, 286.

serenading "is extremely in vogue here now." He and four or five army officers would drink as hard as they could "to keep out the cold" and, attended by a ten-piece band, would sally forth through the streets about midnight, "and play under the window of any lady you choose to distinguish; which they esteem a high compliment." [54]

In the meantime popular songs had been going round by way of broadsides in the British custom, and by simple rote. "I am informed," said Cotton Mather in 1713, "that the Minds and Manners of many People about the Countrey are much corrupted, by foolish Songs and Ballads, which the Hawkers and Pedlars carry into all parts of the Countrey." [55]

The broadside-ballad custom was a part of English town life from the early sixteenth century. It suffered a clean-up campaign at the hands of the Commonwealth, but revived after the Restoration. Broadsides were nothing more than handbills with verse and, usually, a woodcut. The verse was meant to be sung to some specifically designated tune. Until the Restoration most broadside tunes were originally those of folk-songs or folk-dances; after the Restoration they consisted increasingly of "music-hall" art songs as well. On the whole, it may be said that popular songs of both centuries were, oftener than not, "citified" folk-songs, that is, folk-tunes worked over to eliminate their modal char-

PACKINGTON'S POUND [56]

[54] Ibid., XI, 281.

[55] *Diary of Cotton Mather* (2 vols), *Massachusetts Historical Society Collections*, seventh series, II, 242.

[56] William Chappell: *Old English Popular Music*, edited by H. Ellis Wooldridge (2 vols., London, 1893), I, 259; the words: Chappell: *Popular Music of the Olden Time* (2 vols., London, 1859), I, 125, from a song of 1687 in praise of milk.

acteristics and reset as in ballad-opera with words that were patriotic, satiric, sentimental, or bawdy.

How current the broadside ballads may have been in colonial America is uncertain, but clearly not to the extent they were in England. Actual American production of broadsides was small. But the tunes of the popular songs most sung in America before 1725 may be fairly reliably indicated by the tunes most used for British broadside ballads. *Packington's Pound* heads the list. Of the extant seventeenth-century ballads, ninety-nine are known to have been written to this melody, which was familiar also as a lute tune and a country-dance tune, and was extremely popular as a ballad vehicle, especially for political ballads, well into the eighteenth century. The runners-up in seventeenth-century popularity include *Fortune my Foe*, to which ninety-one ballads are known to have been written, *Greensleeves* (eighty), and *Lilliburlero* (thirty-seven).[57]

Seventeenth-century Harvard students were singing such sentimental broadside ballads as *The Love-Sick Maid* — beginning "Begone, Thou fatal fiery fever" — and *The Last Lamentation of the Languishing Squire*. Little manuscript collections of current songs circulated in America from England in the seventeenth and eighteenth centuries called "garlands," "arbors," and "academies." A typical eighteenth-century manuscript book, which went through at least five editions, was called *A Collection of Jigg, Reel, Hornpipe, Minuet, March, Cotillion, Extra, Strathspey, Psalm and Song Tunes*. The tenor of the popular songs whose tunes it included may be indicated from such of their titles as *Kiss Me Quick My Mother's Coming, Bonny Lass under a Blanket, Sweetest When She's Naked*, and *Go to the Devil and Shake Yourself*.

It was the mid-eighteenth century before magazines, newspapers, and broadsides began to circulate freely enough for relatively general song popularization in America. *Sally in Our Alley, Rule, Britannia*, and *The British Grenadiers* were popular songs in eighteenth-century America. Another was *Drink to Me Only with Thine Eyes*, which was known by the tune now exclusively used, but also by others, one of which about 1750 went under the title *The Thirsty Lover*. The first popular song known to have been printed in America (on a broadside in 1759) was the eleven-stanza British ballad, *Brave Wolfe*, which recounted the deeds of the hero of the French and Indian War. The first book of secular songs published in America was Garrat Noel's *The Masque, a new Song Book*, printed in New York in 1767.

The marked influence of the Negro on American popular music awaited the minstrel and showboat era beginning in the second quarter

[57] Cf. Lamson, op. cit.

of the nineteenth century. Music about Negroes or written in a Negro or pseudo-Negro idiom was very rare in America before 1820. Still, before the end of the eighteenth century a consciousness of the Negro had awakened sufficiently for the production of two notable popular songs : *The Desponding Negro* (Philadelphia, 1793) and *I Sold a Guiltless Negro Boy* (Boston, *c.* 1796).

BRAVE WOLFE [58]

In 1768 came the first expression of American nationalism in popular music. It was *The Liberty Song*, by the patriot John Dickinson, which he wrote to a well-known tune *Heart of Oak*, by the English organist William Boyce. The words were widely printed north and south, and the song was officially adopted by the Sons of Liberty, who, according to John Adams's diary, joined in the chorus three hundred fifty strong at their 1769 banquet on the anniversary of the Stamp Act riots.

THE LIBERTY SONG [59]

The chorus, badly fitted to the rhythm of the music, went :

> *In Freedom we're born and in Freedom we'll live,*
> *Our purses are ready,*
> *Steady, Friends, Steady.*
> *Not as slaves, but as Freemen our money we'll give.*[60]

From 1770 on, march music was common in America, mostly to jig-time. American military bands usually consisted of nothing more than drums and fifes, while those of British regiments consisted usually of drums, fifes, and oboes, sometimes with horns and bassoons in addition. The bands of both camps played very much the same selections,[61] of

---

[58] S. Foster Damon, ed. : *Series of Old American Songs* (Providence, 1936), No. 1. This song was still to be found in songbooks as late as the 1840's, and is referred to in many old documents.

[59] Ibid., No. 3, and Chappell : *Old English Popular Music*, II, 189.

[60] Damon, op. cit., No. 3.

[61] Cf. Harry Dichter and Elliot Shapiro : *Early American Sheet Music* (New York, 1941), p. 9.

which without doubt the most popular was *Yankee Doodle*, a tune of uncertain European origin.

Words of every variety were set to it, the verse "Yankee doodle came to town riding on a pony" being fairly current by about 1767, though its origin is as confused as the tune's. The text beginning "Father and I went down to camp" was probably written in 1775 by a Harvard man, Edward Bangs, who was in the Lexington pursuit of April 1775. Lord Percy's troops kept step to the tune when they marched to aid their Concord-routed comrades; but at Concord the colonials seem to have appropriated it as their own, for from that time on, Americans considered it an American air. General Burgoyne surrendered his sword at Saratoga to the playing of *Yankee Doodle*. Lord Cornwallis is supposed to have exclaimed: "I hope to God I'll never hear that damned tune again!" [62] But at his surrender at Yorktown he and his men were obliged to leave the gathering-place while the American band played *Yankee Doodle*. And soon the whole seaboard was singing *Cornwallis Country Dance* — to the tune of *Yankee Doodle*:

> *Cornwallis led a country dance,*
> *The like was never seen sir,*
> *Much retrograde and much advance,*
> *And all with General Greene, sir.*
>
> *They rambled up and rambled down,*
> *Join'd hands, then off they run, sir,*
> *Our General Greene to Charlestown,*
> *The earl to Wilmington, sir.*[63]

The first printed version of *Yankee Doodle* (1782), to which a set of five variations was attached, went:

YANKEE DOODLE [64]

[62] Quoted in Carl Holiday: "American Folk-Songs," *Sewanee Review*, XXVII, 140.

[63] Frank Moore, ed.: *Songs and Ballads of the American Revolution* (New York, 1856), p. 363.

[64] Louis C. Elson: *The National Music of America* (Boston, 1899), p. 318.

A version dated 1790 went : [65]

etc.

The most famous ballad written to *Yankee Doodle* was Francis Hopkinson's *Battle of the Kegs,* inspired by the incident on the Delaware River in 1778 when the Bushnell powder machines alarmed some British crews. The twenty-second stanza concludes :

> *Such feats did they perform that day,*
> *Against those wicked kegs, sir,*
> *That years to come, if they get home,*
> *They'll make their boasts and brags, sir.*[66]

One of the brief contemporary references to this ballad relates that in an army camp "Our drums and fifes afforded us a favorite music till evening, when we were delighted with the song composed by Mr. Hopkinson . . . sung in the best style by a number of gentlemen." [67]

When the battle of Bunker Hill demonstrated that the colonies were committed to a war of doubtful outcome with one of the great military powers of the world, a song, *The American Hero,* became popularly

BUNKER HILL [68]

---

[65] Ibid., p. 321.

[66] Moore, op. cit., p. 214.

[67] Quoted in ibid., p. 210, from Surgeon Thacher.

[68] Olin Downes and Elie Siegmeister : *A Treasury of American Song* (New York : Alfred A. Knopf ; 1943), p. 64. By permission of the publisher. Cf. also Damon, op. cit., No. 3, for a reproduction of this song from a broadside of 1775 that was bound up with a Tate and Brady psalmbook. The melody was meant to be taken by the tenor.

known as *Bunker Hill* and was sung everywhere — in camps, churches, and public meetings of all kinds. Its words were by the eminent patriot Nathaniel Niles, and its music by the same Andrew Law who later introduced the custom in America of placing the melody in the soprano.

The song that became England's national anthem, *God Save the King,* had been sung from about 1740, and was a popular song among the Revolutionaries, who, while the loyalists sang "God save great George our King," countered with such other texts as "God save the Thirteen States." (Smith's words, "My country, 'tis of thee," were of course not written until 1831.)

Practically every regiment in the Revolution had its rhymester, and any significant event of the war called forth a commemorative ballad to some favorite air. Soldiers, to guitar or fife, or to no accompaniment at all, sang of the Boston Tea Party, the shelling of Charleston, the treachery of Benedict Arnold, the victory at Saratoga, or of whatever was the current topic of conversation. The Irish air *Langolee,* the Scotch air *Maggie Lauder,* and the English air *Barbara Allen* are representative tunes that were often employed by the rhymesters. A series of ballads to *Langolee* started in 1775 when an English poet, John Tait, wrote *Banks of the Dee* upon the departure of a friend to America to fight in the British forces. The ballad began :

> *'Twas summer, and softly the breezes were blowing,*
> *And sweetly the nightingale sang from a tree.*

The inevitable rebel parody shortly appeared, attributed to Oliver Arnold of Norwich, Connecticut :

> *'Twas winter, and blue tory noses were freezing,*
> *As they march'd o'er the land where they ought not to be. . . .*[69]

Outside of *Yankee Doodle,* however, probably no melody served more continuous duty than *Derry Down,* with its ending

Of the steady stream of *Derry Down* ballads that poured forth throughout the war, the best probably was *The Heads,* which appeared in several versions from 1776 on. Following is the first of its nine stanzas :

[69] Quoted in Moore, op. cit., pp. 78–81. After *Banks of the Dee* was popular on both sides of the ocean, Tait revised the second line, on remonstrances of Robert Burns that nightingales did not sing in trees and did not exist in Scotland anyway, to "And sweetly the wood pigeon coo'd from the tree."

Ye wrong heads, and strong heads attend to my strains;
Ye clear heads, and queer heads, and heads without brains;
Ye thick skulls, and quick skulls, and heads great and small;
And ye heads that aspire to be heads over all.
Derry down, down, hey derry down.[70]

DERRY DOWN [71]

Ye | wrong heads, and strong heads at- | tend to   my   strains; Ye

clear heads, and queer heads and | heads with-out brains   etc.

At the war's end the great American hero was George Washington, whose glorification in popular music was most conspicuously manifest in an extended line of *Washington Marches* and *President's Marches,* composed in large part by the English-trained musicians who had settled in America and turned their talent to the theater. It was to a *President's March* of one of these musicians, Philip Phile, that Francis Hopkinson's Congressman-jurist son Joseph wrote *Hail Columbia* (1798) as propaganda for John Adams's policy of keeping the American spirit above the interests of either France or England, then at war. It was written at the request of a young actor, Gilbert Fox, who first performed it at an April-evening band concert in Philadelphia. The listeners are said to have yelled themselves hoarse over it, redemanding it nearly a dozen times. By the War of 1812 it had been accepted as a national anthem on an almost equal footing with *Yankee Doodle.*

A tune that was ragingly popular in the late eighteenth century and early nineteenth was that of an English drinking-song, *To Anacreon in Heaven,* the theme-song of several so-called Anacreontic societies on both sides of the ocean named after the hedonist ancient Greek poet.

[70] Ibid., p. 153.
[71] Chappell : *Popular Music of the Olden Time,* I, 350.

TO ANACREON IN HEAVEN

To Anacreon in Heav'n
Where he sat in full glee,
A few Sons of Harmony sent a Petition
That he their Inspirer and Patron would be,
When this Answer arrived from the jolly old Grecian,
"Voice, Fiddle, and Flute, no longer be mute,
I'll lend you my name and inspire you to boot;
And besides I'll instruct you, like me, to intwine
The myrtle of Venus with Bacchus's Vine.[72]

Text after text, usually patriotic in nature, was substituted for these words, from one of which, *For Adams and Liberty,* written by Robert Treat Paine at the request of the Massachusetts Charitable Fire Society, more than $750 profit accrued to the author, showing (for the time) an unusual immediate popularity. The tune was the same as that to which Francis Scott Key wrote *The Warrior's Return* in commemoration of Stephen Decatur's homecoming from the war with Tripoli, and some years later *The Star Spangled Banner,* which, in the practice of the time, was struck off on a broadside and sung at a public tavern within twenty-four hours of its completion.

Once nationalism found an outlet in popular music, in the late 1760's, it remained the dominant theme of that music into the nineteenth century. Popular songs were almost entirely British, or British tunes reworded. In the latter case, however, the tunes were made to serve a purely American expression. Both words and music of one or two of the most serious popular songs were indigenous. *Bunker Hill,* like Billings's *Chester,* was a supreme and sincere effort to express the American mind through a musical medium.

Folk-music

Folk-traditions are so conservative that many tens of thousands of people throughout America today sing and play (alongside later songs and tunes) folk-music of their ancestors of the seventeenth and eighteenth centuries. They sing about characters and settings of fairytale remoteness — knights and ghosts; Robin Hood, Prince Charlie, and Henry V; Londontown, and the banks of Dundee. But the themes of their songs are in the main the fundamental crises and tragedies of life that the singers well understand : adultery (*Lord Orland's Wife*), infidelity (*Lady Isabel and the Elf Knight*), seduction and desertion (*The Gypsy Laddie*), infanticide (*The Cruel Mother*), murder and suicide (*The Brown Girl*). There are a few happier subjects, like the tam-

[72] Quoted in Elson, op. cit., p. 172 (where it is given with the earliest known form of the music, *c.* 1770–5).

ing of the shrew (*The Wife Wrapt in Wether's Skin*) and trouble with the father-in-law (*Earl Brand*); but even when the subjects are saddest, the nature of old English tunes makes the total impression of the songs dramatic rather than tragic. The tunes, which are on the whole far better music than their texts are poetry, and which are much the more important element of the songs, range from high lightheartedness to haunting plaintiveness; they are never really somber or despairing.

Musicological opinion is virtually agreed that the total number of Anglo-American folk-songs is not large — that the most extensively used ballad and song tunes number only about fifty-five separate airs, and that of these as few as five, in many guises, seem to accompany more folk-texts than all the rest put together. Further, nearly all the forms of any widespread tune, with all their small interchanging variant traits, turn up side by side in every district where English folk-music has been collected in any considerable quantity; so that a purely local version of a widespread tune is not often found.[73]

In the great majority of cases folk-songs were kept alive by the women, who sang them as they worked or to entertain or lull to sleep their children. The exacting conservatism of children has been an important factor in the relative changelessness of the songs over so extended a period.

Some of the most affecting of the folk-music has been preserved from distant Elizabethan times; for instance, the tune (though not the words, which are early nineteenth-century) of *My Little Mohee* and the poignant song *Black is the color of my true love's hair,* which retains quaint phrasing like "I love the grass on where she goes." Some of the folk-songs date probably as far back as the time of Chaucer or earlier, such as several of the Robin Hood ballads and *The Hangman's Tree.* In the invariably effective narration of the latter, all the relatives fail to lift a hand to save the damsel on the gallows, but her true love comes through and pays the fine. All love is not fickle or frustrated in the folk-ballads, but most of it turns out so. In the Elizabethan ballad *Greensleeves* the narrator has been rebuffed in love, but, because of the lilting melody, seems not at all disheartened about it. *Greensleeves* has been a morris-dance tune, a song tune, a hymn tune, and a broadside tune; it is found in many lute manuscripts of the sixteenth and early seventeenth centuries, is mentioned twice in Shakespeare's *Merry Wives of Windsor,* and, like *Packington's Pound* and *Lilliburlero,* was incorporated into *The Beggar's Opera.*

---

[73] Cf. Samuel P. Bayard: "Aspects of Melodic Kinship and Variation in British-American Folk-Tunes," *Papers Read at the International Congress of Musicology,* op. cit., pp. 122 ff.

GREENSLEEVES [74]

A - las! my love,-- you do me wrong to cast me off-- dis-cour-teous-ly, etc.

The spirit of *Lord Randall* is in quite another vein. To the question : "What do you leave to your true love, my own true loving son ?" the dying man replies :

> *"The fire and the furnace for to scorch her bones brown,*
> *For she is the cause of my lying down."* [75]

A nostalgic autobiography, *The Foggy, Foggy Dew*, a favorite of the Scotch poet Robert Burns, and another of many fetching folk-songs sung in eighteenth-century America, takes still another attitude toward a specific love affair. The refrain to the first stanza goes :

> *I wooed her in the winter-time,*
> *Part of the summer too,*
> *And the only, only thing that I did that was wrong*
> *Was to keep her from the foggy, foggy dew.*[76]

But among the old English folk-ballads that survive in America today, the most frequently encountered in nearly every section is *Bonny Barbara Allen,* which Samuel Pepys spoke of enjoying in 1666. It tells of a woman who spoke hard-heartedly to her lover as he lay on his death-bed. "The music of the finest singer is dissonance," wrote the eighteenth-century author Oliver Goldsmith, "to what I felt when our old dairy-maid sung me into tears with *Johnny Armstron's last Good-night,* or *The cruelty of Barbara Allen.*" [77]

Barbara Allen exists in the largest number of both tunes and texts of any colonial song, including English, Scotch, and Irish versions and countless variants of each. While the tunes of English folk-songs, regardless of variation, seldom changed so much in America as to lose their essential identity, the words in their adaptation to new environments were sometimes so modified as to obscure any trace of English origin. An extreme example is a twentieth-century version of *Barbara*

[74] Chappell : *Old English Popular Music,* op. cit., I, 239.

[75] Mary O. Eddy, ed. : *Ballads and Songs from Ohio* (New York, 1939), p. 23.

[76] A recording of this song by Burl Ives can be found in Asch album no. 345.

[77] Quoted in Granville Bantock, ed. : *One Hundred Songs of England* (Boston, 1914), p. xx.

BARBARA ALLEN [78]

Allen, in which the heroine has become a Negro desperado named Bobby Allen, whose corpse in shipped out of Dallas, leaving his relatives behind "squallin' and holl'in'" at the station.

Springfield Mountain, which originated during Revolutionary times, is one of the first folk-ballads of which both words and melody are believed to be indigenous; as is usually the case, the American verse is much inferior to the literary level of English folk-song.

SPRINGFIELD MOUNTAIN [79]

[78] Reed Smith and Hilton Rufty, eds.: *American Anthology of Old-World Ballads* (New York: J. Fischer & Bro.; 1937), p. 35. By permission of the publisher.

[79] Downes and Siegmeister, op. cit., p. 38.

The grace notes written in by the musicologist who recorded the song are in approximation of "sudden falsetto quirks," which are but one of the peculiarities of folk-singing, which include vocal catches, scoops, shakes, and slides, the nature of which can only be conveyed by actual performance. Still, folk-singers have oftentimes an amazing sense of intonation, and of enunciation; and accustomed to singing without accompaniment, they achieve a vocal smoothness that usually is lost in trained artists, who subconsciously rely on instrumental background to maintain an even tone.

Folk-songs were not sung communally but by single individuals, often to entertain others. At a neighborly gathering it was customary for those of the party to take turns performing, and an effort was made to sing the least-known ballads rather than the general favorites; for the singers considered a folk-song more as a story to tell than as a pretty tune to sing. The folk-singer, perfectly at ease and with a "dead-pan" expression, matter-of-factly recounted some dramatic, drawn-out, repetitive tale of love and death, in the same high-pitched voice that the English peasant liked to use.

Because of the intimate fusion of words and music in folk-song, the folk-songs of the Swedish, German, and other non-English-speaking minorities tended to die out in America as the younger generations of those minorities adopted the English language. Even of the numerous folk-hymns, only half a dozen tunes survived that were descended from any but British (or Irish) sources. The Methodist folk-singers themselves seemed to hold little basic affinity for the German tunes utilized in their Wesley hymns, and on the frontier reverted, so to speak, to national type. French creole and cajun folk-music is another story; but this development was localized in Louisiana. The English connection with jazz is tenuous; but at least the word "jazz" is a corruption of the Elizabethan "jass," which was perpetuated through the centuries in the brothel vernacular.

The preponderance of British folk-song in America is not fully grasped until it is realized that the songs of childhood, which can be regarded as a fundamental subdivision of a nation's folklore, were almost invariably British: nursery songs like *Billy Boy, Old King Cole, Cock Robin, What Are Little Girls Made Of, A Frog He Would A-Wooing Go, O Dear, What Can the Matter Be,* and the play-songs *Farmer in the Dell, Ring around the Rosy, Needle's Eye, Here We Go round the Mulberry-bush, Green Gravel, Go in and out the Window,* and *London Bridge.*

Not only the landbound but the seafaring Americans sang folk-songs that were British. (The landbound also sang sea-songs.) In particular they sang a sea-song, *The Gallant Victory, or Lowlands Low,* which dates from seventeenth-century England; the oldest surviving version was printed in 1682 from a copy formerly in the possession of Samuel Pepys. The following is from a version that has survived in New England:

THE GALLANT VICTORY, OR LOWLANDS LOW [80]

The cap-tain had a ship in the north— coun-te-ree etc.

(*Blow the Man Down* seems to have been a product of the early nineteenth century, when it was sung by the sailors of the Atlantic packet ships.)

Folk-carols, because their origin antedates the Reformation, and the Protestant Americans reacted against their "popish" content, are comparatively rare in America; but the few that have survived from early tradition are also British. The principal ones include *The Cherry-tree Carol, The Seven Joys of Mary,* and *The Twelve Days of Christmas.*

Though for the most part the folk-music of seventeenth- and eighteenth-century America was British, there were a few native productions prompted by American experience — such as *Springfield Mountain* — and they began to emerge at about the time the American experience was finding expression through other media. But the indigenous folk-song development of significance was less in the invention of new words and melodies than in the deepening of a divergent mood. The struggling, self-reliant frontiersman sang the songs of the English peasant, but he sang them under different conditions from those in which the songs germinated. These different conditions gave him a different outlook on life; and folk-songs are a most intimate and unself-conscious exposition of a national lower-class view of life. The lot of the English peasant may have been hard, but it was insulated with the security that comes of many centuries of familiarity with and adaptation to a pattern of unambitious, humble living. His, too, was a kind of compact life; it was delimited by geographical insularity and an old established population. To judge the peasant of "Merrie England" by his folk-songs, he may have been sometimes pensive and most of the time frankly realistic, but practically never introspective or outrightly melancholy. In the

[80] Eloise Hubbard Linscott, ed. : *Folk Songs of Old New England* (New York : The Macmillan Company, 1939), p. 136. By permission of Mrs. Linscott and the publisher.

American frontier environment — uncertain, isolated, illimitably spacious — the underlying gaiety of English folk-songs, which so often commenced with the cheery line : "As I went out one May morning," tended to be transformed toward mournfulness or longing — a tendency further accentuated in later cowboy ballads and Negro blues, in which the American appeared, in contradistinction to the happily adjusted Englishman on his cozy farm, a person of innate and unbounded loneliness.

Generally speaking, in spite of exceptions like *Greensleeves,* the repertory of the folk-singer was distinct from that of the folk-instrumentalist. The latter seems to have expressed nothing more personal than a lust for life. The most pronounced characteristic of his tunes, at any rate, was their animation, even if they were not exclusively dance music.

The tunes on the whole, as they survive today, seem melodically less complex and technically easier to play than corresponding tunes in the British Isles. And in spite of the strong Scotch-Irish influence on American folk-music, particularly of the frontier, American tunes tend to the simpler English versions rather than the more ornate Scotch and Irish (Celtic) versions. It is probable that the rougher, less leisurely life in America compared to that of the British Isles has accounted for some retrogression in musical skill. But there are a number of American versions of tunes that show no inferiority to the British.[81]

The instruments of the folk-musicians were frequently homemade, notably fiddles, which were the principal folk-instrument ; also primitive zithers, plucked like a harp ; and dulcimers of many varieties. (Dulcimers are guitar-like instruments laid flat on a table or one's knees ; the strings are strummed or plucked with the fingers or a turkey feather, or tapped with small hammers.) There were guitars, but banjos appear not to have come in until the early nineteenth century. Fifes were probably second only to fiddles in commonness of usage, and fifers held playing contests like the fiddlers. End-blown pipes and flutes were also owned. So were jew's-harps ; even the urban Puritans were stocked with jew's-harps on account of their value in bargaining with the Indians. Apparently there were also bass viols and a small proportion of cellos.

Fiddling contests were a featured event at such celebrations as May Day. On a typical May Day in 1727 at Jamestown, as is known from a contemporary letter, four fiddlers played in turn *Greensleeves, Sellinger's Round, Strathspey Reel,* and *Cock of the North* before the queen of the May, whose decision as to the winner is unknown. The quotation

[81] Cf. Bayard : *Hill Country Tunes* (Philadelphia, 1944), p. xxii.

of a few bars of *Sellinger's Round* below is taken from the Elizabethan arrangement of Byrd for virginal :

SELLINGER'S ROUND [82]

There is every reason to believe that the folk-fiddling customs of the present day were those of colonial times. If so, the fiddler, like the folk-singer, usually sat down to perform, and was concerned with the notes and the rhythm, but only incidentally with tone-quality. He may have held his fiddle against his chest, on his left shoulder, against his arm just below the shoulder, on his lap, or on (or between) his knees like a cello. He held the bow toward the middle rather than at the end, and he never learned to use vibrato. He commonly employed the open strings as drones, and often shaved down the top of the violin bridge to make the strings lie on nearly the same plane. His ear was trained in modal scales that would have caused him to think that concert performers of art music were playing out of tune.[83]

The fiddle-dominated country orchestra of colonial times changed little during all the years that followed, and the barn dance it accompanied, still less. The barn dance, also variously called the kitchen whang, kitchen junket, knockdown, and hog-wrasslin', was essentially the same throughout the colonies. Even in New England, although the religious prejudice against dancing did have a considerable penetration into the rural areas, the Puritan minority with its denunciation of "lascivious dancing to wanton ditties" would have found it next to impossible to suppress the country dances. Every cornhusking, apple-paring, harvest, or laying of a new barn floor was a likely occasion for dance celebration.

The small orchestra — often only a fiddler or two — played at the head of the hall, and a "caller" or "prompter" chanted running instructions for the sundry steps of jigs, square dances, and reels. Jigs and reels were usually done to *Yankee Doodle, White Cockade,* or *Irish Washerwoman;* while square dances, which were arranged in square, circular, or longways formations, were done to American adaptations of old English dance tunes, such as *Pop Goes the Weasel, Fisher's*

---

[82] Chappell : *Old English Popular Music,* I, 256.
[83] Cf. Bayard : *Hill Country Tunes,* pp. xxiv–xxvi.

Hornpipe, The Girl I Left behind Me, and *Turkey in the Straw.* The chief difference between American and English country dancing was that the American was more boisterous.

Those dance tunes that were not also songs, originally — it appears — had words to go with them, but the words for the most part were already forgotten before the tunes left England. Dance steps, on the other hand, which once went with songs that ceased to be danced, in some cases survived in England into the twentieth century. A number of the American dances were descended from ancient pagan rituals, the morris and sword dances, which were disappearing in England. Only fragments of the original steps survived in America and, naturally, none of their original meaning. The words that the dance-caller chanted to the various tunes was native doggerel, some of the rhymes of his own devising. The name of a tune would change almost at an individual player's whim, but the tunes themselves remained relatively constant.

Play-party games were dances disguised by terminology. They contained regular country-dance patterns, but were accompanied by singing rather than satanic fiddling. The tunes used were the standard folk-dance tunes, simplified and sometimes abbreviated ; the words were frequently either silly or amorous or both. Ordinarily only the young men sang, as such singing was disapproved for girls. Play-party games were a method of not violating the dance prejudice and also of keeping the youth from kissing-games.

There were of course occasions for dancing among folk who thoroughly approved of both dancing and kissing, who sometimes sang their tunes for mere lack of fiddlers.

Conclusion

Around 1770 Francis Hopkinson was writing art songs in careful conformity to the English aristocratic standard of form and taste ; William Billings was writing fuguing-tunes for the militant middle class ; John Dickinson had utilized an English melody for patriotic expression in popular song ; the Baptists on the frontier were assembling folk-hymns out of the English heritage ; and the hinterland farmers were molding native versions of dance tunes and some of the first indigenous secular folk-songs.

A song need not be composed by those who sing it in order to express the singers' sentiments. But it is remarkable that English music, scarcely modified and unsupplemented, could so long express the American spirit. The colonies had matured nearly to national states before their European music proved no longer adequate for satisfactory expression — an inference being that until very late they remained really more English than American. The American effort to alter the English tradition because it had become inadequate may have brought forth a largely crude result, but the effort in itself is of the greatest significance, as symptomatic of an epochal transition of mind. That the new expression took a place beside the old-world inheritance without displacing it shows how fundamental to the new outlook was the old.

The art musicians in their works and performance confessedly made no attempt before the Revolution to express a new national point of view ; rather the reverse. Francis Hopkinson was by no means a Tory, but he was an aristocrat, and his music expressed the spirit of the aristocratic — largely Tory — class. It showed the same susceptibility to British authority that the aristocracy as a whole showed in the general ordering of its life. That class which was farthest removed from a susceptibility to British influence happened to be the class that evolved a musical expression most radically in disregard of British precedent. Nevertheless, the aristocracy was also American. Its very striving after a high cultural standard disclosed an awakening national pride.

Church-musical practice for early America as a whole was set by New England, which first resorted to lining out and first undertook to overthrow it ; which led in psalm- and hymn-book publishing and in the establishment of singing schools ; and which inaugurated both fugal tunes and standard hymns — even the first folk-hymns — and produced the first sacred-musical composers of English-speaking America. Not only was New England first ; it also generated the most songbooks, the most singing schools, the most hymns and hymn-writers, and the most discussion of every church-musical matter.

Such pre-eminence was due in part to the aims of the Harvard-educated clergy, who had an undisputably magisterial influence in New England ; in part to the Puritan obsession to produce, be purposeful, and see to the welfare of everybody else ; and also in part to the fact that Puritan New England, by virtue of the predominance of its bourgeois stratum of society, was the section of the country which was most vitally concerned about religion, and therefore about religious music.

The worldliness of the southern aristocrats fostered too many pleasurable interests for single-minded attention to religion. These people had less to do with church music than New England because they cared less, as well as because the plantation system hindered close-knit congregational activity. The unlettered country-folk turned away from both aristocratic indifference and bourgeois traditions to suit altogether different religious requirements with folk-hymnody, which, guided by no self-conscious emulative inclinations, diverged farthest from English usage and was the most distinctly American development in church music.

While the southern aristocrats did not challenge New England middle-class leadership in conventional church music, they did assume leadership in art music. And of the rest of the country, they who followed the southern lead were by and large the aristocratic element of the larger cities. Even the sacred art-music in New England — such as organ-playing and oratorio production — was mainly in the hands of Anglican aristocrats. When the southern aristocracy did not exclude any one musical activity, all of the musical activities interacted to the stimulation of art-musical culture as a whole. If, for instance, an opera orchestra presented a concert and then played for the ball that followed, both opera and dancing were fostering orchestral music and a milieu that favored concerts. Aversion to both the theater and dancing in the north not only discouraged the theater and dancing, but also concerts, which theoretically would have been acceptable to the Puritans. The powerful cultural drive of Puritan New England was, in this way and in others, self-confined to church music through the eighteenth century, and even the development of church music felt the constrictions of hold-over Calvinist conceptions regarding worship.

When the Revolution had decided the issue of English loyalty or American independence, art music, especially in operatic composition and concert singing, took on a strong patriotic tinge. Hopkinson's *Temple of Minerva* was one of the earliest examples of this new tendency.

It was a tendency preceded by many years in popular music, which was closer to the pulse of the people as a whole. Before the end of the eighteenth century the largeness of the number of national songs and marches in popular music was hardly credible, considering the state of patriotic expression in music at the outbreak of the Revolution. And before the end of the century the difference in the level and nature of popular music and of art music in American composition was growing indistinguishable. Art music suffered from this near confluence, but not the national consciousness that its cheapened strains glorified.

Still, an equally important constituent of popular music and folk-music — perhaps the more important — was the un-Americanized British music. Certainly it remained more important in art music. Whether it were native or not, it was a part of American culture.

As has been seen earlier, American folk-music tended to develop farthest away from British precedent. Yet, as has also been seen, the development was not divergent by virtue of new creations so much as by virtue of a new interpretation of the old. The frontier probably induced the greatest differentiation between Englishmen and Americans of any single factor ; and the music of the frontiersman reflects this differentiation most clearly, but in a way most subtly, of any class of music. There was significant new creation — notably in hymnody and in an occasional original song — but a more significant nationalization of mood, as the frontier farmer faced away from England and confronted the west with little more than his two hands, a hefty wife, and a large measure of indomitability. The wistfulness of his songs, the exuberance of his dances, and the naïveté of his hymns, grew from the far distances, the restlessness, and the primitive hardship of life in the wilderness.

NOTE TO THE READER

Since music is mainly a matter of sound, the best way to find out about it is to experience it through the sense of hearing.

Much, of varying degrees of merit and scope, has been written pertinent to early American music which contains either no music or music that is not usably presented. To get at the actual music of early America, one step would be to dissect out the early American portions from present-day music and reinterpret it in the olden style. This task may be supplemented and facilitated by phonograph recordings, music scores, song collections, concert-going, and backwoods-visiting.

For conventional colonial church music, the best single anthology is probably William Arms Fisher : *Ye Olde New-England Psalm-Tunes 1600–1820* (Boston, 1930), a small songbook of transcriptions into modern readability. Almost any currently used hymnal will contain the *Doxology, Dundee,* and *O God, our help in ages past,* which might be lined out and dragged, to no accompaniment or to that of perhaps a cello, a flute, and an oboe.

For "unconventional" church music — the folk-hymns — Annabel Morris Buchanan : *Folk Hymns of America* (New York, 1938) is a comprehensive and judiciously selected collection, with apt arrangements and up-to-date annotations. George Pullen Jackson : *Spiritual Folk-Songs of Early America* (New York, 1937) and his supplement to it : *Down-East Spirituals, and Others* (New York, 1943) are two invaluable products of the prodigious scholarship of Dr. Jackson in this field. Although the wealth of selections (which are given unharmonized) is drawn largely from songbooks of the early nineteenth century, many of the songs originated in an earlier unwritten tradition. Nothing would be more instructive of folk-hymnody than to seek out a Primitive Baptist meeting or a country "singing" of a southern Sacred Harp association — and join in.

For art music, the singable arrangements of Granville Bantock : *One Hundred Songs of England* (Boston, 1914) include traditional as well as art songs, most of which were known in early America. A general background orientation may be got from Georg Kinsky : *A History of Music in Pictures*

(London and Toronto, 1930), which is a veritable museum of European musicians, instruments, scores, and art-musical life, much of which, for the eighteenth century, was of course held in common by American cities. Concert works of the baroque and rococo masters are still frequently performed and available in score, such as the symphonies of Haydn, the *concerti grossi* of Corelli, and the clavier suites and vocal music of Handel. Even harpsichords, both on records and in recital, are ceasing to be a rarity.

A choral group of, say, ten or fifteen might perform a dozen or so numbers of the *Messiah, Judas Maccabæus,* or *Samson,* lightly and facilely, in the eighteenth-century manner, rather than in the contemporary Wagnerian manner, and the soloists might also sing lightly and legato — even the female soloists — rather than in the uneven, screechy fashion of oratorio soloists of today. High schools and colleges would find it an interesting experiment — as some have — to present *The Beggar's Opera* instead of the annual musically worthless operetta.

For popular music, William Chappell : *Old English Popular Music,* edited by H. Ellis Wooldridge (2 vols., London, 1893), is a thorough-going, annotated collection of songs, a great number of which were sung in America, in their originals or with other texts. Chappell's volumes of thirty-four years earlier, *Popular Music of the Olden Time,* are better but less accessible. Olin Downes and Elie Siegmeister : *A Treasury of American Song* (2nd ed., New York, 1943) is a large, somewhat unwieldy volume of representative American songs arranged more or less chronologically, with excellent piano accompaniments and attractive background commentary. Otherwise, for popular music, it should be simple to reproduce *Yankee Doodle* with fife and drums in jig-time, to sing the words of the Anacreontic drinking-song to the tune of *The Star Spangled Banner,* and to dance the Virginia reel and cotillion.

In the field of folk-music, the Library of Congress has systematically recorded many of the surviving folk-songs of early America, under the general heading, *Folk Music of the United States.* Catalogues of recordings now available for purchase by the public may be requested of the Recording Laboratory, Division of Music, Library of Congress, Washington 25, D.C. Though wanting acoustically, these albums, recorded for the most part in the field, capture all the subtle and peculiar characteristics of folk-music with utmost authenticity. Also highly recommendable are the commercial phonograph albums of Burl Ives, John Jacob Niles, and Richard Dyer Bennett, who, however, bring some sophistication to the originally unsophisticated material.

Reed Smith and Hilton Rufty : *American Anthology of Old-World Ballads* (New York, 1937) is a careful distillation, tastefully set, of the British heritage of folk-ballads surviving in the United States. The song booklets of Schirmer's American Folk-Song Series are, generally speaking, advisable and appropriate. Number 16 of the series, John Jacob Niles : *Ten Christmas Carols from the Southern Appalachian Mountains,* presents some important fruits of the folk-carol field most acceptably. Many regional compilations of American folk-music are on the market. One of the best, a good source for dances and singing-games as well as folk-songs, is Eloise Hubbard Lin-scott : *Folk Songs of Old New England* (New York, 1939). For the many available works otherwise, the most usable folk-musical bibliography so far is Alan Lomax and Sidney Robertson Cowell : *American Folk Song and Folk Lore, A Regional Bibliography* (Washington, D.C., 1942). It contains brief descriptions and is arranged according to type of music and section of the country. For those to whom folk-music may seem incomprehensible, the well-written and well-reasoned foundation treatise for the study of the Anglo-American variety is Cecil J. Sharp : *English Folk-Song ; Some Con-clusions* (London, 1907) ; his *English Folk Songs from the Southern Ap-palachians*, edited by Maud Karpeles (2 vols., London, 1932) is the founda-tion collection of Anglo-American folk-songs.

A genuine country barn dance might prove a revelation. And in any state, especially in sparsely settled areas and among the old people of those areas, there can be found folk-singers. Ask someone like the county super-intendent of schools, the county farm agent, or home demonstration agent for leads on whom to approach. Be sure to visit awhile with a musical per-son before broaching the subject of singing.

CHAPTER X

Of Loyalties, and of the British-American Nation

"This is thy praise America thy pow'r

"Thou best of climes by science visited

"By freedom blest and richly stor'd with all

"The luxuries of life. Hail happy land

"The seat of empire the abode of kings,

"The final stage where time shall introduce

"Renowned characters, and glorious works

"Of high invention and of wond'rous art,

"While not the ravages of time shall waste

"Till he himself has run his long career;

"Till all those glorious orbs of light on high

"The rolling wonders that surround the ball,

"Drop from their spheres extinguish'd and consum'd,

"When final ruin with her fiery car

"Rides o'er creation, and all natures works

"Are lost in chaos and the womb of night."

PHILIP FRENEAU.

NATIONS AND NATIONALISMS

A NATION is a society. It is a homogeneous group of people, bound together by the ties of common interest, common emotional attachments, and common ideals. It is not to be confused with the state, which is a political institution that may, indeed, be the agent of one or several nations ; but the state has also stood, in many actual historical cases, in a position inimical to the interests of the nation. The nation is thus, figuratively, a social organism ; nationalism is that combination of intel-

[553]

lectual and emotional factors — that psychological force — which holds the parts of the organism together.

Nationalism, as a component element in the "mind" of a people, is a psychological phenomenon. It is not made up of ideas, purely, although the national tradition, literature, and history are the very stuff on which it feeds. On the other hand, it is not purely emotional, either, although it is the emotions of love and loyalty for the aspirations of one's own people that give it the power that has made it such a powerful determinant in the history of modern times. It is a sort of synthesis of idea, emotion, and ideal ; it is an extremely important part of the mind of any nation ; and it has been a profoundly important force in the shaping of the development of this nation, as well as that of all the other national divisions of modern world-society.

This intellectual and emotional phenomenon appeared in Western civilization in the centuries when the peoples of western Europe were being slowly forged into national unities. The English people achieved something approximating social — or national — unity during the Tudor century, and especially under Queen Elizabeth ; but Great Britain (England, Scotland, and Wales) achieved complete political unity only in the eighteenth century, one hundred years after the founding of Jamestown, and spiritual unity much later, even, than that.

The sentiment of nationalism found eloquent literary expression in Shakespeare, although it may be doubted whether Shakespeare's glorification of the English nation represented the feelings of more than a small articulate fraction of the English people ; and Elizabeth and her leaders made a dramatic appeal to it at the time of the Great Armada. From that time on this sentiment of nationalism was growing in England ; the early Stuarts ignored it, to their sorrow, but Cromwell and his poet, Milton, were great patriots ; it reached its eighteenth-century apogee in Henry St. John, Viscount Bolingbroke, who gave it nationalistic sanction in his essays, *The Idea of a Patriot King* and *On the Spirit of Patriotism.*

According to Bolingbroke, societies, or nations, had appeared in the natural order of things as the outgrowth of the "natural" impulse of human beings to form groups. These groups, again in the order of nature, are distinguished by character, language, and government, and the institutions and ideals of each are peculiarly suited to it within the framework or conditions of its natural environment. Thus each nation, applying to itself the principles of right reason and natural law, develops a set of laws and institutions peculiarly suited to its own people and development, but not always applicable to others.

Bolingbroke was certainly read by many Americans ; but his influence as a philosopher of nationalism was probably most effective in the direction of making the Americans more ardent Britishers. Yet his descriptions of the peculiarities of the nation, as they appear in the environment, could hardly have failed to suggest to some of them that America itself, as distinguished from Britain, was developing just such a set of peculiar institutions, customs, and laws as he described.

ORIGINS OF PATRIOTIC FEELING IN AMERICA

That aspect of the American self-consciousness of the 1750's which built the concept of common purpose upon fear of the French and criticism of England was of a negative, defensive sort. Furthermore, that feeling was pretty well contained within the framework of local provincial loyalty, on the one side, and imperial or "British" loyalty on the other.

Yet there is much evidence, scattered to be sure, of a growing, positive American self-assertiveness in the six years following the Peace of Aix-la-Chapelle (1748), which was epitomized by the general intercolonial pride in the feats of other "Americans" and a growing sense of the potential grandeur and power of the America of the future — and this feeling for and pride in America grew quickly, in the fifties and sixties, into a feeling that at the time of the Stamp Act of 1765 could be called "national."

It was in this period that the great expansionists like Franklin, Colden, Archibald Kennedy, Lewis Evans, and others began to sing the manifest destiny of Anglo-America to dominate the continent. Franklin, in his significant *Observations concerning the Increase of Mankind and the Peopling of Countries,* could not resist the temptation to burst into rhapsodies over the swift growth and future glory of America. For the population of America will one day exceed that of England, he said, "and the greater number of Englishmen will be on this side the water. What an accession of power to the British empire by sea as well as land! What increase of trade and navigation! What numbers of ships and seamen! We have been here [in America] but little more than one hundred years, and yet the force of our privateers in the late war [1744–8], united, was greater, both in men and guns, than that of the whole British navy in Queen Elizabeth's time." [1]

And young John Adams, seeing America in 1765 as somehow chosen of God as the instrument of bringing happiness to mankind, wrote : "I always consider the settlement of America with reverence and wonder, as the opening of a grand scene and design in Providence for the illumination of the ignorant and the emancipation of the slavish part of mankind all over the earth." [2] This was a somewhat patronizing sort of de-

---

[1] Franklin : *Works* (Sparks ed.), II, 319.
[2] John Adams : *Works* (C. F. Adams ed.), I, 66.

votion to the great ideal of his nation, in the breast of a confirmed aristocrat; but he was deeply moved by it. For this was his own individual vision of the meaning of America.

This feeling, this intellectual and emotional devotion to the concept of one's nation and its ideals, developed in British America along three lines. For a considerable number of Americans, especially those in economic, social, or political positions that bound their interests closely to the mother country, patriotism and nationalistic feeling revolved about the mother country, and their nationalism was a British Empire, "Tory" nationalism. For many, on the other hand, patriotism meant, or at least included as its chief component element, loyalty to one's own colonial province. For many Americans, however, there had appeared a new loyalty that stood somewhere between these other two, and that was loyalty to "America." The term "Americans" had first been used in this sense; and it certainly was coming to have, at the mid-century, an increasingly clear and distinct meaning for most of the colonists. This new "American" loyalty must be regarded as the earliest manifestation of a genuine American national feeling.

It should always be remembered, however, that all three of these foci of American loyalties were universally assumed to exist within the broad concept of the British Empire. For despite the loudly trumpeted fears of the colonial governors that the continued extension of the powers of the assemblies could only end in independence, and despite the fears expressed by some that the removal of the French from the interior of the continent would hasten the dreadful culmination of that development, no American in the 1750's even dreamed of a separate existence of his colony, or of all the continental colonies, outside of the broad folds of the Empire. All their loyalties, whether to Virginia, to America, or to the King as the symbol of the British nation everywhere, were never even questioned as anything other than the loyalty of a British Virginian, a British American, or a British imperialist. Whatever else he was, the American was always, in the 1750's and 1760's, a British subject. And his pride in himself and his society, or societies, his emotional loyalty to their ideals, his sense of satisfaction and well-being in the enjoyment of his rights, his liberties, his freedom, all these goods and satisfactions, real or fancied, centered upon his thought of himself as a "Briton."

The patriotism of the American Britons

The chief national loyalty of the generation of Americans who flourished *circa* 1750 was a loyalty to Britain and what they imagined to be the British ideal. They thought of themselves as Englishmen, they revered the crown of England as their own, and they glorified in poem and in essay the "British nation," of which they were members.

The idea of a union of any sort, least of all a national union among the English colonies in America, had occurred to relatively few men. To be sure, the idea had been advanced, particularly as a useful means of colonial defense, and a few intercolonial meetings had been held in time of crisis. But the New England Confederation had been the only serious effort at permanent organization by the colonies themselves. The British government, too, had officially experimented with the idea of permanent union, first in the Dominion of New England, which fell apart after the American counterpart of the Glorious Revolution, and again, somewhat half-heartedly, about the turn of the seventeenth century into the next. Finally, the Board of Trade, in its famous report of 1721, had proposed that the colonies be organized as one unified dominion under a governor-general to be seated at New York.

But the colonists had developed no deep or widespread consciousness of common intercolonial interest or loyalty prior to about 1740. On the contrary, such common loyalties as they had were directed toward the mother country; and their emotional outpourings were generally eulogiums upon the glorious British constitution and the sacred ideal of the liberties of Britons. Many essays in this vein appeared in the colonial newspapers in the middle decades of the century, especially in the interim of peace following the Peace of Aix-la-Chapelle, and many of the pamphlets produced in this period express the same "British" patriotic sentiment.

This sentiment was not new. For a sort of nationalistic belief in the superiority of the British way of life had begun to find expression in the glorification of the British constitution early in the century. John Wise, morning star of American democracy, had felt and expressed this sentiment :

It is said of the British empire, that it is such a monarchy as that, by the necessary subordinate concurrance of the lords and commons in the making and repealing all statues or acts of parliament, it hath the main advantages of an aristocracy and of a democracy, and yet free from the disadvantages and evils of either. It is such a monarchy as, by most admirable temperament, affords very much to the industry, liberty, and happiness of the subject, and reserves enough for the majesty and prerogative of any king who will own his people as subjects, not as slaves. It is a kingdom that, of all the kingdoms of the world, is most like to the kingdom of Jesus Christ, whose yoke is easy and burden light.[3]

[3] Wise : *Vindication of the Government of New England Churches*, p. 45.

And in the midst of partisan strife within a colony a "Briton" could appeal beyond the local issue to the loyalty of his readers toward the transcendent verities and unchanging authority and glory of the "British" constitution. Such, for example, was the burden of the complaint of the North Carolina pamphleteer William Smith, who wrote in 1740 : "But blessed be God we live under a *British* Constitution, where Liberty is our undoubted Inheritance, is well understood and ought to be enjoyed in it's full Extent ; in such a Government if any one shall presume to break thro' and violate the common Benefits and Priviledges, secured to us by Law, and trample under Foot the most solemn Oaths, the most binding and necessary Laws . . . is it not high Time for People labouring under such Oppressions and Injuries to look about them?" [4]

God, indeed, had favored Britons above all the other nations of the earth, in the opinion of Jonathan Mayhew — that same Mayhew who had preached so plainly the doctrine of the social contract and the right of revolution : "If we consider ourselves as *British* subjects, and entitled to the liberties and privileges of such, both civil and sacred ; we must acknowledge that providence has, in this respect, favoured us above most *other* protestants : Very few of whom, I might perhaps say none, live under so happy and excellent a form of government as ourselves." [5]

The feeling of "British" nationalism reached its apogee in the Seven Years' War, in which the colonists fought side by side with Englishmen against the French in Canada. "If ever there was a national war," wrote Franklin in 1760, "this is truly such a one ; a war in which the interest of the whole nation is directly and fundamentally concerned." [6] He meant here the British nation all over the world, and it was just as truly British in America as in England. The Americans, he said, were as loyal to the British ideals and objectives in the war as Englishmen themselves : "The inhabitants of [the colonies] are, in common with the other subjects of Great Britain, anxious for the glory of her crown, the extent of her power and commerce, the welfare and future repose of the whole British people. They could not, therefore, but take a large share in the affronts offered to Britain ; and have been animated with a truly British spirit to exert themselves beyond their strength, and against their evident interest." [7]

Franklin's "imperial" patriotism was of a part with the practical

[4] William Smith : *A True and Faithful Narrative of the Proceedings of the House of Burgesses of North Carolina* (Williamsburg, 1940), p. 51.

[5] Jonathan Mayhew : *Two Sermons on Divine Goodness* (Boston, 1761), p. 72.

[6] Franklin : *Works* (Sparks ed.), IV, 21.

[7] Ibid., IV, 17.

proposals he had made up to this time for the more solid political uni-
fication of the Empire, either by the voluntary creation of a colonial
union by act of Parliament that would be closely bound to Britain itself, or by actual representation in Parliament; at the moment, while he
recognized the mother country as the seat of the heart and soul of his
national Empire, he was not averse, in his moments of fancy, to envis-
aging the removal of that seat to America : "I have long been of opinion, that the *foundations of the future grandeur and stability of the
British empire lie in America;* and though, like other foundations, they
are low and little now, they are, nevertheless, broad and strong enough
to support the greatest political structure that human wisdom ever yet
erected." [8]

Franklin's loyalties went through a gradual reorientation as his
thinking about the Empire progressed toward the concept of a commonwealth of autonomous units; and presently he began to define the
differences in loyalties that were being crystallized by the conflicts
following the end of the Seven Years' War. Thus, he said : "When an
American says that he has a Right to all the Privileges of a British Subject, he does not call himself a British Subject, he is an American Subject of the King; the Charters say they shall be entitled to all the Privileges of Englishmen as if *they had been born within* the Realm." [9]

Franklin went on to give his whole loyalty at last to the ideals of
those who thought of themselves as "American subjects of the King,"
and to the sort of Anglo-American nationalism that reached its climax
about 1771 in the poetry of the young Philip Freneau. Many of the
more conservative Americans could not do this, however; their whole
social and political orientation was such as to make even the slightest
diminution of the supremacy of their loyalty to Britain and all things
British intellectually unthinkable and emotionally unbearable.

For this was an aristocratic loyalty, as well as a sort of loyalty to
class, to England; in it was reflected a social and political creed as well
as a loyalty to the British ideal. Obviously, the British Americans of the
1750's who stood at the top of society and in positions of political and
intellectual leadership felt quite profoundly that the British civilization
of which they were members was the finest, noblest, and most nearly
ideal in all the world. They were patriots; loyal, patriotic American
subjects of the British crown. Even young Francis Hopkinson, one of
Smith's young friends who was later to distinguish himself in the cause
of independence, felt the same warm loyalty to the British ideal, and
celebrated the British capture of Louisbourg in 1758 in one of his early
poems :

[8] Ibid., VII, 188.   [9] Quoted in Crane, op. cit., p. 116.

At length 'tis done ! the glorious Conflict's done !
And British *valour has the conquest won !*
Success *our arms, our heroes,* Honor *crowns,*
And Louisbourg an English *monarch owns. . . .*
   Give your loose canvas to the breezes free
Ye floating thund'rers, bulwarks of the sea !
Haste bear the joyful tidings to your king,
And with the voice of war declare 'tis Victory *you bring.*
Let the wild Crowd *that catch the breath of fame,*
In mad Huzzas *their ruder joys proclaim ;*
Let their loud thanks to Heav'n in flames ascend,
Whilst mingling shouts the azure concave rend.
But let the Few, *whom* Reason *makes more wise,*
In tears of Gratitude *uplift their eyes ;*
Oh may their breasts dilate with sober *joy,*
· *Let Pray'r their hearts, their tongues let* Praise *employ !*
To bless our God with me let all unite ;
He guides the conqu'ring sword, he governs in the fight.[10]

This a sort of "Tory" patriotism, in the sense that it held "British valour," and an "English monarch" to be the symbols of the general superiority of the British ideal, and in its assurance that God "guides the conqu'ring sword" for the British. Thousands of Americans who a brief two decades later were to employ their greatest talents to shake off the shackles of the successor to this same "English monarch" felt in 1758 as Hopkinson did, that the British crown was the symbol of a glorious British nation of which they were members, and of the glorious British liberties in which they shared. At the same time it is of interest to notice that Hopkinson's attitude was essentially aristocratic, drawing a sharp distinction between the "wild Crowd" and "the Few, whom Reason makes more wise." It was almost as though British superiority over other nations were one of the manifestations of natural law, along with the more general natural rights of man, and that British superiority was to be identified with the superiority of his class !

Many of these British patriots were even now discovering a new loyalty to America that would one day supplant their loyalty to Britannia. But many others, the unchanging Tories, when the crises came and they had to choose, would sincerely place their loyalty to their King before their loyalty to America. Such a man was Thomas Hutchinson, one of the most truly devoted Americans, who simply could not abandon what was to him a sacred British ideal. Such, also, was Jonathan Boucher, whose whole life and philosophy bound him to the King with a loyalty that was too strong for his growing attachment to America to

[10] Francis Hopkinson : "Poem on the taking of Cap-Breton," *American Magazine,* I, No. 11 (August 1758), pp. 551–4.

break. As he put it, sadly, on the eve of his departure from America at the outbreak of the Revolution :

> It is folly to imagine, that, as an Englishman, interested in the welfare of England, I am not equally interested in the welfare of America. I cannot dissociate the idea of a perfect sameness of interest between the two countries, as much as between a parent and a child. It is true, I had the honor to be born in England . . . yet . . . it is in this country, and in these times, that I have first, or ever, heard it urged as a reproach to any man that he was an Englishman. With respect to America, it has been the country of my choice. I am married in America ; and am settled in it, if I may have leave, most probably for life. I have property here . . . my connexions and friends, whom I love as I do my own soul, are all of this country. Is there a person among you who can produce stronger ties of attachment to any country than these are? [11]

The ideal that Boucher was holding up was a sort of dual loyalty, with loyalty to America embraced in the greater loyalty to Britain. But things being as they were, that was a forlorn hope in 1774, and since he had to choose, he could not but choose what for him was the greater ideal. The American Revolution, in its profoundly significant emotional aspect, was a conflict of loyalties : loyalty to Britain and the Empire versus loyalty to America and an American ideal that had begun to find its first self-conscious being about the middle of the eighteenth century.

It would of course be a mistake to suggest that this conflict of loyalties, or even the appearance of the new American loyalty that precipitated it, was fully self-conscious in the year 1750. But the new loyalty was beginning to show itself, as the bases of economic, social, political, and intellectual homogeneity were being more clearly drawn and firmly laid. Thereafter the dramatic flowering of American nationalism between 1765 and 1770 and the conflict between the new loyalty and the old were only a matter of growth.

Provincial loyalties

The appearance of an American patriotism as an intellectual, emotional, and social force of such power as to be able to force such a leader as Boucher to abandon his pulpit had, however, not only to overcome the retarding effect of the deep American loyalty to Britain but also to supersede the local loyalties and provincialisms of the separate colonies and the bitter intercolonial jealousies and conflicts that sprang from them.

[11] Jonathan Boucher : *A View of the Causes and Consequences of the American Revolution*, pp. 592–3.

It was but natural that there should have appeared a local patriotism, a loyalty of the provincial for "his country," the particular land
and province in which he lived. This pride of place and association
could not but produce invidious comparison and intensified feelings
of self-satisfaction with those things which were one's own. Thus Hugh
Jones, writing in 1724, had extolled the superiorities of Virginia : "If
New England be called a Receptacle of Dissenters, and an *Amsterdam*
of Religion, *Pennsylvania* the Nursery of Quakers, *Maryland* the Retirement of *Roman* Catholicks, *North Carolina* the Refuge of Run-aways,
and *South Carolina* the Delight of Buccaneers and Pyrates, *Virginia*
may be justly esteemed the happy Retreat of *true Britons* and true
Churchmen for the most Part ; neither soaring too high nor drooping
too low, consequently should merit the greater Esteem and Encouragement." [12]

And Franklin, in 1760, in his refutation of the charge that the removal of the French menace might tempt the Americans to become
independent, or dangerous to England, made the mutual rivalries and
distrust between the colonies perfectly clear. For, he said, "If they
could not agree to unite for their defence against the French and Indians
. . . can it reasonably be supposed there is any danger of their uniting
against their own nation, which protects and encourages them, with
which they have so many connexions and ties of blood, interest and
affection, and which, it is well known, they all love much more than
they love one another ?" [13]

Franklin wrote with feeling, for the so-called Albany Plan for a
union of the colonies, of which he was one of the principal authors, had
been rebuffed by the colonies ; and he had had other occasions to observe their mutual jealousies. At the same time, however, he was probably exaggerating the point for the sake of the argument. He was himself a speculator in western lands ; he was an ardent believer in the
"manifest destiny" of the colonies to expand across the continent ; and
he sincerely believed that the French should be eliminated from the
back-country as a necessity for the establishment of a durable North
American peace. Furthermore, he was himself one of the most active
propagandists for a drawing together of the colonies, intellectual as
well as military, and in this same pamphlet he bears testimony to the
fact that many of the colonists were already awake to the desirability
of continental solidarity.

Yet the existence and influence of local provincial loyalties, expressing themselves in petty intercolonial enmities, was a genuine reality. The
differences between the colonies and sections, quite apart from their

[12] Jones : *The Present State of Virginia*, p. 48.
[13] Franklin : *Works* (Sparks ed.), IV, 41–2.

petty squabbles, were deep. The social and cultural make-up of Virginia, for example, was distinct, in many deep and fundamental ways, as must be abundantly evident. William Douglass in his *Summary*, noticed these differences; he even went so far as to express a fear that Pennsylvania, particularly, because of its heavy influx of continental Europeans, might "degenerate into a foreign colony."[14]

Charles Chauncy, writing in 1755, could not restrain his pride in his own native New England: "New England in general, and the Massachusetts-province in particular, are the chief, I may say, the only sources that may be relied on for a supply of effective men, to carry into execution any future designs against the French. There are no men in the American colonies so well qualified, or spirited as these, to engage in warlike enterprizes: and this is so well known, that the other colonies, as well as Great Britain, have their expectations mainly from us."[15]

This bumptious sense of New England's responsibility for the rest of America, this consciousness of provincial differences, with its counterpart, the sentimental loyalty to one's own province of Massachusetts, was complemented, among the forces operating against the formation of any genuine ideal of an American nation, by a budding sectionalism elsewhere. For the sections were, if anything, even more conscious of the differences between them than the individual provinces. The culture of Charleston seemed strange, even "foreign," to the visitor from Boston. Boucher, again, on the eve of the Revolution, appealed to this regional distrust in a warning to the southern colonies to desist from their resistance to England lest they suddenly and to their sorrow discover that they have escaped the mild and benevolent authority of England only to fall into the doleful clutches of New England:

> But consider, we pray you, for a moment in what a case we [of the southern colonies] are likely to be should such an event be permitted for our sins to take place. Wholly unable to defend ourselves, see ye not that after some few years of civil broils all the fair settlements in the middle and southern colonies will be seized on by our more enterprising and restless fellow-colonists of the North? At first and for a while perhaps they may be contented to be the Dutch of America, i.e. to be our carriers and fishmongers; for which no doubt, as their sensible historian [Hutchinson?] has observed, they seem to be destined by their situation, soil, and climate; but had so sagacious an observer foreseen that a time might possibly come when all North America should be independent, he would, it is probable, have added to his other remark, that those his Northern brethren would then become also the Goths

[14] Douglass: *Summary, Historical and Political*, II, 326.

[15] Charles Chauncy: *Two Letters to a Friend, on the Present Critical Conjuncture of Affairs in North America* (Boston, 1755), pp. 16–17.

and Vandals of America. This is not a chimerical conjecture : the history of mankind proves that it is founded in truth and the nature of things. And should the reflection chance to make any such impression on you, as we humbly think it ought, we entreat you only to remember that you are — *from the Southern Provinces.* . . . O 'tis a monstrous and an unnatural coalition ; and we should as soon expect to see the greatest contrarieties in Nature to meet in harmony, and the wolf and the lamb to feed together, as Virginians to form a cordial union with the saints of New England.[16]

This appeal to sectionalism was an appeal to a very real feeling among the colonists — a feeling that supplemented their local provincialisms. Yet the mere formulation of sectionalist self-consciousness may have been a necessary preliminary step toward the growth of the concept of a larger, national entity. In any case, the emergence of an American national sentiment had to await a balancing of local and regional loyalties on the one side, and of the imperial Tory loyalty to Britain on the other, by a newer sense of common intercolonial unity of interest and tradition. In the face of such opposing loyalties, it is at least mildly surprising to discover that "Americanism" appeared at all! Yet it did appear, and that quite definitely and clearly, in these same decades of the 1750's and 1760's.

The genesis of an "American" nationalism

A common loyalty to a common American purpose and ideal was beginning to emerge among the Americans even before 1750. And it was this new American self-consciousness in all things, this new loyalty to America, that was to give the Americans an intellectual and emotional sense of unity of purpose and ideal. It was the conflict with the mother country over the question of taxation, to be sure, that galvanized this American self-consciousness into dramatic literary expression and political action ; but its beginnings lie farther back than that : its roots are deeply embedded in the earliest American experience.

The people of the British colonies in America did not yet, in the year 1750, constitute a homogeneous social entity. For the British Empire in this hemisphere was composed of a congeries of disparate settlements and societies from the primitive trading posts on the shores of Hudson Bay and British Guiana to the highly sophisticated societies of New York, Virginia, or Jamaica. Yet thirteen of the twenty-odd colonies were passing, more or less consciously, through a process that was at once drawing them together toward homogeneity and distinguishing them, as a single unit, from all the others. For these thirteen, located along the eastern seaboard of the continent, were

---

[16] Boucher : *Reminiscences of an American Loyalist,* pp. 132–3, 134.

ᵇeing subtly fused by a number of forces that were daily becoming more powerful.

Among these forces were the influences exerted by increased commercial, social, and intellectual intercourse between colonies. As roads from one colony to another appeared, finally binding them together on one long string from Portsmouth to Savannah, the spreading consciousness of a common cultural tradition could not fail to grow. This development seems to have been an almost inevitable consequence of the expansion of populations that brought the people of one colony to rubbing elbows with the people of the next. As the means of communication were expanded and improved, travel increased; and the traveler from Boston in Charleston, for example, found that the citizens of the two places had much in common. Travel and writing led to intercolonial marriages; and as the number of colleges increased and their fame spread, more and more young men crossed intercolonial boundaries in quest of education. These intellectual and social and economic forces making for closer association were well under way by the middle of the century.

One of the most obvious of these forces was the binding effect of intercolonial trade. And the continued growth of intercolonial economic relations gave impetus to the already well-developed consciousness of the differentness of American economic interests from those of the mother country. The appearance of an American self-consciousness in the realm of economic affairs, in fact, had had its beginning very early in the history of the colonies, and had sprung originally from the realization that their economic interests diverged, at many important points, from those of the mother country. The Navigation Acts and the Acts of Trade had been efforts to force American economic life into the imperial pattern, but they had been only partially successful; and many Americans such as Franklin had begun to question, as early as about 1750, the validity of the entire system. But the formulation of a positive feeling of economic nationalism did not really appear until the conflict with the mother country over the program, initiated about 1764, to make the old imperial system really effective. The colonies, thrown on the defensive, were forced to elaborate reasons for their opposition to the mother country, and some Americans went on beyond their economic philosophy in defense of their liberties to emotional glorifications of the economic grandeur and destiny of America as a whole or of one's own province as a separate unit. Such, for example, was the sentiment of Daniel Dulany, writing in Virginia in 1765:

Let the manufacture of *America* be the symbol of dignity, the badge of virtue, and it will soon break the fetters of distress. A garment of linsey-woolsey, when made the distinction of real patriotism, is more honourable and attractive of respect and veneration, than all the pageantry, and the robes, and the plumes, and the diadem of an emperor without it. Let the emulation be not in the richness and variety of foreign productions, but in the improvement and perfection of our own. . . . I have in my younger days seen fine sights, and been captivated by their dazzling pomp and glittering splendor; but the sight of our representatives, all adorned in compleat dresses of their own leather, and flax, and wool, manufactured by the art and industry of the inhabitants of *Virginia*, would excite, not the gaze of admiration, the flutter of an agitated imagination, or the momentary amusement of a transient scene, but a calm, solid, heart-felt delight. Such a sight would give me more pleasure than the most splendid and magnificent spectacle the most exquisite taste ever painted, the richest fancy ever imagined, realized to the view . . . as much more pleasure as a good mind would receive from the contemplation of virtue, than of elegance; of the spirit of patriotism, than the ostentation of opulence.[17]

The solid intellectual bases for an American national feeling were being laid in the 1740's and 1750's. One of the greatest of the agencies for such a development was the post-office, of which, significantly enough, Benjamin Franklin became the head in 1753. Franklin had actively sought the office of Deputy Postmaster-General for America, partly because he thought it might be remunerative, but also, as he said in his letter to Peter Collinson, because he felt sure the post-office could be made an effective agency for the development of an active intercolonial intellectual exchange. He believed the work of the Philosophical Society would be extended by it, and that Philadelphia might well become the cultural capital of America.

There were probably not many men in America who saw the intellectual maturity of America as Franklin saw it in 1743, or believed that the colonies were culturally so mature. Yet the organization and the success and permanence of the American Philosophical Society may be taken, perhaps, as evidence that in 1743 and the years following there was enough and sufficiently widespread intercolonial interest in intellectual matters to permit of this year being used as the marker of the birth of an American cultural self-consciousness. For the exchange of ideas and associations that resulted must have given considerable impetus to the growth of a sense of a common American intellectual life.

Even if Franklin had been alone in his effort to draw the colonies together culturally, as he was not, his own sponsoring of an intercolonial cultural development was a significant manifestation of his early

[17] Dulany : *Considerations on the Propriety of imposing Taxes in the British Colonies*, pp. 45–6, 48.

"Americanism"; and if in 1743 he was giving form to an American cultural life, twenty years later he was beginning to see in America the very heart and center of the culture of western civilization.

Meanwhile, a cultural self-consciousness was also appearing in other lines of literary production, one of the most notable of which was history. It is probably not without significance, and highly symptomatic of the dawning self-consciousness of the Americans, that Dr. William Douglass's *Summary, Historical and Political, of the British Settlements in North-America,* which was intended to cover the entire Anglo-American colonial area on the continent of North America, appeared between the years 1747 and 1752. The fact that it was not completed does not diminish the significance of the author's conception; for he gave the first important literary and documentary expression to an American continental self-consciousness.

One of the most important manifestations of the awakening cultural self-consciousness of the Americans was the deliberate effort of William Smith and his circle of young littérateurs and artists in Philadelphia to make for America a place in the cultural sun. All of the magazines that were launched between 1740 and 1760 show this cultural objective, in one way or another; and the *American Magazine,* published by Smith and his circle, is full of literary and historical expressions of it.

The Americans, indeed, were slowly but surely awakening to a realization of their own traditions and a sense of their own glorious future as a distinct people, in all the realms of their thinking. Already, for example, American patriots were beginning to extol the humanitarianism of America as a refuge for the poor and the oppressed, and the virtues of "The American, this new man," as the product of the melting-pot. Poor Richard expressed this popular sentiment in 1752 when he sang the praises of this country as a place

> *Where the sick Stranger joys to find a Home,*
> *Where casual Ill, maim'd Labour, freely come;*
> *Those worn with Age, Infirmity or Care,*
> *Find Rest, Relief, and Health returning fair.*
> *There too the Walls of rising Schools ascend,*
> *For Publick Spirit still is Learning's Friend,*
> *Where Science, Virtue, sown with liberal Hand,*
> *In future Patriots shall inspire the Land.*[18]

But the love of one's country inspired by its humanitarian welcome to the poor and suffering of the world was looked upon with a jaundiced eye by those hundred-per-cent patriots who feared the possible

[18] *Poor Richard Improved,* 1752.

un-American activities and influence of the foreigners on our soil. This was the sort of fear which, mixed with religious distrust, led to the passage of the Connecticut "Act Providing Relief against the evil and dangerous Designs of Foreigners and Suspected Persons"; this was the fear, also, that led William Smith to write his diatribes against the Pennsylvania Germans, and William Douglass to pour out the vials of his wrath against the Quakers in his bitter exclamation that "the pusilanimous Doctrine of not defending themselves by force against an invading Enemy is very absurd: PRO PATRIA *is not only a Law of Nations, but of Nature.*" [19]

Even Franklin, in almost the same moment when with the popular voice of Poor Richard he was extolling the national melting-pot, could privately express his fear that the Germans might prove to be too un-American in their influence to be absorbed:

> This will in a few Years become a *German* Colony: Instead of their Learning our Language, we must learn their's, or live as in a foreign country. Already the *English* begin to quit particular Neighbourhoods surrounded by *Dutch* [Germans], being made uneasy by the Disagreeableness of disonant Manners; and in Time, Numbers will probably quit the Province for the same Reason. Besides, the *Dutch* under-live, and are thereby enabled to under-work and under-sell the *English;* who are thereby extreamly incommoded, and consequently disgusted, so that there can be no cordial Affection or Unity between the two Nations. [20]

The split in nationalistic pride between those who glorify the melting-pot and those who fear the un-American activities of foreigners whose ideals do not exactly coincide with their own is no new thing; it has apparently been one of the dialectical strains within American nationalistic feeling almost from the beginning.

The same sort of dialectical strain has also been present in the religious aspects of American patriotism. For, despite the established principle of religious toleration, the nationalistic self-consciousness of the Americans of the eighteenth century expressed itself strongly and repeatedly as committed to the dissenting Protestant way. This was especially visible in the diatribes against Roman Catholic France, but it was also visible even in the resistance of many Americans against the possibility of an expansion of Anglicanism and, most particularly, to the movement for the establishment of an Anglican bishopric here. Jonathan Mayhew had voiced this fear in the preface to his famous ser-

---

[19] Douglass: *Summary, Historical and Political*, II, 152.
[20] Archibald Kennedy: *The Importance of Gaining . . . The Friendship of the Indians . . .*, appendix, p. 30.

mon on unlimited submission in 1750. Twelve years later his convictions had taken on a distinctly nationalistic tinge :

> We [Britishers] are still farther distinguished and favoured of God, by having been born and bred in a *protestant* country, and a *reformed* part of the christian church ; instead of a roman-catholic country, & in the errors, superstitions and idolatries of the church of Rome. For had the latter been our lot, we should probably, the most of us, have been enslaved to those delusions, and the papal tyranny to this day. And those of us, whom God should have given light and courage enough to cast them off, might have suffered a cruel persecution; and " for conscience towards God endured grief" ; as protestants now do, even in France itself, from a pretended most polite, humane and refined, but really *barbarous* people in some respects. . . .[21]

But Americans were favored, even above other Britons, not only on the count of religion, but also because of America's happy isolation from Europe's turmoil and her precious civil liberties :

> If we come to our own country in particular ; we have here enjoyed, of late, almost all the blessings of peace, in a time of war and tumult among the nations of Europe. We have also been favoured with general health. Our invaluable civil rights and privileges are preserved to us. I do not say, that they have even been struck at, in any instance or degree – But if they have, they are not wrested from us : And may righteous heaven blast the designs, tho' not the soul or the body of that man, whoever he be amongst us, that shall have the hardiness and presumption to attack them! [22]

The growth of something approximating a nationalistic religious outlook was accompanied by a corresponding development in concepts of education. For now, to the concept of education as a promoter of social aims, molder of preachers, disseminator of the arts and sciences, and trainer of young people in the skills required for making a living, was added an increasing weight of suggestion that education had a civic duty to perform in the training of citizens ; and since the Americans were coming to have a poignant sense of their own traditions, history was thought of as being the subject most likely to inculcate the civic virtues. Thus in 1749 Cadwallader Colden wrote to Franklin :

> While you keep the great end of education in view, that is, to enable men and incline them to be more useful to mankind in general, and to their own country in particular, and at the same time to render their own life more happy, you cannot be in danger of taking wrong steps, while all of them tend to that end. . . . It is a common opinion, that the power and strength of a nation consist in its riches and money. No

[21] Jonathan Mayhew : *Two Sermons* (Boston, 1763), pp. 71–2.
[22] Ibid., pp. 73–4.

doubt money can do great things; but I think the power of a nation consists in the knowledge and virtue of its inhabitants, and, in proof of this, history shows us that the richest nations, abounding most in silver and gold, have been generally conquered by poor, but, in some sense, virtuous nations. If riches be not accompanied with virtue, they on that very account expose a nation to ruin, by their being a temptation for others to invade them, while luxury, the usual consequence of riches, makes them an easy prey.[23]

Colden was using the language of nationalism and national civic virtue in education. But it must be remembered that his was a "Tory" nationalism; also that he was an aristocrat in education; and that as he grew older and more bitter over the political radicalism of the assembly party in New York, he thought of education as an instrumentality for training aristocratic leaders who would know to whom their supreme loyalty should attach. The important thing to notice here, of course, is that Colden, like so many of his American contemporaries, was feeling his way toward a clear concept of the nation, and was thinking of education as a mechanism for promoting the national civic virtues and national happiness.

Franklin believed strongly in the educational value of history, not merely for the promotion of the social ideal and the virtues of citizenship, but also for inculcation in the student of the peculiar virtues and advantages of his own people : "If the new *Universal History* were also read, it would give a connected idea of human affairs, so far as it goes, which should be followed by the best Modern histories, particularly of our mother country; then of these colonies; which should be accompanied with observations on their rise, increase, use to Great Britain, encouragements and discouragements, the means to make them flourishing, and secure their liberties."[24]

This was written in 1749. Yet there is unquestionably present in this recommendation a consciousness of the peculiar differentness of the colonies, of their common problems, and the preciousness of their liberties. It is this idealization of the abstract qualities of one's own people that is the essence of nationalism. If this was not nationalism itself, then it was surely the psychological germ from which an American nationalism was to grow.

But it was in the face of a common enemy that the nationalistic feelings of the Americans found the freest and most intense expression in the 1750's. For at this point "Tory" feelings and "American" feelings could merge; and the approach of the Seven Years' War was unquestionably the great catalyst that precipitated the most eloquent expressions of America's nascent nationalism. This strong anti-Gallican

[23] Franklin : *Works* (Sparks ed.), VII, 46. [24] Ibid., I, 574.

animosity had been vocal, in fact, since the War of the Austrian Succession (King George's War) and the thrill of general exultation that
ran through all the colonies over the capture of Louisbourg in 1745 by
a little band of New Englanders. Poems and essays in celebration of
that event were published in the newspapers of the south as well as
the north; the following lines taken from a poem in the *Maryland Gazette* are typical of a number of poems like it :

> *And what avail'd their Demilunes,*
> *Their Parapets, and brazen Guns,*
>   *They were but Frenchmen still;*
> *Their feeble Genius soon gave Place*
> *To bold New-England's hardy Race,*
>   *Led on by Pepp'ral's skill.*[25]

As for New England, it was beside itself; and a man so chaste in his
language as Charles Chauncy was impelled to exult : "I scarce know of
a Conquest, since the Days of *Joshua* and the *Judges,* wherein the
Finger of God is more visible. . . . And now as the Conclusion of all,
May it please the good and gracious God to over-rule this glorious Conquest to an happy Issue, the Good of our *Nation* and *Land.* . . . And
may the happy Period come on, when Nation shall no more lift up
Sword against Nation, nor the Alarm of War be heard on Earth."[26]
And Nathaniel Ames poured his patriotic feelings into his almanac in
the form of a prayer to the Goddess of Victory for yet greater favors :

> *Hail, Victory! Thy Aid we still implore,*
> *Thy Britain conquers; send her Thunder o'er :*
> *We only for her moving Castles wait;*
> *But they, alas! have been detain'd by Fate.*
> *Great-Britain's Forests float upon the Floods,*
> *And dreadful Lions dwell within those Woods;*
> *Awake their sleeping Fury, make 'em roar,*
> *And all the Beasts on Canadensis Shore*
> *Shall fear, and all their Native Rage forsake,*
> *And Trembling seize those Coasts, ev'n to Quebeck. . . .*
>   *Proud of thy special Favours heretofore,*
> *Like Beggars once indulg'd we ask for more;*
> *Thou know'st which Way the ridged Fates incline,*
> *If on our Side, give one propitious Sign,*
> *And lo Ten Thousand bold Americans will join,*
> *With chearful Hearts to extirpate a Race*
> *Of Superstitious Papists false and base.*[27]

[25] *Maryland Gazette*, January 14, 1746.
[26] Charles Chauncy : *Marvellous Things done by the Right Hand and Holy
Arm of God in getting Him the Victory* (Boston, 1745), pp. 12, 22–3.
[27] Ames : *Astronomical Diary*, 1747.

This deep and intense fear and hatred of a common enemy, the sentiment that might be called a sense of the "Gallic peril," was expressed in many places and in many ways. It appears again and again in the newspapers and in the pamphlets, especially in the mid-century armed truce between 1748 and 1754. The French were the great enemy of all the colonies except the small, coast-bound provinces like Rhode Island, Connecticut, New Jersey, and Delaware; and as population had expanded even farther and farther westward, the inevitability of eventual conflict had become increasingly apparent to everybody, including the French themselves. The governors of New France repeatedly warned their mother country, especially the Marquis de la Galissonnière, of the irrepressible expansiveness of the British Americans. But the French forts built along the frontier from Crown Point in the north to Fort Toulouse in the south appeared to the British colonists only the visible evidence of an aggressive French determination at least to hem them in along the seaboard. The alarmists, however, saw a greater threat than that and warned their readers that the French would reach out to the coast itself and, it might be, one day drive the British from the Atlantic coastal plain altogether, or, worse still, reduce all the Americans to slavery. One of the easiest ways, obviously, for the French to do this, would be by alienating the "foreigners" along the frontier. The French had lately been active along the Ohio, building forts and establishing control over the Indians; since the Quakers of Pennsylvania were pacifists, it seemed to William Smith that it would be extremely easy, even what the French actually designed, to make, by way of Pennsylvania, a breach in the solid front of the English colonies.

Many Americans were in a state of deathly fear of the French and their iniquitous designs, and the sermons of the period sought to whip their audiences into a fervor of patriotic defense of American soil and liberties. Here is an example from Jonathan Mayhew:

> And what horrid scene is this, which restless, roving fancy, or something of an higher nature, presents to me, and so chills my blood! Do I behold these territories of freedom, become the prey of arbitrary power? . . . Do I see the slaves of Lewis with their Indian allies, dispossessing the free-born [American] subjects of King George, of the inheritance received from their forefathers, and purchased by them at the expense of their ease, their treasure, their blood! . . . Do I see a protestant, there, stealing a look at his bible, and being tak[en] in the fact, punished like a felon! . . . Do I see all liberty, property, religion, happiness, changed, or rather transubstantiated, into slavery, poverty, superstition, wretchedness! [28]

[28] Quoted in Baldwin: *The New England Clergy and the American Revolution*, p. 87.

Freedom of property, freedom to work, freedom of worship, the free pursuit of happiness; these American freedoms were threatened by Louis XV of France, monstrous symbol of dictatorial government menacing the liberty of the world, and especially American freedom! This was an ideological war; and the forces of nationalistic emotion were called upon to defend the American-English ideal of liberty against the rapacious Juggernaut of popish authoritarianism. If there ever was a war of Anglo-American aggressive expansionism, the Seven Years' War in America was that war. Yet that did not prevent the intellectual leaders from preaching, in all sincerity of conviction, and the people from believing, that it was a holy war in the name of an ideal, the ideal of "British" (American) liberty and self-government. Samuel Davies, in Virginia, could pull out all the stops on the organ of his eloquence to stir the Virginians to patriotic self-sacrifice:

> and shall these Ravages go on uncheck'd? Shall *Virginia* incur the Guilt, and the everlasting Shame of tamely exchanging her Liberty, her Religion, and her All, for arbitrary *Gallic* Power, and for Popish Slavery, Tyranny, and Massacre? Alas! are there none of her Children, that enjoyed all the Blessings of her Peace, that will espouse her Cause, and befriend her now in the Time of her Danger? Are *Britons* utterly degenerated by so short a Remove from their Mother-Country? Is the Spirit of Patriotism entirely extinguished among us? And must I give thee up for lost, O my Country! and all that is included in that important Word? [29]

And James Sterling, of Annapolis, "pathetically" urged the Maryland Assembly to patriotic action:

> Let me tell you, my worthy countrymen, the eyes of your constituents are now upon you. . . . The eyes of your sister-colonies are upon you, who will be agitated by shame or rivalship to take their measures from your pattern. Assume then the glory of making your pattern the master-spring of their motion! — The eyes of your venerable mother-nation will be upon you, who requires and expects, that . . . you wou'd imitate her parliaments in a suitable conduct, when French invasions are threaten'd; and no longer be amus'd, like our commissaries in Paris, by the futile and time-spinning wrangles, or by all the stale chicanery of a treaty-making and treaty-breaking race; but crush at a blow the crocodile in the eggshell. — Nay, gentlemen, the Argus' eyes of the very French are upon you, who, by their various and conceal'd emissaries, undisguis'd jesuits, pardoned rebels, and traiterous malcontents, will have dispatched to them at Quebec, or even Paris, the accounts of your proceedings. . . . O then . . . O permit not the zeal of a true public spirit to cool in your breasts; but . . . improve it in

[29] Samuel Davies: *Religion and Patriotism the Constituents of a Good Soldier* (Philadelphia, 1756), pp. 4–5.

yourselves; kindle, increase it in others; and transmit the hallowed principle to your children's children, to latest posterity; till only the day of Judgment and the kingdom of Christ put a period to the British dominion in our *new world;* or till time shall be lost in eternity ! [30]

Many of the Americans, if not all, were being drawn swiftly and deeply into the continental mood of nationalistic self-defense. The Albany Congress, with its plan for intercolonial union, was more a practical effort at defense than a sounding-board of psychological nationalism; yet its members were moved by the same patriotic sentiments that were moving the souls of so many other Americans; and William Livingston reported that "The speakers [at the conference] . . . were

The sentiment for intercolonial union in cartoons: "Join or Die."
[From the *Pennsylvania Gazette,* May 9, 1754]

not many; but of those who spoke, some delivered themselves with singular energy and eloquence. All were inflamed with a patriot spirit, and the debates were nervous and pathetic [fervent]. This assembly . . . might very properly be compared to one of the ancient Greek conventions, for supporting their expiring liberty against the power of the Persian empire, or that Lewis of Greece, Philip of Macedon." [31]

Samuel Davies probably expressed the common mood of most Americans when he said, in 1756: "Now what can be more important, what more interesting, than our country! Our country is a word of the highest and most endearing import: it includes our friends and relatives, our liberty, our property, our religion: in short, it includes our earthly all. And when the fate of our country and all that it includes, is dreadfully doubtfull . . . every mind that has the least thought, must be agitated with many eager, dubious expectations. This is the

[30] James Sterling : *Zeal against the Enemies of our Country pathetically recommended* (Annapolis, 1755), pp. 21–2, 30.
[31] William Livingston : *A Review of Military Operations in North-America* (*Mass. Hist. Soc. Colls.,* VII), p. 77.

present situation of our country. . . ." [32] And Nathaniel Ames, intellectual mentor for thousands of New England almanac-readers, could in 1758, with uncanny prescience, cry down the years to the Americans of the future :

> The Curious have observ'd, that the Progress of Humane Literature (like the Sun) is from the East to the West; thus has it travelled thro' Asia and Europe, and now is arrived at the Eastern Shore of *America*. As the Cœlestial Light of the Gospel was directed here by the Finger of GOD, it will doubtless, finally drive the long! long! Night of Heathenish Darkness from *America* : — So Arts and Sciences will change the Face of Nature in their Tour from Hence over the Appalachian Mountains to the Western Ocean; and as they march thro' the vast Desert, the Residence of wild Beasts will be broken up, and their obscene Howl cease for ever; — Instead of which, the Stones and Trees will dance together at the Music of *Orpheus*, — The Rocks will disclose their hidden Gems, — and the inestimable Treasures of Gold & Silver be broken up. Huge Mountains of Iron Ore are already discovered; and vast Stores are reserved for future Generations : This Metal more useful than Gold and Silver, will employ millions of Hands, not only to form the martial Sword, and peaceful Share, alternately; but an Infinity of Utensils improved in the Exercise of Art, and Handicraft amongst Men. Nature thro' all her Works has stamp'd Authority on this Law, namely, "That all fit Matter shall be improved to its best Purposes." — Shall not then those vast Quarries, that team with mechanic Stone, — those for Structure be piled into great Cities, — and those for Sculpture into Statues to perpetuate the Honor of renowned Heroes; even those who shall now save their Country, — *O! Ye unborn Inhabitants of America! Should this Page escape its destin'd Conflagration at the Year's End, and these Alphabetical Letters remain legible, — when your Eyes behold the Sun after he has rolled the Seasons round for two or three Centuries more, you will know that* in Anno Domini 1758, *we dream'd of your Times.*[33]

The final climax of American nationalistic conviction eventually came in the realm of political thought, which epitomized the whole struggle of the Americans and their culture-complex for self-expression. And this trend toward a political nationalism looked two ways; for while it was expressing itself positively along the lines of the struggle for political self-direction, it was also expressing itself negatively in the increasing resistance to control by the mother country.

Thus in the same years in which the colonists were beginning to sense the reality of their common cause and purpose toward their

[32] Samuel Davies : *Sermons on Important Subjects* (2 vols., Philadelphia, 1794), II, 518.
[33] Ames : *Astronomical Diary,* 1758.

French and Indian enemies, they were also awakening to a consciousness of the common nature of their problems toward the mother country. Hitherto, of course, and even now, the American's highest loyalty was to England and to his King. But these years marked the moment of his awakening, in the course of his struggle over the prerogative, over the regulation of commerce, and over taxation, to the fact of his differentness from Englishmen : the fact that, somehow, the American and the Englishman, though ruled by the same King, were not the same men, that England and America were not the same society ; and that for the American, though he might still be supremely loyal to his King, the society in which he breathed and had his being was American, not English ; and his loyalty to his King was really a symbol of his loyalty to his colony, and through it, eventually, to "America." Jonathan Mayhew's sermon on unlimited submission was a clear warning to the English crown to govern the colonies according to the social compact between them, delivered without for a moment contemplating a reduction of American loyalty. With the same candor within the bounds of "British" loyalty Franklin was criticizing the mother country for her shortsightedness in insisting upon the Navigation Acts. A wise mother he said, would not do it ; and he was speaking for all the colonies, not just one or several.

That some such feeling of differentness was taking shape in Franklin's mind between 1750 and 1755, despite his enthusiastic expansionist imperialism, is clear from his writing during this period touching upon the relations of the colonies to the mother country, economic as well as political. For he not only criticized the unwisdom of Parliamentary restraints upon colonial trade, but, more positively, suggested a greater imperial union, with the colonies enjoying a much more important place in imperial deliberations, representation in an imperial parliament, and greater recognition of the uniqueness of the way of life of the colonies as a distinct unit in the Empire. In his eighteenth-century quest for a natural order in human affairs corollary to the order in the physical universe, he was discovering, or thought he was, the natural processes by which societies are formed. The American society had been formed by the natural process ; it was different from the society from which it sprang ; and it must be respected as being so. There began to be implicit in Franklin's criticisms of England a principle, the nationalistic counterpart of his sociological and economic thinking, of the naturalistic origins and peculiarities of nations. This principle, gradually becoming clearer in his own mind as it found expression in his political thoughts on the nature of the British Empire between 1765 and 1775, did not, as yet, conflict with the principle of loyalty to the King. Franklin was an ardent and patriotic Briton ; but he was also a patriotic American, fired with a sense of the future greatness of his native land.

The growing feeling of criticism of England and the nebular beginning of an intercolonial solidarity were not confined to the struggle of the assemblies against the prerogative, nor even to politics. The manifold activities of the colonial agents in England also reflect the increasing complexity of the problem of forestalling interference in colonial affairs; and the agents were now finding it increasingly to their advantage to present a common front. A very significant case of this sort of co-operative action took place between 1750 and 1753, when the northern colonial agents in London found themselves lined up in a solid front against the sugar-planters of the British West Indies and their agents for the preservation of the trade of the northern colonies with the French West Indies. The proposed restrictions upon that trade, said the northern agents, would paralyze the northern colonies economically; moreover, the restrictions would constitute a violation of the American's rights as Englishmen. Significantly, their protest was based upon the economic differentness of the colonies from England.

This united effort of the agents was successful. The passage of the Sugar Act in 1764 brought the agents together again, and from then on they were regularly instructed to co-operate on questions of common interest; after the Stamp Act of 1765 they met together regularly to formulate joint policies. The significant development here was, of course, the emergence of a united, co-operative front toward the mother country among the colonies through their agents in England. The common front represented in the colonial mind the idea of common interests and a common cause.

During the Seven Years' War in America the feeling of difference between "Americans" and "Englishmen" was heightened by their relationships in military operations. The British soldiers and officers looked down upon their cruder American cousins and infuriated them by their own discrimination and patronizing attitude. This is well illustrated at the time of Braddock's defeat, when, though everybody deplored the disaster itself, there was more than a little grim satisfaction in American commentaries which pointed to it as a lesson to teach the supercilious British that the Americans knew more about warfare in America and claimed that British honor was saved, after all, by the Americans, without whom the disaster would have been far greater than it was.

This mood of American importance in imperial affairs was no passing fancy, either. For there were numerous Americans who felt that it was to the colonials that victory was due, and that the mother country actually owed them a debt of gratitude for making possible so great an expansion of the Empire. This is the theme, for example, in Daniel Dulany's *Considerations on the Propriety of Imposing Taxes on the Colonies,* published in 1765, where he said :

> It is presumed that it was a notable service done by *New England,* when the militia of that colony reduced *Cape-Breton,* since it enabled the *British Ministers* to make a peace less disadvantageous and in-glorious than they otherwise must have been constrained to submit to, in the humble state to which they were then reduced. . . . It is ev-ident that the general exertion of the colonies in North America, dur-ing the last war [1754–63], not only facilitated, but was indispensably requisite to the success of those operations by which so many glorious conquests were achieved, and that those conquests have put it in the power of the present illustrious Ministers to make a peace upon terms of so much glory and advantage, as to afford an unexhaustible subject during their administration, and the triumph of toryism, at least, for their ingenious panegyrists to celebrate.[34]

Dulany demolishes the idea that England protected the colonies out of generosity. Great Britain was fighting for its life, and the colonies were an important factor in saving it. Far from taxing or exploiting the "Americans" (note the use of the term), England should feel only gratitude and respect for them :

> An *American,* without justly incurring the imputation of ingratitude, may doubt, whether some other motive, besides pure generosity, did not prompt the *British Nation* to engage in the defence of the colonies. He may be induced to think that the measures taken for the protection of the plantations, were not only connected with the interests, but even necessary to the defence of *Great Britain* herself, because he may have reason to imagine that *Great Britain,* could not long subsist as an inde-pendent kingdom after the loss of her colonies.[35]

Dulany was an American fully aware of the principle, then current in European diplomacy, that the balance of power among the great commercial states of Europe depended, in large measure if not entirely, upon the possession of profitable colonies in the new world. What he did was to turn that principle to the profit of the Americans by claim-ing that it was they who had preserved and increased England's weight in the international balance of power by preserving and extend-ing England's colonial holdings for her. She had begged the colonies for their aid, and she had got it, with consequent incalculable success and profit to herself ; and she should be grateful. Furthermore, Dulany made so bold as to say that "The frugal *Republicans* of *North-America*

[34] Dulany : *Considerations on the Propriety of Improving Taxes in the British Colonies,* p. 17.
[35] Ibid.

(if the *British* inhabitants there are to be distinguished by a *nick-name*, because it implies that they are enemies to the government of *England*, and ought therefore to be regarded with a jealous eye)"[36] should be acknowledged to know more about their own affairs than anybody in England.

The ideas and sentiments in this curious "Who won the war?" argument are clearly the impulses of a young and bumptious nationalism, the more clearly so because they were the feelings of not just one American, but probably most of them. The Americans were thinking of themselves now as different from their English cousins and as entitled to the respect due to a people that has arrived at political and cultural maturity. As Franklin put it in a letter to Lord Kames in 1767:

> Every man in England seems to consider himself a piece of a sovereign over America; seems to jostle himself into the throne with the King, and talks of *our subjects in the colonies.* . . . But America, an immense Territory, favored by nature with all the advantages of climate, soils, great navigable rivers, lakes, &c., must become a great country, populous and mighty; and will, in a less time than is generally conceived, be able to shake off any shackles that may be imposed upon her, and perhaps place them on the imposers. . . . And yet there remains among that people so much respect, veneration, and affection for Britain, that, if cultivated prudently, with a kind usage and tenderness for their privileges, they might be easily governed still for ages, without force or any considerable expense. But I do not see here a sufficient quantity of the wisdom, that is necessary to produce such a conduct, and I lament the want of it.[37]

Franklin was warning England of the psychological facts. But a subtle and significant change had now taken place in his mind. He no longer spoke of Americans as identical with Britons, or of the colonies as part of England. They were separate; they had only respect and reverence for the great traditions and ideals of the British way of life and all that that could mean; but they were now a separate people, among the other British peoples.

The loyalties of the Americans were becoming more and more sharply divided. The American mentality was growing conscious of this divergence, thinking of itself as a distinct, "American" entity within the Empire, and of England and its people as alien to itself. This was a psychological phenomenon, a factor of profound importance for the future of the Empire and for America. From Franklin's position of 1767 it was but a short step to Jefferson's position of 1774, which spoke of Englishmen as foreigners to America, and to the eloquent Patrick

[36] Ibid., p. 22.
[37] Franklin: *Works* (Sparks ed.), VII, 328–9, 334.

Henry's "I am an American." Or to that of John Randolph, who warned the mother country, on the eve of the Revolution:

> The Histories of dependent States put it beyond a Doubt that America, when she is able to protect herself, will acknowledge no Superiority in another. That she will be capable, some Time or other, to establish an Independence, must appear evident to every One, who is acquainted with her present Situation and growing Strength. But although it must

British-American aspiration in cartoons: wise Britannia releases the dove of American aspiration to fly to the tree of liberty.
[From the *Boston Gazette,* May 14, 1770]

> be apparent to everyone that *America* will, in short Period, attain to a State of Maturity, yet, if *Great Britain* could be prevailed on to govern her Colonies to their Satisfaction, from the force of Habit, and the good Impressions which a pleasing Intercourse must occasion, I am persuaded that she would procrastinate our Separation from her, and carry on an exclusive Trade with us, so long as she is able to maintain her Weight in the political scale of *Europe;* but, on the contrary, if she persevere in her Rigour, and the Colonies will not relax on their Part, the Parent will probably soon be without a Child, and the Offspring become unable to support itself.[38]

What the Americans were driving for was a recognition, by the mother country, of the now self-confident American national personality. The child had grown up and become a man. Psychologically, the American Revolution was a war to force the mother country to admit this basic fact. The Americans were perfectly willing, even anxious, given the mother country's admission of their national maturity, to remain members of the imperial family. But that was just the tragic point at which British nationalism found itself in conflict with British-American nationalism, and since neither one could accept the ideal and

[38] John Randolph : *Considerations on the Present State of Virginia,* pp. 21–2.

the point of view of the other, the British-American mind became the American mind, simply.

THE QUALITY OF AMERICAN NATIONAL FEELING

Thus the ardent national feeling that burst into flame in the Revolution was but the culmination of a long development, the explosion that marked the climax of a long smoldering fire of increasing intensity. It had had its birth within the folds of "British" patriotism; but, beginning as a loyalty to one's province, it had grown into a consciousness of problems and ideals common to all the provinces, first in matters of defense, then in cultural relationships, and finally in the problems of relationship with the mother country. Had Britain been wise enough to understand this aspect of the American mind and to accommodate British colonial policy to it, as it did a century later in the case of Canada, there is every reason to suppose that the colonies might have become the first associated nation in a new British Commonwealth of Nations. But, as Franklin sadly lamented, there wasn't enough of that sort of wisdom in Britain.

The American consciousness of national selfhood that was beginning to show its rudimentary forms by about 1750 was thus not merely allowed to grow naturally, but was actually forced into a flaming patriotic growth by the policies of the mother country. As it existed in its primitive form in 1750 it was a still nebular consciousness of, and loyalty to, the more heroic aspects of American life: the military exploits at Louisburg; the common fear of the common enemies, French and Indian, to the westward; a sense of the glorious manifest destiny of America beyond the mountains and as the future seat of the arts and sciences on this continent. As yet in 1750 and 1760 it was a glorification of Britain in America; by the end of the Seven Years' War loyalty to America was sharply distinguished, by some at least, from loyalty to Britain. As the sixties wore on into the seventies American patriots began to see that there were actually two nationalities involved, with their respective nationalisms.

It was this sense of the ineffable beauty and splendor of America and its promise to the world that inspired Philip Freneau to mark the culmination of American nationalistic felling in his *Poem on the Rising Glory of America* in 1771. Freneau was no rebel; he had no more thought of throwing off British allegiance in 1771 than most other Americans. But he envisioned his America as a nation within a British family of nations. His poem assumed the sort of British Empire that Benjamin Franklin was at that moment beginning to define as a federation of quasi-independent or autonomous states; his patriotism was the prototype of the intra-imperial patriotism of a Canada or an Australia of a later day:

> *To mighty nations shall the people grow*
> *Which cultivate the banks of many a flood,*
> *In chrystal currents poured from the hills*
> *Apalachia nam'd, to lave the sands*
> *Of Carolina, Georgia, and the plains*
> *Stretch'd out from thence far to the burning Line,*
> *St. Johns or Clarendon or Albemarle. . . .*
>
> *And here fair freedom shall forever reign.*
> *I see a train, a glorious train appear,*
> *Of Patriots plac'd in equal fame with those*
> *Who nobly fell for Athens or for Rome.*[39]

It should be emphasized that this American nationalism of 1770 was not a nationalism of independence. It was a nationalism that expected to find self-expression within the framework of the Empire. For conflicts of economic interest and ideologies alone were not necessarily and inevitably productive of civil war; neither, indeed, was conflict in religion, or in culture, or even politics. All these things might be adjusted peaceably; but when pride was pitted against pride, emotion against emotion; ideal of American "liberty" against ideal of an imperial unity to be imposed by force, if necessary, then, and then only, civil war was, in the nature of men and things, inevitable. This germinal American nationalism was nationalism in its best sense — national self-realization, pride in national tradition and achievement, and a sense of the greatness of the national destiny — a sort of national self-respect or pride that made it impossible to submit to the benighted stubbornness of George III and his ministers. Given the men, their convictions, and their mood, given, that is, the self-consciousness and the self-confidence of the American national mind, the outcome could hardly have been otherwise. For these thirteen of the British colonies in America had become a nation. And Patrick Henry, like so many other Americans fired by the discovery of his own America and driven to desperation by the utter inability of Britain to comprehend the nationhood of America, burst out with his famous cry: "The distinction between Virginians, Pennsylvanians, New Yorkers, and New Englanders, are no more. I am not a Virginian, but an American."[40]

[39] Freneau: *Poem on the Rising Glory of America*, pp. 22–3.
[40] William W. Henry: *Patrick Henry, Life, Correspondence, and Speeches* (3 vols., New York, 1891), I, 222.

NOTE TO THE READER

The expressions of American nationalism of the 1750's and 1760's are scattered and largely fragmentary. Of the Tory or imperialist patriots the most articulate were Archibald Kennedy, William Livingston, Jonathan Boucher, Thomas Hutchinson, and William Smith of Pennsylvania. Kennedy's *The Importance of Gaining . . . the Friendship of the Indians* (London, 1751) shows it clearly; Livingston's *Review of the Military Operations in North America* (London, 1757) is an imperialistic tract; his poem *America, or, a Poem on the Settlement of the British Colonies* (New Haven, 1770), was a product of the same mood that produced Freneau's *Poem on the Rising Glory of America*. Boucher's *Reminiscences of an American Loyalist*, already referred to, give a poignant picture of the conflict of loyalties in this sincere Anglican minister; Hutchinson's loyalist convictions are probably best seen in his communications to the Massachusetts Assembly contained in *The Speeches of His Excellency the Governor . . .* already mentioned. Smith's loyalty is fairly clearly to be read in his *Brief State of the Province of Pennsylvania*, also already noted.

Jonathan Mayhew's sermons are full of his religious patriotism, especially the ones published during and after the Seven Years' War, such as his *Two Sermons*, published in Boston, 1763. Charles Chauncy was, if anything, a more fervent nationalist than Mayhew, as may be seen by a reading of his *Marvellous Things done by the Right Hand and Holy Arm of God* (Boston, 1745), or of his later *Two Letters to a Friend . . .* (Boston, 1755). Samuel Davies was one of the great patriotic preachers of the south; one of the best examples is his *Religion and Patriotism the Constituents of a Good Soldier* (Philadelphia, 1756).

The writings of Richard Bland, Daniel Dulany, Benjamin Franklin, Patrick Henry, and William Smith of New York are full of the growing political and economic nationalism of the Americans; and the work of William Smith of Pennsylvania, both in his own writing, and his sponsorship of the *American Magazine*, and in the work of his disciples, is a great monument of self-conscious cultural nationalism.

Of the poets, Francis Hopkinson, Nathaniel Evans, John Maylem, William Livingston, Nathaniel Ames, William Smith of Pennsylvania, James Sterling, and, most of all, the young Freneau brought nationalism into literature in striking fashion. Maylem's poems (see the chapter on literature) and Livingston's *America* were published separately; so was Freneau's *Poem on the Rising Glory of America*. The moods of most of the others can be found in the *American Magazine* of 1757–8. Of all these poems, Freneau's is by far the most eloquent expression of American national feeling, as well as being probably the best poem written by a native American in the colonial period.

CONCLUSION

The Seeds of Liberty

UCH, then, was the pattern of American intellectual and cultural life in the middle of the eighteenth century. It was not an English culture, except superficially, but a new national way of life; a variant within the broad culture-pattern of western civilization as a whole. It seems clear that, as was suggested at the beginning, this American way was neither a reproduction nor a duplication of any other in the world. It was, on the contrary, the product of the fusion of many elements, as operated upon by many formative forces. Inherited ideas, religion, social habits, general racial or cultural background and individual self-interest, whether economic, political, or other, all flowed into the crucible in which this culture was fused. The crucible itself was the environment; but the environment was both physical and sociological. For whereas the formative influence of climate, soil, flora, and fauna was perfectly obvious on the one side, the catalytic force of the presence of French and Indians, in possession of the west, was equally obvious on the other. Less obvious, but no less important, were two other factors, the conservative influence of the mother country and the retarding influence of the tentatively established colonial patterns of the seventeeth century, both of which had to be broken before a pattern native to America and genuinely expressive of the American spirit could emerge.

Those old molds of the Puritan century in north and south had to be broken and new ones set up in their place before the America that was to be could appear. But they were hard to break; and the conflict produced by the attempt to break them grew in intensity throughout the century; until freedom for further development could only be achieved by civil war. For the Revolution was, in a very real sense, a civil war, fought between the determination of the native American genius to break the seventeenth-century framework and the equal determination of the loyal but unenlightened exponents of the first molds that they should not be broken.

In broad, general terms, it may be said that the pattern of the American mind of the middle of the eighteenth century followed the pattern of the economic and social divisions in American society as they overlay the differences between geographic sections. In each section the basic activity was of course economic; and economic ideas tended to run along lines that promoted that activity and rationalized its practices. The forms of society followed the pattern of economic activity, and social thought, generally, rationalized the social scene. Politics followed the pattern of economic and social structure; rival economic or social interests struggled for control of politics and government, and as the partisans organized themselves with increasing effectiveness, "factions," then true parties, appeared to sponsor rival sets of political ideas. Religion rationalized and regulated all three; but the eighteenth century had seen the inroads of science and scientific rationalism upon the old religious systems of ideas; and while religion was still strong enough to dominate philosophy, it no longer dominated literature or art, or even, completely, education. Religion was still, nevertheless, likely to be closely identified, even fused, with the economic, social, and political ideas of its devotees.

But it was not science alone that brought about the dethronement of religion. For this was an increasingly secular age, even without science; and the ultimate effect of the frontier and the melting-pot, despite the strong religious currents in both, was already showing itself in the increasing casualness with which the people as a whole took their religion. And if rationalism attempted to free the minds of men from ignorance and superstition, the frontier freed them from the restraints of the statism and authoritarianism of seventeenth-century religious Calvinism, economic mercantilism, and political oligarchy.

Taken by social class, the American culture-pattern cut horizontally across the vertical sectional lines. For the aristocrats of Boston, Williamsburg, and Charleston had more in common intellectually with each other than they did with the other classes in their own colonies. Similarly, the members of the middle class of the cities had a good deal more in common with each other, from north to south, than they had with the rugged frontiersmen of their own western hills. These north-and-south lines, in fact, were strong ties operating to draw the colonies together.

The north-south lines of interest tended to pit class against class. For the members of the aristocracy, with some exceptions, were likely to belong to the governor's party in politics, to be Anglican in religion, and to be Anglophile in cultural tastes. The middle class, on the other hand, was likely to belong to the assembly party and to be governed by the conservative principles in society and religion that produced the taste in art called American realism. The frontiersman, by contrast, was likely to be a radical in politics, in social outlook, and in religion; radical, that is, for the eighteenth century. As a man who believed in the theory and the practice of democracy, he was suspect, to say the least, to the respectable and the good.

It was the middle class, the assemblymen, the common-sensical in religion, who most substantially represented the mind of the great majority of the Americans. The Anglophile aristocrats, the colonial Tories, looked backward to an England and a culture that were foreign. It was the frontiersmen who held the key to the future; for in the future, still, lay the American way to democracy.

This is not, however, to say that economic and social factors were the only determinants of cultural direction. For it should be clear by now that ideas and ideals, and particularly the ideas and ideals of Puritanism, exerted a formative influence on American culture that cannot possibly be explained in terms of economic and social determinism alone. The human mind unquestionably had an important, if not a decisive, place as a determinant of history in America.

It was all these things combined, or operating concurrently, that constituted the American experience. And it was out of this experience, broadly conceived, that the American mind, or culture, as distinguished from all the others in the world, was generated. But the American experience was a fairly heterogeneous one; its unity was the unity of heterogeneity within a broad, unified pattern. It was only natural that the American mind should also show wide diversity in thought and custom. Above all, however, the American mind of *circa* 1750 was the flowering of a century and a half's growth — a growth of ideas, ideals, and attitudes that was generated in the actual day-by-day living of hundreds of thousands of men, on the land, at sea, and in the forest. As such a flowering, it was a self-conscious, quasi-autonomous fragment of the imperial pattern of British culture round the world; and when it reached full bloom about 1770, it desired nothing more than to be just that. As it stood then, it was a complex product generated of many ingredients in the crucible of the American experience on this continent. But the old pattern had to be broken, at least partially, to make the United States of America. As the generative forces of experience go on, those old patterns may probably have to be broken again and again in order to mold the self-renewing culture of the future. But of this one may be sure, in any case : the pattern of American culture that emerged between 1750 and 1770 was the rationalization of the American experience up to then. But experience goes on : that pattern was not an end; it was only a beginning.

The mind of this new American nation was a complex thing. There were many groups, with many opinions on every subject. And as among a people devoted to the principles of individual freedom of thought there can be no one mind or body of opinion, no "official"

dogma that reduces all thought to one dead level of mediocrity or dull-
ness, or even brilliance, there could be no such uniformity in the mind
of colonial America. Its very diversity was its greatest charm, its greatest challenge to the inquiring mind, its surest sign of health. Yet, for
all its diversity of surface opinion, its most profound current was a
deep, slow-moving stream of thought and conviction that made it
all one.

The formulation of the American culture-pattern of the mid-eighteenth century had been achieved, almost unconsciously, only after the
breaking or the discarding of the old molds, whether those inherited
from Europe or the tentative forms set up in the colonies in the seventeenth century. Both the inherited forms and the tentative American
forms of the seventeenth century were of a relatively rigid, formal,
aristocratic, and authoritarian type. The new pattern, while not yet
completely free from social or political rigidity, was nevertheless
marked by its malleability, its rational approach to life, its tolerance
for new ideas, its fluidity ; in short, relatively speaking, its freedom for
change and growth within itself.

In the century between 1650 and 1750, then, an intellectual revolution had taken place in the British colonies on the continent of North
America. For from the Calvinistic authoritarianism in religion of the
first generations of settlers, the American mind had moved into an acceptance and advocacy of complete religious freedom ; from the mercantilist statism in economics and politics that dominated the first colonies, the Americans had gone over to the philosophies of economic
freedom and the fiercely defended principles of political autonomy
and of government derived from the will of the governed ; from literature, art, and music that were largely confined to the portrayal or
the celebration of the beauty of God and the divine plan with men,
the American arts had freed themselves from religious restraint to become more secular, more humanitarian, more rationalistic : most of
all, from expressing the beauties of the mind of God, they had turned
to an expression of the beauty and the promise of the living experience
of the Americans on the soil of America. The Americans had passed
through an intellectual revolution ; they had created a new culture ;
they knew it, and they were proud of it. For they had brought forth
on this continent a new nation, the keynote of whose thought and literature, to be heard above all others, was liberty, or the principle of human freedom.

INDEX

Abélard, Peter, and medieval Christianity, 18

Acadia, 343; and British claims, 349; and Massachusetts, 349

Adams, John: and class-consciousness at Harvard, 241; and "natural" aristocracy, 280; on an isolationist policy, 348; on a Catholic church service, 508; on the singing at a Presbyterian and a Methodist church, 508; on Francis Hopkinson, 525; and *The Liberty Song*, 534; and *Hail Columbia*, 538; *For Adams and Liberty*, 539; on destiny of America, 555

Adams, John Quincy, on John Adams at Harvard, 241

Adams, Samuel, perception of outmoded political theory, 304–5

Addison, Joseph: and prose of *Spectator* and *Tatler*, 358; 369; Franklin on his emulation of *Spectator*, 370; and southern colonies, 372; 380; Franklin's "Essays of Silence Dogood," 395; 406

Ainsworth, Henry: *Book of Psalmes*, 494

Aix-la-Chapelle, Treaty of (1748), 350

Albany, N. Y.: merchants and King George's War, 345; merchants and isolationism, 347; *see also* Albany Congress

Albany Congress of 1754: and Colden, 329; Franklin's plan of union, 329; Peters's plan, 329–30; Shirley's plan not submitted, 330; Franklin's plan adopted as Albany Plan of Union, 330; and Kennedy's *Serious Considerations*, 330; reasons for rejection of plan by assemblies, 330–2; Albany Plan and struggle of assemblies for autonomy, 330–3; Franklin on Albany Plan, 332–3, 562; English rejection of Albany Plan, 333; Board of Trade transmits plan to Privy Council, 333; Shirley's attitude toward plan, 333, 334–5; and Articles of Confederation, 334; and Franklin's formulation of imperial theory,

Albany Congress of 1754 (*continued*)
334; Albany Plan and isolationism, 348; 383; and cartoon "Join or Die," 455, (illus.) 574; and nationalism, 574

Albany Plan of Union, *see* Albany Congress

Alexander, James, transmits Franklin's plan of 1751 to Colden, 329

Allen, Ethan: and Deism, 42–3, 152, 169–71; on God, 43–4; 53; *Reason the Only Oracle*, 169; on whether he was a Deist, 169–70; advocacy of reason, 170–1; and Witherspoon, 176; and pragmatism, 177

Allen, Joseph, and painting, 431

Almanacs: and Newtonianism, 53; Bridgen's Copernican Almanac, 88; *Poor Richard* on smallpox inoculation, 120; as purveyors of medical knowledge, 130; *Poor Richard* on treatment of dysentery, 130; astrology and quackery, 130; purveyors of scientific knowledge, 137–41; and astrology, 137; "The Anatomy of Man's Body as govern'd by the Twelve Constellations" (illus.), 138; *Poor Richard*, eulogy of scientists, 138–9; "Eclipses of the Sun" and "The Movements of the heavenly bodies" (illus.), 140; Bartram's contribution on the red cedar, 140–1; and pragmatism, 177; "A Table for the more ready casting up of Coins" (illus.), 212; *Poor Richard* on virtues of work and wealth, 220–1, 223, 224; "Father Abraham's Speech," 220, 221, 226; humor in, 392–3; 395; *Poor Richard*, poem on freedom of the press, 396; 397–9; *Poor Richard's Almanack, 1749* (illus.), 397; *Astronomical Diary, 1748* (illus.), 397; literary importance, 399; 403; poetry in, 417–18; woodcut from *Poor Richard* (illus.), 456; woodcuts in, 456; *Poor Richard* on America as a refuge, 567; Ames's eulogy on capture of Louisbourg, 571; Ames on destiny of America, 575